WRITERS
OF THE BLACK
CHICAGO
RENAISSANCE

WRITERS
OF THE BLACK
CHICAGO
RENAISSANCE

EDITED BY
STEVEN C. TRACY

UNIVERSITY OF ILLINOIS PRESS
URBANA, CHICAGO, AND SPRINGFIELD

Library of Congress Cataloging-in-Publication Data
Writers of the Black Chicago renaissance / edited by
Steven C. Tracy.
p.   cm.
Includes bibliographical references and index.
ISBN 978-0-252-03639-2 (hardback)
1. American literature—Illinois—Chicago—History and criticism.
2. American literature—20th century—History and criticism.
3. American literature—African American authors—
History and criticism.
4. Chicago (Ill.)—Intellectual life—20th century.
I. Tracy, Steven C. (Steven Carl), 1954–
PS285.C47W75   2011
810.9'896073077311—dc23   2011029269

CONTENTS

ACKNOWLEDGMENTS

A book like this is, of course, the culmination of a great deal of effort by many people. Most important to this book are the subjects themselves, many of whom have waited a long time to receive this kind of critical emphasis and attention, some receiving it only posthumously. To those who labored in segregated vineyards, drawing insufficient pay and inadequate recognition for their efforts, I have endeavored to provide what I could offer to them: the authors of the entries in this volume. To these critics I extend my heartiest thanks for their insights and remarkable writing skills, their commitment to the project, and their patience as it moved through the process of publication. Of course, I felt much better knowing that these critics were aboard to do justice and honor to their subjects, and through that to themselves. It was also my honor to work again with Joan Mary Catapano, who retired well into her wonderful work on this project, and with Director Willis Regier, Acquisitions Editor Daniel Nasset, manuscript editor Jennifer Clark, Marketing Copy editor Joe Peebles, and the excellent copyeditor Nancy Albright, all of whom reminded me how wonderful it is to publish with University of Illinois Press. Manuscript readers Professors William Maxwell and Amritjit Singh were invaluable as manuscript readers who provided thorough commentaries on the entries. Erica DeJong worked with me for a semester as student assistant on the project, doing some valuable work with the manuscript. My colleagues in the department of Afro-American Studies at the University of Massachusetts Amherst have been supportive throughout my work on the volume, and I particularly acknowledge the involvement of Professor Jim Smethurst, who was certainly there to listen and advise through all the vicissitudes of this project. I also have valued the support and interest of Professor Lianggong Luo of Central China Normal University, Professor Roy Kedong Liu of Harbin Institute of Technology, and the wonderful students at those universities and at the University of Massachusetts Amherst. Sincerest gratitude also goes to the Deans of the College of Humanities and Fine Arts at the University of Massachusetts Amherst: first Lee Edwards, then Joel Martin, and finally Julie Hayes, have been remarkably supportive of all my endeavors while this project has been on the burners. Finally, I offer my thanks for all their love and support to my wife Cathy and children—oh, they are 26 and 19, hardly children anymore!—Michelle and Michael for putting up with a bi-polar and obsessive-compulsive dad. On to my next project.

INTRODUCTION
Steven C. Tracy

Even the seasoned critic writing on the subject under consideration here can fall unconsciously and automatically into writing *Harlem* Renaissance rather than *Chicago* Renaissance. That is how prominent the Harlem movement still is in the minds of scholars of African American literature: it is mere second nature to write "Harlem" with "Renaissance." Not that the Harlem Renaissance is not supremely important. Some scholars believe—though fortunately not all of them—that not much of literary value was written by African Americans before the pivotal era that produced Jean Toomer, Langston Hughes, Claude McKay, Jessie Fauset, Countee Cullen, Nella Larsen, Wallace Thurman, Zora Neale Hurston, Arna Bontemps, Anne Spencer, and others. The literary, indeed cultural, outpouring of the Harlem Renaissance produced unprecedented publishing opportunities in journals like *The Crisis, Opportunity, The Messenger, The Survey Graphic, The Nation, Garvey's Journal, Negro World,* and many others, white- and black-run, as well as journals that had both white and black editors, as did *Liberator* when Mike Gold and Claude McKay were coeditors. Attention that had been experienced previously only by stray African American writers such as Phillis Wheatley, Frederick Douglass, Frances E. W. Harper, Paul Laurence Dunbar, and Charles W. Chesnutt focused on a larger group of African American writers. And when the Harlem Renaissance ended, its destruction fueled by the stock market crash and, in some ways, by attraction to leftist political movements that actually predated the crash and provided positive impetus for a number of social, political, and literary issues in the lives of African Americans, it seemingly left a gulf not filled until the Black Arts Movement of the 1960s. That gulf has been more in African American literary criticism than in actuality.

The late 1930s through the 1950s—roughly the time period of what Robert Bone first labeled the "Black Chicago Renaissance"—were not just years when isolated individuals like Richard Wright or Ralph Ellison or James Baldwin or Gwendolyn Brooks wholly dominated the African American literary scene. But the center that could not hold in Harlem had moved to another prominent destination of the great Black migration—to Chicago. To many, the Chicago Renaissance seemed to be less consciously a "movement," with policies, activities, organs of publication, and purposes of its own. Actually, many critics have regretted the "Renaissance" label, for both Harlem and Chicago, because neither was an actual rebirth or resurgence that brought immediate, profound epochal changes. However, each represented avant-garde political, social, and artistic thinking that eventually produced a stage upon which African American writers could redefine their relationships to American society and the world; therefore, calling each a Renaissance is not really problematical in the sense of the term as a renewal of vigor, energy, or life produced by a newly minted but broad-ranging vision. Indeed, what we call movements are frequently somewhat loose aggregations of writers, few of whom fit all of the criteria later established by critics for the "group," that resist wholly satisfactory definitions. However, the Chicago Renaissance did have its influential major figures (Wright, Brooks), its major influences (Naturalism, Chicago School of Sociology, leftist politics), its clubs (John Reed Clubs, South Side Writers Project), and publishing organs, both black and white (*The Anvil*, *The New Anvil*, the *New Challenge*), and important newspapers like the *Chicago Defender*, the *Chicago Bee*, and the *Chicago Whip*. It also had manifestos such as Wright's "Blueprint for Negro Writing," written in New York and attempting to establish and delineate a sharp break from the Harlem Renaissance, though of course still sharing some values. And, like the Harlem Renaissance, it had an urban scene teeming with important musical and artistic activity, and recording and museum opportunities that were magnets for budding artists.

Perhaps what it lacked that the Harlem Renaissance had was the level of a sense of self-awareness as a group with particular aims and expectations from both within and without. Surely, Black Chicago Renaissance figures knew who they were, knew what cities and neighborhoods they were in, met with each other socially and professionally, and read each others' works. But the milieu of the Roaring Twenties, literary patronage and publisher interest, and postwar optimism and sense of purpose gave way to a movement in Chicago less optimistically galvanized into action. The Harlem Renaissance, after all, had failed to produce the high regard and social equality it was assumed the production of great literature would bring. A more jaded, bitter outlook replaced some of that optimism, and, though there were of course liaisons and associations between white and black artists in the Harlem Renaissance, such interracial liaisons based in leftist political associations were more common in Depression and post–Depression-era Chicago, where Jack Conroy's collaborations with Arna Bontemps and James T. Farrell's support for Richard Wright's works were notable but not uncommon liaisons.

Of course, all literary movements have their antecedents, figures, or even groups that act as precursors or models preparing the way for the new dispensation. Dunbar, Chesnutt, Ida B. Wells, Frances E. W. Harper, W. E. B. DuBois, and James Weldon Johnson, for example, anticipated some elements of the Harlem Renaissance, and in some cases lived to contribute to it. At times such movements, despite the most well-intentioned efforts of literary critics to package them neatly, refuse to hang together as we have seen them or would like to see them. Figures write beyond the "end" of the time frame established by scholars of literature, or challenge the proscriptions of class, race, or gender "boundaries" in ways that demand reconsideration and reappraisal. Such is the case for writers of the Harlem Renaissance, and the Black Chicago Renaissance as well. Still, movements need their definitions and parameters to be as concrete as possible, while recognizing that the natural growth of a grove or garden is to exfoliate or flower in untamed exuberance or under carefully restrained direction.

Unequivocally, Harlem Renaissance writers were important precursors for African American Chicago Renaissance writers in a variety of ways. Their focus on exploring the cultural past and reclaiming it for contemporary lives in a primarily urban setting; the use of blues, jazz, and spirituals by writers such as Hughes, Hurston, and Thurman in their literary creations; the exploration of leftist politics by authors such as DuBois, A. Philip Randolph, McKay, and Hughes; the insistence upon the centrality of African American experiences to any definition of the American character; and the forging of ties with influential white educators, patrons, and publishers—all these elements also figured prominently in the Chicago Renaissance.

In fact, for some writers and critics the term "Harlem Renaissance" was a technical misnomer, as Sterling Brown insisted. There were major outposts of writers associated with the Renaissance elsewhere, for example, in Washington, D.C., where the African American institutions Dunbar High School and Howard University were located, as well as in Virginia, Los Angeles, Boston . . . and Chicago. One major writer, Claude McKay, was in Europe during most of what are described as the "peak" years of the Harlem Renaissance. In fact, in 1920 H. L. Mencken was proclaiming Chicago to be "the Literary Capitol on the U.S." in the London *Nation*, and while what he referred to encompassed primarily the white writers of the earlier Chicago Renaissance, the city clearly had bubbling activity in the black communities that would come to a boil in a few decades.

Because these activities were based in more locations than just Harlem, the term "New Negro Renaissance" more accurately described a movement that had one city as its symbolic spiritual base and hub of activity, just as Chicago functioned similarly in the Black Chicago Renaissance. For example, although Fenton Johnson is sometimes judged a relatively minor poet whose works anticipated Harlem Renaissance themes, his first book, published in 1913, was also a major precursor to the Chicago Renaissance of black writers in the 1930s, with which he later became personally involved as well. Marita Bonner, based in

Washington, D.C., during the Harlem Renaissance years, contributed the important essays "On Being Young—A Woman—and Colored" and "The Young Blood Hungers," along with short fiction and drama, to the Harlem movement before moving to Chicago with her husband in 1930 and being present for the Black Chicago Renaissance later. Indeed, Chandler Owen, cofounder with A. Philip Randolph of the Socialist magazine *Messenger* in 1917, moved to Chicago in 1923 and became editor on the African American newspaper the *Chicago Bee*. Arna Bontemps and Langston Hughes, while rightly associated with the Harlem group, had important ties to the Chicago group as well, as residents, frequent visitors, and, in Hughes's case, as organizer of the Skyloft Players theater group and publisher of the important "Simple" sketches in the *Chicago Defender* beginning in February 1943. Hughes and Bontemps, in fact, lived through the three major African American movements of the twentieth century; though they remain tied by critics to the earliest and were considered elder statesmen/observers of the last—the Black Arts movement—Hughes also made some notable contributions there. These writers should be seen as wholly involved in each movement, not simply anachronistic Harlem Renaissance hangers-on riding the wake of newer boats.

Arna Bontemps is a prime example. Bontemps, a prolific writer in a variety of genres, first published in *The Crisis* in 1924 with the aid of Jessie Fauset, as many important figures of the Harlem Renaissance did, and followed with work in *Opportunity*, *The Messenger*, and *Fire!!*. *God Sends Sunday*, a historical novel by Bontemps, was published in 1931, and he collaborated with Hughes on *Popo and Fifina* (1932), but by this time Bontemps realized that he was not going to make his living as a poet in New York. After leaving Harlem in 1933 and a period of moving around to Alabama and California, Bontemps and family settled in Chicago in 1935, where he worked as a principal at Shiloh Academy and worked on his master's degree.

Ensconced in the city with his job and educational goals, he spent eight years in Chicago and, though he was thoroughly unimpressed with the living environment, he published prolifically under his own name, as a ghost writer for W. C. Handy, and in collaboration with important Chicago writers such as Jack Conroy and his old Harlem friend Countee Cullen. But Bontemps was a public intellectual as well, serving on committees, delivering lectures, and doing radio broadcasts that made him an important public figure at the time. Importantly, he cosupervised the *Negro in Illinois* research project (where he met Conroy) during his Chicago years as well, and he retained contact with Dorothy West and others in the Chicago Renaissance. He left Chicago in 1943 to be the head librarian at Fisk University, but he continued to write and publish until his death in 1973. If he is associated—even by himself—more with the Harlem Renaissance, his work during the time of the Chicago Renaissance in

Chicago made him an important, slightly older figure and a model of public service and publication. His political commitment to his colleagues in Chicago and around the country in his public and literary work—indeed the overlap of the two is clear, as one would expect from a movement driven by politics and thorough sociological grounding—mark him as a complete member of the Chicago Renaissance. Whether writing about slave insurrection in *Black Thunder* (1936) and revolution in *Drums at Dusk* (1939), collaborating with political ally Jack Conroy on the children's book *The Fast Sooner Hound* (1942), working on a book on "the Negro in Illinois" with the support of Rosenwald grants, and writing the important *Story of the Negro* (1948) to narrate the history of black peoples from Egyptian civilization to the present, Bontemps brought inter- and intraracial commitment to his combined political and artistic endeavors, along with a keen sociological eye and a very public, progressive artistic stance. In a larger and more expensive version of this volume, Bontemps would be included among the writers treated in their own essays as well.

Another writer not included here, Waters Turpin, exemplifies the fluid boundaries of various geographically centered "movements" as well. Turpin lived mostly in Pennsylvania and Maryland, never Chicago, but is often grouped with Chicago Renaissance writers by virtue of his discussion of the migration from the South to Chicago of the protagonists in his second novel, *O Canaan!* But Chicago should be seen as a major artistic hub that had associations with other African American midwestern communities. One particularly important center existed in Detroit, where Robert Hayden worked for the Federal Writers' Project and as a professor, and where the *Michigan Chronicle* was published (and where, later, Dudley Randall's *Broadside Press* began publishing in 1965). Cleveland's Playhouse Settlement, later Karamu House, provided cultural centeredness for the African American community there and yet another connection to the Harlem Renaissance and Langston Hughes, who worked with Karamu House beginning in 1936. In *O Canaan!*, Chicago proves not to be a land where milk and honey flows, but his focus on Chicago as an important symbol of the yearning for social, economic, and spiritual freedom would qualify Turpin to be ranked among the figures of the Black Chicago Renaissance. The writers of the Harlem Renaissance provided a thematic and stylistic bridge from one movement to the other and in fact were testimony to the inadequacies of the terms describing what were neither geographically or chronologically isolated movements. The cultural and literary spirit that resided in Harlem lived elsewhere as well. This was also true for Chicago.

Neither were the writers of the Black Chicago Renaissance chronologically or racially isolated. Another confusion in talking about the Black Chicago Renaissance is the existence of another, earlier, Chicago Renaissance of primarily white writers based in Chicago and most active from the 1890s to the 1920s. That earlier Renaissance movement shared any number of important characteristics with the Black movement that reinforces the essential fallacy of considering the Black Renaissance, or indeed any African American literary movements, in isolation from other social, political, and aesthetic currents in the broader American culture. Hamlin Garland, Henry B. Fuller, Theodore Dreiser, Frank Norris, Edith Wyatt, Upton Sinclair, Clara Laughlin, Elia Peattie, Sherwood Anderson, even Hemingway in prose, Vachel Lindsay, Edgar Lee Masters, Carl Sandburg, Eunice Tietjens, Alice Corbin, Mary Aldis, and Florence Kifer Frank in poetry—these and other writers associated with the earlier Chicago Renaissance projected their own urban vision through their contacts with Chicago.

It was a vision that was often crucially associated with American identity. Mencken published *The American Language: An Inquiry into the Development of English in the United States* in 1919, identifying characteristics of American English and calling for employment of vernacular speech in literature as plain and simple as the writing of newspaper journalists such as Ring Lardner and Indiana author George Ade in expression. Mencken was opposed to a concept of gentility that glided gently above the grit and gristle of contemporary existence, preferring a language that was 1) rooted in realistic details but informed by the literary naturalism that was ascendant at the time; 2) socially committed in its direct treatment of social and political problems in works such as Dreiser's *Sister Carrie* (1900) and *The Titan* (1914), Norris's *The Pit* (1902), Upton Sinclair's *The Jungle* (1906), Sherwood Anderson's *Winesburg, Ohio* (1919) and the poetry of Sandburg and Edgar Lee Masters; and 3) unabashedly democratic in scope and spirit. Indeed, William Dean Howells saw this Chicago school of fiction as a crucial reflector of midwestern, and American, democracy. But it was also experimental and modern, mingled with the European modernist experimentation of Pound, Yeats, Joyce, and Stein in Chicago journals such as Harriet Monroe's *Poetry* (with which Fenton Johnson had a close relationship and where Gwendolyn Brooks also published early in her career), Margaret Anderson's *Little Review*, Frances Fisher Brown's *The Dial*, and Floyd Dell's *Friday Literary Times*. In fact, the dual influences of Walt Whitman and Gertrude Stein, particularly with regard to the employment of speech patterns and repetitions in their work, seem to be well represented in the earlier Chicago school in the juxtaposition of Whitman's radical-democratic spirit and technique and Stein's radical Modernist European experimentation.

The earlier Chicago Renaissance aesthetic was, in Whitman's words about his own work, a language experiment aimed at revolutionizing the perceptions of what art is and can do. The movement's aesthetic was born of the rough and often conflict-ridden progress of an urban city beset by battles and broken treaties with Native Americans such as the Dearborn Massacre (1812) and the Blackhawk War (1832). And there were other fits, starts, skirmishes, and eruptions that kept the diverse city in upheaval. There were disastrous fires in 1839 and 1871. At the violent Haymarket Affair of May 1886, a mass protest against the killing of strikers by police during which a bomb exploded killing and wounding several policeman, the antipathies among workers, employers, police, and anarchist Internationalists were played out, the drama treated by Frank Harris in his novel *The Bomb* (1906). Reformer and sociologist Jane Addams, through the Hull House, attempted to deal with the difficulties of inner city immigrants in Chicago beginning in 1889. Labor conflicts such as the Pullman strike led by Eugene V. Debs in 1894 demonstrated an increasingly polarized city, often a result of the challenges precipitated by massive influxes of European immigrants in the late 19th century (the migration of poor white people from the rural Midwest and the South). The major African American migration to Chicago around the time of World War I—blues singer Ida Cox recorded "Chicago Bound Blues (Famous Migration Blues)" in 1923—was also an important historic event. This migration to the "Black Belt" or "Bronzeville" via Highways 41 and 61 and the Illinois Central Railroad line, especially from the time of World War I to around 1950, to work in foundries, stockyards, and steel mills and play in the famed South Side bars and theaters on the Theater Owners Booking Association circuit, produced further anxieties with which the city had to deal. These conflicts contributed directly to the serious "Red Summer" of 1919 race riots in Chicago (reported by Walter White in *The Crisis*) and over two dozen other towns in the United States. Chicago had dealt with multiethnic complications for much of its history. It emerged as a strikingly rebuilt, modern city with issues of trade unionism, suffrage, and the efforts to deal with them foregrounded. The discussions of these issues were infused with the dialect, slang, and oratorical styles of immigrants, which were then integrated into the lexicon and terms of discussion. Chicago was uniquely situated to host such a mélange of influences and issues.

The connection to Whitman is a crucial one. His associations with American identity as the bard, prophet, and sage of democracy, his embracing of a broad variety of dictions and experimentation with the evocative spirit he called "eidolons" in his work, his sexual openness in works like "Children of Adam" and "Calamus," his easy wandering mobility in poems like "Song of Myself," and his work as a reporter seeking to reach a popular audience, all made him a hero to a variety of figures associated with both Chicago Renaissances and the Harlem Renaissance as well. Poets such as the geographically, spiritually, and aesthetically mobile Sandburg of the *Chicago Poems*, Edgar Lee Masters in *Spoon River Anthology* (1915), and Vachel Lindsay were enthralled by Whitman's work. So, too, was the sociologist Robert Park (whose significance for the Black Chicago Renaissance through his thorough criticism and relationship to Richard Wright is well documented), as were American Socialists seeking a model for embracing the American masses. Certainly Langston Hughes demonstrates his connection to Whitman in poems like "I Too" and "Old Walt," as well as his defense of Whitman in the 1950s. The influence is apparent, too, through Sandburg in "Old Timers," which was a clear model for Hughes's "The Negro Speaks of Rivers," and through Lindsay, who boosted Hughes's career in 1925 when Lindsay praised the busboy poet who placed his poems beside Lindsay's plate at Washington, D.C.'s Wardman Park Hotel. Furthermore, Sandburg, as a collector of multiethnic folksongs in *American Song-Bag* (1927), performer on guitar since 1910, and recording artist since 1926, and Lindsay, whose energetic performances were influenced by what he called a "Higher Vaudeville," also demonstrated a crucial connection that ran from Whitman to the Harlem and Chicago Renaissances in relation to sound, speech, performance, and music. Significantly, the venerable poet, critic, and scholar Sterling Brown issued a pointed corrective to Lindsay's famous poem "The Congo," which he entitled "The New Congo," confronting without apology (as he subtitled his poem) what he saw as Lindsay's shortcomings in dealing with the Africanist presence. However, one is also reminded of the acknowledged relationship between Chicago's Sherwood Anderson and Harlem's Jean Toomer, which benefited both writers, and Toomer's references to identity in his letters that are very close to Whitman's ideas, as well as Toomer's explicit reference to Whitman in his fiction, which comes, significantly, in the Chicago section of *Cane*. These writers, who influenced or became part of the Black Chicago Renaissance, share a common ancestry from Whitman, whose influence on the most famous writer of the Black Chicago Renaissance, Richard Wright, is reflected in his early poetry and in his general philosophy. The unfortunate notion of insular groupings or movements in literary history is more convenient than accurate.

As a result, the relationships among black and white writers at the time of the Black Chicago Renaissance should not be ignored. Chicago was, of course, a city where racial segregation was rigidly observed. The enormous black community of Chicago, fed by the WW I–era migrations from the South, was primarily limited to a "Black Belt" that largely isolated the black and white communities socially and politically. One result was that African American cultural productions and institutions were encouraged, formally and informally, within the African American community. Despite this harsh segregation, there were in the white artistic community efforts to integrate socially, politically, and artistically that gave great impetus to the Black Chicago Renaissance. Leftist organizations prominent at the time provided ample opportunities for black and white authors, artists, and activists to interact. Writers such as James T. Farrell, Nelson Algren, Alexander Saxton, William Schenck, and Jack Conroy, the publisher of the proletarian magazine *The Anvil*, were all figures who had frequent contact with or crucial influence on many of Black Chicago Renaissance figures,

Richard Wright among them. The poetry workshop run by Inez Cunningham Stark Boulton at the South Side Community Center had great importance for poets such as Gwendolyn Brooks, Frank Marshall Davis, Margaret Walker, and Margaret Danner. And Studs Terkel's activities on the WPA Writers' Project, as a writer and radio and television interviewer on WEMR, WFMT, and other stations, and especially his interest in jazz, blues, and folk music, contributed to the cultural scene as well. Though these white writers are not included among the entries for this volume, focused as it is on black writers and literary history, they certainly could be in a larger volume, and their influences, acknowledged in a number of essays herein, emphasize that literary, social, and political integration was a hallmark of the Black Chicago Renaissance scene.

The writers who *are* included in this volume, like those of the Harlem Renaissance, came to Chicago from a variety of backgrounds and took a variety of approaches to the style and subject matter of their work, though they were united by the desire to express leftist political and sociological ideals or problems within a frequently realistic and naturalistic mode. Richard Wright was indisputably a central figure in this Black Chicago Renaissance. Wright provided a major impetus for the movement in his essay "Blueprint for Negro Writing," published in 1937 in the seminal issue of *New Challenge* coedited by Wright, Marian Minus, and Dorothy West (yet another connection to the Harlem Renaissance). In it, Wright clearly sought to distance himself and other contemporary writers from what he saw as the failure of the Harlem Renaissance, even as he built in part upon that movement's stylistic and cultural legacy. Wright replaced the Harlem writers' penchant for atavism and optimism in relation to the ability of art to achieve social equality with political activism and a naturalistic emphasis on the modern discipline of urban sociology as a tool for social understanding. Here the influence of Robert Park, Horace Cayton, St. Clair Drake, Louis Wirth, E. Franklin Frazier, and the Chicago School of Sociology is both broad and deep.

But Wright was not alone. A South Side Writers Group consisting of nearly twenty writers including Wright, Margaret Walker, Frank Marshall Davis, Fern Gayden, Theodore Ward, Arna Bontemps, Edward Bland, and others met and wrote regularly. They sometimes met up with each other at meetings of various leftist organizations such as the John Reed Clubs and the League of American Writers, or at the Illinois Writers' Project (Bontemps, Wright, Walker, Fenton Johnson, and Katherine Dunham) or the Federal Theatre Project (Ward) of the Works Project Administration. Important publishing outlets such as the journals *Abbott's Monthly*, *The Anvil*, *The New Anvil*, *The Left Front*, *Negro Digest*, Alice Browning and Fern Gayden's *Negro Story*, *The New Masses*, and Harriet Monroe's *Poetry* (where Margaret Danner eventually became an assistant editor), as well as newspapers such as the *Chicago Bee*, the *Chicago Sun*, the *Chicago Defender*, and the *Chicago Whip* allowed these writers and other social, cultural, and political commentators to espouse their ideas. The Rosenwald Fellowships administered by Edwin Embree provided many writers with financial sponsorship that allowed them, like those involved with the Illinois Writers' Project, to focus on writing. Some figures straddled the literature and visual arts worlds (painters Margaret Goss Burroughs and Archibald Motley), while others straddled literature and music (rent party–style pianist, journalist, and author Dan Burley and novelist William Attaway) or literature and dance (choreographer and author Katherine Dunham). Attaway branched out to write scripts for radio, television, and film. Gordon Parks, a true "Renaissance man" who emerged from the Chicago Renaissance, counted among his genres not only poetry and the novel, but journalism, photography, screenwriting, film directing, ballet, and composing.

This burgeoning local cultural scene assisted in the cross-pollination. The Black Chicago Renaissance was at its core a movement in which a variety of genres and artistic media were in high gear, with no particular genre or medium in the ascendancy. Attempts to separate them out can be dangerous as well, and though our focus here is on writers of the Chicago Renaissance, certainly artists from other arenas also deserve attention, because they are crucial to our understanding of the time and place. Music has been singled out as a genre for inclusion here, in particular because its frequent use of words or texts connects it with the words of our writers. Certainly other artistic genres could well be represented here, too, but space considerations helped produce the decision to explore only the music in detail. There was a strong classical music contingent in the city, including the "all colored" composers concerts organized by William Hackney (1914–16), Nora Holt's founding of the National Association of Negro Musicians (1919), and N. Clark Smith's *Negro Folk Suite* (1924) among the earlier manifestations. Such composers as Margaret Bonds and Florence B. Price also gained prominent reputations in Chicago. In the gospel field, Chicago hosted the songs of William Roberts, Charles Henry Pace, Sallie Martin, Thomas A. Dorsey, Eugene Smith, Mahalia Jackson, the Soul Stirrers, the Caravans, the Lucy Smith Singers, and the Staple Singers. In the blues, the works of architects of the 1930s urban blues Big Bill Broonzy, Tampa Red, Memphis Minnie, Sonny Boy Williamson, and Georgia White, boogie-woogie pianist Albert Ammons, and 1950s electric blues pioneer Muddy Waters, among many others, developed distinctive and burgeoning local scenes. The jazz of pioneers Louis Armstrong, Erskine Tate, Eddie South, and Earl "Fatha" Hines, and such 1940s successors as Red Saunders, Nat Cole, Earl Hines, Budd Johnson, Billy Eckstine, Gene Ammons, and Trummy Young has certainly echoed throughout the history of jazz. And the performances of the American Negro Music Festival were also an important part of a flowering Chicago music scene. There were, in fact, a variety of groups that recorded or appeared under names that included references to Chicago in the title: the Chicago Black Swans, the Chicago Blues Dance Orchestra, the Chicago De Luxe Orchestra, the Chicago Five, the Chicago Footwarmers, the Chicago Hottentots, the Chicago Rhythm Kings, the Chicago Sanctified Singers, the Chicago Sheiks, the Chicagoans, the Windy City Jazzers, and the Windy City Rhythm Kings, among others. There were also some three dozen recorded jazz songs with "Chicago" or "windy city" at the beginning of their titles, not to mention all of those songs that contained references internally. With important labels with studios in Chicago, such as the major outlets Victor/Bluebird, Columbia, and Decca, plus smaller labels like Aristocrat (later Chess), Parkway, JOB, Vee Jay, Chance, and others, the city was well prepared to record its major and minor stars.

And showcase them. One might enumerate the contributors to the visual arts in Chicago at the time as well, such as sculptor Richmond Barthé, who studied in the 1920s in Chicago before moving to New York and becoming associated with the Harlem Renaissance. William Carter, Eldzier Cortor, Charles Davis, Ramon Gabriel, Archibald Motley, Margaret Burroughs, Gordon Parks, Charles Sebree, Elizabeth Catlett, and Charles White, many of whom were associated with the South Side Community Arts Center (opened in December 1940) and/ or worked on Federal Arts Projects, were among others on the active visual arts scene. The Art Institute of Chicago was a drawing card for many African American artists, including William MacKnight Farrow, Charles Clarence Dawson, Richmond Barthé, Willard Motley, and Ellis Wilson, some of whom made their careers in New York after studying in Chicago. Furthermore, in addition to the December 1917 *Paintings by Negro Artists* exhibition and the Chicago Art League exhibition at the Wabash Avenue YMCA in 1923, and numerous Art Institute of Chicago exhibitions, it was in Chicago in 1940 that the "Art of the American Negro, 1851–1940" opened at the American Negro Exposition. Mention should be made, too, of Katherine Dunham and Talley Beatty, who were the most prominent representatives of African American dancers in Chicago; and Sadie and Mary Bruce both had dance studios in Bronzeville as well. Were there more space in this volume, chapters would be devoted to these important visual artists and dancers/choreographers as well.

This large community of African Americans explored their diverse interests in a metropolis that was teeming with excitement, talent, and diversity in a broad array of fields, employing variously the aesthetics and style not only of the African American vernacular, but also a Eurocentric aesthetic, and a hybrid blend of the two. That is not to say that there weren't hard times in Chicago, especially in the Black Belt. Rampant poverty, vice, disease, and housing inadequacies explained the title of the Sparks Brothers 1933 blues recording "Chicago's Too Much For Me," and Sonny Boy Williamson's determination in his 1938 recording "Down South Blues" to leave Chicago and go back where the weather fit his clothes. But the gathering of talent in this urban context in Chicago helped give birth to some of the most exciting and diverse cultural developments of the postwar era.

Clearly, the Black Chicago Renaissance was not a totally unorganized movement, even though it did not have the uneasy but palpable cohesiveness of the Harlem Renaissance. Neither was it composed of only a few towering figures. And the variety of popular and critical successes experienced by various writers makes it somewhat difficult to understand the relative paucity of critical material on Chicago Renaissance writers. For example, Wright's *Native Son* was a Book of the Month Club selection in 1940; Walker's *For My People* won the Yale Younger Poets Award in 1942; Brooks's *Annie Allen* won the Pulitzer Prize for poetry in 1949; and Hansberry's *A Raisin in the Sun* won the New York Drama Critics' Circle Award in 1959—all firsts for African American writers. Two of Willard Motley's novels, *Knock on Any Door* (1947) and *Let No Man Write My Epitaph* (1958) were made into major Hollywood movies. Yerby's thirty-three novels sold more than 55 million copies. Gordon Parks was the first African American to work for *Vogue*, *Life*, the Farm Security Administration, and the Office of War Information. Dunham danced, choreographed, and directed on Broadway, and was the Metropolitan Opera's first black choreographer. It is way past time to revisit the era from the perspective of both the forest and the trees, to correct what has been an oversight of the scope and cohesion of the era. Waters Turpin termed Chicago, ironically, a Canaan. The blues song "Sweet Home Chicago," recorded first in 1937, called it "the land of California" or the "eleven light city." The pop song "Chicago" bragged that evangelist Billy Sunday couldn't "shut [it] down." You might be able to lose the blues in Chicago, but you could always find them again, especially in the Black Belt, and in those artists who came to, were born and raised in, lived in, or left it.

Discussing his return, Frank Marshall Davis asserted that he came back to Chicago in late 1934 for "an increased pace of life, a more dedicated commitment to writing and publishing his poetry, and an immersion into the cultural life he so desperately missed when he was in Atlanta" (Tidwell xviii–xix). Indeed, these elements are important to many writers whose work emerged from a milieu that offered the benefits of urban energy, increased media outlets, and a contemporary cultural vision combining a mix of rural and urban artistic sensibilities with a sense of social imperatives that helped strong art scenes to thrive there. With a heritage of social protest and class consciousness born of an active Socialist and Communist history, Chicago provided an opportunity for black writers to form their own enclaves with a racially based sense of artistry, mission, and commitment, as well as mingle with white writers with similar political ideals and visions. Of course, the gritty realism and naturalistic vision of past Chicago writers, and an urban environment that continued to emphasize the grueling nature of urban existence, reinforced the importance of exploring avenues of class consciousness and social protest, all of which was additionally fueled by the presence of the Chicago School of Sociologists. Rooting literature in sociological ideas and theories both came naturally out of such circumstances and was the result of studious sociopolitical research that helped writers envision and generate their art. The Illinois Writers' Project offered some networking and organizational ties through the Federal Writers' Project and The Federal Theatre Project that helped writers associate with each other as well. Although not all writers evinced these characteristics equally, surely they were touched by the distinctive milieu of Chicago.

The African American literary landscape is much different today because of the aesthetic, focus, and achievement of these writers. The major prizes and attention first won by black writers like Wright, Brooks, and Lorraine Hansberry associated with Chicago has helped bring attention to African American literature, cracking barriers that helped force Americans to take black writers more seriously ideologically and aesthetically. Their syntheses and translations of the African American social, cultural, and political experience into enduring depictions of the struggle to survive, comprehend, and thrive, from Wright's Bigger Thomas to Hansberry's Youngers, exemplify the literature of value that emerged from the crucible of Chicago. The voicing of black rage and portraits of the dehumanizing effects of racism in Wright's work caused critic Nathan Scott to name Wright the presiding genius of the new black urban poetry (323). Cultural critic Larry Neal explored and praised the validity of Wright's assertions in "Blueprint For Negro Writing," asserting that Wright attempted to "lay a theoretical foundation on which future Afro-American writing could be based" (29), and Amiri Baraka has written praising Wright's work and the ways it expressed the views of blacks concerning northern and southern environments. And it was not only Wright whose influence could be felt by subsequent writers, as the influence on and connection to the Black Arts Movement of Gwendolyn Brooks demonstrates. Indeed, James Smethurst asserts that "many from the Popular Front cultural world remained active in Chicago, if on a less prominent level, providing much of the ground on which the Black Arts movement in Chicago would grow" (228). Just as the Harlem Renaissance had laid the groundwork for the Black Chicago movement, so the lingering influence of the Black Chicago Renaissance put elements in place to assist in the birth and growth of the Black Arts Movement.

The Black Chicago Renaissance was not a time when "the Negro was in vogue," as Langston Hughes wrote of Harlem in the 1920s, but it was a time when literature made bold statements that expressed the period in both a timely and timeless fashion, and prepared the way for the literature of the Black Arts Movement and beyond through its bold confrontations, sociological explorations, aesthetic assertions, and unflinching depictions of the lives of African Americans. By the end of the 1950s, many of the writers associated with the Black Chicago Renaissance were no longer in Chicago. Some were dead (Ed Bland, Fenton Johnson); some had moved to other sections of the country (Margaret Walker, Margaret Danner, Arna Bontemps); some had moved out of the country (Wright to France, Frank Marshall Davis to Hawaii, then a U.S. territory). Of the major writers, Gwendolyn Brooks remained to carry the torch, reenergized creativity in the world of Medgar and Malcolm, the Blackstone Rangers, the Wall of Respect, and Broadside Press in Detroit. However, the importance of the spirit and accomplishments of the black writers of the Black Chicago Renaissance, now receiving greater attention from critics who are seeing beyond the Harlem of the phrase "Harlem Renaissance," will become far more apparent as this volume and others like it explore their contributions to American culture. From the focus established by Robert Bone's seminal article on the Black Chicago Renaissance to the groundbreaking studies being contributed today by Bill Mullen, Anne Meis Knupfer, and Davarian Baldwin, writers of the Black Chicago Renaissance are poised to reclaim their unfortunately neglected importance as literary figures who can stand with Langston Hughes and Zora Neale Hurston, Amiri Baraka and Sonia Sanchez in the annals of African American literature.

Works Cited

Baldwin, Davarian. *Chicago's New Negroes: Modernity, the Great Migration, and Black Urban Life*. Durham: University of North Carolina Press, 2007.

Bone, Robert. "Richard Wright and the Chicago Renaissance." *Callaloo* 28 (Summer 1968): 446–68.

Knupler, Anne Meis. *The Chicago Black Renaissance and Women's Activism*. Urbana: University of Illinois Press, 2006.

Mullen, Bill. *Popular Fronts: Chicago and African-American Cultural Politics, 1935–1946*. Urbana: University of Illinois Press, 1999.

Neal, Larry. "The Black Writer's Role I: Richard Wright." In *Visions of a Liberated Future*. New York: Thunder's Mouth Press, 1989.

Scott, Nathan. "Black Literature." In *Harvard Guide to Contemporary American Writing*, edited by Daniel Hoffman. Cambridge: Belknap Press, 1979.

Smethurst, James. *The Black Arts Movement: Literary Nationalism in the 1960s and 1970s*. Chapel Hill: University of North Carolina Press, 2005.

Tidwell, John Edgar, ed. *Writings of Frank Marshall Davis: A Voice of the Black Press*. Jackson: University Press of Mississippi, 2007.

ROBERT S. ABBOTT
(November 28, 1868–February 29, 1940)
Charlene Regester

Robert S. Abbott was editor and publisher of the *Chicago Defender*—one of the longest surviving, widely circulated, and politically active black newspapers in the United States. Abbott was a pivotal force at the turn of the twentieth century because of the power and influence wielded by his paper. He emerged during the first Chicago Literary Renaissance, a movement that was initially launched by white literary figures from around 1912 through the 1930s and included those such as Carl Sandburg, Theodore Dreiser, Edgar Lee Masters, Sherwood Anderson, Edna Ferber, Willa Cather, and Upton Sinclair. A second wave of this movement dominated by black literary figures occurred from the 1930s through the 1950s and included those such as Richard Wright, Willard Motley, Lorraine Hansberry, Langston Hughes (more generally associated with the Harlem Renaissance), Gwendolyn Brooks, and others. Abbott evolved during the first phase of the renaissance, paralleling his white contemporaries in that he shared their vision of radicalism while at the same time being drawn to the more rural life and settings from which he had escaped. Interestingly, some of the literary figures associated with the early movement such as Dreiser and Sandburg had begun their writing careers as journalists prior to launching their literary authorships. Yet, for the black literary figures who emerged in the second phase of this movement, Abbott's newspaper became an important voice in foregrounding issues that plagued the black community, established a sense of race consciousness, and instilled a sense of pride in blacks—themes that would be reverberated in the works of black writers of the Chicago Renaissance. Abbott's newspaper, the *Defender*, and his short-lived magazine, *Abbott's Monthly*, were greatly influenced by this movement as much as they were vehicles that helped to shape the doctrines articulated in the works of the black literary figures produced by this movement.

Abbott established his newspaper to appeal to the masses of blacks who had fled the South and headed northward to seek a better life. His newspaper was designed to elevate these new black immigrants, to give voice to those disenfranchised, and to mobilize the black population facing lives of uncertainty. Promoting social and political change, even while espousing positions that were sometimes unpopular, Abbott had a tremendous impact on the evolution of black progress and development, not only in Chicago but throughout the country.

Robert S. Abbott was born to former slaves Thomas Abbott and Flora Butler Abbott, on November 28, 1868. As a slave, Thomas had been a butler to Captain Charles Stevens of Frederica, Georgia, whose family plantation had been established by Stevens's father in 1784, on St. Simons Island, Georgia. Granted his freedom, Thomas Abbott migrated to Savannah, Georgia, and in 1867 he met and married Flora Butler (born December 4, 1847 to former slaves Harriet and Jacob Butler of Savannah). Returning to Frederica, one year later, Flora and Thomas had Robert (28 November 1868). (Roi Ottley claims that Robert was born November 24, 1870, yet the Parish Register of St. Stephens Episcopal Church where he was baptized reports that he was born November 28, 1868.) Within a year of Robert's birth, Thomas died suddenly of tuberculosis. It was not until 1928 that Robert learned of his father's actual burial place in Frederica, where he erected a monument at the gravesite.

Following Thomas's death, Flora returned to Savannah with Robert, but because of the strained interfamily relationship with the Abbotts, she had to seek legal counsel to retain custody. At this point, John Hermann Henry Sengstacke, a German mulatto immigrant, was also in Savannah, reclaiming his inheritance left by his white father and black mother. Sengstacke assisted Flora and paid for a white attorney to defend her in her custody dispute. On July 26, 1874, Sengstacke became Flora's second husband, and Robert's stepfather; Robert became Robert Sengstacke Abbott. The new family moved to Yamacraw, a black settlement containing property previously owned by John's white father.

John first worked as a translator for the Savannah *Morning News* until his racial identity was revealed. Next, John pursued teaching and preaching and became a missionary in Woodville's Pilgrim Congregational Church in 1876. In Woodville, a suburb of Savannah, Robert spent much of his early years with his new siblings (Alexander, Mary, Rebecca, Johnnah, and Eliza).

At first, young Robert worked as an errand boy at a local grocery and then he worked for *The Echo*, a Savannah newspaper. As an adolescent in preparation for college, Abbott attended the Beach Institute in Savannah (started by the Freedman's Bureau and named after the editor of the *Scientific American*) and worked as a printer's assistant on a local daily newspaper. Encountering some of the most blatant forms of intraracial prejudice, Robert transferred to Claflin University in Orangeburg, South Carolina, on October 6, 1887; six months later, he applied to Hampton Institute, and while awaiting admission, returned to work with *The Echo* and wrote for the *Savannah Tribune*. In 1889, when his stepfather was launching the *Woodville Times*, Abbott entered Hampton Institute, intent upon becoming a printer. While at Hampton, Robert became a member of their quartet, joined the debating society, and founded the Georgia Boys Association. In 1893, he completed his training as a printer; he finished his academic work some three years later in 1896 and became a lifelong member of the alumni association.

After graduation, Robert returned to Woodville, assisted with the publication of Sengstacke's paper, and taught at a nearby school. In the fall of 1897, Robert decided to study law. Enrolling as Robert Sengstacke Abbott, he entered the Kent College of Law in Chicago—a place where he had observed black progress unlike what he had witnessed in the South. In May of 1899, he received a Bachelor of Law degree, but he was never admitted to the Illinois bar. Discouraged from practicing law in Chicago because of racial ostracism, Robert ventured to Topeka, Kansas, where he again met racial obstacles. He returned to Chicago, but this time with a contract to distribute copies of the *Topeka Plaindealer* newspaper, and received help from a Chicago politician, Louis B. Anderson, who assisted Robert in obtaining employment with the Loop printing house of Chicago.

On June 23, 1904, Robert's career was briefly interrupted when his stepfather, John Sengstacke, died of nephritis. Abbott, desiring to carry out his stepfather's mission by providing legal counsel to those who remained deprived while continuing to provide education to indigent blacks, returned to the South. Having gathered the necessary funds from his siblings and obtaining assistance from a former teacher, he established the Sengstacke Memorial Military and Mechanical Academy in the Pilgrim Academy, formerly operated by his stepfather.

Returning to Chicago shortly thereafter, Robert pursued his dream of starting his own newspaper. First working as a printer and typesetter for local papers, he ingratiated himself with Chicago's social world and joined the Choral Study Club, which proved to be central to the establishment of his paper. He boarded with Henrietta Lee (a widow and mother of three and a strong supporter when he established his paper). Renting office space from a local businessman, and relying on his landlord's daughter for assistance, Abbott printed the first issue of the *Chicago Defender*, May 5, 1905, with the "oft-repeated pledge that his paper would be a defender of his race, [James] Scott [an associate suggested the name] 'The Defender.' [As] Abbott [added] the word 'Chicago,' the paper acquired the name that was to become a torch to thousands."[1]

From May 1905, the *Defender* was published continuously, and it is still being published today. Examining its issues over the years (the earliest extant issue of the paper is September 16, 1905), its format and style paralleled that of the *Woodville Times* started by Sengstacke and the early issues were devoted to "community and Negro achievement."[2] According to Ottley, "If Negroes had problems of a social or racial character, they were not apparent in the *Defender*; nor were there any accounts of accidents, suicides, murders, trials, or incidents of racial discrimination, lynching or conflict—sensational news which was eventually to distinguish Abbott's journalism."[3] Initially, Abbott intended to appeal to the 40,000 blacks who resided in Chicago and printed some 300 copies of a 4-page paper, in handbill size. Until 1912, Abbott served as writer, editor, journalist, and distributor; then the paper expanded to newsstand sales. Struggling to survive financially, he had to move the office to his landlady's home. In later years, Abbott placed the operations of his now expanded paper into that same building, but on the second and third floor, attributing his success to this location.

Not until 1909, when Abbott "launched his first muck-raking crusade did his paper actually begin to catch on with the public,"[4] and eventually outstrip his competitors such as the *Broad Ax, Illinois Idea, Conservator, Indianapolis Freeman*, and *New York Age*. Abbott's exposure of the crime and corruption that infiltrated Chicago—as when prostitution, supported by alliances that existed between politicians and criminals, invaded black neighborhoods—now took a "stand," and solidified the black community. "The *Defender* utilized the 'wages of sin' theme in several editorial cartoons. One depicted a venomous snake bearing the name 'Social Degeneration' as it uncoiled itself menacingly from a can of beer."[5] In opposing such degradation and working to prevent the moral decay and decline of the community, Abbott recognized that his paper had become a vehicle of empowerment.

As circulation increased, Abbott solicited the assistance of additional (but unpaid) workers, such as R. F. Spriggs (assistant editor), L. N. Hogatt (cartoonist) and H. H. Byron (theatrical editor). He also recruited community members including Henry Middleton (covering political and social events), Julius Nelthrop Avendorph (sports reports), Noah Thompson (news from Los Angeles), Fon Holly and Langston Mitchell (cartoonists), Alfred Anderson (editorials), Frank George (news relevant to blacks outside of Chicago), and W. Allison Sweeney (exploring information about the antiblack politicians in Chicago).

The *Defender* had become a centrifugal force of the Black Press, which by 1910 totaled some 288 periodicals throughout the United States, with a combined circulation of some half million. Because of the *Defender* in particular and the Black Press in general, illiteracy rates in 1910 had declined from 44.5 percent in 1900 to 30.4 percent. Expanding his operations, in 1910 Abbott added J. Hockley Smiley to his staff as managing editor. By adopting Chicago newspapers' daily paper style and introducing techniques of yellow journalism, the *Defender* achieved a new level of success. Smiley encouraged Abbott to change the format of the paper, adopt banner headlines, provide a sensational treatment of news, and express black concerns and fears. Abbott's competitors reacted with contempt to these changes—for example, his use of headlines printed in red ink—but it was these changes that had increased circulation, and his paper was hailed as the "the world's greatest weekly."[6] Despite these changes, Abbott did not deviate from his basic principles that included eliminating discrimination; lobbying for black admission into trade unions; supporting black representation in the president's cabinet; promoting equality in public service positions, government jobs, and schools; abolishing lynching; and securing the full enfranchisement of all Americans. It is such principles that would later permeate the writings of black literary figures. Smiley encouraged the paper to address relevant issues: for example, how blacks should refer to themselves—Negro, Colored, Afro-American, Aframerican, African, or Black. They often resolved this dilemma by employing the term "Race," though the paper would use many of the aforementioned terms interchangeably as long as they did not diminish the dignity of the race.

Adopting this new format and exploiting issues of relevance to the black community propelled the paper to explore a wide range of topics. One topic was the July 4, 1910, victory of the first black heavyweight champion of the world, Jack Johnson, over his white opponent, Jim Jeffries. The *Defender* called Johnson a symbol of black defiance to counter the white supremacists' views. Although the paper exacerbated the divide between blacks and whites and reportedly encouraged altercations between the two groups, the paper gained in popular appeal and found Johnson newsworthy throughout his career.

By 1915, increasing newspaper sales again forced Abbott to expand his operations. He hired Phil Jones, Fay Young, Sylvester Russell, and others and began a crusade to defend the black screen image. When *The Birth of a Nation* (1915), a motion picture based on *The Klansman* authored by Thomas Dixon and produced by D. W. Griffith, was released, the *Defender* played an active role in the protests staged to halt the picture's exhibition and reported on riots erupting in many northern cities. Among those who joined the *Defender* in publicly denouncing the film was Jane Addams, the prominent white Chicagoan who had established the Hull House, which was designed to improve the plight of the impoverished.

During this same year, the *Defender* reported on the death of Booker T. Washington, one of Abbott's mentors. And although he supported Washington, he did not alienate Washington's adversary W. E. B. DuBois, choosing rather to establish a compromise between the two. As Ottley pointed out, "While Washington urged Negroes 'to cast down your buckets where you are'—meaning remain in the South—Abbott cried: 'Come North, where there is more humanity, some justice and fairness!' And while DuBois sought to create a 'talented tenth,' or educated elite, to lead the race, Abbott declared himself, 'for the masses, not the classes!'"[7]

Interested in the women's suffrage movement, Abbott crusaded to have black women become members of the Chicago police force. By 1916 three black women had passed the police examination and one was eventually appointed to the police force. This action was part of the *Defender's* overall endorsement of women's suffrage as it urged black women to become more involved in this movement.

Centering itself in the struggle for equal rights, in 1916, the *Defender* expressed outrage at the fact that members of the Tenth Cavalry Regiment (an all-black regiment) had been subjected to hostility in Houston, Texas, on their return from Mexico. The paper warned that race riots might ensue. A rampage did occur in Houston, when black troops of the Twenty-fourth Infantry Regiment engaged in an altercation with whites; whites were killed, blacks were hanged, and other blacks were imprisoned for life. The reporting on this event allegedly increased the paper's circulation by some 20,000, a number that continued to increase with the *Defender's* exposure of atrocities such as the lynchings of blacks, and with the encouraging of blacks to defend themselves. In addition to such reporting, Abbott's practical management strategies such as hiring newsboys to distribute his paper, further heightened circulation figures.

Abbott's campaign to encourage blacks to leave the South and migrate northward was endorsed by Pullman porters, dining car waiters, and stage performers. According to Metz Lochard (Abbott's first foreign editor), "The South was a bad place, Abbott told them, and he flooded his columns with vivid descriptions of the most distasteful aspects of living in the South. Abbott dared to articulate in print what southern Negroes were afraid to whisper. He gave them courage to acknowledge their dissatisfaction, and some sense of security by telling them that others were championing their cause and could give them protection in the city that was the home of the *Defender*."[8] With 65,000 blacks migrating to Chicago between 1917 and 1918, its black population jumped from 40,000 to 150,000 within a short period of time, causing whites to view Abbott and his paper as subversive.

When Abbott lobbied against the paucity of black soldiers during WW I, the War Department itself investigated the paper's policies. Although the newspaper surveillance began earlier "in the fall of 1916 when a reporter for the *New Orleans Times-Picayune*, probing allegations that the Chicago weekly was inciting blacks against whites, passed his suspicions on to the Bureau of Investigation, . . . the *Defender* immediately came under renewed scrutiny once the United States declared war on Germany on 6 April 1917."[9] Interrogated by the Bureau's Chicago office, Abbot claimed that despite his exposure of racial atrocities, there was no intent of disloyalty to the government and that he had encouraged blacks to purchase war bonds. Abbott's paper by now had developed a nationwide reputation.

On September 10, 1918, Abbott married a widow from Athens, Georgia, Helen Thornton Morrison. A woman thirty years his junior, she was so fair in complexion that she was often mistaken for white. Their childless marriage lasted fourteen years.

In 1919, the "Red Summer" ensued in Chicago—heightened racial tensions and lynchings resulted in riots as blacks competed with whites for low-wage jobs. Riots were precipitated by a black swimmer crossing the racial line in Chicago's Lake Michigan, being stoned by whites, and drowning. A series of riots occurred and involved some 10,000 persons and lasted for nearly twelve days. The politically astute *Defender* assumed the authority to speak *for*, as well as *to*, the African American community and called for blacks to engage in restraint. The liberal *Daily News*, by commissioning Carl Sandburg, "attempted to speak for the assured political and cultural leadership of a white post-immigrant community."[10] In a Commission on Race Relations (viewed with suspicion by DuBois), the Governor, Frank O. Lowden, appointed Abbott among others to examine the issues that caused these riots.

In the year following the riots (1920), the *Defender*'s 30,000 circulation represented the largest circulation ever achieved by a black paper, with two-thirds of its circulation outside of Chicago. The *Defender* expanded to thirty-two pages, with city and national editions. To accommodate its expanding operations, Abbott purchased a three-story building that had been a former synagogue and hired Clarence Brown (white) as plant foreman. Brown then established a union shop (a union that refused admission to blacks) and hired a crew of white workers, a move that initially fared well but would later cause anguish for Abbott, even though his paper in 1921 was evaluated at $500,000, with sixty-eight paid workers and branch offices in New York, Detroit, Toledo, Louisville, Philadelphia, Los Angeles, and New Orleans, in addition to foreign offices in London and Paris.

With an ever-expanding work force, Abbott continued broadening his publishing, in content as well as circulation. Each decade he concentrated on the focus and issues of the period—social, political, and cultural. As for the political, during this period, the *Defender* paid particular attention to Marcus Garvey, founder of the UNIA (Universal Negro Improvement Association) and *The Negro World*. Garvey's views on black nationalism and his back-to-Africa movement appealed to millions of blacks disillusioned with race as it existed in the United States. Though in some respects, Garvey and Abbott shared many similarities as well as differences, when Abbott suspected and implied that Garvey paralleled another black leader who had defrauded blacks with his scheme to return blacks to Africa, there was a sharp split. Garvey filed a libel suit against Abbott for one million dollars but, as Ottley pointed out, "The New York courts awarded him [Garvey] a one-cent victory, but he was obliged to pay court costs."[11] When Garvey tried to launch his campaign in Chicago, he was promptly arrested for selling stock in the Black Star Steamship Line; this was a violation of Illinois law. Garvey accused Abbott of conspiring in his arrest; later the *Defender* reported on Garvey's legal struggles and his deportation.

Meanwhile, Abbott, now a self-made millionaire, enjoyed many luxuries, including a Rolls Royce (an automobile disallowed to blacks). He also traveled to South America, about which he wrote a series of articles for his paper. Abbott became one of the few black journalists in the United States to cover this region. According to Lochard, "He . . . indulged in somewhat fanciful sentimentality in recalling his trips to Europe and Latin America. He especially liked the fact that these people did not refer to him as a 'Negro,' and he wrote glowingly of the 'unity, peace, and contentment' that resulted, he reasoned, from the lack of racial distinctions. He wishfully generalized from his limited experiences, but he was justified in his accusation that the United States discriminated more abominably than any nation outside of perhaps South Africa."[12]

Abbott's successes were often followed by failures and disappointments, some resulting from financial abuses by staff. He was forced to dismiss members of his staff including his manager, Phil Jones, to whom he had entrusted his paper's operation while he temporarily abandoned publication of his magazine. But he recovered from these setbacks, and continued to publish issues relevant to the black community.

As for the cultural aspect, the 1920s that coincided with the first Chicago Literary Renaissance, and specifically, the 1920–25 period, was a beginning of the rise in and acknowledgment of black writing and black films—the black literary figures authoring the books upon which the films were scripted; the black actors and actresses taking lead roles; and the black producers, publicists, and theater-owners paving their way. It was at this time that black author Charles W. Chesnutt's novel, *The House Behind the Cedars* (1900), was being produced by black filmmaker, Oscar Micheaux, and was being serialized in the *Defender* as a promotional device for the similarly titled film.

The *Chicago Defender* was also instrumental in influencing literary figure Willard Motley, a native of Chicago who, at the age of thirteen, submitted a short story to the *Defender* that was printed in some three installments in 1922. Later, Motley as a youngster, wrote the Bud Bulliken column designed to appeal to the *Defender*'s young readers from 1922 to 1924. Some of his columns reflected his race pride as well as an acknowledgment of human suffering. That Abbott's paper provided such literary figures with the opportunity to cultivate their writing talent speaks to Abbott's support of black literary figures in the Chicago Renaissance.

Black authors, essayists, dramatists, poets; black actors, actresses, filmmakers; singers, musicians; artists—all took their place alongside their white colleagues, equals in talent, and equals as participants, to give rise to the consecutive movements of the Chicago Renaissance. And the *Chicago Defender* was there to take note, to report, to disseminate their views.

In the 1925–30 period, the *Defender* continued to focus on political issues as well as turned its attention to the Pullman porters' struggle for equitable wages. In 1925, A. Philip Randolph attempted to organize the Pullman porters and formed the Brotherhood of Sleeping Car Porters. When reports surfaced that bribes were offered to civic leaders and ministers to oppose the union organization, Randolph criticized the *Defender* for its antiunion policy. Later, Abbott retreated from his original position and supported the porters' union while applauding Randolph's efforts, and thus, extending the *Defender*'s power and influence.

It was during this period, that the *Defender* noted the achievements of those associated with the Chicago Renaissance as well as the Harlem arts movement and extensively covered prominent artists such as Josephine Baker and Paul Robeson, as well as literary figures Motley and Langston Hughes, who was gaining prominence as a writer publishing his first book of poetry, *The Weary Blues* (1926), *Fine Clothes to the Jew* (1927), and the novel, *Not Without Laughter* (1930). These artists and literary figures paved the wave for a subsequent generation.

Emulating these artists whose writings were often informed by their travels, Abbott interrupted his career to engage in travel. In June 1929, he and his wife toured Europe; Abbott reported discrimination (being barred from hotels) but also pleasant experiences, such as laying a wreath at the tomb of the Unknown Soldier at the Arc de Triomphe in Paris. Yet, when he returned to the United States in October 1929, Abbott's publishing enterprise had become a victim of the 1929 stock market crash.

The years 1930–35 were troubling for Abbott, despite his new magazine venture, *Abbott's Monthly* (a forerunner to *Ebony Magazine*), which achieved an initial circulation of some 100,000. "It contained eight poems; four lengthy, illustrated romance stories; fifteen well-written 'Special Features' articles of varying lengths; and numerous photographs, illustrations, news items, book reviews, and bawdy jokes."[13] Some of the magazine's prominent contributors were Arthur Schomburg, bibliophile and collector of black history; Salem Tutt Whitney, stage performer; and Dr. C. Leon Wilson, physician. Later issues featured works by attorney Clarence Darrow, Langston Hughes, and Chester Himes. The first issue of the magazine was dedicated to Abbott's stepfather and dissolved after some thirty-six issues—due to the impact of the depression and, some argue, to its overzealous mission. This decline was similarly witnessed by the newspaper, because between 1930 and 1932, the *Defender*'s circulation decreased from 200,000 to less than 100,000 and the paper lost money for the first time since its widespread growth. At the same time, Abbott was diagnosed with tuberculosis and on September 21, 1932, his mother, Flora, died.

All of these difficulties coincided with Abbott's divorce from his first wife, Helen, finalized June 26, 1933. The *Defender* reported the costs: Helen's award, the largest award ever made to a black woman, was $50,000 cash, an automobile, furnishings from their mansion, and $5,000 in lawyer's fees. Within a year, Abbott married Edna Brown Denison, a widow (former wife of a distinguished army officer) and the mother of five. Abbott's divorce also signaled a final-ditch effort at magazine publishing; *Abbott's Weekly* and *Illustrated News*, initially a sixteen-page weekly publication, ceased to exist after March 1934.

Forced to invest $260,000 of his own money in 1935, Abbott kept the *Defender* financially solvent. The paper's financial problems were compounded when it became known that while blacks remained unemployed at the *Defender*, the paper continued to employ whites. This caused consternation for many, forcing Abbott to replace white workers with blacks. Added to this was Abbott's discovery that the paper's mismanagement of financial affairs had resulted in a $300,000 loss. Abbott then appointed his nephew, John H. H. Sengstacke, as vice president and treasurer, an appointment which proved vital to the *Defender's* continued existence.

The *Defender's* change in management did not cause it to shy away from political issues, reporting extensively on the Scottsboro Boys case (involving nine black males who were tried and convicted of raping two white women in Alabama). The Scottsboro case received considerable attention in the *Defender*, as the paper assumed that the judgment in this case was not just an indictment on these individuals but an indictment on the entire black race.

In this period, Abbott's paper continued to promote its political views, which often coincided with those of the literary figures who ushered in the Chicago Renaissance such as Hughes, Motley, Richard Wright, and Gwendolyn Brooks. To convey the importance of Abbott's influence on these literary figures, Hughes revealed that, "As a child in Kansas I grew up on the *Chicago Defender* and it awakened me in my youth to the problems which I and my race had to face in America. Its flaming headlines and indignant editorials did a great deal to make me the 'race man' which I later became, as expressed in my own attitudes and in my writing. Thousands and thousands of other young Negroes were, I am sure, also affected the same way by this militant and stirringly edited Chicago weekly."[14] Hughes, compelled to visit and interview the Scottsboro boys so that he could expose the racial injustice of this case, may have been influenced by the *Defender's* coverage of the case.

Although Hughes became a *Defender* columnist in 1942 after Abbott's leadership ended, he undoubtedly was influenced by the views of the paper. When Hughes accepted the offer from the *Defender* as a columnist (an association that continued until the early 1960s), his appointment served two purposes— one, to expose his writings to a broader audience and popularize his works and two, to provide a steady income to a black writer who did not have the financial opportunities afforded to white writers despite his literary success. It was as a columnist for the *Defender* that Hughes's political views resounded in the press, and he expanded the exposure of his artistic talent by introducing his well-known fictional character, Jesse B. Simple. Hughes utilized this character to articulate the views and concerns of the working class, which were not so frequently exposed in the daily press: "Through the voice of Simple, Hughes could convey the peculiar experience of being black in America while retaining the emotional distance that fiction allows, a distance perhaps necessary to alleviate some of the pain he felt in his own life."[15]

The *Defender* may have been equally influential in shaping the ideas and providing the social milieu from which Willard Motley's novel, *Knock on Any Door* (1947), which focused on an Italian immigrant facing a life of crime and juvenile delinquency, was conceived. Assuming a variety of jobs to sustain his career as a writer, Motley worked for the Chicago Housing Authority—an experience that also might have informed the circumstances faced by his protagonist in the novel and an experience likely exposed on the pages of Abbott's *Defender* providing the impetus for his novel. When the novel was transformed on screen, the film was covered extensively by the *Defender* and Motley was highlighted as a writer.

Such influence can be similarly observed in Richard Wright's novel, *Native Son* (1940), a novel for which Wright received widespread literary acclaim, a novel that also focused on a character paralyzed by the circumstances that surrounded him and a novel based on Wright's own experiences in Chicago. The *Defender* likely foregrounded the impoverished conditions reconstructed in Wright's novel and may have helped to expose the environment created in the novel. Aside from the newspaper's influence on Wright, the *Defender* provided reviews of Wright's controversial novel, reported on the novel when it became a play, covered the novel's film production, and frequently covered Wright's literary career. The thematic content of the novel often reverberated the ideas and principles articulated by the *Defender.*

Again, the newspaper's influence on shaping the ideological views of Gwendolyn Brooks (the first African American to win a Pulitzer Prize for poetry) cannot be understated. The *Defender* published some of her early works (her first seventy-five poems) between 1934 and 1936, attesting to the paper's commitment to exposing the talent of black literary figures as well as the determination to give voice to those literary figures associated with the Chicago Renaissance. Brooks's writings addressed many of the same issues and conveyed a similar political tone that the *Defender* appropriated and embraced.

During the 1930s, celebrating the paper's 35th anniversary, Abbott reiterated the objectives he had established for his paper by stating, "I have been relentless in my campaign against discrimination, lynching and industrial exploitation. I have initiated drives for legislative reforms, battered down regional or sectional segregation, censured members of the Race who would auction off our social and political rights, and condemned Nordism, Ku Klux Klanism and all who would pervert the masses by making the blacks the sick men of American democracy."[16] Abbott's paper continued its mission during this period, chronicling the careers of black men outstanding in their careers, such as black boxing champion Joe Louis and black jazz musicians Cab Calloway, Duke Ellington, Lionel Hampton, Louis Armstrong, and others—black men who impacted this period. The *Defender* covered the struggles of the NAACP (National Association for the Advancement of Colored People) and the Urban League, and it highlighted leaders such as Mary McLeod Bethune (who was appointed to a governmental position during the Franklin D. Roosevelt administration).

As he attempted to elevate the masses by delineating the struggles they endured, Abbott was equally critical of blacks themselves: "By telling them what whites did to them, he showed them who and what their common enemies were; by telling them what they were doing for themselves, he demonstrated how they should prepare for the fight."[17] Abbott was widely known for promoting race pride and for urging that black accomplishments and black history should be celebrated—a creed that he adhered to by celebrating black literary figures associated with the Chicago Renaissance.

Abbott, however, while celebratory of blacks, also faced scrutiny from those he defended: "Though he was frequently criticized for taking advertisements to straighten hair and lighten skin, he severely attacked the setting of a standard of desirability for white features."[18] Such outspokenness invited criticism of Abbott himself. Added to these criticisms, Abbott's class politics were questioned. Lochard contends that, "Despite his urgings for a strong class structure in the Negro community, his friends insist that Abbott remained a humble man close to the people all his life. But others, especially whites and upper-class Negroes, thought him a pompous, conspicuous spender, having a baronial home with a corps of servants and three automobiles."[19]

As Abbott's health declined, suffering with tuberculosis and Bright's disease, he finalized his last will and testament on December 19, 1939, and died some two months later, on February 29, 1940. Abbott's body lay in state at his home, 4742 South Parkway; his funeral was held at the Metropolitan Community Church in Chicago, and he was buried at the Lincoln cemetery. A large number of dignitaries—Governor Henry Horner; Mayor Edward J. Kelly; A. Philip Randolph; entertainer Noble Sissle; Dr. Emmett J. Scott, former secretary to Booker T. Washington; and NAACP Executive Secretary Walter White—served as honorary pallbearers.

As specified in his will, the *Defender* was continued by his nephew, John Sengstacke, who operated the paper from 1940 until his death in 1997. Under Sengstacke's leadership, the paper recovered from its financial troubles and even expanded its operations. In 1956 the paper became a daily newspaper representing the largest black-owned daily paper in the world. Sengstacke was also instrumental in establishing a chain of papers that included the *Gary Defender*,

National Defender, Tri-State Defender, Michigan Chronicle, Louisville Defender, Pittsburgh Courier, and *New York Age Defender.* On the newspaper's fiftieth anniversary, under the direction of Sengstacke the *Defender* serialized Roi Ottley's biography of Abbott, *Lonely Warrior.*

Sengstacke would continue the tradition established by his predecessor of commemorating, applauding, and showcasing the talent of black literary figures. Sengstacke featured many of the black literary figures who were contemporaries and beneficiaries of the Black Chicago Renaissance established by Hughes, Wright, Motley, and Brooks, and he noted the achievements of a later generation such as Lorraine Hansberry (popularized because of her award-winning play *A Raisin in the Sun,* 1959, based on black life in Chicago) and Chester Himes who, although a contributor to *Abbott's Monthly* in the 1930s, would not gain noticeable acclaim as a literary figure until the 1940s with his novels *If He Hollers Let Him Go* (1946) and *Lonely Crusade* (1947).

In establishing the newspaper, the *Defender,* which "combined the conservative tendencies of approval of middle-class values and self-help with radical agitation for civil and political rights,"[20] Abbott established himself as one of the single most important forces in journalism, particularly in the Black Press. Because of the power and influence wielded by his paper, he was a significant figure in the Chicago Literary Renaissance. As Abbott challenged the status quo, championed the cause of those disenfranchised, and heralded the achievements of blacks in the Chicago area, he created a significant impact on the Chicago political, social, and artistic landscape—the background for the Chicago Literary Renaissance. A citing of this movement, the Chicago Literary Renaissance, would be less complete without acknowledging the role that Abbott and his paper played in its development.

In addition to the local influence of the *Defender,* the newspaper was also greatly responsible for national changes and achievements of blacks in the early years of the twentieth century. The publishing enterprise that Abbott established in Chicago and developed over the course of his lifetime throughout the United States is a testament to his will, conviction, and intelligence. Thus, his own words signify his legacy as he stated, "I built up the *Defender* not only by printing all the news, but also by clinging to the ideas that success could be achieved by recording contemporary documents and public utterances, and by contending for social justice, political rights and industrial equity. . . . These are things that I have contended for and obtained at the cost of personal sacrifices, against cross current of opposition and intrigue from without and betrayal of trust from within. . . . For greater love hath no man than to lay down his life for his people and of humanity at large."[21]

Notes

1. Ottley, Roi. *The Lonely Warrior: The Life and Times of Robert S. Abbott.* Chicago: Henry Regnery Company, 1955, 87.

2. Ibid., 90.

3. Ibid.

4. Ibid., 97.

5. Stovall, Mary E. "The *Chicago Defender* in the Progressive Era." *Illinois Historical Journal* 83 (Autumn 1990): 166.

6. Ottley, *The Lonely Warrior*, 188.

7. Ibid., 126.

8. Lochard, Metz T. P. "Phylon Profile, XII: Robert S. Abbott—'Race Leader,'" *Phylon* 8, 2 (Second Quarter 1947): 125.

9. Kornweibel Jr., Theodore. *"Investigate Everything": Federal Efforts to Compel Black Loyalty during World War I.* Bloomington: Indiana University Press, 2002, 119–20.

10. Doreski, C. K. "From News to History: Robert Abbott and Carl Sandburg Read the 1919 Chicago Riot," *African American Review* 26.4 (Winter 1992): 638.

11. Ottley, 217.

12. Lochard, "*Phylon* Profile, XII" 129.

13. Amana, Harry. "Robert S. Abbott." In *Dictionary of Literary Biography* Vol. 91. Detroit: Gale Research Inc., 1990, 4.

14. De Santis, Christopher C., ed. *Langston Hughes and the Chicago Defender: Essays on Race, Politics, and Culture, 1942–62.* Urbana: University of Illinois Press, 1995, 13–14.

15. Ibid., 15.

16. Abbott, Robert S. "Looking Back," *Chicago Defender*, March 2, 1940, 8. This article is a reprint of that which appeared in the *Chicago Defender* on May 4, 1935, when the newspaper celebrated its thirtieth anniversary.

17. Lochard, "*Phylon* Profile, XII,'" 131–32.

18. Ibid., 131.

19. Ibid., 132.

20. Stovall, "The *Chicago Defender* in the Progressive Era," 172.

21. Abbott, "Looking Back," 8.

For Further Reading

"A Busy Life Come to a Close," *Chicago Defender*, March 2, 1940, 8.

Abbott, Robert, S. Robert S. Abbott Papers are primarily located in the *Chicago Defender* archives. Reports on Abbott appear in other collections such as at the University Archives, Hampton University, Hampton, Virginia; National Newspaper Publisher Association Collection, Black Press Archives, Moorland-Spingarn Research Center, Howard University, Washington, D.C.; Schomburg Research Center in Black Culture, New York City Public Library, New York; Claude A. Barnett Papers, Chicago Historical Society; Mary McLeod Bethune Collection; John H. H. Sengstacke's (stepfather) diary is housed with the Savannah Historical Society.

Botkin, Joshua. "Abbott, Robert Sengstacke." In *Encyclopedia of African-American Culture and History Vol. I.*, Salzman, Jack, David Lionel Smith, and Cornel West. New York: Simon and Schuster, 1996, 2–3.

Briggs, Johnathon E. and Rob Kaiser. "Whirlwind of Change Blows In at *Defender*," *Raleigh News and Observer*, October 12, 2004.

Chicago Public Library, Journalism, Chicago Renaissance 1932–1950, http://www.chipublib.org/.

Cooper, Caryl A. "The *Chicago Defender*: Filling In the Gaps for the Office of Civilian Defense, 1941–45." *Western Journal of Black Studies* 23.2 (Summer 1999): 111–18.

DeSantis, Alan D. "A Forgotten Leader: Robert S. Abbott and the *Chicago Defender* from 1910 to 1920." *Journalism History* 23.2 (Summer 1997): 63–71.

"Editor Abbott an Inspiration Abroad," *Chicago Defender*, March 2, 1940, 9.

Hill, George H. "Robert Abbott: Defender of the Black Press," in *Bulletin of Bibliography* 42.1 (March 1985): 53–55.

Jemielity, Sam. "Challenging the *Defender*: The Nation's Last Black Daily Struggles to Survive," http://weeklywire.com/.

Johns, Robert L. "Robert S. Abbott." In *Notable Black American Men*, edited by Jessie Carney Smith. Detroit: Gale, 1999, 3–6.

"Making an Impact in Real Time: Real Time Inc. Assumes Ownership of *Chicago Defender*," http:www.leadingedgealliance.com/issues_old/2003/spring/realtimes.

"Robert S. Abbott Is Dead: Funeral Rites Monday at Metropolitan Church," *Chicago Defender*, March 2, 1940, 1.

"Robert S. Abbott, 69, A Chicago Publisher," *New York Times*, March 1, 1940, Schomburg Center Clipping File.

Snorgrass, J. William. "Abbott, Robert Sengstacke." In *Biographical Dictionary of American Journalism*, edited by Joseph P. McKerns. Westport, Conn.: Greenwood Press, 1989, 4–6.

Strother, Ella. "The Black Image in the *Chicago Defender*, 1905–1975." *Journalism History* 4:4 (Winter 1977–78): 137–41.

Taylor, Rebecca Stiles. "N.A.C.W. Official Lauds Editor Abbott," *Chicago Defender*, March 2, 1940, 9.

WILLIAM A. ATTAWAY
(November 19, 1911–June 17, 1986)
Richard Yarborough

William Attaway's literary reputation rests upon two novels—*Let Me Breathe Thunder* (1939) and *Blood on the Forge* (1941)—that establish him as an exceedingly important black fictive voice of his generation. Most notably, his depiction in *Blood on the Forge* of the tragic physical and spiritual toll taken by the Northern industrial mills on black laborers from the South remains one of the most vivid and compelling dramatizations of the underside of the Great Migration in U.S. literature. In addition, even though he never published another novel in the wake of this magnificent accomplishment, Attaway did not, in fact, give up creative writing; rather, he embarked upon a long and fruitful career in television, music, and film. Neither of his novels is set in Chicago and he spent relatively little of his adulthood in that city. Nonetheless, it is crucial to understand Attaway as very much a product of the rich creative outpouring termed the "Black Chicago Renaissance" and to attend to the ways in which his fiction reflects the literary and ideological impulses informing the work of other African American artists identified with Chicago of the 1930s and 1940s.

Born in Greenville, Mississippi, on November 19, 1911, William Alexander Attaway was raised in a family of no mean distinction. His father, William A. Attaway, was a physician, an entrepreneur, and a leader in the region's black community. After earning his medical degree at Meharry in 1902 and setting up a successful practice, Dr. Attaway launched a number of business initiatives that gained him considerable notoriety. In 1906 he assumed the presidency of a black savings bank not far from Indianola, Mississippi. Then, two years later, he headed the formation of a firm that eventually became the Mississippi Life Insurance Company, the first such venture owned and operated by African Americans.

In an article in the *Daily Worker* in 1939, Attaway comments on the motivation behind his family's move from Mississippi to Chicago: "My father . . . had a notion that Negro kids brought up in the South unconsciously accept the whites' estimate of them, and they never get to know what it is to be a human among humans. He brought us north hoping we wouldn't absorb these false

Southern ideas."[1] Although that explanation is no doubt accurate, there are also indications that Dr. Attaway had occasionally run afoul of powerful white interests in Mississippi because of both his commercial ambitions and his political views. Accordingly, his decision to leave the South may well have been driven by a range of concerns, some more pressing than others. Regardless, probably around 1918, Attaway's father relocated the family to Chicago, where he built a new medical practice and his wife, Florence Perry Attaway, took a position as a school teacher.[2] In short order, the Attaways established themselves as important members of the local black elite. Just how quickly Dr. Attaway rose to a position of prominence was apparent during the racial unrest in the city in July of 1919. As reported in the *Chicago Daily Tribune*, he was one of a handful of "representative business and professional men" who issued a public statement urging African Americans "to be the first to cease all acts of violence," even if provoked by white attacks. He articulated his views on the matter this way: "Our policy ought to be to do everything we can to stop the rioting, and not depend upon reprisals and violence to right any wrongs."[3] Moreover, in the early 1920s he was a member of the Chicago Business League and a group called "the Mississippi club," the purpose of which was to unify and advance the community of African American transplants from that state. On her own part, Mrs. Attaway was also a significant figure in black Chicago, serving around this time as an officer of a settlement organization in the city. Even the two Attaway daughters, Florence and Ruth, received notice in the *Chicago Defender* for their social activities.

Attaway's parents were as ambitious in the goals that they set for their three children as they were in their own lives, and they hoped that their son would enter a profession that might solidify a place for him in the black bourgeoisie. Attaway, however, was pulled in other directions. On the one hand, he was fascinated with machines, and he attended Tilden Tech High School in Chicago with the goal of becoming a mechanic. Particularly captivated by airplanes, he remembered paying visits to a nearby airfield, where he performed odd jobs in exchange for free flights. On the other hand, Attaway developed a lasting interest in literature after encountering the poetry of Langston Hughes in school. His sister Ruth, an aspiring actress, encouraged his early attempts at creative expression, and he wrote a number of plays for her drama group.

Known for its trade curriculum under the guidance of Principal Albert Evans, Tilden Tech was racially integrated, and its black students helped to solidify the school's reputation as an athletic power. Indeed, one of the most celebrated Tilden alumni from that period was the African American sprinter Ralph Metcalfe, who starred in the 1932 and 1936 Olympics and who later became a successful Chicago politician. It also may well have been at Tilden Tech that Attaway developed into a skilled tennis player; by the fall of 1930 he was competing in local tournaments, and he continued to do so for several years. Despite the prominence of blacks in the student body, however, Tilden was hardly free of racial tension. For instance, in 1929 the *Chicago Defender* published an article protesting its plans to hold a whites-only junior prom.

In the wake of his father's sudden death in the late summer of 1929, Attaway reportedly dropped out of school and "spent much time hoboing to the exasperation of his mother."[4] After returning to Chicago, he graduated from Tilden in January of 1932, and one month later he followed in the footsteps of his two older sisters and entered the University of Illinois. From the outset, his conflicted goals had a deleterious impact on his academic performance, with his growing investment in creative writing proving a particularly serious distraction. Attaway recalled that he "spent the mornings sleeping through anatomy classes and the nights writing stories and one-act plays" and that he changed his major to pre-law because those courses were in the afternoon.[5] In May of 1933, he also participated as an actor in a dramatic production on campus headed by his sister Ruth. Attaway later observed that all of this extracurricular activity "led to trouble with the dean, who was unimpressed when I exhibited a sociological novel as a substitute for prescribed work. In disgust I left college."[6] Other possible factors here may have been the lingering, destabilizing impact of his father's passing and an urge to rebel against the strictures of his middle-class upbringing.

By the end of the spring semester of 1933, Attaway had turned his back on school; and at some point that year, he embarked on a wandering journey across the United States. After gambling away what funds he had in Kansas City, he made his way to San Francisco, where he worked as a stevedore and as a hand aboard cargo ships. Attaway traveled as an agricultural laborer through the West and Midwest as well, once riding a railroad car into Mexico, where, as Milton Meltzer puts it wryly in the June 26, 1939, *Daily Worker*, "his college Spanish failed him." Attaway claimed that he had written a book while on a farm near Topeka, Kansas, during this period and that he had even gone to New York City in an attempt to find a publisher. Unsuccessful, he subsequently resumed "hoboing" and ended up on the West Coast, where he lived with a Japanese American family for several months.[7] Finally, Attaway returned home to Chicago, nearly freezing to death in a freight car en route. After roughly a year and a half away from college, Attaway reenrolled at the University of Illinois for the fall semester of 1934. Wasting little time completing his degree requirements, he graduated in June 1936 with a BA in pre-law.

During this second stint in college, Attaway continued his creative work, most notably producing "Carnival," described in the *Chicago Defender* as a "Negro one-act folk" play.[8] The piece was staged on campus on January 25, 1936, by Cenacle, a black theater group in which Attaway participated as both a writer and an actor. In addition, his short sketch entitled "Tale of the Blackamoor" appeared in the June 1936 issue of *Challenge* magazine. A scant three pages in length, the story is a dreamlike fable that focuses on a black boy's longing for the attentions of the "proud duchess" whom he serves. By the end of the tale, the youngster has projected his romantic urges onto a "Dresden china doll" that magically comes to life in his imagination.[9] Although there is little in the piece that stylistically foreshadows Attaway's more mature fiction, one can identify a number of themes that do, in fact, emerge in his later writing: first, the power of music; second, the connection between social hierarchy and race; and third, the use of fantasy as a way to transcend emotional distress. Ultimately, however, "Tale of the Blackamoor" is revealing as much for where it was published as for its actual content. Founded in March 1934 and edited by Dorothy West, *Challenge* provided a crucial forum for both established and aspiring African American authors, including Langston Hughes, Owen Dodson, and Arna Bontemps. And although its editorial posture was not as explicitly Marxist as that of *New Challenge* (its later incarnation, for which Richard Wright served as associate editor), *Challenge* was nonetheless radical in its ideological orientation.

Another important factor in the shaping of Attaway's career during this phase was his relationship with Richard Wright, whom he recalled initially encountering when he heard him deliver an address on labor issues. Attaway subsequently arranged for Wright to speak before a campus literary group. On that occasion, Wright presented a draft of "Big Boy Leaves Home" and, as Attaway later observed, he ended up alienating virtually all of his listeners: "He started to read that swell story . . . and when he got to the second paragraph, half the audience had fled. Dick went on, set on giving it to them, and at the end, the room was empty of the literary set and only Dick and I were there."[10] Over the course of these interactions, Attaway befriended Wright, and the two Mississippi natives kept in touch at least into the 1940s.

One also cannot underestimate the impact of Chicago itself on Attaway's life at the time. In the 1930s, the city was an extraordinarily vibrant and energetic site of artistic and political activity, and both Attaway and his sister Ruth were part of it. For instance, the famed African American dancer and choreographer Katherine Dunham considered Ruth Attaway and her brother to be among her closest Chicago friends in the 1930s. Moreover, Attaway was one of several black authors who gathered at the South Side (George Cleveland Hall) branch of the Chicago Public Library that had opened in 1932, and he may have had been involved as well in the South Side Writers Group, which Richard Wright helped to form in May 1936. Whether Attaway was actually a member of that organization is unclear however, and the majority of researchers who have published on the South Side Writers Group do not list him as such.

Indeed, there appears to be a degree of uncertainty regarding Attaway's activities more generally during these years. For example, a number of scholars state that he worked on the Illinois Federal Writers' Project (FWP), offering dates ranging from late 1935 through 1936. Michel Fabre posits that Richard Wright and Attaway may have interacted, or even possibly first met, in the Chicago office of the FWP. (Wright had been appointed to the Illinois FWP in 1935, and he remained employed on it until his transfer to the New York City unit in the late spring of 1937.) Yet Attaway himself does not mention the FWP in his autobiographical comments in the late 1930s and early 1940s. Furthermore, although he was quite familiar with Attaway's fiction, Arna Bontemps does not include him in his article on "Famous WPA Authors" in the June 1950 issue of *Negro Digest*. Finally, in a letter to the head of the Illinois Federal Writers' Project in September 1937, Sterling Brown, the FWP's Editor on Negro Affairs, identifies Attaway as someone who might be tapped for the Project, which suggests that the young, aspiring writer had not been formally involved to that point. Attaway's participation in the Illinois FWP may have been unofficial, and he certainly was close to individuals whose service with that unit has been documented—Richard Wright and Katherine Dunham, to name but two. However, his college transcript indicates that he was enrolled at the University of Illinois in Champaign-Urbana from the fall semester of 1934 through the spring semester of 1936 (including the summer session of 1935), which would likely have limited the time he could spend in Chicago primarily to breaks in the academic year and weekends.

Similarly, questions persist about whether Attaway, like Richard Wright, joined the Communist Party in the 1930s. Drawing upon interviews with Attaway's black activist contemporaries, Alan M. Wald contends in *Exiles from a Future Time* that he "was a committed Communist from the late 1930s well into the Cold War era."[11] Other scholars simply note his radical Left affiliations. What is, at the very least, undeniable is that, as William J. Maxwell puts it, Attaway and many of his fellow Chicago black authors "wrote or edited or apprenticed within the Old Left's literary networks."[12] Particularly after the Communist Party's launching of its Popular Front phase in 1935, it actually would have been unusual for an ambitious, politically progressive black writer like Attaway not to have turned for his closest associations to artists on the Left, some of whom were Party members and some of whom were not.

With his college degree in hand, Attaway planned to move to New York City, where his sister Ruth was establishing herself as an actress; he reported spending the summer of 1936 working in a mint field to make money for the trip. Once in New York, he held a range of jobs, including stints as a labor organizer in Harlem and as a clerk in a dress shop. In 1936 Ruth Attaway joined the cast of *You Can't Take It with You*, a Pulitzer Prize–winning Broadway comedy by Moss Hart and George Kaufman that opened in December of that year. A road company was being assembled, and Attaway's sister convinced him to audition. He later commented, "I never wanted to be an actor . . . I was so scared reading those lines they all thought I was very funny. I got the part."[13] Attaway's self-deprecating remarks do scant justice to the real accomplishment that his being hired represented. Indeed, the man for whom he was employed as understudy, James Carl "Hamtree" Harrington, was a relatively well-known vaudeville, musical theater, and film veteran. The production in which Attaway participated met considerable success, especially in Chicago, his hometown, where it had a record-breaking run from early February 1937 through mid-January 1938. In the midst of the demands of the touring schedule, he found time to continue his writing, and he recalled completing *Let Me Breathe Thunder* in three and a half months while in Philadelphia. He submitted the manuscript to the publishers Doubleday, Doran and Company and was with the play in Texas when he learned that his novel had been accepted.

Released in June of 1939, *Let Me Breathe Thunder* focuses on Ed and Step, two white migrants traveling through the American West looking for work during the Depression. Told from Ed's point of view, the narrative traces the men's experiences, first, with Hi Boy, a young Mexican whom they encounter in New Mexico and take with them to Washington; and then with a landowner named Sampson, whose daughter, Anna, impulsively enters into an ill-fated romantic relationship with Step. Appropriately, the text opens with Ed, Step, and Hi Boy riding a freight car; and for a large portion of the book, the main characters are in transit—either by train, on foot, or by automobile. This motif of men in motion lends the social world that Attaway creates a powerful sense of instability that aptly represents the lives led by Ed and Step. And Step's habit of carrying a set of keys that are useless to him signifies the fact that while his and Ed's easy mobility constitutes a sort of freedom, the cost is the absence of home, of domestic connection. The bonds that matter the most in *Let Me Breathe Thunder* are clearly male-centered, and they are marked by an often ruthlessly enforced emotional self-suppression that shields the two young men and their fellow wanderers from their own vulnerability. This passage in which Ed describes traveling in a cold boxcar with Step and Hi Boy reveals the code of behavior that he and Step endorse: "The kid moved up against me. His body was hot against my side. It would have been better for all of us to have snuggled together in a heap, but Step and me were funny about things like that. We were always so anxious to prove to each other how much we could stand. So he sat apart, and I was glad it was too dark for him to see me enjoying the heat of the kid's body."[14] While understandable, this restraint can find expression, Attaway indicates, as callousness that, in turn, can lead to casualties—most notably, Anna, whom Step takes advantage of sexually and then abandons, and Hi Boy, who ultimately dies from a hand injury that he inflicts on himself in an attempt to demonstrate his toughness to Step, whom he idolizes.

For much of *Let Me Breathe Thunder*, the plot mimics the wayward nature of Step and Ed's journey, with the narrative constructed of a series of nearly freestanding set pieces. Among the most effective are a conversation among a group of migrants riding a freight train and a moving depiction of the confusion and embarrassment that Ed and Step feel in a railroad dining car on the sole occasion in the novel when they can actually afford to pay for their passage. Once they and Hi Boy arrive at the Sampson farm, however, the pace and structuring of the book change as new interpersonal bonds begin to develop between Step and Anna and between Anna's father and Hi Boy. The social network afforded the two men during this period also encompasses a black prostitute-turned-property-owner named Mag and her former pimp, Cooper. Although issues of race certainly arise, Attaway seems to be implying via Step and Mag's warm friendship that the color line can be more porous the lower one descends in class, a point made explicitly by the one black man in the aforementioned freight-car conversation ("Guys on the road ain't got prejudice like other folks," he contends[15]). The peaceful, near idyllic life on the Sampson farm is finally violated by the trouble that follows in Step's wake. Unwilling to accede to Step's imminent departure, Anna arranges a tryst at Mag's house, where she gets caught up in a violent conflict involving the pitifully insecure Cooper and a fiercely jealous Mag. Not only is Anna seriously hurt but local whites take Mag into custody in a scene that ominously resembles the early stages of a lynching. Although Ed and Step appear to escape this tragic turn of events unscathed, their return to the familiar life on the rails does not bring comfort, as they have to watch helplessly while Hi Boy slowly and excruciatingly dies from the infection that has spread from his hand wound. At the end of the novel, the two men are virtually where they were at the outset, disconnected from everything and everyone but each other, and still unable to express their pain, their neediness, and, now, their deep sense of loss.

One of the book's real strengths is the direct simplicity with which Attaway limns his multiethnic cast of characters, for while Ed and Step are white, he includes several significant African American and Mexican American figures. Another is the power with which, like other proletarian fiction of that era, *Let Me Breathe Thunder* highlights the quotidian reality and importance of labor as well as the psychic cost entailed when people are unmoored from stable, meaningful jobs. Yet Attaway is careful to maintain his distance from the understated drama that his narrative unfolds. There is undeniable tragedy in the failed relationship between Step and Anna and especially in the fate awaiting Hi Boy, who embodies innocence in a world corrupted both by harsh economic realities and by the inevitable failings of human nature. However, Attaway renders no easy moral judgments in the text, and he strives to preclude the reader's doing so as well.

A number of contemporaneous reviewers voice reservations about *Let Me Breathe Thunder*. The most negative dismiss it as imitative, linking Attaway's approach to that of John Steinbeck in *Of Mice and Men* (1937). Others identify the stylized language and an indulgence in sentimentality as flaws, and one blames what he sees as weaknesses on Attaway's having previously been a writer for the stage. In contrast, some critics note with approval both the force and realism of his dialogue and also the skill with which Attaway, a black author, brings to life his white protagonists. In the *New York Post*, May Cameron lauds his prose this way: "The novel is tightly, economically and cleanly written"; and Alain Locke highlights "the strong naturalness of [Attaway's] characterization."[16] The most thorough review was that by Ulysses Lee in the journal *Opportunity*. Lee pays considerable attention to the black figures in *Let Me Breathe Thunder*, describing them as "among the best-realized characters in the book." Moreover, he argues, "Attaway's race proves itself of distinct advantage" in that his experiences as an African American afforded him insights into the alienation and hardship suffered by Ed and Step.[17] Lee closes with this optimistic prediction about Attaway: "When he turns to a novel primarily of Negro life, he should produce one which will do much for Negro literature."[18] Other reviewers likewise anticipated a bright future for the young writer.

Despite the mostly favorable reception met by *Let Me Breathe Thunder* upon its release in 1939, the book has elicited relatively scant notice since then. Ralph Ellison gives it a reservedly complimentary mention in "Recent Negro Fiction" in the August 5, 1941, issue of *New Masses*; and in *Negro Voices in American Fiction* (1948), Hugh Gloster touches briefly upon it (but, oddly, not *Blood on the Forge*). More typical is G. Lewis Chandler's neglecting of Attaway entirely in his 1948 overview of African American novels in *Phylon*. In 1952, Lion Books reissued *Let Me Breathe Thunder* in a pulp paperback edition called *Tough Kid* (with a second printing in 1956). However, it was not until Robert A. Bone's *The Negro Novel in America* (1958; revised edition, 1965) that Attaway's work finally began to undergo close scrutiny. Starting in the late 1960s, there has been an increase in scholarship on Attaway's writing, but the bulk of it has centered on *Blood on the Forge*. One factor here may be the tacit critical consensus that of his two novels, Attaway's second constitutes the richer artistic achievement. Another is the extent to which much of the fiction by African Americans in the 1940s and 1950s that focuses on whites—or at least on figures not clearly identifiable as black—has been overlooked by scholars. (Other examples include Willard Motley's *Knock on Any Door* [1947], Ann Petry's *Country Place* [1947], Chester Himes's *Cast the First Stone* [1952], Richard Wright's *Savage Holiday* [1954], and most of the books by the prolific Frank Yerby.)[19]

The sense that *Let Me Breathe Thunder* manifested but the initial flowering of Attaway's considerable creative promise was shared by the administrators of the Rosenwald Fund. Founded by Julius Rosenwald, who had earned his fortune via mail order sales and his part-ownership of Sears, Roebuck and Company, the

Fund supported a wide range of projects. Of crucial importance were the many fellowships given to African Americans between 1928 and 1948, with the largest cluster of such grants allocated in the fine arts. William Attaway received one of these awards in 1940, and it facilitated the completion of his second novel, *Blood on the Forge*, which appeared in August of 1941. By that time, Attaway had established himself as a notable figure on the African American cultural landscape in New York City. He was a part of a remarkable cohort of black artists, musicians, and authors (the "306 Group") who met regularly at 306 West 141st Street in Harlem; and in 1940 he resided in an apartment building at 33 West 125th Street along with, among others, Jacob Lawrence, Claude McKay, and Romare Bearden. [20] The news of his forthcoming novel was significant enough for Arna Bontemps to write the following to his close friend Langston Hughes on August 19, 1941: "See where Attaway and Dick [Richard Wright] both have books coming up, entitled 'Blood on the Forge' and '12 Million Black Voices Speak' respectively. Looks like this will be a heavy fall for our crowd."[21]

Coincidentally, both of the works mentioned by Bontemps focus on the phenomenon termed the "Great Migration." (Jacob Lawrence's celebrated sequence of paintings called *Migration Series* appeared in 1941 as well.) From early in the twentieth century, commentators like R. R. Wright Jr., W. E. B. DuBois, Ray Stannard Baker, Herbert W. Horwill, George E. Haynes, and Carter G. Woodson had noted the remarkable "Negro Exodus" from the rural South to the urban and industrialized sections of the North and Midwest. There were many forces driving this unprecedented movement of African Americans—among them, crop failures, the restrictions on European immigration during World War I, ongoing Jim Crow practices and other forms of racial oppression in the South, and appeals disseminated both by Northern companies (often via labor agents sent into Southern communities) and by such black publications as the *Chicago Defender*. By 1920, the burgeoning African American population in the North had become concentrated in several manufacturing areas, one of which was Pittsburgh and its environs in western Pennsylvania. It is in this locale that William Attaway sets his powerful narrative about three black half-brothers who escape a degrading existence in rural Kentucky only to find themselves in the mind- and body-numbing hell of a mill town where steel is valued more than human life. Incorporating into his plot the dramatic steelworkers' strike that took place in the region in 1919, Attaway examines the complex effects of the Black Migration in the context of the labor conflicts that marked the postwar period in the United States.

Blood on the Forge is organized into five sections. The first focuses on the Moss family—Mat, Melody, Chinatown, and Mat's wife, Hattie—who are struggling to survive on a barren, worn-out farm in the spring of 1919. In Part 2 (the shortest in the novel), the three men flee the South in a freight car after Mat strikes a white overseer who had insulted their mother. Part 3 opens with the brothers' arrival in the Allegheny County steel town and describes their sense of dislocation in the face of not just a new material and economic reality, but also a confusing multiethnic community where little of the Southern Jim-Crow racial protocol to which they are accustomed applies. Attaway reinforces the assaultive character of this world by highlighting the horrific sounds and sights of the factory: "The shaping mills were far down the river, but he could hear the awful screams when the saws bit into the hot metal. The blast was a million bees in a drum. The open hearth was full of agony. The daylight was orange yellow with the droning flames of the Bessemers."[22] Over the course of the final three sections of the novel, we see the brothers attempt to adapt to their brutal, dehumanizing new environment, only to fail in a tragedy that transcends the fate of any single individual or even that of the Moss family as Attaway levels a broad sociopolitical critique that indicts the values infusing a system so wasteful of life.

Attaway dramatizes the failure of the Moss brothers in terms not just psychic but also corporeal. Indeed, the physical loss that each man suffers literalizes the effects of the unnatural forces unleashed in the corporate drive to produce steel: Chinatown, who gains pleasure from the sensory surface of things, loses his eyes; Melody, who has coped with hardship though the art of his guitar-playing, smashes his hand; and Big Mat, who has heretofore overcome the trials of his life through his sheer brute strength and masculine vigor, is killed by a white striker while Mat is misguidedly acting as an enforcer for the mill owners. However, the Moss brothers are not the only characters who are damaged in this vicious, unyielding world. By rendering disturbing images of adolescent incest and of dismemberment and bodily deterioration, Attaway effectively conveys the extent to which the steel mill and the corrupting interests it represents consume and undermine the humanity of many of the workers and their families.

Particularly noteworthy among the victims in the novel are the women, who often resort to marketing their bodies in the desperate attempt to survive in a social order that commodifies nearly everyone in the community and that too frequently accords females value primarily in sexual terms. At one point, it appears that a young Mexican woman named Anna might free herself from her life as a prostitute when she and Mat move in together, establishing the rudimentary beginnings of what could conceivably evolve into a stable domestic home space. Unfortunately, Mat's insecurity and violence and Anna's obsession with the superficial trappings of class status ensure that their relationship will disintegrate. When Mat finally confronts Anna over her infidelity, she assails him with the insult "black peon."[23] In retaliation, Mat beats her unmercifully in a scene that both echoes his explosive rage upon his mother's death that Attaway describes early in the novel and also foreshadows his brutal attack on the striking workers toward the end.

Just before he dies, Mat is groping toward an awareness of his true relationship to the exploitative economic powers that have manipulated and ultimately destroyed him, but the harshness of the fictive vision in *Blood on the Forge* remains unrelieved by any dramatic shift in consciousness on the part of the main characters. When seeking a counter to the book's sobering pessimism, one should rather look first at the simple fact that in the final pages Melody and Chinatown are alive and on a train leaving the mill town. Second, Attaway does present members of the European immigrant community who have found ways to build coherent family structures. (That the black male migrants in the novel have come North without women and children may explain the absence of a corresponding African American community here.) Third, while Attaway keeps his authorial intrusions to a minimum, the ideological thrust of the book toward a qualified endorsement of the labor strike is evident, even as he shows how racism can leave many blacks alienated from both the management of the mill and the predominantly white union.

The reviews of *Blood on the Forge* were even more favorable than those earned by *Let Me Breathe Thunder*. In particular, the majority of the critics emphasize the persuasive evocation of the inhuman conditions in the steel factory and of the toxic life in the mill town. The verisimilitude to which commentators allude apparently derived from personal experience. In 1980 Attaway recalled that he "spent 1 ½ years as a steelworker—at the Republic plant in South Chicago, at U.S. Steel in Youngstown, Ohio, and at other mills in Pittsburgh and Gary."[24] Although it is difficult to pinpoint exactly when in his life he held these jobs, the firsthand knowledge that he tapped in producing *Blood on the Forge* contributed to the convincing nature of the narrative, and many saw the novel as marking the fulfillment of the potential manifested in *Let Me Breathe Thunder*. Typical of such praise is that of Drake de Kay in the *New York Times Book Review*: "Written by a Negro author with notable objectivity, this is a starkly realistic story involving social criticism as searching as any to be found in contemporary literature."[25] George Schuyler lauded the book as "thoughtful, penetrating, brilliant" and he placed Attaway in the front rank of contemporaneous black authors: "With the exception of Arna Bontemps, no Negro novelist has made his characters come so alive and painted his background with such authenticity."[26] Where several observers felt *Let Me Breathe Thunder* to be derivative of Steinbeck's *Of Mice and Men*, some now linked *Blood on the Forge* with Richard Wright's best-selling *Native Son*, which had appeared the previous year. For instance, George Sanford describes *Blood on the Forge* as "reminiscent of Wright because the book is fraught with frustration and suffering."[27] However, if the unprecedented success of *Native Son* overshadowed Attaway's new novel, Doubleday, Doran and Company took full advantage of Wright's notoriety by including his imprimatur in an advertisement for *Blood on the Forge* in the

September 9, 1941, issue of the *New York Times*. In his comments, Wright urges, "If there are people who are baffled by the conduct of the Negroes, then they should read this novel, and they will be better people for having done so, for it will add unto them a new and better knowledge of the processes of American civilization. The reality that Attaway depicts is not beautiful, but it is nonetheless moving and human for that."[28] Similarly impressed with Attaway's achievement, Sterling Brown, Arthur Davis, and Ulysses Lee included an excerpt from the book in their groundbreaking anthology, *The Negro Caravan* (1941).

The strong support for *Blood on the Forge* expressed by Richard Wright, a well-known Communist author, indicates the extent to which Attaway was perceived as an important radical political voice at the time. Not surprisingly, his novel garnered its most detailed evaluations from reviewers influenced by leftist ideological perspectives. In the December 1941 *Crisis* magazine, James W. Ivy describes the book as effectively engaging "the eternal problem of capital and labor and race as we find it everywhere in industrial America."[29] However, both Ivy and James O. Hobson (in the November 1941 *Opportunity*) judge the portrayal of the Moss brothers to be limited. In the November 8, 1941, issue of the Communist Party's *Daily Worker*, Ralph Warner contends that although Attaway dramatizes the oppression of African American laborers, he does not display their ability to come to self-awareness regarding the complexity of their situation and to discern the route to liberation through the "final unity of black and white workers." Warner emphasizes the fact that "there is no Mr. Max [Bigger Thomas's Communist lawyer in *Native Son*] to evaluate the social significance of Big Mat's plight."[30] This omission, Warner contends, makes it all the more imperative that Attaway develop his proletarian characters further. The single most elaborate and lengthy review of *Blood on the Forge* was by Ralph Ellison, writing in the spring 1942 *Negro Quarterly*, a journal edited by Angelo Herndon. Fully sharing Warner's sense that Attaway fails to deliver the ideological payoff that the novel so compellingly sets up, Ellison opines, "There is no center of consciousness, lodged in a character or characters, capable of comprehending the sequence of events." He further complains that "Attaway grasped the destruction of the folk, but missed its rebirth on a higher level."[31] Ultimately, Ellison can appreciate the skill with which Attaway sketches the painful dilemma confronting black workers like Mat and his brothers. However, what he had clearly hoped to see and did not is Attaway's commitment to demonstrating how Mat's "motivation, the intense desire to live and maintain a sense of dignity, has also produced the most conscious American Negro type, the black trade unionist."[32] Attaway's willingness to engage such critiques from the progressive community in a public forum reflects the seriousness with which he took them. In December 1941, a few months after the release of *Blood on the Forge*, Attaway was featured in the "Evenings with Negro Authors" series at the New York Public Library branch in Harlem. The *Chicago Defender* quotes a portion of Attaway's defense of his novel at the event: "I'm not interested in writing about those Negroes who succeed. . . . I'm looking for the major trend of the masses, not the talented tenth." His respondents at the event were "Dr. Samuel Sillen of New York University, Editor Roy Wilkins of *The Crisis* and short story writer Ralph Ellison of the League of American Writers."[33]

Although Carl Milton Hughes treats Attaway's second book briefly in *The Negro Novelist* in 1953, the first in-depth scholarly examination of *Blood on the Forge* was Robert A. Bone's close reading in *The Negro Novel in America* (1958; revised edition, 1965). A major shift in the treatment of Attaway generally and of *Blood on the Forge* in particular was then ushered in by Edward Margolies's chapter on the writer in *Native Sons: A Critical Study of Twentieth-Century Negro American Authors* (1968) and by the release of two new editions of *Blood on the Forge*: a hardback reprint by Chatham Bookseller in 1969 and a paperback by Collier-Macmillan in May 1970 with an introduction by Margolies. (In 1953 *Blood on the Forge* had been issued as a inexpensive paperback by Popular Library in a run of 300,000; as in the case of *Tough Kid*, the cover art of this pulp edition was designed to highlight and exploit the sexual relationship in the narrative.)

The late 1960s and early 1970s witnessed the rediscovery of a whole raft of African American texts, and it is hardly surprising to come across several scholarly analyses of *Blood on the Forge* during this period. One of the most striking is that by the black cultural nationalist Addison Gayle Jr. in *The Way of the New World* (1975). Although Gayle acknowledges Attaway as "the most important of the novelists to view the black problem in Marxist terminology," like some earlier reviewers he finds the characterization of Mat to be deeply flawed.[34] However, in contrast to Ellison, who argues that Attaway fails to dramatize the Communist ideal of interracial class struggle, Gayle contends that Attaway's hewing to a Marxist line is itself the problem insofar as it precludes his accepting Mat "as the black outsider become rebel."[35] In the wake of Gayle's evaluation, one encounters in the 1980s useful treatments of Attaway and his fiction by such scholars as Jane Campbell, Bonnie J. Barthold, Lawrence Rodgers, Bernard Bell, and Samuel B. Garren, to name a few.

Another shift in the critical commentary on Attaway dates roughly from the paperback reprint of *Blood on the Forge* issued in 1987 by Monthly Review Press with an introduction by novelist John Oliver Killens and an afterword by Richard Yarborough. The 1970 Collier edition had fallen out of print, and the novel's rerelease by Monthly Review, a leftist publisher, brought the book to the attention of a new generation of readers while situating Attaway firmly within a radical literary tradition.[36] The burgeoning body of research over the past two decades on the impact of Left politics on African American authors has proven beneficial in the case of William Attaway, because it has led to a more detailed and nuanced sense not just of his career and writings but also of the historical context in which he worked and the ideological strains that shaped his fictive vision. Especially noteworthy in this regard is the scholarship on black artists and the Left by Alan M. Wald, Barbara Foley, Timothy R. Libretti, William J. Maxwell, Gerald Horne, Bill V. Mullen, James Edward Smethurst, and Mary Helen Washington. As the 1950s Red Scare—with its public pillorying of Communists, former Communists, and alleged Communists—recedes further into the past, these and other scholars will, no doubt, shed new light on the complex ways in which American radicalism influenced black writers, thereby enhancing our appreciation of Attaway's contribution.

The entry of the United States into World War II led to Attaway's enlisting in July 1942 in the military, where he served until the end of the conflict. In the October–November 1944 issue of the periodical *Negro Story*, the editors observe, "In spite of the fact that WILLIAM ATTAWAY is in the army now, he is writing continually, and we should soon be hearing from this fine young author who, like [Charles W.] Chesnutt, is a writer first and then a Negro."[37] If Attaway was, in fact, writing during this time, little of what he produced appears to have survived. Indeed, in October 1947 a new journal entitled *The Tiger's Eye* carried a short story of his that may have been the last fiction that he published. Included in an issue with pieces by Thomas Merton, Owen Dodson, Marianne Moore, and Anaïs Nin, "Death of a Rag Doll" recalls Attaway's "Tale of the Blackamoor" (as well as sections of Jean Toomer's *Cane* and Sherwood Anderson's *Winesburg, Ohio*) far more than it does either of his two novels, which are grounded firmly in the conventions of proletarian realism. As in "Tale of the Blackamoor," Attaway here adopts a suggestive, almost dreamlike tone in his depiction of the psychological bond between a woman named Mina Smith and her half-brother, Cal, whose mental disabilities and peculiar appearance cause some in the community to dub him "that witless boy at the Smith farm."[38] To Mina, however, Cal is "like my rag doll after the rain," and Attaway poignantly examines the strain on the siblings' relationship brought on by Mina's impending wedding as she ultimately decides to turn her back on her doting half-brother to enter what appears to be a loveless marriage. Although Attaway describes Mina as "the dark child of the wife's first husband," there is no explicit invoking of race or racial conflict in the story, and it is unclear whether this piece indicates a direction in which Attaway might have gone had he continued to produce fiction.[39] One can also only speculate regarding the possibility that Attaway's impressionistic tracing of a troubled family tie in "Death of a Rag Doll" might speak in a veiled way to his own relationship with his sister Ruth (who had, by that point, married the prominent writer and editor Allan Morrison). What is certain is that this story signaled the close of the initial major phase of his writing career. A number of factors could explain why he chose to turn away from fiction. First, there were the negative judgments of *Blood on the Forge* rendered by some of his peers on the Left. Second, his books were, at best, modest successes in terms of sales, and Attaway was to find other, more lucrative creative outlets. Finally, he was evidently sensitive to the high expectations spawned by his two novels, and the burden of meeting those expectations may have proven too daunting and discouraging to overcome. Regardless of the reasons for the shift, Attaway's next major artistic accomplishments were in the arenas of music, television, and film.

After the war, William Attaway struck up a close friendship with the talented singer Harry Belafonte, who had taken acting classes with Attaway's sister Ruth. Both men were involved in progressive political circles in New York, and both men shared a great interest in music as well. In December 1950 Attaway and an acquaintance named Ferman Phillips opened the Sage, a restaurant in Greenwich Village. Belafonte joined them in what turned out to be a fascinating but financially unrewarding venture that cemented the connection between Attaway and Belafonte. According to Arnold Shaw, author of *Belafonte: An Unauthorized Biography*, the restaurant was patronized by "indigent Village-ites, jazz musicians, dope addicts, theater people, alcoholics, folk singers, and hoods."[40] In spite of the tribulations that managing the Sage entailed, the place served as an energizing creative environment, and Attaway remembered "working out arrangements" for folk songs with Belafonte and others after hours at the establishment.[41] By the late summer of 1951, the friends had sold the restaurant; however, the musical collaboration that took seed there would bear considerable fruit.

In the early 1950s, Harry Belafonte's artistic career began its rapid, upward trajectory. He became a fixture as a singer on the club scene in New York City, and he cut his first recordings for RCA Victor in the spring of 1952. He made his film debut in 1953 in *Bright Road*, and that same year he won a Tony Award for his role in the Broadway play *John Murray Anderson's Almanac*. Then, in 1954 he starred with Dorothy Dandridge in the movie *Carmen Jones*. As Belafonte's celebrity grew, William Attaway accompanied him on his travels around the country. Attaway saw this relationship as not just professional but personal, and he later mentioned his awareness of the sense of isolation that his good friend experienced on the road. Attaway recalled that he once had his sister Florence meet Belafonte upon his arrival in Chicago "just so that he would not feel he was coming alone into a strange city."[42]

By the mid-1950s, Attaway's own career was again on the rise. However, he was now making his mark as a writer for television, a medium then still in its infancy. One especially notable TV project on which both he and Belafonte worked was "Winner by Decision," an episode of *The General Electric Theater* series. Broadcast by CBS in late 1955 and based on a teleplay by Attaway, this show featured Harry Belafonte in his first dramatic TV role and the well-known African American singer and actress Ethel Waters. Attaway appreciated how the two stars delivered his lines; but because of "this effort on the part of both principals to outdo one another, the show ran long" and his scripting credit never made it to the screen.[43]

Around this time, Attaway and Belafonte also collaborated on a stage musical entitled *Sing, Man, Sing*, a production fueled by the latter's powerful engagement with *The Family of Man*, a celebrated photographic exhibition curated by Edward Steichen in 1955 at New York's Museum of Modern Art that resulted in a best-selling book of the same title. The relatively disappointing response to *Sing, Man, Sing*, which premiered in April 1956, paled in comparison to the stunning success of Belafonte's appearance only months earlier in the October 2, 1955, episode of NBC's *The Colgate Comedy Hour*. A staff writer at the network, Attaway had been assigned to help prepare the segment featuring Belafonte, and the initial plan had been to focus it on the black folk hero John Henry. However, the two decided on a Caribbean music theme instead, and they brought on board the singer-songwriter Irving Burgie, who performed under the name "Lord Burgess." Although Burgie appears to have been partly responsible for alerting Belafonte and Attaway to the potential appeal of calypso, it is crucial to stress that they both had long been interested in black folk material and that Belafonte had previously sung and recorded Caribbean music. The three men developed several pieces for the television program, among them the now well-known "Banana Boat Song" (or "Day-O"); and the Belafonte segment, entitled "Holiday in Trinidad," was "a smash," as Burgie put it in 1996.[44] They soon thereafter went into the studio to produce an entire album, and Attaway was involved throughout the process, including providing liner notes for the record. Released by RCA Victor in the fall of 1956 and featuring such numbers as "Jamaica Farewell" and "Banana Boat Song," *Calypso* brought Harry Belafonte unprecedented global popularity as a singer and was the first long-playing album in the United States to sell a million copies. Moreover, it triggered what *Time* magazine dubbed "Calypsomania"—"the biggest thing in the pop-music business since rock 'n' roll started rolling."[45]

Astutely capitalizing on the fad, Attaway published *Calypso Song Book: Authentic Folk Music of the Caribbean* in November 1957. A large-format volume aimed at young readers, it contains tablature for twenty-five songs along with an introductory discussion of the history of calypso. Although brief and simply written, this essay manifests a conception of black culture that represents a telling strain in Attaway's thought. Highlighting the roots of calypso in Africa, he contends that the music is dramatic proof of the power and durability of the artistic practices that Africans brought with them across the Atlantic. In addition, Attaway links calypso to strategies of resistance developed by the slaves as mechanisms for both psychic nurturance and practical subversion in the face of racist attempts to dehumanize them. This reading of African American folk cultural production as a complex response to oppressive conditions informs Attaway's treatment of the blues in *Blood on the Forge*. It also belies any superficial reading of calypso generally, and it complicates considerably one's sense of the ideological impulses driving Attaway and Belafonte's remarkable musical project.

Although his involvement in Belafonte's appearance on *The Colgate Comedy Hour* in 1955 constituted a landmark in Attaway's postwar career, it was hardly an isolated case. According to Arnold Shaw in 1960, Attaway had generated "more than 400 TV scripts" by that point.[46] One of his most important subsequent achievements in the medium was the episode of *ABC Stage 67* entitled "A Time for Laughter: A Look at Negro Humor in America" and broadcast on April 6, 1967. Produced by Harry Belafonte and written by Attaway, this program featured an extraordinary collection of black actors and comedians, including Redd Foxx, George Kirby, Moms Mabley, Richard Pryor, Pigmeat Markham, Sidney Poitier, Dick Gregory, Diana Sands, Godfrey Cambridge, and Diahann Carroll. Indeed, "A Time for Laughter" probably represented the first opportunity for many non-black Americans to see some of these performers, and the show earned a 1966–67 Emmy Award nomination in the category of "Outstanding Variety Special."

In 1967 William Attaway published *Hear American Singing*, his final book and his second on music. With an introduction by Harry Belafonte, this volume is an ambitious, if compact, historical overview of folk music in the United States. As was his goal with *Calypso*, Attaway is clearly trying to reach a mass, most likely youth audience; and as was the case with that earlier text, his engagement with folk culture is shaped by his refusal to take either a narrowly aesthetic or an ethnographic approach to the topic. The fact that the volume is bookended by an opening chapter on American Indians and two closing chapters on, respectively, African American music and contemporaneous popular music suggests both the range of Attaway's interests as well as his attempt to decenter white bourgeois culture in the narrative that he constructs. If the multicultural assumptions undergirding this text might seem familiar to twenty-first-century readers, Attaway's organizational strategy was certainly ahead of its time in 1967.

Throughout the fifties, sixties, and seventies, Attaway also wrote steadily for film, often on an uncredited basis. In 1957 Attaway was said to have been penning the script for an all-black version of Dostoevsky's *Crime and Punishment*, to be directed by Robert Rossen.[47] This project, along with a proposed movie adaptation of *Let Me Breathe Thunder*, apparently never came to fruition. However, Attaway's relationship with Rossen reportedly led to his working on the script for the award-winning film *The Hustler* (1961) even though his contributions ultimately received no public acknowledgment. Shortly after the release of *Hear America Singing*, Attaway became involved in what potentially could have been two of the most significant movie projects of his career. Published in September 1964 by the bestselling author Irving Wallace, *The Man* is a speculative novel about an African American senator who unexpectedly becomes president of the United States. Although the controversial book, like most of Wallace's fiction, was exceedingly popular, major studios were wary of investing in a film version for fear of alienating Southern theater-owners. By 1968, however, plans for a cinematic adaptation were in place, and Attaway took on the job of writing the screenplay. Samuel B. Garren notes that Attaway submitted two drafts in 1968 and 1969, making major changes in the portrayal of blacks in the text. Wallace himself met with Attaway in Los Angeles and was impressed with his insights and his intense commitment to the story. Nonetheless, the studios ultimately paid Attaway for his work and dropped him from the movie, supposedly because of dissatisfaction with his scripts. *The Man* was completed without his further participation and released in mid-1972 to a decidedly lackluster reception. That same year, Attaway was tapped by the actor Anthony Quinn to produce the screenplay for a possible film about Henri Christophe, the Haitian revolutionary leader. In the wake of heated protests by black actors when Quinn, a Mexican American, indicated that he planned to play Christophe himself, this project was aborted.

Attaway's personal life underwent major changes during the sixties. In 1962 he married longtime friend Frances Settele in a ceremony in Harry Belafonte's house. In 1964 their son, William, was born; their daughter, Noelle, followed two years later. Then in 1966 he and his family traveled to the Caribbean for what was to have been a short vacation; they ended up remaining there for about a decade, mostly in Barbados. Until that point, Attaway had been active in the Civil Rights movement, taking part, for instance, in the famous march from Selma to Montgomery, Alabama, that Reverend Martin Luther King Jr. led in March 1965. However, for a range of professional and personal reasons, Attaway may well have needed distance from the American scene. A few observers suggest that he found Barbados especially appealing since it offered him the opportunity to live in a country run by blacks.

After returning to the United States (where he resided in Berkeley before moving to Los Angeles), he was hired to write for a new dramatic series on NBC entitled *Skag*, which ran for a handful of episodes in early 1980 before its cancellation. Soon thereafter, Attaway joined the production team of *Grambling's White Tiger*, a made-for-TV movie featuring the Olympic decathlon champion Bruce Jenner in the role of a quarterback recruited as the first white player on the football team at Grambling, a historically black college. Broadcast by NBC on October 4, 1981, *Grambling's White Tiger* also marked a professional reunion of Attaway and Harry Belafonte, who was cast to play Eddie Robinson, Grambling's celebrated coach. Attaway's final project was another television movie, *The Atlanta Child Murders*. Helmed by Abby Mann (with whom Attaway had collaborated on *Skag*), this docudrama focused on the serial killings of black children and young adults that had drawn extensive national attention in the early 1980s. Before he could complete the assignment, however, Attaway was stricken with cancer, and he died in Los Angeles on June 17, 1986.

In evaluating the literary accomplishments of William Attaway, one might reasonably argue that he was the victim of bad timing. Most notably, *Blood on the Forge* appeared but a year after Richard Wright's *Native Son*, a text that cast a dense shadow over virtually every novel published by an African American in its immediate wake. Furthermore, World War II interrupted Attaway's career soon after the release of his second book, and then the 1950s saw a shift in readers' tastes away from proletarian fiction, a mode in which he had made a name. Later, at the peak of new scholarly and popular interest in African American literature in the late 1960s and early 1970s, Attaway was living outside the United States. By the time he returned, mainstream America had begun to turn in a conservative ideological direction, and the white fascination with black literature had subsided. All that said, any characterization of Attaway's artistic career as one thwarted by lost opportunities and unfulfilled potential is, in fact, inaccurate. Although different circumstances may conceivably have encouraged him to continue to produce fiction, it is undeniable that he remained a strikingly resourceful and deeply political writer throughout his adult life. If, on the one hand, he merits no little recognition for his complex, innovative engagement with issues of labor, power, race, and masculinity in *Let Me Breathe Thunder* and the exceptional *Blood on the Forge*, he may, on the other hand, ultimately deserve even more accolades as a pathbreaking creative force in film and television in a period when there were few black voices to be heard in those predominantly white media. When viewed as a whole, Attaway's artistic life was distinguished by real and sustained achievement in a remarkably diverse set of venues.

Acknowledgments

My research benefited immeasurably from the staffs at the Chicago Historical Society, the University of Illinois Library, the Newberry Library, the National Archives, the University of California-Berkeley Library, the Carter G. Woodson branch of the Chicago Public Library, the Chicago Public Schools alumni website, and the Young Research Library of the University of California-Los Angeles. I also want to thank Mary Helen Washington and Alan Wald for their valuable input and the following individuals for their diligence as research assistants: Neetu Khanna, Aneeka Henderson, Denise Cruz, Rychetta Watkins, and Mary Lou Fulton. Finally, I must express my special gratitude to Mrs. Frances Attaway and to her children, William Attaway and Noelle Attaway Kirton.

Notes

1. Meltzer, Milton. "William Attaway, Negro Novelist," *Daily Worker*, June 26, 1939, 7.
2. Attaway recalled that he was five when his family moved, which would have placed their arrival in Chicago between November 1916 and November 1917 (see Meltzer, "At-

taway," 7). However, there are reports of his father's involvement in Mississippi politics through early 1918. In July 1918, the *Chicago Defender* notes that Dr. Attaway was now residing in the city.

3. "'End Riots Ere It's Too Late,' Negroes Advise," *Chicago Daily Tribune*, July 31, 1919, 3.

4. Burley, Dan. Review of *Let Me Breathe Thunder*, by William Attaway, *New York Amsterdam News*, August 12, 1939, 6.

5. "Autobiographical Note," *Illinois Alumni Newsletter* (December 1939) (clipping identified and dated by hand), J. Kerker Quinn Papers, record series 15/7/30, box 20, University of Illinois Library; Meltzer, "Attaway," 7.

6. "Autobiographical Note."

7. Meltzer, "Attaway," 7.

8. "Illinois State News," *Chicago Defender*, February 1, 1936, 21, National edition.

9. Attaway, William A. "Tale of the Blackamoor." *Challenge*, 1 (June 1936): 3.

10. Meltzer, "Attaway," 7. Meltzer's article specifies neither the college where Attaway first heard Richard Wright speak nor the location of Wright's reading. In his biography of Wright, Michel Fabre observes, "The *Daily Worker* reported that the only exception [to the positive responses to "Big Boy Leaves Home"] had been the Literary Society at the University of Chicago where, as he was reading the manuscript, he saw the audience gradually leave the room, apparently shocked by his language." In a footnote, Fabre adds, "In an early version of *Black Boy* . . . [Wright] says this took place in Evanston, where he had been invited to read his works and talk, and that the Communists who denounced him as a Trotskyite at the time spread the word that the audience had to leave because Wright was speaking without their permission. Wright found himself alone with William Attaway, who took him to a party among black people where they had a wonderful time" (Michel Fabre, *The Unfinished Quest of Richard Wright* [New York: William Morrow, 1973], 133, 547–48). It may well be that Attaway witnessed this incident during one of his trips home to Chicago. If so, he may have somehow been involved with the literary society at the University of Chicago since Meltzer credits him with inviting Wright to address the group.

11. Wald, Alan M. *Exiles from a Future Time: The Forging of the Mid-Twentieth-Century Literary Left*. Chapel Hill: University of North Carolina, 2002, 281. Wald continues, "At the height of the Cold War he hid and transported Black Communist Party leaders who went underground" (Wald, *Exiles*, 283).

12. Maxwell, William J. *New Negro, Old Left*. New York: Columbia University Press, 1999, 2.

13. Meltzer, "Attaway," 7.

14. Attaway, William. *Let Me Breathe Thunder*. Garden City, N.Y.: Doubleday, Doran, 1939, 50–51.

15. Attaway, *Thunder*, 57.

16. Cameron, May. "New Negro Writer Makes His Bow," review of *Let Me Breathe Thunder*, by William Attaway, *New York Post*, June 29, 1939, 15; Alain Locke, "Dry Fields and Green Pastures." *Opportunity* 18 (January 1940): 8.

17. Lee, Ulysses. "On the Road." *Opportunity* 17 (September 1939): 283.

18. Lee, "On the Road," 284.

19. See Gene Andrew Jarrett, *Deans and Truants: Race and Realism in African American Literature*. Philadelphia: University of Pennsylvania Press, 2006.

20. The illustration on the original dust jacket for *Blood on the Forge* was produced by African American artist Charles Alston, one of the leaders of the "306 Group."

21. Arna Bontemps to Langston Hughes, August 19, 1941, *Arna Bontemps-Langston Hughes Letters, 1925–1967*, edited by Charles H. Nichols. New York: Dodd, Mead, 1980, 87. Bontemps also commented on Attaway's novel in a radio program entitled *Of Men and Books* ("To Interview Arna Bontemps on Radio," *Chicago Defender*, November 15, 1941, 12, National edition).

22. Attaway, William. *Blood on the Forge*. Garden City, N.Y.: Doubleday, Doran, 1941, 67.

23. Attaway, *Blood*, 262.

24. Deeb, Gary. "'Skag,' A Real Ground-Breaker May Bring TV into the 1980s," *Chicago Tribune*, January 24, 1980, A8. Romare Bearden spent some of his youth in Pittsburgh with his maternal grandmother, who had black laborers from the South lodging with her. In the December 1937 issue of *Opportunity*, Bearden published an article about the role of such workers in the struggle to unionize the remaining mills in the Midwest after the CIO's victory in its dealings with the massive U. S. Steel (Romare Bearden, "The Negro in 'Little Steel,'" *Opportunity* 15 [December 1937]: 362–65, 380). Attaway and Bearden were close in the late 1930s—in the summer of 1939, for instance, Attaway took his friend along on a trip to visit his mother in Michigan. Bearden's knowledge of the steel industry and interest in the union movement likely provided considerable reinforcement for Attaway's current project. It may even be the case that Bearden supplied Attaway with information for *Blood on the Forge* to which the latter would not have otherwise had easy access. In 1968 Bearden acknowledged that Attaway had positively affected his own work as well by urging him to focus on "Southern themes" in his art. He recalled Attaway telling him, "Why don't you draw—you know, just let yourself go and draw some of the things that you know about!" (Romare Bearden, interview by Henri Ghent, June 29, 1968, in the Smithsonian Archives of American Art, http://www.aaa. si.edu/collections/oralhistories/transcripts/bearde68.htm).

25. de Kay, Drake. "The Color Line," review of *Blood on the Forge*, by William Attaway, *New York Times Book Review*, August 24, 1941, 18.

26. Schuyler, George S. "Kingdom of Steel," review of *Blood on the Forge*, by William Attaway, *Pittsburgh Courier*, October 18, 1941, 15.

27. Sanford, George. Review of *Blood on the Forge*, by William Attaway, *Chicago Defender*, November 8, 1941, 9, National edition.

28. Advertisement for *Blood on the Forge*, by William Attaway, *New York Times*, September 9, 1941, 21. A second such ad appeared in the *Chicago Defender* but with a differently worded statement by Wright and a brief comment from Walter White (Advertisement for *Blood on the Forge*, by William Attaway, *Chicago Defender*, November 1, 1941, 2, National edition).

29. Ivy, James W. "Trouble in Canaan." *The Crisis* 48 (December 1941): 395.

30. Warner, Ralph. "'Blood on the Forge' Is Story of Negro Brothers," review of *Blood on the Forge*, by William Attaway, *Daily Worker*, November 8, 1941, 7.

31. Ellison, Ralph. "Transition." *Negro Quarterly* 1 (Spring 1942), 90. Ellison's review is a revision of his earlier piece on Attaway's novel (see Ralph Ellison, "The Great Migration," *New Masses*, December 2, 1941, 23–24).

32. Ellison, "Transition," 91.

33. "'Blood on the Forge' Author Replies to Book's Critics," *Chicago Defender*, December 13, 1941, 9, National edition.

34. Gayle, Jr., Addison. *The Way of the New World: The Black Novel in America*. Garden City, N.J.: Anchor Press/Doubleday, 1975, 159.

35. Gayle, *Way of the New World*, 163.

36. The Monthly Review edition is now out of print, as is that issued by Anchor-Doubleday in 1993 with an introduction by Nicholas Lemann. The novel is currently available on the New York Review of Books imprint (2005), with an introduction by Darryl Pinckney.

37. "Current Town Talk." *Negro Story* 1 (October–November 1944), 60.

38. Attaway, William. "Death of a Rag Doll." *The Tiger's Eye*, 1 (October 1947): 87.

39. Attaway, "Rag Doll," 86.

40. Shaw, Arnold. *Belafonte: An Unauthorized Biography*. Philadelphia: Chilton, 1960, 75. In a recent interview, Belafonte suggests that Sidney Poitier was also involved in the Sage (Misani, "A Talk with Harry Belafonte," part 2, *New York Amsterdam News*, December 29, 2005–January 4, 2006, 17).

41. Shaw, *Belafonte*, 78.

42. Ibid., 118.

43. Ibid., 171.

44. Jay Orr, "Music City: Singer Greets Music City with Legendary Sound of 'Jamaica Farewell,'" *Nashville Banner*, November 14, 1996, C3.

45. "Calypsomania," *Time*, March 25, 1957, 55.

46. Shaw, *Belafonte*, 171.

47. An Academy Award winner for *All the King's Men* in 1949, Rossen had been blacklisted after testifying before the House Un-American Activities Committee in 1951; then, two years later, he agreed to provide the Committee with names of individuals with Communist Party affiliations.

For Further Reading

Attaway, William. *Blood on the Forge*. Garden City, N.Y.: Doubleday, Doran, 1941.
———. *Calypso Song Book: Authentic Folk Music of the Caribbean*, edited by Lyle Kenyon Engel. New York: McGraw-Hill, 1957.
———. "Death of a Rag Doll." *The Tiger's Eye* 1 (October 1947): 86–89.
———. *Hear American Singing*. New York: Lion Press, 1967.
———. *Let Me Breathe Thunder*. Garden City, N.Y.: Doubleday, Doran, 1939; London: Robert Hale, [1940].
———. "Tale of the Blackamoor." *Challenge* 1 (June 1936): 3–4.
Barthold, Bonnie J. *Black Time: Fiction of Africa, the Caribbean, and the United States*. New Haven: Yale University Press, 1981.

Bone, Robert A. *The Negro Novel in America.* 1958; rev. ed. New Haven: Yale University Press, 1965.

Campbell, Jane. *Mythic Black Fiction: The Transformation of History.* Knoxville: University of Tennessee Press, 1986.

Foley, Barbara. *Radical Representations: Politics and Form in U.S. Proletarian Fiction, 1929–1941.* Durham, N.C.: Duke University Press, 1993.

Garren, Samuel B. "'He Had Passion': William Attaway's Screenplay Drafts of Irving Wallace's *The Man.*" *CLA Journal* 37 (March 1994): 245–60.

———. "Playing the Wishing Game: Folkloric Elements in William Attaway's *Blood on the Forge.*" *CLA Journal* 32 (September 1988): 10–22.

———. "William Attaway." In *Dictionary of Literary Biography. Vol. 76: Afro-American Writers, 1940–1955,* edited by Trudier Harris and Thadious M. Davis, 3–7. Detroit: Gale Research Inc., 1988.

Gayle, Addison, Jr. *The Way of the New World: The Black Novel in America.* Garden City, N.J.: Anchor Press/Doubleday, 1975.

Hamilton, Cynthia. "Work and Culture: The Evolution of Consciousness in Urban Industrial Society in the Fiction of William Attaway and Peter Abrahams." *Black American Literature Forum* 21 (Spring–Summer 1987): 147–63.

Libretti, Timothy R. "U.S. Literary History and Class Consciousness: Rethinking U.S. Proletarian and Third World Minority Literatures." PhD Dissertation, University of Michigan, 1995.

Margolies, Edward. *Native Sons: A Critical Study of Twentieth-Century Negro American Authors.* Philadelphia: J. B. Lippincott, 1968.

Maxwell, William. *New Negro, Old Left: African American Writing and Communism between the Wars.* New York: Columbia University Press, 1999.

Morgan, Stacy I. "Migration, Material Culture, and Identity in William Attaway's *Blood on the Forge* and Harriette Arnow's *The Dollmaker.*" *College English* 63 (July 2001): 712–40.

Rodgers, Lawrence R. *Canaan Bound: The African-American Great Migration Novel.* Urbana: University of Illinois, 1997.

Wald, Alan M. *Exiles from a Future Time: The Forging of the Mid-Twentieth-Century Literary Left.* Chapel Hill: University of North Carolina, 2002.

Papers

Various of Attaway's page proofs, scripts, and correspondence can be found in collections at the University of California-Los Angeles Library, the Schomburg Center for Research in Black Culture, the University of Minnesota Library, and the University of California-Berkeley Library.

CLAUDE A. BARNETT
(September 16, 1889–August 2, 1967)
Bill V. Mullen

Claude Barnett, along with the founders of the *Chicago Defender* and *Ebony* magazine Robert S. Abbott and John Johnson, respectively, stands as one of the three most important African American media entrepreneurs in Chicago in the twentieth century. The founder of the Associated Negro Press, the first Black news service in the country, Barnett significantly advanced the role of the Black Press in Chicago and nationally from 1919 to after World War II. An innovator in press coverage, news sharing, advertising, and public relations, Barnett professionalized Black journalism and displayed a middle-road commitment to racial progress and civil rights. He was also friend, correspondent, and publisher to many of the most important African American writers of his day. Up until his death in 1967, Barnett arguably played the single largest role in nurturing the modern Black Press we know today.

Barnett was born in Sanford, Florida. His father, William Barnett, was a hotel worker. His mother, Celena Anderson Barnett, worked as a housekeeper. He moved to Chicago as a child, where he attended elementary schools and Oak Park High School and worked as a houseboy in the home of Sears Roebuck and Company founder Richard W. Sears. In 1904, he began attending Tuskegee Institute in Alabama, where he became enamored of the self-help Black capitalist ideology of Tuskegee founder Booker T. Washington. After graduation he returned to Chicago and took a job at the post office. Subsequently, he took a number of jobs, selling photographs and working in advertising before setting up his own agency, C. A. Barnett Advertising, and shortly thereafter Kashmir Chemical Company, manufacturer of Nile Queen cosmetics. His commercial ventures, reminiscent of the barnstorming entrepreneurship of Madame C. J. Walker, foreshadowed his sound instincts for entrepreneurship and a savvy understanding of the emerging African American market for products and issues surrounding African American identity.[1]

Barnett was working for the *Chicago Defender* selling advertising on commission in 1919 when the idea for the Associated Negro Press (ANP) was born.

Barnett recognized that many small Black newspapers across the country were in desperate need of a centralized news service that could regularly provide stories for publication on issues relevant to Black Americans. The ANP began as a tiny office on Chicago's South Side with a small staff providing news releases and other noteworthy materials to Black newspapers through the mail for publication. In return, the newspapers paid modest fees and provided ANP credit lines. ANP news releases initially concentrated on Black joblessness and problems of political representation. The ANP's rise coincided with the proliferation of new Black newspapers not just in Chicago but in other large cities such as Norfolk, Virginia; Houston; and Oklahoma City. Barnett provided for those papers the valuable service of news by and about Black Americans. Barnett also innovated advertising techniques, offering ANP service to newspapers in exchange for advertising space paid for by Black-owned businesses, especially successful cosmetics businesses, including his own. This allowed the ANP to profit and began to challenge the white domination of American commercial advertisers who tended to shun the Black Press. It also linked the rise of the Black Press to commercial prosperity in various sectors of the Black economy. During the 1920s Barnett was also active in Republican Party politics earning minor appointments from then Secretary of Commerce Herbert Hoover.[2]

During the 1920s, the ANP was directed in large part by Percival L. Prattis. The first editor of ANP was Nathum D. Brascher. Yet in the early days of the ANP, Barnett himself wrote and revised many of the company's news releases. He was a skillful and efficient writer and used as his model the wire service reports of the established white press services like Associated Press. The ANP also promoted black achievement in all areas of life and encouraged mass education, a recurring theme in Barnett's own life. The ANP paid special attention to news about Black churches and fraternal organizations while also covering Black entertainers. Internationally, the Press paid special attention to Black Americans traveling overseas, giving coverage to W. E. B. DuBois's efforts to organize the Fifth Pan-African Congress in Tunis in 1929 and reporting on James Weldon Johnson's trip to Japan in the same year to attend a conference at the Institute of Pacific Relations. Regular coverage was also paid to events in Liberia, the Philippines, India, the Caribbean, and South Africa. In 1929, the ANP gave regular coverage to the occupation of Haiti by U.S. Marines. Barnett's tendency to broaden the horizons of readers helped to predict his interest in the affairs of Africa to which he traveled frequently in the later years of his life.[3]

By the onset of the Depression, the ANP was well-established and Barnett was becoming an important figure in Black political and social circles in Chicago. In 1932, he became one of the first graduates of Tuskegee Institute to be elected to its board of trustees. He also assumed a political voice and role, lobbying the National Negro Business League to encourage attention of advertisers to Black consumers and lobbying the Roosevelt administration to pay more attention to the needs of Black colleges. In Chicago, he served as president of the board of Provident Hospital and became a director of the Supreme Liberty Life Insurance Company. In 1934, he married Etta Moten, a widely popular concert singer and actress. Moten helped direct Barnett's attention to the role of Black arts and artists. Meanwhile, as the ANP expanded its coverage, it began to be challenged for the attention of the major Black daily newspapers. Irked by Barnett's role as competitor, the *Chicago Defender* for a short time canceled ties to ANP. Later in the mid-1930s, Barnett was one of a group of investors who attempted, unsuccessfully, to buy the *Defender*. Even into the 1940s the relationship between the ANP and the *Defender* could be testy. In 1949, Barnett complained in a letter to publisher John Sengstacke that the *Defender* "unlike most any other paper, has a habit of using ANP material without credit lines." Yet generally speaking the ANP and *Defender*, Chicago's two journalistic titans, coexisted peacefully in the common pursuit of building a stronger national Black Press.[4]

The growth of the ANP also mirrored and was driven by the increasing attention paid to Black American life by the Roosevelt administration. In 1939, Alvin E. White became the ANP's first full-time representative in Washington. During World War II, as the Black Press increased demand for access and recognition, Ernest Johnson represented the ANP in Washington without the benefit of full press credentials. Barnett supported a National Conference of Negro Publishers meeting held in Chicago in March 1940. Also in 1940, Barnett was one of the primary organizers of the important American Negro Exposition, a showcase for national Black writers and artists held in Chicago. During the war he wrote for the CBS radio broadcast "The Negro Press in America's War Effort," which argued that the Black Press was the most powerful institution in Black America outside of the church. In 1942, Barnett was appointed special assistant to the U.S. secretary of agriculture. During the war he also became a trustee of the Phelps-Stokes Fund, a foundation sponsoring programs to improve race relations. Also in 1942 Barnett lectured at the annual convention of the Negro Newspaper Publishers Association, a national network of Black publishers. On June 6, 1942, at their annual meeting, Barnett urged the publishers to develop a cooperative plan that would directly boost the role of the ANP and expand its territorial base to New York and Washington. He also encouraged Black papers to increase their photographic coverage of news. On the political war front, Barnett demanded that papers continue their coverage of racism suffered by Black soldiers and underscored the need for coverage of Africa. "Africa is the real prize in this war" he argued, "and our contact with Africans and African papers show us that we are far more than cousins to them."[5] In 1945, the ANP printed an annual report with an extensive list of "Membership Newspapers." They included almost all of the major Black newspapers of the day: *Baltimore Afro-American, Atlanta Inde-*

pendent, Amsterdam News of New York, Birmingham Reporter, Portland Times, Phoenix Tribune, Kansas City Call, St. Louis Argus, Tuskegee Student, Washington Bee, and *Indianapolis Recorder.* At one point the ANP included *The Negro World,* published by Marcus Garvey, on its membership list.

Among the special features developed by the ANP during the 1930s and 1940s were opinion columns by William Pickens, field secretary of the NAACP, and Fisk University President Charles S. Johnson's "A Minority View" column. Pickens wrote a series of articles on Cuba and the difficulty African Americans had earning visas to travel there. The ANP also provided limited but regular coverage of international events. Marian Anderson's concert tour to Germany earned coverage, as did efforts by the U.S. Commission sent to study allegations that slavery was being practiced in Liberia. Prattis, an ANP correspondent, wrote a series of articles on Haiti as a member of the Hoover Commission sent to study educational conditions there. The ANP regularly received requests by newspapers overseas for stories and news releases on Black American life. The ANP had as many as eight war correspondents stationed overseas during World War II and shared a correspondents' pool with the National Negro Publishers Association. Among the correspondents was the white literary impresario Nancy Cunard, who was stationed in Paris. By 1944, ANP subscribers were at an all-time high, its member newspapers reaching a combined circulation of more than one million a week.[6]

Politically, Barnett and the ANP held to a solid middle-ground position during a period of political turbulence and increased federal monitoring and surveillance of the Black Press. Barnett boasted that the ANP had "no axes to grind" and often skirted politically volatile issues in their newspaper coverage. Barnett remained vigilant that the ANP be a bridge-builder between and among different Black newspaper entities and that it retain an editorial policy wedded to the production of profits. In June of 1943, for example, Barnett wrote to *Chicago Defender* publisher John Sengstacke vowing to improve the relationship between the National Negro Publishers Association and the Associated Negro Press. This concept was tied to Barnett's plans to raise rates and profits, a benefit, he argued, for all parties to the Black Press. At the same time, Barnett remained committed to improving mass education for Black Americans and reversing or ameliorating what he perceived as widespread economic dissatisfaction. This calculated, progressive agenda, marked by a Washingtonian premise that economic uplift was a key to the future of the race, helped the ANP avoid some of the more strenuous harassment and monitoring directed against other Black papers and media organizations by the federal government. The ANP generally gave necessary attention to egregious acts of racism against blacks while leaving more militant editorializing against lynching and job discrimination to subscriber clients like the *Defender* and *Pittsburgh Courier.*[7]

As the ANP grew, Barnett did assume an increasingly large public role as gadfly and promoter of African American culture, especially literary culture. Barnett organized the exhibits and programs on the Black Press, art, and theater for the 1940 American Negro Exposition. The ANP features editor throughout the 1930s and up until the end of the war was the poet, jazz critic, and photographer Frank Marshall Davis. Davis was one of a number of book reviewers for the ANP who helped to promote new Black writers and titles like the work of Melvin Tolson and Margaret Walker. Davis, who was openly progressive in his writing and politics, may also have been responsible for encouraging the more conservative Barnett to make room for more sharply political commentary and criticism. For example, in September, 1944, Chicago painter and poet Margaret Taylor Goss Burroughs reviewed Howard Fast's *Freedom Road* for the ANP. The ANP also produced reviews of new books by poet Owen Dodson and Chicago writer Willard Motley's *We Fished All Night*. Frank Marshall Davis, who published several books of poems while employed by the ANP, reviewed Margaret Walker's groundbreaking collection *For My People*, calling it "far and away the best book of poetry by a Negro to be published in the last five years," as well as Melvin Tolson's *Rendezvous with America* in 1944.[8] The ANP trumpeted the arrival of Chicago writer Theodore Ward's new play *John Brown* in 1950 and promoted popular genre novelist Frank Yerby into the 1950s. Langston Hughes, a friend and regular correspondent with Barnett, developed a unique writing relationship to the ANP, writing poems on political themes for direct distribution by Barnett's news service. Poems like "Governor Fires Dean" and "The Mitchell Case" were submitted directly to Barnett and then distributed for publication in newspapers like the *Defender*. Richard Wright and Zora Neale Hurston also were Barnett's friendly correspondents. In 1941, Barnett responded favorably to a proposal by Wright to write ten articles at 1,000 words each on the Soviet Union and China. Hurston shared intimate political views with Barnett in letters about the atomic bomb, World War II, and American racism. The Wright and Hurston correspondence helps to reveal how broad-ranging Barnett's influence was whether as a journalist entrepreneur or a sympathetic supporter of writers, who often implicitly trusted him with their opinions and ideas.[9]

At war's end the ANP, like other figures and institutions in Chicago, found itself in rapid transition. The birth of large commercial Black periodicals like *Ebony* created instant competition for Barnett and loosened his hold on Black news distribution. Barnett also lost a key member of his editorial staff when writer and editor Frank Marshall Davis left the ANP and Chicago to move to Hawaii. In 1947, Barnett made his first trip to Africa and both Barnett and Etta Moten lectured on Africa in the United States He began regular travels there and increased coverage of Africa in the ANP. In 1959–60 Barnett organized a World News Service (WNP). The WNP operated out of Chicago and provided

African newspapers with new releases in English or French. At one point the ANP posted stringers, part-time writers, in more than ten countries, including Russia, France, and Ghana. The ANP meanwhile continued its biweekly news releases even as the *Chicago Defender* moved to a daily edition. Barnett also used the ANP during the 1950s to voice modest support for the anticolonial movement being led by more vociferous voices in the United States like Paul Robeson and W. E. B. DuBois. By the late 1950s, competition with other media was reducing Barnett's subscription base. In 1964, Barnett retired and sold the ANP to Al Duckett, a Black journalist from New York. Not longer after, in July 1964, the ANP ceased operations. Barnett's health began to decline, and he suffered a stroke that caused partial paralysis. He died on August 2, 1967.

Claude Barnett played a crucial mediating role in Chicago's Black Renaissance. He provided news coverage, work opportunities, and cultural contacts for African Americans, especially in Chicago, and helped to build a national Black media and readership that forecast the rise of the Black commercial press after World War II. His tireless promotion of Black culture and Black capitalism put him at the center of efforts to increase Black participation in a liberal democratic society. His tolerance of and support for leftist writers and editors and his willingness to publish poetry on explicitly political themes was in keeping with the general spirit of militancy in the Black Press, especially during World War II. It contributed to the swell of Black reading interest in Black newspapers in particular, which during the war saw a rise in combined weekly circulation of nearly 43 percent. At the same time, Barnett also institutionalized and foreshadowed the explosion of Black-owned, Black-operated publications from the end of World War II until the 1960s proliferation of small magazines, journals, and other cultural outposts such as theater. While it would be unfair to call Barnett simply a Black capitalist, his savvy, groundbreaking strategies for producing Black wealth while holding aloft the banner of self-respect and decency make him, at the least, a key "race man" of the twentieth century. In 1963, *Ebony* magazine, appropriately, ranked Barnett among the 100 most influential Black Americans. Barnett's legacy will only grow as scholars continue to study the still underexplored body of his personal and professional work, including the Claude Barnett Papers, one of the most important archives of Black journalism in the United States

Notes

1. See Linda J. Evans. "Claude A. Barnett and the Associated Negro Press." *Chicago History: The Magazine of the Chicago Historical Society.* Spring, 1983. V. XII, N. 1, 44–56.
2. Ibid.
3. Ibid. See also Lawrence D. Hogan. *Black National News Service: The Associated Negro*

Press and Claude Barnett, 1919–1945. Rutherford, N.J.: Fairleigh Dickinson University Press, 1984.

4. Evans, 48–50.

5. Ibid., 50–51.

6. See James Johnson. *The Associated Negro Press: A Medium of International News and Information, 1919–1967*. Ann Arbor: UMI, 1982.

7. Evans, 47.

8. Davis, Frank Marshall. "For My People Best Poetry Volume in Five Years." In *Writings of Frank Marshall Davis: A Voice of the Black Press*, edited by John Edgar Tidwell. Jackson: University Press of Mississippi, 2007, 67.

9. See Martin Schipper. *The Claude A. Barnett Papers: The Associated Negro Press News Releases, 1928–1964*. Frederick, Md.: University Publications of America, 1986.

For Further Reading

BlackPressUSA.com.

Cayton, Horace and St. Clair Drake. *Black Metropolis: A Study of Negro Life in a Northern City*. New York: Harper and Row, 1962.

Finkle, Lee. *Forum for Protest: The Black Press during World War II*. Rutherford: Fairleigh Dickinson University Press, 1975.

Washburn, Patrick S. *A Question of Sedition: The Federal Government's Investigation of the Black Press during World War II*. New York: Oxford University Press, 1986.

Papers

The Claude A. Barnett Papers are housed at the Chicago Historical Society and are open to public view. They include correspondence, news clippings, and other papers for the years 1918–67 and Associated Negro Press news releases from 1928–64.

HENRY LOWINGTON BLAKELY II
(1916–1996)
Lovalerie King

In Henry Blakely's poem, "What If," the speaker poses the dual question, "What if the atoms of my breath / be galaxies, / and all man's great philosophies / his fear of death?"[1] Like so many of his other poems, "What If" displays the poet's deeply contemplative nature, his need to pose the existential question. Blakely was born in 1916 to Henry Lowington and Pearl Telley Blakely; his maternal family background included Kentucky slavery. His mother's family settled in Chicago where Pearl met Henry Blakely I at Wendell Phillips High School. Their marriage yielded three sons, Henry, Julius, and Edgar. The elder Henry Blakely was a dreamer and an inventor, which led to some problems on the domestic front. While he could earn a good income in the steamfitting trade, the dreamer in him drove him to spend time on a variety of inventions. Pearl Blakely was more practical. Blakely would contrast his parents in the poem, "My Daddy": "Mother was earth / and nourished us. / But Daddy saw earth / as mire / trapping the feet and movement / and promises of far journeys."[2]

When Blakely was thirteen years old, his father left the family and moved in with another woman. In his biography of Gwendolyn Brooks, George Kent writes that Henry seems to have been the most affected by his father's desertion. Not only did Blakely have to endure the fact of the desertion, but he also knew that his father had children with other women. With irregular support from the father, the family moved often and Henry, for a time, came to associate hunger with his father's domestic failures. In "My Daddy," he writes, "Hunger I came to not care for, / nor for Daddy, / before I was old enough to see / that dreams / must be paid for, / that it is as right / to want fuel for flight / as for boiling beans."[3] The poem, really an epic salute to his father, reveals the breadth and depth of the family anguish the father's desertion caused. Still, his "single" mother raised him with love and discipline. George Kent writes that in characterizing his relationship with his "single" mother, Blakely recalled both the tender times when his mother read poetry to her sons and the times when she bestowed severe whippings on them to instill discipline.

Like his father and namesake, Henry Blakely was also a dreamer. At Tilden High School in Chicago, young Henry found an outlet for the technical aptitude he inherited from his father and, later, he found an outlet for the sensitive poet part of himself in writing classes at Wilson Junior College. By 1937, he called himself a writer and hoped to find a partner who also wrote. He struck gold when he met Gwendolyn Brooks at the YWCA on Forty-Sixth and South Park (later MLK Drive). Brooks wrote that upon taking note of Blakely, she immediately declared, "There is the man I am going to marry."[4] Against his mother's (perhaps somewhat prophetic) protests that Henry was not ready to take on the responsibilities of husband and father, the couple married two years later, on September 17, 1939, with the Reverend T. C. Lightfoot officiating. While his mother had argued practically that Henry was still in college and a dreamer who had no real way of supporting a family, Henry proved a resilient amalgam of his mother's practicality and his father's technical ability and dreamy, questing nature. Nevertheless, some of Pearl Blakely's wisdom was realized in hindsight because Henry and Gwendolyn struggled to deal with the myriad tensions that married life can bring even in the best of circumstances; there were several separations. In his biography of Brooks, George Kent writes that the couple later discussed their separations casually enough. Blakely felt that marriage had "required him to lose innocence and toughen up immediately, whereas Gwendolyn could retain a certain innocence." As they had both been poets, Blakely felt he understood her situation much "better than she could understand the realities he faced outside the home."[5] Blakely's literary life clearly came in second behind the role of family man. Brooks writes of Blakely in the introduction to *Windy Place* (1974) that he was not someone who "cared to rush into print."[6] No doubt the immediacy of attempting to provide for home and family forestalled the development of his craft and, thus, his literary production, particularly given his own family history and the limited opportunities for economic advancement available even to college-educated black men during the early decades of his adult life.

During the first fifteen years of marriage, Blakely worked at a variety of jobs and professions, including a driver, an estimator of automobile repair costs for his co-owned repair shop, and part owner of a consumer consultant buying corporation. Later, he would work as an insurance adjuster. The couple lived in a series of apartments, including their honeymoon kitchenette in the Tyson Apartments on Forty-Third and South Park, 6464 Champlain, 5412 Indiana, and 623 East Sixty-Third. Brooks provides a vivid description of the Forty-Third Street kitchenette in *Maud Martha* (1953). Their son, Henry III, was born October 10, 1940, at the Champlain address and, according to Brooks, contracted bronchopneumonia at the Indiana Street address where they lived in a drafty converted garage. Clearly, the housing and overall socioeconomic situation created tensions in the family that came to a head in July of 1941, when Brooks took their child and left the marriage.

This first separation was short-lived, however, Brooks having been persuaded by her parents to return. Later, the family would settle in for some seven years at the Sixty-Third Street address, the mice-infested home where (as Brooks tells us in *Part One*) they gave their best parties, including one for Langston Hughes. The family's housing problems did not end there, and they devised a number of ways to cope—including sharing living quarters with a family friend and living under separate roofs. At one point, Brooks and son Henry lived in an apartment in the 6800 block of South Evans, while Blakely slept in the downtown garage he was helping to manage. In 1950, Brooks won the Pulitzer Prize for *Annie Allen* (1949), a circumstance that helped to ease temporarily some of their economic woes. In 1951, the family was able to move into a place together at 32 West Seventieth Street, and daughter Nora was born that year on September 8. The family moved into their own home finally on October 10, 1953, the feat being accomplished in part by the selling of a Kalamazoo, Michigan, rental property.

In the 1940s, the couple became associated with socialite Inez Cunningham Stark's writing workshop at the South Side Community Arts Center. Margaret Walker, Margaret Esse Danner, Frank Marshall Davis, and several others joined the workshop. According to Brooks, Starks "loved poetry and valued the minds that made it."[7] The workshop, along with the WPA's Illinois Writers' Project, The Rosenwald Fund, the Chicago Unit of the Federal Theatre Project, the South Side Writers Workshop (which began years earlier), the Great Migration beginning decades before, and the intellectual energy emanating from the "Chicago School" (a group of scholars based at the University of Chicago that included Horace Cayton, Charles S. Johnson, Robert Park, E. Franklin Frazier, and Louis Wirth), all fed life into the Chicago Black Renaissance (later called the Negro People's Front to reflect its Socialist ideological underpinnings). Its early years identified largely with Richard Wright's work and his seminal essay, "Blueprint for Negro Writing," the broader cultural movement flourished in the (roughly) two decades from the early 1930s to the early 1950s and included writers, scholars, and performers, including those mentioned above and others such as Dorothy West, Fenton Johnson, Arna Bontemps, Willard Motley, Katherine Dunham, Theodore Ward, and Frank Yerby. (Frank London Brown, who served as Director of the Union Leadership School at the University of Chicago, was a close Blakely family friend with whom Henry Blakely had numerous discussions about his work.) According to Brooks, Langston Hughes was also present in Chicago for a time, providing assistance to a number of the younger, struggling writers. Some see the Chicago Black Renaissance as an artistic movement equal to the Harlem Renaissance because it produced novels, poetry, drama, music, and literary journals. Although Gwendolyn Brooks achieved great recognition as a poet during the Chicago Black Renaissance—publishing two award-winning collections—Blakely published little in comparison. Kent notes in his biography of Brooks that Blakely had submitted some good poems to Harper, but they were too few in number for a collection. Blakely also circulated some stories and completed a novel, which George Kent describes as massive, "The Dry Well Papers." Two poems, "Dread Automaton" and "Earthworm," were published in 1940 and 1950, respectively. Both poems (with "Dread Automaton" changed to "Automaton") were included in *Windy Place*.

A commentary on the age of machines, "Automaton" depicts machines used in construction collectively as a huge mechanical beast that blocks out the sun and crushes beauty "beneath his iron feet," with "vibrant life" oozing "redly out / through crushing fingers of steel." The monster's "voice" emits sound that drowns out the sounds of the natural world; the poem's mood is one of inevitable doom for the natural world overcome by the onslaught of the man-made steel monster: "Bird song, / sky song, / music of wind and water, / against the booming cadence / of his voice, trilled to nothing." Blakely's use of words such as "oozed," "crushing," and "booming" breathes life into the otherwise dead steel, its artificial "booming cadence" displacing the natural music of bird, wind, and water.[8] "Earthworm" displays a reverence for the natural world; the poem's earthworm functions in a Dickinsonian manner as a metaphor for the unsung of the world who go about the necessary work of living and producing future generations "without formal statement of law, / without science or art, / and, seemingly, without awe."[9] The poem references faith in the unseen, the routines of living, and the diligence with which the masses at the bottom layer of society confront life day after day, year after year, and generation after generation.

Blakely was finally able to publish the poems he had written and honed over many years in *Windy Place*. The collection of sixty-three poems appeared around the time that he and Brooks reconciled after a separation that began in 1969. Brooks recalls that the reconciliation actually began when she invited Blakely to her mother's eighty-fifth birthday party in 1973. In her introduction to *Windy Place*, she explains that the work reveals Henry Blakely's Chicago, particularly Sixty-Third Street: "We get to know Club Arden, which became a vacant lot. We leap over time and see the tavern wall graffiti. We know Lucy, Club Arden's queen." We also "meet Sixty-Third Street pigeons who, 'too tired for flight,' move 'slow / with glassy eye,' the pigeons reminding us of "old men 'moving slow, with glassy eye.'" *Windy Place* contains "salutes to heroes, romantic songs, tributes to the varying voices and faces of nature."[10] The poems express themes that dealt with the often harsh realities of growing up black and poor in the hostile environment that was Chicago at the time.

Like George Kent, Brooks recognized "My Daddy" as the major achievement of *Windy Place*. Brooks called it his masterpiece, "a little epic."[11] Kent wrote in *Phylon* that "My Daddy" was deservedly the "opening and separately sectioned poem" that "takes the black father of unstable family relationships from his frozen place in sociological cliché and restores him to the density of reality."[12] "My Daddy" is composed of some forty stanzas of varying lengths with irregular rhyming schemes. The use of "daddy" rather than "father" casts the speaker as a young boy. The opening stanzas, as Kent notes, project "swift movement and concreteness":[13]

> My Daddy died age sixty-seven,
> one Saturday night,
> hale at nine,
> gone at eleven.
>
> Tall for his time,
> my Daddy,
> and quick and lean
> as men must be when
> lithe and alive
> and on the move.
>
> "Came in and took a bath,"
> they said.
> "And then went out."
> And that was that.[14]

In these early stanzas, the poet constructs his father as a manly hero. At sixty-seven, the father showed no signs of slowing down, and the poet reinforces this point in a later stanza explaining that the woman he was with when he died was even too young for the son.

The next stanzas are softer; the speaker begins to recollect childhood memories. He remembers his father's magic tricks, "making nuts and candies" appear.[15] He recalls an intelligent man who could explain the physics of "why air collapsed a can in which the steam had turned to water," a man who knew how to spell words and who understood math. He depicts a man among men, for when his daddy spoke, "men listened." Even his deserted mother reflects awe in referring to him as "so mighty" on the day of his funeral.[16]

The speaker casts mother and father elementally as earth and air, respectively; his mother was the grounded, practical entity and his father the dreamer for whom the earth was "mire / trapping the feet and movement / and promises of far journeys." In other examples from everyday life, he recalls wrestling matches with the three sons—Henry, Julius, and Edgar—who tried but never could "hold an arm down." The speaker clearly identifies with the father; seeing his own name on the funeral directory "made time bunch up, / rubbed out the little space / separating him from me / and for a moment let me know / how it was to be dead." The father was also an inventor, who made clocks, scooters, airplanes, boats, and a barbecue grill "'that did everything but buy the meat.'"[17]

The recital of his father's greatness segues into a discussion of his human failings, his infidelities to wife and sons: Gracie, the too young woman that had been with his father the night he died, and Helen (mother of Howard, his father's other son). He recalls the family angst at having to endure their presence at the funeral, forced to share even their grief with them. The speaker continues to alternate among funeral memories, memories of the immediate family, and the broader paternal and maternal histories—his maternal roots being much wider and deeper. In the end, the speaker tries to come to terms with his father's act of desertion, and even questions why his mother in her obvious enduring love for him did not see that the man "feared to die / and felt that death could not come / if he was up and moving on"; he concludes simply that "Daddy was his own man, / no clocks, nor gate, nor stall."[18] Even after recounting the hunger, the drafty basement apartments, and the other deprivations that the father's desertion caused the family, the speaker can say,

> "Strange now
> that I remember him kindly,
> see him
> as more right than wrong.
> Strange now
> that I see Mother wanting bread,
> needing it—for us,
> and know that bread
> was not enough.[19]

Ever the existentialist, Blakely cannot end on that note, however, and adds one last stanza positing that perhaps the now dead man has some things to work out in the spiritual realm. Kent notes importantly that, "in a poem of very simple diction the reader moves among many tensions, complexities, shadows, lights." In the descriptions of the various family relationships and "the father's life and his relationships with the family and others, there are the lines which . . . project the terrible mixtures of emotions the powerful figure occasions within us, even when he disappoints our most elemental needs."[20] "My Daddy" puts the poet's soul on display, and we travel with him back through a most difficult part of his life in his quest to come to terms with his own personal history, to understand the man that gave him life and his name.

In other poems, such as "Autumn Perspective," the poet considers the fleeting nature of existence. The poem moves quickly, mediated by its language and delivered in short lines that form a series of questions making abundant use of the sibilant. It begins with a stanza of seven lines and the simple statement that "Henry Blakely's beard is gray," followed by the question, "When did this happen?" The central stanza is the longest, composed of fifteen short lines that form four questions. The longest line is the sixth, composed of five words:

> Where are the winds
> And wines,
> The girls
> And melodies?
> What journeying
> is tracked in this gray?[21]

In the autumn of life, what aspects of the person's life journey are revealed (or hidden) in gray hair? By the end of the central stanza, girls are no longer girls, they are "only women, / co-predators."[22] The final stanza contains one question, the less than optimistic question of whether death is not only possible but also wise under the circumstances.

In "Lucy," the poet pays tribute to a Club Auden regular, the type of fun-loving party woman that might be found in a Langston Hughes poem, even as her name invokes the prehistoric hominid Lucy whose remains were discovered in 1974. Lucy becomes both real and representative. Contemporary graffiti becomes hieroglyphics. Club Auden's Lucy is engaged in the world's oldest profession, but she is always fair in her dealings. Blakely alternates between the three four-line stanzas (with an aaba rhyme scheme) and two (unrhymed) nine-line stanzas. The quick rhythm of the short stanzas—"Club Arden is a vacant lot / where Lucy shook it, lush and hot, / as does her shade now, / like as not"—gives way to the more conversational tone of the longer stanzas that expand and elaborate. The final stanza leaves us with the idea of Lucy's "feet" as the *trace* of the woman and of the representative (ancient) figure: "Graffiti leaving, but no concrete / ritualed by the Lucy feet."[23]

"Windy Place" closes the volume and is composed of six stanzas of free verse in four or five lines each. The speaker reflects on the passing of a friend, whose name is Gerard Lew. The friend's passing distracts the speaker from "press-of-living thoughts, mortgage, job, / Goddam-car's-in-the-shop-again thoughts." The speaker ponders the workings of the wind in the Windy City as he goes about his morning routine, seeing the wind take hold of a bottle cap that has been flicked into the air by the motion of a car's wheels. The bottle cap and its wind-propelled path serve as collective metaphor for individual human journey propelled by the winds of destiny, but it also reminds us of physics and the poet's technical bent: ". . . A car passed, / its wheels flicking a bottle cap on end, / and with the wind the cap was set in motion." The speaker wonders how the wind could take hold of the small, erratically shaped object and set it in motion. He follows the path of the cap: " . . . it wheeled the intersection / through traffic mindless and immense / to its own somewhere on the other side, / itself mindless, and perhaps, immense." The fifth stanza questions what trick of fate and circumstance coming together propelled the cap's journey, and the sixth stanza responds, playfully and optimistically:

> I did not know, but I was glad
> to taste the wind thresholding April
> and to consider that a friend,
> while waiting at some windy place,
> might also have marveled and surmised.[24]

The poem ends Blakely's collection on that optimistic, spiritual, and existential ponderance, confirming that Henry Blakely was indeed a serious dreamer.

In *Part One*, Gwendolyn Brooks described her husband as "a man of intellect, imagination, and dynamic 'constitution,' the old folks' name for a certain physical indomitableness, an on-going strength that resists, again and again threats to its proud survival."[25] Such a characterization pays tribute to Blakely's demonstrated resilience and resolve in the face of the poet's personal, professional, and artistic struggles. On June 7, 1987, Brooks presented a poet laureate award to Blakely designating him an outstanding black poet of Illinois.

Notes

1. Blakely II, Henry Lowington. "What If?" In *Windy Place*. Detroit: Broadside Press, 1974, 69.

2. Blakely, "My Daddy." In *Windy Place*, 12.

3. Ibid.

4. Brooks, Gwendolyn. *Report From Part One*. Detroit: Broadside Press, 1972, 57.

5. Kent, George. *A Life of Gwendolyn Brooks*. Lexington: University Press of Kentucky, 1990, 59.

6. Brooks, "Introduction," in *Windy Place*, 9.

7. Brooks, *Report from Part One*, 65.

8. Blakely, *Windy Place*, 46.

9. Ibid., 31.

10. Brooks, "Introduction," in *Windy Place*, 9.

11. Ibid., 9.

12. Kent, George. "Notes on the Black Literary Scene." *Phylon* 36, 2 (Second Quarter 1975): 182–203.

13. Ibid., 194.

14. Blakely, *Windy Place*, 11.

15. Ibid., 11.

16. Ibid., 12.

17. Ibid., 11–18.

18. Ibid., 15.
19. Ibid., 18.
20. Kent, "Notes on the Black Literary Scene," 194.
21. Blakely, *Windy Place*, 19.
22. Ibid., 19.
23. Ibid., 20.
24. Ibid., 70.
25. Brooks, *Report from Part One*, 58.

For Further Reading

Blakely, Henry Lowington, II. "The Dry Well Papers" (unpublished novel).
Bone, Robert. "Richard Wright and the Chicago Renaissance." *Callaloo* 28 (Summer 1986): 446–68.
Brooks, Gwendolyn. *Annie Allen*. New York: Harper Brothers, 1949.
———. *Maud Martha*. 1949. Chicago: Third World Press, 1993.
Mullen, Bill V. *Popular Fronts: Chicago and African-American Cultural Politics, 1935–46*. Urbana: University of Illinois Press, 1999.
Woolley, Lisa. *American Voices of the Chicago Renaissance*. Dekalb: Northern Illinois University Press, 2000.

ALDEN BLAND
(1911–1992)

Joyce Hope Scott

In the early 1930s, as the famed Harlem Renaissance of black cultural achieve-ment was winding down, a new surge of African American creativity, activism, and scholarship began to flower in the South Side Chicago district. This new "Chicago Renaissance" was fueled by two unprecedented social and economic conditions: the "Great Migration," mass movement of Southern blacks to Chi-cago in search of economic opportunity and perceived safety from lynch mob rule, and the crisis of the Great Depression that followed. They were fleeing the pervasive white violence and racism of the South, which kept African Americans endangered, impoverished, and dispossessed.

Over the preceding two decades, Chicago's black population had soared; from 44,000 in 1910, the community grew to more than 230,000 by 1930. For the most part, the new migrants were confined to a rigidly segregated zone. Richard Wright called its miserable, overcrowded housing "the world of the kitchenettes." The migrants went to work in meatpacking plants and steel mills, garment shops and private homes. After 1929, however, many people lost their jobs as the Great Depression hit the African American community hard. Out of this crisis emerged new ideas and institutions, new political activism, and a revitalized community spirit. By the early 1930s, the South Side black com-munity began to call itself by a new name, "Bronzeville."

Alden Bland was one of the thousands of migrants who came to Chicago from the South. He was born in New Orleans, Louisiana, in 1911. Alden, his brother Edward, and his mother migrated north at the end of WW I when his father, Edward Bland Sr. brought the family to Chicago in order to evade the draft. According to Alden's nephew, Edward Bland III (son of Edward Bland Jr. who reports having known his uncle Alden better than he knew his own father), Alden, and Edward's mother, Philomene Murray Bland, came from a New Orleans family that passed for white. Philomene, being too dark to pass, was given to Edward Bland Sr. in a marriage arranged between her family and the Bland family. Philomene's family origins were rarely mentioned in the Bland households, but Edward Bland III remembers his grandmother as being an extremely intelligent and resourceful woman (Interview with Edward Bland III of Smithfield, Virginia, June 20, 2005).

Alden Bland attended the Illinois Institute of Technology and the University of Chicago but did not graduate from either. After the Depression, he got a job as a postal inspector, his only job but one that he hated because "it stole time from [his] writing." However, he was well respected in his position and even honored at the White House, along with other postal inspectors, during the Johnson administration (Edward Bland III).

The whole Bland family was "quite dysfunctional," according to Edward Bland III. Alden wrote to his editor in December of 1946 that he was "married with one son, Alden Jr." However, he gained a reputation as quite a womanizer and was married seven times during his lifetime. There was talk as well of his having fathered an illegitimate child. His last marriage was to Dr. Alma Jones Bland, now a retired teacher and school principal living in Chicago. His son, Alden Jr. also lives in Chicago, but remains aloof from the family (Edward Bland III).

Alden and his brother, Edward Bland, were members of the South Side Writers Group "organized by Richard Wright in 1936," of which Gwendolyn Brooks, Richard Wright, Frank Marshall Davis, Theodore Ward, and Margaret Walker, among others, were members. In his biographical work on her, George Kent points out that Gwendolyn Brooks knew both Alden Bland and his brother Edward, a poet and critic: "Alden and Edward . . . patiently helped teach Henry [her husband] and me to think." Edward Bland III remembers visits to his home from South Side artists such as Ralph Ellison, Margaret Walker, and Richard Wright, and that Gwendolyn Brooks was a very good friend to his uncle Alden and his father, to whom Brooks dedicated the poem in the Introduction to *Annie Allen*.

Behold A Cry (Charles Scribner's Sons, 1947) was Bland's first and only published work. It was written, as Bland says, "in streetcars, on elevated trains, in wash rooms and public libraries" during the Depression while Bland worked as a porter, street-sweeper, dishwasher, salesman, and accountant. Bland took the title for the book from the Bible, Isaiah: "and he looked for judgment, but behold oppression; for righteousness, but behold a cry." Set in 1918 Chicago, the novel is among a large number of other "migration novels," as Lawrence R. Rodgers refers to them in *Canaan Bound: The African-American Great Migration Novel*. In Rodgers's opinion, *Behold A Cry*, like Ralph Ellison's *Invisible Man* and James Baldwin's *Go Tell It on the Mountain*, "constitute[d] a more optimistic, more nuanced perspective on migration than [its] fugitive migrant forerunners."

Behold A Cry, which is very much an autobiographical account of the Bland family's experiences during Alden and Edward's childhood, fictionalizes the Great Migration experience of blacks coming from the South to the North. The narrative focuses on Ed Tyler, a black man who, like thousands of other black men, left the Mississippi Delta looking for a better life in the North. Ed has left his wife and sons behind saying that he would send for them when he has earned enough money to support them. This similarity to Alden and Edward Bland's own family is unmistakable. The fictionalized Edward Bland Sr., Ed Tyler, is a very tall, strikingly handsome man who has become mesmerized by the high-living, nightclub, and pool-hall life, and the streetwise, classy "colored women" of Chicago's urban ghetto. His slaughterhouse wages make it possible for him to dress stylishly and live in an apartment that he shares with his mistress.

In order to escape the draft, however, Ed Tyler (like Edward Bland Sr.) is obliged to send for his wife and sons, something that he is not anxious to do. He is "disgraced by their fresh-from-the country appearance" (12–13). He casually moves them into the apartment he shares with his mistress, Mamie. Even though Phom, his wife, is not happy with the arrangement, the living conditions seem relatively good. Ed continues to sneak off to be with Mamie, however, while trying to keep the truth of their relationship from Phom and their children (Dan and Son). Like Claude McKay in *Home to Harlem*, Bland succeeds in capturing the street life and the "liberating" and transforming influence it has on Ed Tyler, who radically changes from a simple country peasant to a womanizing "dandy." Yet, unlike McKay's work, which portrays characters submerged in drifting, ad hoc relationships and the easygoing nightlife of Harlem, *Behold A Cry* depicts the harsher realities for blacks in northern cities.

The novel also foregrounds the Chicago race riots of 1918 and 1919, which, in Bland's representation, are provoked by an incident at a public beach where a young black man is killed by whites after blacks attempt to integrate a section of the beach usually off limits to them. However, murderous rioting erupted in the spring and summer of 1919 in twenty-two American cities and towns. The rioting in Chicago was among the most severe in the country. The narrative focuses on the disastrous outcomes for blacks as a result of the riots that followed when black men like Ed Tyler and his friends were used as strikebreakers. Also a focus of the narrative are the varied attitudes of blacks toward unionization:

> "Crop failures, high rents, epidemics, Negroes got plenty reason for leaving the South . . . And there was good jobs waiting in the cities . . . But the war is over now. Things can't stay like this . . ."
>
> "So the union's going to straighten all this out," Tom said derisively.
>
> "But where you going to find more prejudice than in unions?" Joe asked. "Now take us, in the sheepkill, here. We knife men, ain't we? And knife men is supposed to join the Butchers.' Can we? Hell no! All Negroes join 651, All *niggers*—not butchers!"(61)

In the turning point of the narrative, Ed decides to break the strike by going to work at the slaughterhouse. He is badly beaten by whites on his way home and, as he recovers, starts to feel even more trapped in his marriage and his home life. True to his unstable nature, seen throughout the novel, Ed ultimately runs away with the young wife of his protégé whom he has taken into his home. The novel ends with Phom (the fictionalized Philomene Murray Bland) and the children left to face their fate in Chicago's South Side as she remarks that, "The old Ed [who had left her in the South] was broken to bits" (52). She fears for the future of her sons wondering: "When they come face to face with what it means to be black, what then? What happens to [their lives] after that? But how can you get a child ready for it? . . ."(52).

From September 1946 to April 1947, Alden Bland and his editor, Maxwell Perkins, wrote a series of letters to each other concerning Perkins's and others' thoughts on the novel itself, other issues relative to the book's reception, and Bland's potential literary career. The letters indicate that Perkins and Scribners were committed to working with Bland on promoting *Behold A Cry*, as well as possibly publishing other works. Bland instructed Perkins to send copies of the book to a number of influential literary people, among them Richard Wright, Sinclair Lewis, Erskine Caldwell, Frank Tannenbaum at Knopf, Lillian Smith, and Langston Hughes. Bland sent Perkins excerpts of a letter he received from William Carlos Williams about *Behold A Cry*. In it Williams offers glowing praise as well as advice to Bland about being a writer:

> I finished your *Behold A Cry* last evening . . . I don't think you will ever write a book that will give you greater satisfaction . . . I am avoiding all sorts of comments as you may guess, comments thoroughly justified by the book's general excellence . . . I wish you all the courage in the world—for with your own authentic and beautifully realized materials you may, . . . just . . . raise your whole paraphernalia of personal, intimate inescapable world of thought and feeling up to a level of expression that *can* be truly liberating to the mind, to men and women of all races . . .

According to George Kent, who interviewed Alden Bland as well as reviewed the novel, Alden deferred to his brother Edward as a decisive force among the South Side Writers group. Edward Bland's description of the black community as "pre-individualistic" is instructive and seems to have influenced Alden's portrayal of his central character, Ed Tyler. According to Edward Bland, " . . . the Negro stress is on group. Instead of seeing in terms of the individual, the Negro sees in terms of 'races,' masses of people separated from other masses of people according to color." Alden's character, Ed Tyler, articulates this "pre-individualistic" thinking to his sons after he is beaten by whites in the riots:

> . . . Ed opened one eye. It glittered with hate.
> "Look good!" he said . . .

"Look good!" he commanded. "Because I want you to remember what you see. Think about this when you hear all that fancy talk about white folks and how much a friend they is!"

" . . . You too young to understand, I guess. But first and last, remember you a nigger. Look at me and see what it means. I'm your father, yes, but we tied together in another way. We all niggers together! That's something special because it only happens to us . . . being niggers is most important of all!" (163–164)

Alain Locke makes reference to *Behold A Cry* in "A Critical Perspective of the Literature of the Negro for 1947" observing about the work that, "It is a novel of the personal triangle of wife, mistress and desertion as well as of the economic triangle of labor, capital and race, set in World War I Chicago," indeed an exposé of the social realism embraced by Richard Wright and others of the South Side Writers Group. Horace Cayton labeled it "A convincing portrait of Negroes against the rising racial and labor unrest of 1918 . . ." and goes on to note that: "Although not outstanding, perhaps because of its failure to focus on one character that holds the reader's sympathy, this story is convincing in its portrayal of a southern Negro's attempt at adjustment in Chicago . . ."

Theodore Pratt's review of the novel (*New York Herald Tribune Weekly Book Review*, March 9, 1947) is one of the most comprehensive of those given. In "Southern Negroes in Chicago," he characterizes the novel as "a warm human story . . . a novel of Negro life in which the characters are people and not stock figures . . ." Rosenberger continues:

> His subject is one which has been little explored in American fiction: the urban Negro worker who has migrated from the South, and the accompanying personal and social tensions. . . . The author examines clinically the amalgam of hatred and Ignorance and suspicion which makes [Ed Tyler] and hundreds of his neighbors in the crowded Negro section more than Willing to become strike-breakers against the white workers . . . [The novel] has about it no sensationalism to attract an audience, but in its quiet maturity it introduces a new writer of distinction. (7).

Robert Bone gives slight mention of *Behold A Cry* in *The Negro Novel in America* by commenting that it contains "psychological subtlety" (159). Another reviewer, Robert E. Fleming, wrote that "*Behold a Cry* offers, among other things, an examination of the black man's relationship with unions; it presents a black view of the major race riot that erupted in the summer of 1919 . . ."(75).

In one of Bland's letters to Maxwell Perkins, he wrote that he was "interested in doing a novel of the South an open examination of what is happening to the Negro and white personality . . ." However, the project never came to fruition. After retirement, Bland went into real estate where he did extremely well, "becoming nearly a millionaire," (Edward Bland III). Although *Behold A Cry* remains a little-known novel today, overshadowed by the works of Richard Wright and other giants of the South Side Writers group, it does merit "rediscovery" and reconsideration by students and scholars of the New Negro Renaissance in general and the Chicago Renaissance in particular.

Behold A Cry is important, as Robert E. Fleming points out, not only as "an examination of the black man's relationship with unions" and an African American view of "the major race riot that erupted in the summer of 1919," but also as an exposé of the transformative experience of the Great Migration and its ensuing problems for black people in 1947, as well as its consequent legacy inherited by blacks living in American ghettos today. Alden Bland died in Chicago in 1992.

For Further Reading

Alden Bland Letters. A. Pauls Rare Books & Special Collections. Princeton, N.J.: Princeton University Library.

Barnes, Deborah. "'I'd Rather Be a Lamppost in Chicago': Richard Wright and the Chicago Renaissance of African American Literature." *Langston Hughes Review* 14, 1,2 (1996): 52–61.

Bone, Robert. *The Negro Novel in America.* New Haven: Yale University Press, 1958.

———. "Richard Wright and the Chicago Renaissance." *Callaloo* 28. Richard Wright: A Special Issue (Summer 1986): 446–68.

Cayton, Horace. "Behold A Cry." *Booklist* (May 1, 1947)43: 272.

Fleming, R. E. "Overshadowed by Richard Wright: Three Black Chicago Novelists." *Negro American Literature Forum* 7, 3 (Autumn 1973): 75–79.

Giles, James R. and Jerome Klinkowitz. "The Emergence of Willard Motley in Black American Literature." *Negro American Literature Forum* 6, 2 (Summer 1972): 31–34.

Griffin, Farah Jasmine. "Canaan Bound: The African-American Great Migration Novel." Review, *African American Review* 34, 3 (2000): 531–33.

———. "Migration." *Oxford Companion to African American Literature.* New York: Oxford University Press, 1997, 497–98.

Grossman, James R. *Land of Hope: Chicago, Black Southerners, and the Great Migration.* Chicago: University of Chicago Press, 1989.

Kent, George E. *A Life of Gwendolyn Brooks.* Lexington: University Press of Kentucky, 1990.

Kinnamon, Keneth, ed. *New Essays on Native Son.* Cambridge: Cambridge University Press, 1990, 24.

Locke, Alain. "A Critical Retrospect of the Literature of the Negro for 1947." *Phylon* (1940–19), 9, 1 (First Quarter 1948): 3–12.

Melhem, D. H. *Gwendolyn Brooks: Poetry & the Heroic Voice.* Lexington: University Press of Kentucky, 1987.

Okafor-Newsum, Ikechukwu. "Review of Lawrence Rodgers' *Canaan Bound: The Afri-*

can-American Great Migration Novel." *Research in African Literatures* (Winter 1998): 204–5.

Pratt, Theodore. "Behold A Cry," *New York Herald Tribune Weekly Book Review*, March 9, 1947, 7.

———. "Behold A Cry," *New York Times*, March 23, 1947, 18.

Rodgers, Lawrence R. *Canaan Bound: The African-American Great Migration Novel.* Urbana: University of Illinois Press, 1997, 8, 104, 132–33, 141–42.

———. "Dorothy West's *The Living Is Easy* and the Ideal of Southern Folk Community." *African American Review* 26, 1, Women Writers Issue (Spring 1992): 161–72.

Rosenberger, Coleman. "Behold A Cry." *Library Journal* (March 1, 1947): 72, 387.

Rowley, Hazel. *Richard Wright: The Life and Times.* New York: Henry Holt and Co., 2001.

EDWARD BLAND
(February 2, 1908–March 20, 1945)
Lawrence Jackson

As a phenomenon of American literary history, the Chicago Renaissance that began in the second half of the 1930s is most significant for its articulation of an almost complete break with the "Harlem" or "New Negro" Renaissance of the 1920s. The radical tenor of the artists associated with the Chicago movement developed in two distinct forms: the social realism and literary protest of the 1930s and early 1940s, and the high modernism of the second half of the 1940s. The early work of Richard Wright, the early short stories of Frank Yerby, Frank Marshall Davis's poetry, the novels of William Attaway, and the plays of Theodore Ward represent well the efforts of protest realism; the later work of Richard Wright, beginning with "The Man Who Lived Underground" of 1944, the poetry of Robert Hayden, and the poetry of Gwendolyn Brooks best characterize the second movement. These achievements culminated with the efforts of the best-known high modernist novelist, Ralph Ellison. This momentous break from the literary strains of the 1920s and 1930s required a series of radical judgments to refine and transform the literary aesthetics of African American writers.

The first black writer who developed a body of criticism that made a departure from a straightforward doctrinaire Marxist analysis, but who captured the dissident spirit of the new generation, was Edward Bland, brother to novelist Alden Bland. Black critics had been conscious of the tension to assimilate into the white American mainstream, but rarely had they looked analytically at the structure of Western literary evolutions and their place as a formerly enslaved racial minority within that structure. In 1935 and 1937, the black Marxist critics Eugene Gordon, Eugene Holmes, and Richard Wright presented a broad refutation of what they saw as a tendency towards romanticism and assimilation in African American writing. Of these, Wright's "Blueprint for Negro Writing" (1937) is the best known and recognized as the most definitive. And yet, the essays do not strike a completely compelling note; there is a dogmatic formulism in them that lacks complete freshness and originality. Bland's major works, "Social Forces Shaping the Negro Novel," and "Racial Bias in Negro Poetry," introduced key literary terms that produced new revelations about the value of African American literature and culture and its relation to the American mainstream.

Edward Bland was born in New Orleans, Louisiana, on February 2, 1908. His father, Edward Bland III, had moved to Chicago seeking work and sent for his wife Philomene and his two sons Edward and Alden from Louisiana in 1919. Edward and his brother grew up on the South Side, and Edward attended Wendell Phillips High School. After high school Bland married Althea McCoy, and began a career at the U.S. Post Office in Chicago. Bland had four children, two of whom survived: Geraldine, and Edward O. Bland, the noted composer, director of films, and maker of the tour de force documentary "The Cry of Jazz."

During the Depression Bland lived at 5951 Indiana Avenue, where he collected thousands of books, from John Dewey and Bertrand Russell to Karl Marx. The neighborhood was culturally and intellectually alive and included institutions such as the Carter School, Englewood High School, and Wilson Junior College. Self-taught and active in politics, Bland pursued a career as a disciplined adherent to the philosophy of dialectical materialism. He believed in developing his own talents but he also engaged in local cultural associations. Bland was an original member of the South Side Writers Club, formed immediately following the National Negro Congress of February 1936. The club was created by Richard Wright and held its first meeting at the home of Robert Davis, Bland's best friend, and then the group maintained regular weekly meetings at the Abraham Lincoln Center on Oakwood Blvd. While Davis went on to become a Hollywood actor under the name Davis Roberts, Bland turned himself into a literary critic. At the meetings, Bland developed his ideas, criticism, and fiction alongside Wright, Margaret Walker, Frank Marshall Davis, Theodore Ward, Russell Marshall, Fern Gayden, Robert Davis, and Arna Bontemps. Among such distinguished peers, Bland was considered a leader in matters of literary criticism, and he was especially close to Fern Gayden. On occasions when the group met at his home, Bland required his adolescent son to listen to Richard Wright read his short stories.

After Wright departed in the late spring of 1937, according to Margaret Walker, the original club fell apart. Bland continued to remain active on the Chicago art and writing scene, which held unique opportunities for vibrant intellectual exchange and artistic exploration. He was a close friend of the composer Ulysses Kay, and at that time, several blacks were studying for degrees at the University of Chicago—Marian Minus, Arna Bontemps, Frank Yerby, Lawrence D. Reddick, St. Clair Drake, Horace Cayton, and Ulysses Lee among them. Both the Abraham Lincoln Center and the Good Shepherd Community Church Center on 57th Street (which became the South Parkway Community Center) served as forums for original dramatic and artistic expression alongside regular community-based classroom instruction. Bland also took an occasional class at the University of Chicago.

The pivotal moment for Bland's development and influence, however, was probably the 1941 opening of the South Side Chicago Community Art Center, located in the Old Comiskey Mansion on South Michigan and 39th Street. Fern Gayden sat on the board of trustees and was planning a regular journal that would appear in early 1944 called *Negro Story*, a journal that carried the work of world-famous Richard Wright and the earliest work of a completely unknown Chicago poet and Wilson Junior College graduate named Gwendolyn Brooks. In this milieu, Bland, by now quite confident in literary matters, took a personal interest in instructing Brooks, nearly ten years his junior. She was talented, shy, and curious, but her work showed vivacity, technical astuteness, and powerful insight. Bland expressed particular concerns about the weaknesses of the black middle class' point of view in literature, which he thought too narrow and a weak formula for public relations. On the other hand, he resisted the efforts of his cadre's writers to write exclusively in the vein of social protest without revealing the richness of African American heritage. According to his brother Alden, Edward was socratic in his critical method during group sessions, enabling others to embark upon a "voyage of self discovery."

The movement of Richard Wright and Langston Hughes between New York and Chicago increased the contacts between radical black writers of both cities. In Manhattan in 1941, a new journal, *Negro Quarterly*, appeared, put out by the Negro Publication Society of America. Similar to Carter G. Woodson's Associated Publishers in Washington, D.C., the New York–based Negro Publication Society promoted historic works by black writers and about African American history, but with a left-wing political edge. According to Saunders Redding, the society did not survive because it was targeted by a "red-smear" campaign, but the editors of the *Negro Quarterly* were two of the most important figures for black political organization and literary criticism: Angelo Herndon and Ralph Ellison.

Ellison served as the managing editor of *Negro Quarterly* for nearly two years, and in that capacity he introduced the work of Edward Bland to American audiences. In the third issue of the journal Bland published his most important work, "Social Forces Shaping the Negro Novel," one of *Negro Quarterly's* most distinguished essays. The essay was outstanding for two reasons. It was one of the earliest examples of thoroughgoing, modern criticism of black literature in ideological terms, and it sharply and openly criticized black American literary craftsmanship from a nonaligned point of view, outside of the central orbit of both the Communist Party and black American racial-uplift magazines, newspapers, and journals.

Bland's crusading spirit sprang from the opening line: "One of the outstanding features of the Negro novels that appeared during the twenties was their literary incompetence." Paying close attention to the "new criticism," unleashed in 1938 with Brooks' and Warren's *Understanding Poetry*, Bland focused on the technical poverty of the novelist, who had shown poor competence in literary technique and "in integrating these devices to meet the fullest demands of theme." "Artistically they were more absorbed in what they were doing than in how," said Bland. Black writers during the 1920s and later had privileged content over form, a disastrous mistake.

A dismissal of the writers as individuals did not concern Bland; he wanted to analyze their defects as a strata. Black isolation from American institutions had not produced "conscious craftsmen," but rather a group of middle-class scribblers frustrated by their status.

> Briefly, it might be said that the Negro writer of the twenties was pre-disposed to an inferiority in literary artisanship because of his utilitarian conception of the purpose of literature; because he neglected the mechanics of writing out of his confidence in the expressional skill of Negro folk culture (which fixed at a lower level of display talents which might have been more fruitfully trained), and because those social forces which might have activated a lively interest in writing strategy were absent from the Negro situation.

The "social forces" Bland drew his reader's attention to were grounded in the historic cleavage that had produced the engine of modernity in the modern Western world—the overthrow of the feudalistic regime of the landed gentry by the bourgeoisie mercantile class. For Bland, the resulting material dominance by the middle class had caused their artistic consciousness to sunder the world into a dualism between Man and Nature, according the latter adversarial power. Granting almost no agency to blacks during the Civil War, Bland faulted the urban and minute African American middle class that had "emerged within this world as its creation rather than its creator" as coming into existence too late to respond to this dynamic. By the time black business emerged in any numbers, Bland thought the middle class had become dependent upon the "social environment" for its consciousness, rather than the awe-inspiring power of Nature.

For Bland, this ecological condition of the inchoate black intellectual class produced novelists "reticent about the patterns and meaning of existence," and bereft of consciousness of "the wider dimensions of life." The implications for the novel were great: "The creation of a sensibility whose contact with Man created only occasional and temporary feelings of inadequacy, this novel spurned the larger interests of the mind as seen through the major traditions of the West." Black writers from the middle class had produced Victorian-era–style romantic dramas, but they were unconcerned with the "overtones of significance" that had spurred the romantic tradition's revolt of individualism, and instead wrote with an emphasis on "conformity to civilized practices." The result of the imitation was an empty novelistic form.

Bland turned his attention to the history of black efforts in poetry in March of 1944, when Harriet Monroe's Chicago-based magazine *Poetry* published his essay "Racial Bias and Negro Poetry." In the essay, Bland again offered what was becoming his trademark bracing analysis, as evidenced by the essay's very beginning: "A provincial view of life and a tremendously slanted approach mark almost all poetry by Negroes, and these factors operate as serious limitations." In this work also, Bland explored the yawning gap of social difference between the way blacks viewed themselves and the way that they were understood by white Americans. Instead of an orientation in commonly available social values, such as "the humanistic notion of the natural dignity of man and the Christian stress on human brotherhood," Negro poetry was characterized by "the defensive maneuverings of a minority against a hostile group." Black poets sought to shape the understandings of whites but were ineffectual, in some regard, because they lacked a community of shared assumptions. When the poet Countee Cullen's poem "Incident" reaches its climactic moment and the narrator recoils at being called "nigger," could whites who saw nothing offensive in the term understand the meaning of the poem? For Bland, "Lack of rapport leaves inaccessible to whites the Negro's attitudes toward life." Bland never doubted the importance of the interracial audience, but, because of difficulties of reception across racial lines, he thought the most effective verse crossing the racial divide were works that focused on desperation and revolt, enabling even a remote reader to participate in an emotional catharsis. Frank Horne, who had written "Nigger," and Claude McKay, who had produced "If We Must Die," "Tired," and "Is It Because I Am Black," had offered poems that were completely direct and "announce[d] [their] orientation before racial prejudice interposes itself." Unfortunately for the poets, "It is this bigoted white world that Negro poetry seeks to come to grips with, a world that would limit the breadth of its meaning."

But Bland's most stimulating and influential insight lay in his surmise of the "internal" condition of black poetry. He found black poets, and black writers more generally, holders of "pre-individualistic values," a belief system nearly opposed to the Western tradition of distinctive, individual humanistic examination: "Instead of seeing in terms of the individual, the Negro sees in terms of 'races,' masses of peoples separated from other masses according to color." Bland decided that the "limitation" caused by this situation, "detracts from whatever poetic skill may be otherwise present." Bland hoped that, in keeping with the American propaganda, the Second World War's successful conclusion would advance the humanistic elimination of white prejudice. And he also hoped that the "self-conscious 'race values'" that "impair and delimit the vision of the artist" would also find their end.

Bland did not live to see the results of his critical efforts. Anxious to leave Chicago, he volunteered for the Army around 1943 and worked in a segregated special services unit in the European theater of operations. In early 1945 he sacrificed his rank and seniority to volunteer for the racially integrated 394th combat infantry regiment of the 99th division, an outfit created as the U.S. Army pushed its way into Germany anticipating heavy losses. A bazookaman, Bland led an attack and was killed on March 20, 1945, six weeks before the end of hostilities in Europe.

His reputation however, should not be underestimated. With his razor-sharp judgments against mediocrity and his wide-ranging intellectual project that unceasingly demanded that African American letters be understood in relation, albeit often antagonistic, to a larger Western humanistic tradition, Bland spearheaded the transformation from literary works of social protest and sentimental romantic fiction to high modernism. In his own groundbreaking essay of 1945, "Richard Wright's Blues," a review of *Black Boy*, Ralph Ellison borrowed heavily from Bland's "Racial Bias and Negro Poetry" work and its exploration of preindividualistic values, even as Ellison acknowledged the work of Booker T. Washington in the essay as well. The work enabled Ellison to frame properly Richard Wright's *Black Boy* for a multiracial and politically diverse audience. Ellison of course went on in his own work to take with religious seriousness Bland's dictum that Negro literature must formidably take on the intellectual challenges of Western writers and reject the narrow identity of minority literature with an accompanying narrow bed of concerns. After his death, the South Side Community Center began to give an annual Edward Bland Prize for Literature. Even more deeply influenced than Ellison was the high modernist poet Gwendolyn Brooks, who freely admitted that at the South Side Community Center and the soirees and artistic parties at Margaret Burroughs's loft, Edward and Alden Bland "patiently taught me and Henry [Henry Blakely, Brooks's husband] to think." Brooks published an elegy memorializing Bland in 1945, a poem that she used to open her famous 1949 collection *Annie Allen*. The book was also dedicated to Bland. The ode to Bland and his "cool twirling awe" in the first book written by a black American to win the Pulitzer Prize served as a fitting tribute to one of Chicago's most exciting and influential critics.

References

Bland III, Edward O. Telephone interview, April 26, 2005.
Brooks, Gwendolyn. *Annie Allen*. New York: Harper and Brothers. 1949.
———. *Report from Part One*. Detroit: Broadside Press, 1972.

Ellison, Ralph. "Richard Wright's Blues." *Shadow and Act.* (1964) New York: Quality Paperback Club, 1994, 77–94.

Gordon, Eugene. "Social and Political Problems of the Negro Writer." *American Writers Congress*, edited by Henry Hart. New York: International Publishers, 1935, 141–45.

[Holmes], Eugene Clay. "The Negro in Recent American Literature." *American Writers Congress*, ed. Henry Hart. New York: International Publishers, 1935, 145–53.

Kent, George. *A Life of Gwendolyn Brooks.* Lexington: University Press of Kentucky, 1990.

Mullen, Bill. *Popular Fronts: Chicago and African-American Cultural Politics, 1935–1946.* Urbana: University of Illinois Press, 1999.

Walker, Margaret. *Richard Wright, Daemonic Genius.* New York: Amistad, 1993.

Wright, Richard. "Blueprint for Negro Writing." *New Challenge* 2.1 (Fall 1937): 53–65.

———. Essays: "Social Forces Shaping the Negro Novel." *Negro Quarterly* 1.3 (Fall 1942): 241–48.

———. "Racial Bias and Negro Poetry." *Poetry* 53.6 (March 1944): 328–33.

———. "Southside Art Center Gives 7 Poetry Awards," *Chicago Daily Tribune*, July 19, 1942: sw5.

MARITA BONNER (OCCOMY)
(June 16, 1898–December 6, 1971)
Kimberly N. Ruffin

Born in 1898, Marita Bonner's life and writing career are marked by the imprint of three different cities: Boston, Washington, D.C., and most extensively, Chicago. Rather than focus on the lives of the middle-class Blacks that her own life mirrored, Bonner chose to highlight the lives of the Black working class, leading critics to characterize her work as "proletarian fiction." The New Negro discourse of the early 1900s from intellectuals such as W. E. B. DuBois and Alain Locke encouraged Black writers to counteract racist thinking and institutions with "racial uplift," which provided upstanding portraits of Black life. Bonner chose to concentrate on the desperate situations in which the masses of Blacks found themselves. Her writing embodies a keen sensitivity to the experiences of those who transformed their lives with movement from rural, southern locales to northern and western cities during the Great Migration (one of the largest voluntary movements of people in history). Blacks seeking improved employment opportunities and less exposure to racist oppression and violence carved out new lives in northern cities such as Chicago (which was a common destination for Blacks from Mississippi) and western cities such as Los Angeles. While their expectations were sometimes met, most would endure immense environmental and cultural dislocation that caused anxiety, discord, and economic uncertainty. Published in *The Crisis* magazine (funded by the National Association for the Advancement of Colored People) and *Opportunity* magazine (funded by the National Urban League), Bonner was a strong presence in artistic efforts to document, publicize, and improve the lives of African Americans whose lives were forever altered by this switch from rural to urban life. As an early contributor to the Black Chicago Renaissance, she amplified the struggles of new arrivals to urban worlds that had demanding circumstances and emphasized the power of environmental influence to shape and sometimes determine human potential.

Bonner's upbringing by her parents, Joseph Andrew and Mary Anne (Noel) Bonner, shielded her from the severe consequences of racism experienced by most of her characters. Benefiting from the economic buffer of a middle-class home, Bonner's movement from city to city was relatively smooth. Throughout her childhood education in the Boston area, she demonstrated academic excellence and artistic accomplishment as a pianist. Her writing career blossomed during her years at Brookline High School where she contributed regularly to a student magazine. Noticed for her writing skill, she was encouraged to apply to Radcliffe College, where she majored in English and comparative literature (she was fluent in German). Bonner, along with other Black students, was not allowed to live on campus, so she commuted from home. During her college years she was able to secure a position in a prestigious writing seminar with Charles Townsend Copeland and win two Radcliffe song competitions (1918, 1922). Before graduating from college (in 1922) she began a teaching career, which she continued with a position at the Bluefield Colored Institute in Bluefield, Virginia, after obtaining her degree. Bonner's first nationally published short story, "The Hands," appeared in *Opportunity* magazine in 1925; her first nationally published essay, "On Being Black—a Woman—and Colored," appeared in *The Crisis* magazine that same year.

These two inaugural publications signal thematic foci that recur in Bonner's later work. In "The Hands" the narrator develops a brief story about the hands of a fellow bus rider playing a game the narrator calls "Christ-in-all-men."[1] The game inclines the narrator to ennoble and embellish the life of the man based on the appearance of his hands. The sketch the narrator paints is of a hardworking male laborer whose life the narrator anchors in the action of his hands, following him from his youth, adulthood, marriage, fatherhood, and death with actions such as "shoveled," "patted," "soothed," "smoothed," and "steadied."[2] Along with the focus on a member of the Black working class, the story includes theological references that resurface in Bonner's writing.

"On Being Black—a Woman—and Colored," an essay that has received much attention since 1989, takes an autobiographical detour into discussing the lives of the Black working class. Bonner begins this essay with second-person narration broadly describing the idealistic expectations of the young, middle- or upper-class, Black woman who is "covered with sundry Latin phrases"[3] after her college graduation. Her all-inclusive hopes for career, home, and husband (foreshadowing the "have-it-all" dilemma identified in later feminist movements) are fueled by a youthful energy. However, the young middle-class Black Everywoman feels compelled to "test" her hopes and dreams of the world in the "ghetto" of a Black community. Ideologies of racial uplift and solidarity circulating at the time from thinkers and activists such as W. E. B. DuBois, Booker T. Washington, Anna Julia Cooper, and Nannie Helen Burroughs encouraged Blacks of all socioeconomic classes to work together to dismantle institutional racism and to increase Black progress. Along with uneasiness about the potential success of racial solidarity, the "young Colored woman"[4] must also confront the ignorance of racism. Caught between the prodigal relationship she has with the masses of Black people because of her relative socioeconomic privilege and her despisement of mainstream society burdened by the legacy of racism and slavery, the persona in Bonner's essay wonders about the perception of Black women by White society and the impact of racism on those who are discriminated against suggesting that "every part of you becomes bitter."[5] She contemplates the accumulation of wealth this discrimination provides ("a stupendous mass of things"[6]) and juxtaposes this conspicuous accumulation and consumption with ancient civilizations in Greece and Rome that also had "possessions" and "culture" but lacked "Wisdom." At this point she personifies "Wisdom" as the twin sister of "Understanding," saying that they will not aid those who discriminate.[7] In closing, she draws on the image of Buddha sitting quietly to console women whom she believes can, after they lend themselves to silence and preparation, "swoop" to their feet and take advantage of better circumstances.[8] Bonner's work from the 1930s and 1940s is set exclusively in Chicago, and she is artistically devoted to the lives of the Black working class. This is foreshadowed in both "The Hands" and "On Being Young—a Woman—and Colored" in which her own, relatively uncommon and privileged upbringing shows little sustained attention. This essay also features other themes recurring in Bonner's later work: the questioning of racial categorization, highlighting of class divisions among African Americans (comparing them to "live fish in a basket" with the "apathetic" poor on the bottom and the better off on top eager and striving to get out of the basket entirely), and focusing on the conditions and perspectives of women.[9]

In the year after her writing debut on the national stage, Bonner had two short stories published in *The Crisis*. "The Prison-Bound" paints the picture of a couple in an unnamed city who endure lives of utter despair. The plea to "God" at the beginning and end of the story underscores Charlie's and Maggie's desperate situation. Their absentee, negligent landlord who lets property fall into disrepair was a common feature in the lives of working class Black migrants who were trapped in slums because of housing discrimination. The environmental stress of living under such conditions exacerbates Charlie and Maggie's relationship, leaving Maggie to loathe her mate and long for more. The narrator presents stressors affecting both Charlie and Maggie, but the primary focus is on Maggie's frustration with not only her marital discontent but also the intracultural discrimination she experiences from a "citified" neighbor who calls her "green and countrified."[10] Seemingly without any other recourse, Maggie longs for tomorrow and the narrator closes with a "prayer heard in a country church": "God, help the prison bound—Them within the four iron walls this evening!"[11] Like Bonner's story, most naturalist literature depicts the environment as a primary factor in determining the success of its characters. However, Bonner suggests the environment does play a crucial role that may be somehow mitigated by the presence of a sympathetic God. At the same time, the parallel she draws between the substandard living conditions in a northern city and prison stands in stark contrast to the claims in Black periodicals of the time such as the *Chicago Defender*, which encouraged Blacks to abandon unsafe, racist locations in the South for new lives in industrial, northern cities.

Even though Bonner still resided in Washington, D.C. in the 1920s, she employed Chicago as the setting for her other short story published in 1926, "Nothing New." Although Chicago has been described as one of the most segregated cities in the United States, it appears, initially, as a "melting pot" of cross-cultural promise in Bonner's description of the multicultural "Frye Street" with its mix of immigrants from Europe and Asia and Black immigrants from the American South. Denny, the son of hardworking, religious parents fresh from their Georgia home, confronts the racial tension that looms around the multicultural community, ultimately killing a White male student that attacks Denny for having a romantic relationship with a White female fellow student. Denny's actions have immense consequences: he is sentenced to death, and although there is a favorable consensus among the Frye Street neighborhood when evaluating Denny's parents (they "tried to raise Denny right"), the multicultural promise in the opening of the story is polarized into "White Frye Street" and "Black Frye Street" in the end. Occomy attributes regressive notions about race to both factions. As with "The Prison-Bound," this story is framed with a theological reference. Here Bonner suggests those on Frye Street missed an opportunity to see "God" in themselves only if they "had looked deeper."[12]

A vibrant community of Black authors existed in Washington, D.C., which is the home of Howard University, a historically Black institution where Black theater thrived. Georgia Douglas Johnson's "S Street" literary salon attracted not only Bonner but writers such as Zora Neale Hurston, Mary Burrill, and Angelina Grimké as well. Johnson encouraged her to write plays, and Bonner also participated in the theater group the Krigwa Players. Despite their critical acclaim, Occomy's plays were never produced while she was alive. In fact, her first play is entitled *The Pot Maker (A Play to Be Read)*; in it Elias Jackson has been "called from the cornfields" to serve as a minister. Bonner describes Elias's wife, Lucinda, and her lover Lew with utter contempt, calling Lew an "over fat, over facetious, over-fair, over-bearing, over pleasant, over-confident creature."[13] The moral hollowness of Lucinda and Lew is apparent in their bold disregard for Elias; they flirt in front of Elias and his parents. The title stems from Elias's biblically inspired sermon in which he compares God to a pot maker who can repair sinners who have "cracks" in them if they will only ask God to be healed. This sermon's theme anticipates the action that follows an eruption between Lucinda and Elias: Lew has fallen into a well and is drowning. "Full of mad agony," Lucinda tries to save Lew, but she too falls in the well. Initially Elias leaves his wife alone to try to save her lover; however, once Lucinda falls in the well, he goes to the well and tries to save her. It would appear that in a morality play such as this, the righteous Elias would save his wife at the play's close. Instead, Bonner intimates that Elias falls in the well after admitting that "I got a crack in me too!" The open ending leaves the situation unresolved except for a cryptic conclusion that reads, "That's all there will be. A crack has been healed. A pot has spilled over on the ground. Some wisps have twisted out." The play's startling close adds moral complexity to characters that at first seem to be drawn as flat and unlayered.[14]

Bonner takes her readers from the southern dialect and country setting of *The Pot Maker* into two different locales in the short stories she has published in 1927, "One Boy's Story" (published under the pseudonym Joseph Maree Andrew) and "Drab Rambles." The young boy's voice that narrates "One Boy's Story" is unique in Bonner's stories. Living in an affluent White neighborhood in upstate New York with his single mother, Donald is a believable, young biracial protagonist, who does not understand that the married White doctor who occasionally visits his mother ("Louise Gage") and him is actually his father. Donald finds great pleasure in a book that Dr. Swynburne gives him which contains Greek mythology, Greek tragedies, and biblical narratives, including the story of David and Goliath. As with *The Pot Maker*, this reference to biblical literature foreshadows the story's climax. Distraught about a fight between Dr. Swynburne and his mother, which exposes his true parentage, Donald defends his mother and accidentally kills his father with a slingshot, which was also the biblical David's weapon. The cataclysmic encounter with Donald and his father is followed by the graphic cutting of Donald's tongue so he will not reveal his involvement in his father's death. Donald compares himself with Orestes and Oedipus saying, "I am bearing my Furies and my clipped tongue like a Swynburne and a Gage—'cause I am both of them."[15] A mainstay of several of Bonner's works, violence underscores the dramatic inequalities many of her characters face and the moral shortcomings of individuals.

"Drab Rambles," anticipates the predominant focus on Chicago of her later work and provides two portraits of city life through the lens of gender difference. Bonner provides an introduction that works to universalize the experience of her two protagonists by emphasizing the environmental influences on their lives saying, "close all men in a small space, tinge and touch the Space with one blood—you get a check-mated Hell."[16] "The First Portrait" profiles the life of a Black male day laborer who faces discrimination during a hospital visit when an insensitive doctor tells him he must quit his job because of his heart condition and whose alternative solution is a prescription for medicine he cannot afford. The doctor blames the man for staying on his job despite the detriment to his health, and the laborer strikes back with comments that stress the racial discrimination he experiences saying, "I had to dig ditches because I am an ignorant black man. If I was an ignorant white man, I could get easier jobs. I could even have worked in this hospital."[17] "The Second Portrait" profiles the life of a female worker, Madie Frye, with a similar skill level as the male day laborer in the first portrait. Her experience of racial discrimination involves sexual exploitation as well. After a sexual encounter with her employer that leaves her pregnant, she loses her job as a domestic worker. She struggles to find another job as a domestic worker but has a hard time because she cannot afford day care. The child care she does find is questionable—to quiet the child the elderly child-care worker gives the baby paregoric. Fear influences the protagonist's submission to the sexual exploitation of another boss; jobless and left with another child, the protagonist is distraught and despondent with city life. The apostrophe Bonner uses to conclude these two portraits accentuates the casual disregard some give to workers in these situations. Bonner warns, in the second person narration she so commonly employed, "somewhere in God's day of measuring full measures overflowing—the blood will flow back to you—and you will care."[18]

By far the most critically acclaimed piece of Bonner's work written in the late 1920s is her experimental, allegorical, and surreal play *The Purple Flower*, which won the 1927 *Crisis* prize for "Literary Art and Expression." The play clearly represents a break with her earlier reliance on naturalism and social realism. Contemporary critics have remarked that the play's abstract approach to racial conflict and strong division between the multifaceted imagery of "Us" and the "Sundry White Devils" leaves open a broader scope to address other social injustices. For instance, the "Sundry White Devils" are described with soft hair that flows around horns that glow red all the time, and the "Us's" have a shifting appearance that is sometimes "white as the White Devils, as brown as the earth, (or) as black as the center of a poppy." At the same time, "they may look as if they were something or nothing."[19] This physical elusiveness makes the play difficult to cast and also gives her message an epic quality that is part of its stellar reputation. The "purple flower" itself is an image that Occomy incorporated in her earlier short story "Nothing New": the symbolism is similar here in that the flower serves as an image of "Flower-of-Life-at-Its-Fullest." The privileged White Devils do everything in their power to keep the flower on the hilltop where they live prohibiting the "Us's" from leaving the valley, climbing the hill, and taking the flower despite the work that the "Us's" have done to beautify not only their own valley but also the White Devils's area. This battle is easily applied to the dilemma faced by disenfranchised people in any society who often work hard to obtain a lifestyle of the upper classes but who face serious structural problems that do not reward their work in a manner that would support such goals. Various theories on how to address the problem of racial discrimination circulating at the time ranged from self-imposed exile, accommodation, legal agitation, and economic self-determination. The most surprising departure from the ideologies of the "race men" (and women) of the day is the play's prediction that the resolution for the battle between the have and have-nots can be found only in blood.

In Bonner's last published essay, she returns to the question of religion. "The Young Blood Hungers" (1928) is a candid reflection on how much of an earlier conception of God should be inherited by a younger generation, more specifically how much of Christian theology is pertinent to youth. This essay includes an image popularized by W. E. B. DuBois in his book *The Souls of Black Folk*. In part, DuBois's "Veil" described the barrier that mainstream White society faced in acknowledging the experiences of Black Americans. Here the veil refers to barriers to intellectual/spiritual curiosities that prohibit young people from important answers about religious understanding. Bonner writes, "The Young Blood knows that growing means a constant tearing down of Illusory Veils that lift themselves thin—filmy—deceptive—between you and truth."[20] Rather than suggest an appropriate manner to obtain these answers, Bonner devotes the essay to documenting this aspect of young people's lives suggesting that "perhaps . . . God must be sought in new ways."[21]

Bonner's last published play, *Exit, An Illusion* (1929) returns to the domain of domestic relationships and the naturalism found in her earlier work. It includes a character common in the literature of the Harlem Renaissance—the biracial, or "mulatto," person who may appear to be White. Dot is the female member of the couple with the physical ability to "pass" for White. Her jealous lover Buddy is angry because he disapproves of Dot's plans to go on a date with an old childhood friend named Exit Mann, who is apparently White; his name is more than a flourish. In this naming, Bonner draws the reader's attention to the actual dilemma faced by Dot: Buddy's jealously about her date is fueled not only by the fear that Dot has betrayed their romantic bond but also by his recognition that Dot longs to be part of White culture instead of Black culture. Buddy conveys a sense of self-loathing in his threats to Dot. In Buddy's eyes, Exit Mann is an opportunity for Dot to "exit" Black culture. Bonner frames this play dramatically with an opening and ending scene with much in common. This similarity puts the play's actions and meaning well beyond Buddy and Dot's relationship; the commentary extends to the realm of race relations and the sociopolitical ramifications of cultural affiliation.

Bonner would eventually meet her husband William Almy Occomy in Washington, D.C., marrying him in 1930. For several years, she traded her work as a teacher for her work as a mother of their three children: William Almy Jr.,

Warwick Gale, and Marita Joyce Occomy. She continued to write and used her multicultural Chicago neighborhood as the inspiration for the fictional "Frye Street," making Chicago the setting of most of her remaining work. In fact, she planned to write an artistic "map" of Chicago called "The Black Map" but never completed the project. Her work was published again in 1933 with an installment of stories in *Opportunity* called "A Possible Triad on Black Notes" (including "Part One: There Were Three, " "Part Two: Of Jimmie Harris," and "Part Three: Three Tales of Living: Corner Store"). "There Were Three" and "Three Tales of Living: Corner Store" are the strongest of the three stories and show Bonner's maturity as a writer. Beyond the series of simple sentences that summarized the action of her early stories, the longer short stories here unfold their plots more smoothly and develop their characters more thoroughly. "There Were Three" returns to a prevalent concern—the economic and psychological well-being of single mothers and their children. Lucille is a White-looking mother with two children who, unbeknown to Little Lou and Robbie, works as a sex worker in a hotel at night so that she can support her family. Feeling the need to support the family economically as well, Robbie obtains a job as a bellboy at the same hotel without his mother's knowledge. Peril is the result of the family secret-keeping after Robbie is called to a room where he discovers his mother and one of her "johns." Once the White "john" discovers that Lucille is indeed the mother of Robbie and that she is Black, he strikes Robbie. Robbie, near a window, falls to his death. In one of the dramatic conclusions characteristic of Bonner's work, Lucille resides in an asylum and the whereabouts of Little Lou are undetermined. The family in "The Corner Store" benefits from greater economic stability, and yet they face conflict born out of the cultural tension of migration and racial difference. Making a departure from her other work, Occomy uses three German Jews as her central characters and illustrates her fluency in German to convey the speech of the recent immigrants to Frye Street. The action of the story pivots on a mother-daughter conflict that pits Esther and Meta against one another: Esther, the mother, yearning for the stone homes and cultural familiarity of her Jewish ghetto in Germany; Meta, the daughter, buoyed by the multicultural community and freedom from German anti-Semitism she finds in Frye Street.

A Black family in conflict is the subject of Bonner's next published story, "Tin Can" (1934). *Opportunity* awarded her with the 1933 fiction prize for this story, and as a testament to the merit of her writing during this time, she was the runner-up in the contest as well. Pa is depressed and withdrawn from parenting while Ma's efforts to take an active role in raising their two boys is thwarted by long work hours, a street culture that cultivates delinquency, and a truncated turn to church culture. Bonner makes a scathing commentary on other adults in positions of leadership who may be able to help parents and children in need in her depiction of the Black principal at Jimmie Joe's school who is simply called the "Black Bass Drum." Rather than address any of the community problems that surface in the school: teenage pregnancy, academic underachievement, violent gangs, and "the spread of social diseases," the Black Bass Drum is enthralled with his own accomplishments. Bonner reveals high expectations of the Black middle class; perhaps she expected them to act as she did and mute the anomaly of her own achievements and lifestyle to broadcast the dire conditions of the Black poor. Her employment of violence in this and other stories stresses the urgency of alleviating the poverty and racism that so many of her working-class characters endured: Jimmie Joe is sentenced to death for his murder of a romantic rival. Caught in her grief, Ma faints on a sidewalk. The misinterpretation of her actions by a patrol wagon driver who asks of a cop, "Where the devil do you 'spose these nigger women go to get drunk so early in the morning?" represents the stereotypical attitudes poor Black people face from those charged to help the public.[22] Continuing a period of high productivity, Bonner takes up the perilous end result of romantic rivalry again in her 1936 story "A Sealed Pod." Frye Street has many interracial relationships that make cross-cultural attractions clear; however, the economic instability of many characters and the impact of racism magnifies the consequences of romantic/sexual competition and companionship. Frye Street has the presence of a character in Bonner's Chicago-based stories. Her urban environmental consciousness recognizes the extreme impact poor living conditions can have on individuals and communities and serves as an artful reminder of human frailty.

Bonner was not only an author whose social realism spotlighted the lives of city residents but also the lives of women, anticipating the renaissance of Black women's writing in the 1980s and 1990s. Her treatment of female characters is complex and evenhanded. While she describes frequently the gendered aspects of society that made being female a disadvantage, she also creates Black women characters who are fully human, with a range of attributes that make their behavior no better or worse than anyone else's. The 1938 stories present Black women with clear faults: "Black Fronts" first presents a pretentious Black couple who use a lavish lifestyle as a front for their economic desperation and moral emptiness. The second front is a playfully written interchange between a housewife and her maid. The audience initially reads a monologue from the perspective of the maid who believes she can steal from her employer because of the employer's relative wealth. The next monologue takes the audience through the perspective of a pampered housewife whose overallegiance to politeness prevents her from firing the thieving maid immediately. Written under the pseudonym Joyce N. Reed, "Hate Is Nothing" addresses the serious topic of colorism within Black communities. As a dark-skinned woman, Bonner applied her personal experience of color discrimination (she faced at the hands of light-skinned women in

Chicago's Black middle-class communities) to her depiction of a mother-in-law "most heavily cursed by the old inferiority hangover left from slave days."

The institution of slavery exacted immense damage on the Black family. Bonner's 1939 stories ("The Makin's," "The Whipping," and "Hongry Fire") suggest that the Black family still faces vulnerability well after slavery has been ended. Their lives on Frye Street, far away from plantations in the South, have still not yielded the "promised land" millions of Blacks sought during the Great Migration. The inability of the urban environment to encourage progress is perhaps best symbolized in "The Makin's" by David's futile attempt to get a dime from his mother and father to fund his school project planting seeds. Instead, his mother and father only fund David's errands: placing a bet in the underground lottery and buying cigarettes. David's parents are oblivious to the hope their son's project represents, and their addictive behaviors serve as coping mechanisms for their lives of misery and diminished vision.

Despite Bonner's sober view of life in the city, she does not embrace a pastoral view of rural life. "Patch Quilt," written in 1940, returns Bonner's reader to the South and depicts the rapid disintegration of preparations for celebration into preparation for revenge. Here a female character reacts violently to adultery and forever alters the lives of those involved. "One True Love" (1941) is the final story Bonner published during her lifetime. Here the central romantic relationship fares better than the doomed love triangles in other stories, but Nora, the protagonist, still encounters racism and economic burdens that derail her attempts to be a lawyer.

Although she maintained a fondness for the craft in which she demonstrated so much talent and dedication, Bonner stopped writing in 1941. Interestingly, considering the prominence of theological subject matter and biblical reference in her writing, she and her husband joined the First Church of Christian Scientist the same year. However, there is no critical consensus about a correlation between the end of her published work and the beginning of her membership in this congregation. After her youngest child was close to school age, Bonner resumed her teaching career in Chicago, sometimes teaching students with special needs. She continued teaching until the late 1960s. In 1971 an apartment fire contributed to her death; she was rushed to the hospital but died after she experienced a slight recovery.

A notebook with several stories unpublished during Bonner's life was found after her death. The seriousness with which Bonner took her artistic endeavors is apparent in the marginal critiques she made of the stories. Six of these stories were included in a 1987 collection of her work, *Frye Street and Environs: The Collected Works of Marita Bonner*. The Black female protagonist and permutations of gender take center stage in most of these stories (with some set on Frye Street), but they also include the familiar terrain of class and race issues. The warped aspirations of women in a Black middle-class family anchors "On the Altar." "High Stepper" chronicles the life of a woman who gradually uncovers the courage to express her pain and anger through a wide range of narrative techniques, with stream of consciousness and interior monologues among others. A woman spoiled by her parents in childhood meets with a rude awakening during her marriage in "Stones for Bread." "Reap It As You Sow It" advocates the biblical dictum of "You shall reap as you sow" through the story of a couple's choices that come back to haunt them. Finally, "Light in Dark Places" depicts the importance of a tenacious, crafty, and blind grandmother as a much needed help to a naive teenage girl. These unpublished works highlight the lives of Black women with just portrayals that give depth to the characters and light to their circumstances.

While she lived in three distinct urban centers, Bonner's most consistent muse and the setting for the finest writing of her substantial and well-regarded career was Chicago. The Chicago Renaissance benefited from her ability to convey her characters' humanity even when they faced conditions that could reduce them to faceless statistics. The fictional Frye Street bubbles with the multicultural challenges of contemporary life across the globe, which demands movement and cross-cultural encounters of innumerable kinds. Against the problems and promise of the multiethnic Frye Street, Bonner drew her readers' attention to the structural conditions that made class and gender important elements of her characters' lives as well as race.

Notes

1. Joyce Flynn and Joyce Occomy Stricklin, eds. *Frye Street and Environs: The Collected Works of Marita Bonner*. Boston: Beacon Press, 1987, 60.
2. Ibid., 60–63.
3. Ibid., 3.
4. Ibid., 5.
5. Ibid., 6.
6. Ibid., 6.
7. Ibid., 7.
8. Ibid., 8.
9. Ibid., 4.
10. Ibid., 67.
11. Ibid., 68.
12. Ibid., 76.
13. Ibid., 18.
14. Ibid., 29.
15. Ibid., 91.
16. Ibid., 92.

17. Ibid., 92.
18. Ibid., 101.
19. Ibid., 30.
20. Ibid., 10.
21. Ibid., 13.
22. Ibid., 139.

For Further Reading

Berg, Allison and Meredith Taylor. "Enacting Difference: Marita Bonner's *Purple Flower* and the Ambiguities of Race." *African American Review* 32.3 (1998): 469–80.

Flynn, Joyce. "Marita Bonner Occomy." *Dictionary of Literary Biography 51: Afro-American Writers from the Harlem Renaissance to 1940*. Farmington Hills, Mich.: Thomson Gale, 1987.

Flynn, Joyce and Joyce Occomy Stricklin, eds. *Frye Street and Environs: The Collected Works of Marita Bonner*. Boston: Beacon Press, 1987.

Johnson, Georgia Douglas. "Review of *Autumn Love-Cycle*." *Opportunity* 7 (April 1929): 130.

Musser, Judith. "African-American Women and Education: Marita Bonner's Response to the 'Talented Tenth.'" *Studies in Short Fiction* 34.1 (1997): 73–86.

———. "'The Blood Will Flow Back to You:' The Reactionary Proletarian Fiction of Marita Bonner." *Canadian Review of American Studies* 32.1 (2002): 53–80.

[Occomy] Bonner, Marita. *The Purple Flower*. *Black Theater USA*, edited by James Hatch and Ted Shine. New York: Free Press, 1974, 202–7.

———. "The Whipping." *Writing Red: An Anthology of American Women Writers 1930–40*, edited by Charlotte Nekola and Paula Rabinowitz. New York: Feminist Press at CUNY, 1987, 70–78.

———. *The Purple Flower* and *Exit, An Illusion*. *Black Female Playwrights: An Anthology of Plays before 1950.*, edited by Kathy Perkins. Bloomington: Indiana University Press, 1989, 191–99, 200–205.

———. "On Being Young—a Woman—and Colored." *Invented Lives: Narratives of Black Women 1860–1960*, edited by Mary Helen Washington. New York: Anchor Press, 1987.

———. "The Hands—A Story." *Calling the Wind: Twentieth-Century African-American Short Stories*, edited by Clarence Major. New York: Harper Perennial, 1993, 30–33.

———. "One Boy's Story," "Drab Rambles," and "Nothing New." *The Sleeper Wakes: Harlem Renaissance Stories by Women*, edited by Marcy Knopf. New Brunswick: Rutgers University Press, 1993, 95–123.

———. "The Hands—A Story." *Opportunity* 3 (August 1925): 235–37.

———. "On Being Young—A Woman—and Colored." *The Crisis* 31 (December 1925): 63–65.

———. "The Prison-Bound." *The Crisis* 32 (September 1926): 225–26.

———. "Nothing New." *The Crisis* 33 (November 1926): 17–20.

———. *The Pot Maker (A Play to Be Read)*. *Opportunity* 5 (February 1927): 43–46.

———. "One Boy's Story," as Joseph Maree Andrew. *The Crisis* 34 (November 1927): 297–99, 316–20.

———. "Drab Rambles." *The Crisis* 34 (December 1927): 335–36, 354–56.

———. *The Purple Flower. The Crisis* 35 (January 1928).

———. "The Young Blood Hungers." *The Crisis*, 35 (May 1928): 151, 172.

———. *Exit, An Illusion. The Crisis* 36 (October 1929): 335–336, 352.

———. "A Possible Triad on Black Notes, Part One: There Were Three." *Opportunity* 11 (July 1933): 205–7.

———. "A Possible Triad on Black Notes, Part Two: Of Jimmie Harris." *Opportunity* 11 (August 1933): 242–44.

———. "A Possible Triad on Black Notes, Part Three: Three Tales of Living: Corner Store." *Opportunity* 11 (September 1933): 269–71.

———. "Tin Can." *Opportunity* 12 (July 1934): 202–5; 12 (August 1934): 236–40.

———. "A Sealed Pod." *Opportunity* 14 (March 1936): 88–91.

———. "Black Fronts." *Opportunity* 16 (July 1938): 210–14.

———. "Hate is Nothing," as Joyce N. Reed. *The Crisis* 45 (December 1938): 388–90, 394, 403–4.

———. "The Makin's." *Opportunity* 17 (January 1939): 18–21.

———. "The Whipping." *The Crisis* 46 (June 1939): 172–74.

———. "Hongry Fire." *The Crisis* 46 (December 1939): 360–62, 376–77.

———. "Patch Quilt." *The Crisis* 47 (March 1940): 71–72, 92.

———. "One True Love." *The Crisis* 48 (February 1941): 46–47, 58–59.

Roses, Lorraine Elena and Ruth Elizabeth Randolph. "Marita Bonner: In Search of Other Mother's Gardens." *Black American Literature Forum* 21.1–2 (1987): 165–83.

Spahr, Heather E. "Marita Bonner (1898–1971)." *African American Authors, 1745–1945: A Bio-Bibliographical Critical Sourcebook*, edited by Emmanuel S. Nelson. Westport, Conn.: Greenwood Press, 2000. 30–35.

Papers

A collection of Marita Bonner's manuscripts and correspondence is at the Arthur and Elizabeth Schlesinger Library on the History of Women in America, Radcliffe College, Harvard University, Cambridge, Massachusetts.

GWENDOLYN BROOKS
(June 7, 1917–December 3, 2000)
Stephen Caldwell Wright

The second decade of the twentieth century gave rise to tumultuous activity, global and national. The United States, like most of the world, was reeling from the aftermath of war and what was portrayed as the ultimate quest for freedom, making the world safe for democracy while the democracy itself was flawed. For most Americans, this was a time of hope for prosperity. Many other Americans, however, faced a different scenario, one of struggle for redemption and mere acceptance as Americans. Foremost among these, in a severely race-conscious culture, were people of color, particularly Americans of African heritage. In many ways, this climate of ambivalent approaches to race-separation clouded and, in some instances, tainted the artistic endeavors by both blacks and whites and frequently resulted in a "white" standard as the dominant factor in criticism. This is especially evident among the poets and writers of the time. On one hand, writers of color striving for success in the mainstream of publishing were expected to adhere to "universal" themes and to avoid "social themes," relevant to the condition and struggle of people of color desirous of being seen as equally creative and legitimate in comparison to any other artists.

On the other hand, near the end of the second decade of the 1900s, a highly committed cadre of writers of color were involved in igniting the invincible energy of the Harlem Renaissance, perhaps the most noted but not the only cultural, social, artistic, and intellectual movement engineered by people of color in the United States. This kind of renaissance activity was visible in a number of urban cities, not the least of which was Chicago, the home of Gwendolyn Brooks, the first Black to be awarded a Pulitzer Prize. She received the award in 1950 for *Annie Allen*.

Born on June 7, 1917, in Topeka, Kansas, Gwendolyn Brooks was the first child of Keziah and David Brooks. While she was still a very young baby, the young couple returned to Chicago, which Brooks considered home and where she lived all her life. The family eventually moved into a home on the South Side, and she and her brother Raymond, who was born in 1918, grew up sharing a strong bond of mutual respect and admiration that would last until Raymond's death in 1976.

At the time of Brooks's birth, the racial climate in Chicago, as in most of America, was tense, and two years later came the summer of 1919, which James Weldon Johnson referred to as the "Red Summer" because of the high passions and spilling of much African American blood after proud black soldiers returned to the irony of Jim Crow. Across America, disenchanted Blacks responded to the harsh intimidation and flagrant discrimination at the hands of disgruntled whites, particularly the Ku Klux Klan who remained set against any semblance of racial equality for people of color. Subsequently, at an early age Brooks was exposed to the social restrictions of the time and began to formulate her deep thinking about the vicissitudes of black life and its challenges in the City of Chicago and in America. After graduating from Englewood High School and earning an associates degree from Wilson Junior College in 1936, Brooks continued to expand her literary interests and joined various writers' groups.

The conflicting experiences of her youth and young adulthood would continue to inform her thinking and her writing. Brooks viewed the world as a place of varied possibilities, and she possessed the sensibilities of one who was opposed to all forms of unfairness and inequity. This consciousness would prevail throughout her career, including the 1960s and 1970s when she acknowledged she had been "introduced" to a radical approach to race-consciousness. In fact, Brooks's collective experiences shaped her vision to such an extent that even her earliest writing is rarely without the direct focus of race-consciousness and the call for positive self-identity. In this context, the willing reader does not confuse Brooks's concentration on race with racism. Brooks regularly addresses in her work the injustice that accompanies and drives the negative consequences of a race-based society.

Focusing on life in Chicago, the thriving center of the Midwest, the breadth of Brooks's writing highlights an entire community and its cross-cultural diversity. As a young adult, Brooks continued to read widely and seek the wisdom of established writers, living and dead. She studied the works of T. S. Eliot and Ezra Pound, and was deeply immersed in the works of Emily Dickinson. Not too many readers and critics acknowledge Gwendolyn Brooks's deep interest in many white writers. Brooks was, in fact, quite open in her appreciation of all humanity and embraced broadly the importance of world literature. Thus even as a self-conscious black artist, Brooks was able, at the same time, to maintain a DuBoisian dual consciousness—the ability to thrive in a world separated by cultural and social expectations. Brooks was also impressed and inspired by the work of James Weldon Johnson and Langston Hughes, and she continued to cultivate an open and lasting affinity with strong black writers who were compelled to portray blacks in a positive light. While a young girl, Brooks met Johnson and Hughes. According to Brooks, the scholarly, aristocratic Johnson was not as warm and welcoming as Langston Hughes, the poet of the "low down folks." Johnson, whom she met in a Chicago church, offered the young Brooks some general commentary and polite salutations. Hughes, on the other hand, encouraged Brooks to continue writing. In subsequent years, Brooks cultivated a professional relationship with Hughes, whom she first met at the South Side Community Center, where Brooks and other aspiring writers met on a regular basis, under the philanthropic tutelage of white benefactress Inez Cunningham Stark.

Being involved with the many cultural and civic activities in her community, Brooks met her husband, Henry Blakely, also a poet, at an NAACP meeting. It was a meeting, as Brooks often stated, that was sealed by fate. In 1939, they married and had two children, Henry III and Nora. Brooks, however, continued the serious pursuit of writing as a vocation. Throughout her writings, it is apparent that Brooks's relationships with her family and her community informed the poet's vision of the universe. Her works frequently focus on the lives and experiences of children, adult male and female relationships, and the day-to-day struggles of everyday life in the Black community. Brooks's father, David, was a porter for the McKinley Music Publishing Company, and her mother, Keziah, worked as a domestic for white families. Coming from a working class family, Brooks was quite aware of living in an often hostile social, cultural, and economic environment.

As poet-celebrity, Brooks enjoyed a prolific writing career, beginning with the poet's earliest fascination with words and ideas and resulting in the publication, as George Kent acknowledges, of her first poem "Eventide" in *American Childhood* (October 1930). Even at an early age, Brooks's intentions were firm and her success eminent as she moved into a life of poetry. Brooks went on to become one of the signature voices included in mainstream American literature. Her ability to speak in her own voice while respectfully adhering to "established form" afforded her a respectability that led to a broad acceptance of her verse and sonnets. Her earliest poems were published in the *Chicago Defender* and soon in more publications, including anthologies of American poetry. An avid student of the local literary scene, she participated in workshops and was introduced to influential resources such as *Poetry* magazine. Her exposure continued at the Midwestern Writers' Conference, sponsored by Northwestern University, and her success in these endeavors proved beneficial to her reputation as a writer.

As do most poets with national and international acclaim, Brooks found herself, at different times, in the center of many debates on the role of poetry and, indeed, of the function or duty of the poet. This attention highlights the polemics involved even today—rightly or wrongly—in any discussion of Brooks's works. Two topics become quite apparent. The first of these, which seems to propagate others, is Brooks's affinity for Blackness and the Black Aesthetic. The other issue is her refusal to continue to go "mainstream" despite her apparent genius and the effects of this decision, presented by supporters and detractors alike, on the currency of Brooks's poetry and her status as a world class poet.

Brooks is equally acute in bringing to the surface the life of a community that is separated and suppressed, yet thriving and surviving. In 1945, Gwendolyn Brooks's first collection of poetry, *A Street in Bronzeville*, was published by Harper and Brothers. When *A Street in Bronzeville* appeared in 1945, Brooks began the fulfillment of her lifelong ambition of becoming recognized as a poet. The themes of her first book echo the challenges of people of color. For "Blacks"—the term preferred by Brooks—America was often an inhospitable place of existence and struggle that proved a relentless challenge for survival. The setting for *Bronzeville* was an actual historic community in South Chicago. *A Street in Bronzeville* brings to life and makes accessible the real world of "Negro life" at that time in Chicago. In this book that was so well received nationally, Brooks provides for the world a revealing glimpse into the urban life of Black America in one of its most notably populous cities.

The poems in *A Street in Bronzeville* capture the private and public concerns of Blacks. In several poems, Brooks highlights issues that the community relates on a daily basis. In "a song in the front yard" and in "Negro Hero," the poet touches on themes to which whole generations might refer in the recollection or research about a people in constant transition, hope, and renewal. In "a song in the front yard," she opens the poem with the revealing and challenging lines: "I've stayed in the front yard all my life / I want a peek at the back."

These lines suggest the decorum, the control, and sometimes defiance of those locked in a disciplined society, and are indicative of those individuals in the early Black communities in Chicago and those scattered across America: North, South, East, and West. Brooks brings to focus larger issues concerning the status and contributions of Blacks in "Negro Hero." Though speaking, suggestively, of Dorie Miller, "Negro Hero" chronicles in a convincing way the ability of Brooks to reckon with the past and to chart the future struggles of people of color. The persona in the poem states and highlights the openness of those seeking positive change: "Naturally, the important thing is, I helped to save them / them and a part of their democracy." In this poem, Brooks strikes a noticeable historical chord as she accentuates the racial and economic divide that greeted Black soldiers returning from every American war.

Focusing on urban Chicago as a thriving center in the Midwest, Brooks portrays an entire community and its varied cultural diversity. This appreciation for the lives in the community can be seen in a sampling of the poems in the collection. The poem "kitchenette building," for instance, discloses the daily life of those who, in search of a better existence, must yield to priorities of survival. This poem cleverly chronicles the sacrifices of people in search of a dream, and, in some ways, echoes sentiments of Hughes's famous poem "Dream Deferred" (also known as "Harlem") that also influenced and provided the title for Lorraine Hansberry's play, *A Raisin in the Sun*. The cultural climate of urban Chicago is captured convincingly in "southeast corner," the poem that allows the reader to experience the full breadth of community life, including the possibly reproachable "Madam." In "southeast corner," as in the other poems, Brooks passes no judgment on the persona; she simply portrays the characters as they live. Perhaps, in "Mathew Cole" the reader is, again, provided insight to life in the city and, beyond that, revelation of the raw life of the elderly in isolation and desperation in the typical urban dwelling.

A *Street in Bronzeville* also echoes the mores of her Chicago community and other urban cities and the challenge to live the straight and narrow and not yield to the "wild life." These observations that Brooks witnessed from afar, as a child, are later presented graphically in her writings as an adult. In so doing, the poet uncovers the unpretentious language of the women "at the hairdresser's" and the shadowy club life in "Queen of the Blues," a poem in which the persona, living the fast life, also grapples for self-esteem and respect from others. Brooks is no stranger to controversy, and two poems included in *A Street in Bronzeville* certainly confirm that reputation. The poem "the mother" is among the most controversial of Brooks's poems. The poem covers the subject of abortion. Brooks, however, does not announce her feelings, pro or con. Again the poet states without judgment the case of the persona, a woman speaking to her unborn children in a voice filled with remorse and compassion but also with resolute determination and full acceptance for her decisions that are not in any way cavalier. The other poem that solicits reluctance from many readers is the "Ballad of Pearl May Lee." In graphic detail, Brooks recounts the subdued agony and vocal outrage of Pearl May Lee, who mourns in mocking, bittersweet fashion her Black lover, whose fascination for white women results predictably in his hanging. This ballad echoes the crisis of racially motivated murders and the sordid history of the past, particularly in terms of the forbidden practice of intimate mixing of the races.

As Brooks continued to explore the larger world of writing and to fulfill her goals, she was awarded a Guggenheim Fellowship in 1946 and was also named a Fellow of the American Academy of Arts and Letters. She won her second Guggenheim Fellowship in 1947 and continued to write literary reviews. Brooks published *Annie Allen*, her second volume of poetry, in 1949. By this time, Brooks's reputation as a serious, capable writer was becoming widespread and her accomplishments more notable. *Annie Allen* is perhaps as comprehensively characteristic of the breadth of Brooks's abilities as any of her lengthy collections.

Annie Allen generated exciting though mixed commentary, most of which related to the poet's treatment of the urban life and the people in her community. While some suggested Brooks was limited artistically by her choice of subject matter, others applauded the poet's ability to portray successfully the real life of her subjects in the city of Chicago. Actually, in *Annie Allen*, Brooks continues the revelations begun in *A Street In Bronzeville*, and she demonstrates her dedication to mastering "form" while also exercising a voice that is fresh in its delivery. The sense of honesty that permeates all her works, early and late, allows the reader to travel through known but often unacknowledged or untold cultural and social territory. A milestone in her life and career, *Annie Allen* reveals the commonplace while preserving, through formal presentation, significant cultural and social observations. Published by Harper and Brothers, *Annie Allen* was awarded *Poetry* magazine's Eunice Tietjens Prize, a distinctive honor for Brooks and her Chicago community. In 1950, Brooks proudly accepted the Pulitzer for *Annie Allen.*

Annie Allen, presented basically in three parts, comprises: "Notes from the Childhood and the Girlhood"; "The Anniad"; and "The Womanhood." The first section of *Annie Allen*, "Notes from the Childhood and the Girlhood," is an exceptional grouping of poems that addresses in clear, accessible yet demanding language the pithy reality of growing up. This growth comes through the eyes of a young girl caught on the brink of "almost womanhood." Annie, the persona, strives to discover herself within the boundaries of home, community, and society. Throughout the trials of childhood, Annie learns many of the lessons it takes to cope and survive in a world of added challenges. The poems cover the broad spectrum of youthful discovery. In "old relative," for instance, Annie witnesses the dead, and she does so within the capabilities of her mind and station as a young person viewing adult issues. Likewise, in "downtown vaudeville," the reader is provided a view of the complexity surrounding those awkward "reminders," especially for Blacks in the larger society, of the continuing need for awareness of the worth and value of being Black—in terms of human dignity.

The second section of Annie Allen centers on "The Anniad," an assortment of poems that echoes and highlights the continuing quest for "clarification" in an emerging adult world of promises and obstacles common to those who lived on the South Side. In these poems, everyday occurrences are recognized and presented in substantive contexts. In presenting an examination of life for those fully embracing or merely adjusting to living, Brooks addresses insightfully the matters of birth, marriage, and death, not necessarily in that order.

"The Womanhood" consists of views of urban life, told from varying perspectives. The poems are diverse in subject matter and powerful in diction and conviction. Brooks continues to explore the unadorned life of determined, seasoned inhabitants in situations often requiring vigilant struggle for survival and adaptation to the demands of urban life, particularly among the diverse racial populations in Chicago. This mix of cultures in Chicago is captured succinctly in "I love those little booths at benvenuti's." The poems range from issues related to "the children of the poor" and matters highlighting the defensive mode of daily life in "first fight. then fiddle." In "beauty shoppe" Brooks provides the reader with a revealing glimpse into the mind-set of Blacks, urban and rural. The women in "facial," "manicure," and "shampoo-press-hot-oil-&-croquignole," the three poems that comprise "beauty shoppe," demonstrate powerful use of language, in this case, the idioms of black speech. Beneath the casual tone of the language rests Brooks's serious message that people have difficulty accepting who they are, their natural attributes. Brooks is already proclaiming, "Black Is Beautiful," the slogan that would become popular during the turbulent 1960s.

The poems in "The Womanhood" also assert Brooks's diversity. In this regard, there are poems that seem to echo Brooks's acknowledged interest in Emily Dickinson. These include "a light and diplomatic bird," "and if sun comes," and "Exhaust the little moment." The trained reader recognizes in the Brooks poems the similarity in uniqueness of phrasing and austere sensibility so often associated with the poetry of Dickinson. This similarity echoes Brooks's appreciation of Dickinson as well as Brooks's independent spirit and devotion to her own artistic inclinations. These poems also demonstrate that Brooks could write about the world as well as she could about Chicago, as noted by many and eloquently voiced early on by Paul Engle. In one of the first and most meaningful reviews of Brooks's *A Street in Bronzeville*, Engle observed what is also applicable to *Annie Allen*: "The finest praise that can be given the book is that it would be a superb volume of poetry in any year by any person of any color. This is the kind of writing we need in this time."

On the whole, in sonnet-laden *Annie Allen*, Brooks skillfully preserves the authenticity of her subjects. In poems from the section "The Womanhood," Brooks pays tribute to the people of the earth. She does so in the year 1949, a season of critical urgency for the future of Blacks in Chicago and in America. The poet opens this section with "the children of the poor." In the first two lines to this sonnet, she asks: "What shall I give my children? Who are poor / Who are adjudged the leastwise of the land . . . ?" *Annie Allen* addresses community life of neighbors in touch with each other and with each other's conditions, including the sufferings and the celebrations. Her view of Chicago translates to the world, where the poet becomes visionary in her anticipation of the struggles of the 1950s and the daunting 1960s. In the poem "old laughter," the lines "The bamboo and the cinnamon / Are sad in Africa" intimate the ongoing struggles in Africa, a land that became increasingly important to Brooks and others in the decades that followed the publication of *Annie Allen*. In this light, the essence of Brooks's early works provides relevance to the Civil Rights struggles of the 1950s, the 1960s, and beyond.

Chicago remained a proud focus of Brooks's writings. Two years after her second child, Nora, was born, her novel *Maud Martha* was published in 1953. The novel is an entertaining and engrossing yet loosely constructed account of urban life, representative of the experiences of the writer. It portrays in an essential way the subtleties of "Negro" life at a time when the color line within the race and other demarcations such as job status and parental heritage held a stronghold on the possibilities of freedom within one's home and the larger community. The subject matter is comprehensive, from personal relationships to the color line within the Black community. The probing novel also uncovers hidden layers of devastating effects of the color line's endangering reaches into America at large. Brooks honestly and courageously explores this territory and comments on the social implications of the position of women, particularly women of color. *Maud Martha* is a daring book, coming at a time before society at large was willing to discuss the prevalent issues of race, gender, and socioeconomic equality. A careful reading of *Maud Martha* reveals one of the earliest discussions on the color line in America, which W. E. B. DuBois said would plague the twentieth century. Gwendolyn Brooks lived the experiences she wrote about, and her personal experiences informed the progression and focus of her works.

In reading *Maud Martha*, the reader travels through the daily affairs of Maud, a Black woman confronting the harsh realities of her life. Unique in its format and renderings, the novel explores the human motivations apparent and not so apparent in societal affairs and accentuates the search for self-esteem. Although significant in its original presentation, its probing revelations, and its universal assessments, in many ways the novel remains a neglected manifesto on Black reality in the United States. Brooks is known primarily as a poet, not as a novelist, and few know of her interest in writing stories of her life in Chicago. Nevertheless, *Maud Martha* offers a realistic portrayal of tenement life and the larger community. It draws on the lives of people who struggle daily and who, for the most part, ultimately survive in their search for validation.

Loosely autobiographical, *Maud Martha* is clever in its design, employing a series of brief scenarios to tell Maud's story. Maud, in fact, becomes the embodiment of an individual's search for identity and validation. The simple structure of *Maud Martha* belies its thematic complexities: raw portrayals of love and death, the advent of racial and interracial prejudice, and the struggle for intellectual independence. The mere titles of the vignettes underscore the visceral and psychological issues relevant to the times. In Section Four, the understated title "Death of Grandmother" augments the reader's sense of the narrative and confessional connection of the event to Brooks's own life, her personal and communal reverence for the power of life and community. Similarly, "We're the Only Colored People Here" exposes the awkwardness of race relations publicly, and the failure of so-called integration to ameliorate confused and confusing relations. In this brief episode and in "The Self-Solace," the author portrays the anger and ambivalence that prevent meaningful cooperation. Furthermore, "The Self-Solace" explores, with rare and daring scrutiny, the lasting sting of pejorative language that emerges, consciously or otherwise, from social isolation and subjection.

As evident in *Bronzeville Boys and Girls* (1956), Brooks's concern for future generations is another major motif in her works. This brief collection of poems highlights Brooks's mastery of the compelling voices and minds of young black children, and addresses childhood experiences related to issues of image and esteem. Brooks speaks through the characters, who remain positive in outlook and carry the optimism Brooks held for all young people. This hopeful concern for the young remained central to Brooks's creative spirit and commitment, and this collection advances a "youthful optimism," to which many of her later works attest. In fact, Brooks uses children's names as titles for poems again thirty-five years later in *Children Coming Home*. The use of the names not only allows the reader to see the children as living characters, but also it allows the reader to witness the writer's compassion for and devotion to the children as people and poetic spirits themselves with moving voices of their own. Brooks creates and caresses these precious works of art, innocent and youthful, and at the same time she chronicles the realities many young individuals face in a South Side Chicago world where, unfortunately, they cannot control or even meaningfully divert their lives from a system of low expectations and achievement. Still, as is common in Brooks's life and artistic aesthetic, she writes *for* them and speaks *as* them so that the voices blend with hers and receive the strength of support they deserve.

As a Chicagoan, Brooks continued her portrayal of Black life in Chicago and its connection to the South. *The Bean Eaters* (1960) opens with a poem of dedication to David Anderson Brooks, the poet's father, who had died in 1959. This collection, appearing at the beginning of one of the most turbulent decades of the twentieth century, foretells the transformations of the coming years. Brooks would increasingly seek out controversial issues and subject matter outside the poetic boundaries of contemporary white literature. This volume contains some of the more popular poems by the author: "The Bean Eaters" and, perhaps her most anthologized poem, "We Real Cool."

Also included in *The Bean Eaters* are other poems that address the culturally historical connection between the City of Chicago and the State of Mississippi. After more than a century of Black migratory connections between the two geographical regions, Brooks recounts, at a critical point in U.S. history, the sordid social and cultural interrelationship that connected the people of color in the South and those in the more northern Midwest. The poems "A Bronzeville Mother Loiters in Mississippi. Meanwhile, a Mississippi Mother Burns Bacon" and "The *Chicago Defender* Sends a Man to Little Rock" are some of the author's most compelling works related to the Civil Rights struggles and mayhem of the 1950s. These two poems address unabashedly the horrible ills of an American society gone mad with unlearned lessons from the past and a continuing imbalance of justice and freedom for all citizens. These poems point to the teeming issues of race that served as precursors to the modern Civil Rights Movement that would last through the 1960s and beyond. Chicago has had its share of uprisings, and these continue to influence the cultural milieu of the city.

Perhaps, however, the most telling of accounts of people of color in a hostile land is the story of one of America's most brutal chapters in history; it is the story of Emmett Till. In "The Last Quatrain of the Ballad of Emmett Till," Brooks uses soft strokes of diction to assert one of America's greatest tragedies: the murder of a naive fourteen-year-old black boy from Chicago who was spending the summer in Mississippi, and who was accused of whistling at a white woman. The brutal torture, murder, and mutilation of this young boy visiting the south frame the poem, whose message still permeates the national conscience.

In 1963, *Selected Poems*, perhaps the most widely distributed of the author's collections, was published by Harper and Row. It was largely appreciated by college students and avid followers of Brooks for including many "favorites" among Brooks enthusiasts, such as poems from *A Street in Bronzeville*, "Negro Hero," and a section titled "New Poems," including "Of Robert Frost" and "Langston Hughes." During this time, the early 1960s, Brooks was also involved in college and university teaching. She conducted workshops at Columbia College in Chicago and taught classes at, among others, Elmhurst College, City College of New York, Northeastern Illinois State College, Columbia University, and the University of Wisconsin. A year later, in 1964, Brooks received her first honorary Doctor of Humane Letters from Columbia College. She would go on to receive more than seventy-five honorary degrees from various colleges and universities worldwide.

In the late 1960s, during the critical stages of the Black revolution in America, Brooks would rise to the occasion. To many college students and other writers and activists, Brooks became an established literary voice who added to the legitimacy of a cadre of young Black writers speaking in rebellion at a turbulent time when the social, cultural, and intellectual activities demanded urgent responses across the United States, particularly in Chicago. Brooks is known to have given credit to the young Black writers for engaging her "consciousness." While this may be true, a careful reading of Brooks's earlier works evidences a preexisting "consciousness" akin to the later "transformation" that is often evidenced by Brooks herself and acknowledged by others. It is safe to say, nevertheless, that a stronger vocalization of "Blackness" can be seen in the works of Brooks after her participation at the Fisk University Second Black Writers' Conference in 1967. It was here that the writers spoke from a Black Aesthetic that was becoming the mantra for black writers and artists across America, with the Chicago area as one of the focal regions. Brooks was already seen as an influential figure in both the black and white literary communities. Over time, however, it became increasingly clear that she viewed her kinship to the black community as paramount, and this allegiance would have lasting influence on the focus of her writing.

Living in Chicago, Brooks remained a part of her community, and, as such, she waged a relentless campaign to educate the young writers in the city she loved. She participated in activities sponsored by Chicago's Organization of Black American Culture, and she connected with and assisted, intellectually and financially, many writers in Chicago and elsewhere, as she traveled around the United States. In her home city, she enjoyed the support not only of the up-and-coming writers of the time such as Haki Madhubuti (then Don L. Lee) but also the respect of established figures such as, among others, Hoyt Fuller, writer and editor; Lerone Bennett, prolific scholar and writer; Val Gray Ward, actress; and Larry Neal, poet and critic. Brooks was seen as the accomplished voice of wisdom and experience as Brooks and other writers, who gravitated toward her and who participated in the many workshops held in the black Chicago communities, reached consensus on their duty as Black writers.

In 1968, Gwendolyn Brooks's long literary journey reached a peak when she was named Poet Laureate of Illinois. In the same year, she published *In the Mecca*. This collection came at the height of Brooks's more noticeable immersion in "things black." It was a time of self-awareness and cultural appreciation in the Black community, and Brooks was eager to be a viable part of the movement in which she believed and to which she became more visibly committed. Essentially, *In the Mecca* chronicles life in the historic Mecca Building in its days of decline from showplace to slum tenement. The Mecca building is typical of countless other buildings in cities throughout the United States. Most will agree, however, that the larger cities experienced a more pronounced version of such phenomena of buildings and neighborhoods abandoned after decades of having served the middle class well. Poverty-level replacements moved in and dealt the best they could with their literal and figurative marginalization—economic, social, and cultural. Life in Chicago provided Brooks with endless provocation and inspiration to tell the stories of those individuals and collective citizens of color living under varied and long-standing questionable conditions. At the same time, Brooks celebrates these individuals' resolve to respond honestly and to survive bravely. *In the Mecca*, issued by Harper and Row, was to become Brooks's last collection of new poems by a major white publisher.

After her ascension to poet laureate, Brooks, who always believed in "sharing the wealth," continued her long-standing supportive relationship with the young people in her community. She was convinced that they needed to know and appreciate their heritage. To this end, she sponsored trips to Africa for several youths from her block on the South Side of Chicago. Her humanitarian inclinations did not stop there. In 1969, she began the Annual Poet Laureate Awards, held at the University of Chicago. Each year she invited, at her own considerable expense, elementary and high-school poets from across Illinois. She awarded each poet a monetary award of at least fifty dollars. In addition, it was not unusual for Brooks to award even higher monetary awards, usually five hundred dollars, to adult poets from Illinois and other states to which she had traveled. Furthermore, it was not uncommon for Brooks to pause during her reading, wherever she was, and announce monetary awards to poets she had met during her visits to high schools, colleges, campuses, and community centers across the United States.

By 1969, when her book *Riot* was published by Broadside Press, Brooks had decided to use only Black publishers, and this decision reflected her resolve to support the concept that being black was as positive as being white. It was a major decision requiring extraordinary courage and devotion. Brooks, nevertheless, took the leap and, once she had taken it, she made good on her word. *Riot* addresses all the mixed emotions of everyone involved in the act of rioting—those rioting and the sometimes outsiders who are perceived as the causes of the rioting. The book, in three parts, focuses on the human and inhuman responses to the upheaval following the death of Martin Luther King Jr. Firmly grounded in historical time and feeling, the volume nonetheless expresses ideas of loss, anguish, anger, and resolve in the voices of characters whose language and points of view make the volume a riveting and instructional read.

Riot is dedicated to Dudley Randall, the owner of Broadside Press. A longtime friend, Randall eventually published a number of Brooks's works. *Riot* is historically significant in that it chronicles the climate of the 1960s and the turbulence and unrest particularly in black urban neighborhoods. Brooks was witness to the chaos in her city and in other cities across the United States, and she generated in this small collection moving and insightful poems, including the title poem "Riot" and "The Third Sermon on the Warpland." "Riot" highlights the necessary sociopolitical connection between Brooks and all the constituents within her neighborhood and community. In this poem, Brooks depicts the prelude to a new stage of activist response in "The Young Men Run" and "The Law Comes Sirening across the Town." Subsequently, the community pivoted to a time when "the poor were sweaty and unpretty" and "were black and loud.

/ And not detainable. And not discreet." Charting the arc of outrage, Brooks closes *Riot* using the words of Martin Luther King Jr.: "A riot is the language of the unheard." Through her works, Brooks provided a polyvocal articulation for the disenfranchised, and a unified resolve to address grievances.

As Brooks continued to develop her intensified focus on Black Power issues and responses, she again turned her attention to the empowerment of youth in a world where they would need to be self-assured in order to survive. In the eight poems of *Family Pictures* (1970), Brooks continues her skillful unveiling of cultural lessons affecting both people of color and others in the community. "The Life of Lincoln West," clear evidence of Brooks's continued attention to the "color-line" so aptly explained in 1903 by W. E. B. DuBois, does not oversimplify her view of humanity. As in previous collections, she amplifies the social issues and causes of the Civil Rights struggle by concentrating on the "integrated" community experience and daring to explore the crudest of negative associations with blackness in social and cultural terms. In this long poem, Brooks, again, uses the child's innocent persona to express with increasing poignancy the child's experiences with the brutality of racism. Brooks, nonetheless, seizes the ugliness of the actions against Lincoln and turns the negativism into an opportunity for a celebration of enlightenment and acceptance, prevailing themes throughout the body of Brooks's works. The young Lincoln in the poem is granted an emblem of lasting pride. Through the ironic twist of his assailants' ignorance and hatred, as well as young Lincoln's brilliant creativity and sensibilities, the young black boy learns and internalizes unadulterated love of self. Of equal importance, Brooks focuses not only on individuals but on how self-acceptance can help produce general acceptance among youth, the hope for the future, as demonstrated in "Speech to the Young. Speech to the Progress-Toward." Dedicated to her two children, this poem is a plea as much as it is a visionary anthem of hope that not only her children but also all children will live their lives fulfilling their promise: to "Live not for The End of the Song / Live in the along" (lines 12–13). The year 1971 also proved to be rather prolific for Brooks. Besides other literary projects with which Brooks was associated, another book written for children, *Aloneness*, appeared, consisting of a single poem that exemplifies her nurturing spirit and her dedication to young people. Her continued focus on the subject is reminiscent of one of her mentors, Langston Hughes, who made children's works a priority in his career as well.

Two years after Brooks decided to use only Black publishers, Harper and Row, the original publisher of her work, negotiated release of a collection of previously published poems. Thus, *The World of Gwendolyn Brooks*, 1971, became the poet's final book issued by a major publisher and serves as a pivotal point in the public's access to Brooks's printed works. At the same time, Brooks began a schedule of more public readings and engagements after the official resolution of her relationship with Harper and Row. This separation from Harper and Row was perhaps the most dramatic and courageous decision Brooks would make in her literary career. The decision proved to be the beginning of a positive adventure; Brooks became more independent in decisions related to her literary aspirations. On the other hand, however, this break with a major publisher in some ways limited the access to the works of a poet of national renown. Brooks, nevertheless, was resolute in her willingness to undergo the sacrifices and the rewards precipitated by a decision of conscience. After 1971, her works were published by Broadside Press in Detroit and Third World Press in Chicago, as well as, from time to time, her own publishing entities: Black Position Press, Brooks Press, and The David Company.

Brooks kept Chicago as her base but continued to spread her influence. *Report from Part One*, 1972, an autobiography, appeared a year after Brooks's trip to Africa in 1971. This account of the poet's life acknowledges all the influences and associations relevant to her evolvement as an individual and as a poet. *Report from Part One* was perceived as less autobiographical than readers had anticipated, yet Brooks was pleased with what she offered in the book. In *Part One*, Brooks chronicles her early years and those people, including her parents, who influenced her choice to become a writer. Of particular interest is Brooks's discussion of her growing affinity for Africa as a homeland and the role of the artist, particularly the artists of African ancestry. This book also includes the rather substantively revealing interview of Brooks by educator and historian Paul M. Engle. The interview valuably complements any assessment of Brooks and her writing philosophy at that point in her life. Brooks always remained generous to those with whom she had had meaningful literary and cultural contact. It is not surprising, then, that she would devote so much of her own story talking about others who made meaningful contributions to her life experiences. Essentially, *Report from Part One* traces the advent of Gwendolyn Brooks and, more importantly, chronicles her transformation from beginning poet to master poet. In *Part One*, Brooks provides a history of her work as a reviewer, her teaching experiences, and her introduction to the young black voices of the 1960s. Perhaps the most engrossing spiritual and intellectual experiences were her trips to Africa and her continual dedication to furthering the young voices that she said "influenced" her and prompted greater dedication to her less than favorably received activist posture in the white-dominated literary world.

Following the autobiography, Brooks continued with a spate of children's books centering generally upon themes of the necessary search for a moral, ethical, and useful identity in the contemporary world frequently beset by violence and racism. *The Tiger Who Wore White Gloves, or What You Are You Are* (1974), is, as with most celebrated children's books, full of messages for all ages, not just children. The story explores the universal theme of the need to search for, recognize, and embrace personal identity, developing from insecurity and denial to ultimate acceptance. This time the stories are explicitly related to African subject matter and art forms, richly portrayed through the African folk tradition of using animals in the telling of stories and skillfully illustrated by Timothy Jones. Dedicated to her children Nora Blakely and Henry Blakely III, Brooks nurtures her own biological children and those of the reading community by encouraging them to recognize, accept, and laud positive self-identity.

As a result of this focus, Brooks remained cognizant of the activities in her neighborhood and remained in touch with the people on the South Side. *Beckonings* (1975) builds on Brooks's interest in issues relevant to her community and reiterates the concept of establishing and, in some instances, restoring positive self-identity, especially among young Blacks. Brooks generates hope that the young in her community and everywhere will fulfill their potential in becoming whole in a hostile or seemingly indifferent society. Her convictions and desires can be measured in her laments for those in her community. In "The Boy Died in My Alley," the poet addresses not only the violence but also the transformation of her neighborhood from a community living in illusory accord to one rife with inherited and fresh cultural, political, social, and economic differences. Still, by claiming the alley, the speaker recognizes the responsibility of those in the community to own their streets, houses, neighbors, and lives. Brooks does not avoid the lighter side of life, the common and enjoyable experiences that people share, as in "Steam Song," a poem centering on singer Al Green, and "Horses Graze." "Horses Graze" focuses explicitly on horses, but, as in *The Tiger*, the animals' experiences serve as a commentary on the human, the sad wasting of human capabilities. Likewise, in the poem "Boys. Black," Brooks makes a probing, passionate appeal to black boys to "forge through the sludge" of false promises and personal miscalculations about the society in which they must live. She "beckons" to them to overcome. In another voice, Brooks announces "A Black Wedding Song," perhaps one of the leading displays of positive interaction and reciprocation between men and women of color in works by Brooks. In this poem, the speaker calls upon the participants to reach to a place beyond mere unconscious, automatic parroting. Black people need to inform their sacred rituals with words that express themselves. Brooks closes each of the two stanzas in confirmation: "Come to Your Wedding Song," as if a journey will discover what has been awaiting the awakened consciousness. As expected, Brooks concludes the collection with positive expectation. In this volume, the reader discovers Brooks's love of Chicago and her devotion to promise of a better world for those she knows will come years after her.

As Brooks continued to refine her focus and her literary goals, in 1975 she also coedited, with Keorapetse Kgositsile, Haki Madhubuti, and Dudley Randall, *A Capsule Course in Black Poetry Writing* (Detroit: Broadside Press), designed to assist writers in their craft and in their literary and social consciousness. This work proved to be a harbinger for many emerging scholars of the Black Movement, who were beginning to access "the movement" and its impact on American culture, at a time when the prevailing cultural and political energy in America had grown more conservative. Brooks also seized this publishing opportunity to echo her concern that poetry should not be nor appear "too studied," a term she liked to use to describe even some of her own early poems. Rather, for Brooks, a feeling of improvisation, spontaneity, and cooperation leading to excitement and evocation of the spirit directly related to African communal practices, helps to express the energy of humanity. In this practice she attempted to explain and champion the creation of Black literature by rooting it in African communal aesthetics, which in turn made literature, especially poetry, relevant to "average" people, particularly those of color. Through this, the work motivated cycles of creativity and action that were interactive and affirmative.

Brooks increased her speaking engagements across the United States, but her family remained her foremost priority. In 1976, Brooks lost her brother, Raymond Brooks, and in 1978, Keziah Brooks, her mother, also died. This was a critical time in the poet's life. It is, therefore, understandable that Brooks did not publish another volume until *Primer for Blacks* in 1980. The poems "Primer for Blacks," "To Those of My Sisters Who Kept Their Naturals," and "Requiem before Revival" that comprise *Primer for Blacks* all echo Brooks's long-standing determination to move as many as possible of her people to a point of pride and self-determination. She felt that she had much to say and offer during this waning period of the Black Pride Movement that had risen to prominence in the late 1960s. This thin volume offers enduring moments of encouragement to beginning writers of any age or race. In "Primer for Blacks," the poet uses the symbol and essence of "Blackness" to connect American Blacks with the universe of Blacks. "To Those of My Sisters Who Kept Their Naturals" echoes Brooks's sustaining appreciation of the steadfast warriors who remained relentless, who kept their natural hair, and who had "not wanted to be white." The poem salutes Black pride, a staple in all of Brooks's poems related to daily life in her native Chicago and elsewhere.

Brooks was ever the generous benefactor and mentor.

She was noted for her impressive impromptu literary awards to deserving students and for her advice to the writers she met. Brooks often wrote letters to many young, aspiring writers and other individuals she met during her travels. Thus it is understandable that, in 1980, she would publish *Young Poet's Primer*, a poetic text of guidelines for young writers. The thin volume provides, in accessible language to the young, poetic insights to the art of human expression. In similar fashion to *Young Poet's Primer*, another volume for budding poets, *Very Young Poets*, was published in 1983. Brooks remained current in her views and quite aware of the social and cultural shifts of the day. Being informed on gender issues, she also was aware of the many challenges young children faced in their daily lives. In *Very Young Poets*, for instance, Brooks's poem "Computer" reminds the young: "I conduct a computer / A computer does not conduct me" (27). These two volumes sustained Brooks's willingness to invest her dreams in the nurturing of the young people in Chicago and around the world.

In terms of her extending her fame, a year after her trip to the Soviet Union, Brooks published *To Disembark* (1981). The collection comprises previously published poems, including "In Memoriam: Edgar William Blakely," "Family Picture," "To Prisoners," and "To Disembark." The poems highlight Brooks's relentless desire to uplift the downtrodden and the disenfranchised, but with a nuance of focus as a nod to her recent international travel. In the poem "To Prisoners," Brooks appeals to the prisoners to put forth diligent efforts, which result in a sense of decorum that contributes to their survival. To a greater extent, Brooks takes a more pronounced stance in presenting her concerns in a global context, outside the urban setting and beyond Chicago. *To Disembark* is a collection that crystallizes the significance of the African Diaspora through its international context, prompting a continued focus among informed scholars and intellectuals of color, and reinforcing this as an essential characteristic of African American Studies departments. The connection of American Blacks to African culture was vital to any affirmation of positive self-identity, and Brooks remained a part of this growing crusade. *To Disembark* is, as she says in "In Memoriam: Edgar William Blakely," a plea for all to " . . . Be sane. Be / Neighbor to all people in the world." Neighbor, community, country, and world.

Remaining reliably attuned to current events, Brooks especially kept abreast of the events in her culturally enriching Chicago. In 1983, Brooks, having published *Very Young Poets*, continued to inspire as many young writers as possible and still fulfill her official responsibilities as the Poet Laureate of Illinois and a major literary voice of Chicago. Therefore, in 1983, Brooks also published the salutary *Mayor Harold Washington and Chicago, the I Will City*. This tribute to the first Black mayor of Chicago comprises three distinct poems: "Mayor Harold Washington," "Chicago, the I Will City," and "A Hymn to Chicago." The energy that drives this tribute is rooted in the long history of Chicago as a political lightning rod in American politics. Chicago, long known as one of the most segregated cities in America, finally elected a Black mayor in 1983. Brooks, who was an active supporter, wrote this volume in honor of Harold Washington. Brooks found Washington's election just cause for celebration, signaling a redemptive moment for the people of Chicago who had moved a great distance from old politics. More importantly, Brooks recognized and celebrated this achievement as a worthy triumph for people of African descent in the City of Chicago and as an emblem of pride for Blacks across the nation. The poet's inclusion of "A

Hymn to Chicago" in this volume echoes the long-standing concerns that helped to drive the efforts of Brooks in correcting inequities and injustices for the good of all involved on all sides of any concern related to making real the "promises of democracy" in Chicago and for all Americans.

Brooks's views on humanity are evidenced through her apparent appreciation of individual awareness and social responsibility in a universe of constant social, cultural, and political change. In *The Near-Johannesburg Boy and Other Poems* (1986), Brooks's international perspective sits beside local Chicago matters in a seamless blend of Pan-African social awareness and responsibility. Where "The Near-Johannesburg Boy" and "In Nairobi" explore world matters, Brooks also includes previously published poems that entail life in the Chicago region and across America, cleverly uniting the essence of African struggles with those of Blacks in America. "Early Death: 'Of the Young Dead;'" and "To the Young Who Want to Die" reiterate Brooks's long-standing appreciation of the challenges presented to young and older members of Black communities. In "The Chicago Picasso," Brooks, as Illinois Poet Laureate and one of Chicago's leading literary figures, addresses the power and broad appeal of modern art through her reference to Picasso, a towering figure whose use of "primitive" African masks and aesthetics helped him revolutionize art around the world. "The Chicago Picasso" ironically reclaims the tradition and greatness that has been associated with that artist. The poem demonstrates Brooks's ability to function effectively in relation to different strands of the social fabric, but with a principled vision. In addition, with the inclusion of the memorably ironic poem "Infirm," the collection becomes a tribute to universal acknowledgment of human equality and dignity. The closing poem "Infirm" echoes the need to recognize the larger commonalities connecting all members of the human race. Overall, the poems in *The Near-Johannesburg Boy*, "dedicated to the students of Gwendolyn Brooks Junior High School, Harvey, Illinois," demonstrate Brooks's commitment to recognizing a common humanity.

The breadth and wealth of Brooks's literary contributions is made clear through the body of her literary offerings, and this is quite noticeable in her impressive collection *Blacks* (1987). Through this seminal collection by Brooks, consisting of a representative sampling of the poet's works—*A Street in Bronzeville, Annie Allen, The Bean Eaters, In the Mecca, Riot, Maud Martha* (novel), and excerpts from *Primer for Blacks, Beckonings, To Disembark*, and *The Near-Johannesburg Boy*—these works were assured due prominence among scholars and other Brooks enthusiasts. It is a comprehensive collection for many who otherwise would not have convenient access to works by Brooks. In this edition, new and longtime readers encounter a tenacious Brooks preferring the term "Black" to any others in the long-standing quarrel over preferred terms for people of color, including but not limited to "colored," "black," "Negro," "Afro-American," and

"African American." Brooks preferred the all-inclusive term "Black" because she felt the term included people of color everywhere. Black is less literally a deterministic color than it is a proactive and empowering manner of dealing with a world frequently bent on outright control and manipulation of its perceived threatening differences.

Blacks is the closest thing to a definitive collection of Brooks's works, coming at a time, in 1987, when the poet began to enlarge earlier themes and to add new ones. The collection presents 512 pages of challenge, struggle, and triumph. The writings are spiritually and intellectually integrated to quintessential accuracy in accounting the many nuances that continue to shape the black search for the Pan-African (American) dream and universal freedom. *Blacks* embodies the growing stature and the poetic life of Gwendolyn Brooks. Equally important, as indicated earlier, the collection sustains the understanding that Brooks was always intellectually concerned and involved with all people of color and, in fact, echoed many of the themes that younger poets, years later, would come to announce more loudly as the mantra during the days of the turbulent years of civil unrest and cultural revolution, primarily during the late 1960s and the early 1970s. *Blacks*, then, represents a substantive portion of the career of one of America's most lauded poets, expressing her long-standing awareness of the engrained issues facing people of color, Americans more broadly, and brethren around the world.

Following up *Blacks*, *Gottschalk and the Grande Tarantelle* (1988) comprises four poems: "Gottschalk and the Grande Tarantelle," "Winnie," "Thinking of Elizabeth Steinberg," and "Michael, Young Russia." This collection reflects, as clearly as her other later collections, Brooks's ability to express in an international context the nuances of black involvement not only in the black world but in the white one as well. "Gottschalk and the Grande Tarantelle" provides a history lesson on the customary misappropriation of the wealth—gifts and talents—of blacks by some whites. The scathing, satirical poem uses Gottschalk, U.S. pianist and composer, to highlight the genius of African American music and to call attention to America's fascination with the power and influence of this universally recognized genius, but interestingly employs "European" terms in the title to emphasize how European music is not "a white thing" and how knowledge should not be avoided under any circumstances. It may lead one back to oneself. On the other hand, in "Thinking of Elizabeth Steinberg," Brooks demonstrates her compassion and dread at the death of any child, closing *Gottschalk* with the moving salute, again to the young—but this time to "Michael, Young Russia." These poems go a long way in dispelling the frequently cited notion that Brooks was totally indifferent to the plight of people other than those of her race. The long poem "Winnie," first published in the 75th Anniversary issue of *Poetry*, also appears in this collection. In 1988, Brooks published *Win-*

nie, dedicated to her daughter Nora Blakely and focusing on Winnie Mandela, as a separate publication. *Winnie* confirms Brooks's devotion to world issues and to championing heroic people, whoever and wherever they are. For Brooks, Blackness does that.

Brooks remained optimistic as she focused on the childhood of the innocent young and the childhood experiences in urban settings. *Children Coming Home*, 1991, written about children, focuses on the plight of children and also posits the importance of adults properly engaging and nourishing not only their young but also all of the young people within their care and influence. Fittingly, Brooks opens the book with a quote from poet Mari Evans: "Speak the truth to the people." Accordingly, *Children Coming Home* is a realistic portrayal of the life issues of children and consists of poems bearing children's names and corresponding titles. Brooks uses this array of names and children to present a cross section of the issues affecting America's children. The children include, among others, Tinsel Marie, Kojo, and Nora. In "The Coora Flower," Tinsel Marie is in a household where her mother is on drugs, and Tinsel Marie has to sleep uneasily because there might be a strange man in the house. Brooks makes it clear that she is a delicate flower in need of protection and whose nurturing has been neglected by a mother who is caught in a cycle of sex and drugs that unfortunately too often overwhelms and destroys young women. In contrast to The Coora Flower," "Kojo: I Am A Black" features Kojo, who is negotiating the world of racial politics by advocating for his own sense of the world, wanting to be called "Black," not "African-American." Articulating Brooks's preference to use "Black" for race identification, Kojo still comes from an environment where, like Tinsel Marie, he faces forces that attempt to limit and define him, requiring increased strength and endurance to survive and prevail. Nora, the persona in "I'll Stay" speaks to the ambitions of a child fulfilling her dreams of success wherever she happens to be living. The poem is oddly reminiscent of Brooks's own desire "to stay" in her neighborhood despite the shifting demographics and declining sense of community occurring in her later years. Reluctantly, Brooks had to move, eventually, from her old neighborhood to a safer environment on South Shore Drive.

In *Children Coming Home*, Brooks remains current with the issues of the times, and she establishes in a unique way the authentic presentation of the life of those she portrays. Each poem delicately translates the emotions of each child. Annye L. Refoe observes: "The uniqueness of this volume lies in the tone that each poem assumes. The inhibitions that accompany adults are usually absent in children; therefore, what is stated and attributed to the children is exactly what is on 'their' minds without embellishment or self-pity." Coming late in Brooks's life, *Children Coming Home* is a lasting presentation of all the fervor that went into Brooks's earlier books for children: *Bronzeville Boys and Girls* and

Aloneness. In *Children Coming Home*, however, Brooks covers every subject of conversation and most of the unspoken challenges faced by the youth of today. With this volume, Brooks steps into the modern age with graceful scrutiny and steadfast alertness. Brooks manages to cover the compelling issues facing the young, and the book becomes an appeal to save all children without the maudlin sentimentality that usually accompanies this subject.

It is auspicious that *Children Coming Home* is the last collection Brooks published while she was alive. This collection provides one of the broadest spectrums of Brooks's vision and talent. The collection further evidences Brooks's ability to adapt to the times while not losing her enthusiasm for life. She nurtured the uncanny ability to remain interested in new things and new ways of expressing old ideas and concepts, and she kept a balanced view of modern culture, including television, movies, and contemporary music. She was a strong supporter of spoken word poetry and selective rap. Brooks liked children as well as poets, young and old, who brought freshness to the universe of ideas, formal and informal. Likewise, due in large part to her Chicago savvy and her world exposure, she embraced a range of literary expression and remained dedicated to encouraging new voices in poetry. And she always came home.

In writing and speaking of herself, Brooks was reserved yet honest and forthright: she measured her revelations in conversation and in print. *Report from Part Two*, the second part of the autobiography of Gwendolyn Brooks, published in 1996, is more a record, a report, than a full autobiography, as many have cited. In *Part Two*, Brooks continues where *Report from Part One* closed. Brooks affirms her relationships with those who remained faithful through the years and acknowledges her associations with those who, casually or otherwise, made a lasting difference in her life. The sketches she re-creates are revealing and memorable. The details of her travels to Africa and other events, personal and public, unveil the full dimension of Brooks as a humane individual. The book also includes the sentimental. She devotes a chapter "Keziah" to her mother, Keziah Brooks, who remained a life-force in the poet's life and greatly influenced the poet's sensibilities. Another chapter of import is "The Day of the Gwendolyn," which recounts Brooks's role as 1985–86 Consultant in Poetry to the Library of Congress (the title "Poet Laureate" was legislated the following year). Building on the familiar practices of her life in Chicago communities and elsewhere, Brooks continued to reach out to "the people" on all stations of life. Brooks brought to this office the enviable notion that the position of Consultant in Poetry should be one of activity and involvement. Brooks clearly produced one of the earliest, most active and inclusive tenures as Consultant in Poetry and helped to establish the tradition of an interactive poet laureate.

Part Two becomes for Brooks a celebration of her life and remains an informative survey of incidents, people, and personalities deserving of her commentary. It provides insight to her gracious nature as she seizes opportunity to demonstrate her appreciation for friends and acquaintances at a late stage in her life, including many famous contemporaries. During her introductions of writers she invited to read at The Library of Congress, she offers insight on two respected colleagues: poet Donald Hall, whom she identified as having courage and conviction, and William Golding, author of *Lord of the Flies*. While there are times when students and scholars can have a tendency to isolate Black artists from white, Brooks clearly took her place among black and white writers of her time. The final section, "I'm Here!," fittingly complements Brooks's benevolence. In this closing section, the poet acknowledges those who remained spiritually and intellectually faithful. Foremost among these is her longtime manager and friend, Beryl Zitch of The Contemporary Forum. It was through Zitch's office that America could contact Brooks, Poet Laureate of Illinois. Essentially, *Part Two* remains a memorable and enlightening self-assessment by the author.

In Montgomery: And Other Poems (2003) is the first volume of Brooks's poetry published after her death—on December 3, 2000, at her home in Chicago. The collection includes "In Montgomery," which resulted from an assignment arranged by *Ebony*'s Executive Editor, Herbert Nipson, and first appeared in *Ebony Magazine* (August, 1971). "In Montgomery," a poem of over six hundred lines, addresses the racial climate in Montgomery during the seminal years of the Civil Rights Movement in the Deep South. The other poems include, among others, previously published "Gottschalk and the Grande Tarantelle," "Winnie," "Song of Winnie," "Thinking of Elizabeth Steinberg," "Michael, 'Young Russia,'" and "Jane Addams." It is clear to those who followed the career of Brooks that she was always writing and had plans for many other works. This collection is a lasting reminder of how much more the readers need to see the yet unpublished works of this author, one of America's most highly venerated poets.

Gwendolyn Brooks came to the end of her career as she began it—with accolades. She garnered a list of many "First Achievements," including the first black recipient of a Pulitzer Prize, 1950; an invitation from President John F. Kennedy to read at a Library of Congress Poetry Festival in 1962; the first Black Poet Laureate of Illinois, 1968–2000; the first to receive an Honorary Doctorate from Western Illinois University, 1971; the first Black woman to serve as Poetry Consultant to the Library of Congress (Poet Laureate of the United States), 1985–86; and recipient of the Society for Literature Award, University of Thessaloniki, Athens, Greece. Her other honors include being named the 1994 Jefferson Lecturer for The National Endowment for the Humanities, the highest Federal Government Intellectual Achievement Honor, and the 1999 Academy of American Poets Sixty-Fifth Fellowship for Distinguished Poetic Achievement and election by the Academy's Board of Chancellors. In addition, the Gwendolyn Brooks Cultural Center at Western Illinois University and the Gwendolyn

Brooks Cultural Center for Literature and Creative Writing at Chicago State University honor the legacy of Brooks. Although the Brooks Center at Chicago State serves as a repository of the poet's works, her personal papers are a part of the African American Writers Collection at the University of California, Berkeley's Bancroft Library. There remain wide admiration for and growing scholarly interest in the literary life of Gwendolyn Brooks.

Brooks, who always wanted to be a poet, published a few poems as a child. Her first book of poems, however, was *A Street in Bronzeville* (1945). Being quite inquisitive, she grew up pondering the issues of her time: talent, race, and culture. In her writings and interviews, it is clear that she preferred the term "Black." She found it inclusive and fully embracing. This concept is nowhere more apparent than in "Kojo: I Am A Black," the poem in *Children Coming Home*, in which Kojo says:

> I am a Black and a Black forever.
> . . . .
> I am other than hyphenation.
> . . . .
> Do not call me out of my name.

Brooks gave a voice to the multitude of the disenfranchised in her "native" city of Chicago, but she became and remains a voice for people of color everywhere and certainly an equally qualified voice for all those who love humanity and know of its promise. Thus, it is understandable that in closing "Requiem before Revival" in *Primer for Blacks*, Gwendolyn Brooks says:

> I continue my old optimism. In spite of all the disappointment and disillusion-ment and befuddlement out there, I go on believing that the Weak among us will, finally, perceive the impressiveness of our numbers, perceive the quality and legitimacy of our essence, and take sufficient, indicated steps toward defi-nition, clarification.

Brooks remained steadfast in her convictions and was noted for her integrity as an individual and as an artist.

One of the long-standing concerns about Brooks's career as a writer is the scarcity of access to her works in printed form. What is more redeeming, how-ever, is the awareness that Brooks, wherever she appeared, with her exceptional voice and unfaltering energy, provided to each audience a memorable record of personal performance, delivered with intense conviction and a style, hers alone. Those who heard her will always remember the grasp and authenticity of her assertions to preserve all things living and to accentuate all things im-portant within the arena of human endeavor and survival. Brooks remains a voice whose conscience guided her consciousness. Likewise, her poems echo, in clear and memorable tones, the challenges and aspirations of those on the South Side of Chicago as well as those other increasingly varied and troubled voices across the United States and around the world. Perhaps her spirit and character are best encapsulated in her mantra for the world in her poem "The Second Sermon on the Warpland": "Conduct your blooming in the noise and whip of the whirlwind."

References

Davis, Arthur P. *From the Dark Tower: Afro-American Writers, 1900–1960*. Washington, D.C.: Howard University Press, 1981.

Engle, Paul. "Chicago Can Take Pride in New, Young Voice in Poetry," *Chicago Tribune Books*, August 26, 1945, 11.

Franklin, John Hope and Alfred A. Moss Jr. *From Slavery to Freedom: A History of Negro Americans*. New York: Alfred A. Knopf, 2000.

Kent, George E. *A Life of Gwendolyn Brooks*. Lexington: University Press of Kentucky, 1990.

Kufrin, Joan. "Gwendolyn Brooks." *Uncommon Women*. Piscataway, N.J.: New Century Publishers,1981.

Loff, Jon N. "Gwendolyn Brooks: A Bibliography." *College Language Association Journal* 17 (September 1973): 21–32.

Melhem, D. H. *Gwendolyn Brooks: Poetry and the Heroic Voice*. Lexington: University Press of Kentucky, 1987.

———. *Heroism in the New Black Poetry: Interviews and Interviews*. Lexington: University Press of Kentucky, 1990.

Mootry, Maria K. and Gary Smith. *A Life Distilled: Gwendolyn Brooks, Her Poetry and Fiction*. Urbana: University of Illinois Press, 1987.

Refoe, Annye L. "Children Coming Home: A Tribute to Survival." *Revelry: The Literary Voice of the Gwendolyn Brooks Writers Association of Florida* 5 (Spring 1992): 17–21.

Shaw, Harry B. *Gwendolyn Brooks*. Boston: Twayne, 1980.

Spear, Allan H. *Black Chicago: The Making of a Negro Ghetto: 1890–1920*. Chicago: University of Chicago Press, 1967.

Wright, Stephen Caldwell, ed. *On Gwendolyn Brooks: Reliant Contemplation*. Ann Arbor: University of Michigan Press, 1996.

See also Brooks entries in *DLB 5: American Poets Since World War II*, 1980.
DLB 76: Afro-American Writers, 1940–55, 1988.
DLB 165: American Poets Since World War II, Fourth Series, 1996.

Books

A Street in Bronzeville. New York: Harper and Brothers, 1945.
Annie Allen. New York: Harper and Brothers, 1949.
Maud Martha. New York: Harper and Brothers, 1953.
Bronzeville Boys and Girls. New York: Harper and Brothers, 1956.

The Bean Eaters. New York: Harper and Row, 1960.
Selected Poems. New York: Harper and Row, 1963.
In the Mecca. New York: Harper and Row, 1968.
Riot. Detroit: Broadside Press, 1969.
Family Pictures. Detroit: Broadside Press, 1970.
Aloneness. Detroit: Broadside Press, 1971. Children's Book.
The World of Gwendolyn Brooks. New York: Harper and Row, 1971.
Report from Part One: Autobiography. Detroit: Broadside Press, 1972.
The Tiger Who Wore White Gloves, or What You Are, You Are. Chicago: Third World Press, 1974.
Beckonings. Chicago: Third World Press, 1975.
Primer for Blacks. Chicago: Brooks Press, 1980.
Young Poet's Primer. Chicago: Brooks Press, 1980.
To Disembark. Chicago: Third World Press, 1981.
Mayor Harold Washington and Chicago, the I Will City. Chicago: Brooks Press, 1983.
Very Young Poets. Chicago: Brooks Press, 1983.
The Near-Johannesburg Boy and Other Poems. Chicago: The David Company, 1986.
Blacks. Chicago: The David Company, 1987.
Gottschalk and the Grande Tarantelle. Chicago: The David Company, 1988.
Winnie. Chicago: The David Company, 1988.
Children Coming Home. Chicago: The David Company, 1991.
Report from Part Two: Autobiography. Chicago: Third World Press, 1996.
In Montgomery: And Other Poems. Chicago: Third World Press, 2003.

FRANK LONDON BROWN
(October 7, 1927–March 12, 1962)
Michael D. Hill

Whether depicting a young girl's suicidal reaction to an unwanted pregnancy or a family's desperate attempt to integrate a neighborhood, Frank London Brown writes about everyday folks and their revelatory encounters with crisis. His works show the sociological imprints that mark his predecessors, Nelson Algren and Richard Wright; however, Brown's faith in black culture tempers his blunt portrayals of alienating industrialization and institutional racism. His is one of the most celebratory voices in the Chicago Renaissance. Where others stress the city's ability to erode the individual's will, Brown unearths the rituals that prepare a hurting soul for redemption. His writings never evade the difficulties of blackness or urbanity, yet using his intimate knowledge of Chicago's musical and working-class landscapes, he multiplies the perspectives from which a reader may view a dilemma and reveals the durable life-ways and the resilient spirit that nourish the potential for triumph.

Brown achieves literary force through what Ruth Miller calls an "unvarnished atmosphere of immediacy."[1] Often treating circumstances that he has experienced firsthand, the writer transforms the crude poetry of survival into poignant testimony. Like James Baldwin, whose spiritual odyssey acts as a multivalent prism for his creative output, Brown confronts the anonymity and the camaraderie, the random treachery and the unexpected sustenance that emanates from urban experience. Facing this reality he emerges as a prophet of a secular gospel, embracing jazz, the blues, and affection as antidotes to the absurdity that threatens modern life. Brown's command of vernacular speech convincingly evokes his characters' sensibilities, and his shrewd social awareness compellingly creates the environment that they inhabit. Despite his regionalist tendencies, Brown scrutinizes Chicago's cultural particularities as a vehicle for comprehending heroism, death, and love in broader African American life. He prizes the city because it vigorously sates his curiosity about the achievement of liberty amid unremitting coercion.

Brown, the eldest child of Myra Myrtle and Frank London Brown Sr., was born in Kansas City, Missouri, but in 1939, his family moved to Chicago, seeking relief from racial discrimination and financial difficulty. The Browns discovered a city filled with bittersweet possibilities. As a youngster, Frank attended Colman Elementary School. After Colman, he went to DuSable, Chicago's first high school built for an African American population. DuSable High, named in 1935 to honor the black city father, John Baptiste Point DuSable, featured a high-quality musical program. Under the direction of Walter H. Dyett, this program included a concert band, a marching band, and a jazz band. Dyett also initiated an annual production, the Hi-Jinks show, which spotlighted the varied talents of the student body. Brown's appreciation of jazz and the blues certainly benefited from these conspicuous resources in his formal education. He also imbibed from his DuSable peers a determination to pursue lofty ambitions. In an environment that nurtured Harold Washington, the first black mayor of Chicago, and renowned publisher William H. Johnson, Brown undoubtedly sensed the need to live meaningfully. He refined his views of that necessity through an unorthodox tutelage on the South Side streets.

If 1938 South Wabash Avenue, the address of DuSable High School, represents one pole of Brown's adolescent enlightenment, then the Fifty-Eighth Street "Stroll" is the other. From Morrie's Record Shop, where the teenager listened to Dizzy Gillespie, Thelonious Monk, Charlie Parker, Muddy Waters, and Joe Williams to the ubiquitous tenements that housed "a dark nether-world of crime," addiction, and despair, the Stroll embodies the irreducible contradictions in black urban life.[2] Sterling Stuckey asserts that Brown's adventures along this "grinding, dehumanizing" thoroughfare form an "apprenticeship."[3] Introducing the inescapable simultaneity of beauty and ugliness, this environment exposes Brown to the disparate experiences that cohabitate the human spirit. Even in high school, he imagined writing might be a way to order these impressions. Sixteen-year-old Brown, in the spring of 1944, visited the offices of Johnson Publishing Company and requested a job as an editor. Since he had no qualifications other than his desire, the episode ended disappointingly; however, it showed Brown's vague conviction that writing and publishing mattered. As he furthers his education, this conviction strengthens.

Brown graduated from DuSable in January 1945. Following a brief stint at Wilberforce University in Ohio, he joined the army in January 1946. While in the service, perhaps inspired by fond memories of the Hi-Jinks shows, he sang baritone in a group. His courtship of Evelyn Marie Jones, his high-school sweetheart, intensified, and on November 30, 1947, the two were married. Their union produced three daughters and a son who died a short time after birth. Taking advantage of the GI Bill, Brown registered at Roosevelt University in downtown

Chicago. Opened in 1945 after a controversy over prejudicial admissions policies at the Central YMCA College, Roosevelt quickly became an attractive destination for what Dempsey J. Travis termed "education-hungry black veterans."[4] There, Brown discussed the plight of Chicago with future power players such as Gus Savage, who would serve in the United States Congress, and Harold Washington. Brown's enthusiastic participation in debates and strategizing showed his commitment to social change and his investment in the city's development. As his associations widened and his job history diversified, he concentrated his political energy on Civil Rights and labor issues.

While completing his undergraduate studies, Brown provided for his family with an intriguing array of jobs. Spending time as a machinist, a postal clerk, a loan interviewer, and a tavern owner, he not only developed an interest in the labor movement, but also honed the observational skills that prepared him to represent Chicago. After graduating from Roosevelt with a BA degree in 1951, Brown registered at Kent College of Law in Chicago. His interest in the law flagged, leading him to leave Kent in 1954, but during this same interval, his writing career gained momentum. Appearing at the Gate of Horn, a landmark music club, Brown became one of the first writers to read short stories to jazz accompaniment. He supplemented these experiments with work for the *Chicago-Sun Times*, the *Chicago Tribune*, and the *Chicago Defender*. Later, he resumed his education, enrolling in a master's program at the University of Chicago. Brown's intellectual drive was formidable, and it is telling that throughout his studies, he worked continually. Wary of withdrawal from everyday realities, he sought positions and pursued research that ensconced him in common living. This commitment, along with his upbringing, made him prize the obscured struggles of hidden personalities, a disposition that influenced his creative writing.

Brown's early publication, the short story "Night March" (1957), explores the obligations that an imminent lynching creates. Set in an unnamed Southern community, it functions somewhat like a parable. Geeter, a black man who got caught with his white mistress, is imprisoned in a henhouse awaiting the murderous retaliation of the town's white men. Buster, the conflicted protagonist, alerts other black men to Geeter's plight, but when the group, chafed by prior inaction, commits to violent intervention, he laments, "I didn't think we was going to commit suicide. I just thought that we might get together and ask Mr. Gunison nice-like not to kill Geeter."[5] Dramatizing how racism impels ordinary black folks to epic decisions, Brown dwells on intraracial barriers to action. Buster's proposal not only reflects bizarre reasoning, but also a troubling willingness to make someone else responsible for Geeter's release. When the group commences its night march, going to rescue Geeter, they leave Buster behind "in [a] darkened room."[6] The story ends as Buster's "whining broken cry"[7] rises around the others, who walk "in single file."[8] Crisp dialogue propels this story, but its real strengths are delicate characterization and a spare, yet striking plot. The theme of noble confrontation that emerges here becomes a staple in Brown's oeuvre.

In 1958, *Down Beat* magazine published "More Man Than Myth," Brown's profile of the iconoclastic jazz pianist, Thelonious Monk. A widely cited article, this piece, filled with sharp insights and impeccable scene-setting, foreshadows the writer's bolder experiments with multivoiced, single-subject narration. Monk fascinates Brown, nevertheless, as the writer observes, "one interview or 10 cannot shatter the wall that Monk has built around himself."[9] To address this dilemma, Brown multiplies his views of his subject. Combining the perceptions of Nellie, Monk's wife; Harry Colomby, his manager; Robby Barnes, a singer; and Baron Bennerson, a bartender with Monk's own observations, the writer captures the pianist as a montage of uniquely illustrative impressions. This technique shows how the collaborative impulses of small-group jazz coexist with the fully realized individuation of the solo, and it unlocks for Brown a literary aesthetic that suits his portrayals of modern urban existence.

Chicago's sociocultural reality saturates Brown's imagination, but he rejects the idea that placing characters in the city insures their destruction. By studying bebop artists like Monk, the writer discovers that the interplay between context and individual potential need not be fatal. As Maryemma Graham argues, bebop, "an abstract extension of the historical forms of jazz," acknowledges external forces like poverty, sickness, and oppression; however, instead of succumbing to them, the bebop artist internalizes these forces and uses them to form a mature self that resists "the victimization process."[10] Once Brown assimilates bebop's conviction that heroic exertion can transform despair, he creates Chicagoans, who although harried, always have the option of pursing dignity.

Trumbull Park (1959), Brown's first novel, explores the menace that prompts a black family to leave the slums and the hostility that envelops them as they move into a white housing project. Named after the residential development that Brown and his family lived in from 1954–57, this book, as Charles Tita has noted, engages "the national thrust toward racial integration"; nevertheless, its writer insists on telling a uniquely local story.[11] References to landmarks like the Owl Theater and Club DeLisa situate readers in Chicago's musical milieu, and elevated stops and streets evoke the city as a distinct physical space. Even the housing crisis at the center of this novel bespeaks the peculiar history of overcrowding, restrictive covenants, and racial diversity that make Chicago a midwestern industrial immigrant city. Brown embraces the simultaneously national and local significance of *Trumbull Park* because he sees in it an adjunct to the public and the personal quality of human duress. For him, literature should confront this complexity in life's discordances, and his initial novel examines one family's response to its own customized chaos.

At the beginning of *Trumbull Park*, Louis "Buggy" Martin, the novel's protagonist and first person narrator, watches two-year-old Babydoll fall off a disintegrating porch and "hit the ground four stories down."[12] Capturing the absurd volatility that permeates his family's present home, the dilapidated Gardener Building, Babydoll's death becomes an immediate catalyst for the Martins' relocation. If their old building contains rotting banisters, indomitable vermin, and premature death, their new apartment, in segregated Trumbull Park, quickly reveals an impressive set of perils. Incessant bombing, mobs chanting racist epithets, and an indifferent police force are everyday realities for Buggy and his wife, Helen, and their two daughters. Initially their reaction is grim endurance, but as they form closer relations with other black couples who live in the neighborhood, the Martins realize that planned collective action not only provides physical and psychological fortification, but also a more efficient path to liberty.

Much of *Trumbull Park* considers what a meaningful response to racial intimidation looks like, and at the center of its meditations are questions about black manhood similar to those asked by Richard Wright in *Uncle Tom's Children*. When angry whites chase Buggy into his apartment, he tearfully says to Helen, "I should have stayed out there and fought . . . I should have stayed out there and died . . . What kind of man am I?"[13] Although they do not face the same situations, each of the black men who live in the project confronts a similar quandary: what is masculinity when the safety, the sanity, and the dignity of my family are threatened? Buggy's inclination to martyrdom appears noble, yet Brown tinges it with abdication. By juxtaposing Buggy's musing with the image of his pregnant wife and his two children, the writer suggests that simple sacrifice will not resolve this crisis. Brown emphasizes marriage and parenthood as integral parts of the solidarity that grows between the black families, and in doing so he hints at the magnitude of the transformation that these folks must undertake. Their lot involves a willingness to face mortality, yet their deepest calling is preparing the world for their living.

Throughout *Trumbull Park*, police escorts humiliate the black families. When the men go to work, they must request a paddy wagon. If the women want to shop, visit their parents, or even give birth to their children, they must be transported via a police vehicle. Ostensibly this arrangement protects them from harm, but its chief effect is to reinforce the circumscribed quality of their existence. In the novel's final chapter, Buggy refuses the ride from the police and stages a "walk-in." He plans a solo entry, but Harry Harvey, the most recent arrival in Trumbull Park, joins him. Singing Joe Williams's song, "Every Day," the men walk through a brick-hurling, "nigger"-chanting mob not only signaling their discovery of a path to freedom, but also hinting at how Brown's view of Chicago dialogues with those offered by Richard Wright and Gwendolyn Brooks. Whereas the former, in *Native Son*, emblematizes the city through the ineffable terror of the tenements, the latter's novel, *Maud Martha*, evokes the suffocating quality of kitchenette buildings even as it celebrates the quiet, private embrace of self. Brown's presentation of the Gardener acknowledges that certain spaces swallow lives; nonetheless, his novel's conclusion suggests a city whose unique beat enables a loud and public black identity, one that delivers entire communities instead of solitary souls.

According to Mary Helen Washington, *Trumbull Park* "sold more than 25,000 copies,"[14] and Clarence Major remarked that "when the book came out the publisher actually promoted it."[15] Despite these facts and a string of positive reviews in the *Chicago Sunday Tribune*, the *Christian Century*, and the *New York Times Book Review*, Brown's novel has received very little long-term notice. Washington discusses it as a "'repressed' text of the 1950s,"[16] suggesting that Brown's trade-union, left-of-center politics may have harmed the book's reception. Whatever the reasons, any objective estimate must conclude that scholars, whether of regional or African American literature, have neglected *Trumbull Park*. Despite their indifference, in March of 2004, *Eight Forty-Eight*, an award-winning Chicago Public Radio program, included the novel on its "essential book list for anyone who wants to truly understand Chicago."[17] This honor demonstrates that, at least for some Chicagoans, the work still captures something essential.

Brown began working at *Ebony* in November 1958, and by March 1959, he realized his teenage ambition when he was promoted to associate editor. While with the magazine, he completed an interview with Mahalia Jackson entitled, "Mahalia the Great" (1959). He dwells, in this article, on the singer's authenticity, stressing the sincerity of her Christianity. When he writes that "no sensitive man can escape the life cry in her song,"[18] Brown, in part, supplies the celebratory overstatement that such profiles demand, but he also reveals a genuine appreciation for Jackson's artistry. In her singing, he saw an unpretentious profundity and a conviction that he aspired to in his own work. Despite receiving recognition because of *Trumbull Park*, Brown did not slow his pursuit of other publications. He revisited the site of prior success, placing "A Cry Unheard" (1959) in *Chicago Review*. Getting into his first non-Chicago–based journal, he published "In the Shadow of a Dying Soldier" (1959) in the *Southwest Review*. When Robin Cuscaden and Arnold Kaye started *Vigil* at Brown's alma mater, he contributed "Tuesday 10:31 AM" (1959). These three short stories capture an oscillation between documentary realism and modernist experimentation that reveals an intriguing development in Brown's literary aesthetic.

The Southern setting and combat undertones of "In the Shadow of a Dying Soldier" link it with "Night March," as does its evocation of lynching. Still, where the latter dramatizes an abstract circumstance, the former explicitly represents the trial of Emmett Till's murderers, J. W. Milam and Roy Bryant. Following

Frank, a union program coordinator from Chicago, the story chronicles a reverse migration that starts in the Midwest and ends in Sumner, Mississippi. Initially, Frank's first person narration evinces a journalistic precision, presenting characters, settings, and attitudes with certainty; however, the longer he stays in the South, the more he understands that "the facts were beginning to betray" his "well-thought-out generalizations."[19] At the trip's start, Frank believes that the conviction of the accused men would constitute the sole terms of victory. When he departs Sumner, speeded by warnings from his landlady, he holds a different perspective. Frank, on his plane ride home, discovers that Milam and Bryant have been acquitted, and he becomes sick. Recovering from his disappointment, he realizes that notwithstanding the outcome of the trial, "something BIG had been won"[20] even in black folks' willingness to publicly name their wrongdoers.

In "A Cry Unheard" twenty-two-year-old Maggie, with her baby in her arms, jumps from a window. While her act reverberates through the text, this story, a rambling monologue, focuses on her brother's response to the tragedy. His statements ostensibly express his inability to comprehend what his sister has done, yet they betray fear that his and his parents' reaction to her out-of-wedlock pregnancy may have contributed to her death. Even as he insists that Maggie could have turned to her family, he remembers his mother's embarrassment, his father's anger and his own suggestion that she "put the baby in an orphanage."[21] Equally damning are his references to the letters that his sister wrote him, letters filled with pain that he did not answer. As the story ends, Maggie's brother remarks, "She didn't have to do it." His sentiment partakes more of self-recrimination than external indictment.

"Tuesday 10:31 AM" details the plight of Bob, "the only living being,"[22] after an atomic bomb hits Chicago. Filled with stream of consciousness narration that intermittently shifts from third to first person, this story literalizes urban destruction, using the nuclear threat associated with the Cold War as a subtle, yet crucial, subtext. Bob, who floats on a "mattress in the uppermost room of the Pershing Hotel," wonders about his family, his infidelity, the bomb shelters of the rich, and God, but ultimately he wants to die. Although his injuries and his entrapment insure eventual death, Bob, alternately praying and ranting, seeks to speed up the process. He tries to summon the will to roll off the mattress and drown; however, he balks at suicide, returning instead to ask God to end his life. Bob's situation begs the question of how humans should comport themselves at the extremes of existence. Whereas Brown's earlier work engages this theme via concrete dilemmas, here the writer creates a philosophical case study, a technique that recurs later in his career.

In 1960 Brown completed his master's degree at the University of Chicago. As part of the requirements, he submitted a thesis that ultimately became his second novel, the posthumously published *The Myth Maker* (1969). Reminiscent of Richard Wright's *The Outsider* (1953), this book explores death and the meaninglessness of life in the context of African American urban existence. Set in Chicago, it draws intensely on Brown's familiarity with the city's South Side. Ernest Day, the novel's protagonist, abandons Phyllis his wife and Helen his daughter protesting that his "routine of morning noon and night" as a husband and a father destroys his "chances of ever knowing what life is all about."[23] Filling his rented room with books that comfort "him in his loneliness,"[24] he seeks vast truths to ease his "great ache."[25] Ernest's quest occasionally exhilarates him, but more often it inspires "dryness,"[26] an agonizing frustration that fixates him on death. As *The Myth Maker* opens, he struggles with a dry episode.

Standing on Fifty-Eighth Street, the "Stroll," Ernest watches as an old man "smelling like gin and talcum powder"[27] walks past. When the man smiles at him, showing "even, yellow teeth," the protagonist experiences an inscrutable rage, and after chasing him down an alley, he chokes him to death. Momentarily, this murder relieves Ernest's dryness, but for the remainder of the novel, he struggles to determine the significance of his act. A junkie, who witnesses the murder, tries to blackmail Ernest, and Officer Blimp, a corrupt policeman, encourages Ernest to join his drug ring. These men suggest the vulnerability that the protagonist's crime produces, but he gains the greatest insight into the murder's meaning when he interacts with an informal group of racial strategists.

Initially Ernest's bookishness alienates him, but when he is introduced to Willard, Gary, Richard, and Freda, he finds a group of black folks who also earnestly seek vast truths. This group lacks a consensus position; they represent ideologies as disparate as Communism, Black Nationalism, and capitalist pragmatism. Despite their heterogeneity, they remind Ernest that his need not be a solitary journey. In particular, he gravitates toward Willard because he sees in the young man a burgeoning dryness that resembles his own. During a car ride, Ernest confesses to Willard that he has killed a man. Willard, when he discovers that Ernest took a black man's life, chides him for his misdirection. As he, Ernest and Richard are having a beer, Willard explains, "I don't want to kill a man to be a bird in my own private sky. I'm going to kill a man to create a mass sentiment . . . a mass conception of the Negro by the Negro."[28] Ernest, by now, rejects Willard's notion that violence can create a whole consciousness. He sees the moral equivocation that his own act occasions, and he senses that other avenues have been neglected.

Richard, a young black student, dates Rhea, a white coed, and at a crucial moment in the novel, she discovers that she is pregnant with his child. After overhearing Richard talk stridently about the inevitability of conflict between blacks and whites, Rhea decides to get an abortion. When complications arise following that procedure, Richard enlists Willard and Ernest to help him get her to a hospital. The couple's tenderness as they work through the crisis reminds Ernest that love teaches seminal lessons about life. Discussing it with Willard, he relates that he left his family for "a great big, smoky dream of the wild blue yonder" only to discover "the dark place"[29] of his ideal existence. He tries, in the final pages of *The Myth Maker*, to redeem what Richard and Rhea have taught him.

An unspoken bond immediately emerges when Ernest meets Freda, Willard's sister, and he senses within her glances a question about when he would "make himself whole again with her body and her again whole in a new and perhaps this time sanctified way."[30] Their connection occurs very early in the novel, but they act upon it only in the book's final chapter. After sharing all the misguided ways that they attempted to remind the world that "life [is] real,"[31] the couple starts their lovemaking. Officer Blimp smashes Freda's door, coming to hold Ernest responsible for the murder, yet he cannot penetrate the cocoon of Ernest's enlightenment.

Shot through with references to Sophocles, Dante, and Virgil, *The Myth Maker* also alludes to Ornette Coleman, Thelonious Monk, and John Coltrane. Brown makes this conglomeration effective by embracing the philosophical without abandoning the concrete context of Chicago. This book presents politically engaged black characters who read voraciously, yet they occupy cultural spaces, like the Stroll, that daily emblematize the conundrums that they ponder. Thus, like Ernest, they continually retain the resources for correcting misperception.

In 1961 Brown unsuccessfully pressed Roosevelt University to hire Gwendolyn Brooks. Despite his failure, he did express his admiration for her in a *Negro Digest* article entitled "Chicago's Great Lady of Poetry" (1961). At the University of Chicago, Brown worked toward his doctorate in political science. The Committee on Social Thought, under John U. Nef, honored him with a fellowship, and continuing his concern for labor issues, he directed the university's Union Leadership Program. During the summer of 1961, Brown discovered that he had leukemia. Unlike the protagonist of "Tuesday 10:31 AM," he seemed to view imminent death as a call to more vigorous action. Sterling Stuckey remembers that Brown, late in 1961, decided "to pay his dues"[32] by participating in a wade-in at Chicago's Rainbow Beach and by taking part in a sit-in against discriminatory practices in University of Chicago–owned apartment buildings. These actions suggest that Brown never tired of pursuing justice; his final publications show a similar impulse.

"McDougal" (1961), a much anthologized work, is almost identical to "The Whole Truth" (1964). Building up to a trumpet solo from the story's namesake, a "tall worried looking white man,"[33] the text registers the impressions of his black bandmates as they shift from ridiculing McDougal's appearance to acknowledging the emotion within his playing. Brown avers that circumstance rather than race informs righteous sound.

The South recurs as a setting in "A Matter of Time" (1962), a story that captures the last moments of Willie Lee, a laid-off mill hand. Certainly, the specter of his own demise influences Brown's theme; nevertheless, even as he portrays his protagonist's death, the writer frames it with a layoff, an indication of volatility in a laborer's life. The supreme irony is that Willie Lee dies not while unloading a bale of cotton, but while listening to his children argue. The Monday after his funeral, "the plant called the men back to work."[34]

On March 12, 1962, Brown died at the University of Illinois Educational Research Hospital. Gwendolyn Brooks read the poem "Frank London Brown: A Tenant of the World," at his funeral, and many mourned his passing. In "An Unaccountable Happiness" (1962), an essay published less than a month after his death, Brown reinforces his belief that irreducible contradictions define human existence. He writes, "The fault is believing that the world can be park all the way through."[35] Chiding naiveté, Brown's remark also implicitly endorses empathy. His two posthumously published short stories pick up this meditation on fellow feeling.

The Northern laborer takes center stage in "Singing Dinah's Song" (1963), a first person account of technology and its enigmatic effect on the worker. While the narrator, an employee at Electronic Master, Incorporated, views his punch press as an ugly machine that "bangs and screams,"[36] his buddy, Daddy-O, who sometimes stands amid the presses singing Dinah Washington songs, asserts, "That is my machine . . . Me and this machine is blood kin."[37] Daddy-O's speech punctuates an episode in which he confronts a manager and is taken away by the police, but in the aftermath, the narrator realizes that he knows his punch press "better than . . . most live people."

"The Ancient Book" (1964) contemplates the unpredictable shape of deliverance. Living in a condemned building, Maggie, the protagonist, wields her departed boyfriend's .38 automatic to fend off rats that attack her sleeping baby. Driven into the snow-filled streets by the rodents' boldness, she seeks shelter in a tavern. A man, claiming to be "the di-rect kin of an African chief" offers her a book, "from before the Bible," that will change her life.[38] Giving him her last dollar, Maggie discovers that the book was published in 1957. She falls asleep reading the book and a young girl slips a "hat-collected cluster of bills down her bosom."[39]

Clarence Major, in *The Dark and Feeling* (1974), states that Frank London Brown "will remain a minor writer occupying a small place in the literary history of black Chicago."[40] Major's assessment contains a disarming frankness; however, his judgment of Brown's legacy is both prescient and myopic. *Trumbull Park* generates a season of notoriety for Brown, yet the following decades deliver virtual obscurity. In part his plight stems from the shortness of his life; however, his literary career reveals not only the politics of American publishing, but also the benefits and drawbacks of a man committed to a single locale. Brown devotes himself to Chicago, touching lives in literary, social, and political circles. This choice affords him unbounded good will within the city and makes him a significant figure in the Chicago Renaissance, but it cost him a broader reputation. In the end this trade-off probably would have satisfied him, and still the book on his worth is not closed. In October 1998, Brown was posthumously inducted into the National Literary Hall of Fame for Writers of African Descent. In 2005, Northeastern University Press published a scholarly edition of *Trumbull Park*, with a foreword by Mary Helen Washington. Thus, the man Gwendolyn Brooks called a "scrupulous pioneer"[41] is still conquering new terrain.

Notes

1. Miller, Ruth. "Frank London Brown." In *Black American Literature 1760–Present*, edited by Ruth Miller. Beverly Hills: Glencoe Press, 1971, 625.

2. Stuckey, Sterling. "Frank London Brown." In *Black Voices*, edited by Abraham Chapman. New York: New American Library, 1968, 670.

3. Ibid., 670.

4. Travis, Dempsey J. *An Autobiography of Black Chicago*. Chicago: Urban Research Institute, 1981, 119.

5. Brown, Frank London. "Night March." In *Short Stories by Frank London Brown*. Chicago: Frank London Brown Historical Association, 1965. This volume does not number its pages; thus, I have identified all quotations from it by indicating the page of the individual story on which it appears. This quotation is taken from the third page of "Night March." All further references will follow this format.

6. Ibid., 4.

7. Ibid., 5.

8. Ibid., 4.

9. Brown, Frank London. "More Man than Myth." *Down Beat* 25 (October 30, 1958): 16.

10. Graham, Maryemma. "Bearing Witness in Black Chicago: A View of Selected Fiction by Richard Wright, Frank London Brown, and Ronald Fair." *CLA Journal* 33 (March 1990): 289.

11. Tita, Charles. "Frank London Brown," In *Contemporary African American Novelists: A Bio-Bibliographical Critical Sourcebook*, edited by Emmanuel S. Nelson. Westport, Conn.: Greenwood Press, 1990, 59.

12. Brown, Frank London. *Trumbull Park*. Chicago: Regnery, 1959, 1.

13. Ibid., 142.

14. Washington, Mary Helen. "Desegregating the 1950s: The Case of Frank London Brown." *The Japanese Journal of American Studies* 10 (1999): 23.

15. Major, Clarence. *The Dark and Feeling: Black American Writers and Their Work*. New York: The Third Press, 1974, 102.

16. Washington, "Desegregating," 16.

17. Chicago Public Radio, "A Chicago Birthday Book Bag," http://www.wbez.org/programs/848/series_features/848_040304books.asp (11 July 2008).

18. Brown, Frank London. "Mahalia the Great." *Ebony* 14 (March 1959): 74.

19. Brown. "In the Shadow of a Dying Soldier," in *Short Stories*, 2.

20. Ibid., 16.

21. Brown, Frank London. "A Cry Unheard." *Chicago Review* 13 (Autumn 1959): 120.

22. Brown, Frank London . "Tuesday 10:31 AM." *Vigil* 1 (Spring 1959): 6.

23. Brown, Frank London. *The Myth Maker*. Chicago: Path Press, 1969, 78.

24. Ibid., 23.

25. Ibid., 21.

26. Ibid., 12.

27. Ibid., 15.

28. Ibid., 163.

29. Ibid., 162.

30. Ibid., 60.

31. Ibid., 176.

32. Stuckey, "Frank London Brown," 671.

33. Brown, Frank London. "McDougal." In *Black Voices*, edited by Abraham Chapman. New York: New American Library, 1968, 204.

34. Brown, "A Matter of Time," in *Short Stories*, 3.

35. Hauke, Kathleen A. "Frank London Brown." In *Dictionary of Literary Biography*, edited by Trudier Harris. Detroit: Gale Research Inc., 1984, 76.

36. Brown, "Singing Dinah's Song," in *Short Stories*, 1.

37. Ibid., 5.

38. Brown, Frank London. "The Ancient Book." *Negro Digest* 13 (March 1964): 60.

39. Ibid., 61.

40. Major, *The Dark and Feeling*, 103.

41. Brooks, Gwendolyn. "Of Frank London Brown: A Tenant of the World." *Negro Digest* 11 (September 1962): 44.

For Further Reading

"Backstage." *Ebony* 14 (April 1959): 20.

Brown, Frank London. "Night March." *Chicago Review* 11 (Spring 1957): 57–61.

———. "More Man than Myth." *Down Beat* 25 (30 October 1958): 13–16, 45–46.

———. "Mahalia the Great." *Ebony* 14 (March 1959): 69–76.

———. "Tuesday 10:31 AM." *Vigil: New Writing by New Writers* 1 (Spring 1959): 6–8.

———. "A Cry Unheard." *Chicago Review* 13 (Autumn 1959): 118–20.

———. "In the Shadow of a Dying Soldier." *Southwest Review* 44 (Autumn 1959): 292–306.

———. *Trumbull Park*. Chicago: Regnery, 1959.

———. "McDougal." *Phoenix Magazine* (Fall 1961): 32–33.

———. "Chicago's Great Lady of Poetry." *Negro Digest* 11 (December 1961): 53–57.

———. "A Matter of Time." *Negro Digest* 11 (March 1962): 58–60.

———. "An Unaccountable Happiness: For Kermit Eby." *New City Magazine* (April 1, 1962): 14–15.

———. "Singing Dinah's Song." In *Soon One Morning: New Writing By American Negroes, 1940–1962*, edited by Herbert Hill. New York: Knopf, 1963, 348–54.

———. "The Ancient Book." *Negro Digest* 13 (March 1964): 53–61.

———. "The Whole Truth." In *Black Orpheus: An Anthology of African and Afro-American Prose*, edited by Ulli Beier. Ikeja, Nigeria: Longmans, 1964, 71–73.

———. *Short Stories by Frank London Brown*. Chicago: Frank London Brown Historical Association, 1965.

———. *The Myth Maker*. Chicago: Path Press, 1969.

———. *Trumbull Park*. Hanover, N.H.: Northeastern University Press/University Press of New England, 2005.

Brownley, Les. "Frank London Brown: Courageous Author." *Sepia* 8 (June 1960): 26–30,

Dyett Academic Center, "The History of Walter H. Dyett," http://www.dyett.cps.k12.il.us/whdyett/ (July 11, 2008).

Fleming, Robert E. "Overshadowed by Richard Wright: Three Black Chicago Novelists." *Negro American Literature Forum* 7 (Fall 1973): 75–79.

Fuller, Hoyt W. "The Departed." *Negro Digest* 11 (September 1962): 50.

Hawkins, B. Denise. "Interview with Gwendolyn Brooks." *Black Issues in Higher Education* 11 (November 3, 1994): 16, 20–21.

Neal, Bessie L. "A Brief History of the Chicago Jean Baptiste Point DuSable League, October 2001," http://www.artic.edu/~apalme/duslea.htm (July 11, 2008).

Serebnick, J. "New Creative Writers." *Library Journal* 84 (February 1, 1959): 507.

Papers

A few letters mentioning Brown are included in Willard Motley's papers at the University of Wisconsin-Madison's Memorial Library. The Path Press archives include the manuscript of *The Myth Maker*, and the papers of the Frank London Brown Historical Association contain photos and correspondence related to a memorial service at the Parkway Ballroom. These materials are housed in the Vivian G. Harsh Collection of Afro-American Literature, part of the Woodson Regional Library, Chicago. Most of Brown's papers remain private.

ALICE C. BROWNING
(November 5, 1907–October 15, 1985)
Bill V. Mullen

Alice Browning's cultural entrepreneurship and dedication to local literary production provided important contributions to Chicago's Black Renaissance. A shrewd literary gadfly, and a modestly gifted writer, Browning symbolized the inclusive spirit of the Renaissance as well as its paradoxical tendencies toward both critical engagement with pressing social issues of the day and overt commercialization of African American culture. Her primary work as editor and publisher also signifies the rise and expanding impact of the Black Press during and after World War II.

The daughter of a minister, Browning was a graduate of Chicago's Englewood High School, Chicago Normal School, and the University of Chicago. Published records and private files from Ms. Browning do not disclose her maiden name (her mother's surname was Marshall). In an unpublished autobiographical sketch written in 1961, Browning wrote that she wanted to be an author from the age of eight when she began to read the classics. She cited the influence of British novelists like Thackeray and George Eliot, but also noted the impact of reading Paul Laurence Dunbar, Charles Chesnutt, and Jessie Fauset at an early age. Fauset's work, she wrote, motivated her to try to represent the Black middle class, an ambition realized in her later short stories. At nineteen, Browning began study at the University of Chicago in pursuit of her bachelor's degree. There she began writing short stories and took a home-study course in writing from the University. After graduation, she worked as an elementary school teacher and married Charles Browning, then director of the Division of Works Projects of the Illinois National Youth Administration. Her byline first appeared in a fashion column in the *Chicago Defender* in March, 1938, where she was described as a "young socialite-teacher." In 1941, she took a sabbatical from her teaching position at Forestville Elementary School to work on a master's degree in literature at Columbia University, where she came under the direction of Vernon Loggins. Loggins, a pioneer in African American literary history, was the author of *The Negro Author: His Development in America to*

1900, as well as a biography of musical composer Louis Moreau Gottschalk. He became friend and mentor to Browning and later published short fiction in *Negro Story*. Originally intending to write an MA thesis on the Negro novel before 1900, she began writing short stories and showed them to Loggins, who encouraged her to submit for publication. In 1941, she submitted a short story called "Tomorrow" to *Esquire*, which rejected it. In 1942, she published her first story, "New Year's Eve 1942," in the *Pittsburgh Courier* under the pen name Lila Marshall. She also began work on a novel, never published. Browning pursued the ambition to publish a novel well into her adult life, at one point receiving publishing advice from Nelson Algren, who attempted to help her find an agent. She also endeavored to publish her MA thesis but was not able to do so. Later in life she took writing courses at Northwestern University in hopes of finding a publisher for her work.[1]

Eager to expand publishing opportunities for Black writers, herself included, Browning returned home and founded *N.Y.P.S.* (*Negro Youth Photo Script*), a glossy magazine dedicated to publishing photographs and stories about Black life in Chicago. Shortly thereafter, she began discussion with her friend Fern Gayden about the possibility of starting yet another magazine, one that would provide opportunities for Black short story writers. Thus was born *Negro Story*, Alice Browning's most important and singular contribution to Chicago's Black literary renaissance. *Negro Story* was imagined by Gayden and Browning to be the African American equivalent to *Story* magazine, the leading mainstream, and predominantly white, literary journal of short fiction begun in 1933 by Whit Burnett. But how to build a new magazine? Browning and Gayden had no national literary reputations to speak of and virtually no publishing experience. Gayden, a social worker from Kansas, had entered Chicago literary circles through her relationship to Richard Wright. In 1935, Gayden had helped move Wright and his family into a South Side apartment. The two became friends, and Wright invited Gayden, herself an aspiring writer, to join the newly formed South Side Writers Group.

To cover start-up costs of publication, Browning borrowed $200 from her husband Charles, now working as vice president for public relations for the *Chicago Defender*, and the two set to work on the production of their new magazine. Vol. I, N. 1 appeared as the May–June issue in the summer of 1944. The simple, inexpensive and unadorned sixty-four–page issue had been assembled by Browning and Gayden in Browning's home at 4019 Vincennes Avenue. Subtitled "A Magazine for All Americans," the first issue was prefaced by "A Letter to Our Readers" coauthored by Browning and Gayden. "For a long time, we, the editors," they wrote, "have been attempting to improve our writing techniques and to express ourselves through the short story. The other day, the idea struck us that among thirteen million Negroes in America, there must be many who were eager to write creatively if they had a market." The letter also bespoke editorial principles significant of larger currents of Chicago's Black Renaissance. Gayden and Browning argued that "good writing may be entertaining as well as socially enlightening."[2] They encouraged contributors to write well-crafted stories on timely themes that would reflect the desire of African Americans to both assimilate into and change for the better the social fabric of the United States. They also encouraged novice writers to see the magazine as their first opportunity to publish.

Their combination of marketing pluck, grassroots consciousness, and commitment to literature as social engagement marked the diverse currents and influences that had brought Browning and Gayden to their collaboration. The contents of the first issue reflected this as well. Contributors included Browning herself, still writing under the pen name Lila Marshall; Langston University Professor and literary critic Nick Aaron Ford, and West Indian writer Roger Mais, a member of Norman Manley's People's Socialist National Party. Also included were prose contributions by Gwendolyn Brooks, a friend to both Gayden and Browning, and Richard Wright's "Almos' a Man," originally intended for publication in his proletarian-style novel, never completed, *Tarbaby's Surprise.* Wright's appearance in the magazine was in part serendipitous. Wright had purchased a house for his mother just two doors down from the Browning home on Vincennes Avenue; Browning and Gayden visited Wright at the apartment of Horace Cayton during a visit by Wright to Chicago in early 1944, seeking his permission to use a story for their inaugural issue.[3]

The balance of *Negro Story*'s premier issue were contributions by largely unpublished friends of the editors, many of them working women and teachers from Chicago's South Side. This blend of writers—established, emergent, and amateur—became the magazine's hallmark during its two-year run from 1944 to 1946. Among the contributors to *Negro Story* were Langston Hughes, Frank Marshall Davis (already a published poet), Ralph Ellison, and Chester Himes. Himes was perhaps the magazine's most popular contributor. He published six stories in the magazine, many anticipating the themes of his 1945 debut novel *If He Hollers Let Him Go.* Other stories by less heralded local writers highlighted important social and political themes such as the racist treatment of black soldiers during the war and the conditions of black women domestic workers. The magazine was also a home for contributions by radical and progressive white writers. They included Chicago proletarian novelist Jack Conroy, author of *The Disinherited* and a fixture on Chicago's progressive interracial South Side culture scene, and ex-Communist Earl Conrad, also a columnist for the *Defender.* Indicative of the interracial atmosphere of collaboration generally during the Chicago Renaissance, Conrad replaced Fern Gayden as "associate editor" when she left the magazine after the publication of its fourth issue in early 1945. In addition, Black visual artists such as WPA painter and lithographer Elton Fax and Chicago painter and organizer Margaret Goss Burroughs published visual and literary work in the magazine.

Negro Story was circulated by hand on the South Side, by mail to Black soldiers overseas, and to a select number of libraries at Historically Black Colleges and Universities. Browning's entrepreneurial and activist energies, meanwhile, were ever-expanding. In 1945, she was appointed president of the National Negro Magazine Publishers Association, a sister organization to the National Negro Newspaper Association. On July 30 and 31, 1945, the NNMPA met at Harlem's Hotel Theresa, where Browning led a call for "adaptation in story and article form of case histories of Negro life to cover civil liberties, housing, individual health, socialized medicine, and fascism—native and foreign." She was joined by editors of *Opportunity, Color,* and other black periodical editors who vowed that "magazines and newspapers should work together in a united front for the Negro." In July, 1945, Browning initiated a plan for "Negro Story Book" clubs and announced publication of a new children's magazine, *Child Play,* published by the new Negro Story Press, her own enterprise. In August, 1945, the Press published Lionel Hampton's *Swing Book,* a glossy commercial magazine modeled after *Vogue* intended to capitalize on Hampton's status as the recurring winner of *Chicago Defender* reader polls on favorite swing band leaders. Browning also continued to publish commentaries and stories in *Negro Story* under a variety of surnames, most commonly the anglicized, and male, name "Richard Bentley." She simultaneously sent photographs and press releases heralding new issues to the *Defender,* and rose to modest celebrity in South Side cultural circles.[4]

Browning's contributions as a writer to *Negro Story* also merit attention as reflective of social and literary concerns of both African American and African American women writers of her time, as well as reflecting the ambitions of a broad range of Chicago writers to participate in the short story genre. Browning's stories appeared regularly in *Negro Story.* Nearly always she wrote under the pseudonym "Richard Bentley." This possibly reflected her desire to mask her role as editor and writer for the magazine. It also was a symbolic reminder, for readers and friends who knew her, of the impetus for starting the journal: namely the feeling that Black women and women writers in particular were being shunned by mainstream literary markets. The pseudonym also gave Browning perhaps playful free rein to write and publish stories that foregrounded taboo gendered and racial themes. For example, in the March-April 1945 issue of *Negro Story* Browning published "The Slave," a short story featuring as protagonist a white woman named Sue who is the daughter of a plantation master and privileged child of the slave system. Sue returns home from college one summer and for the first time takes physical notice of a fair-skinned slave named Dan, whom she has known since childhood and alongside whom she has grown up. The two begin a covert courtship and then love affair. They plan Dan's escape and a reunion in the North where they hope to carry on their illicit relationship. The story turns when Sue becomes pregnant. She confides her secret, including her relationship to Dan, to her familial Mammy, and vows to her to be with Dan forever. The import of slavery, race, and her affair come crashing down when Mammy reveals to her that Dan is her half-brother. Sue's "lovely Southland of sunshine," as Browning describes it, becomes a site of deep mourning and recognition. The story, anticipating both potboiler romance novels of a later era and more serious engagement by African American writers with the quagmire of miscegenation is also notable for Browning's efforts to write about slavery from a white, and white female, perspective.

Browning also situated gendered themes in more contemporary settings, as in her story "Tomorrow" published in the December-January, 1944–1945 issue of the magazine. The story centers on Jack, a tall, handsome white soldier desperate to find female companionship after an extended tour of duty with the eighteenth regiment in New York. Browning refers to the soldier as "Corporal Bryant" to underscore his rank and secure social standing. At the beginning of the tale he picks up a kindly woman named Helen for a date. She is initially awed by his good looks, uniform, and grace. This brief reverie quickly gives way as Jack tries to rape Helen on their first date. The description of the attempted rape is visceral and, by standards of the era, explicit. Helen fends him off by biting his arm. The soldier curses her, and women, and the story ends by invoking the title, "Tomorrow," as Bryant's optimistic promise to himself that another day and another girl are just around the corner. The story weaves a complex subtext of nationalism, chauvinism, violence, and aggression that was consistent with *Negro Story*'s larger editorial commitment to point out the abuses of World War II against all but white men.

Yet by early 1946, *Negro Story* was also losing readership ground to larger, better-financed publications like John Johnson and Johnson Publishing Company's *Negro Digest*, which first appeared in 1943, and Johnson's watershed *Ebony*, modeled on Henry Luce's *Life* Magazine. Browning had in fact anticipated the emergent black middle-class readership Johnson famously captured and helped to create, as well as its mixture of integrationism, social protest, and commercial savvy. She had also helped to demonstrate the need for a Black periodical market to cater to that readership.

Negro Story published its final issue in April, 1946. What is the legacy of Alice Browning and *Negro Story*? Chester Himes, Ralph Ellison, and Gwendolyn Brooks all clearly profited from exposure provided by the magazine prior to the publication of their first books. No fewer than seven stories first published in 1945 editions of *Negro Story* were also listed in Martha Foley's 1946 edition of *Best American Short Stories*, including Ralph Ellison's "The Birthmark," Chester Himes's "The Song Says 'Keep on Smilin,'" and two pseudonymous stories by Browning herself: "The Slave" and "Tomorrow"—the same story turned down by *Esquire* that motivated Browning to begin the magazine. In part for this reason, Robert Bone has called the magazine "for a brief moment . . . the focal point of black writing in America." In 1947, Earl Conrad described *Negro Story* as the fulcrum of a "Blues School of Literature." "*Negro Story*," he wrote, "frankly presents all of the issues of segregation and protest, the complexities of Negro-white labor relationships, intermarriages, and all matters of color, 'race,' caste, class and sex." Conrad aptly summarizes the stated objectives of Gayden and Browning in 1944. Clearly, the magazine crystallized not just the literary entrepreneurship of Chicago's Black Renaissance, but more especially the central role aspiring Black writers, publishers and artists played in advancing their own version of cultural rebirth.[5]

Alice Browning's career and public visibility in Chicago recessed with the end of the war and the end of *Negro Story*. Both were temporarily revived by the Black Arts Movement in Chicago. In 1970, Browning formed two new literary ventures inspired by the upsurge in Chicago Black Arts: the International Black Writers Conference in Chicago, an annual meeting of poets and authors, and Browning Press, a small publishing company. In 1972, Browning Press published *New Voices in Black Poetry*, an anthology of poems written by members of the annual conference. When she died in 1985, Gwendolyn Brooks wrote an eponymous tribute poem to Browning.

Browning's public and behind-the-scenes work as a cultural worker, writer and organizer bespeaks the significant pioneering role played by Black women in Chicago's Black Renaissance. Her desire to change the production, publishing, and consumption habits of Black writing and reading dovetails neatly with the Chicago Renaissance's practical goal of fostering autonomous networks of local cultural production and cultural pride. Browning's bourgeois standing in Chicago's rapidly evolving Black social hierarchy of the 1930s and 1940s and her shrewd use of economic and cultural capital also bespeaks the commercial empowerment that attended Black literary culture in the wake of the sensation of Richard Wright's 1940 novel *Native Son*. Indeed, Browning's major contribution to the Renaissance is perhaps as a reminder of how widespread and contagious was the spread of literary culture in Chicago during the 1930s and 1940s.

Notes

1. Mullen, Bill V. *Popular Fronts: Chicago and African-American Cultural Politics, 1935–1946*. Urbana: University of Illinois Press, 1999, 106–7.
2. *Negro Story*, V. 1, N. 1. Westport, Conn.: Negro Universities Press, 1970, 1–2.
3. Mullen, *Popular Fronts*, 106–26.

4. Ibid., 121.
5. Ibid., 121–26.

For Further Reading

Bone, Robert. "Richard Wright and the Chicago Renaissance." *Callaloo* 9.3 (1986): 446–68.

Browning, Alice C. Interview with Horace Cayton. Horace Cayton Papers. Vivian G. Harsh Collection. Carter Woodson Library, Chicago, Illinois.

Browning, Alice C. *Black n' Blue.* Chicago: Browning Press, 1972.

———, ed. *Child Play: A Magazine for boys and girls 4 to 14.* V. I, N. 1, Negro Story Press, July–August, 1945.

———, ed. *Lionel Hampton's Swing Book.* Chicago: Negro Story Press, 1945.

Browning, A. C. and H. Honore, eds. *New Voices in Black Poetry.* Chicago: Browning Press, 1972.

Conrad, Earl. *Jim Crow America.* New York: Duell, Sloan and Pearce, 1947, 59–60.

Negro Story Magazine. V. II, N. 1–3. Westport, Conn.: Negro Universities Press, 1970.

Travel News. V. 1, No. 2. *Zip Magazine.* Zip Publishing Company (Dec.–Jan., 1968–1969).

DAN BURLEY
(November 7, 1907–October 29, 1962)
Kimberly Stanley

Now I stash me down to nod;
My mellow frame upon this sod.
If I should cop a drill before the early toot,
I'll spiel to the Head Knock to make all things root.[1]

The "hepcat" that reworked the famous children's nighttime prayer "Now I Lay Me Down to Sleep" was Dan Burley, an integral figure in Chicago during the 1930s. The outburst of creativity that took place during the Chicago Renaissance was often linked if not compared to the Harlem Renaissance. The cultural and creative achievements that had taken place in Harlem, by the mid 1930s, seemed to be taking shape in Chicago as well. Music, art, literature, and journalism were part of Chicago's growing urban environment. Journalism, in particular, kept blacks, some who had recently migrated to Chicago from such states as Alabama, Mississippi, and Georgia, in touch with their southern relatives and friends and updated them frequently on current events. The *Chicago Defender* and the *Chicago Bee* were just two of the few black papers at the center of black journalism during the Chicago Renaissance, and Dan Burley was a key fixture at both newspapers.

As a journalist, Burley covered a gamut of subjects in regards to African American life and culture. He reported on sports and entertainment and kept his readers up to date with current events by chronicling the racial conflict in America and the military conflicts abroad. Yet, Burley did not just reserve his creative energies to journalism. He channeled his love of language, prose, and African American culture into writing and publishing two books that took preoccupation with the language of jive, *Dan Burley's Original Handbook of Harlem Jive* (1944) and *Diggeth Thou?* (1959). Burley's knowledge and preoccupation with jive stemmed, in part, from his status as a musician. Burley was known around the South Side of Chicago and in New York for his own unique style of jazz, where the music reflected the energy and originality of the language about which

Burley wrote. As an integral figure during the Chicago Renaissance, Dan Burley personifies the creative richness that emerged during the 1930s in Chicago.

Daniel Gardner Burley was born in Lexington, Kentucky, on November 7, 1907, to Anna and James Burley. Burley's father, born a slave, was a Baptist minister and thirty-five years older than his wife. One of the few memories that Burley could recall regarding his father was that he enjoyed "'tinkering with objects and communicating with the Patent Office in Washington.'"[2] Anna Seymour Burley, prior to her marriage, taught at Tuskegee Institute under the tutelage of Booker T. Washington. When Burley was three years old, his family left Kentucky and moved to Texas. Unfortunately, two years after this move, the senior Burley died while in the pulpit of his church. By 1917 Anna Seymour Burley remarried, and the family moved again, this time to Chicago. Burley's mother was active in Chicago politics and was considered influential in rallying blacks to vote. Burley recalled politicians, such as Mayor William "Big Bill" Hale Thompson and Governor Len Small frequenting their South Side home.[3]

Although Burley would eventually inherit his father's ingenuity and his mother's political activism, as a youngster and a teenager Burley's interests centered on journalism and music, specifically on blues and the emerging genre of jazz. Burley, similar to many early performers of jazz, had no formal musical training. Hersal Thomas, a child prodigy and a fellow classmate of Burley's at Douglas Elementary school, "taught Burley to play his first blues piece on the piano."[4] Thomas would subsequently teach Burley other arrangements to which Burley would master and play at parties held around the South Side of Chicago.

Burley's aversion to formal training stemmed from his belief that it was too concerned with technique instead of innate ability, raw emotion, and improvisation. Burley would later assert "if it is supposed to be jazz, it must perform the function of reporting on a condition of life, always on a corridor of human existence which the player must have experienced or understands through the works of others."[5]

Burley attended Wendell Phillips High School, a school that was famous for producing talented blacks who would later make their mark in literature, science, sports, and music, such as Nat "King" Cole, Eddie Cole, and Milt Hinton. Milt Hinton, who was known as the "Judge" among jazz bassists, recalled having after-school jam sessions with Burley, saxophonist Scoville Brown, and trombonist Edward Burke.[6] Having grown up around 31st Street in Chicago, which was the nexus for many of the nightclubs, Burley and his classmates were undoubtedly influenced by the types of sound and style emerging from this area.

Yet, music was not Burley's only passion. He was editor of the school newspaper, *Phillipsite*, involved with the student council, and at one time, president of the Pen and Ink club. In high school, Burley's musical interest was now being split with his love for writing. Yet, despite his involvement with extracurricular activities, Burley had very little interest academically in school.

At seventeen years old, Burley got his first professional break in the newspaper industry working as a copy boy for the *Chicago Defender* while still a student at Wendell Phillips High School. Along with making twenty-five dollars a week at the *Defender*, Burley continued to play piano in some of the roughest establishments in Chicago. Though still a teenager, Burley appeared older and was already known for being quite sociable, and he was not intimidated by the people who frequented these joints. In addition, playing in these establishments allowed Burley the opportunity to associate and learn from "authentic barrel-house musicians," which was key for a man who often played "by ear."

Burley soon developed a reputation as a semiprofessional musician. He performed in barrelhouses and nightclubs, and was also able to draw a crowd to social events, such as "rent parties." Rent parties were very popular during the Depression era when jobs and money were scarce. A "low-on-the-rent-money" tenant would host a party and charge admittance, hoping that the money that they made would help pay the monthly rent. In exchange for a nominal fee, the tenant was expected to provide beverages, good food, and good dance music for the guests to ensure a large turnout. Hinton recalled hearing Burley play "many times" at rent parties in Chicago, which of course is a testament to Burley's abilities as a pianist and, possibly, at drawing a crowd to these gatherings.[7] At these events, Burley honed his skills as a barrelhouse and "skiffle" musician. Skiffle music became almost synonymous with the name Dan Burley in later years. He is not only credited with popularizing the term "skiffle" but also the music, as a genre, during the 1930s, and he helped it to reemerge during the 1950s.[8]

In 1927 Burley left school and the *Chicago Defender* and traveled to several destinations, making his money as a lumberjack and piano player. However, by 1931 Burley returned to the *Defender*, taking on more responsibilities and writing duties, and eventually becoming a columnist and sports editor. The first indication of a "Burley" article appeared in the *Defender* on March 21, 1931. It was a series of local high school sports updates and the byline read "Daniel."[9] Two weeks later, the April 4 edition of the weekly had a new column, "'Sports Squibs' Doped by Daniel."[10] On April 11, 1931, "Sports Squibs by Dan Burley" appeared in the *Chicago Defender*. "Sports Squibs by Dan Burley" was Burley's first byline column for the *Defender*. Burley, an avid sports fan, would occasionally write his column with his trademark lyrical flare and humor:

> Bill Shakespeare, bard of the Dark Ages, was something of a scribe, we'll all admit and while my memory of his lines in "Julius Caesar" may be somewhat bedimmed by too much intermingling with lowlifer sports bugs, I still am wide awake enough to see the connection between Cassius and one Leroy "Satchel"

Paige, especially in the case of the American Giants playing the Kansas City Monarchs at Comiskey Park on Sunday.[11]

Burley wrote extensively on the Negro League and was an avid proponent for the desegregation of baseball, a cause he continued to advocate for and write about even when he began working for the *New York Amsterdam News* in late 1937.

In 1932, Burley left the *Chicago Defender* and became editor and columnist for the *Chicago Bee* while concurrently working as a correspondent for the Associated Negro Press. After spending approximately three years at the *Bee*, Burley returned to the *Chicago Defender*. It was during his brief return to the *Defender* that Burley created his column "Back Door Stuff." Originally intended as a borderline risqué-gossip-entertainment column, the purpose of "Back Door Stuff" was to expose the dirty little secrets of Chicagoans. In his May 1, 1936, column, Burley cited the "preamble" of "Back Door Stuff's" constitution:

> This column, herein . . . shall be dedicated to the principles of telling the truth and nothing but the truth, on what goes on after dark; what transpires behind closed doors and what hubby and wifey do when apart during the day and night, whatever the case may be. It shall be forever the ideal for this column to stand on the theory that what a man does is our business if we find out, and Lawd help his wife if she sings off-key.[12]

"Back Door Stuff" was Burley's sounding board—a vehicle for him to express his concerns regarding current political and racial contradictions, a literary space for him to wax poetic, and a medium for him to name-drop. Similar to many artists who emerged during the Chicago Renaissance, Burley was also a social commentator, taking note and writing about social ills he witnessed. Burley would later be known for his other controversial columns, "Confidentially Yours" and "Talkin' Out Loud."

At the *Defender* Burley tackled other serious topics. In 1935 he did an extensive report on the war in Ethiopia and penned several columns in the *Chicago Defender Foreign News Section*, a section devoted to world news. Yet Burley would also address human interest stories and accomplishments of African Americans around the country and provide political and historical information to his readers. Burley wanted his readers to be informed and knowledgeable on historical and current political and social events.

Burley's love for writing and his flare with words took a different twist in 1944 when his first book, *Dan Burley's Original Handbook of Harlems Jive* was published. Although living in New York at the time *Handbook* was written, Burley's decision to write this dictionary of slang was undoubtedly inspired by the creative milieu of Chicago. The literary atmosphere was very rich during the period of the Chicago Renaissance, producing many poets and writers. Burley's literary flare, and his love for black history and culture, which was evident in many of the newspaper columns that he wrote, was now gathered in book form.

Burley, who often wrote "Back Door Stuff" in jive, normally limited his use of the language to those columns directed specifically to African Americans who considered themselves "hep." But in *Original Handbook*, Burley's target audience was not specifically those familiar with the language of jive. Indeed, the *Handbook*, in addition to locating the origins of the term "jive" in Chicago, is a pedagogical tool aimed at teaching the language of jive. As one of the first "dictionaries" of jive, Burley presents a thoroughly researched text on the evolution of a language spoken in the inner city and how this dynamic language reflected the dynamism of the culture.

After he explicates the history of jive, Burley proceeds to explain the rudiments of the language. In this, Burley becomes a semiotician. He provides a glossary of jive terms and demonstrates how words can mutate from noun, verbal noun, adjective, and simile to hyperbole. Burley then suggests that his "students" try to construct a sentence based on all the information that is given. *Dan Burley's Original Handbook of Harlem Jive* was well received and lauded for its comprehensive study of African American culture and language. Burley wanted to give credence to jive and in the process celebrate black culture. His hope when he published the book was that one day,

> the cats who lay that larceny in the book of many pages (dictionary) will give the jivers a break and substitute the phrase, "twister to the slammer," for the word, "key"; use the word "jive" in their definition of "slang"; and, otherwise, give notice to those hipped studs who have collared such a heavy slave to add color to the American language.[13]

Burley's motivation for writing the *Handbook* was possibly twofold. He seemingly wanted white audiences to accept this lyrical and complex language and to see the merits of jive and African American culture; and he wanted his black audience to take pride in their rich American heritage. Burley was praised as a "scholar of merit" and his legitimization of jive as a language "elevated [him] to the status of semanticist: historian, linguist, and lexicographer, all in one."[14] His *Handbook* was considered a true reference source. It was translated into four languages and could be found on any reference shelf.[15] Although the *Handbook* had been out of print for several years, it was republished in 2009 and is still considered a modern reference source because of its thorough examination of jive.

Burley's legacy and contribution to the Chicago Renaissance and black culture would not be complete without mentioning his professional accomplishments in the realm of jazz. Burley was friends with many great entertainers in the world of jazz, such as Lionel Hampton, Sticks and Brownie McGhee, Leonard Feather, and Dizzy Gillespie, and he appeared on some of their recordings. Burley also had his own band, "Dan Burley and His Skiffle Boys," who recorded a number of 78 rpm records. As a composer, he wrote and cowrote several jazz tunes, including "They Raided the Joint," "Pig-Feet Sonata," and "Chicken Shack Shuffle," the latter two with Lionel Hampton. In 1948, filmgoers witnessed Burley's musical talent in cinematic form when he appeared in Dizzy Gillespie's musical variety film, *Jivin' in Bebop*. Burley was featured in two segments of the film, playing alongside fellow jazz musician Johnny Taylor.

In a tribute to Burley, A. S. "Doc" Young recalled the moment when he first heard Burley play skiffle music on a jazz piano. According to Young, to watch Burley play was to witness "the reincarnation of an age when jazz was a feature of the speakeasy."[16]

> He'd play 32 bars, probably, and then perspiration would cascade from his pores. His large, brown eyes would stare out in ecstasy, yet mischievously, and Dan, like Hamp, would grunt or groan or, like Dizzy, start a humorous conversation with a listener.[17]

Burley had a passion for jazz. He witnessed the evolution of the genre from boogie-woogie in the 1920s to swing, to bebop in the 1940s. Gillespie, Earl Hines, and Burley were just a few of the bop musicians known around Bronzeville or the South Side of Chicago. Bop is considered a more stylistically challenging form of jazz. It avoids a melody line and conformity, yet it consists of fast tempos and complex harmonies. This along with the language of jive that many boppers spoke, set bop apart from the more polished Swing performers. Bebop was said to have emerged as a response to Swing. Burley believed jazz was "three quarters biographic and the rest heresy" and that it symbolically reflected the condition of life in the inner cities.[18] Jazz, similar to jive, was a form of emotional expression. It was this emotional expression and cultural richness that Burley sought to communicate in his performing and writing.

Burley, similar to Wright and other social commentators that emerged during the Chicago Renaissance, recognized that art needed to reflect and represent the social conditions of its urban environment. As an artist, Burley who mingled with the social elite, also kept company and spoke the language of the people who dwelled in some of the most impoverished places in the inner city. Burley was a cultural icon who was informed of every facet of African American culture, from history, folklore, and music, to politics, and he felt the desire to keep all blacks informed with not just current events, but also with historical events that would impart knowledge and education.

In late 1937, Burley left to Chicago for New York and worked as a journalist and editor for *New York Amsterdam News*. In New York, Burley continued his music career and was also a disc jockey at two New York radio stations. During

World War II, Burley traveled with the first USO tour and would occasionally pen columns from his locale. However, by 1949 Burley left New York and returned to Chicago where he continued to work in journalism. At Johnson Publishing Company (JPC), the black-owned business started by John H. Johnson, Burley wrote and was associate editor for both of JPC's magazines *Ebony* and *Jet*.

After leaving JPC, Burley started his own short-lived men's magazine, *Duke* in 1957. *Duke*'s format was similar to both *Ebony* and *Playboy*: it showcased black athletes, jazz musicians and black women. Burley's popularity and notoriety as a journalist and then as publisher continued, so much so that in 1960, when The Nation of Islam decided to start their own newspaper to spread their message, they recruited Burley to help launch their endeavor. Burley's first publication for the Nation of Islam was *Salaam*, a short-lived magazine that was formatted similar to *Jet*.[19] Nevertheless, despite the failure of *Salaam*, Burley's editorial knowledge and Malcolm X's political message helped to make the Nation's next vehicle, *Muhammad Speaks*, one of the most widely circulated black newspapers of its day.

Burley's second book, *Diggeth Thou?* was self-published around 1959. *Diggeth Thou?*, similar to the *Handbook*, is a book that showcased the language of jive. However, whereas the *Handbook* could be used as a reference tool, *Diggeth*'s primary preoccupation was the reciprocity between jive and jazz. In 1962, after working for the *Chicago Crusader*, Burley published and edited his own weekly newspaper, *The Owl*.

Dan Burley died in October 1962 leaving behind his wife Gladys, daughter D'Anne, and two stepchildren. The tributes to Burley that were published after his death mentioned his humor, wit, and ability to embrace and report on the ironies of African American life. Burley's legacy, similar to the legacies of all the Renaissance artists, is that he was able to express the struggles and the triumphs of African Americans in the inner city and blended it with his own distinct creativity to create art.

Notes

1. Burley, Dan. "The Techniques of Jive." In *Mother Wit from the Laughing Barrel*, edited by Alan Dundes, 206–21. Englewood Cliffs: Prentice-Hall, Inc, 1973. For those not familiar with the nighttime prayer: Now I lay me down to sleep. I pray the Lord my soul to keep. If I should die before I wake, I pray the Lord my soul to take.

2. Nowakowski, Konrad. *Dan Burley, South Side Shake: 1945–1951.* Compact disc. Vienna: Wolf Records, 1991, WJB-CD-008, 12.10.

3. Ibid., 12.

4. Ibid., 12.

5. Tamony, Peter. "Funky." *American Speech* 55, 3 (Autumn 1980): 212.

6. Hinton, Milt. "Foreword." *Dan Burley, South Side Shake: 1945–1951*. Compact disc. Vienna: Wolf Records, 1991, WJB-CD-008, 12.10.

7. Nowakowski, 13.

8. Major, Clarence. *Juba to Jive: A Dictionary of African-American Slang*. New York: Penguin Books, 1994, 420.

9. *Chicago Defender*, March 21, 1931, 8.

10. *Chicago Defender*, April 4, 1931, 9.

11. *Chicago Defender*, September 8, 1935, 13.

12. Burley, Dan. "Back Door Stuff," *Chicago Defender*, May 2, 1936, 23.

13. Burley, "The Techniques of Jive," 208.

14. Ibid.

15. Burley, Dan. *Diggeth Thou?* Chicago: Burley, Cross, & Co., 1959, 3.

16. Young, A. S. "Doc." "The Legend of Dan Burley." *Sepia* (January 1963): 5.

17. Ibid., 76.

18. *Norfolk Journal and Guide*, November 10, 1962, 18.

19. Muhammad, Askia. "*Muhammad Speaks*: A Trailblazer in the Newspaper Industry." *Final Call* Special Edition, October 3, 2000; April 16, 2004. www.finalcall.com/national/savioursday2k/m_speaks.htm

For Further Reading

Burley, Dan. "Back Door Stuff," *Chicago Defender*, May 2, 1936, 23.

———. *Blackman in America*, "The Truth about Burley, Dan." "The Vacant Chair: A Short Story with a Thrilling and Unexpected Climax." *Abbott's Monthly* 1, 1 (October 1930).

———. *Dan Burley, South Side Shake: 1945-1951*. Compact disc. Vienna: Wolf Records, 1991, WJB-CD-008, 12.10.

———. *Dan Burley's Jive*, edited by Thomas Aiello. DeKalb: Northern Illinois University Press, 2009.

———. *Dan Burley's Original Handbook of Harlem Jive*. New York: Jive Publishing, 1944.

"Daniel," *Chicago Defender*, March 21, 1931, 8.

———. "Demon Balu." *Abbott's Monthly* 2, 6 (June 1931).

Burley, Dan. *Diggeth Thou?* Chicago: Burley, Cross, & Co., 1959.

———. *Diggeth Thou? and Dan Burley's Original Handbook of Harlem Jive*. edited by Thomas Aiello. Dekalb: Northern Illinois University Press, 2009.

———. "He Ballyhooed a Race." *Negro Digest* 1, 2 (December 1942).

———. "Jim Crow Train Pulls Out." *Negro Digest* 2, 3 (January 1944).

———. "My Favorite War Hero." *Negro Digest* 4, 7 (May 1946).

———. "Sports Squibs by Daniel," *Chicago Defender*, April 11, 1931, 9.

———. "Sports Squibs Doped by Daniel," *Chicago Defender*, April 4, 1931, 9.

———. "The Strange Will of Colonel McKee." *Negro Digest* 10, 1 (November 1951).

———. "What Became of Negro Humor?" *Negro Digest* 10, 8 (June 1961).

———. "What's Ahead for Robinson?" *The Crisis* 52, 12 (December 1945).

Jivin' in Bebop. Movie, 1948. idem idvd 1018.

"Muhammad." *Message to the Blackman in America*, by Elijah Muhammad. Chicago: Muhammad Mosque of Islam No. 2, 1965.

Reisler, Jim. *Black Writers/Black Baseball: An Anthology of Articles from Black Sportswriters Who Covered the Negro Leagues*. Jefferson, N.C.: McFarland and Company, 1994, 127–44.

Rusinack, Kelly E. "Dan Burley." *Dictionary of Literary Biography*. Detroit: Thompson Gale, 2004.

Magazine: *Duke* (1957).

Newspapers Edited/Published: *South Side Civic Telegram*, 1932; *The Owl*, 1962.

MARGARET ESSE DANNER
(January 12, 1915–May 1, 1986)
Keith D. Leonard

Though she is not as well-known as some of her contemporaries and has not received as much critical attention, poet, editor, and activist Margaret Danner was a central figure in the emergence out of the Midwest of the Black Arts Movement of the late 1960s and early 1970s. In her five volumes of poetry, Danner was among the first African American poets to celebrate a continuity between African American culture and West African art and to treat the multiple African, European, and American heritages of African American people as a source of strength for the artist, not a liability. Such affirmation was to become a defining ideal for the radical Black Aesthetic of the late 1960s. Also, Danner has consistently been praised for how, through her careful craft, she used distinctive subtlety, irony, and evocative imagery and symbolism to link ethnic cultural heritage, spirituality, and beauty as the manifestation of political resistance. Finally, as the editor of two anthologies and as the founder of two writers' workshops in Detroit and Chicago, Danner joined poets such as Gwendolyn Brooks, Dudley Randall, and Haki Madhubuti in fostering community among African American writers in Detroit and Chicago and in bringing a new generation of African American writers to the public eye. In these ways, Danner offered an innovative sense that communal heritage was a source of imaginative and social freedom that could be realized through the spiritual meaning of artistic beauty, ideals that placed her at the center of the Chicago Renaissance.

Multicultural arts and identity seemed always to be intertwined for Margaret Esse Danner, who was born to Caleb and Naomi Esse of Pryorsburg, Kentucky, on January 12, 1915. Although she would not publish poetry until much later in her life, Danner cultivated her poetic talent as early as junior high school, winning first prize in a poetry contest for her poem "The Violin" when she was in the eighth grade. The poem is an early instance of Danner's career-long interest in using Stradivarius and Guanerius violins to symbolize her knowledge and appreciation of European art, from the violin to the ballet, alongside her innovative concerns about African culture.

Danner's public career as a poet began once she joined the socially conscious artistic community of Chicago, where her family had relocated by the time Danner had entered high school. She attended Englewood High School in Chicago before enrolling at Loyola and Roosevelt Universities. During this time, she was selected as one of the top ten African American poets as part of the University of Michigan's contribution to "Patterns in American Culture." Also, at the 1945 Midwestern Writers Conference at Northwestern University, Danner won second prize in the Poetry Workshop. She also received guidance and support from established editors and poets Karl Shapiro and Paul Engle, as well as African American writers Richard Wright, Owen Dodson, and Brooks, all of whom in turn had been influenced by sociologists such as Robert Park who saw culture as a means to social integration and equality. Such idealism about integration would soon have a place in Danner's vision of ethnic affirmation.

As a poet of place, Danner began at this time to use her neighborhood and her family as the foundation for her innovative ideals of heritage and community. She was married twice, first to Cordell Strickland and then to Otto Cunningham. She and Strickland have a child, Naomi, who is the mother of Sterling Washington Jr., Danner's grandson and one of the chief inspirations for her poetry. He is the young boy in Danner's many "Muffin" poems in which she shows not only her joy and pride in being a grandmother and her admiration for the child's innocent wisdom, but also her sense that one role of poetry is in conveying wisdom to succeeding generations. Muffin becomes her ideal audience for her meditation on how artistic beauty is the principal means to affirm cultural heritage. These "Muffin" poems include "Black Power Language," about a child's perspective on Black Vernacular English, and "For Muffin," about a gift to the child of an Ashanti stool as a token of race pride. Ethnic community becomes a family for Danner, and its heritage is mirrored in its commitment to beauty and cultural memory.

Early in her career, like her fellow Chicago writers Brooks, Wright, Theodore Dreiser, and Carl Sandburg, Danner used the Chicago setting of her poems to reveal her concern that the social and economic forces of this brutal urban life destroyed the African self, a self that could potentially be healed through art like hers. Poems like "Garnishing the Aviary," "The Dance of the Abakweta," "The Visit of the Professor of Aesthetics," "Edna Moten's Attic," "Best Loved of Africa," and "The Painted Lady" exemplify her approach. All six of these poems explore the alienation that descendants of Africa feel when moving either from Africa or the South of the United States to Chicago. In "Garnishing the Aviary," for example, the Africans who were adapting to the city were compared to birds who had feathers that, "though still exotic / Blend in more easily with those on the wings / Of the birds surrounding them."[1] Acknowledging the loss of distinctiveness this blending implies, the poet fears for "The Painted Lady," "a small

African / Butterfly gayly toned deep tan and peach." The lightness of the colors is emblematic of the poet's anxiety as the poem ends: "is there strength enough in my / Peach paper rose or lavender sea-laced fan?"[2] Unlike Brooks and Wright, then, Danner is not sanguine about the alleged historical inevitability of integration that many Chicago writers imbibed with optimism from the "Chicago sociology" of Robert Park. Instead, Danner emphasizes what is potentially lost in this process, as in the end of "Best Loved of Africa": "in Lincoln Park / Lies Bushman, best loved of Africa, huge / And beautifully black as he ever was, but dead."[3] Such a lament anticipates the radical Black Aesthetic of the 1960s, the ideal that African American writers should claim an ethnically distinctive and politically radical art based in African American and African cultures.

This distinctive vision of the need for cultural preservation led Danner to prominence in the 1950s. In 1950, she won a grant from the Women's Auxiliary of Afro-American Interests. Also, in 1950 and 1951, respectively, Danner won the Harriet Tubman Award and the John Hay Whitney Fellowship for *Far From Africa: Four Poems*, with the latter fellowship intended to support a trip to Africa scheduled for that year but which she did not take until 1966. Between 1952 and 1956, the four poems for which she won the Whitney Fellowship, along with two others—the six mentioned above—were published in the Chicago-based *Poetry: A Magazine of Verse*, a journal known for its commitment to the avant-garde and to introducing new writers to the public. Moreover, between 1951 and 1955, Danner served as an editorial assistant for that journal and, in 1955, apparently at the urging of Karl Shapiro, who was editor of *Poetry* at the time, was promoted to assistant editor. She was the first African American to hold the position, in which she served from 1956 to 1957. Finally, in 1956, she won the Native Chicago Literary Prize and, in 1960, a grant from the American Society of African Culture.

By the 1960s, Danner had combined her editorial work with her maturing poetry to become one of the most important figures in African American literary culture both in Chicago and in Detroit. Critics generally agree that Danner's first full-length volume, *Impressions of African Art Forms in the Poetry of Margaret Danner*, first published in 1960, is her most important because of its distinctive emphasis on the value of African culture for African American art and identity and for its representation of the poet's shift in perspective from the anxiety of poems like "Best Loved of Africa" to greater, more explicit affirmation. She is also praised for the way in which she suggests that such a shift is necessary for all Americans. In the volume, much of which was written while she was in Chicago, Danner reclaims the ideal cultural continuity between African art, generally exemplified for Danner by Benin sculpture, and African American as a remedy to the sense of cultural discontinuity caused by slavery and racism. The volume contains some of Danner's best-known poems, including "The Small Bells of

Benin," about the symbolic tolling of literal bells of Benin sculpture calling for African American cultural self-awareness; "The Dance of Abakweta," about how a presumably white American ballet instructor would misunderstand an African dance by trying to conceive of it in terms of that Western dance form rather than in terms of African spirituality; and "Etta Moten's Attic," about a friend's collection of artifacts that helped inspire Danner's own developing appreciation of African art. As Broadus N. Butler suggested in his introduction to the volume, Danner's poems "probe into the social body and perform a kind of midwifery to assist the present rebirth and transformation of appreciations African American art."[4] In Danner's own words, as quoted by June M. Aldridge in an article on Danner's poetry, her verse was meant "to cause men, especially Blacks, to realize that Black roots are as deeply planted and authentic as those of other people with whom we must deal in creating this New World."[5]

This ideal of transforming perceptions of African American people through African culture and this desire to make a "New World" from multiple cultural roots fed Danner's leadership in the artistic communities in Chicago and Detroit. In 1961, in large part due to the success of this volume, Danner started as poet-in-residence at Wayne State University in Detroit, the first of several such posts she held throughout the rest of her life, including at historically black colleges Virginia Union in Richmond, Virginia, and LeMoyne Owen in Memphis, Tennessee. While in Detroit, Danner came to work closely with Dudley Randall, producing their collaborative volume *Poem Counterpoem* in which the two poets included poems on common subjects and alternated them on facing pages. Their paired poems dealt with issues ranging from the death of the four little girls in the infamous church bombing in Birmingham to the value and potential compromises of the Civil Rights Movement strategy of passive resistance. In her poem "Passive Resistance," Danner declares "I want no more of this humility" and worries in "This is an African Worm" that such humility leads black people to "crawl and wait" rather than to stand up against oppression and actively claim equality.[6] The fact that established presses were reluctant to publish the volume contributed to Randall's desire to start Broadside Press in 1965, the black-owned and -operated publishing house that made *Poem Counterpoem* available in print in 1966, along with the works of many well-known and new African American poets. The press also reissued Danner's first volume, *Impressions of African Art* in 1968. In 1962, Danner helped to establish the most prominent African American writers' community in Detroit by converting an empty parish house of the King Solomon Church into Boone House, named after the minister whom Danner persuaded to open the space for a workshop for children. Boone House brought together poets like Randall, Owen Dodson, Robert Hayden, Hoyt Fuller, and Naomi Long Madgett, in addition to serving its area youth so that, as Randall put it, "we created a poetry community to inspire each other."[7] In this endeavor, Danner fostered the talents and careers of writers like Hoyt Fuller who would be instrumental in formalizing the ideals of the Black Aesthetic, making her, as Paul Breman put it, "the doyenne of Detroit's black letters."[8]

Spirituality became the final component of Danner's art as her Baháʼí faith provided a basis for and terms by which to reconcile her knowledge of and commitment to African American culture and history with ideals of transracial and transnational unity. Danner even served from 1964 to 1966 as the touring poet with the Baháʼí Teaching Committee. Though this aspect of her verse has received practically no commentary, this spirituality transformed cultural anxiety into spiritual unity. For example, her consistent use of lace as a symbol for unity, including in the title of her 1968 volume *Iron Lace*, derives in part from the Baháʼí doctrine of the interconnected nature of all of the world's major religions through their worship of the same divinity and the consequent Baháʼí belief that all humanity is therefore united despite national and cultural divisions. In "Today Requires a Lace of Truths," Danner declares that ideals of human unity need to be "as eclectic as the lace that Truths form / in the stone of the temple of Baháʼí" and "as forever enduring in grace / as the intermolding of / the Benin Bronze."[9] African heritage and a religion rooted in the Middle East constitute the twin, "eclectic" and "intermolded" pillars of this ideal "New World" and therefore are twin sources of African American self-affirmation. Although some of her poems contain explicit references to the Baháʼí faith, Danner achieves her greatest spiritual effects when using the lace symbolism, to suggest that beauty derives from an aesthetic unity that is an analogy for social and spiritual harmony.

These effects are best demonstrated in her last volume, *The Down of a Thistle* (1976), a collection of new and previously published poems that, critics agree, constitutes her crowning achievement. Enhanced by the illustrations of Fred Weinman, the volume opens with two poems that elaborate upon the symbolism of the title thistle, a plant native to Africa where it is "accorded reverence" and transplanted to the United States where it grows thornier for self-defense in its new, hostile climate. The title poem, "The Down of a Thistle," lays out a symbolic middle passage by implying the plant's analogy to black people and asserting "that few get near enough / to enjoy the down."[10] "Endowned," the second poem about thistles, concludes with the image of a hummingbird who gets past the thorns and "knows / that the down of a thistle is as soft / as the petal of a rose."[11] Using both traditional literary images, spiritual symbols, and African culture, these poems set the terms of alienation, alternative notions of beauty, and fundamentally shared humanity that necessitate the shift in perspective that would allow the beauty of the thistle to be appreciated.

This last volume makes quite clear the balanced terms of ethnic affirmation and human unity, political commentary and spirituality, by which Danner offers her beautiful protest of racism and her validation of black identity. These ideals also therefore guide the poems about the Illinois and Michigan locales in which Danner explores the new habitat of the thistle. For example, the fact that the first letters of the names of the Great Lakes spell "HOMES" gives Danner the chance to explore the meaning of her American locale for her emerging African sensibility. With a great deal of nature imagery, the second section of the volume offers poems like "Detroit Michigan" about willow trees that do not weep but bow respectfully and that follow the nonracial "green man," who is loved by black and white, into a meeting of the "Eastern religion" of the Bahá'í.[12] That section also contains most of Danner's explicit Bahá'í poems and includes "The Lady Executive Looks at a Mangbetu Palm Wine Jug," in which the speaker refrains from criticizing a white American's misunderstanding of this African artifact until she herself understands its significance.

This tension between affirmation and alienation gets played out fully in the volume's next section, called "Endangered Species." In "Endangered Species," a black pearl—the souls as well as the bodies and the culture of African American people—is disparaged for being black. But that same pearl—a reference to the pearl of great price in the Bible—gets aid from the "Caster"—a figure for God—who "stoops to groom it" and "intercedes / to help it shine full bloom" only after those who recognize its beauty also seek to give assistance.[13] In "The Elevator Man Adheres to Form," a man with a PhD runs an elevator, a clear criticism of a society that prevents educated black men from opportunities commensurate with their education. But as the title of the poem suggests, the speaker is not satisfied with the elevator man's apparent acceptance of this "form" of life accorded to him and his people either. The speaker wishes instead that the elevator man—whose potential for uplift is implicit in his name—would "turn his lettered zeal / toward lifting them above their crippling storm."[14] The implication of both poems is that an oppressive society disparages African Americans in large part by not appreciating their beauty and that perhaps the most important gestures African Americans can make in response is to appreciate their own beauty and seek to help themselves, the result of which will be divine assistance. In this way, African Americans can resist the "modern pigs" (presumably including misguided black people) who, in "Endangered Species," "can't quite see the utter need / there'll be for such a sooty stone." By recognizing and acting on their commonality both within the race and across racial lines, the black pearls should bring about their own spiritual and cultural well-being.

Because of this emphasis on positive self-perception and communal unity and on the artistic celebration of African American people, Danner's poems on African art and African heritage remain her most important poems even in this volume. A central example is "And Through The Caribbean Sea." The poem opens by suggesting that "we" African Americans "have been forced to exist in a huge kaleidoscope world" and have "been shifting with time and shifting through space," experiencing "whimsical" turns of the kaleidoscope "until any pattern or place / or shade is our own."[15] As Don L. Lee observed, the "references or allusions which are not African are meant to indicate a loss of identity."[16] The poem reads, "Until, who questions whether we'd be prone to yearn / for a Louis Quinze frame, a voodoo fire, / Rococo, Baroque, an African mask or a Gothic spire / or any style of any age or any place or name."[17] The transit through the Caribbean Sea to the "New World" has forced an adoption of Western culture and therefore confusion about which culture to claim, leaving the descendants of Africa susceptible to "any place or name."

But as the title of the volume implies, this thorny problem has its soft, shared, and affirming down, its petals as soft as any rose, which is art. And for Danner, that affirmation has to do with how art helps to create the new identity in this New World, one in which, contrary to Lee's assertion, the non-African references do not necessarily indicate loss. Those places and names do sometimes become "our own." For example, in "The Slave and Iron Lace," Danner celebrates the creativity by which a slave named Samuel Rouse transformed the materials of his enslavement—metal—into a self-affirming mode of expression. According to the poem, "The craving of Samuel Rouse for clearance to create / was surely as hot as the iron that buffeted him. / His passion for freedom so strong that it molded / the smouldering fashions he laced." Artistic expression and freedom become synonymous for Danner and, in the context of the lace image, analogous to both social and spiritual unity. "How else," the poem asks after listing several patterns the slave created in his metalwork, could he "create all this in such exquisite, fairyland taste, [so] that he'd / be freed and his skill would still resound / one hundred years after?"[18] African American art, when developed in response to the craving for freedom and an awareness of history, validates the self of the artist and becomes validating heritage for the community. Her art places her in what Richard Barksdale describes as the African continuity, that "immense shining cultural highway leading from Beale Street down through the stressful centuries back to Benin."[19]

It is precisely this eclectic heritage that, paradoxically, makes possible the creativity of Samuel Rouse and, the poem implies, of the Black Nationalist Margaret Danner herself. In one of her most important poems, "In a Bone White Frame," Danner symbolically suggests that a unified and culturally affirming vision of African American culture can emerge for the poet herself even though she is "framed" by a potentially deadening white Western culture. Providing an artistic image for W. E. B. DuBois's well-known concept of double consciousness, the poet "must make two paintings. / No spending all of my time acquainting / myself with ming blue, peach pastel." To be whole, she must acknowledge the "huge mahogany oil" that "occupies me through every cell." In other words, she must address both sides of her competing selves and the divided audience by accepting the "oil" of her biological and cultural inheritance. That mahogany painting of an African and the poem in which Danner discusses it both serve as counterweights to the possibility of the black artist losing herself in Westernized and abstracted beauty: "I won't release this oil, / it goes where I go. / So, it will not be easy for us to fly."[20] But being grounded in the black past is neither deadening to creativity nor a rejection the West altogether but the best way for African Americans to realize that Black roots are deep and authentic in both traditions. This is why, in "Inheritance for Muffin," Danner declares that she cannot leave Muffin monetary gold but she can leave him "this exquisitely carved Benin Bronze," "this Senufo Firespitter mask," "these modern bones so superbly carved" that they remind misguided viewers of "'Rome' and other classic places" though they were made on Beale Street and, finally, "these eclectic laces and lattices of the writings of Baháí / in the temple in Wilmette."[21] In short, she can give her grandson a heritage through her art, and therefore a positive sense of self.

In these ways, her art comes full circle, going to history and back to the family. For example, in "From Esse to Handy to Hayes":

It is Black Art that leaps, churning up,
flaming out from the Esse furnace
within us, wherever we are flung.
Exploding into the streets and cities
of Black men,
from the beginning of our Benin past
to the blessed estate of Baha'u'llah.[22]

In this poem, Danner links her personal past to an African past by linking her maiden name to a city in Nigeria of the same name, a process of personalizing history and finding one's meaning that she wanted her black readers to do. The individual poet's creativity is but a species of the creativity of all "Black men" and comes to the surface in expression "wherever we are flung." And that expression, Danner concludes, links the African American's African past to the future "blessed estate" of human unity that was part of the prophecy of Bahá'u'lláh, the most holy figure of the Baháí faith. Integration here is not the loss she implies it to be in her apparent questioning of the ideals of Chicago sociology in her early work. It is self-affirmation. And in the intricate lace of this vision, Danner as artist becomes part of the heritage she so uniquely claimed and espoused.

It is no wonder, then, that Danner enjoyed continued public accolades in the late 1960s and early 1970s, during which time she published two more volumes and two anthologies. In 1966, Danner finally took her trip to Africa to attend the World Exposition of Negro Arts in Dakar Senegal, where her friend Robert Hayden won the prize for his volume *A Ballad of Remembrance* (1962) and where Danner herself read some of her poetry. She also used the trip to visit an African art exhibit in Paris. In 1968, in addition to *Iron Lace*, mentioned above, Danner also produced *Brass Horses*, an anthology published by Virginia Union University and, in 1969, a second anthology called *Regroup*, also published by Virginia Union. Throughout this period, Danner appeared at various writers conferences, including the Phillis Wheatley Poetry Festival at Jackson State College (now University) organized by fellow Midwestern poet Margaret Walker (Alexander) in November 1973. Perhaps the most important of Danner's many appearances, this conference featured eighteen prominent African American women poets reading from their work and discussing contemporary poetry. The conference garnered significant attention, with a feature article in *Black World* in February 1974 and a photo essay in *Ebony* in March of the same year.

Throughout her eclectic and impressive career, Margaret Danner developed a distinctive vision that combined an awareness of African heritage, an appreciation of European art, a thorough examination and critique of the ideals of integration and assimilation and, ultimately, the ideal of spiritual unity to produce a powerful collection of verse affirming human unity through ethnic difference. Seeing African Americans and artists as communities with shared heritage, she fostered the success of a new generation of African American writers. Although Danner did not have any other major publications between *The Down of a Thistle* and her death in 1986, her work anticipates the most important trends of cultural heritage in African art since her first published poems, establishing her as something of a prophet for cultural unity and spiritual wholeness.

Notes

1. Danner Margaret. *The Down of a Thistle: Selected Poems, Prose Poems, and Songs.* Waukesha, Wisc.: Country Beautiful, 1976, 47.

2. Ibid., 78.

3. Ibid., 73.

4. Butler, Broadus N. "Introduction." *Impressions of African Art Forms in the Poetry of Margaret Danner.* Detroit: Broadside Press, 1960, 2.

5. Aldridge, June M. "Benin to Beale Street: African Art in the Poetry of Margaret Danner." *College Language Association Journal* 31 (2) (December 1987): 202.

6. Danner, *The Down of a Thistle*, 86, 98.

7. Boyd, Melba Joyce. *Wrestling with the Muse: Dudley Randall and the Broadside Press.* New York: Columbia, 2003, 105.

8. Aldridge, "Benin to Beale Street," 205.

9. Danner, *The Down of a Thistle*, 41.

10. Ibid., 12.

11. Ibid., 14.

12. Ibid., 20.

13. Ibid., 59.

14. Ibid., 68.

15. Ibid., 117.

16. Madhubuti, Haki (Don L. Lee). *Dynamite Voices I: Black Poets of the 1960s*. Detroit: Broadside Press, 1971, 41.

17. Danner, *The Down of a Thistle*, 117.

18. Ibid., 103.

19. Barksdale, Richard. "Margaret Danner and the African Connection," paper delivered at the annual meeting of the National Council of Teachers of English, Cincinnati, Ohio, November 2, 1980, 3.

20. Ibid., 70.

21. Ibid., 76.

22. Danner, *The Down of a Thistle*, 108.

For Further Reading

Adoff, Arnold, ed., *The Poetry of Black America: Anthology of the 20th Century*. New York: Harper and Row, 1973. Includes poems by Danner.

Aldrich, June M. "Langston Hughes and Margaret Danner." *The Langston Hughes Review* 3 (2) (Fall 1984): 7–9.

Bailey, Leonard Pack, ed. *Broadside Authors and Artists: An Illustrated Biographical Directory*. Detroit: Broadside Press, 1974.

Barksdale, Richard and Keneth Kinnamon, eds. *Black Writers of America: A Comprehensive Anthology*. New York: Macmillan, 1972. Includes poems by Danner.

Bontemps, Arna, ed. *American Negro Poetry*. New York: Hill and Wang, 1963. Includes poems by Danner.

Boyd, Melba Joyce. "'Prophets for a New Day': The Cultural Activism of Margaret Danner, Margaret Burroughs, Gwendolyn Brooks and Margaret Walker." *Revista Canaria de Estudios Ingleses* 37 (November 1998): 55–67.

Brown Johnson, Patricia L., et al., eds. *To Gwen with Love*. Chicago: Johnson Publishing Company, 1971. Includes poems by Danner.

Danner, Margaret. *Impressions of African Art Forms in the Poetry of Margaret Danner*. Detroit: Broadside Press, 1960.

———. *Iron Lace*. Millbrook: Kriya Press, 1968.

———. *To Flower: Poems*. Nashville: Hemphill Press, 1963.

———, ed. *Brass Horses*. Richmond: Virginia Union University, 1968.

———, ed. *Regroup*. Richmond: Virginia Union University, 1969.

Danner, Margaret and Langston Hughes. *Writers of the Revolution*. Black Forum (BB 453).

Danner, Margaret and Dudley Randall. *Poem Counterpoem*. Detroit: Broadside Press, 1966.

Hayden, Robert, et al., eds. *Afro-American Literature: An Introduction*. New York: Harcourt Brace Jovanovich, 1971. Includes poems by Danner.

Henderson, Stephen, ed. *Understanding the New Black Poetry*. New York: Morrow, 1973. Includes poems by Danner.

Pool, Rosey E., ed. *Beyond the Blues: New Poems by American Negroes*. Lympne: Hand and Flower Press, 1962. Includes poems by Danner.

Randall, Dudley ed. *The Black Poets*. New York: Bantam, 1971. Includes poems by Danner.

Redmond, Eugene. *Drumvoices: The Mission of Afro-American Poetry, A Critical History*. Garden City, N.Y.: Anchor/Doubleday, 1976.

Stetson, Erlene, ed. *Black Sister: Poetry by Black American Women, 1746–1980*. New York: Morrow, 1973. Includes poems by Danner.

Thompson, Julius E. *Dudley Randall, Broadside Press, and the Black Arts Movement in Detroit, 1960–1995*. Jefferson, N.C.: McFarland, 1999.

Ward Jr., Jerry Washington. *Trouble the Water: 250 Years of African American Poetry*. New York: Signet Books, 1997. Includes poems by Danner.

See also the Margaret Danner entry in DLB 41.

FRANK MARSHALL DAVIS
(December 31, 1905–July 26, 1987)
Kathryn Waddell Takara

In Chicago, between 1934 and 1948, Frank Marshall Davis embodied a Renaissance figure who played multiple roles: a poet, newspaper reporter, editor, columnist, labor and Civil Rights activist, photographer, radio personality, humanist, and often unacknowledged leader of the Chicago progressive community. As a Renaissance man and an African American writer, his professional task was to use the written and spoken word to expose and break down social and political barriers, destroying the construct of a preordained subordinate place for blacks in society, and to create and cultivate a literary and social consciousness. The indictment of white America as imperialistic, paternalistic, and racist remained a common theme in his writing. Davis was a courageous figure in Chicago's radical urban renaissance experience from 1927, when he began his job as the editor of the *Chicago Evening Bulletin*, until his departure for Hawaii in 1948. There, he lived, raised his family, wrote, and experimented with a few business ventures for almost 40 years until his death in Honolulu in 1987.

Frank Marshall Davis was born in Arkansas City, Kansas, in 1905. When his parents divorced the following year, he lived alternately with this grandmother and mother and stepfather, J. M. Boganey—a surname he would later use for an editorial column. Unlike many blacks, he lived in a predominately white working-class neighborhood where attitudes reflected the Jim Crow pattern of the day. To escape his loneliness and a low self-esteem due to isolation and alienation during his formative years, Davis developed a passion for books.

His stepfather (who worked the railroad and got Davis summer jobs there) introduced him to the Black Press by sharing black newspapers with Davis at an early age. After graduation from Arkansas City High School in 1923, Davis worked for a summer on the railroads in secondary service jobs, worked as a busboy in an exclusive club, and in the fall took classes in nearby Wichita at Friends University. However, he left the school when he could no longer afford to attend due to the death of his grandfather. The following year Davis moved to Kansas City and enrolled at Kansas State Industrial and Agricultural College (now Kansas State University) where he began to study journalism. He wrote and published his first poems in 1924, having received encouragement from one of his English teachers, Miss Ada Rice, who recognized his talent.[1]

In 1927, Davis moved to Chicago where he got a job as night city editor and columnist for the *Chicago Evening Bulletin*, and wrote short somewhat sensational stories for the popular market under the name of Frank Boganey. In 1928 he wrote for the *Chicago Whip* before he accepted a position at the *Gary American* in Indiana where he was a reporter, editor, editorial writer, and columnist, writing sociopolitical columns under the pseudonym "Raymond Harper."[2] He also introduced "Jazzin' the News," which was to reappear as a column when he was an editor at the *Atlanta World*.

During his first break from Kansas State Industrial and Agricultural College at the beginning of the Depression, Davis went to Gary, Indiana, for his first job in the newspaper field. Unfortunately, because of segregation (also known as Jim Crow), many blacks were denied access to most administrative and professional jobs outside of limited African American institutions and entertainment, the railroad industry, or sports.

Consequently, some of the most gifted Black intellectuals like Davis found themselves in these alternative careers. A few chose traditional careers in medicine, science, teaching, and the arts, and still others, like Davis, chose journalism. He quickly experienced another kind of alienation when he discovered the rampant corruption of big city politics, and the exploitation of employees by factory owners and "Big Bosses." His frustrations and feelings of impotence expanded as he began to understand the enormity of the problems of race and poverty.[3]

The tragic circle of domination and degradation encouraged whites to strengthen segregation and relegate African Americans to declining expectations of success. By 1929, Davis returned to Kansas State on a scholarship and resigned his position at the *Gary American*, only to return in 1930, when he wrote a column entitled "A Diplomat in Black."

In 1931, Davis was recruited by W. A. Scott to be managing editor of the biweekly *Atlanta World*, which he turned into a daily newspaper in 1932. While in Atlanta, he wrote editorials on many controversial race issues such as lynching and violence in the black community, and he had two columns: "Touring the World" and "Jazzin' the News."[4]

Davis resigned from the *Atlanta World* in 1934 and accepted a part time position at the *Gary American*, where he again used the pseudonyms "Raymond Harper" for editorials, and "Frank Boganey" or "The Globe Trotter" for his sports columns.[5]

Even before his career changes, Davis was writing poetry based in part on his experiences in the South. His poetry also reflected his love for and belief in the power of jazz. Davis used the rhythms and discordant tones and improvisation in jazz to express alienation and pain. For Davis, jazz spread like a wildfire across the country and around the world, affirming the active, creative, and rebellious presence of African Americans. Davis deemed the music of jazz and the blues unique and culturally and historically significant.

In 1933, he met with an editor in Chicago about publishing a book of poems. When Davis returned to Chicago from Atlanta, he was happy to return to this haven for musicians and national center of jazz and the blues. One could listen to Louis Armstrong, Fletcher Henderson, Jelly Roll Morton, Teddy Wilson, Lionel Hampton, and W. C. Handy, "the father of the blues," all in one night by visiting the many clubs, theaters, and cabarets on Chicago's predominantly black South Side.

Davis described jazz as "musical militancy" in an age when African Americans found it hard to speak out openly about whites. In his poem "Jazz Band," he writes:

> Play that thing, you jazz mad fools!
> Boil a skyscraper with a jungle
> Dish it to 'em sweet and hot -
> Ahhhhhhhh
> Rip it open then sew it up, jazz band![6]

Davis revealed his command of language, imagery, world culture, and history, as well as his perception that music transcends individual and national differences. The ironic tones, the cultural references, and the use of sounds to imitate jazz were common to African American writers of the period, especially Langston Hughes. Such juxtaposed themes were evident in the jazz and blues music as well as in poetry: the bittersweet tones, the staccato anger, and the raging riffs. Indeed, much of Davis's life and writing reflect the notable influence of jazz.

Davis also wrote book reviews and made innumerable speeches about town. Slowly, he gained more legitimacy and respect in the white community, expanding his voice and empowering himself through his writings and lectures. He included an African American historical context in his editorials, which were informed and occasionally erudite, and he discussed the contributions of women in his columns whenever possible. Meanwhile, in 1935, he wrote several columns like the editorial, "Behind the Headlines," and a theater column under the pseudonym "Franklyn Frank" which allowed him to "chronicle the show world and bathe in hot jazz."[7]

Through his creative writing, Davis joined the South Side Writers Group and the Allied Arts Guild, which included a variety of creative people from various fields including writers, dancers, singers, pianists, photographers, and painters. Between the years 1933–1948, he met or became reacquainted with other black intellectuals, activists, and outstanding individuals like Jack Johnson, Richard

Wright, Langston Hughes, Paul Robeson, and Gwendolyn Brooks. Davis, like Hughes, belonged to a small group of intellectuals and artists who had a deep appreciation for the common people, their colorful and original art, lifestyles, resilient spirit, dynamic energy, and oral history.[8]

As a poet, Davis's first book, *Black Man's Verse* (1935), appeared a few months before he joined the staff of the *Associated Negro Press*. By 1948, Davis had added three more books of poetry: *I Am the American Negro* (1937), and *Through Sepia Eyes* (1938), that was later incorporated into *47th Street* (1948). Davis received excellent reviews nationally by such writers and critics as William Rose Benet, William Allen White, Alain Locke, and George Schuyler. Sterling Brown also wrote in *Opportunity* (July 1936) of Davis's "strong and vivid revelations of the American scene." Davis enjoyed the positive reviews, but remained broke.

His writing exemplified the new Black Aesthetic, which valorized indigenous African American creative expressions. He urged writers to continue the quest to create, define, expand, refine, and articulate a black aesthetic. There is also a political aspect of the African American Aesthetic which has usually been characterized by an ideological and moral quality that Davis embodied. Davis recognized the need to create a language devoid of negativity directed toward African Americans. For example, he sifted through old words such as "savage," "black," "heathen," "power," "love," "friendship," "community," and "sexual" to understand their contextual usage in relation to African Americans. It was necessary to explore the worlds of white supremacy and black inferiority to better understand the reasons for their continuing oppression. This act of critique guided the central acts of perception and informed the subject matter of African American writers.

In his 1937 poem "Christ is a Dixie Nigger," Davis attacked institutional racism, the politics of domination, injustice, and patriarchal assumptions found in Christianity as an illustration of this process:

> You tell me Christ was born nearly twenty centuries ago . . . your artists paint a man as fair as another New White Hope. Well, you got it all wrong . . . facts twisted as hell . . . see?[9]

Davis rebels against traditional religious subservience. He sets forth a new discourse reflecting and re-creating the social organization in the minority voice. To Davis, African American literature, then, is often a literature of survival and necessity, a literature produced to perform a political function as much as to embody an aesthetic one. This political function has been to critique white racism and simultaneously, to demonstrate the intellectual capacity of all African American people through the agency of the artistic products of the writer, who becomes a voice of the group, presuming a collective "I" or "we."

As had other African American writers before him, Davis experimented with images, borrowing from the visual arts, music (especially jazz and jazz rhythms) and musical instruments, science, and philosophy. Like Carl Sandburg and Vachel Lindsay, Davis often used the city as a metaphor of urban life, a locus that he captured, personified, and bestowed with character, moods, and authority—a giant dwarfing human beings. In the 1948 poem "Chicago Skyscrapers," he writes:

> Here in this fat city
> Men 72 inches short
> Have frozen their dreams
> Into steel and concrete
> Six hundred feet tall.

Davis, soon became known as a social realist, writing of the pathos of frozen dreams of black immigrants from the South, and the insignificance of people dwarfed by a steel and concrete city that depersonalizes individuals. He created poetry, sometimes using rhetoric, in order to disown and sometimes destroy the lying figures of speech, the disguise of "civilized, artistic" forms, and the insidious masks of poetic diction that denigrated and segregated African Americans from the rest of society. To counter the blatant and subtle verbal attacks by white writers, Davis sometimes used critical and emotionally charged language as a counterforce to the dominant discourse, a challenge to white abusive authority and the tradition of patriarchal power.

After the publication of his first book, during the mid to late 1930s in Chicago, Davis was in contact with other African American intellectuals such as Arna Bontemps, Countee Cullen, A. Philip Randolph, and Margaret Walker.[10] Like Davis, most of these black artists were concerned with the material and emotional lives of the ordinary people that influenced the content of the African American aesthetic. Those creative writers he most respected held to a radical approach to culture and art as he did and were not afraid to speak out in a writing style that became known as social realism.

During the 1930s and 1940s, the voice of the African American writer, including Davis, often had similar tones of frustration and outrage. Common themes ranged from racism, the politics of color, miscegenation, corruption, crime, exploitation of power, big business to slave insurrections, folk tales, "passing," gender issues of African American men and women, Northern upper-class urban life, the influence of the West Indian presence in African American life, racial violence and discrimination, urban life, and the plight of the much darker-skinned person in the color-conscious community. The voice and themes also reflected the social origins, education, styles, preoccupations, daily employments, and attitudes toward the problems of living and writing in a white patriarchal society.

Bearing in mind this racial aesthetic spectrum, Davis used his writing to re-vision and reinterpret the world from a new and positive perspective of black courage and strength in order to formulate an ideology of collective hope and survival. Putting aside the "victim" mentality, Davis saw that the writer can explain and interpret the African American reality against a modern back-ground of oppression. Davis focused on exploring themes dealing with survival, environmental racism, poverty, the disorder and decay of cities, the threat of war and effect of war on the African American community, environmental destruction and decay, political repression, economic stagnation, the declining role of religion and the church, and of values such as unity, courage, persever-ance, patience and philosophical inquiry. Through deconstruction of traditional metaphors, paradigms, and ideologies—such as the word "black" and its de-rivatives, which function as a metonym for evil and negativity—Davis saw that the African American writer can reconstruct reality with African Americans as active positive forces.

When he published *I Am the American Negro* in 1937, he included a "Fore-warning" to the reader:

> Fairy words . . . a Pollyanna mind
> Do not roam these pages.
> Inside
> There are coarse victuals . . .
> Companions who seldom smile . . .
> For being black
> In my America
> Is no rendez-vous
> With Venus . . . [11]

This cosmology suggests alienation and loss but also stresses a variety of values including the various interrelationships between humans and the universe. His poem included an appreciation for the body and physical pleasures (eros), the roles of the individual and group in society, the role of the extended fam-ily, the valuation of the ancestors, and the exalting of fertility, intuition, music, rhythms, and dance.

Usually, he preferred the raw, vibrant, and sometimes explosive energy and folk tradition of the masses. He wrote poems about women ("Horizontal Cam-eos"), musicians ("Lady Day & Cabaret"), the policy man, and the exploited workers ("Mojo Mike's Beer Garden"). Davis wrote of the familiar warmth of common folk and places like the bars, poolrooms, barbershops, and other in-formal institutions. He respected the colorful dialect of the people, the new black music of jazz and the blues with its staccato rhythms and angry tones, which he incorporated into his writing style. In "47th Street," he uses dialect and standard English to show familiarity and offer commentary on a slice of life in the neighborhood with few hopes of escaping from poverty:

> "Five cents'll git you five dollars
> A dime brings ten iron men
> So gimme your gigs
> An' hope t' God you hits."[12]

Davis explored the dynamics and philosophy of black culture in order to contextualize the black experience. This will to balance, to re-create images, and to deconstruct a paradigm of white superiority was his way to help heal the bruises and wounds of racism, an almost invisible destructive force in the fabric of society, incorporated and institutionalized into American literature. He felt the need to rescue "native" culture from prejudged imaginary myths and texts that exploit and trivialize the lives of those people with darker skins and little education. He felt it was the responsibility of the writer to destroy the colonialist discourse and negative stereotypes sometimes embodied in the plantation tradition of black inferiority and misrepresented identity. Indeed, Davis observed the values of democracy subverted almost daily by callous competition, the dominant upper class, and the profit motives of capitalism in various institutions in American society.

In addition to his love of poetry, Davis also understood the value of having an African American press to construct a positive group identity and to balance the colonial themes and white perspectives of wealth, power, and status. Like other African American editors and activists, he chose to construct an alternative paradigm to white supremacy. Through the African American press, Davis presented a variety of views, including news of the African Diaspora, and analysis about and for African Americans and their communities. His columns were based on the principles of a democratic society that he fought for with each column he wrote. Not surprisingly, while Davis worked for the Associated Negro Press (ANP) in 1934, he was interested in the survival of the Black Press during hard economic times. But, he couldn't accomplish his aims if the newspaper folded.

Indeed times were hard and he came to rely on the Republican Party for extra money. Despite his reformist attitude, Davis stuck with the GOP a bit longer than most blacks and liberals who were aware of continuing discrimination and wage discrepancies between African Americans and whites in many of the New Deal programs. Davis was realistic about the pressures of survival, but he was seduced by the GOP perks and paid advertisements that he could rely on, not to mention the cash payoffs given for newspaper publicity promoting the GOP within the African American community.

Although an African American intellectual and journalist known for his militancy, Davis continued to believe in and support the principles of democracy and publish news to promote it. When an African American student, Lloyd Gaines, with the help of the NAACP, sued for admission to the law school of the University of Missouri in 1938, Davis characteristically covered the story:

> The U.S. Supreme Court in 1937 rendered its historic Gaines case decision, establishing the precedent that a state must provide equal educational opportunities for all citizens within its borders—a break in the dike of discrimination paving the way for the high court decision seventeen years later outlawing segregated schools . . . And again I want to stress that this drastic change came about only through militancy on the part of Afro-Americans.[13]

Davis then recounts how he was approached by segregationists to help establish and possibly head a professional regional school "for Nigras," even though it was in direct violation of the recent decision: "State officials had the choice of admitting Gaines to the law school or establishing a completely equal separate law school within Missouri borders. They chose the latter and shelled out taxpayers' funds to start a law school at Lincoln University, the state's Jim Crow institute of higher learning."[14] Davis publicly deplored the role of the legal system as a whore to social tradition in the perpetuation of inequality. Intellectuals like Davis met at workshops, rallies, conferences, jazz clubs, and the Allied Arts Guild where they discussed issues and strategies on combating segregation in the armed forces, the fight against fascism, the struggle against poverty, and the various federal work programs. By joining their voices and efforts, African American strength and political clout grew. They participated in the National Negro Council, the National Negro Congress (a coalition of about 40 African American organizations, which was infiltrated by the Communist Party in 1936), and the National Negro Exposition in Chicago, which included many distinguished African Americans.

The Communist Party, which appealed to many black intellectuals, encouraged a proletarian art that changed American cultural history by publishing and promoting working class and African American artists. The Communist Party's influence rendered the thirties and forties a very exciting and creative period in the development of diversity in American culture and the arts. There was a sense of excitement and solidarity between artists and political activists.

During the forties, Davis's slow, intense voice made him a much sought-after public speaker in Chicago at events both political and cultural. His network of African American and white radical friends was as extensive as an African American "Who's Who," ranging from those in the most influential communities to the regulars at Mojo's Cafe. Davis credits Richard Wright for acquainting him with a number of white writers, almost all militantly leftist, who encouraged Davis in his forthright writing and oratorical style. Davis was known and respected as an outspoken editor and critic of Jim Crow, white supremacy, and the inequalities of capitalism. He managed to live fairly well during this period in spite of many obstacles, not the least of which was his low salary, standard for the African American newspaper business.

Davis became another significant pioneer in the long history of African American journalism following a tradition which began in the early 1800s when abolitionists used the printed word and the power of circulation to communicate freedom and equality among the public.[15] Confronted with hostility and rejection, lacking access to most power organizations, the African American press and its writers had a critical role. They had to analyze their situation, indicate possible solutions, mediate between various factions, and transform a negative self-image by educating the public to African American successes and failures.

White-superiority theories advanced by leading white anthropologists and sociologists fed African American intellectuals' discomfort. The many legal tentacles of justice attacked self-esteem and served to detract from a positive sense of identity. Even in the havens of home, library, and job, there was no easy escape from such theories.

To counter these spurious theories, Davis used journalism to document the movements of individuals and the community, reporting on oppression, liberation, failure, and success during the Chicago Renaissance. There were major breakthroughs in race relations in sports, which he recorded and commented on in his forums, poetry, prose, and editorials in the Associated Negro Press. For example, Davis attacked the color bar in sports. Since African Americans could traditionally aspire to earning a decent living and a measure of success in only a limited number of fields, Davis wrote of the difficult obstacles even in those fields for promising talent. He wrote about trials and tribulations of the heavyweight boxing champion Joe Louis, who, like Jack Johnson before him, was an early symbol of success and power to African Americans, especially youths.[16]

Davis even documented the segregation in most sports, especially football, basketball, and boxing. In 1939 he covered the first annual National Professional Basketball Tournament played by the two best African American teams in the nation: New York Rens out of Harlem, and the Harlem Globetrotters out of Chicago. He also wrote about how outstanding players on these African American teams met their demise once the teams were integrated, or how they were lured away to formally all-white teams with promises of higher salaries, better publicity, and more power.[17] Furthermore, journalism provided Davis with a forum for his ironic commentaries, analyses, and critiques of society. Although his salary was often minimal, the press card gave him access to almost any event, as well as free drinks, invitations to parties and dinners, and even occasional bribes, which ranged from booze and cash to women and clothes, all "customary" in Chicago, a city known for its graft and corruption.

Between 1933 and 1945, Davis was a reporter for, and later executive editor of, the Associated Negro Press. Along with his columns, he often handled publicity for other organizations, such as the National Negro Congress and the Republican Party. As a columnist, he had access to famous musical and sports personalities: Ray Nance, Cab Calloway, Oze Simmons, and Joe Louis.[18] He also penned stories on dancers and even a few impersonators. Davis was also a Pan-Africanist who often reflected upon the ideologies of Marcus Garvey and W. E. B. DuBois. Davis prided himself on extensively reading national and international newspapers on a daily basis to inform his editorials and essays concerning blacks globally. Clearly, Davis's particular responsibilities at the ANP were enormous, but by all accounts, he was an excellent editor.[19]

One of his more significant contributions as an editor during the Chicago Renaissance was his input to the 1941 National Conference of Negro editors in Washington, D.C., ironically scheduled the day after the attack on Pearl Harbor. Although Davis was unable to attend, his associate and colleague, Claude Barnett, presented his suggestion for volunteer integrated fighting units during World War II to General George Marshall, chief of staff, in the presence of representative editors and members of the NAACP gathered from all over the country. Even though the proposal was initially vetoed, "the question of an integrated army was officially on the record before many witnesses. Immediately after the close of the conference, the NAACP launched a nationwide petition campaign, creating strong sentiment for the proposal and obtaining thousands of signatures demanding mixed army units."[20]

Not surprisingly, Davis's talent and commitment to the African American community were most evident when he was working as editor of the ANP. It was here that he showcased his "versatility as a newspaperman."[21]

The Second World War and its aftermath produced peculiar tensions with American race relations to which Davis was acutely sensitive. Davis continued to observe and comment on racism on a regular basis through the news stories he covered, editorials, and poetry. In poems like "Nothing Can Stop the People," he observed how the rise of fascism in Europe brought early concern to African Americans, especially after Italy invaded Ethiopia. The irony of the color bar for African American troops serving in a war to combat (among other things) fascist racism struck Davis as particularly absurd. He exposed the ill treatment of African Americans, such as lack of promotions, inadequate training, and quick assignment to active combat duty. Consequently, during the Battle of the Bulge when the American army integrated its first group of voluntary soldiers, both white and black who were willing to downgrade their rank to private, Davis liked to take some of the credit for the breakthrough.[22] Like most African American men, Davis smoldered daily at his exclusion from the social order, the lack of economic opportunities and political power available to African Americans. He raged at the hypocrisy of a democratic "system" that bred corruption at all levels regardless of color. He observed that greed and the desire for power, bribes, and perks were as abundant as restaurants in the city but recognized that it always seemed to be the whites who became wealthy. To soothe the barbs of racism and injustice, he turned to musical entertainment in the evenings where he found solace and others like himself, seeking to forget the pain and humiliation of daily living. The blues and jazz vibrated between the rhythms of exhilaration and despair.

To help relieve the tensions and disparities of race and class, Davis wrote, began to drink more, and unconsciously laid the foundation for what later evolved into an Epicurean philosophy of life. In a poem called "Creed for Hedonists," Davis wrote:

> Yesterday is a bucket of bones . . .
> Tomorrow stirs in the womb of Now . . .
> Only today is real! . . .
> For who can surely say . . .
> He will be around . . .
> To dine tomorrow?[23]

He embraced or slipped into a "seize the day" philosophy and a hedonistic lifestyle when he was not working, perhaps in part to erase the humiliation of exclusion and to compensate on the individual level for the inequalities of a society where African Americans anchored the socioeconomic scale.

In the North, in large cities like Chicago, some African Americans who became too disillusioned with the system often turned to various forms of hedonism. Others found hope in black nationalism and various brands of separatism, espoused by early emigrationists like Martin Delany, and later Marcus Garvey and the Black Muslims. Even the Communist Party for a while advocated self-determination and a separate region for African Americans in answer to the strong nationalistic sentiment that was sweeping the masses in the community. Davis, however, disagreed because "at that time the prevailing goal was complete integration, not separation into a black nation."

Many Black nationalists sought to relocate African Americans somewhere away from whites, either in a separate state or country; some, like Garvey, preferred to think of returning to Africa. The significance of Garveyism on the Chicago Black Renaissance and the African American intellectual cannot be ignored. Garvey's message to the urban masses was one of black awareness and self-esteem, and the "race men" who followed in the 1930s and 1940s, including Davis, saw the necessity of the race to be aware of its history, heritage, and culture. Garvey's injunction, "Black man, know thyself," was a theme that was to appear in various ways in Davis's life and writings. However, Garvey's message of racial purity did not find a place in Davis's ideology.

Nevertheless, Davis resented being deprived of full participation in the democratic system, which had been so liberating for most Euro-Americans and so hypocritically oppressive and confining to most African Americans. Indeed, he was forever seeking more effective ways to fight racism and injustice in a system where the laws, angels, and God from which they came, seemed to be all white. The African American cosmology reflected in the discourse of the intellectuals became more and more accusatory and mistrustful of white America.

Eventually, despite his independent efforts as a journalist, Davis came to believe that an individual, even through poetry and editorials, was not strong enough to effect change in American society's racial politics. Then he decided to join hands with others fighting racism like the labor movement. When Davis joined the powerful Chicago labor movement, he took a large risk by calling attention to himself in a period rife with suspicion and censorship by the federal government. Although involvement with the labor movement was Davis's opportunity to promote better wages and conditions for both African Americans and whites, most significantly this movement allowed Davis and other African American intellectuals to mix freely in interracial situations, thereby opening doors for those who came after. It was a chance to heal some of racism's wounds.[24]

During the Chicago Black Renaissance, there was yet another arena besides music, labor, and government where African Americans and whites could meet and share on intellectual and social levels. This was in liberal political circles and coalitions, which often included Socialists, Communists, university types, and representatives from labor unions. Like many creative and intellectual African Americans of the thirties and forties, Davis regularly circulated in these so-called "radical political groups," which sponsored rallies, forums, poetry readings, and petitions, and generally declaimed the existing inequalities of class and race. These activities served in the long run to effect a change in the national political consciousness of the public, heighten the awareness of the values and issues of democracy, and lay the groundwork for the Civil Rights Movement which was yet to come. Davis inevitably associated with people connected with the Communist Party, since they were most likely to be involved in civil rights, labor, art, and the fight for equality.[25]

Around 1943, Davis became interested in photography thanks to his friend and neighbor, Leo, who provided him with inexpensive equipment and a camera. He quickly and proficiently learned how to develop and print, and soon turned his attention to the human body, especially nude women. Considering that the African American female tended to be less constrained by African American men and her community in the personal realm of sex, Davis was not surprised to have an ample supply of African American women models when he began to develop his passion for photography. Although promiscuity was frowned upon, and the family structure was respected, circumstances (historically and contemporarily) often created a more independent attitude in poor black communities toward sexual expression.[26]

Davis enjoyed the power of controlling people's images and observing their vanity and desire possibly to be immortalized in film. His preference for African American women at this point in his life seems obvious, or perhaps it is no more than his appreciation of the beauty of the human form. He was later to distinguish himself in this field and win several national awards.

In 1944, Davis began teaching in a university setting as a guest lecturer. He participated in an annual series of outstanding lectures on race relations at Northwestern University and spoke to the sociology classes of Dr. Melville J. Herskovits, author of *The Myth of the Negro Past* (1941) and renowned anthropologist. Davis was fascinated by the complexities and issues of American identity and acknowledged that African Americans were "culturally and biologically . . . a goulash of Europeans, Africans, and American Indians, with African dominant." Imprisoned by the politics of color, he was understandably most fascinated by the carryovers of surviving Africanisms, represented in rhythms and atonalities.[27]

Not surprisingly, Davis taught the first classes on the history of jazz offered at the Abraham Lincoln School in 1945, commonly known as the Little Red Schoolhouse, because so many controversial events occurred there. In his lectures, he enjoyed explaining how the African musical traditions blended with European melodic concepts. The connectedness of traditions and experience are evident when Davis explains how the European instruments and the African American rhythms and tone combined to create a syncretistic expression evident in jazz.[28]

The Chicago Renaissance afforded artists the access to information so that they could present correspondences, explore cross-cultural connections, and study world history and cultures. He was aware that composers like Stravinsky and Bartok were influenced by jazz. Davis attributed the uniqueness of African American expression called "soul" to the emotional content that was created by a people who had suffered, both economically and racially: "This music vividly illustrated how these Baptist hymns originating in England had been completely transformed by African musical patterns retained." He also taught about the functional aspects of African and African American music, the role of the work song, the blues, and the political role of spirituals in the Underground Railroad. He unveiled the creativity and genius of the often poor, self-taught, African American musicians.[29]

Although Davis distinguished between New Orleans Jazz as African American and Dixieland as white jazz, he felt strongly that this period of history was one of the first stages of integration and true democracy in America. Davis credited John Hammond, a white liberal who fought against discrimination in the music industry, for helping to integrate the jazz bands. Not only did Davis write poetry, give lectures, teach classes, and write columns about jazz, but in 1945 he also developed and hosted a popular jazz radio program that he called "Bronzeville Brevities" on WJJD in Chicago.[30]

Ironically, due to the location of Northwestern University, his students were almost all white. Since the course was offered at night, most African Americans were afraid of getting harassed for being found in a white community after dark. Not only was the African American community denied access to his courses due to the politics of race and place, but Davis observed that jazz also soon fell victim to exploitation as white musicians copied and softened the rebellious rhythms and tones of the African American musicians, rendering it more palatable and less offensive to the white public. Soon, with a modified product, white jazz artists were making much better money than most of the African American composers, musicians and performers.[31]

As Davis moved within liberal and radical circles in 1945, he soon discovered that many white women and men wanted integration, but perhaps for dubious reasons. Both secretly and openly harbored desires to have sexual contact with educated African American males. This was perhaps due to sexualized and primitive stereotypes about African Americans that were carryovers from slavery time when blacks were used as breeders and sexual objects. Davis himself was curious about sexual contact with whites, and this inquisitiveness led him on a path that was eventually to end in marriage and exile in Hawaii.[32]

Davis saw the need for unity between the working class and wealthy of both races as well. Being an optimist and a social realist, he tried to bridge this economic gap between both groups. In 1944, he wrote "Peace Quiz for America":

> Say, Mister, you with the white face, you toiler
> Come over here and let's talk.
> Maybe we both got the same disease
> But different symptoms;
> Mine pops out in humiliating race discrimination
> Yours is a rash of class distinction and poverty
> Coming from the same infection;
> Fascism and profit grabbing [33]

The original poem titled "War Quiz for America" offended the white power structure and Communists alike, although most African Americans, even the more conservative ones like Roy Wilkins of the NAACP could relate to Davis's attack on white supremacy, patriarchy, discrimination, and the hypocrisy of democracy, fascism, poverty, sharecropping, perpetual debt, exploitation, violence, colonialism, and imperialism. Unfortunately, for too many African Americans, the trauma and psychological damage of this cultural isolation and economic alienation manifested in a neurosis of inferiority and socioeconomic impotence, sometimes juxtaposed with a fierce determination to succeed and assimilate into the dominant white society, despite catastrophic rejection.

However, with the growing consciousness of the New Negro and the international movement of negritude, the significance of color in the African American community declined in proportion to education. Nonetheless, Davis seemed to exclude himself from the social gatherings of the African American bourgeoisie, perhaps because of his democratic idealism and global vision, his unwillingness to become involved in trivia, competition, gossip, vanity, false pride, and hypocrisy.[34] Being a "race man," Davis saw the compelling need to lift up the masses, and for the group to work together as a whole. When Davis decided to align himself with political groups, he knew that his life was going to change from the comfortable immunity of being a reporter. Although he did not belong to the John Reed Club as did Richard Wright, Davis joined the League of American Writers, a national united front organization which was mobilized by the alarming rise of power of Hitler and Mussolini. It published a controversial booklet, *Writers Take Sides*, which soon drew the attention of the House Un-American Activities Committee (HUAC) to those involved, including Davis. Davis said all the writers in the League were listed in Washington as "un-American" for opposing the Rome-Berlin Axis. Since he considered himself a free thinker and was obviously not afraid to speak out against what he thought was wrong, Davis did not want to forget the struggle against racism at home for the sake of national unity.[35]

However, having lived in the Deep South, Davis could not see the relevance of the Communist plan for self-determination and nationalism in the Black Belt. He knew that the majority of southern African Americans had never heard of Communism or Stalin. Indeed, the prevalent view at that time expressed by most Civil Rights groups was that the way to equality was through integration and assimilation, not the Communist brand of nationalism and a separate black nation. Eventually, the African American newspapers became as anti-Communist as the rest of the white press, but Davis was not so quick to dismiss the Communist Party and their call for equality and brotherhood.

Davis's public activities were numerous, and he was often associated with groups considered to be radical. He spoke on anti-Semitism for the Democratic and Republican Platform Committees in 1944, was on the National Committee to Combat Anti-Semitism, the National Civil Rights Congress, and the Board of Chicago Civil Liberties Union which fought bigotry in the public schools.

Bigotry was particularly bad in Chicago because many European immigrants in the area adapted and maintained the national pattern of prejudice. Being the lowest on the social totem pole due to their recent arrival, European immigrants looked for a scapegoat to elevate themselves, gain status and favor with the dominant whites, and justify their usurpation of African American jobs.

Davis also frequently spoke to young members of American Youth for Democracy, organized and chaired conferences on black-white unity, helped to organize white collar workers, addressed mixed audiences on African American history, worked with the Boy Scout movement, and spoke before various CIO unions. Davis even shared panels with Adam Clayton Powell, Paul Robeson, Marshall Field, and Mike Quill, head of the Transport Workers Union.

In 1944, FBI agents were asking others about Davis, as they had previously questioned him about other African American leaders who were perceived as a threat to national security. He made a game out of misleading them, and when asked about specific individuals whom he considered conservative, Davis would tell the agents that they were "dangerous" and a "rotten security risk." On the other hand, if the subject were militant, Davis would again mislead the agent as much as possible, labeling the individual in "glowing terms." The FBI continued to keep an eye on Davis and to monitor his activities even after the "Red scare" and his move to Hawaii.[36]

Moreover, the Office of Censorship kept an eye on African American newspapers across the nation and scrutinized Davis's editorials, especially during the war years, since he regularly reported on discrimination, race riots, inequality of promotions, inferior training, and disproportionate casualties in the armed forces. However, with the death of Roosevelt in 1945, the progressive coalition of liberals, leftists, and African Americans broke up.

By 1946, the FBI tried to curb Davis's controversial editorials about racism and violence in the armed forces, alleging that his stories eroded national unity and gave the enemy propaganda to be used against the United States. They regularly questioned Davis's friends, producing a "dossier" on him and alleging activities that Davis was to have attended in an attempt to frighten or intimidate him. Davis says he was quick to respond, "Stop the prejudice and the stories will stop themselves." He exposed the inefficiency of the FBI agents in his writing. Davis was not easily intimidated; however, most people cowered in fear for their families and careers and, if they found themselves on the blacklist, they sometimes sacrificed others for their own freedom. Davis stood up, condemned HUAC and called their intimidation fascist. However, his irreverence and hard-hitting racial candor marked him for the HUAC and the FBI, influenced his subsequent career choices, and eventually evoked in him a kind of nihilistic attitude toward the world of politics.

With the rise of African American nationalism and growing race pride, instability between African Americans and whites became increasingly evident, except in a few liberal and radical integrated circles. Even labor unions split under the pressure, as anti-Communist pressure started to build. Before long, Republicans regained control of Congress and national policy.

The rapid deterioration of relations between the United States and Russia and the increased Red-baiting again created tension and suspicion between former allies. Davis appealed to Ben Davis Jr. of the Communist Party, encouraging his efforts to maintain a connection with the African American press since both opposed racism and supported civil rights, equal opportunities, antilynching legislation, and abolition of the poll tax. The idea was apparently not accepted and soon the African American press was almost as violently anti-Communist as the general press.[37]

One bright spot amid this oppressive atmosphere was the creation and promotion of *The Chicago Star* in 1946, a citywide labor weekly, financed by various labor unions, progressives, liberals, and ghetto dwellers. Davis was the editor until 1948, while maintaining his editorial position at the *Associated Negro Press*. The editorial column "Frank-ly Speaking" began at *The Chicago Star*. The aim of this publication was to heal the rift between the various groups and promote a policy of cooperation and unity between Russia and the United States. The paper backed Henry Wallace, whose platform included full employment for all citizens in peacetime, as an independent candidate for president in 1948. However, when it seemed that too many Democrats would desert the Party and vote on the Independent ticket, Truman spoke out for an innovative Civil Rights program, and many African Americans turned back to the Democratic Party, affording Truman a victory. Unfortunately, under Truman, old antagonisms at home and abroad flared and the Cold War began. Conservative forces of the "industrial-military complex," a term coined by Eisenhower in his Inaugural Address ("Military-Industrial Complex"), regained control, and thus support for Civil Rights subsided.[38]

Because it had been common for almost everyone with a conscience to associate with the Civil Rights struggle, labor, and or leftist intellectual thought, the HUAC felt compelled to censor anything or anyone they could not control. In 1947, Davis again began to receive pressure from Rankin's House Un-American Activities Committee. He writes: "With the rapidly deteriorating political situation and the growth of the witch hunts during the Joe McCarthy period, a number of libraries removed my books from their shelves and stored them in the basement along with other controversial literature until the nation began returning to sanity."

When Davis decided to move to Honolulu in December 1948, he escaped the open antagonism—hostile stares, jeers, and insults—toward his interracial marriage. Several articles in Hawaii's newspapers, the *Honolulu Star-Bulletin* and the *Honolulu Advertiser* announced the imminent arrival of Frank Marshall Davis and his wife, Helen Canfield. He was tired of being hounded for his association with radicals and the discrimination of white supremacists. He was tired of African American Nationalists, the Hearst press, and racist propaganda. Perhaps more importantly he fled the unbearable insularity in his desire to evolve toward a more collective, objective human communication. He moved to a place where he did not have to always be on guard or feel impotent in his repudiations of injustice. In Hawaii, Davis found dignity, a sense of belonging and acceptance, and a new dimension of freedom, which permitted him to experiment further in the realm of a multicultural, seemingly more democratic, environment.[39]

In December 1948, several articles in Hawaii's newspapers, the *Honolulu Star-Bulletin* and the *Honolulu Advertiser*, announced the imminent arrival of Frank Marshall Davis and his wife Helen Canfield. Upon his arrival to the islands, Davis had at last found dignity and respect as a man and as a human being. Although Davis realized that race relations in Hawaii were not perfect, he enjoyed "the shifting kaleidoscope" of people. He became familiar with the subtle forms of discrimination and, on occasion, the more blatant ones as well, like the segregated housing facilities at Pearl Harbor, particularly with Civilian Housing Areas 2 and 3.[40] Davis also became familiar with the hostilities between Okinawans and Japanese, and various other inter- and intraethnic group prejudices and discrimination. That year he also sent a series of Associated Negro Press articles from Hawaii.

After a few months' stay, Davis and his wife decided to settle permanently in Hawaii, and they bought a house on Mt. Tantalus overlooking Honolulu. Davis had already contacted labor leaders Harry Bridges and Koji Ariyoshi. He felt welcome and assumed that finding a job would not be difficult, especially with all of his experience and expertise in journalism. Shortly thereafter, Davis tried to get a salaried job with the large local daily, but when word got around that Davis was prolabor, the paper, controlled by the big Five quietly ignored him; the huge International Longshoreman's Workers Union (ILWU) strike was imminent, pitting labor against the Big Five.[41]

Economically, this did not bode well for Davis because he was soon to have five children to support and Helen's inheritance was at risk if her mother were to discover she had married an African American. However, because he felt that, since his arrival in the islands, he had at last found dignity and respect as a human being, Davis was slow to complain. He had resolved that even politics was never to take his dignity away from him again. Fortunately, he was soon offered a weekly column, his reprised "Frank-ly Speaking," in the *Honolulu Record*, the local labor newspaper affiliated with the International Longshoremen's Warehousemen's Union edited by Ariyoshi, and he continued to write until 1958.[42]

When Davis became a columnist for the *Honolulu Record*, the newspaper was just beginning to document the imminent strike of the ILWU and the subsequent breaking up of the monopolistic power of the Big Five over the various immigrant labor groups, including the Japanese—the most powerful and radical—Chinese, Filipino, and Portuguese. For Davis, this was the kind of political ferment and struggle between the powerful and powerless that he thrived upon and enjoyed writing about. He commentated on the impact of the union movement on the plantation economy in the postwar Honolulu scene.[43]

His eye for class analysis led him to discern quickly the exploitative role of big business and landowners in the lives of the ethnic nonwhite minorities, and Davis wrote several strong poems expressing his observations and analyses. While living in Chicago, he had already written an editorial on the infamous Massie case, where a white wife of a military officer stationed on Oahu falsely accused local men of rape, so Davis knew that Hawaii residents experienced virulent episodes of racism. He observed the discrimination in certain bars and restaurants and the reluctance of the legislature to pass a Civil Rights law with the excuse that by passing such a law, it would admit to having a problem.[44]

Because his job as a columnist at the *Honolulu Record* did not include salary and benefits, Davis started a paper supply business, Oahu Papers, on Sand Island, in 1959, which sold advertising items (calendars, novelties, gifts) to local business firms. But when the warehouse mysteriously burned in 1961, he lost his assets. Davis experienced the forced sale of his property on Tantalus to cover the losses. This coincided with the labeling of Davis as a labor sympathizer and Communist. He wrote a formal response to the increased pressure from the House Un-American Activities Committee.

After the fire and the Tantalus fiasco, and to escape the negative forces pressing upon him in Honolulu, the Davises invested in property on the Windward side of Oahu, first in Kahaluu, then in Hauula where the family remained for seven years, during which time the couple had several children. Davis seemed to feel welcome in Hauula, and only moved to the leeward Kalihi valley in 1956 for its convenience and proximity to hospitals, schools, and work in Honolulu. Ironically, even within the relative freedom of Hawaii, a world away from Chicago, there were still racial tensions, again within the islands' peculiar mixture of race and class origins, and continued pressure on Davis from the HUAC on Communism charges. Davis and Helen struggled to survive in the cosmopolitan lifestyle they preferred. In 1963, he announced to ANP owner, Claude Barnett, that he had begun working on his autobiography, *Livin' the Blues: Memoirs of a Black Journalist and Poet*, which was published posthumously in 1992.

Since his job prospects grew no brighter and his wife's inheritance dwindled, Davis finally decided to write a sex novel, *Sex Rebel: Black*, to earn extra money. Helen went to work part-time between pregnancies creating illustrations for an advertising agency. Davis worked as a correspondent for the ANP, wrote and published a few poems, and tried to complete his explicit manuscript, all the while wrestling with alcoholism.

Consequently, when Davis decided to stay permanently in Hawaii, he concomitantly chose a life of isolation from the continent and much he had previously considered valuable: his illustrious career and the African American struggle for freedom and equality. Nevertheless, he did not stop writing. Blacks living in Hawaii at this time had a certain fluidity between several ethnic groups that afforded Davis a unique platform from which to observe and discuss the consequences of the post–WWII Hawaiian economy. He wrote of the parallels of laws and influences between the southern plantation system and plantations in Hawaii, as well as parallels between Blacks and Hawaiians. His writing provided insight into colonial techniques and strategies for dividing minority groups, and on discrimination and racism in Hawaii. Davis provided a significant voice in the historical process of Hawaii's economic development, intergroup relationships, and changing social consciousness.[45]

In 1973, he returned to visit the mainland United States for the first time in twenty-five years and read poetry at Howard University; Atlanta University; Chicago's DuSable Museum, sponsored by his old friend, Margaret Burroughs; the University of California at Berkeley; and San Francisco's African American Historical Society. The following year, he returned again to read poetry in Southern California's Orange County. In 1976, Margaret Burroughs produced a small chapbook of Davis's jazz poems, *Jazz Interludes: Seven Musical Poems*, and in 1978 another chapbook, *Awakening and Other Poems* appeared.[46]

Davis moved to Waikiki in 1969. Between 1979 and 1987 when he died, Davis was a largely ignored figure in the Hawaiian Islands, except for his family (five grown children and his ex-wife Helen) and a few friends. He continued to write, working on his autobiography, *Livin' the Blues*, published posthumously; an unpublished manuscript that he called *That Incredible Waikiki Jungle*; and his mostly unpublished collection of poems on "working women" called *Horizontal Cameos*. He kept up with the world and local news by keeping his TV constantly on, and finally moved to a small cramped apartment on Kapiolani Boulevard, where he received a few favored friends and for whom he occasionally cooked. He died suddenly of a massive heart attack one bright July night, and his ashes were scattered from a familiar mountain near the University of Hawaii.

Davis is a representative of the African American intellectual of his time. He was informed by and spoke to the concrete human issues of his immediate ethnic community and of the larger world. He also was concerned with the search for identity and his place in the world. His works have included a significant political discourse similar to the multimedia responses of most African American artists; indeed, many great artists have made political statements. As a mentor to the young Barack Obama in the 1970s, as described in Obama's *Dreams from My Father*, Davis posthumously entered the media debates surrounding Obama's social and political backgrounds during the 2008 presidential campaign. In most of his works, Davis speaks out against racism and discrimination, and his readers have been multiethnic, multicultural, and multinational.

His world view remained leftist in intention and execution. Davis was antibourgeois, anticapitalist, anti-imperialistic, and revolutionary—not only in language, style, and form, but in his presentation of capitalism, communism, fascism, and sexism in a poetic genre. He was a militant poet whose sociopolitical work anticipated that of many contemporary young rap singers and jazz musicians.

The quest for physical independence, spiritual wholeness, economic power, and equality were predominant themes in the life and writings of Frank Marshall Davis. He refused to conform to reified roles of class behavior. He felt no obligation to illustrate the race's potential in his every move. He did not fear and avoid gaucheries, vulgarities, and other behavior patterns typically associated with "black behavior." The act of writing for many African American writers is still a political action, a protest, and condemnation ("writing is fighting") of Eurocentric domination.

The African American writers of the 1930s and 1940s have served as models for those to come. Davis's vision has lasted because he was neither imitator, nor eunuch, nor Lazarus. His irreverent humor, vituperative tongue, stark pictures, occasional disillusionment, and distilling interpretations did not hide the optimist he was until the time of his death in July 1987. His broad thoughts and primordial connections will survive his reputation as a gruff cynic. In his death, Davis left a secret for those who remain: rhythm, movement, and creative acts. His spirit in living has transcended the anger and bitterness of his past. He has become the embodiment of a transformative experience. African Americans like Frank Marshall Davis have sought to affirm their own humanity through writing and to provide new themes of equality, pluralism, reconciliation, humanity, and healing to literature, at the same time striving to maintain ethnic integrity and to preserve positive cultural differences.

Notes

1. Davis, Frank Marshall. *Livin' the Blues: Memoirs of a Black Journalist and Poet*, edited by John Edgar Tidwell. Madison: University of Wisconsin Press, 1992, 79.

2. Ibid., xx.

3. Ibid., 57, 174–75.

4. Ibid., 180.

5. Ibid., 235.

6. Davis, Frank Marshall. *Black Man's Verse*. Chicago: Black Cat, 1935, 34–34.

7. Davis, 1992, 228.

8. Ibid., 238.

9. Davis, *I Am The American Negro*. Chicago: Black Cat, 1937, 28–29.

10. Davis, 1992, 239.
11. Davis, 2002, 57.
12. Davis, *47th Street: Poems*. Prairie City, Ill.: Decker Press, 1948, 15.
13. Davis, 1992, 260.
14. Ibid., 259.
15. Bardolph, Richard, *The Negro Vanguard*. New York: Vintage, 1959, 62.
16. Davis, 1992, 255.
17. Ibid., 231–33.
18. Ibid., 229.
19. Ibid., 250, 267.
20. Ibid., 270.
21. Ibid., 231.
22. Ibid., 231.
23. Davis, 2002, 171–72.
24. Davis, 1992, 277.
25. Ibid., 278.
26. Ibid., 230–31.
27. Ibid., 290.
28. Ibid., 287–89.
29. Ibid., 288.
30. Ibid., 286.
31. Ibid., 284.
32. Ibid., 199–200.
33. Davis, 2002, 137.
34. Davis 1992, 34.
35. Ibid., 279, 283.
36. Ibid., 323–26.
37. Ibid., 282.
38. Ibid., 298.
39. Ibid., 312.
40. Ibid., 314.
41. Ibid., 323–24.
42. Ibid. 313.
43. Ibid., 312–13.
44. Ibid., 313.
45. Ibid., 320.
46. Davis, 2002, xix.

For Further Reading

Bardolph, Richard. *The Negro Vanguard*. New York: Vintage, 1959.
"Betty," "Arline," Frances," "Louise," "Olive," "Rita." *Ramrod 7*, edited by Joe Balaz. Honolulu: Iron Bench Press, 1986, 16–21.
Davis, Angela. *Women, Culture, and Politics*. New York: Vintage, 1990.

Davis, Frank Marshall. *Black Man's Verse*. Chicago: Black Cat, 1935.

———. *I Am The American Negro*. Chicago: Black Cat, 1937.

———. *Through Sepia Eyes*. Chicago: Black Cat, 1938.

———. *47th Street: Poems*. Prairie City, Ill.: Decker Press, 1948.

———. *Sex Rebel: Black Memoirs of a Gash Gourmet*. Published as Bob Greene. San Diego: Greenleaf Classics, 1968.

———. *Livin' the Blues: Memoirs of a Black Journalist and Poet*, edited by John Edgar Tidwell. Madison: University of Wisconsin Press, 1992.

———. *Black Moods: Collected Poems*, edited by John Edgar Tidwell. Urbana: University of Illinois Press, 2002.

DuBois, W. E. B. *The Souls of Black Folk*. New York: Signet, 1968.

Duffy, Bernard I. *The Chicago Renaissance in American Letters*. East Lansing: Michigan State University Press, 1964.

"Duke Ellington," "Louis Armstrong," "Billie Holiday." *Black World* (February 1974): 22–25.

Fanon, Frantz. *Black Skin, White Masks*. New York: Grove, 1967.

Foner, Eric. *America's Black Past*. New York: Harper, 1970.

"Frank Marshall Davis." Interviews with Davis and others. *Rice and Roses*. Audiotapes and transcripts prior to edited version, 1986 [completed in 1987] Honolulu: PBS.

"Frank-ly speaking." *Honolulu Record*, 1949–52.

Frazier, E. Franklin. *Black Bourgeoisie: The Rise of a New Middle Class*. New York: Free Press, 1957.

Gennari, John. "'A Weapon of Integration': Frank Marshall Davis and the Politics of Jazz." *The Langston Hughes Review* 14: 1,2 (1996): 16–33.

Hellman, Lillian. *Scoundrel Time*. Boston: Bantam, 1983.

Herskovits, Melville Jean. *The Myth of the Negro Past*. New York: Harper, 1941.

Horizontal Cameos. Unpublished typescript. n.p., 1970s.

Killens, John O. *Black Man's Burden*. New York: Trident, 1965.

Lemelle, Anthony J. "Beyond Black Power: The Contradiction between Capital and Liberty." *The Western Journal of Black Studies* 10: 2 (1986): 70–76.

Obama, Barack. *Dreams from My Father*. New York: Crown Publishers, 1995.

Record, Wilson. *Race and Radicalism: The NAACP and the Communist Party in Conflict*. Ithaca: Cornell University Press, 1964.

Redding, Jay Saunders. *On Being Negro in America*. New York: Bobbs-Merrill, 1951.

———. *The Lonesome Road*. Garden City, N.Y.: Doubleday, 1958.

Reed, Ishmael. *Mumbo Jumbo*. Garden City, N.Y.: Doubleday, 1972.

Rodgers, Lawrence R. "Richard Wright, Frank Marshall Davis and the Chicago Renaissance." *The Langston Hughes Review* 14: 1, 2 (1996): 4–12.

———. Personal interviews with Kathryn Waddell Takara. 1983–87.

This Is Paradise. Comp. by Kathryn Waddell Takara. Unpublished poems, 1986.

Tidwell, John Edgar. "Ad Astra Per Aspera Frank Marshall Davis." *Kansas History* 18: 4 (1995–96): 270–83.

Tidwell, John Edgar, ed. *Black Moods*. Urbana: University of Illinois Press, 2002.

———. "I Was a Weaver of Jagged Words": Social Function in the Poetry of Frank Marshall Davis." *The Langston Hughes Review* 14: 1,2 (1996): 65–78.

"To a Young Man" and "Black American." *Black World* (May 1975): 46–48.

"To a Young Man," "Moonlight at Kahana Bay," "Tale of Two Dogs." *Ramrod 8*, edited by Joe Balaz. Honolulu: Iron Bench Press, 1987, 2–5.

"Touring the World." *Atlanta World*. Editorial column. *Atlanta Daily World*. His other columns included "Speakin' bout Sports" and "Jazzin' the News," 1931–33.

Werner, Craig Hansen. *Playing the Changes*. Urbana: University of Illinois Press, 1994.

West, Cornel. *Prophesy Deliverance!* Philadelphia: Westminster, 1982.

West, Stan. "Tip-Toeing on the Tightrope: A Personal Essay on Black Writer Ambivalence." *African American Review* 32: 2 (1998): 285–91.

See also the Davis entry in *DLB 51: Afro-American Writers from the Harlem Renaissance to 1940*.

RICHARD DURHAM
(September 6, 1917–April 24, 1984)
Patrick Naick

voice: (On cue) Oh freedom, oh freedom
  Oh freedom over me
  And before I'd be a slave
  I'd be buried in my grave
  And go home to my Lord and be free.
announcer: (On cue) *Destination Freedom.*
(music: Theme up and under)
announcer: In cooperation with the *Chicago Defender*, WMAQ
  brings you *Destination Freedom*, new radio series dramatizing the
  great democratic heritage of the Negro people, part of the pageant
  of American history.

Thus began each episode of *Destination Freedom*, Richard Durham's most significant contribution to the annals of African American history. In its two-year broadcast, *Destination Freedom* celebrated the achievements of African Americans both past and present in an effort to counter the racist stereotypes dominating the airwaves. From this program and much of Durham's earlier work, one sees an avocation for civil rights years before the formal start of the Civil Rights Movement. What is also apparent is his commitment to the city of Chicago, a city with its own legacy of racial segregation and discrimination, in his attempts to educate his audience and encourage social change. Durham's relationship to Chicago embodies the atmosphere then surrounding much of the South Side's "Bronzeville." Culturally, Black Chicago was in the midst of a renaissance, burgeoning with literature, art, the social sciences, and the institutions serving as their forums. His work attests to the renaissance objective that improved race relations might emerge from artistic endeavors, and thus throughout his career, Richard Durham depicted the lives and accomplishments of numerous African Americans in a medium largely devoid of an African American presence. Concerned with more than the injustices faced by African Americans as a group, Durham specifically addressed those offenses inflicted upon women, and his writing portrays strong women who battled against discrimination. Although his programs were locally broadcast and his listeners were exclusively Chicagoans, he wrote of issues recognizable around the world, and his contributions to the renaissance helped to define the local cultural aesthetic.

Born September 6, 1917, in Raymond, Mississippi, as Isadore Richard Durham, Richard Durham moved with his family to Chicago's South Side in his youth. As with many other African American families, the Durhams were among the waves of Southern migrants moving to the northern industrial centers of Detroit, Cleveland, and Chicago in search of better opportunities and a life free of Jim Crow. Raised in Chicago and a resident until his death in 1984, Richard Durham attended Hyde Park High School and later Northwestern University. His interest in writing began when he won first prize in a poetry contest conducted jointly by Northwestern University and Mundelein College. This interest was encouraged through his friendship with Langston Hughes, who urged him to polish and publish his poetry. Consequently, several of Durham's poems appeared in print on the pages of such publications as the *Pittsburgh Courier*, the *Chicago Defender*, *New Masses*, and *Opportunity*. The September 1939 issue of *Opportunity* featured his poem "Death in a Kitchenette," of which Langston Hughes commented, "What a swell subject for tremendous poetry the South Side is! I want to live there sometime & write a whole series of South Side poems."[1] The poem, which typifies the lives of many impoverished African Americans living in South Side tenements, places Durham as a contemporary of Frank Marshall Davis and Gwendolyn Brooks. In its content, Durham's commitment to local social change is obvious, and this continued attention to the South Side and the plight of its residents firmly situates his work in the canon of Chicago writing.

Richard Durham began his formal writing career as a writer for the Illinois Writers' Project (IWP), a branch of the Works Progress Administration established to support writers during the Great Depression. During his time with the project, Durham wrote, "Don't Spend Your Money Where You Can't Work," an essay highlighting the campaign for equal employment opportunities led by the Black Press. Perhaps most importantly, he received training as a radio scriptwriter writing for the IWP program, *Legends of Illinois* (1940), which recounted "true events in Illinois history" and was heard locally on WCFL radio. While writing for *Legends*, Durham was also employed by the Art Institute of Chicago to write a program dramatizing the lives of world-renowned artists. Broadcast on WMAQ as *Art for Art's Sake* and on WGN as *Great Artists* (1940–1941), Durham wrote forty scripts dealing with artists and the works they produced. Though not a formal historian, Durham did substantial research on his subjects in preparation, creating scripts rooted in historical scholarship and possessing a literary dimension. "The Story of Auguste Rodin," "Goya: The Disasters of War," and an adaptation of Nathaniel Hawthorne's *The House of Seven Gables* were among several of the fifteen-minute episodes airing on Saturday mornings from 9:15–9:30 CWT.

While with the IWP, Durham's scripts began to show signs of a strong political consciousness. One example is, "A Matter of Technique," a sketch set in France shortly after Nazi occupation that uses the life of Pablo Picasso to comment boldly on issues of violence and domination under fascism. This political consciousness motivated him to write a letter to the editor of the *Chicago Sun* six months later. As a reaction to their "Parade" article, "What will we do with the children of fascism?" Durham asserts, "But suppose our postwar leaders did not think it necessary to teach tomorrow's children that no race is inherently superior or inferior. Suppose that after the war the races of the world were not given equal freedom or equal rights. Then plainly the dying and suffering being done in Europe and Asia is worse than useless. Our victory would be empty and senseless."[2]

The war years were a time of uncertain optimism for African Americans. The "Double V" campaign, a campaign originating in the *Pittsburgh Courier* calling for an end to fascism at home and abroad, was strongly supported in Chicago by many who felt the U.S. government's hypocrisy of fighting to secure the rights of the oppressed overseas while denying equal rights to African Americans could no longer endure. Influenced by this political climate, Durham's work, like that of much of the art emerging from Bronzeville, began to speak of injustice and often reflect this sense of hope.

After his time with the Illinois Writers' Project, Richard Durham spent the year 1942–1943 at work on *At the Foot of Adams Street.* This program, cosponsored by the Art Institute of Chicago and the *Chicago Tribune*, and heard locally on WMAQ radio 670, showcased current artists on exhibit. Following *Adams Street*, Durham worked for two of the nation's leading African American publications, as an editor for *Ebony* and as a feature writer and page editor for the *Chicago Defender.* In the four years Durham worked for the *Chicago Defender* he wrote a total of 508 special articles and stories, many of great significance including his coverage in 1945 of the birth of the United Nations at the San Francisco Conference. That same year, he won a Page One Award given for outstanding newspaper stories by the American Newspaper Guild for his series of *Chicago Defender* articles on race discrimination in war plants, an issue of particular relevance to Chicago because such plants had initially lured many African Americans to the city.

Durham continued to hone his craft during what is hailed as radio's Golden Age (1930s–1950s), when radio was being used as both source of entertainment and as a political medium. As radio was becoming more popular and more powerful, many African Americans hoped the medium would promote positive images of black America and black American life. To their dismay, most of the depictions of African Americans broadcast on the radio relied on and further propagated prevalent racial stereotypes. As African Americans migrated to northern urban industrial centers and developed distinct communities, they soon began seeking accurate portrayals of themselves on the air. This was, co-incidentally, a time when the radio industry itself was in flux, becoming less a national and more a local medium as networks turned their attention to television. Because radio was slowly being usurped by national television in the late 1940s, programs designed specifically for black audiences began appearing as advertisers realized the local market potential. Chicago, Philadelphia, and New York City broadcast programs pertaining to the collective experience of African Americans. The local media provided the platform, where the national media ignored the situation as African American artists strove to promote positive race relations in a time of racial tensions. These changes within the radio industry afforded Durham the opportunity to use his post-IWP programs, *Democracy U.S.A.* and *Destination Freedom*, as vehicles to replace negative representations with more realistic depictions of African Americans.

In 1946, Richard Durham began *Democracy U.S.A.* Produced in cooperation with the *Chicago Defender* and CBS-owned WBBM's Department of Education, this weekly fifteen-minute series sought to tell the "living story of American unity" by dramatizing the lives of exceptional African Americans. The program, Durham's first major radio experience, presented biographical sketches of people such as Dr. Ulysses Grant Dailey, chief attending surgeon at Chicago's Provident Hospital; Dr. Charles Wesley, president of Wilberforce University; and Albert W. Williams, president of Unity Mutual Insurance Company, all of whom made important contributions to the African American community. In the episode, "Albert W. Williams, the president of Unity Mutual Insurance Company," Durham relayed experiences in Albert Williams's life that led to his resolve to provide insurance to all in need regardless of race. At the end of the episode, Williams appeared to advocate for the creation of a Fair Employment Practices Law in Illinois. Such stories were characteristic of the type Durham wanted to tell—accounts of black individuals who were confronted with and overcame social and political injustice. These stories, as lived experiences or artistic retellings, were the essence of the renaissance. Although he gained valuable experience writing scripts for *Democracy U.S.A.* and the program won sixteen awards and a special citation from Harry Truman, Durham would later disapprove of the program over what he viewed was a demeaning representation of African Americans. It was with this that he turned his attention to new projects.

In 1947, Durham began writing a black soap opera for WJJD entitled, *Here Comes Tomorrow.* Sponsored by the Metropolitan Insurance Company of Chicago and airing three times weekly, *Here Comes Tomorrow* told the story of the Redmonds, an African American family and their everyday struggles with racial prejudice and discrimination. At the time, it was the only Black serial in existence. The political consciousness that emerged with *Democracy U.S.A.* had solidified as Durham used the series to stage direct attacks on racism. In its short run, it was hailed by critics. One critic observed: "*Here Comes Tomorrow* might well be one of the best things that has come along to further understanding between the races."[3] Acclaim also came in the form of *Billboard Magazine's* award for best dramatic show on the radio in 1948.

Destination Freedom premiered on June 27, 1948. It is undeniably Richard Durham's most mature radio series. Durham, then in his midtwenties, was even bolder in expressing his social agenda than he had been in his prior work. The thirty-minute program aired weekly in Chicago on NBC-owned WMAQ. However, after the program's first few months, its sponsor, the *Chicago Defender* withdrew its financial support. *Destination Freedom* continued to air because the Urban League of Chicago assumed sponsorship in an attempt to further positive race relations. In the series' original run, 1948–1950, Durham wrote 105 scripts, all which were produced by Homer Heck and performed by an interracial ensemble cast of young actors that included Oscar Brown Jr., Janice Kingslow, Fred Pinkard, and Wezlyn Tilden. All of the actors were members of Chicago's liberal Du Bois Theater Guild, and they, along with Durham, brought to the series a sense of "crusade," a passion indicative of the renaissance. As Durham stated, "at that time you were running with the wind in your face [so] there was that thing of a crusade spirit—of a drive to get the story over."[4]

The purpose of the *Destination Freedom* was didactic—to demonstrate the achievements of African Americans past and present while contradicting the black caricatures offered by radio programs such as *Amos and Andy* and the *Jack Benny Show*. At the same time, it advocated civil rights. Through strong storytelling and characters providing positive examples of self-achievement, Durham attempted to lessen the inequalities of race and gender.

For *Destination Freedom* as with *Democracy U.S.A.*, Richard Durham wrote biographical sketches based on the experiences of prominent African Americans. Selecting historical and contemporary subjects, Durham dramatized the accomplishments of Crispus Attucks, Mary McLeod Bethune, Jackie Robinson, and Gwendolyn Brooks, among others. Durham's accounts lacked sentimentality; facts took precedence over emotions in order to advance freedom and equality. *Destination Freedom* was particularly striking in its concern for gender discrimination and women's rights. Durham saw parallels between the exploitation of women and the exploitation of African Americans and felt that women could identify equally with his characterizations of men as those of his women. As he told an interviewer, "The women of the world of all races and creeds in their upward swing toward real emancipation, find it natural to identify their striving with the direction and emotional realism in Negro life today."[5] He selected as subjects strong, independent women such as Sojourner Truth, Ida B. Wells, and Katherine Dunham because of their determination to battle intolerance founded on racism and sexism. He also tackled issues pertinent to African Americans living locally in Chicago, such as housing and the origins of the Chicago Urban League. In "Housing: Chicago," the realities of the inadequate housing of many of the city's African Americans is portrayed. At one moment in the episode, the protagonist Jack Warren and his family seeking new housing are refused because of their race, a common scenario for many Black Belt families, "Thus were, the Jack Warrens denied the right to rent; the right to move and live and grow and stretch out free not only for one man, but for his children born and yet to come."[6]

Destination Freedom won awards from the Institute for Education by Radio, the City of Chicago's Commission on Human Relations, and the National Conference of Christians and Jews, and it received a special citation from Illinois Governor Adlai Stevenson. These accolades speak to the importance of the program in combating racism, as well as granting recognition to the artistic creativity occurring among Chicago's Black artists. In view of radio broadcast history, the forcefulness and revolutionary tone of the scripts is impressive. The quality and content of these scripts speaks to the new direction African American art was assuming in the city. As a product of the renaissance, *Destination Freedom* is an imaginative channel to positive racial representation. As J. Fred MacDonald rightly asserts, "Throughout the last half of the 1940s, then, Richard Durham wrote and produced what undoubtedly was the most consistent and prolonged protest against racial injustice by a single talent in all the popular arts."[7]

Destination Freedom as a series was discontinued in 1950. Facing an increasingly conservative Cold War climate, WMAQ canceled the program and replaced it with a revised version hosted by "Paul Revere," who lauded the accomplishments of whites rather than African Americans. After the cancellation of the original *Destination Freedom*, Durham remained in Chicago but left radio work to become the National Program Director for the United Packinghouse Workers of America. Intent on advancing the cause of African Americans within the union, Durham's agenda was met with resistance and he was forced to resign in 1957.

From 1964–1970, Durham worked with Elijah Muhammad as editor of the newspaper column, *Muhammad Speaks*. In the early 1970s he began editorial work for Muhammad Ali on what would become Ali's autobiography, *The Greatest* (1975) and created and wrote scripts for the local television show, *Bird of the Iron Feather*, funded by the Ford Foundation. Debuting in 1970 and airing on WTTW television, the show captured the tense relationship between police and local residents that existed in the mid-1960s. Though airing for only thirteen weeks, the importance of the program was recognized and it later received an Emmy Award. Richard Durham spent the remainder of his life living on Chicago's South Side, living in the same section of the city he had moved to as a child. He died April 24, 1984.

Richard Durham's work was, in many ways, ahead of its time. His collaborations with Elijah Muhammad and Muhammad Ali clearly situate him as a prominent figure in the radical phase of the Civil Rights Movement. However, his prior work, with its attention to the civil rights of African Americans and those abroad, displays an enduring interest and critique of inequity. Using this interest as the basis for much of his radio scripts, Richard Durham exemplifies the prolonged process that culminated in the modern Civil Rights Movement, demonstrating that such concerns emerged prior to the 1950s. His varied characterizations and political aims epitomize the mission of the Chicago Renaissance. Broadcasting in an era when radio programming was almost exclusively operated by whites, Richard Durham gave a voice to the voiceless and replaced racial stereotypes with historically accurate accounts of African American achievements.

Notes

1. Richard Durham Papers. Richard Durham's papers, including the transcripts from *Democracy U.S.A.* and *Destination Freedom*, are in a collection at the Vivian G. Harsh Research Collection of Afro-American History and Literature, Woodson Regional Library, Chicago. Tapes of the *Destination Freedom* broadcasts are held at the Schomburg Center for Research in Black Culture, New York Public Library, and the Museum of Broadcast Communications, Chicago.

2. Ibid.

3. Ibid.

4. MacDonald, J. Fred. "Radio's Black Heritage: *Destination Freedom*, 1948–1950." *Phylon* 39 (1960): 66, 67.

5. Durham interview with Cordier, Cordier, 25.

6. Durham, "Housing: Chicago," in *Destination Freedom*, 7.

7. MacDonald, J. Fred, ed. *Richard Durham's Destination Freedom: Scripts from Radio's Black Legacy, 1948–50.* New York: Praeger, 1989, 7.

For Further Reading

Art for Art's Sake/Great Artists. Radio Series. (1940–41).
At the Foot of Adams Street. Radio Series. (1942–43).
Bird of the Iron Feather. Television Series. (1970).
Cordier, Hugh. *A History and Analysis of Destination Freedom.* Evanston, Ill.: Northwestern University Press, 1949.
Democracy U.S.A. Radio Series. (1946).
Destination Freedom. Radio Series. (1948–50). 32 episodes available on 1 mp3 CD at OTRCAT.com.
Here Comes Tomorrow. Radio Series. (1947).
Legends of Illinois. Radio Series. (1940).

MacDonald, Fred J. *Don't Touch That Dial!: Radio Programming in American Life, 1920–1960*. Chicago: Nelson-Hall, 1979.

———, ed. *Richard Durham's Destination Freedom: Scripts from Radio's Black Legacy, 1948–50*. New York: Praeger, 1989.

Savage, Barbara Dianne. *Broadcasting Freedom: Radio, War, and the Politics of Race, 1938–1948*. Chapel Hill: University of North Carolina Press, 1999.

Editorial Work

Chicago Defender (1943–46).
Ebony (1945–46).
Muhammad Speaks (1964–70).
The Greatest (1975).

LORRAINE HANSBERRY
(May 19, 1930–January 12, 1965)
Lisbeth Lipari

Although chiefly known as an award-winning dramatist and author of the classic Broadway hit *A Raisin in the Sun* (produced in 1959), Lorraine Hansberry was a significant voice in the Civil Rights era. Beyond her playwriting, Hansberry wrote journalism, essays, and public letters, and gave speeches as well as radio and television interviews. Her chosen genre of drama, however, may have been shaped at least in part by the Chicago Renaissance school's stylistic emphases on urban speech and spoken language. Like the Chicago Renaissance's principal figure, Richard Wright, who wrote for the *Daily Worker* and *New Masses*, Hansberry's early work as a journalist enabled her to draw upon underlying Black aesthetic traditions that employ spoken language as a means of producing what Lawrence Rodgers claims as Chicago's unique heritage as the home base of the "new vocabulary of documentary realism, sociological detail and violent black agency"[1] with which to portray Black urban America. As a younger member of the Chicago Renaissance, Hansberry's work drew upon both aesthetic and political traditions of the city such as the poetic inspirations of blues and jazz, the political and sociological realism of Wright, and the modernist, womanist breadth of Marita Bonner. Doris Abramson notes the similarity between Hansberry's *A Raisin in the Sun* and Wright's *Native Son* by observing that both works are set in Chicago's South Side, that both of the central male characters (Walter Lee Younger and Bigger Thomas) work as chauffeurs and that in reaction to racism both characters explode, albeit in different ways.[2] Like Bonner, and her Chicago predecessor Ida B. Wells-Barnett, Hansberry's writing took on the triple jeopardy of race, class, and gender oppression with uncompromising vitality and conviction. Whether exploring topics such as African colonialism or American racism, her writings spoke against the poison of all oppressions, including sexism and homophobia. Jewelle L. Gomez writes that "many critics have neglected the full ramifications of Hansberry's life as a cultural worker" and that contemporary scholars have yet to "rediscover the depth and breadth of Hansberry's social and political concerns and to see how they are manifest in her work."[3]

Although Hansberry died tragically in 1965 of cancer at the age of 34, her dramatic writing continues to be read, produced, and discussed throughout the world. In addition to her plays *A Raisin in the Sun* (1959), *The Sign in Sidney Brustein's Window* (1965), Robert Nemiroff's posthumous adaptation of her writings *To Be Young, Gifted and Black* (1969), and her posthumously published *Les Blancs* (1972), *The Drinking Gourd* (1972), and *What Use Are the Flowers* (1972), Hansberry was an active writer and speaker. As a public intellectual, she wrote public letters to *The Ladder*, the *New York Times*, and *The Village Voice*. Her writings, interviews, and speeches were published in the the *Black Scholar*, *Commentary*, *Cross Currents*, *Ebony*, *Esquire*, *Freedom*, *Freedomways*, *Liberation*, *Masses and Mainstream*, *The Monthly Review*, *Negro Digest*, *Theater Arts*, and *The Village Voice*. She gave speeches at New York's Town Hall, the American Academy of Psycho-Therapists, the American Society of African Culture, the United Negro College Fund, and, at age 22, to the Inter-Continental Peace Congress in Uruguay. In 1959, her television interview with journalist Mike Wallace was broadcast on national television. That same year, a Chicago station broadcast a debate between Hansberry and the film director Otto Preminger about his direction of the film *Porgy and Bess*. That year she was also interviewed by Chicago radio host Studs Terkel who inquired extensively about her political views as well as her hit play, *A Raisin in the Sun*. In 1961 she participated in a radio symposium on "The Negro in American Culture" with, among others, James Baldwin and Langston Hughes. In 1963 she took part in a historic meeting between civil rights leaders and U.S. Attorney General Robert F. Kennedy. According to James Baldwin (1979), Hansberry ended the meeting after Kennedy denied her request for a moral commitment. Baldwin describes that "The meeting ended with Lorraine standing up. She said . . . 'I am very worried about the state of the civilization which produced that photograph of the White cop standing on that Negro woman's neck in Birmingham.'"[4]

Born May 19, 1930, Hansberry's middle-class family lived in Chicago's South Side Black neighborhood where the minority middle-class and professional Black population lived in ghettos side by side with Blacks of all classes. She was the youngest of four children and her father, Carl Augustus Hansberry, was a real estate broker and businessman who founded one of the first Black banks in Chicago. Her mother Nannie Perry Hansberry was a former school teacher originally from Tennessee whose father had been born a slave. Both parents were active in community life, politics, and civil rights organizations such as NAACP and the Urban League. Carl Hansberry was a U.S. Marshall who also ran for Congress, and both he and Nannie were, as were most northern Blacks of their generation, Republicans. In fact, when Hansberry was four years old, Chicago Democrat Arthur W. Mitchell, the first Black democrat elected to Congress in American history, defeated incumbent Republican Oscar Stanton De Priest, who was the first African American elected to Congress in the twentieth century. Throughout her youth, the Hansberry home was a gathering place of influential African American leaders and artists such as W. E. B. DuBois, Langston Hughes, Duke Ellington, and Paul Robeson. Another frequent visitor to the home was Hansberry's uncle, William Leo Hansberry, a professor of African history at Howard University and widely considered a distinguished scholar of Africa. Professor Hansberry, aka "Uncle Leo," often brought African students and exiles with him on his visits to the Hansberrys' home and later had a university in Nigeria named after him. The frequent visits of these prominent figures influenced the development of the young Hansberry's intellectual, political, and artistic sensibilities and commitments.

Hansberry's life underwent significant transition when in 1937 her father bought and moved the family into a home in the racially restricted White Chicago neighborhood of Woodlawn. Not long after the Hansberrys moved to the new home, the neighbors responded with violence, forming a mob in front of the house and throwing bricks, one of which nearly hit the eight-year-old Hansberry. At one point, the NAACP had to provide armed guards to protect the family. With the assistance of the NAACP, Carl Hansberry proceeded to fight assiduously against the restrictive racial covenant. In his legal case, *Hansberry v. Lee,* Carl Hansberry claimed that the Woodlawn covenant infringed upon his Fourteenth Amendment rights to due process. Initially both the District and State Supreme Courts evicted the Hansberrys and upheld the neighborhood association's claim to maintain a racially restrictive covenant that barred African Americans from owning or living in the neighborhood. But in 1940 the lower court decisions were overturned by the U.S. Supreme Court, which ruled that White neighborhoods cannot legally exclude African Americans. Unfortunately, because the case was resolved on a legal technicality having little to do with the Hansberrys' claim, other race-based housing restrictions continued in Chicago. Bitter over continuing racism in the United States and especially over the racial discrimination and segregation of the U.S. military during World War II—where Lorraine's brother Carl Jr. served in a segregated unit—Carl Hansberry bought a home in Mexico City, where he planned to move the family. Unfortunately, he died of a cerebral hemorrhage in 1945 at the age of fifty-one before the family could move out of the country. The family had returned to South Side Chicago where Hansberry graduated from segregated Englewood High School in 1948. These experiences of race hatred were deeply formative for Hansberry, who, twenty years later, drew upon the Woodlawn incident to form the basis of her play *A Raisin in the Sun.*

In 1948 Hansberry left Chicago to attend college at the predominantly white University of Wisconsin in Madison, unlike the rest of the Hansberry family who had attended Howard University. At Wisconsin she studied journalism, theater, and the visual arts. Racism prohibited her from living in the women's dormitory, so she lived off-campus in a residence called Langdon Manor, where she was the first Black student resident.[5] Although she enjoyed the personal independence and political opportunities college offered, she was less enthusiastic about science courses and preferred instead art and writing courses. In her extracurricular activities, Hansberry was powerfully influenced by a production of Sean O'Casey's play about Irish peasants, *Juno and the Paycock*, as well as her readings of Henrik Ibsen and August Strindberg. While in college she also joined the Young Progressives of America, with whom she worked on the 1948 presidential campaign of third-party candidate Henry Wallace. Although she was disillusioned with politics when democrat Harry Truman was elected, she herself was elected chair of the Madison chapter of the Young Progressives. She also joined the Labor Youth League. During this period, Hansberry began cultivating an interest in theatrical stage design and also studied painting in Chicago and Mexico. In 1950 she left college for New York, where she believed her prospects as a writer lay. Hansberry's first publication was a 1950 poem published in *Masses and Mainstream* and titled "Flag from a Kitchenette Window." In the poem, the twenty-year-old Hansberry depicts the contradictions between American racism and its hypocritical ideals of freedom and democracy from the perspective of a South Side Chicago on Memorial Day: "Southside morning / America is crying / In our land: the paycheck taxes to / Somebody's government / Black boy in a window; Algiers and Salerno / The three-colored banner raised to some / Anonymous freedom, we decide / And on the memorial days hang it / From our windows and let it beat the / Steamy jimcrow airs."[6] These sociopolitical themes, including the nascent critique of African colonialism, persisted as central concerns of her writing throughout her career.

After moving to New York City in 1950, Hansberry soon joined with radical Black and Communist activists (including her future husband), and in 1951 began working at *Freedom*, the progressive Black paper founded by Paul Robeson and edited by Louis Burnham. In 1952 she was named an associate editor of the paper. She served first as writer and reporter and for a short while as associate editor, until 1955. John Oliver Killens, who worked at Robeson and DuBois's Council on African Affairs (which was housed in the same building as *Freedom* on 125th Street in Harlem) describes her when she first came to New York. "I remember her as a brilliant young woman . . . as an artist she saw the paradox and irony of every human being's sojourn on this earth, especially where Black Americans are concerned."[7] *Freedom* was a short-lived Black newspaper started in 1950 at a time when both Robeson and DuBois were being harassed, ostracized, and silenced by fallout from the fanaticisms of Cold War McCarthyism.[8] In his biography of DuBois, Manning Marable's[9] description of *Freedom* suggests that it may have been one of the few, if only, Black newspapers of the 1950s not capitulating to the censorious pressures of the red scare. The paper featured regular columns by Robeson, DuBois, and Alice Childress. Nevertheless, it was a small paper with meager financial resources. In spite of holding fundraisers and putting out frequent desperate pleas for support, the paper folded in 1955. During her career at *Freedom*, Hansberry wrote on a wide variety of topics including book and theater reviews, local labor and civil rights news, and international news, including articles about burgeoning independence movements in Africa, including Ghana, Egypt, and Kenya. These news stories, in addition to the influences of her Uncle Leo's scholarship and DuBois's Pan-Africanism, may have influenced the later writing of her unfinished play about African colonialism, *Les Blancs*. She took a year-long seminar on Africa with DuBois and wrote a paper entitled "The Belgian Congo: A Preliminary Report on Its Land, Its History, and Its People."

In 1953 Hansberry married Robert Barron Nemiroff, a son of Russian Jewish immigrants, graduate student in English at NYU, political activist, and song-writer, whom she met on a picket line protesting racial discrimination in college athletics. After the marriage, the couple moved to an apartment in Greenwich Village. At that time Hansberry quit her full-time job at *Freedom* (although she continued to write articles) in order to focus on playwriting. While working at a variety of temporary jobs such as typist, department store clerk, waitress, host-ess, cashier, and theatrical production associate, she worked on several plays, a novel, and an opera. In 1956, Nemiroff and his friend Burt D'Lugoff wrote a hit song, "Cindy, Oh Cindy," that generated enough income to enable Hansberry to quit her temporary jobs and focus on writing full-time. One year later, in 1957, she completed her first play, *A Raisin in the Sun*. When she read the draft to Nemiroff and D'Lugoff, as well as their mutual friend, the theatrical impresario Philip Rose, the response was overwhelmingly positive. Rose agreed nearly im-mediately to produce the play and began soliciting financial investments, actors, and directors. After considerable struggle to raise enough money to produce the play, wildly successful productions were staged in New Haven, Philadelphia, and Chicago, and finally New York. Janet Tripp quotes the play's director Lloyd Richards reflecting on how close the play came to not being produced: "It took more than a year to raise the money. There were more investors in *A Raisin in the Sun* than in any production that has ever appeared on Broadway. The big-gest investment was $750; the average was $250 . . . several times the project was almost jettisoned."[10] When the play finally opened at Broadway's Ethel Bar-rymore Theater on March 11, 1959, it ran for an astonishing 538 performances and Hansberry won the New York Drama Critics' Circle Award for Best Play of the Year, becoming the first Black playwright and fifth woman to win the pres-tigious award. The 1959 production of *A Raisin in the Sun* was the first play in Broadway history to be written by an African American woman, as well as the first to be directed by an African American, Lloyd Richards. The cast included future film star Sidney Poitier making his first Broadway appearance, as well as Ruby Dee, Claudia McNeil, and Diana Sands. Since its 1959 opening, *A Raisin in the Sun* has been translated into dozens of languages and performed thousands of times in hundreds of cities all over the world. In the United States, the play has had five significant runs: two theatrical Broadway runs in 1959 and 2004, a 1973 run as a musical, a 1961 film, and a PBS TV production in 1989. Each of these five productions garnered great critical acclaim and not an inconsiderable number of award nominations and awards.

Written when Hansberry was twenty-seven years old, the play *A Raisin In the Sun* tells the story of a five-member intergenerational African American, South Side Chicago family. The family are at odds about how to spend the $10,000 life insurance benefit of their recently deceased father who had been a railroad porter. The family matriarch, Mama (Lena) Younger (played by Mc-Neil), wants the family—which includes her college-student daughter Beneatha (played by Sands), her son Walter Lee (played by Poitier) who works as a chauffeur, her daughter-in-law Ruth (played by Dee) who works as a maid, and her adolescent grandson Travis (played by Glynn Turman)—to move out of their cramped ghetto apartment and into a spacious home in a White neighborhood surrounded by trees and grass. Referring to inadequate ghetto housing and usurious ghetto prices, Lena says the home "is the nicest place for the least amount of money."[11] Although three of the four adults in the family work fulltime, collectively they can barely afford the dingy two-bedroom apartment in which Travis must sleep in the living room on the couch. Mama also wants to use some of the money to support Beneatha's plans to attend medical school. Walter Lee, however, is opposed to Mama's plans and wants instead to invest the life insurance money in a liquor store business and from there climb what looks to him like the ladder of sweet success. The central conflict of the play occurs when, after Mama had placed $3500 as a down payment for the house in the White neighborhood, Walter Lee is swindled out of the remaining $6500 that Mama has entrusted to him for bank deposit. In the face of this tremendous financial loss, the family is next confronted with the insulting "offer" of the White neighborhood association to buy the family out of their contract on the house and thereby keep them from moving into the neighborhood. The climax of the play revolves around the family's decision—delegated to Walter Lee by Mama—either to surrender to racism and sell the house or to reject the offer and move toward an uncertain and contested future in the segregated and racist neighborhood. In addition to the central conflicts of racism, the play also explores themes such as African liberation (introduced through Beneatha's revolutionary Nigerian suitor, Asagai), Black class snobbery (introduced through Beneatha's rich boyfriend George Murchison), abortion (introduced through

Ruth Younger's unwanted pregnancy), sexism (woven throughout the play), and intergenerational tensions that followed the great migration of southern Blacks to Chicago. These tensions are introduced, for example, by Mama's slapping Beneatha for doubting the existence of God and for Mama's observation, in response to Walter Lee's claim that money is "life," that: "Once upon a time freedom used to be life—now it's money. I guess the world really do change."[12]

Remarking on the play's surprising success, James Baldwin wrote that "I had never in my life seen so many Black people in the theater. And the reason was that never before, in the entire history of the American theater, had so much of the truth of Black people's lives been seen on the stage."[13] The play was often performed to standing-room–only audiences that, Abrams notes, frequently included as many Black as White audience members. Theater producer and director Woodie King Jr. describes how the play "opened doors within my consciousness that I never knew existed. There I was in Detroit's Cass theater, a young man who had never seen anywhere a Black man (Walter Lee) express all the things I felt but never had the courage to express—and in a theater full of Black and White people, no less!"[14] Yet in spite of the play's longstanding success, the critical reception of *A Raisin in the Sun* was mixed. On the one hand, thousands of audience members, Black and White, enthusiastically celebrated the play. Some White critics from major New York newspapers described the play as "honest drama" that "has no axe to grind" and "will make you proud of human beings." Harold Cruse quotes a *New York Times* reviewer who wrote that "The leading character is, to be sure, a Negro, but his principal problems have nothing to do with his race. They are pre-eminently the problems of the human being as such, for this is, so far as I can recall, one of the first consciously existentialist novels [sic] to be written by an American."[15] Scholars such as Lloyd W. Brown in 1974 and, later, Ben Keppel in 1995, note how these universalist interpretations obscured the play's criticism of racism as well as of capitalism itself. As Keppel notes: "*A Raisin in the Sun* is an intriguing play, one that appropriates a traditional narrative form to press a point entirely alien to the mainstream of 1959: that the liberation of the American Negro required confronting economic forces and arrangements that according to Hansberry, racism exists to perpetuate. This, however, was not the reason for the enthusiasm with which the play was greeted by the White critical establishment."[16]

Contrary to the majority of White critics, Black Arts critics such as Amiri Baraka (then Leroi Jones) and Cruse as well as some White critics and writers such as Nelson Algren, criticized *A Raisin in the Sun* as bourgeois and assimilationist drama. Baraka wrote that "young militants" like himself "thought Hansberry's play was part of the 'passive resistance' phase of the movement, which was over the minute Malcolm's penetrating eyes and words began to charge through the media with deadly force. We thought her play 'middle class' in that its focus seemed to be on 'moving into White folks' neighborhoods.'"[17] Critic Harold Cruse, author of *The Crisis of the Negro Intellectual*, wrote that the play's very success as well as the "patronizing critical exhuberance" of theater critics itself was proof that it was unthreatening to White racism: "Not a dissenting critical note was to be heard from Broadway critics, and thus the Negro made theater history with the most cleverly written piece of glorified soap opera I, personally, have ever seen on a stage."[18] Even as recently as 1990, the Black film scholar Donald Bogle claimed that "the film celebrated integration and ultimately paid homage to the America of free enterprise and materialism."[19] This struggle over the interpretation of *A Raisin in the Sun* reflects similar struggles experienced by African American writers of both the Harlem and Chicago Renaissance, who were torn between politically conservative but aesthetically radical choices and aesthetically conservative but politically radical choices.

At the time of the play's opening run, Hansberry objected to both the majority White and the Black Arts interpretations of the play and said so in a number of published essays and interviews. She argued that the tensions between the characters of Mama and Walter Lee in the play should not simply be seen, as some White critics suggested, as the expression of "typical" U.S. intergenerational struggle. Nor should they merely be seen, as some Black critics suggested, as the expression of integrationist and assimilationist aspirations. Instead, she argued that the tensions evoke the complex and historically grounded experiences particular to Black Americans that emerge at the intersection of capitalism, slavery, reconstruction, northern racism, and sexism. When Studs Terkel asked how she would answer the critics' claim that *A Raisin in the Sun* is not *really* a Negro play, she said: "I believe one of the soundest ideas in dramatic writing is [that] in order to create the universal, you must pay very great attention to the specific. Universality, I think, emerges from truthful identity of what is. In other words, I have told people that not only is the play about a Negro family, specifically and culturally, but it's not even a New York family or a southern Negro family—it is specifically South Side Chicago. To the extent we accept them and believe them as who they're supposed to be, to that extent they can become everybody. So I would say it is definitely a Negro play before it is anything else."[20] In a letter to her mother, Hansberry writes that *A Raisin in the Sun* is "a play that tells the truth about people, Negroes and life and I think it will help a lot of people to understand how we are just as complicated as they are—and just as mixed up—but above all, that we have among our miserable and downtrodden ranks—people who are the very essence of human dignity."[21]

In more recent times, former Black Arts critic Amiri Baraka has rescinded his earlier criticisms of the play. In a 1995 essay commemorating the twenty-fifth anniversary of *A Raisin in the Sun*, Baraka wrote: "The truth is that Hansberry's dramatic skills have yet to be properly appreciated—and not just by those guardians of the status quo who pass themselves off as drama critics."[22] In his 1972 introduction to *Les Blancs*, Julius Lester noted that Malcolm X had placed a down payment on a suburban home just "a few weeks before he was murdered. And one surely can't accuse Malcolm of bourgeois aspirations."[23] Lester commented on the play's criticisms of materialism and the "American Dream": "As Blacks acquire more and more of America's material offerings, are they, too, going to be transformed by their acquisitions into mindless consumers like the majority of Whites? Or are they going to continue to walk the path of righteousness like their forebears?"[24] Lester argues that contrary to arguments made by former Black Arts critics, the play in fact rejects the myth that Blacks want to be integrated with Whites. He says the fact that the neighborhood the Youngers plan to move into "is White is the least important thing about it. It merely happened to be the neighborhood in which Mama Younger could find a nice house she could afford."[25] Other recent scholars have further explored the play's political criticisms of race, class, and gender. Neal A. Lester explores how the play offers a critique of sexist Black manhood and male chauvinism "at a time when collective Black identity was couched in the values of rhetoric and Black manhood."[26] Lester argues that both Walter Lee and Asagai press Beneatha to adopt traditional gender roles, such as when Walter Lee ridicules Beneatha's desire to become a doctor and Asagai sees her as "his American cultural conquest, a symbol of his own vainglory."[27] Keppel describes how the play explored the relationship between racism and economic exploitation and "sought to re-establish the salience and legitimacy of the leftist and Marxian critique that had been publicly purged from American discourse during the early fifties . . . The crux of the problem as Lorraine Hansberry saw it was American capitalism itself."[28]

Two days after the 1959 production of *A Raisin in the Sun* opened, one of the play's producers, David Susskind, began soliciting interest in a film version of the play. By the fall of 1959, Columbia Pictures had bought the rights to *A Raisin in the Sun*, hired Hansberry to write the screenplay, and was in search of a director. According to Steven Carter, Hansberry's first choice of director was Sidney Lumet who had directed the award-winning courtroom social drama *12 Angry Men* in 1957 and later went on to direct three play-to-cinema translations, two by Eugene O'Neill and one by Tennessee Williams. But the studio ultimately contracted with the young film director Daniel Petrie as well as the original cast.

Hansberry's original screenplay of *A Raisin in the Sun*, which was not published until 1992, takes full advantage of cinema as a story-telling medium. The screenplay opens by directing the camera to pan across the exterior of the South Side Chicago city landscape, backyards, boulevards, and kitchenettes while superimposing lines from Langston Hughes's poem "Harlem" in *Montage of a*

Dream Deferred over panning shots of the city. The lines from the poem read "What happens to a dream deferred? / Does it dry up / like a raisin in the Sun / Or fester like a sore—/ And then run?"[29] Later, the screenplay directs the camera to capture a series of montage scenes depicting the Calumet Highway at night, the steel mills of Chicago, the stockyards, the Chicago Loop at midday, the South Side, and the Negro Soldier's monument. Her notes for the screenplay describe the Younger family's apartment, its weary furnishings, the tiny kitchen, and the single window that is the apartment's sole source of natural light. She describes how, in Chicago's South Side ghetto, rents are disproportionately higher than in any other places in the city and that to move to a larger apartment would "exhaust them financially since the hard-earned combined wages of the three income-making members must feed, clothe, and house five people.[30]

Throughout the screenplay, Hansberry directs the camera to illustrate how, in Margaret Wilkerson's words, "the many subtle ways in which racism invades the characters' lives on a daily basis."[31] The script relies on mise-en-scene and cinematography to chronicle some of the myriad ways that racism manifests in everyday life. For example, the screenplay contains a new scene depicting Mama's last day of work at her employer's household, the Holidays. The scene illustrates the complexity of interracial and interclass relations such as Mama's uncompromisingly loving attachment to her young White charge and Mrs. Holiday's dawning awareness of Mama's humanity and the economic injustices that keep Blacks available to Whites as low-wage workers. Mrs. Holiday's complicity is revealed when Mama describes to Mrs. Holiday's "innocent" surprise, the harsh conditions of her working life, which include a story about a former employee who says, after Lena asks for a raise, "Why, Lee-na! I never thought to hear you-ou talk as if you thought of this as a job."[32] Another new scene involves Walter Lee in a park observing a political orator on a ladder who exhorts a crowd of listeners with revolutionary rhetoric. He says, "Everywhere on the African continent today the Black man is standing up and telling the White man that there is someplace for *him* to go—back to that small cold continent where he came from—Europe! Well then—how long before this mood of Black men everywhere else in the world touches us here? How long!"[33]

In another new scene of Walter at work, Hansberry directs the camera to pan the elegantly furnished dining room of his employer where Walter's employer's wife, Mrs. Arnold, lounges comfortably at home. The camera contrasts the Arnold home with the Younger home, the leisure and affluence of Mrs. Arnold with the hardworking exploitation of the two Mrs. Youngers, and the life of White privilege through the angry eyes of Walter. With close-up shots of four of the characters' hands, the camera links consecutive scenes of Mama and Walter at work, from "extreme close shot of Lena's hands fixing bedding" and "extreme close up of Lena's hands working at buttons on a coat,"[34] to close-ups of Walter

Lee buttoning up his livery. Subsequent shots direct the camera to deep focus backgrounds that maintain foreground focus on Walter's hands, his employer Mrs. Arnold's "manicured hand," and then a close-up of Mr. Arnold's hands moving back his cuff to look at his watch. The screenplay also includes another new scene to illustrate ghetto price-gouging. In the scene Lena encounters a surly White clerk. The script reads:

> Got the nerve to be askin' people thirty-five cents for them apples look like they was on the scene when Moses crossed over. Just think the Southside is the garbage dump of this city where you can sell all the trash don't nobody else in America want. Wouldn't be tryin' to sell 'em over yonder where I work.[35]

After Lena refuses the purchase, the camera follows her to a streetcar and then shifts to an extreme close-up of "large, red, voluptuous apples" in Chicago's famous "open markets" enjoyed primarily by White shoppers. Another important and brief addition to the screenplay occurs when the family travels to Clybourne Park (the "White neighborhood") to visit the new house Mama has bought. Hansberry's directions instruct the camera to roam the neighborhood:

> There is an imposed starkness in the shot, reflecting these surroundings as they seem to Ruth and Walter. These are American homes where rather ordinary types and varieties of Americans live; but at the moment something sinister clings to them. At some windows curtains drop back quietly into place, as though those who are watching do not want to be seen; at others, shadowy figures simply move back out of view when they feel that Walter and Ruth's gaze is upon them; at still others, those who are staring do so without apology. The faces—the eyes of women and children, in the main—look hard with a curiosity that, for the most part, is clearly hostile.[36]

In the end, however, over one-third of the original screenplay was cut and little of the original screenplay's cinematic exposition was incorporated into the 1961 film, which was screened as a virtual twin of the play. In her introduction to the unfilmed screenplay, Margaret Wilkerson[37] hypothesize that political objectives were behind the editing of Hansberry's film script, and Spike Lee describes how "After I finished reading the screenplay, I went out and rented the video cassette. It seems to me that all the cuts had to deal with softening a too defiant Black voice."[38] Instead of the original screenplay's opening montage of South Side ghetto scenes superimposed with the Langston Hughes poem, the film opens with title and credits on a gray background reminiscent of early 1950s television graphics. The poem appears neither on the screen nor the sound track. In a 1961 newspaper article, the director Daniel Petrie expressed disappointment at the time of *A Raisin in the Sun*'s receipt of a special Gary Cooper Award for "Outstanding Human Values" at the 1961 Cannes Film Festival. Petrie describes European "complaints" about the film including excessive dialogue, limited location, and inappropriate mise-en-scene, and attributes these complaints to the final cutting of the film:

> There was so little visual emphasis on the poor living conditions of the Chicago Negro family that foreign audiences didn't see what they had to complain about. . . . To shorten it, most of the visual description of the neighborhood was removed, while almost all of the play's dialogue remained. When I saw the foreign audience grow restless, I was convinced that the wrong things had been cut out.[39]

Similarly, Hansberry is quoted in a 1961 news article as saying that the screenplay was cut because it made the film too long and this claim is repeated in the 1992 publication of the original screenplay. However, Lisbeth Lipari[40] investigates how memos and letters of studio executives suggest that the cuts were made not simply because the screenplay was too long, but because the executives thought Hansberry's original screenplay made her criticisms of racism all too visible.

In 1973 the play was resurrected as a musical adaptation, *Raisin, The Musical*, and ran for 847 performances and won the Tony Award for Best Musical in 1974. The musical version starred Joe Morton as Walter Lee and Debbie Allen as Beneatha. In 1989, the PBS American Playhouse produced a twenty-fifth anniversary TV version of *A Raisin in the Sun* starring Danny Glover as Walter Lee and Esther Rolle as Lena, and was nominated for three Emmy Awards. Like the 1959 version, the 1989 television version enjoyed awards and accolades as well as some muted criticism. In an examination of contemporary racial representations in media, bell hooks severely critiques the PBS production: "I was stunned by the way in which the contemporary re-visioning of Hansberry's play made it no longer a counter-hegemonic cultural production but a work that fit with popular racist stereotypes of Black masculinity as dangerous, threatening, etc. Attempting to make this play accessible to a predominately White mass audience, the work was altered so that the interpretation of specific roles would correspond with prefabricated notions of Black identity, particularly Black male identity."[41] hooks goes on to describe how although she had personally talked with many Black artists and intellectuals who had serious criticisms of the play, "no one made it the subject for extensive public cultural critique."[42]

Most recently, a 2004 revised Broadway version of *A Raisin in the Sun* boasted a nine-week run at Broadway's Royale Theater and starred hip-hop artist and mogul Sean Puffy "P. Diddy" Combs as Walter Lee, former Cosby Show star Phylicia Rashad as Mama, Audra McDonald as Ruth, and Sanaa Lathan as Beneatha. The $2.6 million production was directed by Atlanta-based director Kenny Leon and in nine weeks recouped not only its production cost but also earned a profit of $700,000, one of the biggest weekly takes for a nonmusical play in Broadway history. The revision also earned four Tony nominations and two Tony awards. Phylicia Rashad became the first African American woman to win the Tony Award for best performance by a leading actress in a play and Audra McDonald won the Tony Award for Best Featured Actress in a Play. The audience reception of this production was as enthusiastic as the original 1959 production, and the critical reception far less mixed. Many critics noted that the cast, especially Sean Combs, drew younger than typical audiences to Broadway. In a 2004 radio interview with Tavis Smiley, Michael Eric Dyson said the play continues to be relevant today because Black audiences "can identify with the play's themes of identity, of struggle for self-determination in a culture that continues to be racist."[43]

During the period between the completion of *Raisin in the Sun* in 1957 to 1960, Hansberry was actively writing plays as well as essays, letters, and speeches. She also, as a lesbian, began exploring the nascent homophile movement and dating women. Carter quotes Nemiroff as saying that "Hansberry's homosexuality was not a peripheral or casual part of her life but contributed significantly on many levels to the sensitivity and complexity of her view of human beings and of the world."[44] In 1957 she attended at least one meeting of the New York Chapter of the Daughter's of Bilitis (DOB), a national lesbian organization that had been founded in San Francisco in 1955.[45] Elise Harris describes Hansberry as making her "debut in to a small, almost cotillion-like lesbian set"[46] that included writers Louise Fitzhugh, Patricia Highsmith, and lesbian literary pioneer Marijane Meaker, who wrote over forty novels under the pen names M. E. Kerr, Mary James, Vin Packer, Ann Aldrich, and M. J. Meaker. Hansberry soon began dating Renee Kaplan, who lived around the corner from Hansberry's Bleecker Street apartment in Greenwich Village. Although Hansberry was the only African American in this white set of lesbians, she also lived a few blocks from her close friend, the openly gay James Baldwin, with whom she also spent a great deal of time. In the spring and summer of 1957 Hansberry wrote anonymously, as was the convention at the time, two long letters to *The Ladder*, a lesbian publication published by DOB. Her two letters, more like mini-essays of 840 and 1340 words respectively, reflected many of Hansberry's political concerns about racism and class oppression. But in the letters, Hansberry linked those concerns to gender and sexuality as well. Her letters sketched her concerns with separatism and assimilation, sexual ethics, and the economic and intellectual subjugation created by sexism. In May 1957, she wrote: "I feel that women, without wishing to foster any strict separatist notions, homo or hetero, indeed have a need for their own publications and organizations. Our problems, our experiences as women are profoundly unique as compared to the other half of the human race. Women, like other oppressed groups of one kind or another, have particularly had to pay a price for the intellectual impoverishment that the second class status imposed on us for centuries created and sustained."[47] This point echoes arguments she made in her unfinished essay, "In Defense of the Equality of Men," that articulates a feminist position and celebrates 19th century feminists who "set a path that a grateful society will undoubtedly, in time, celebrate." The point is also echoed two years later in 1959 when, in an interview with Studs Terkel, she states that "Obviously the most oppressed group of any oppressed group will be its women who are twice oppressed."[48] These themes are also discussed in her unfinished essay, "Simone De Beauvoir and the Second Sex: An American Commentary, an Unfinished Essay-in-Progress,"[49] where she discusses pornography, women's economic position in society, and the politics of housework. And while scholars have noted that none of Hansberry's plays revolve around a central female protagonist, earlier versions of *The Sign in Sidney Brustein's Window* and of the play *Les Blancs* centered around female characters who were later rewritten as male—Sidney Brustein was first written as Jenny Reed, and Tshembe Matoseh from *Les Blancs* was first written as Candace.

Hansberry's August *Ladder* letter closes with a tentative exploration of the link between homophobia and sexism: "In this kind of work [women's intellectual labor] there may be women to emerge who will be able to formulate a new and possible concept that homosexual persecution and condemnation has at its roots not only social ignorance, but a philosophically active anti-feminist dogma."[50] This theme also appears in 1961 in an unpublished letter to the West Coast–based homophile publication *One* where Hansberry links the oppression of homosexuality to the oppression of women:

> The relationship of anti-homosexual sentiment to the oppression of women has a special and deep implication. That is to say, that it must be clear that the reason for the double standard of social valuation is rooted in the societal contempt for the estate of womanhood in the first place. Everywhere the homosexual male is, in one way or another, seen as tantamount to the criminal for his deviation; and the woman homosexual as naughty, neurotic, adventurous, titillating wicked or rebellious for hers.[51]

In her other speeches and writings, Hansberry also expressed these concerns. In a 1959 speech to the Society for African Culture, Hansberry deconstructs what she calls the political "illusions" of her day "fostered by a year's steady diet of television, motion pictures, the legitimate stage and the novel."[52] Among the topics Hansberry takes on in this speech are the illusions "most people who work for a living are executives, women are idiots, people are White, negroes do not exist . . . sex is very bad, sex is very good . . . war is inevitable, so are armies . . . any form of radicalism (except conservativism) is latent protest against Mom, toilet-training, or heterosexuality." Later in the speech she asserts: "And as of today, if I am asked abroad if I am a free citizen of the United States of America, I must say only what is true: *No*."[53]

During this period of her life, Hansberry and Nemiroff had begun to grow apart. In 1960, the two bought a house on Waverly Place in Greenwich Village, and Harris writes that Dorothy Secules, who had rented an apartment in the house since the 1930s, remained in the apartment while Hansberry settled into the top floor.[54] Not long afterwards, the two women fell in love and remained secretly together until Hansberry's death. In 1961, Nemiroff and Hansberry bought a second property—a home in Croton-on-Hudson, a small village on the Hudson River about fifty miles from New York City. Hansberry named the home *Chitterling Heights* (after the southern dish of fried hog intestines more informally known as *chitlins*), as a whimsical allusion to her southern heritage. In order to concentrate fully on her writing, Hansberry spent many long weeks alone in the country house, eventually filling three file cabinets with work. Tripp describes Hansberry's study as filled with images of artists, writers, and thinkers who inspired her, including a photo of Paul Robeson above her desk, a bust of Albert Einstein on the desk, and in the hallway, a picture of Sean O'Casey.[55] Shortly after the success of the film version of *Raisin in the Sun*, Hansberry was contacted by NBC producer Dore Schary about the prospect of writing a play about the Civil War. Schary's idea was to commemorate the 100th anniversary of the Civil War with an NBC series of five ninety-minute teleplays. Hansberry was inspired by the idea and as a result in 1961 wrote the play *The Drinking Gourd* about "the peculiar institution" of slavery. Although NBC agreed to fund research and development of the series (and Hansberry says she was well paid for her efforts), the corporation later backed out due to lack of sponsorship—advertisers were dubious about the economic prospects of the series. *The Drinking Gourd*, titled after the name slaves on the underground railroad called the Big Dipper, explores the brutality of slavery from the perspective of both slaves and slave owners. The play tells the story of two slaves, Rissa and her son Hannibal, who are owned by an ailing "master" Hiram Sweet. Although Hiram struggles with his conscience about the mistreatment of slaves, his son Everett is a sadistic tyrant who blinds Hannibal for learning to read. Hiram, at death's doorstep, seeks Rissa's forgiveness claiming that he had nothing to do with Hannibal's torment. But in the act of Hannibal's blinding, the formerly docile and "blind" Rissa's eyes are opened and she turns her back to the dying old man to instead care for her son. Speaking about *The Drinking Gourd* in a radio discussion in 1961 on the "Negro Writer in America" with James Baldwin, Langston Hughes, and others, Hansberry said in reference to the teleplay: "We've been trying very hard . . . in America to pretend that this greatest conflict didn't even have at its base the only thing it had at its base. . . . Person after person will write a book today and insist that slavery was not the issue."[56] During this time, Hansberry also completed work on *What Use Are the Flowers*, a play about life on earth after a nuclear holocaust. The play describes an interaction between a dying hermit and a few surviving children whom he teaches to cherish beauty and, literally, reinvent the wheel.

Battling severe illness that was to be diagnosed as pancreatic cancer only shortly before her death, Hansberry secretly divorced Nemiroff in the spring 1964. By that time the couple had been living apart for several years, but only a few close friends were told of the divorce. Throughout this period, Nemiroff and Hansberry had maintained a close working relationship, and three months after the divorce she named him her literary executor. Near the same time, the play *The Sign in Sidney Brustein's Window* opened and ran for exactly 101 days, until her death in January. A day after the play opened, Hansberry was hospitalized after losing her sight and falling into a coma. Although she eventually awoke from the coma and regained her sight, she spent the remaining months of her life in the hospital while friends struggled financially to keep the play open. In the play Hansberry's gaze turns from her focus on Black American life to focus on the contradictions and moral ambiguities of White liberalism. The play follows five characters living in the Bohemian and ethnically and racially mixed New York neighborhood of Greenwich Village. Sidney Brustein, the title character, is a left-wing Jewish intellectual cynic and disengaged from his prior political commitments. Although ostensibly progressive, he fails to take his wife Iris, a "Greco-Gaelic-Indian hillbilly," seriously. The other central characters struggle with their own forms of disillusion and blindness as the play weaves through a range of topics including racism, Marxism, and political corruption. In one of the central threads of the play that eventually leads to a suicide, Sidney's Black friend Alton Scales rejects Gloria, his White fiancée. This ill-fated relationship explores the economic dimensions of race and gender oppression when, after Alton discovers that Gloria earns her living as a high-class call girl, he tells Sidney he won't accept a wife who is "White man's leavings," and explains his reasons for breaking the engagement:

> Alton: Someone who has coupled with my love . . . used her like . . . an . . . inanimate object . . . a thing, an instrument . . . a commodity. . . . Don't you understand, Sidney? Man, like I am spawned from commodities . . . and their purchasers. Don't you know this? I am running from being a commodity. How do you think I got the color I am, Sidney? Haven't you ever thought about it? I got this color from my grandmother being used as a commodity, man. The buying and the selling in this country began with me.[57]

But while the character Alton recognizes his own oppression and the price paid by women slaves, like the other characters in the play he is oblivious to the ways in which he is implicated in the oppression of others. This point is made by Gloria when she describes to Sidney how easy it is for women to be lured into prostitution out of economic necessity. "I was a nineteen-year-old package of fluff from Trenersville, Nowhere, and I met this nothing who took one look at the baby face of mine and said, 'Honey, there's a whole special market for you.'"[58] Another encounter between the Brustein's gay neighbor David, a writer, and Gloria illuminates the blindness of gay men to sexism. David, oblivious to the fact that Gloria has just been beaten, blithely declares that "Isn't it the great tradition for writers and whores to share the world's truths?" In response, the wincing and angry Gloria says "Look, little boy—I've never met you before, but I have met them like you a hundred times and I know everything you are about to say; because its been asked and written four thousand times."[59] In another scene, Alton illuminates the hostility of some Black men to gays when after telling David to "Turn off, fag face!" he storms out of the apartment saying, "I'm sorry if it makes me unsophisticated in your eyes; but after a while, hanging out with queers gets on my nerves!"[60] This complex blending of the intersection of oppressions was not well received by critics, who were surprised that Hansberry should write a play not centrally concerned with matters of race. Moreover, they felt the play was too difficult and complicated and, apparently, audiences agreed. Despite its lukewarm critical reception, friends from the theatrical, literary, and political communities, including James Baldwin, Sammy Davis Jr., Ruby Dee, Shelley Winters, Ossie Davis, Anne Bancroft, and Mel Brooks, kept the play running until Hansberry's death on January 12, 1965, when it finally closed.

Although she was very ill at the time, in 1964, Hansberry was invited to write the text for a photo documentary book titled *The Movement: Documentary of a Struggle for Equality.* The book chronicles the history of activism and voter registration in the South and was put together by the Student Nonviolent Coordinating Committee (SNCC). Written while she was in and out of the hospital for radiation treatments for the cancer that would kill her in the very near future, Hansberry's text narrated photographs of marches, lynchings, prayers, as well as segregated water fountains, countryside scenes, and poverty-stricken communities. Commenting on a photograph of armed police with attack dogs, she wrote: "What the dogs and guns and hoses have proved is that the entire power structure of the south must be altered."[61] In several places, Hansberry links racism to wider systems of economic and social exploitation. Next to a photograph of White policemen in helmets, she writes that they are "from a class of Southerners who are themselves victims of a system that has used them and their fathers before them for generations."[62] And beneath a photograph of an industrial slum, she writes: "The coming of industry into the Southland has not changed the problems of many of its people—White or Black—for the better."[63] The book concludes with photographs of young activists. Hansberry writes: "They stand in the hose fire at Birmingham; they stand in the rain at Hattiesburg. They are young, they are beautiful, they are determined. It is for us to create, now, an America that deserves them."[64]

One of Hansberry's last projects was the play *Les Blancs*, a work she had begun in 1960 and left unfinished at the time of her death. The play was written partly in response to French author Jean Genet's drama *Les Negres*, a "clown-show" about Black nationalism that many Black critics, including Hansberry, had objected to as ignorant and derisive. As Philip Effiong writes, "Genet perpetuates the minstrel dynamic by using Black characters to lampoon Black nationalism."[65] Although Hansberry had written the thematic development, plot outline, and major speeches, the play was completed by Nemiroff and opened at the Longacre Theater in 1970. The play received wildly divergent reviews and closed after forty-seven performances. However, *Les Blancs* has been produced in regional theaters across the country ever since. Drawing on her lifelong interest in Africa and African history, *Les Blancs* presents an unambiguously powerful critique of colonialism that takes place in the mythical African country of Zatembe on the eve of revolution. Loosely based on the so-called "Mau-Mau" (a derogatory term devised by European colonists) uprising in Kenya, the play recounts the story of an African expatriate, Tshembe Matoseh, living in England who returns home for his father's village funeral to experience imminent anticolonial revolution. Upon returning home, Tshembe encounters a range of morally compromised if not corrupt characters such as the Albert Schweitzer–like White missionary Rev. Torvald Neilsen and his wife; a White "liberal" American journalist, Charlie Morris, who had traveled to Zatembe to interview the "great" Neilsen; the brutally oppressive White colonist, Major Rice; and Tshembe's own two brothers, Abioseh, a Catholic priest who sides with the White colonists, and Eric, a lost gay biracial man born of the rape of their mother by Major Rice.

While clearly drawing on historical events of the period as well as Hansberry's own study of Africa, John Gruesser[66] contends that *Les Blancs* is Hansberry's attempt to rewrite the Eurocentric image of Africa and Africans that had long been portrayed by European writers. To do this, Gruesser claims that Hansberry draws on both African and European traditions—the oral and folk art traditions of African as well as the literary traditions of paternalist European writers whose distorted portrayals of African "natives," be they noble or savage, equate Africa with ugliness. Hansberry herself wrote that when she was a child "everything distasteful and painful was associated with Africa. This came from school, from the movies, and from our own people who accepted this." And while Philip Effiong explores Hansberry's use of African customs and aesthetic practices in music, costume, and folklore in the play, Gruesser argues that *Les Blancs* is, among other things, an Afrocentric rendition of Joseph Conrad's *Heart of Darkness:* "Hansberry not only reassigns the blame for the falsehood and corruption of Africa to colonialism and Africanist thinking but shows that this is only the first step. As Tshembe tells Morris, merely exposing colonialist sentiments as a lie, as Conrad does in *Heart of Darkness*, is not enough because such falsehoods kill people."[67] In the play Tshembe argues that, like religion, or ethnicity, race is a justification for exploitation: "I am simply saying that a device is a device, but that it also has consequences: once invented it takes on a life, a reality of its own. So in one century, men invoke the device of religion to cloak their conquests. In another, race. Now, in both cases you and I may recognize the fraudulence of the device, but the fact remains that a man who has a sword run through him because he refuses to become a Moslem or a Christian—or who is shot in Zatembe or Mississippi because he is Black—is suffering the utter reality of the device."[68]

Thomas P. Adler explores how Tshembe, like Sidney Brustein, is a character who moves from disengagement to commitment. Tshembe, Adler writes, is "another of Hansberry's existential heroes who makes a series of choices that redefine him as a human being."[69] While Tshembe has a new life and a White wife in England and longs to stay removed from the uprisings, he is impelled to join the fight for independence after witnessing the open wounds of colonialism that had virtually enslaved and deracinated his people and plundered the hills for silver and gold. Tshembe understands the connection between colonialism and capitalism and, as Adler notes, "understands, too, that Whites need the hatred of Blacks to assuage their guilt for having oppressed them."[70] For example, when the "nonviolent" Morris asked Tshembe if he hates all White men, Tshembe replies "I do not 'hate' all White men—but I desperately wish that I did. It would make everything infinitely easier. But I am afraid that, among other things, I have seen the slums of Liverpool and Dublin and the caves above Naples. I have seen Dachau and Anne Frank's attic in Amsterdam. I have seen too many raw-knuckled Frenchmen coming out of the Metro at dawn and too many pop-eyed Italian children to believe that those who raided Africa for there centuries ever 'loved' the White race either. I would like to be simple-minded for you, but, I cannot. I have, seen."[71] Like her character Tshembe, Hansberry understood all too well the moral paralysis engendered by White liberalism. In her 1964 speech to New York's Town Hall, Hansberry urges Whites to stop being liberals and work side by side with African Americans in the struggle for Civil Rights. "The problem is we have to find some way with these dialogues to show and to encourage the White liberal to stop being a liberal and become an American radical."[72]

When Lorraine Hansberry died on January 12, 1965, hundreds of friends and family, including Paul Robeson, Langston Hughes, Malcolm X, and other intellectual and theatrical luminaries attended her funeral at a small church in Harlem presided by Rev. Eugene Callendar. Her past and present partners Renee Kaplan and Dorothy Secules served as pallbearers. McKissack and McKissack[73] describe how, after the congregation sang "Abide with Me," messages from James Baldwin (who was in France at the time) and Rev. Dr. Martin Luther

King Jr., were read aloud by the Reverend. The telegram from Martin Luther King read, in part: "Her commitment to spirit, . . . her creative literary ability and her profound grasp of the deep social issues confronting the world today will remain an inspiration to generations yet unborn."[74] Other speakers, including Paul Robeson, praised her contributions to the Civil Rights Movement and extolled her work as "a precious heritage." Julius Lester notes the irony of Hansberry's death falling a little more than a month before Malcolm X's assassination: "Somehow it seems like more than a coincidence that the two should die within less than a month and a half of each other and scarcely nine months before the 'deferred dream' exploded in the streets of Watts."[75] She is buried in Bethel Cemetery in Croton-on-Hudson, and the inscription on her tombstone quotes selections from *The Sign in Sidney Brustein's Window*. One selection is from a speech made by Sidney where he says: "The why of why we are here is an intrigue for adolescents; the how is what must command the living. Which is why I lately have become—an insurgent again!"[76]

At the time of her death, Hansberry left a number of unfinished essays and plays including *The Arrival of Mr. Todog*, a satire of Samuel Beckett's existentialist *Waiting for Godot*; a play about the eighteenth century feminist and author of the 1792 *A Vindication of the Rights of Women*, Mary Wollstonecraft; as well as a libretto about the Haitian revolutionary Toussaint L'Ouverture. As with her Black Chicago Renaissance predecessors, writing was to Hansberry a political as well as an artistic act. This is evident in all her writings regardless of genre— whether it be in the full-blown critiques of racism, sexism, and capitalism in *A Raisin in The Sun*; of racism, homophobia, and colonialism in *Les Blancs*; or of capitalism and racism in her documentary text *The Movement*. Describing her work with *Freedom* editor Louis E. Burnham she says: "The things he taught me were great things: that all racism was rotten, White or Black, that everything is political."[77] And like other writers of the Chicago Renaissance, her politics and art arose from the streets of South Side. As she writes in her 1961 tribute to the Chicago painter Charles Wright in *We Are of the Same Sidewalks*, "Like him I came to adolescence in a community where the steel veil of oppression which sealed our ghetto encased within it a multitude of Black folk who endured every social ill known to humankind: poverty, ignorance, brutality and stupor. And, almost mystically, beside all of it: the most lyrical strengths and joys the soul can encompass. One feels that the memories of that crucible, the Chicago South Side, must live deep within the breast of this artist."[78]

Notes

1. Rodgers, Lawrence R. "Richard Wright, Frank Marshall Davis and the Chicago Renaissance." *The Langston Hughes Review* 14, 1, 2 (1996): 4–12.

2. Abramson, Doris E. *Negro Playwrights in the American Theater: 1925–1959*. New York: Columbia University Press, 1969.

3. Gomez, Jewelle L. "Lorraine Hansberry: Uncommon Warrior." In *Reading Black, Reading Feminist*, edited by Henry Louis Gates Jr. New York: Meridian, 1990, 307–17.

4. Baldwin, James. "Lorraine Hansberry at the Summit." *Freedomways* 19, 4 (1979): 269–72.

5. Cheney, Anne. *Lorraine Hansberry*. Boston: Twayne Publishers, 1984.

6. Hansberry, Lorraine. "Flag from a Kitchenette Window" (poem). *Masses and Mainstream* 3 (September 1950): 38–40.

7. Killens, John Oliver. "Lorraine Hansberry: On Time!" *Freedomways* 19, 4 (1979): 273–76.

8. Duberman, Martin Bauml. *Paul Robeson*. New York: Knopf, 1988.

9. Marable, Manning. *W. E. B. Dubois, Black Radical Democrat*. Boston: Twayne Publishers, 1986.

10. Tripp, Janet. *The Importance of Lorraine Hansberry*. San Diego: Lucent Books, 1998.

11. Hansberry, Lorraine. *A Raisin in the Sun*. New York, Ethel Barrymore Theatre, March 11, 1959.

12. Ibid.

13. Baldwin, James. "Sweet Lorraine." In *To Be Young, Gifted, and Black*, edited by Robert Nemiroff. New York: Vintage, 1995, xvii–xx.

14. King Jr, Woodie. "Lorraine Hansberry's Children: Black Artists and A Raisin in the Sun." *Freedomways* 19, 4 (1979): 219–22.

15. Cruse, Harold. *The Crisis of the Negro Intellectual*. New York: New York Review, 1967, 275.

16. Keppel, Ben. *The Work of Democracy: Ralph Bunche, Kenneth B. Clark, Lorraine Hansberry, and the Cultural Politics of Race*. Cambridge: Harvard University Press, 1995.

17. Baraka, Amiri. "A Critical Reevaluation: *A Raisin in the Sun*'s Enduring Passion." In *Lorraine Hansberry, A Raisin in the Sun*, edited by Robert Nemiroff. New York: Vintage, 1995.

18. Cruse, *The Crisis of the Negro Intellectual*, 278.

19. Bogle, Donald. *Toms, Coons, Mulattoes, Mammies, & Bucks: An Interpretive History of Blacks in American Films*. New York: Continuum, 1990, 198.

20. Terkel, Studs. "An Interview with Lorraine Hansberry," by Studs Terkel. *WFMT Chicago Five Arts Guide* 10 (April 1961): 8–14.

21. Nemiroff, *To Be Young, Gifted, and Black*, 91.

22. Baraka, *Lorraine Hansberry, A Raisin in the Sun*, 10.

23. Lester, Julius. "Introduction." In *The Collected Last Plays of Lorraine Hansberry*, edited by Robert Nemiroff. New York: Random House, 1972, 8–9.

24. Ibid., 9.

25. Ibid., 11.

26. Lester, Neal A. "Seasoned with Quiet Strength: Black Womanhood in Lorraine Hansberry's *A Raisin in the Sun* (1959). In *Women in Literature: Reading through the Lens of Gender*, edited by Jerilyn Fisher and Ellen S. Silber. Westport, Conn.: Greenwood Press, 2003, 248.

27. Ibid., 247.

28. Keppel, *The Work of Democracy*, 202.

29. Hughes, Langston. "Harlem." In *The Poems: 1951–1967: The Collected Work of Langston Hughes, Volume 3*, edited by Arnold Rampersad. Columbia: University of Missouri Press, 2001, 74.

30. Hansberry, Lorraine. *A Raisin in the Sun: The Unfilmed Original Screenplay*, edited by Robert Nemiroff. New York: Signet, 1992, 5.

31. Ibid., xxxv.

32. Ibid., 40.

33. Ibid., 132–33.

34. Ibid., 31.

35. Ibid., 53–54.

36. Ibid., 155.

37. Wilkerson, Margaret. "Introduction." In *A Raisin in the Sun: The Unfilmed Original Screenplay*, edited by Robert Nemiroff. New York: Signet, 1992, xxix–xliv.

38. Lee, Spike. "Commentary: Thoughts on the Screenplay." In *A Raisin in the Sun: The Unfilmed Original Screenplay*, edited by Robert Nemiroff. New York: Signet, 1992, xlv–xlvii.

39. Archer, Eugene. "Raisin Director Plans Two Films," *New York Times*, June 10, 1961, 12.

40. Lipari, Lisbeth. "'Fearful of the Written Word': White Fear, Black Writing, and Lorraine Hansberry's *A Raisin in the Sun* Screenplay." *Quarterly Journal of Speech* 90, 1 (2004): 81–102.

41. hooks, bell. *Yearning: Race, Gender and Cultural Politics*. Boston: South End Press, 1990, 2.

42. Ibid., 2.

43. "Michael Eric Dyson Commentary: 'A Raisin in the Sun'" *The Tavis Smiley Show*," June 17, 2004. http://www.npr.org/templates/story/story.php?storyId=1961517.

44. Carter, Steven R. *Hansberry's Drama: Commitment amid Complexity*. Chicago: University of Illinois Press, 1991, 6.

45. Lipari, Lisbeth. "The Rhetoric of Intersectionality: Lorraine Hansberry's Letters to *The Ladder*." In *Queering the Public Sphere*, edited by Charles E. Morris. Columbia: University of South Carolina Press, 2007.

46. Harris, Elise. "The Double Life of Lorraine Hansberry." *Out Magazine* 70 (September 1999): 96–101, 174–75.

47. Hansberry, Lorraine. "Readers Respond." *The Ladder* 1, 8 (May 1957): 26–28.

48. Terkel, Studs. "An Interview with Lorraine Hansberry," by Studs Terkel. *WFMT Chicago Five Arts Guide* 10 (April 1961): 8–14.

49. Hansberry, Lorraine. "Simone De Beauvoir and the Second Sex: An American Commentary, an Unfinished Essay-in-Progress." In *Words of Fire: An Anthology of African-American Feminist Thought*, edited by Beverly Guy-Sheftall. New York: The New Press, 1995, 128–42.

50. "Readers Respond." *The Ladder* 1, 11 (August 1957): 26–30.

51. Carter, *Hansberry's Drama: Commitment amid Complexity*, 6–7.

52. Hansberry, Lorraine. "The Negro Writer and His Roots: Toward a New Romanticism." *Black Scholar* 10, 4 (1981): 4.

53. Ibid., 10.

54. Harris, *Out Magazine*.

55. Tripp, *The Importance of Lorraine Hansberry*.

56. Hansberry, Lorraine. *The Negro Writer in America*. Audio-Forum 23062. Recorded 1961 from a WBAI-FM radio broadcast originally titled "The Negro's Role in American Culture."

57. Hansberry, Lorraine. *The Sign in Sidney Brustein's Window*. New York: Samuel French, 1965, 84.

58. Ibid., 106.

59. Ibid., 104.

60. Ibid., 56.

61. Hansberry, Lorraine. *The Movement: Documentary of a Struggle for Equality*. New York: Simon and Schuster, 1964, 60.

62. Ibid., 68.

63. Ibid., 13.

64. Ibid., 122.

65. Effiong, Philip Uko. "History, Myth, and Revolt in Lorraine Hansberry's *Les Blancs*." *African American Review* 32, 2 (1998): 274.

66. Gruesser, John. "Lies That Kill: Lorraine Hansberry's Answer to Heart of Darkness in *Les Blancs*." In *New Readings in American Drama*, edited by Norma Jenckes. New York: Peter Lang, 2002, 44.

67. Ibid., 45.

68. Hansberry, Lorraine. *Les Blancs: The Collected Last Plays of Lorraine Hansberry*, ed. Robert Nemiroff. New York: Random House, 1972, 92.

69. Adler, Thomas P. *American Drama, 1940–1960: A Critical History*. New York: Macmillan International, 1994, 198.

70. Ibid., 199.

71. Hansberry, *Les Blancs*, 102–3.

72. Hansberry, Lorraine. "The Black Revolution and the White Backlash." In *Black Protest: History, Documents, and Analysis 1619 to the Present*, edited by Joanne Grant. New York: Fawcett Premier, 1968, 447.

73. McKissack, Patricia and Fredrick L. McKissack. *Young, Black, and Determined: A Biography of Lorraine Hansberry*. New York: Holiday House, 1998.

74. Ibid., 134.

75. Lester, "Introduction," *Les Blancs*, 3.

76. Hansberry, *The Sign in Sidney Brustein's Window*, 283–84.

77. Hansberry, *To Be Young, Gifted, and Black*, 79.

78. "We Are of the Same Sidewalks," Catalogue of the ACA Gallery's Charles White exhibition, 1961, published in *Freedomways* 20 (Winter 1980): 198.

For Further Reading

Abell, Joy L. . "African/American: Lorraine Hansberry's *Les Blancs* and the American Civil Rights Movement." *African American Review* 35, 3 (2001): 459–70.
Brown, Lloyd W. "Lorraine Hansberry as Ironist." *Journal of Black Studies* 4 (March 1974): 237–47.

Lorraine Hansberry

Books

A Raisin in the Sun. New York: Random House, 1959; London: Methuen, 1960.
The Sign in Sidney Brustein's Window. New York: Samuel French, 1965. In *Three Negro Plays.* London: Penguin: 1969.
To Be Young, Gifted, and Black: Lorraine Hansberry in Her Own Words, adapted by Robert Nemiroff. Englewood Cliffs, N.J.: Prentice-Hall, 1969.

Play Productions

To Be Young, Gifted, and Black, adapted by Robert Nemiroff. New York, Cherry Lane Theatre, January 2, 1969.
Les Blancs, adapted by Robert Nemiroff. New York, Longacre Theater, November 15, 1970.
The Sign in Sidney Brustein's Window, The Musical, adapted by Robert Nemiroff, music by Ray Errol Fox. New York, Longacre Theater, January 17, 1972.
Raisin, The Musical, adapted by Robert Nemiroff, music by Judd Wolden. New York, 46th Street Theater, October 18, 1973.
———. Adapted by Robert Nemiroff, music by Judd Wolden. New York, Equity Library Theater, May 17, 1981.
A Raisin in the Sun. New York, Royale Theater, April 26, 2004.

Screenplay

A Raisin in the Sun, Columbia Pictures, 1961.

Television

To Be Young Gifted and Black, adapted from Nemiroff's play based on Hansberry's writings by Robert M. Fresco, WNET, January 1972.
A Raisin in the Sun, PBS American Playhouse Television Production, February 1989.

Recording

Lorraine Hansberry Speaks Out: Art and the Black Revolution, selected and edited by Robert Nemiroff, Caedmon Records (TC 1352) 1972.

Other

"The Negro in American Culture." *Cross Currents* 11, 3 (Summer 1961): 205–24. Transcript of 1961 WBAI-FM radio symposium.

"A Challenge to Artists." In *Voice of Black America: Major Speeches by Negroes in the United States 1797–1971*, edited by Philip S. Foner. New York: Simon and Schuster, 1972, 954–59.

"In Defense of the Equality of Men." In *The Norton Anthology of Literature by Women*, edited by Sandra M. Gilbert and Susan Gubar. New York: Norton, 1985, 2056–68.

"Village Intellect Revealed," *New York Times*, sec. 2 (October 31. 1964): 26–29.

"The Beauty of Things Black—Toward Total Liberation: Mike Wallace Interviews Lorraine Hansberry (1959), *Lorraine Hansberry Speaks Out: Art and the Black Revolution*," Caedmon Cassette.

Selected Periodical Publications

"An Author's Reflections: Willy Loman, Walter Lee Younger and He Who Must Live." *Village Voice* 4 (August 12, 1959): 7, 8.

"Genet, Mailer and the New Paternalism." *The Village Voice* 1 (June 1, 1961): 10, 15.

"The American Theatre Needs Desegregating, Too." *Negro Digest* 10 (June 1961): 28–33.

"A Challenge to Artists." *Freedomways* 3 (Winter 1963): 33–35.

"The Black Revolution and the White Backlash" (transcript of Town Hall Forum). *National Guardian* (July 4, 1964): 5–9.

"The Nation Needs Your Gifts." *Negro Digest* 13 (August 1964): 26–29.

"The Legacy of W. E. B. DuBois." *Freedomways* 5 (Winter 1965): 19–20.

"The Negro Writer and His Roots: Toward a New Romanticism." *Black Scholar* 12 (March/April 1981): 2–12.

"All the Dark and Beautiful Warriors." *Village Voice* 28 (August 16, 1983): 1, 11–16, 18–19.

Kaiser, Ernest and Robert Nemiroff. "A Lorraine Hansberry Bibliography." *Freedomways* 19, (Fourth Quarter 1979): 285–304.

Rich, Adrienne. "The Problem with Lorraine Hansberry." *Freedomways* 19, 4 (1979): 247–55.

Papers

The Lorraine Hansberry archives are held at the Schomburg Center for Research in Black Culture, part of the New York Public Library system.

FENTON JOHNSON
(May 7, 1888–September 16, 1958)
James C. Hall

By some measures, Fenton Johnson is a marginal figure to the Black Chicago Renaissance. He published nothing during its most vibrant period and after the late 1920s seemed to willfully slide into complete and total obscurity; his loyalty to a sardonic, imagist poetic technique, similar to that of fellow Chicago poet Carl Sandburg, would, on the surface, make him out of step with either the general critical social realism or modified high modernism that generally held the day in black Chicago through the 1930s and 1940s. African American poet Arna Bontemps worked diligently to ensure that later work by Johnson had a presence in a late 1940s anthology of African American poetry that he edited, but that brief and tantalizing selection of four poems had to stand for what remained of a once real and vibrant ambition. Indeed, from another angle, that very ambition may make Johnson indispensable to the emergence of a substantive cohort of black artists, writers, critics, and entrepreneurs in Chicago that could command national and international attention. By a similarly reasonable measure, then, Fenton Johnson could be remembered as black Chicago's pioneering literary entrepreneur such that without his modest successes and significant failures, the energy behind the South Side Writers Group, the South Side Community Arts Center, and *Negro Story* are simply unimaginable. Much recent attention to the Black Chicago Renaissance has focused upon its foregrounding of a critical realism within the Popular Front, an intimate relationship between literary and civil rights activity, and the integration of urban and literary concerns that lead to the emergence of a vital "black arts" scene. If the black Chicago Renaissance had a future, it most certainly had a past, and Fenton Johnson is a crucial part of that history.[1]

Fenton Johnson was born in 1888 to Elijah and Jessie Johnson and into a comfortable, if complex, middle-class existence on Chicago's South Side. Elijah was a Railway Porter, a distinctly respectable and secure position for African American men of the time, and had had some success purchasing real estate. The late 1880s and 1890s were transitional times for black Chicago. Patterns of permanent residential segregation had not wholly settled in and it would not be unusual for someone like Johnson to have had an upbringing that included contact with the great diversity of Chicago's immigrant communities, and, moreover, it most certainly would have been an upbringing that included class ambition and expectation. By the time of Johnson's high-school years at Englewood and Wendell Phillips High Schools, however, Chicago would be gradually formulating its own version of Jim Crow, and thus laying the groundwork for a nascent and necessary cultural nationalism by its black inhabitants. Johnson's maturity would coincide with the establishment of an important network of schools, hospitals, clubs, banks, businesses, theaters, and newspapers, a virtual black metropolis, eager to serve a thriving and growing community uneasily surrounded by nonblacks often equally eager to scapegoat Blacks as they were faced with the hardships of industrialization and modernization.

Regardless of whether or not Johnson was shaped most completely by either the assimilationist hopes of one portion of the black middle class, or the nascent nationalist dreams of another, he had no difficulty imagining for himself a thoroughly literary existence. By twelve years of age, he had published his first poem, and by nineteen by some accounts (no record has yet been found) had plays produced at black Chicago's important playhouse, the Pekin Theatre. Arna Bontemps recalls Johnson telling of his family's electric car and the scene he made driving the vehicle around the city; he was a literary man, most certainly, if not a self-conscious dandy and dreamily (if not realistically) upwardly mobile. The fluidity of Johnson's (if not the whole community's) class experience can be marked by the rumors that some of his earliest literary and theatrical ventures were funded by his uncle John "Mushmouth" Johnson, black Chicago's most accomplished cabaret operator and suspected gambling kingpin. As in troubled decades to come, the line between underground and traditional economies was not impervious. If racism sought to circumscribe black opportunity, talented entrepreneurs would simply sidestep respectability altogether to gather wealth and other trappings of success.

Not unlike his contemporary, African American poet and fiction writer Jean Toomer, and perhaps because of the complexity of his family support and network, Johnson seemed permanently restless and actively tried on different middle-class identities. He spent time studying at Northwestern University and the University of Chicago and seems to have considered at various moments a career in the clergy and in teaching. The clergy was probably never a realistic life choice, and, after one year at the State University of Kentucky at Louisville (now Simmons University), he was quite sure that teaching was also not to be his calling or vocation. After publishing his first volume of poetry, *A Little Dreaming* (1913), he headed to New York to study journalism. There were opportunities as a stringer for the Eastern News Service and as a theater correspondent for the New York *Daily News*, but there is no indication that these efforts settled him or satisfied his literary and intellectual ambitions. He returned to Chicago at the height of the First World War and into the ferment of the first Chicago literary renaissance. It is unclear how he decided to focus his attentions in magazine publishing, or how he began to enter into conversations with influential anthologist and critic Harriet Monroe and the crowd around *Poetry* magazine, but in 1916 he established *The Champion Magazine* and was firmly part of the Chicago literary universe.

The Champion is most certainly Johnson's most significant and lasting contribution to African American cultural history, and is perhaps so because he somehow surrounded himself with a significant range of literary, political, and financial intelligence. Ironically, given that Johnson's later reputation was for introversion and withdrawal, he had managed to gather up a goodly portion of the black and Pan-African intelligentsia for his venture. Critic Lorenzo Thomas, noting the magazine's debt to W. E. B. DuBois's *The Crisis*, speculates that it is the presence of writer William Ferris, the future editor of Marcus Garvey's *The Negro World*, who as associate editor gave the magazine credibility and vision.[2] It is also reasonable to assert that it was once again the presence of close family members that gave Johnson confidence. His cousin, Henry Binga Dismond, a successful athlete and aspiring poet, edited a section in the magazine on sports, while their uncle, the famous Chicago financier and entrepreneur Jesse Binga provided significant financial advice, support, and guidance. Johnson's New York journalism contacts were also no doubt crucial in his securing contributions from historian Benjamin Brawley, writer Alice Dunbar Nelson, and poets Georgia Douglas Johnson and Joseph Seamon Cotter, among others. The magazine was a lively collection of essay, opinion, poetry, and reportage from Chicago and throughout the diaspora. Despite its urgency, relevance, and intellectual diversity, it was either never able to solidify a significant circulation or was never financially backed to the extent that it could find firm footing. It ceased publication a little over a year after it began.

While he now had a firm foothold in literary life, and had married Cecilia Rhone, there was no indication that this was to translate into any kind of economic or intellectual security. He was willing, and perhaps needed, to give magazine publishing another try. *The Favorite Magazine*, which ran from 1918 through 1921, seemed more clearly a vanity vehicle. It did not have the same access to or coverage by the Pan-African intelligentsia (although it included at least one contribution from popular historian J. A. Rogers) and was more desperate and pleading in tone. It is not wholly surprising that in the aftermath of the 1919 Chicago race riot Johnson seemed to get pulled into the unproductive vortex of postmortem social diagnosis and had his optimism for the future of the African American community and race relations in the city deeply wounded.

The magazine alternately and not cohesively pleaded for "racial reconciliation" (a mainstay of Johnson's social vision) and simultaneously railed against the perceived threat of left-inspired agitation within the African American community. A partial source of this ideological confusion and anger is most probably J. Edgar Hoover's *Report on Negro Radicalism*. There is some indication that *The Favorite* (if not Johnson's whole network of "bohemian" contacts) had caught the future FBI director's attention and that subsequent observation had discomfited Johnson. The irony is that if there was a strong strain of cultural radicalism in Johnson's past, he was no economic threat or prophetic voice against capitalism. Whatever the reality of political duress or pressure from "red panic," there is no evidence that Johnson had any vision for or ability to provide the more personal venture of *The Favorite* with editorial clarity. More and more of the magazine content was provided directly by Johnson himself, and much other writing not delivered under his byline may have been pseudonymously presented.

His rapidly changing career goals and his increasing personal frustration with a disintegrating racial dialogue was in some ways matched by a rapidly changing aesthetic sensibility. At worst, such change could appear to be a desperate search for approval; this need for endorsement can be seen in his slim correspondence with Harriet Monroe, but it would be too cynical to conceive this search entirely as mere opportunism. There is evidence that he (and, for that matter, much of the cohort of emerging African American literary artists) was confused as to the most productive way to ground their poet aesthetic. In his first three books, poetically, Johnson had moved from repetition of genteel themes, classical reference, and biblical allusion, to a belated consideration of dialect and cultural distinctiveness, and finally to a partially realized folk sensibility. These changes, and indeed each stop along the way, were not without intellectual substance or accomplishment. African American poet Robert Hayden's judgment in his anthology *Kaleidoscope* that these early efforts by Johnson were miserably incompetent may be too harsh, but it is fair to suggest that patience was not a Johnson strong suit. While open to the charge of a kind of poetical tourism, and even relentless amateurism, he is better accused of unchecked ambition.[3] Still, at each step along the way, there are important, and pioneering, signs of a thoroughly modern cultural pride and enthusiasm. Johnson had nothing if not good instincts about opportunities for the black artist and intellectual in the first quarter of the twentieth century.

Having opened with a plea to his reader to see him as a "poor minstrel," *A Little Dreaming* (1913) is often overwrought with mundane and uninteresting odes to nature and moral platitudes but also stepped out toward a vibrant Africanist sensibility. "The Ethiopian's Song" and "To an Afro-American Maiden" are suggestive of what he would eventually come to refer to as the rich racial treasure of the African past. Somewhat melodramatic in its orientation, "Rich

222 JAMES C. HALL

old Ethiop and Greece are there / In the swarthy skin and dreamy eye, / And the red man of the forest grants / Raven hair and figure tow'ring high." "To an Afro-American Maiden" is at least direct in its willingness to take up the opportunities of racialized identity. Somewhat predictably, this cultural turn backward is marked first off by a poem for and about African American poet Paul Laurence Dunbar, an almost inevitable influence and obstacle. Of course, the book also contains an ode to and about the Victorian sentimentalist Charles Swinburne and, despite its efforts to break away from Victorian and genteel modes, seems to want to hedge its bets. The volume also hints at the future vers libré style in the "The Plaint of the Factory Child" ("Mother, must I work all day? / All the day? Ay, all the day?") and is suggestive of at least a more restrained sensibility, a controlled modern cool that will eventually embrace a variety of social realism with a nod toward existential angst. In some ways, such jarring juxtapositions are indeed what remain memorable about the volume. It is an introduction to an ambitious but profoundly inchoate consciousness.

There is little question that Johnson was urgently in need of a strong editorial hand, or, perhaps more pointedly, access to a critical, supportive, and active group of friends with real literary sensibility. Over the course of the three volumes published between 1913 and 1916, he included over 160 poems. This is a straightforward path toward mediocrity and points to the dilettantism with which Johnson constantly flirted.

Indeed, it is crucial to an appreciation and criticism of Johnson that we acknowledge that we have few resources by which to measure changes at this early formative moment. There are hints in the slim archival record that he received some support and mentorship from the journalist William H. A. Moore in Chicago but no details about their relationship. Similarly, there is no question that Johnson had made literary and cultural contacts in his switch to New York, but we currently have no way of knowing whether these contacts translated into sustained conversations about craft, aesthetics, or politics.

Somewhat cynically, one might suggest that Johnson may have received more marketing than stylistic advice. *Visions of the Dusk* (1915), his second volume, turns in an interesting and belated way to the question of dialect and the overworked territory of the plantation and ante- and postbellum romance. Given Johnson's time in New York theater circles this is not wholly unsurprising; there is the distinct hint of the minstrel show and its more modern theatrical "coon show" derivative, although no poem in this mode is so distant or neutral as to not express clear sympathy (if at the same time withholding identification) with the black grassroots. The dialect experiments were themselves multiple; he posed in a Scots-Irish voice on occasion and invoked the specter of Scottish folk poet Robert Burns. Johnson's experiments with the African American spiritual are of much greater interest and lasting impact than his ventures into folk dialect.

Whether or not Dunbar is regarded as so strong a poet and forerunner that readers inevitably sense derivation and repetition, the dialect poems seem un-original and unimportant. The poems influenced or inspired by the spirituals, however, are distinctive because they self-consciously mean to allude to a broad cultural mode rather than assert authenticity. Johnson wrote in presenting these first experiments: "These songs we offer, not as genuine Negro spirituals, but as imitations. We attempt to preserve the rhythm and the spirit of the slaves, and to give a literary form and interpretation to their poetic endeavor. Here and there we have caught a phrase the unlettered minstrels used; here and there we have borrowed of that exquisite Oriental imagery the Africans brought with them."[4] Whatever discomfort we might have with the invocation of "Oriental" and its imperial overtones, there is no question that this combination of "imitation" and "interpretation" is an important breakthrough. In the third "Jubal" poem, Johnson wrote

Ring the church bells, honey,
Jubal's free;
Set the chimes a-pealing,
Jubal's free;
God above is shouting,
Devil goes a-pouting,
Earth and sky is meeting,
Freedom is their greeting,
Jubal's free.

Like African American anthropologist and novelist Zora Neale Hurston and others to come, Johnson intuits that significant poetic work can be accom-plished by seeking to recover the force or meaning of a particular form rather than meeting a crasser audience desire through mere replication. Given how this kind of reflection and research grounded much of the African American artistic accomplishment during the years of the Harlem Renaissance, this was an important experiment.

Songs of the Soil (1916) pushes further down this road toward a vital encounter with the folk and anticipates the poets Langston Hughes and most especially Sterling Brown. What is distracting and confusing is that Johnson seems unwill-ing to wholly commit himself to the radically interpretive gesture of the spiri-tual experiments. He continues to produce an undistinguished body of dialect poems, and does so because of the endorsement he receives from some portion of the white critical establishment. While the goal is to produce something that is distinctly not anthropological in its meaning, the work of this final complete volume of poetry is ultimately limited by the poet's very limited contact with the "soil" that he would represent or conjure. In his preface to the volume, Johnson correctly writes that "Behind the Negro there is a wealth of buried tradition," which has added "droll racial instincts" to "Americanism." He's more energetic still when he writes that "To the Negro, slavery is his epic hour. The freedom from restraint he enjoyed in his own circles kept alive those qualities he brought with him from Africa." And Johnson recognized the dangerous ground he was upon and wrote "I do not hope to complete my career as merely a singer of the plantation." Whether by luck or instinct, this final volume includes another poem that seems distinct and different from what came before. In "Harlem: The Black City," perhaps the earliest known poem to describe the Manhattan neighborhood as an emergent black metropolis, Johnson not only sounds resonant and prophetic, with a powerful vision of what became the Harlem Renaissance a few years later, but is also on the verge of a stylistic and tonal breakthrough that will serve him especially well. After pointing to an emerging urban life that is ruled by a perverse dialectic of respectable work and destructive pleasure, he concludes

> We ask for life, men give us wine,
> We ask for rest, men give us death;
> We long for Pan and Phoebus harp.
> But Bacchus blows on us his breath.
> O Harlem, weary are thy sons
> Of living that they never chose;
> Give not to them the lotus leaf,
> But Mary's wreath and England's rose.

The poem remains distant from the great breakthroughs of Langston Hughes and Sterling Brown in the 1920s because it still feels ruled by the discourse of "respectability" but it is inching toward a resonant respect and concern for the absurdities of city life.

Johnson's three published volumes are of primary importance for what they tell us about the challenges facing the black writer in the pre–Harlem Renaissance years. Haunted by the strong presence of Paul Laurence Dunbar and minstrel-rooted poetics on one side, and the class promise of a more genteel literary manner on the other, at the very moment when both the minstrel and genteel modes were collapsing upon themselves, it took real courage to imagine new modes of creative expression with little critical feedback from the community. His continued exploration of black cultural forms, his unapologetic "Ethiopianism," his instinctive Pan-Africanism, and especially his experiments with the spiritual tradition are noteworthy for their vision and enthusiasm. Having noted that innovation, it is, however, neither surprising nor unjust that none of the poems from the three published volumes was ever regularly anthologized or became part of the emergent African American literary canon. Whatever the nature and depth of the crisis in his personal and intellectual life that grew out of his magazine publishing ventures and the Red Scare, it is only during the late years of the second decade of the century that real poetic distinction began to emerge. Enveloped within the energy of the imagist and free-verse–driven Chicago Renaissance, and perhaps observing both the plain speaking of Carl Sandburg and Midwestern poet Edgar Lee Masters and a broad and general spirit of cross-cultural experimentation, Johnson began to produce a poetry reduced to an interesting set of essentials. "Aunt Hannah Jackson," "Aunt Jane Allen," "The Banjo Player," "The Barber," "The Drunkard," "The Gambler," "The Minister," "The Scarlet Woman," and "Tired," are Johnson's very best work and are especially noteworthy for asserting a deep moral and human complexity at the heart of urban black life. The influence of Masters's *Spoon River Anthology* is most certainly there, as are Sandburg's odes to Chicago working life. These separately published free-verse poems that appear between 1919 and 1927 are the legitimate basis of an ongoing poetic reputation and are regularly anthologized as exemplary of the best of non–Harlem-based black writing from the 1920s. In African American poet Frank Marshall Davis's estimation, Johnson emerges at this moment as the foremost black pioneer of free-verse poetry in the United States.[5]

It is possible to argue that Dunbar also looms here again as an influence. The tone of some of these poems can be discerned within Dunbar's pioneering naturalist novel, *Sport of the Gods* (1903), but Johnson's accomplishment is perhaps more daring still. The poems are deeply and simultaneously sardonic and meditative, and sometimes work by way of understatement and irony and sometimes by the most straightforward and disarming pessimism. They speak to the ways in which common ambition and social expectation are undone by the constrictions of a city increasingly defined and organized by race. "All the stock I had," says the narrator of "The Scarlet Woman," "was a white girl's education and a face that / enchanted the men of both races." Sometimes Johnson's skillful irony is not rooted in intercultural restriction so much as intracultural expectation. The less anthologized poem, "The Minister," tells of a highly educated black pastor who loses his charge "because I could not make my congregation shout." But the best simply communicate an accumulation of wear and tear on the spirit:

> For rubbing on other people's clothes Aunt Hannah
> Jackson gets a dollar and fifty cents a day and worn
> out dress on Christmas.
> For talking to herself Aunt Hannah Jackson gets a
> smile as we call her a good natured fool.

Johnson's "Tired" predates Langston Hughes's "The Negro Speaks of Rivers" and an argument can be made that it is Johnson's poem that most urgently clears the last remains of the genteel tradition so that Hughes's blues sensibility can come to the fore. It is most certainly the poem that has the firmest hold in the African American literary canon. Poet, critic, activist and historian James Weldon Johnson included "Tired" in his pioneering 1922 anthology of "Negro Poetry" even though the poem's sensibility deeply disturbed him. The poem begins by invoking a term highly charged in the early decades of the twentieth century: "I am tired of work: I am tired of building up somebody else's civilization." Fenton Johnson's invocation of "civilization" recalls the resurgence of eugenicist and racialist thinking and systematizing that marred a common social philosophy of the early twenties even as he points to its dismissal. The narrator's voice goes on to a reverie upon the end of his enforced work and an end to remembering. Its infamous conclusion, with its sense of resignation to defeat, has been jarring to generations of readers:

Throw the children into the river; civilization has given
us too many. It is better to die than it is to grow up
and find out that you are colored.
Pluck the stars out of the heavens. The stars mark our
destiny. The stars marked my destiny.
I am tired of civilization.

It speaks to the power of the poem that a reader as skilled as James Weldon Johnson might be distracted by the common critical error of assuming that the poem's speaker was transparently the voice of the author. Lorenzo Thomas argues instead that "Tired" exemplifies the "hyperbolic dramatization" that is consistent with and characteristic of the blues, and, as such, Johnson is voicing a real energy within the black community, but hardly making a political argument.[6] African American literary and cultural history records the stories of many individuals and groups who considered suicide or even infanticide as a response to slavery, but Johnson's poetic suggestion was jarring to many not ready to capitulate. The poem speaks to a focused, total, and even pragmatic pessimism that can be both an individual cry and a collective gesture by the community that is meant to undermine a culture of official optimism. Fenton Johnson is never again so total or destructive as he is in "Tired," but his series of portrait poems begins to build the poetic equivalent to the urban fictional space shaped by African American writer Rudolph Fisher. As Johnson figures it, the Great Migration—in combination with Jim Crow segregation—is costly in terms of the isolation, disappointment, and often false promise it offers to African Americans.

Johnson's plan seems to have been to gather all this work into a manuscript to be called *African Nights*. Despite the change in tone and strategy, the title suggests real continuity with the cultural nationalist project he seemed to invoke on many occasions in the prior decade. (In an account of the history of African American poetry that he wrote for the WPA's Writers' Project, he specifically asserted that he belonged in a group with other "nationalist poets.") The manuscript has never surfaced in its totality, but, if it was meant to include work produced for Harriet Monroe's *Poetry* magazine, for critic Alfred Kreymborg's *Others* magazine, and other occasional pieces from the 1920s, it would have most certainly by far have been his most successful volume.

Johnson also collected a series of essays and short stories into two volumes, *For the Highest Good* and *Tales of Darkest America*, both published in 1920, but, like the early poetry volumes, these were sloppily done, despite often revealing his increasingly dark humor and disappointment with the contemporary cultural scene. In a preface unlike any other in the African American literary tradition, Johnson wrote desperately in his introduction to *Tales* that "I know that I am facing ruin and starvation . . . I know that my dream of success in literature is fading." It is important to keep in mind that Johnson's eventual retreat from the public sphere has meant that there is a significant dearth of information about events that may help us understand the aesthetic and cultural distance between texts, and even less information on the very specific personal and financial crises that seemed to dominate his thoughts in these years. There is no reliable information as to how Johnson lived the last years of his fully active literary life; we know he had married in the late 1910s, but we have no information on the success of this marriage or how long it may have endured. Given his class and social roots, an inability to build for himself (and his wife) a comfortable existence must have been personally devastating.

Poet, critic, and memoirist Frank Marshall Davis arrived in Chicago around 1927 and recalls meeting Johnson at "writing club events" but has no details to deliver. This certainly suggests that Johnson's reclusiveness was perhaps never as total as some commentators have suggested. Indeed, a report for the "Negro in Illinois" group of the Illinois Writers' Project of the WPA (IWP) placed Johnson amid at least one writing and reading group of black Chicagoans. Known as the "Letters" circle, none of the individuals within the group were distinguished as literary artists, but it did include journalist and social worker Dewey Jones and educator and Civil Rights activist Horace Bond. However this alters our understanding of Johnson supposedly abandoning literature sometime in the late 1920s, we still know nothing about how Johnson made a living after the collapse of *The Favorite*, until he resurfaces in the offices of the Illinois Writers' Project of the WPA in the late 1930s. Given the centrality of the "Negro in Illinois" project to the Illinois team, his arrival was opportune. Johnson was assigned tasks related to black literary and theatrical traditions in Chicago from the early part of the century, as well as more particular assignments to draw biographical profiles of significant African American figures in the city's history.

228 · JAMES C. HALL

He pursued these tasks with some vigor and also seemed to become a prime informant to other writers seeking to complete entries on aspects of the city's black cultural history.

The most compelling historical puzzle now facing critics and historians is determining whether Johnson's work with the project led to significant inter-action with figures from what we now call the Black Chicago Renaissance who had WPA connections (novelists Richard Wright and Frank Yerby, dancer and anthropologist Katherine Dunham, and poet Arna Bontemps), or relations to other major cultural configurations such as the South Side Community Arts Center or the South Side Writers Group. The other possibility, of course, is that Johnson's own participation in the emergence and activities of these organi-zations and collectives actually led to his work with the Writers' Project. It is quite provocative to reflect on the kinds of advice, guidance, and caution that Fenton Johnson would have given a new generation of black artists and intel-lectuals full of Popular Front fervor. Johnson was well-positioned to deliver a cautionary tale about permanence and the lack of a direct connection between respect and personal wealth. If there is no clear aesthetic inheritance to the Black Chicago Renaissance to be found, there are most certainly compelling family resemblances. Through the poetry of Frank Marshall Davis, and, to a lesser extent (and much less directly), the work of poet Gwendolyn Brooks and fiction writer and journalist Frank London Brown, we see the emergence of rich imagist techniques toward the construction of complex (and often dark and foreboding) urban profiles. Each writer hovers around or deeply shares a suspicion of the effects of modernity, and can be seen repeating and extending Johnson's troubling alienated contemporary consciousness. Black writers and artists of 1920s and 1930s Chicago may have taken from Fenton Johnson a deep commitment to irony as a fundamental literary mode. Because Johnson had deep roots in that community, his and their use of that mode does not displace social criticism so much as direct greater attention to the emotional and per-sonal aspects of African American existence.

In somewhat dramatic or melodramatic fashion, after having been released from the FWP, Johnson left a manuscript of poems on the desk of fiction writer and project staffer Jack Conroy. The manuscript was eventually titled (but not published) by Arna Bontemps as *The Daily Grind: 42 WPA Poems*. Bontemps eventually used five poems from the manuscript for his mid-1960s anthology *American Negro Poetry*. *The Daily Grind* is alternately moving and morbid. There are moments when Johnson is able to recapture the striking detachment associated with the best poems of the 1920s, when he reveals himself to be a skilled observer of urban life and sensitive to the complex nexus of urban life, ambition, and survival, especially as it was framed by the economic depres-sion and the New Deal. In "The WPA Gang Foreman," more than twenty-five

years after Hoover's wrongheaded assertion that *The Favorite* might harbor
radicalism, Johnson does meditate upon the nearness of revolution: "I shudder not for these men I command, / I shudder for those who scoff at them. /
I am human, even as they are human. / When one leans on a shovel he thinks.
/ There is dynamite in your thinkers." As it was at the beginning of his career,
however, he was desperately in need of sharp and impartial editorial guidance
and the quality of the work varied greatly. Critic Hammitt Worthington Smith
has argued that the final gathering of poems is significant in that they represent
a novel and sustained attempt by Johnson to shape a continuous meditation
on the concept of love. There is indeed evidence of such an investigation and
it is not simple pathos, but, as in earlier volumes, Johnson has never been at
his best when pursuing a more philosophic lyrical mode. The meditations on
love, however insistent as theme, are rarely successful. Much more successful
are those lyrics that operate as theological meditation. In the title poem, "The
Daily Grind," Johnson adapts the sardonic voice that has previously served the
short, imagistic urban profiles:

> Naught can you do
> but watch that eternal battle
> between Nature and the System.
> You cannot blame God,
> you cannot blame Man
> for God did not make the System
> neither did Man fashion Nature.
> You can only die each morning
> and live again in the dreams of the night.
> If Nature forgets you,
> If the system forgets you,
> God has blest you.

Other poems, like "Dust" and "The Old Repair Man" also operate successfully
in this mode and are suggestive of what Johnson might have been capable if he
had been surrounded by able critics and editors.

The volume's most coherent and sustained attention is paid to the situation of
a writer enveloped by the WPA itself, which appears in Johnson's poetic vision
as simultaneously safety net and prison. "Producers," "Rewrite Man," "Rookie
Field Worker," "The Senior Writer, Professional," "Rosemary for Chicago Poets,"
"The Artist's Chicago," and "A WPA Director" make up a lucid meditation upon
the paradox of "writing" to serve government demand. Given few, if any, alternatives, the opportunity to work as writer, as idea producer, is crucial to survival.
At the same time, for Johnson, there is incoherence, even punishment in the
placement of the writer in the midst of an evolving bureaucracy. Some of this

anxiety seems consistent with a longstanding ambivalence in Johnson toward the coming of a full modernity, while there is also some hint of a slightly less noble complaint that this work is just somehow beneath him. In the final manuscript, Johnson can be seen settling scores old and new. Kicking back at "supervision," he is also replaying the past and trying to make sense of the circumstances that led to the complex trail of loss and disappointment. "'We're getting somewhere on the road to Art'" says the narrator of "The Re-Write Man," "Sixty thousand words of field workers' copy—/ Grind it down, Bussel, into twenty lines," where the speaker of "Rookie Field Worker," says "I have trod many, many miles for a foolish job." In "An Artist's Chicago," and in a voice that feels more transparently that of Johnson, we hear that "I was only a dreamer, / and you broke me as easily / as you break brittle straw."

The single best poem in the volume is modest and sad and, perhaps, a literal transcription. "A Negro Peddler's Song" harks back to Johnson's hopeful nationalist project and recalls too the powerful urban profiles of the 1920s:

> Good Lady,
> buy for Mary and for John,
> and when the work is done
> give a bite to Sadie.
> . . . .
> Good Lady,
> I have corn and beets
> onions, too, and leeks
> and also sweet Pota-ty

This brief, even ethnographic fragment, most importantly reminds us what a good eye and ear Johnson had. While he is never able to conjure a full *or* ironic nostalgia, the final manuscript does help to explain the fragmented perspective of earlier efforts. Johnson on the one hand craves a previous utopian and organic construction, the rich "racial tradition," but he remains on the other an unreconstructed lonely urbanite at heart.

Fenton Johnson died mostly alone in a Chicago nursing home in 1958. His legacy to African American literature is a diverse and experimental poetics that provided the basis for future poets to build a sophisticated synthesis of modernism, nationalism, and existentialism. The best of his work has a rich interest in the possibilities of the African American past even as he came to a moment in his career where he recognized the necessity of an urgent experimentation and forward-looking aesthetic. He innovated as a black intellectual and as a cultural entrepreneur even as his experience in those areas was fundamentally cautionary.

Notes

1. Relevant archival materials are to be found at Special Collections, Fisk University Library; Cullen-Jackman Collection of the Arnett Library, Atlanta University; Harriet Monroe Collection at the Regenstein Library, University of Chicago; Vivian Harsh Collection at the Woodson Branch of the Chicago Public Library. Professor Hammett Worthington-Smith of Albright College in Pennsylvania worked for decades on a project to document Johnson's life and was gracious enough to give me his research notes and files. Some of the biographical details related here have come from the correspondence with early black Chicago literary and cultural figures that are in his collection.

2. Thomas, Lorenzo. *Extraordinary Measures Afrocentric Modernism and Twentieth-Century American Poetry.* Tuscaloosa: University of Alabama Press, 2000, 18–19.

3. Hayden, Robert, ed. *Kaleidoscope: Poems by American Negro Poets.* New York: Harcourt, Brace and World, 1967, 40.

4. Johnson, Fenton. "Introduction." In *Visions of the Dusk.* New York: Trachtenberg, 1915, n.p.

5. Undated letter, Frank Marshall Davis to Hammett Worthington-Smith, in the author's possession.

6. Thomas, *Extraordinary Measures*, 34.

For Further Reading

Brown, Sterling. *Negro Poetry and Drama.* Washington, D.C.: Associates in Negro Folk Education, 1937.

Hutchinson, James P. "Fenton Johnson: Pilgrim of the Dusk." *Studies in Black Literature* 7 (Autumn 1976): 14–15.

Johnson, Fenton. "Absalom's Death." *Chicago Broad Axe*, February 24, 1900, n.p.

———. *A Little Dreaming.* Chicago: Peterson Linotyping Co., 1913.

———. "The Black Fairy." *The Crisis* 6 (1913): 292–94.

———. *Visions of the Dusk.* New York: Trachtenberg, 1915.

———. *Songs of the Soil.* New York: Trachtenberg, 1916.

———. "De Witch 'Ooman." In *The Chicago Anthology: A Collection of Verse from the Work of Chicago Poets*, edited by Charles G. Blanden and Minna Mathison. Chicago: Roadside Press, 1916, 104–5.

———. "The Call of the Patriot," "The Sunset," and "Rulers." *The Liberator* 1 (1918): 25.

———. "War Profiles." *The Crisis* 16.2 (June 1918): 65.

———. "The Last Love," "How Long, O Lord," and "Who Is That A-Walking in the Corn?" *Poetry* 11 (June 1918): 136–37.

———. "The New Day." In *Victory! Celebrated by Thirty-eight American Poets*, edited by William Stanley Braithwaite. Boston: Small, Maynard, 1919.

———. "Tired." *Others* 5 (January 1919): 8.

———. "Aunt Hanna Jackson," "Aunt Jane Allen," "The Gambler," "The Barber," and the "Drunkard." *Others* 5 (February 1919): 17–18.

———. "The Artist" and "Dreams." *Others* 5 (April–May 1919): 20.

———. *For the Highest Good.* Chicago: Favorite Magazine, 1920.

———. *Tales of Darkest America.* Chicago: Favorite Magazine, 1920.

———. "A Dream," and "The Wonderful Morning." *Poetry* 19 (December 1921): 128–29.

———. "The Lost Love," "How Long, O Lord," and "Who Is That A-Walking in the Corn?" In *The New Poetry: An Anthology of Twentieth-Century Verse in English,* edited by Harriet Monroe and Alice Corbin Henderson. New York: Macmillan, 1923, 218–19.

———. "Sweet Love O' Dusk." *The Crisis* 34 (October 1927): 265.

———. "The Banjo Player," "The Drunkard," and "The Minister." In *An Anthology of American Poetry: Lyric America, 1639–1930,* edited by Alfred Kreymborg. New York: Tudor Publishing, 1930, 537–38.

———. "Children of the Sun," "The New Day," "Tired," "The Banjo Player," "The Scarlet Woman," and lines from "The Vision of Lazarus." In *The Book of American Negro Poetry,* edited by James Weldon Johnson. New York: Harcourt, Brace, 1931, 141–46.

———. "Rulers," "The Banjo Player," "The Scarlet Woman," "Tired," "Aunt Jane Allen," "When I Die," "The Lonely Mother," and "Who Is That A-Walking in the Corn?" In *The Poetry of the Negro, 1746–1949,* edited by Langston Hughes and Arna Bontemps. Garden City: Doubleday, 1949, 61–64.

———. "The Daily Grind," "The World Is a Mighty Ogre," "A Negro Peddler's Song," "The Old Repair Man," and "Counting." In *American Negro Poetry,* edited by Arna Bontemps. New York: Hill and Wang, 1964, 25–28.

———. *The Daily Grind.* Heritage black poetry pamphlet 2. London, U.K.: The Heritage Press, 1994.

———. *42 WPA Poems.* Unpublished ms. c. 1935–40.

Kerlin, Robert. *Negro Poets and Their Poems.* Washington, D.C.: Associate Publishers, 1935.

Lumpkin, Shirley. "Fenton Johnson." In *Dictionary of Literary Biography, Volume 45: American Poets, 1880–1945, First Series,* edited by Peter Quartermain. Detroit: Gale Group, 1986, 214–20.

Redding, Jay Saunders. *To Make a Poet Black.* Chapel Hill: University of North Carolina Press, 1939.

Redmond, Eugene. *Drumvoices: The Mission of Afro-American Poetry, A Critical History.* Garden City, N.J.: Anchor/Doubleday, 1976.

Wagner, Jean. *Black Poets of the United States from Paul Laurence Dunbar to Langston Hughes.* Urbana: University of Illinois Press, 1976.

Woolley, Lisa. "From Chicago Renaissance to Chicago Renaissance: The Poetry of Fenton Johnson." *Langston Hughes Review* 14(1–2) (1996): 36–48; see also Joseph Harrington, "A Response to Lisa Wooley," 49–51.

Worthington-Smith, Hammett. "Fenton Johnson." In *Dictionary of Literary Biography, Volume 50: Afro-American Writers before the Harlem Renaissance.* A Bruccoli Clark Layman Book, edited by Trudier Harris. Detroit: Gale Group, 1986, 202–5.

———. "The Poetry of Fenton Johnson." Unpublished ms. in possession of the author. n.d.

JOHN H. JOHNSON
(1918–2005)
Jamal Eric Watson

During World War II, African Americans found themselves battling two very different wars as part of what was known as the "Double V" challenge: a war against fascist forces in Europe and a war on the home front against racism in the United States. Even as African Americans enlisted in the U.S. military to defeat the Nazi's occupation in Europe, they knew that life under a set of regimented Jim Crow laws would prevent them from achieving recognition as full citizens in America. When they returned to America after fighting abroad, these heroic African American soldiers were prohibited from drinking from certain water fountains and eating at various restaurants.

The Black Press, which had had a long tradition of advocating for African Americans dating back to 1827 in New York with the publication of *Freedom's Journal*, quickly emerged as an important resource in articulating the interests of African Americans in the early 1940s. In major cities like Chicago, where the Chicago Renaissance was well under way, Black newspapers like the *Chicago Defender*, which was founded in 1905 by Robert Sengstacke Abbott and later passed down to his nephew John H. Sengstacke, boasted an impressive circulation of 82,059. The newspaper challenged the discrimination that had become so pervasive throughout the country.

It was in this tradition that John Harold Johnson created what would later become a multimillion dollar enterprise: Johnson Publishing Company. It is no coincidence that Johnson would build his company in the same city where Sengstacke's firm was headquartered, thus making Chicago a popular destination spot for African American writers looking to begin careers writing for Black-owned publications.

Born on January 19, 1918, in rural Arkansas City, Arkansas, to Leroy Johnson and Gertrude Jenkins Johnson, an impoverished Black family, John H. Johnson suffered a series of devastating setbacks as a child. His father was tragically killed in a sawmill accident when he was just eight years old, and Johnson was quickly forced to confront the harsh realities of segregation in the South. He attended the community's overcrowded, racially segregated elementary school because Blacks were unable to enroll elsewhere. Following the path that took many African American southerners from the South to the North, young Johnson and his mother set out for Chicago in 1933 in a journey as part of the African American Great Migration. Johnson's mother decided that the Jim Crow South was not a good place to raise a Black child from whom she expected greatness. There were no Black high schools in the town of Johnson's birth. In fact, Johnson repeated the eighth grade just to keep learning. To give her only son an opportunity for a better life, Johnson's mother worked as a camp cook on a levee for two years to save up enough money for the train trip to Chicago, where she and her young son lived with a friend to keep costs down. Johnson's stepfather joined the family later.

Early on, Johnson credited his mother with providing him with self-discipline and motivation that helped him to remain focused despite the racial discrimination he later felt and witnessed as a young boy. "My mother was the influence in my life," said Johnson in an interview a year before his death from heart failure. "She was a strong woman and believed in justice. She believed that if you worked hard, you would achieve," he said. "I knew very early on that I stood on the shoulders of many who came before me and I came to understood very quickly that these heroic Black men and women helped to carve out a space for me to grow and succeed."[1]

Johnson honed his intellectual skills at DuSable High School in Chicago, eventually emerging as a student leader among his peers. Among his classmates were singer Nat King Cole, actor Redd Foxx, and future entrepreneur William Abernathy. Though he was later offered a scholarship to attend the University of Chicago, he never completed his studies there, focusing his energy instead on working for Chicago's Supreme Liberty Life Insurance Company. One of Johnson's duties at the insurance company was to collect news and information about African Americans while preparing a weekly digest for Harry Pace, the company's president.

It was while working at the insurance company that Johnson became convinced that there was an untapped market for an African American magazine. Over a period of several years, he worked tirelessly to try and develop a marketing and business plan for such a publication. He wanted his magazine, like the *Chicago Defender*, to have a national audience, read by political newsmakers as well as ordinary African Americans. He did not favor an "objective" magazine. From the very beginning, he wanted the publication to be driven by an advocacy agenda.

A year after marrying Eunice Walker, a native Alabaman whose father was a doctor and whose mother was a high-school principal and a college instructor, Johnson mortgaged his mother's furniture for a meager $500 so he could pay for his first direct mail advertising about his magazine, *Negro Digest*, which he launched in 1942. The letter that Johnson sent out to the public offered subscriptions at two dollars each and he eventually managed to bring in 3,000 subscribers. When the 5,000 printed copies did not sell out, he asked thirty of his friends to inquire about the magazine at local newsstands in order to create a demand. Modeled after the popular *Readers' Digest*, within eight months, *Negro Digest* reached $50,000 a month in sales. The magazine featured articles about the growing social inequities in the United States and provided a platform for African Americans to read about a wide range of critical issues such as housing discrimination and the reported cases of lynchings in the South. Still, with few resources, Johnson set up his publishing company on the second floor of Chicago's Supreme Life Insurance Company building and assumed the title of both editor and publisher. Though he had no journalistic background, he would assign and edit the news stories and actively run the business operation, which primarily focused on generating advertising revenue.

By October 1942, the readership of *Negro Digest* continued to soar, with 100,000 copies of the magazine being sold. It had a readership that extended far beyond Chicago, an extended audience for which Johnson had hoped. Johnson was even able to convince First Lady Eleanor Roosevelt to write a column entitled "If I was a Negro." In the piece, Roosevelt conceded that if she were Black, she would have experienced great bitterness as a citizen in the United States. After the column was published, people attacked *Negro Digest* as a Communist magazine and the column highlighted the racial plight that African Americans were forced to endure. Despite the controversy over the publication of Eleanor Roosevelt's column, a young Johnson was also startled by the success that the magazine had generated and, over time, he convinced Norman Thomas, Marshall Field, and other white political leaders to pen essays for the growing publication. "I was both surprised and shocked by its success, but realized that we had developed something extremely important to America. People were reading us," he said.[2]

Soon after the magazine gained national prominence, writers began to flock to Johnson looking for an opportunity to publish their work. Freelance photographers followed in tow. They came from far and near for an opportunity to be published in the country's most premier Black magazine. Among writers associated with the era are Richard Wright, Gwendolyn Brooks, Frank Marshall Davis, William Attaway, Frank London Brown, Willard Motley, Theodore Ward, Frank Yerby, and Lorraine Hansberry, all of whom either published in or sought to publish in Johnson's magazine. The Black Chicago Renaissance was fueled by two unprecedented social and economic conditions: the "great migration" of Southern Blacks to Chicago in search of economic opportunity and perceived safety from lynch mob rule, and the crisis of the Great Depression that followed. Johnson's *Negro Digest* provided a valuable local and national outlet for a number of writers associated with the Chicago Renaissance to express their ideas.

By this time, there were dozens of Black newspapers across the country like the *Chicago Defender,* the *Pittsburgh Courier* and the *New York Amsterdam News,* but the idea of a Black national magazine was relatively new. While *Crisis,* the publication of the NAACP and *Opportunity,* the publication of the National Urban League existed, some viewed these publications as mere tools for the civil rights organizations that were deeply political and some did not feel that the magazines adequately portrayed Black life in the United States outside of the struggle for civil rights.

The widespread support that Johnson received from African Americans ultimately enabled him to purchase the company's first building at 5619 South State Street in Chicago. It was there that he launched the magazine *Ebony,* named by his wife Eunice. *Ebony* is currently the oldest continuously running African American magazine in the country. The magazine, which was launched in 1945, was initially targeted to the Black middle class, but quickly became a popular item in most Black homes, as well as in barber shops, beauty salons, and the offices of Black physicians and dentists. The magazine transcended class differences. Its mission specifically was to train a spotlight on the achievements and successes of African Americans at a time in which Black accomplishments were largely ignored by mainstream media. The magazine prominently featured pictures and long-range profiles of African Americans graduating from college and Black couples getting married, and showcased African American births, as well as their academic and scientific achievements. Johnson broke new ground by bringing positive portrayals of Blacks into a mass-market publication and encouraging corporations to use Black models in advertising aimed at Black consumers.

Early on, *Ebony* was barely surviving when Johnson's pursuit of advertisers landed him ads from Zenith Corporation. With a major white radio manufacturing firm on board, others soon followed and the magazine thrived, so much so that it was joined by other Johnson Publishing Company products: *Jet, Ebony Man, Tan Confessions, Copper Romance, Ebony Jr.,* and *Ebony International.* Today, only *Ebony* and *Jet* are published.

As a show of his persistence, in the mid-1940s, Johnson sent an ad salesman to Detroit every week for ten years before an auto manufacturer agreed to advertise in *Ebony.* "We couldn't do it then by marching, and we couldn't do it by threatening," Johnson said of gaining advertisers. "We had to persuade people that it was in their best interest to reach out to Black consumers in a positive way. We knew that we had a product that was not inferior."[3] By the mid-sixties *Ebony* was riding a crest, featuring articles by Dr. Martin Luther King Jr., journalist Carl T. Rowan, and Lerone Bennett Jr., whose scholarship and reputation as a public historian gave the publication additional cachet. There was some derision in the late sixties from activists, however, and eventually *Black World,* formerly *Negro Digest,* was shut down in April 1976.

The demise of one element of the Johnson Empire was soon replaced by other ventures, including the increasing popularity of the Ebony Fashion Fair, a division of Johnson Publishing Company that was started from scratch. With an idea and twenty bottles from a chemist, Johnson created the largest Black-owned cosmetics company in the world. The logic behind Johnson's new venture was his belief that Black women's needs had been ignored by the major cosmetics industries. He had argued that existing products were not marketed or sold to meet the particular needs of women of color. Many women with deeper skin tones were to choose from products that were clearly made with fair skin tones in mind. When Johnson noticed that models in the Fashion Fair, the company's traveling fashion show, mixed foundations to create the right blend to match their hues, he was driven into action. First, Johnson approached existing cosmetics companies and urged them to create a line specifically to meet the needs of Black women. When no one took up the challenge, Johnson and his wife decided instead to take the matter into their own hands. They went to a private lab that created permanent formulas out of the mixtures the models had been making.

After experimenting by using the makeup on the models in the fashion show, the Johnsons produced a mail-order package called the *Capsule Collection* in 1969. The response was overwhelming. It became clear almost immediately that there was a market for a Black cosmetics line. Fashion Fair Cosmetics was born in 1973, named after the fashion show that inspired it. The line was marketed to high-line department stores and opened its first counter in Chicago at Marshall Fields on State Street. Today, Fashion Fair is the world leader in the field of cosmetics for all women of color and its products are sold in stores across the United States as well as in Canada, Africa, the Caribbean, England, France, and other countries around the world.

Though Johnson ventured into cosmetics, his passion remained publishing. He had transformed the industry so much that he was affectionately called the godfather of African American publishing. In this capacity, he built *Ebony* from a circulation of 25,000 on its first press run in November 1945 to a monthly circulation of 1.9 million in 1997. *Ebony* was launched just after World War II, as African American soldiers were returning home. At the time, there were no African American players in major league baseball and virtually no Black political representation holding city, state and national office. In fact, civil rights leader Roy Wilkins of the NAACP strongly encouraged Johnson not to enter the publishing world, predicting failure for his venture. Wilkins later recanted and apologized to Johnson, telling the publisher that he underestimated his skills.

The success of *Ebony* was followed six years later by the creation of yet another magazine, which Johnson felt he could successfully market and sell to African Americans. In 1951, *Jet*, a pocket-sized weekly publication that highlighted news of African Americans in the social limelight, political arena, entertainment business, and sports world became popular almost immediately. The magazine, which is still in existence along with *Ebony*, has a readership of over eight million.

Jet's coverage of Emmett Till's killing is considered a major development in the civil rights movement. The magazine's one photograph of Emmett Till, his body mutilated after being beaten by white men after he allegedly whistled at a white woman, exposed the entire Black community to the challenges of life for Blacks in the South, Johnson recounted. Johnson said that at the time, some on the *Jet* staff were squeamish about using the Till funeral photographs. "I had reservations, too, but I decided finally that if it happened, it was our responsibility to print it and let the world experience man's inhumanity to man."[4]

The popularity of *Jet* further pushed Johnson into other enterprises, adding to his lucrative empire. He would later start new magazine ventures, and publish books, including Lerone Bennett Jr.'s groundbreaking bestseller *Before the Mayflower*, a classic text. Additionally, he built several radio stations and became the majority owner in Supreme Liberty Life Insurance, the company that gave him his first career opportunity. In the 1950s, Johnson expanded his profile and became active in national politics. He began a long career of serving in special positions in both Republican and Democratic administrations. In 1957, he accompanied Vice President Richard M. Nixon on a special goodwill tour to nine African countries and was a part of his delegation two years later when he toured Russia and Poland. President John F. Kennedy appointed Johnson as Special U.S. Ambassador to the Independence Ceremonies of the Ivory Coast in 1961, a position he would serve for two years until he was appointed in 1963 as Special U.S. Ambassador to the Independence Ceremonies of Kenya.

Johnson was an investor in *Essence* magazine, founded in 1970, which soon became the most successful magazine for African American women, one of the last Black-owned magazines with a national following. In 2002, the magazine was sold to Time Warner Corporation. The sale of *Essence* essentially left Johnson as the lone African American publisher of a major publication. In 1972, Johnson was named Publisher of the Year by the Magazine Publishers Association. In 1974, the National Newspaper Publishers Association, a consortium of Black publications, named him the "Most Outstanding Black Publisher in History." In 2003, Baylor University named him the "The Greatest Minority Entrepreneur in U.S. History." In that same year, Howard University named its communications school the John H. Johnson School of Communications after Johnson made a financial donation of $4 million to the historically Black college.

Despite his ailing health, Johnson did not slow down. He occupied the top floor of the office building that he purchased in downtown Chicago. In fact, Johnson was also the first African American to build a major building in downtown Chicago where his publishing empire is housed. In 1982, he became the first African American to appear on the Forbes list of 400 wealthiest Americans, though, as he liked to remind people, back in the 1930s in Chicago his family made only the welfare list. He was recognized for his philanthropy and lauded for his giving to Black organizations and also served on many advisory commissions at the local, state, and federal levels. In addition, he served on the boards of a number of major corporations and educational, cultural, and philanthropic organizations. In his 1989 autobiography, *Succeeding Against the Odds*, Johnson wrote: "no matter where I am or what I'm doing, I'm always looking for opportunities to make money."[5] By 1990, Johnson's personal wealth was estimated at $150 million, making Johnson's Publishing Company the largest Black-owned publishing company in the world.

In 1995, on the 50th anniversary of the founding of *Ebony*, Johnson received the Presidential Medal of Freedom, America's highest civilian honor, from President Bill Clinton. At the ceremony, Clinton asserted that Johnson gave "African-Americans a voice and a face, in his words, 'a new sense of somebody-ness,' of who they were and what they could do, at a time when they were virtually invisible in mainstream American culture." Johnson's business success and his involvement in the community won him invitations to serve on the board of directors of major American corporations. He served first on the board of Twentieth Century Fox Film Corporation and later on the boards of companies such as VIAD, Chrysler, Zenith, Conrail, Bell and Howell, Continental Bank, and Dillard Department Stores. He served as a trustee of the Art Institute of Chicago, the United Negro College Fund, and the National Conference of Christians and Jews. Time after time, he was credited as one of the trailblazers in business and international media and is acknowledged as the first entrepreneur to recognize the colossal buying power of Black America.

"Retirement is not in this company's vocabulary," said Johnson. "I am firmly of the belief that if you are well and able to work, you can stay at the company and that's what I plan to do. I have never imagined doing anything but working. Quite frankly, I wouldn't know what to do." On August 8, 2005, Johnson died at the age of 87. He was working in his office just a few days before he was hospitalized and died.

His funeral at Rockefeller Memorial Chapel in Chicago drew over 2,000 people, including President Bill Clinton. But the news coverage of Johnson's death was also scrutinized. African Americans leaders felt that mainstream media did not adequately cover Johnson's death. Only a handful of newspapers placed Johnson on the front page. Most newspapers, however, had no front-page story but referred to a piece on Johnson inside the paper, sometimes using a front-page photo. Those papers included the *Los Angeles Times*, California's *San Jose Mercury News*, Florida's *Tampa Tribune*, the *Detroit Free Press*, Minnesota's

St. Paul Pioneer Press, Mississippi's *Biloxi Sun-Herald*, the *Kansas City Star*, the *New York Times*, the *Democrat and Chronicle* in Rochester, N.Y., Texas's *Austin American-Statesman*, the *Dallas Morning News*, and *USA Today*.

Papers that gave Johnson no front-page presence at all included many of the mainstream papers that have African American editors in top positions. They included the *Arkansas Democrat-Gazette* in Little Rock, which had initiated coverage, three months before his death, of Johnson's return to Arkansas City, where he grew up in the 1920s, and where his hometown and state helped turn his childhood home into a museum. The state of Arkansas turned his boyhood home into a museum. The John H. Johnson Delta Cultural Entrepreneurial Learning Center was designed to educate youngsters about Johnson's life. Of the three broadcast networks, "CBS Evening News" and "NBC Nightly News" both gave Johnson short mentions on the nightly newscasts Monday—57 words on CBS and 66 on NBC. There was no mention on ABC's "World News Tonight."

Johnson, who retained the titles of chairman and publisher until his death, made Johnson Publishing a family business. His mother, Gertrude, was a vice president of the firm until her death in 1977; her office remains as she left it. His wife, Eunice W. Johnson, is secretary-treasurer. His daughter, Linda Johnson Rice, held several positions before she became CEO.

Like other powerful men, Johnson had his fair share of critics. Some former employees said he was a tough, hard-driven boss who spent too much time focused on the bottom line. In fact, he was once quoted as saying, or joking, as he offered later in his defense, that he would push over a ten-story building on a baby if it meant stopping a threat to his business. And despite his success, over the years some Blacks complained that *Ebony* was too oriented toward the middle class and skirted hard news in favor of success stories. In recent years, the magazine has largely focused on covering Black celebrities. Johnson himself acknowledged that "we don't rush to print critical things about Black leaders— even if it's true,"[6] acknowledging that the magazine ignored the missteps and shortcomings of Black political leaders.

Despite his detractors, however, Johnson received an impressive list of honors from America's most prestigious educational institutions. During his lifetime, he received honorary degrees from thirty-one colleges, including Harvard, Howard, and Northwestern Universities, a major recognition for someone who did not even graduate from college.

"The tallest tree in the history of African American journalism has fallen, but has fallen gracefully," said civil rights leader Rev. Jesse L. Jackson who spoke at Johnson's funeral. "The tree that stood tall for over sixty years and a tree that planted a forest, a tree with widespread limbs and full of fruit. He connected to Africa and African Americans. He shared the pain of Emmett Till, the development of Martin Luther King Jr., and was a source of information and inspiration. He was the number one black publisher for sixty years. His impact had been felt through the whole world of journalism."[7]

Notes

1. Interview with John H. Johnson, July 17, 2004.
2. Ibid.
3. Ibid.
4. Ibid.
5. Johnson, John H. *Succeeding Against the Odds: The Autobiography of a Great Businessman.* New York: Amistad, 1993.
6. Johnson, interview with author, July 17, 2004.
7. Interview with Jesse L. Jackson, September 13, 2005.

For Further Reading

Finkle, Lee. *Forum for Protest: The Black Press during World War II.* Rutherford, N.J.: Fairleigh Dickinson University Press, 1975.

Johnson, John H. *Succeeding Against the Odds: The Autobiography of a Great Businessman.* New York: Amistad, 1993.

Interview with Jesse L. Jackson, September 13, 2005.

Interview with John H. Johnson, July 17, 2004.

Simmons, Charles A. *The African American Press: With Special References to Four Newspapers, 1827–1965.* New York: McFarland, 1998.

Streitmatter, Roger. *Voices of Revolution: The Dissident Press in America.* New York: Columbia University Press, 2001.

"MATTIE" MARIAN MINUS
(1913–1973)
Donyel Hobbs Williams

"Mattie" Marian Minus was a prolific writer who invested a significant portion of her life in uplifting the African American race. Although Minus was born in South Carolina, her parents, Laura Whitener Minus and Claude Wellington Minus, moved the family to Ohio around 1920. Eventually, Minus left Ohio to attend Fisk University in Tennessee; she graduated magna cum laude in 1935. Between 1935 and 1937 Minus attended graduate school at the University of Chicago where she majored in social anthropology.

During her stay in Chicago, Minus met Richard Wright, and in 1936 she became a member of the South Side Writers Group. Members of the group included poet and journalist Frank Marshall Davis, poet and novelist Margaret Walker, playwright Theodore Ward, poet Robert Davis, social worker and activist Fern Gayden, and others. The group's prime directive involved the responsibility of Black writers to a literary heritage that embraced European and white American influences as well as the social and political components of Black American life. After the South Side Writers Group disbanded in mid-1937, Minus returned to New York.

In addition to strengthening her personal relationship with Harlem Renaissance alumna Dorothy West, Minus also worked with West on the *Challenge* journal. Contributors to the journal included Langston Hughes, Sterling Brown, Margaret Walker, Alain Locke, Bruce Nugent, Ralph Ellison, Arna Bontemps, Frank Yerby, and Richard Wright. The journal was an important bridge between writers associated with the Harlem Renaissance and those who followed in its wake and sought to establish a new spirit in African American writing, including a number of writers associated with the Chicago Renaissance.

Minus's writing career began with "Present Trends in Negro Literature," which was published in *Challenge* in the Spring 1937 issue. In "Present Trends in Negro Literature" Marian Minus argued for an African American literature that reflects human nature, i.e., characterization and social situations, via an immortalized universal appeal. In other words, Minus imagined an African

American literature in which characters and social situations are universally identifiable and due to an invariable human nature, these self-same characters and social situations achieve immortality. In order to achieve this universality, Minus examines the evolution of African American writing as well as the role or task of the African American writer.

Minus likens the African American writer's development to the stages of human development. Whereas in infancy, the writer's creation may reflect symbolic "puppet-figures" who lack "the vitality of distinct characters," during the transition from "adolescence" to "adulthood" the writer's creations progress and the nondistinct characters morph into fully "embodied fellow-men and then the objects who reflect the social scene in terms of its operation upon them and their reaction to these forces." As she explains the task of the African American writer, Minus emphasizes the dichotomy of an African American heritage and perceptively acknowledges that the African American writer embraces a double-consciousness where the writer attempts to "holds close to him . . . his exclusive cultural heritage." Minus entreats the African American writer to "return to the earthy, burning, vital forces which typify the greater proportion of Negro existence" as this becomes a necessary "phase" toward universality and moralization. Furthermore, Minus suggests that the African American writer "look carefully to the legends, myths and ballads" because the "immortalized . . . culture heroes . . . will last for ages . . . [and] because they are people . . . who reflect the aspirations and failures of all humanity," these people embody "elements of universality."

The second consciousness, according to Minus, must be cognizant of the inherent likenesses of human nature—"human emotions, ideals and struggles." That being the case, Minus cautions the African American writer that even though "centuries of oppression are still to be exhausted" in African American literature, the "continued creation of [racialized] symbols" mar the likelihood of universality and immortalization due to perceptions of exclusion by some, while others may perceive "colorless mediums, . . . shibboleths, detached clichés, and . . . routine . . . stereotyped expressions." In addition to overshadowing the intent of African American literature, the danger in mass perceptions of the stereotypicality of literature lies in an ensuing restrictiveness, which threatens other "greater creative possibilities" and "the end of literary attainment for the Negro." In other words, Minus expresses apprehension at saturating the literary arena with the conventional, racialized protest literature that already prevailed. Minus believed that, eventually, the "consistent creation of poetry and prose out of prejudice" would result in a mass disregard for African American literature. Minus also evokes the belief that, perhaps, the most dangerous repercussion of literature of this style, is the possibility that it thwarts both the creation and the reception of the "great Negro novel." Ultimately, Minus stipulates that only through a "fusion" of the two consciousnesses, in which the African American writer identifies himself as "a member of a world-society," can the African American writer effectively meet his task of universality.

Criticism surrounding *Challenge*'s "nonpolitical aesthetic" initiated an editorial restructuring. The Fall 1937 issue of the journal bore a new name, *New Challenge*, and Richard Wright secured an associate editorship and West and Minus were coeditors. With Richard Wright at its helm, *New Challenge* assumed a more political stance. For this maiden issue, Wright collected entries from Sterling Brown, Frank Marshall Davis, Robert Davis, Ralph Ellison, Langston Hughes, Alain Locke, and Margaret Walker. Wright's manifesto, "Blueprint for Negro Writing," which incites terms such as "humble," "prim," "decorous," and "bourgeoisie" to describe the Black writers of the Harlem Renaissance, first appeared in *New Challenge*. Wright's scathing assessment of the Harlem Renaissance and its writers led Minus to write a positive review of Zora Neale Hurston's *Their Eyes Were Watching God*. Thus, Wright's dogma, verily at odds with West's and Minus's, along with financial difficulties, halted further publication of *New Challenge*.

As the journal publication came to an end, Minus's and West's struggles for survival eventually led West to the New York Works Progress Administration (WPA) and Minus to the New York Consumers Union where she worked as a correspondent. Minus related her experiences in the article, "The Negro as a Consumer," which appeared in the September 1938 issue of *Opportunity*. In "The Negro as a Consumer," Minus apprises consumers of the "poor merchandise"— "inferior food," "inferior clothes," and ineffective patented medicines that resulted in a "high" "mortality rate among Negroes"—that is "forced upon the buying public." Minus charges that the main goals of consumer organizations are "to make more palatable and easy the exploitation of purchasing groups." Thus, Black consumers make up this group due to their inabilities to save money and to make intelligent choices based upon complete and accurate product information. Minus further adds that withholding knowledge of food value and comparative shopping in all expenditures also contributes to this exploitation. In addition to ascertaining the quality of household expenditures—clothing, food, medicine, insurance, etc.—Minus entreats consumers to be aware of the working conditions of employees. Disproportionate wage rates based on race, "bootleg child labor," and substandard employment conditions and/or discrimination of any kind, may be relieved, according to Minus, if consumers embrace the concept of "boycotting." Minus cautions that only through consumer awareness can prejudicial marketing strategies be effectively eradicated; however, in order for consumers to receive adequate information, "unbiased" consumer research organizations must be established "which are in no way connected with distributors, manufacturers, or commercial interests generally."

Subsequent to the publication of "The Negro as a Consumer," between 1938 and 1952 Minus wrote for *The Crisis, Opportunity,* and *Woman's Day*. The body of writings Minus produced from the late 1930s to the early 1950s reflected an adherence to both the principles outlined in "Present Trends of Negro Literature" as well as the creed of the South Side Writers Group—the belief that African American literature must reflect the European and white American influences on the Black literary tradition. Minus's first published short story, "The Fine Line," appeared in the November 1939 issue of *Opportunity*. Part of a tradition from which Zora Neale Hurston and Frank Yerby, to name a few, would eventually follow, "The Fine Line," subtitled "A Story of the Color Line," analyzes race relations from the perspective of white characters.

The story's poor, white protagonist, sixteen-year-old Cadie Culkey, harbors contempt for those "of her kind" and herself as she associates them, and by extension, herself, with a bleak future. Cadie is reminded of her dreary existence as it is her four-dollar-per-week job as a mill worker that makes her the sole supporter of her family's seven members—a consumptive-stricken father who could not work; a mother who "couldn't go out and work" because "thirty cents a day wasn't worth it since the young ones had to be looked after"; and four "sallow"-faced sisters and brothers. Despite a poverty-filled existence—barefoot children, an inadequate diet and insufficient food, and the wooden shack called a home—imprinted in Cadie's psyche, primarily by her father, is the belief that her "status" as a white person makes her superior to "niggers."

However, following an encounter with a Black couple, Cadie reassesses her father's teachings. Instead of meeting lowlife Blacks whose living conditions, family ethics, and morals were beneath her own, this family introduces Cadie to a Black life where not only does politeness and hospitality toward one's fellow man prevail, the family possesses materialistic amenities that Cadie can only wish for. Additionally and, perhaps, most importantly, this concept of Blackness exemplifies an organized family structure—one comprised of order, ethics, morals, admiration, and love of family—a concept that is completely absent from Cadie's life. "The Fine Line" concludes with Cadie's uncertainty toward her father and his racist doctrine—one justified by religion. Cadie concedes that these Blacks are more than her equal; both economically and emotionally, they "were better off than the Culkeys had ever been." Primarily, "The Fine Line" functions are Minus's vehicle of illustrating the absurdity, irrationalism, and humiliation associated with racial prejudice.

Minus further conveys the concept of racial prejudice's humiliating consequences in "Girl, Colored," a short story published in the September 1940 issue of *The Crisis*. Carrie Johnson, a domestic in search of work, endures a humiliating interview from a potential white employer. Mrs. Cado P. Clark consistently taunts Johnson—throughout the interview process—with the prospect of rescinding the position and employing a "German girl" in her stead. Additionally, the proposed salary which undercompensates the workload, Clark's stinginess with time off and the meager living accommodations with which Clark expects Johnson to contend stem from Clark's knowledge of her advantage over Johnson's predicament—the "woman knew she needed the job." However, neither Mrs. Clark's threats of hiring someone else to fill the position nor her "prudence" with wages, time off, and accommodations compares to the dubious manner in which she scrutinizes Johnson's character—her reliability, her propensity to tell the "truth" as well as her trustworthiness—and the credibility of her references. And even though Johnson genuinely needed this position, Minus empowered her and allowed her some measure of advantage over her would-be employer. Mrs. Clark's need for domestic assistance rivaled Johnson's need for employment because, upon her arrival, Johnson noted that Mrs. Clark's disheveled appearance matched the state of disarray in the house. Thus, Johnson's demeanor during the interview process was not one of complete acquiescence. With facial gestures and verbal expressions, Johnson also expressed reservations about accepting the position. In effect, Minus endeavors to point out in "Girl, Colored" that in situations where African Americans may seem powerless or nonthreatening, in actuality an interior or internalized empowerment often exists waiting for the precise moment to present itself.

Such is the premise of "Half Bright," a short story published in the September 1940 issue of *Opportunity*. "Half Bright" tells the story of Sonny Blue, a twelve-year-old described as "good-natured" and quite big for his age. Many, including Sonny's parents, Jim and Hattie, believed "that Sonny Blue wasn't quite bright." In other words, a number of people suspect that Sonny may be developmentally challenged.

As the story unfolds, Jim Blue returns from town excited about a new plow the town's white store owner advanced him on credit. Blue's elation also stems from the owner's hospitality; following Blue's down payment, Mr. Simpson, in a gesture to treat his Black customers as equal to the white ones, carries the plow out to Blue's wagon. However, upon returning home, Blue discovers the plow missing and his wife states the likelihood that Simpson never placed it in the wagon. Sonny volunteers to uncover the truth regarding the plow's whereabouts, goes into town, and confronts Simpson.

The forcefulness of Sonny's confrontation, resulting in "his eyes los[ing] their childish, good-natured light," his "incredible" behavior, and his declaration, "I ain't near crazy as folks think I am. I ain' crazy one bit . . .," strikes enough fear in Simpson that the man and two others attempt to beat Sonny. Sonny bravely informs Simpson that he is not scared but he "jus' can' stan' bein' hit" because "it hurts me inside." Sonny dodges the offenders' blows and flees from Simpson and the mob that ensues and finds safety under a dangerous railroad trestle. Upon returning home, Sonny receives a beating from his mother as she perceives his disheveled appearance to mean he has been playing on the trestle in spite of her warnings against such behavior.

One of the implicit concepts in "Half Bright" is that due to the racism and the strained relationships between Blacks and Whites, Blacks' desire for equality often leaves them openly gullible. Conversely, Sonny's role in the short story also serves as a reminder that that which we perceive completely weak and susceptible may possess a strength and depth of force unlike any other. The "thing" inside Sonny that hurts him when stricken is Minus's metaphor for humaneness; with each blow to that childlike innocence, with every strike against that good-naturedness, humanity bring itself closer to its own ruin.

In addition to issues of race prejudice, Minus also directs attention to gender concerns and women's empowerment. In "The Fine Line" Cadie Culkey, the sixteen-year-old, sole provider for a family of seven and on the verge of womanhood, discovers one must form opinions of people based on one's experience. Cadie obtains empowerment as she understands that a person's idealized or romanticized concept of people may wholly differentiate from that which is real. Minus returns to this theme in "If Tom Were Only Here" published in the June 1945 issue of *Woman's Day* magazine. Following her father's death and her brother Tom's desertion, only through her job as a factory worker does Vivian Kent support herself and her mother, who suffers from a debilitating heart condition. Vivian's mother, and to some extent Vivian herself, believe that Tom's presence insures them a better standard of living. Vivian's workload would lessen and perhaps she could date and eventually marry. However, upon Tom's return twenty years later, Vivian realizes that her mother's, as well as her own, idealized version of an adult Tom significantly contradicts the makeup of the real-life man.

Whereas Vivian excelled in high school, graduating as class valedictorian, and graduating college with honors, Tom's lead a noncommittal life with connections to nothing, no place, and no one. Whereas Vivian adheres to a strict work ethic, one of which costs her the opportunity to begin a family of her own, Tom wallows in excuses to keep himself from a job. For Tom, first, too little compensation and then an injury prevents him from working. Upon acknowledging that the only way to initiate change lies with herself, Vivian understands her naiveté at the loyalty she bestowed upon an undeserving person; thus, she commits herself to reclaiming and proceeding with her life on her own terms.

In sync with the concept of universality, Minus utilizes winter as a metaphor for aging. In "Another Winter," published in the May 1946 issue of *Woman's Day*, Nella Adams is confronted with the reality that as one ages, nothing remains the same. As Nella returns to her summer vacation home each person whom she encounters refers to winter and the changes that have taken place in their lives during that period. The most profound impact, however, comes from Nella's neighbor, Mrs. Pearson. Pearson explains that in an attempt to maintain some measure of youthfulness, she discarded the "old-fashioned" items, as they remind her of times gone past.

Mrs. Pearson's belief—that beginning again, i.e., by replacing the old with the new, staves off the changes of aging—frightens Nella as this idea forces her to confront the impending changes in/to her own life. Nella informs Mrs. Pearson of her aversion to change, stating that "change makes me feel like life is rushing past me." As the story closes, Minus, through Nella, reminds humanity of its own mortality; she simultaneously cautions that winter—old age and death—may be an "enemy," "lurking" at the heels of every man and woman, but urges humanity to go "out into the . . . sunshine," i.e., live life to its fullest.

Steadfastly committing to exploring universal issues, Minus's short story, "Mr. Oscar Goes to Market," published in *Woman's Day* July 1947 issue, addresses the boundless debate over the importance of "men's work" versus "women's work." Mr. Oscar, a zealous contractor, trivializes his homemaker wife's dedication to maintaining a well-balanced household. Mr. Oscar fails to differentiate between his need to secure necessary construction supplies and his wife's need to secure the necessary household supplies. Just as Mr. Oscar repeatedly visit's the same lumber yard to obtain the building components necessary to ensure satisfaction to his customers, Mrs. Oscar makes repeated visits to the market to acquire the ingredients needed to ensure her husband's contentment; however, Mr. Oscar fails to discern any correlations between his and his wife's needs. With Mr. Oscar's final comment, " . . . men just go about things different from women," Minus indicates a certain pointlessness to attributing more importance to one partner's responsibilities over the other's. Moreover, Minus appears to imply that men and women adopt whatever strategy necessary to insure the success of their respective tasks.

Minus continues to delve into the male/female relationship in "Twice in His Lifetime" published in *Woman's Day* December 1949 issue. Here, Minus evokes an incident from a man's teenage years to foreshadow his relationship with his wife. After a six-month trial separation at his wife's behest, Stan Morgan's reconciliation day dawns with a memory from his youth. Morgan was forced to pawn a prized watch—even though his body's magnetic current prevented the watch from keeping accurate time. As time passed, a youthful Morgan realizes that the watch, while ineffectual to himself, may better suit someone else. Morgan reaches the same decision as he contemplates resuming a relationship with his wife. Fundamentally, Minus emphasizes the vital importance in recognizing the psychological and emotional benefits of detaching oneself from unfavorable situations.

In "Lucky Man," published in *Woman's Day* in the June 1951 issue, Minus distinguishes between "luck" and "diligence." For years, Charlie Faria dreamed of owning a boat. However, various family responsibilities thwarts Charlie's efforts. This same obligation to family causes Charlie to purchase a raffle ticket; upon learning that first prize is a boat, Charlie increases his ticket purchase by a dozen. After winning the prize, however, Charlie realizes that owning a boat and operating a boating business requires more revenue than it would generate; subsequently, Charlie sells the boat. In addition to expensive operating costs, Charlie understood that his dreams and his reality contradicted each other; however, Charlie also recognizes the rewards of diligence to one's dreams.

Throughout her literary career, Minus maintained employment with the New York Consumers Union. In the early to mid-1950s Minus became a full-time office supervisor; her final appointment was that of personnel director of the Union in 1958. Minus held this position until her retirement and died in New York in 1973.

For Further Reading

Gable, Craig. *Ebony Rising: Short Fiction of the Greater Harlem Renaissance Era*. Bloomington: Indiana University Press, 2004.

Minus, Marian. "Present Trends in Negro Literature." *Challenge* (Spring 1937).

———. "The Negro as a Consumer." *Opportunity* (September 1938).

———. "The Fine Line." *Opportunity* (November 1939).

———. "Girl, Colored." *The Crisis* (September 1940).

———. "Half Bright." *Opportunity* (September 1940).

———. "If Tom Were Only Here." *Woman's Day* (June 1945).

———. "Another Winter." *Woman's Day* (May 1946).

———. "The Threat to Mr. David." *Woman's Day* (June 1947).

———. "Mr. Oscar Goes to Market." *Woman's Day* (July 1947).

———. "Ambitious Mr. Trueworthy." *Woman's Day* (June 1948).

———. "Twice in His Lifetime." *Woman's Day* (December 1949).

———. "Woman and Mr. Oscar." *Woman's Day* (February 1951).

———. "Lucky Man." *Woman's Day* (June 1951).

Mitchell, Verner D. and Cynthia Davis, eds. *Dorothy West. Where the Wild Grape Grows: Selected Writings, 1930–1950*. Amherst: University of Massachusetts Press, 2005.

Rowley, Hazel. *Richard Wright: The Life and Times*. New York: Henry Holt and Company, 2001.

WILLARD MOTLEY
(July 14, 1909–March 14, 1965)
Alan M. Wald

Willard Motley was in all likelihood the most prolific novelist associated with the concluding years of the Black Chicago Renaissance. Nonetheless, two features pivotal to a discernment of the intricacies his life and work remain nebulous in biographical and critical scholarship. One is Motley's convoluted political connection to the city's principal tradition of African American literary radicalism; only in his late thirties did Motley emerge as a committed leftist, and his fiction was largely concerned with European ethnic groups and, later, Mexicans. The second enigmatic peculiarity is the presence of a degree of biographical mystery; Motley was a gay man who did not identify himself as such, and, for sundry reasons, guarded and even dissimulated about his private life.

More precisely, Motley was a determined young writer coming of age in what is commonly called "The Red Decade," yet he had no link to Black literary networks such as the South Side Writers Group, nor is there any evidence of his association with the traditional political causes of the Great Depression during the 1930s. Moreover, despite the traces of Marxist thought and a fidelity to the left-wing protest tradition of social realism in his novels, Motley's African American fictional characters are customarily subsidiary and African American culture only superficially and even stereotypically represented.

Motley was, furthermore, chronically hostile to suggestions of what he perceived to be militant Black nationalism, whether he detected it in the radical fiction of Chester Himes in his review of Himes's *Lonely Crusade* in 1947,[1] or James Baldwin's attitude toward white liberals which he protested in a letter to *Time* magazine in 1963.[2] Confounding his identification with the Chicago Renaissance, Motley relocated permanently to Mexico in 1951, a few years after the issuance of his first novel, publishing three quarters of his oeuvre from exile.

Nonetheless, an examination of Motley's life and writings, enhanced by new research and extended contextualization, renders an emended appraisal that roots him more securely in the Chicago Black radical tradition. Notwithstanding the thematic focus of his published fiction, Motley was unquestionably immersed in African American culture due to family and social connections. Starting in his teenage years, he wrote for the African American newspaper *Chicago Defender*, and in 1940 issued an influential essay on "Negro Art in Chicago" in the National Urban League's journal *Opportunity*.[3]

Moreover, in the early 1940s, Motley developed friendships with left-wing Euro-American writers residing in Hull House, the social work settlement founded in 1889 by Jane Addams and Ellen Starr, as well as with radicals on the Federal Writers' Project. Then, in the late 1940s, Motley emerged as a crusading revolutionary, variously associating himself with a range of Communist and Trotskyist causes. Despite the expatriatism of his last fifteen years, Motley's second and third novels, as well as volumes of unpublished fiction, were set in the city of Chicago, and he maintained personal contacts with emerging Chicago writers such as Frank London Brown.

Unquestionably a consequential source for many themes and strategies of Motley's novels, his personal life is marked by exceptional features that have been misunderstood or unrecognized by critics and scholars; the result has been a channeling of his accomplishment into the more limited categories of sociological, documentary, and "raceless" writing.[4] Most notably, Motley was actively complicit in promoting false information about the Motley family history, much of which was repeated in newspaper items, and then in scholarship and reference books up until the late twentieth century. An illustration of this appears in the 1955 autobiographical entry that Motley supplied to Stanley Kunitz for the first supplement of *Twentieth Century Authors: A Biographical Dictionary*.[5] Here Motley gave his birthdate as 1912 and stated that the painter, Archibald Motley Jr., was his older brother. Moreover, *Knock on Any Door* was dedicated "To Mary, My Mother," and *Let No Man Write My Epitaph* "To Sergio, My Son." In fact, Motley was born three years prior to 1912, Mary was not his mother, the painter Motley was not his brother, and there is no evidence of any biological children or legal adoptions.

My own research indicates that Motley was born Willard Francis Bryant in 1909.[6] His mother was Florence "Flossie" Motley, the fourteen-year-old daughter of Archibald John Motley, a Pullman porter who worked on the New York–Chicago "Wolverine" train, and Mary ("Mae") Frederica Huff Motley, a school teacher. Nothing is known of his biological father, Bryant, other than that he was a thirty-six-year-old boarder in the Motley family home on the South Side of Chicago. A marriage between Flossie and Bryant was hastily arranged, and then quickly annulled, so that the birth would not be illegitimate. Motley was told that his grandparents were his parents, that his mother was his sister, and that his uncle (Archibald Motley Jr. born in New Orleans in 1886) was his brother. Bryant managed to impregnate Flossie a second time, resulting in the birth of Rita Motley. Rita was also raised as a child of Mary and Archibald Sr., and the sister of Willard and Archibald Jr. The subject of one of the latter's most distinguished paintings, Rita died of diphtheria in 1927.

Motley was raised Roman Catholic, serving as an altar boy, and grew up in a predominantly white, middle-class, German American and Irish American neighborhood. Between December 1922 and January 1924, he published a children's column in the African American newspaper *Chicago Defender* under the name "Bud Billiken."[7] Around that same time he apparently learned the true identity of his mother inadvertently, due to an angry outburst from his grandmother, Mae. Flossie, however, had remarried and was beginning to raise her own family; she never accepted Willard as a son.

The revelation of this secret family history was traumatic for the teenage boy whose head was filled with romantic ideals. Over the years Motley's anguish about the circumstances of his birth gnawed away at him and was the subject of family quarrels. His tangle of emotions about Flossie was combined with a suspicion that the strong moral professions of his grandparents actually masked questionable behavior on their own part, although his devotion to Grandmother Mae was abiding. In the end, though, Motley was convinced of the profound hypocrisy of the Black middle class, a principal ingredient in his proud self-identification as an outcast and partisan of all those on the bottom rung of society.

Following his 1929 graduation from Engelwood High School, where he played on the football team and wrote for the school newspaper, Motley had hopes of attending the University of Wisconsin. Nevertheless, financial limitations interfered with this dream; so, after a visit to Madison, he decided to return to living in the family home. From Engelwood he plotted a series of adventurous travels in preparation for becoming a popular novelist in the vein of Alexander Dumas.

In 1930 Motley launched himself on this project by taking a bicycle trip to New York City, and in 1936 he made his first automobile trip out West. In between, Motley devoted himself to the craft of establishing himself as a published writer, producing a large number of short stories and articles that met with steady rejections from local and national publications. His grandfather and uncle grew discouraged with him, but Mae remained supportive. She provided financial aid while Willard passed through a succession of odd jobs in a brewery, neighborhood store, and dress factory.

Motley's aim in traveling West was to gather material for future writing, and he recorded activities in his journals. One episode from which he kept notes was a month spent in jail in Wyoming, after he was arrested for stealing gas. He also chronicled experiences with numerous odd jobs on the route down to Southern California from Oregon. In Los Angeles he immersed himself in the Mexican American community and then took a twenty-five-day trip to Catalina Island. There Motley encountered an elderly British man, Wlliam Rix, who gave

Motley advice on writing and subsequently carried on a vigorous correspondence with him. An even more momentous meeting occurred during Motley's
return to Chicago via Denver. Motley had a chance encounter with a Mexican
American reform school inmate named Joe Nuaves, who became the subject
of several articles that would be published by Motley in the *Ohio Motorist*. Joe
also became one of several prototypes for his chief protagonist in *Knock on Any
Door*, Nick Romano.[8]

After minimal success with publications from his first trip to the West, Motley
launched a second expedition in 1938. This time Motley worked throughout his
travels on a large manuscript, which he called alternately "Adventure" or "Adventures and Misadventures." Moreover, for his production of shorter pieces, he
targeted less literary publications. These included *The Highway Traveler*, *Out-
doors, Automobile and Trailer Travel Magazine*, and the *Ohio Motorist*, where
his success rate of acceptance was considerably higher than before. When passing through Denver, Motley met with Joe once more and gathered information
about his reform school life and friends that would eventually become reworked
into *Knock on Any Door*.

In 1939 Motley made a dramatic decision to leave his family home and relocate to a Chicago slum area known as the "Maxwell Street Neighborhood," in
the vicinity of Fourteenth and Union Streets. There he befriended other young,
aspiring writers who lived in or were attracted to Hull House on South Halsted
Street, such as Alexander Saxton and William P. Schenk. They encouraged him
to engage in a wide reading of nineteenth- and twentieth-century novelists,
including John Steinbeck, John Dos Passos, Ernest Hemingway, James Joyce,
Leo Tolstoy, Upton Sinclair, Jack London, and Sherwood Anderson. Motley
also became familiar with the work of playwrights such as Anton Chekhov
and Henrik Ibsen and fell under the spell of poet Carl Sandburg. Motley's own
production of short fiction now turned more directly toward realist techniques.

Chicago's *Hull-House Magazine* was launched in mimeographed form in the
autumn of 1939, with Schenk listed as editor and Motley and Saxton as associate
editors. Motley had by this time abandoned the paying market that he sought
for his travel writings. Now he was experimenting with plotless sketches of the
Maxwell Street neighborhood under titles such as "Hull-House Neighborhood,"
"Pavement Portraits," and "Handfuls."[9] Some of Motley's contributions would
later be adapted into his published fiction. Soon after the demise of *Hull-House
Magazine*, Motley began drafts of *Knock on Any Door*, which he originally titled
"Leave Without Illusions."

Motley was brought into the Federal Writers' Project of the Works Progress
Administration in the spring of 1940. He worked there for two years, during
which time he evolved through the ranks to the status of Professional Writer.
One of Motley's assignments was to prepare a report on an Italian American

neighborhood in Chicago called "Little Sicily." He carried this out in March 1941 and produced a report in which he combined his own photographs with captions and a text.

Among the most important literary acquaintances of Motley at the Federal Writers' Project was Jack Conroy, a Missouri-born figure in the proletarian literature school. Conroy, author of the novels *The Disinherited* (1933) and *A World to Win* (1935), had edited the left-wing journal *Anvil* between 1933 and 1937. At the time that he and Motley became friends, Conroy was revamping the publication as *The New Anvil*. Motley submitted a piece of fiction, "The Beer Drinkers," to the magazine. Conroy admired it, but he determined the story to be too many pages for his little journal. The two became lifelong friends, and Conroy offered crucial encouragement to Motley's literary labors.

When the Selective Training and Service Act was passed in 1940, Motley declared that he would not serve in a segregated military, and he wrote an unpublished essay ("I Discover I'm a Negro: Selective Military Training in Defense of American Democracy Places the Negro Just Outside of the Democracy"[10]) announcing his plan to be a conscientious objector. In April 1943, the Selective Service in Chicago agreed to assign this classification to Motley. He was then appointed to Civilian Public Service in Maryland, entailing physical labor. However, by that time Motley was already employed as a lab technician on a government job and thus was able to appeal the assignment so that he could remain in Chicago.

Besides Motley's Hull House and Federal Writers' Project activities, many other personal adventures lay behind the making of the early drafts of *Knock on Any Door*. Most important, Motley continued his special relationship with Joe, who moved from Denver to Chicago for a while, and he developed friendships with other young men who had criminal associations. One of those, who would also become a model for Nick Romano, was referred to only as "Mike" in Motley's private papers. Mike stole from Motley and was the subject of a short story, "The Beautiful Boy," that was never published.[11]

In 1941 Motley attended the trial of Bernard "Knifey" Sawicki, a juvenile killer of four people, including a police officer. Afterward Motley met the defense attorney, Morton Anderson, an advocate for the poor, who appears under his own name in *Knock on Any Door* as Romano's lawyer. Motley also conducted firsthand research at the county jail. His aim was to understand the operations of the electric chair and procedures for execution. Moreover, he arranged for a judge to review his fictionalized narrative of Nick's sentencing.

Nancy Jill Weyant's 1975 doctoral dissertation contains an entire chapter devoted to describing Motley's mostly unpublished "Short Fiction, Drama, and Miscellaneous Writing" of the years leading up to *Knock on Any Door*.[12] Weyant counts over fifty items of unpublished short fiction alone, between 1938 and

1947. Moreover, Weyant notes that, after 1940, these writings tend to become less sentimental and increasingly realistic, and more focused on Chicago. One of Motley's most sustained efforts, a 1942 three-act play called "The Keepers of the Wall," is the first fictional work by Motley to offer an explicit political stance. The drama features Dave, an African American opponent of World War II, who refuses to take up arms against Hitler by serving in a segregated army. Moreover, unlike Motley himself, Dave even rejects conscientious objector status because segregation was enforced among pacifists as well. Dave identifies himself as neither an American nor "a Negro, but just one of two and a half billion, insignificant little creatures crawling across the face of the globe."[13]

In the spring of 1943, Motley thought that he had finished his novel, still called "Leave without Illusions" and immediately began a new one, "Of Night, Perchance of Death." However, the process toward the publication of "Leave without Illusions" would be grueling. The manuscript was 1,951 pages after he typed the final version over the summer, and it was quickly rejected by Harper & Brothers publishers only two months following his mailing it to them in September. Early the next year he made an attempt to get it accepted by MacMillan publishers, which eventually resulted in a contract but also a demand on the part of the editors for major cuts in length and to eliminate many of the sexual (and especially homosexual) references. After a year-and-a-half of revision, MacMillan canceled its contract and declined to publish the novel. The editors were still unhappy with the remaining sexual passages and aspects of the revised narrative.

In yet another emotional turn of events, Appleton-Century publishers immediately accepted the new manuscript, requesting only that the title be changed. As an alternate, Motley readily adapted the phrase "knock on any door" that had already occurred at both the beginning and end of the novel. In 1947, Motley's *Knock on Any Door* was issued, and remained on the *New York Times* best-seller list for ten months. It stayed consistently in print until the 1970s, selling over two million copies in hardback and paperback. A condensed version, comic strip serialization, and a 1949 Columbia Pictures film, starring Humphrey Bogart and John Derek, were also produced.

The reaction to *Knock on Any Door* in the book reviews of leading publications was sensational. The *New York Times* hailed the debut of "an extraordinary and powerful new naturalistic talent" and the *Saturday Review of Literature* wrote that "not one [of its pages] is dull and many are calculated to make the heart beat faster." Yet the *Times* also referred to the novel as "a dramatized slice of sociology" and the author as a "Disciple of Dreiser"; this introduced a theme, regarding Motley's alleged lack of artistic skill and a dated, derivative style, that would be repeated in harsher forms in response to his subsequent novels.[14]

The published version of *Knock on Any Door* came out at 504 pages. The narrative concerns an Italian American youth, Nick Romano, originally from

Denver, whose family descends into financial ruin in the 1920s. Nick's father, called Pa Romano, loses his grocery store and the family relocates to a poorer neighborhood. There the good-looking Nick, whose mother thought he might become a priest, falls under the spell of tough guys and delinquents. Following the false accusation of his having stolen a bike, Nick serves a period in reform school when he is fourteen. The experience is transformative and creates the foundation for Nick's succumbing to something of a naturalistic view of society as a jungle where the strong dominate the weak. Nick concludes that the moralistic claims of the adult world and its institutions are merely masks for a struggle for power and control.

Thus Nick rejects adult society, and what he views as the hypocritical righteousness of his family, and is ineluctably drawn to the life of a street hustler and petty criminal. In making this choice, Nick achieves immediate gratification for his material and physical desires. Yet in selecting various gang members with whom to associate, he also satisfies a need for companionship based on mutual trust, attraction, and admiration. Although the criminal subculture is actually antisocial in its actions, it does allow for the feeling that one is building a new family and community based on comradeship uncorrupted by pretense.

The move of the Romano family to Chicago, in the hope of finding industrial work for Nick's father, acutely accelerates Nick's trend away from family and toward the street, despite the concern of two older men who befriend him. One is Grant Holloway, a liberal journalist who progressively moves farther Left in the course of the novel. The other is identified only as Owen, a lonely homosexual who becomes ardently devoted to Nick. Toward the climax of the novel, Nick, feeling that something is missing in his life and that he may be heading for a disastrous end, makes an effort at self-reform. He embraces the fantasy of successfully honoring a marriage to Emma, a German American woman who falls in love with him. Emma is markedly unlike Nick's habitual associates on the street; in a sense Emma represents a vestige of the lost dreams of his youth for a moral and honorable life according to conventional institutions. Moreover, he is under the illusion that Emma's personal love might be sufficient to induce him to abandon his addictive attraction to promiscuity, deceit, and easy money.

Yet it is quickly evident that Nick's life in the gang has caused him to become so undisciplined that he cannot hold down a job, so he steadily yields to criminal pursuits. Even worse, Nick suffers sexual impotence with Emma and soon reverts to seeing prostitutes and Owen. These episodes culminate in a jail sentence and a confession to Emma of his bisexual promiscuity. Subsequently Emma commits suicide and Nick plunges even further into the criminal underworld.

Ultimately, Nick, pursued after a robbery attempt, explodes in rage and frustration by repeatedly shooting a sadistic police officer, Riley. Following a manhunt, where he is hidden briefly by a woman who had once protected him from

the police during his Denver childhood, Nick is captured. Yet he refuses to con-
fess. Although he is ably defended by Andrew Morton, and supported by Grant,
Owen, and the multiethnic members of his gang, Nick breaks down when the
suicide of Emma is raised by the prosecutor. In a conclusion with strong parallels to Richard Wright's *Native Son*, Morton provides a powerful closing oration
declaring that society is guilty for the transformation of Nick into a criminal,
but his efforts fail and Nick goes to the electric chair at age twenty-one.

In its form and style, *Knock on Any Door* bears many features of canonical literary naturalism. Assuredly, the socially determined features of Nick's behavior,
the courtroom defense, and even the title suggesting that society and culture,
not the individual, are to blame, recall Theodore Dreiser's *An American Tragedy*
(1925). Equally notable, however, is the legacy of social realist fiction of the 1930s
radical movement, such as James T. Farrell's *Studs Lonigan Trilogy* (1932–1936).
In the works of Farrell, John Dos Passos, Jack Conroy, Richard Wright, and
others, there is often a revolutionary, usually quasi-Marxist, underpinning to
the plot and perspective. Yet markers of such a perspective emerge with varying degrees of directness.

Closest to Motley's approach is Farrell, who juxtaposes the fully drawn Studs
Lonigan to the more thinly sketched Danny O'Neill. The former is a lower-mid-
dle-class youth aspiring to become a "tough guy," while the latter a prototype of
a revolutionary intellectual. At the climax of the third volume of Farrell's trilogy,
Studs lies dying while Danny appears in a Communist-led May Day parade.
The juxtaposition hints at the potentiality of an alternative response, through
Danny's behavior, to the failures of the same capitalist institutions and culture
that crushed Studs. In parallel fashion, Motley contrasts the evolution of the
fully drawn Nick Romano to a character named only "Tommy." Nick generally
accommodates to the culture that brutalizes him, while Tommy turns his rage
derived from poverty and repression into militant union activism.

When both Nick and Tommy are faced with the brutalizing reform school
environment, Nick is disoriented, but Tommy proceeds according to a principle
of social solidarity based on human rights. This is chiefly demonstrated when
Tommy defies the racism of the reform school and its toughest inmates. Unlike Nick, whose first reaction is to defer to commands from racists, Tommy
insists that he will associate with African Americans and anyone else whom
he pleases. Tommy also organizes a mass escape of the youngest boys from the
reform school.

Both Nick and Tommy end up being physically assaulted in the last pages of
Knock on Any Door. Yet Nick is executed for his futile murder of Riley, while
Tommy is beaten by antiunion thugs for his attempt to organize a strike. Moreover, Tommy lives to see another day and to shed tears for Nick, about whom
he reads in a newspaper. In effect, notwithstanding the focus of Motley on the

criminal underclass, the role given to Tommy is a sign that Motley was affiliating himself with the left-wing literary tradition that had battled its way into U.S. literature during the 1930s.

Despite the many naturalist motifs of the novel and Nick's own appropriation of a quasinaturalist outlook, the theme of *Knock on Any Door* is not so much that Nick is without choices or free will. Rather, Motley wishes to demonstrate that, beneath its proclamations of equality and opportunity, capitalist society is a relentlessly oppressive structure for the majority and that one of its most powerful weapons is to obscure effective means of revolt. For the most part, the reform school events in Denver set the pattern for the remainder of the novel.

Upon entrance to the reform school, Nick is depicted as a potentially good and caring person who is stunned by the cruelty he witnesses. Although he is personally drawn to Tommy, and later on he remembers some of Tommy's words and actions, Nick can neither formulate nor sustain a vision of fulfillment. In a reified world, without access to a means of understanding the actual sources of his brutalization or the means of change, Nick pragmatically slips into a way of life that offers short-term pleasures but ultimately a miserable end.

In the reform school, the thuggish Bricktop is presented as a fascistlike figure, one who embodies the corrupt, power-hungry desire of the adults to dominate the world of the younger boys. Furthermore, the key to Bricktop's authority is the capacity to set youth against each other, preeminently by employing racism to divide them. At the opposite pole from Bricktop in the reform school is Jesse, a Christlike Mexican American who is in frail health and eventually beaten to death by the guards. In the picture is also Allen, a tough African American who has gained acceptance because of his physical prowess. In contrast, another African American, Sam, is smaller and weaker, protected only by Tommy. The blond, fatherless Tommy and Sam carry out a close, homosocial relationship, with frequent physical contact. Nick is trapped among the contending forces; he often feels sympathy for the physically weaker characters, such as Jesse and Sam, but he lacks self-confidence and a vision that can lead to decisive action. Eventually Nick is pressured into fighting Bricktop and surprised to find himself the winner.

In the most crucial episode in the reform school, Tommy is captured by the authorities following the escape that he engineers with a group of younger boys. As an example to terrorize the rest of the reform school population into cooperation, Tommy is subjected to a humiliating public beating that suggests a sadistic anal rape. With his pants pulled down and naked buttocks exposed, Tommy is forced to bend over while a powerful, one-armed man named Fuller whips his backside brutally. The image haunts Nick for the rest of his short life, and it is the very last image in Nick's mind a decade later as he sits in the electric chair: "Nick shut his eyes against the blackness of the head hood. Again he saw

WILLARD MOTLEY • 259

the circle of cloth and Tommy grabbing his ankles with the skin taut across his small behind . . . saw the hard light beating down, Fuller's arm raised with the strap, like a coiled snake, ready to strike. Ready to cut the flesh, ready to bring blood and screams and sobbing, whimpering, blubbering."[15] Although Motley's fiction is often treated as a species of sociology, such crucial episodes indicate that he astutely perceived a psychosexual component to the institutionalized forms of oppression and social control in capitalist society. The suggestion in the image is not that Fuller is a homosexual; rather, that Fuller's sanctioned brutality indicates that he, and the society he represents, are sexually maimed or crippled, and achieve compensation through rapelike domination of the younger and weaker.

Thus the reform school provides a microcosm of the coercive institutions of capitalist system, stripped of all illusions and pretenses. The claim that the re-form school actually aims to "reform" its inmates is openly treated as a joke by the institution's physical education instructor. In fact, the constant unleashing of adult male physical power on boys is the actual instrument of attempted behavior modification. As Nick concludes: "He knew how men treated boys. And he knew how they reformed them. He hated the law and everything that had anything to do with it. Men like Fuller were behind it. He was against them."[16] Among the inmates, gangs form in imitation of and in opposition to this adult power, and each gang develops its own culture of resistance. The pattern continues once Nick and the others are returned to the world outside the reform school.

Thereafter, Nick, in choosing the friends and associates that will comprise his various gangs, will try to reject the model provided by Bricktop, with its racism and authoritarianism. Yet he is incapable of seeing anything further, of going beyond petty crime to channel his justified rage into oppositional politi-cal activity. Despite their good will and desire for Nick to reform, Grant, Owen, Emma, and also his sympathetic Aunt Rosa, are unable to articulate a course of action that makes sense and seems viable to Nick. Instead, he becomes locked into a pattern of criminal life, of seducing women and taking money from ho-mosexuals, from which he cannot tear himself away.

This evolution is certainly bolstered by the workings of the social and eco-nomic system, although Nick's evolution is not foreordained; Tommy, after all, moves in a very different direction. Moreover, Nick's brother, Julian, just a few years older, escapes the pattern and appears to be moving toward success within the conventional social model of marriage and a career. Indeed, Julian's apparent escape from the fate of becoming a criminal or living in desperate poverty might raise the question of whether Tommy's route, that of working-class organization and collective struggle, is merely one of several options that Motley presents. Is Motley also suggesting that, with focus and diligence, one might still lead a satisfactory life within the social order?

Actually, due to the puritanical and hypocritical culture of Nick's society, Julian's marriage is based on a potentially devastating lie; his wife, Rosemary, has never told Julian that she was earlier seduced by his own brother, Nick. Although Nick dies without disclosing this damaging secret, Rosemary was surely taking a great risk in hiding the truth about her past from her husband. The information might have been revealed during one of the many angry exchanges between Nick and his brother, just as Motley's own family secrets had inadvertently come to the fore with hurtful consequences. Or Rosemary might have become haunted by guilt to the point of confessing or acting self-destructively. All in all, there are few signs that any marriage can provide a happy ending in Motley's world; even Grant lives under the threat that his possible marriage to a wealthy woman might result in his corruption.

Thus *Knock on Any Door* provides little avenue for optimism within the existing social order. Nick may not be entirely unanswerable for his criminal behavior, but the odds are stacked against his ever fully realizing the humane impulses that came so naturally in his youth. Rather, circumstances combine with his growing personal weaknesses to produce the fatal outcome. Nick's addiction to quick and easy money is certainly a trait that he fails to bring under control; the quality is rooted in the deprivations of his childhood that escalated so considerably when the family's economic status plummeted. A more important part in Nick's evolution is played by his uncommon good looks. "Pretty-Boy Romano," as the newspapers will eventually label him, is able to gain the instantaneous sympathy of strangers, effortlessly deceive people who love him, and quickly seduce an abundance of women and men. A triumph of the novel lies in Motley's ability to render Nick's powers of attraction convincing and credible.

Still, although the political logic of *Knock on Any Door* is revolutionary in terms of a suggesting the author's fundamental opposition to a class society, explicit political references rarely appear. These are chiefly in the background and customarily available only by inference, especially in the dim character of Tommy. Motley's principal strategy is to demonstrate how society progressively beats down Nick's intrinsically positive qualities. The reader is frequently reminded that, before the reform school experience, Nick's potential for behaving virtuously was authenticated by his rescue of a mouse from the jaws of a cat. On the other hand, Nick's propulsion toward the criminal life most often occurs on the heels of his witnessing or experiencing brutality by the social system. In particular, Nick's fatal decision to carry a gun, once he is located in Chicago, is the consequence of a depraved beating that he receives from the police. Understandably, he concludes that he must arm himself so that he will never be forced to undergo such a beating again.

The politics of the novel occasionally evoke the philosophy of French Romantic Jean-Jacques Rousseau; social institutions, such as the reform school, are depicted as if they are imposed upon and deform nature. Yet there are several traditional concerns of the Marxist Left that appear in passing. The reader is reminded in the course of Nick's trial that the Chicago Police Department is linked to the infamous massacre of workers during the strike at Republic Steel in 1937. The police, the prosecuting attorney, the fascistlike Bricktop, and even Nick's mother express the racist and ethnocentric opinions associated with notorious capitalists of the era such as Henry Ford. In contrast, the poor community of Chicago is depicted as a happy melting pot, complete with multiethnic street dances:

> The crowd ringed a drunken Irishman who danced in the street, his hat sliding over his eyes. Then a colored boy and girl did a jitterbug dance while the crowd clapped hands, keeping time with the music. . . . Then a Jewish girl in a high school sweater with bumps and her skinny partner in loud-colored trousers and glasses took over. . . . A lean young Negro, black as the hat he wore, came out of the crowd and asked a pretty Italian girl in her teens for a dance. She smiled and nodded. . . . They whirled across the dirty asphalt and back. . . . The crowd, three-fourths white, watched, applauded when they were finished.[17]

The internationalism of the Left is also explicitly recalled in the composition of Nick's own gang in Chicago, which is Italian American, Polish American, African American, and Mexican American. Nick is even called an "anarchist" by the prosecutor, and it is the one true proletarian on Nick's jury, a truck driver, who holds out longest against conviction.

While the novel contains substantial data about Italian Americans and German Americans, and there are a number of references to Mexican Americans and African Americans, the intelligence about ethnicity in *Knock on Any Door* is not eminently revealing or original. Most often a stereotypical character from a group is balanced by another one with opposite features; for example, among Mexican Americans there are Juan the womanizer and Jesse the saint; and among African Americans there are the loyal yes-man Sunshine and the independent Allen. Motley rather mechanically makes the point to the reader that each ethnic group consists of different sorts of people.

Naturally, with the presence in the novel of extensive narratives about the European American families of Nick and Emma, Motley provides abundant details about Italian American and German American ethnic food and tradition. Yet even here, Motley's principal burden in regard to educating his readers about ethnicity is political. He wishes to emphasize the universality of diverse cultures in order to militate against organizing one's values around a mythical norm. He also wishes to substantiate the omnipresence of discrimination suffered by most groups—not just African Americans and Mexican Americans. Moreover, Motley aspires to demonstrate the devastating effects of poverty and loneliness that cross ethnic lines, although he does not want to suggest that wealth and power solve these problems. What is required is a culture of solidarity among humanity.

Although Motley has been declared a "raceless" author by some critics such as Robert Fleming and Gene Jarrett, the phrase can be misleading. In his novels set in Chicago, Motley certainly fails to focus primarily on groups marked by race, or to see the world from the perspective of any particular such group. Moreover, the information he imparts about the culture and life experience of such groups—in this instance, mainly African American and Mexican American—is not especially profound. Yet Motley's choices in theme, subject matter, and approach are likely motivated by a keen consciousness of the tenets of white supremacism.

As can be documented by Motley's private papers, diaries, and correspondence, Motley was acutely attentive to the irrationality of ideologies of racial difference as well as the pain produced by racism upon its targets. His response, however, was to demonstrate that the shared characteristics among the poor of different ethnic groups are stronger than differences, and less meaningful than are class inequalities. Race and ethnicity are not to be ignored; to the contrary, they are ubiquitous. Yet they are not the definitive cleavage in regard to choosing communities of association. In Motley's philosophy, people are just people, and the rage of the have-nots should not be aimed at ethnic and racial minorities but at those who engage in economic exploitation and domination.

To understand the literary achievement of *Knock on Any Door*, it may ultimately be more rewarding to interrogate the consequences of Motley's dramatization of the sundered sensibility of the author in the text than to herald the authenticity of the ethnic cultures depicted. Grant and Owen, two characters who try to rescue Nick, seem to share features of a divided consciousness of Motley; one is the aspiring crusader for reform, and the other is the lonely gay man. Concurrently the perceptions and behavior of Grant and Owen aid in creating the near-mesmerizing persona of Nick as victim and victimizer, sex object and object of sexual exploitation, mouse and cat, and killer and scapegoat.

Motley, of course, is also very much present in the omniscient narrator. This is the case especially in the italicized poetic effusions, which appear sporadically in the novel; many more of these were cut during the course of editorial revision. Motley's views, too, seem to be expressed in the courtroom orations by attorney Morton. Moreover, Grant is probably modeled somewhat on Motley's novelist and Communist friend Alexander Saxton, to whom the novel is partly dedicated, and Owen, according to Motley's diaries, was inspired by a man he observed in a bar.

Nevertheless, some of Grant's experiences are grounded in Motley's own. In particular, Grant's meeting with Nick at the Denver reform school is a re-creation of Motley's encounter with Joe Nuaves. Owen, too, reproduces some of Motley's behavior. Like Motley, Owen is a homosexual and not effeminate, and he offers living space in his apartment to Nick in the manner that Motley himself took in young men with criminal pasts. Moreover, Owen remains loyal to Nick as Motley did to Joe and Mike.

Without a doubt, neither Grant's nor Owen's personal biographies correspond to Motley's, and neither is African American. Yet Motley is linked to the two by features of personality. In the mid-1940s Motley was in the process of transforming himself into a social crusader such as Grant pledges himself to be at the end of the novel; moreover, like Motley, Grant's efforts to change doomed individuals like Nick doesn't involve preaching, and Grant, like Motley in the 1940s, enjoys traveling to Mexico. Then there is Owen's ultimate loneliness, his apparent state of being without what he regards as a real family, his frustrated search for love—all recall Motley during much of his life.

Knock on Any Door's status as a gay novel has yet to be assessed. On the one hand, Motley introduced gay subject matter in popular fiction at a time when such information was risky, even though Nick doesn't acknowledge being bisexual, except to Emma, and Owen never discusses his own sexual orientation. Moreover, the novel is to some limited degree a social document of aspects of the male homosexual experience in Chicago at that time. What may be most vital is that Motley doesn't reduce homosexuality to merely a personal problem of eccentric individuals. He tacitly raises sexual orientation as a question of social justice in the sense that homosexuals are akin to other excluded ethnic groups.

In truth, there are suggestions in the novel that homosexuals might be regarded as in particular respects the group against which there is the most discrimination. After all, despite the varying economic status of homosexuals in the novel, social prejudice is depicted as virulent and widespread. Moreover, the legal status of homosexuals is depicted by Motley as so flimsy that homosexual victims of "jackrolling" and other violence can't go to the police, protest, or fight back. Motley, of course, fails to treat any homosexual character as a complete human being, but this is comparable to his approach to characters who are African American and from other minority groups, apart from his chief protagonists. As with most minority groups in the novel, Motley's cardinal strategy is to subvert simple stereotyping by presenting several types of homosexuals. Thus Owen, especially in his patience and near passivity in relation to sex, is contrasted with a range of other gay men who appear in passing in the novel.

Might *Knock on Any Door* be adjoined to any kind of "gay literary tradition"? As in the instance of James Baldwin's *Giovanni's Room* (1956), Motley's inaugural explicit discussion of homosexual life in his published fiction involves Euro-American characters, and even one of Italian ancestry who is doomed. For both African American authors, this strategy may have served to distance the consideration of homosexuality in the books from immediate biographical correlation to their own lives. More than Baldwin, however, Motley shows the gay subculture as something of a loveless meat-market. In *Knock on Any Door*, homosexual social life seems sordid, unattractive, and desperate; except for the idyllic time spent in Owen's room, existence as a homosexual brings one close to the criminal underworld. In contrast to Baldwin's later novel, *Another Country* (1962), there is no example of the homosexual as a redemptive figure. Such an approach would be inconsistent with Motley's refusal to elevate a particular minority group above others.

On the other hand, Owen does grow in stature from a pathetic hanger-on to loyal friend. Nick's ultimate acceptance of Owen, after first denying to friends that Owen is a homosexual, is intended by Motley to be seen as a positive step, comparable with Nick's earlier expressions of antiracism. The statement that Nick makes to Owen pointedly recalls Tommy's sentiments about Sam: "I don't care what you are. You're all right."[18] As Nick's feelings for Owen grow stronger, Owen is identified with that small circle of friends in whom Nick confides about his feelings for Tommy. Eventually Nick declares: "Owen was somebody who understood. Maybe because Owen, in his own way, lived outside the law, too."[19] Thus Motley places homosexuals squarely in the new community of human solidarity that he is constructing outside the system, alongside of criminals created by poverty and middle-class revolutionaries who take their side.

Such was the point of the compass of Motley's own life, after his transit to the Chicago slums in 1939. Rooting himself in the poor communities of Chicago, and partaking in a midwestern gay milieu that also embraced Madison, Wisconsin, Motley retrospectively assumed an identification with the Left literary heritage of the 1930s. Initially, his decision to announce himself a conscientious objector in opposition to World War II detached him from the hegemonic radical movement in Chicago, that led by the Communist Party. However, by the early 1940s Motley was attending classes taught by Communists at the Party-led Abraham Lincoln School and thinking about the 1930s "causes" that had escaped him at the time, such as the formation of the Congress of Industrial Organizations (CIO) and the Spanish Civil War.

Although Motley in the mid to late 1940s had some traits of a Communist fellow traveler, he was not a liberal attracted to illusions about the Soviet Union. More precisely, he was a self-reliant revolutionary who was delighted to act jointly with others who avowed themselves in opposition to class exploitation and ethnic prejudice. This independence helps explain why Motley's most spectacular emergence as a political crusader came about by way of his association with the Trotskyist movement in Chicago in 1947.

This occurred when Motley played a leadership role in the sensational defense case of James Hickman, not long after the publication of *Knock on Any Door*. Hickman was a fiercely religious Southern sharecropper who participated in the

Great Migration to Chicago. Although Hickman found employment in the steel industry during World War II, he had great difficulty in locating an affordable apartment for his wife and seven children. Eventually he found a Black landlord, David Coleman, who accepted a bribe to let the Hickman family squeeze into an attic atop a three-story apartment.

Soon after, Coleman reached a decision to convert the entire structure into kitchenettes, which would liberate him from rent control laws and also allow him to rent out more space. When Hickman refused to leave the apartment building in order to allow this transformation, Coleman threatened to burn out the Hickman family, and several small fires were set on the stairway leading to the attic. Finally, in January 1947, a larger fire erupted on the third floor and spread to the attic, killing four of Hickman's children. Convinced that Coleman was responsible, Hickman shot and killed Coleman.

As it turned out, the other beleaguered tenants of Coleman's building were working with the Chicago Tenants League, an organization led by members of the Socialist Workers Party, a small Trotskyist political party. The result was that Hickman was offered a radical attorney, Mike Meyer, and a Chicago Defense Committee was established that included the well-known labor activist Sidney Lens, previously an acquaintance of Motley. Motley, in turn, stepped forward as a leading spokesperson for the case. He wrote about Hickman for the newspapers, and he personally convinced Marshall Field, owner of the *Chicago Sun-Times*, to give Hickman's side of the case fair play.

According to Lens's autobiography, *Unrepentant Radical*, the labor of Motley and the Hickman Defense Committee created immense empathy for Hickman in the Black community; the population deemed the situation as indicative of the overall housing crisis suffered by African Americans.[20] Motley and the others on the Committee did not apologize for Hickman's shooting of Coleman, which they attributed to temporary insanity. They did argue, however, that blame for creating the conditions of the shooting should rest with racism, landlords, and the refusal of the government to provide a decent public housing program. The trial resulted in a hung jury and an arrangement was afterward reached for Hickman to plead guilty in return for a sentence of two years on probation.

Motley also sponsored the national defense committee for James Kutcher, a member of the Socialist Workers Party who had lost his legs fighting in World War II, and who was in 1949 fired as a "subversive" from the office of the Veterans Administration in Newark, New Jersey. Yet Motley was more frequently involved in radical activities in the milieu of the Communist Party. Most notably, in 1948, Motley supported the Progressive Party campaign of Henry Wallace for president and was involved with a number of Communist and fellow-traveler intellectuals in public activities. In 1949 Motley, along with many pro-Communist intellectuals, sponsored the Cultural and Scientific Conference for World

Peace held at the Waldorf-Astoria Hotel in New York City, and the National Non-Partisan Committee to Defend the Rights of the Twelve Communist Party Leaders who had been indicted under the Smith Act.

In 1951 Motley relocated to Mexico, from where he published *We Fished All Night*. This 560-page novel was designed to be his political and moral manifesto for the post–World War II era. From the onset of the violent events in Europe and the deployment of U.S. troops, Motley was acutely conscious of the effects of the violence and killing on the consciousness of participants. His rudimentary plan for the book was to track the fate of five men from Chicago in two volumes that would showcase the occurrences of the war in one and the postwar era in another.

We Fished All Night aggregated this data into one passionate volume that treated only three main characters, with one of the original ones mentioned just in passing. Those featured include a Polish American, Chet Kosinski, who changed his name to Don Lockwood during an amateur theater career in the late 1930s. After losing a leg while fighting in North Africa, Lockwood exploits his stature as a wounded veteran to ascend in the Chicago political machine. The second protagonist, Aaron Levin, aimed to be a poet prior to the war, but he returns to Chicago in humiliation, following a mental breakdown and abandonment of his unit under fire. Growing ever more deluded about his writing talent, Levin embraces various religions and then Communism before acceding to full dementia. The third leading man, Jim Norris, commences as a visionary labor organizer in the prewar years. Although a valiant warrior in battle in Europe, Norris subsequently finds himself traumatized by an encounter he has there with a very young prostitute. Returning to Chicago, his marriage crumbles and his belief in the labor movement disintegrates as he conducts an inner war with feelings of pedophilia.

We Fished All Night is a singular work in the tradition of the Chicago Renaissance for its detailed anatomy of the inner political structure of the city. This focus is expedited by the narrative of Don Lockwood, because the reader is given an interior look at the political engine functioning by payola and kickbacks. Ballots are incinerated and fraudulently signed, and voters are purchased. The proprietor of a large enterprise, the Haines Corporation, manipulates his leverage as a campaign contributor to devise for city police to disrupt a strike. As in Motley's other novels, ethnic prejudice—in this instance, especially against Polish Americans and Jewish Americans—remains a puissant cultural force. Racism against African Americans is broached, but predominantly as a constituent of the larger representation of ethnocentric intolerance.

For the most part, critics responded to Motley's second massive tome (fifty pages longer than his first novel), as if it lacked a coherent narrative. In the *New York Times*, writer James M. Cain called it "tormentingly bad" because Motley "neglected to give any discernible thought to the art of building a tale."[21] Another novelist, Harvey Swados, wrote in the *Nation* magazine that "it is harder to discover what Motley is driving at than if he had written an experimental or avant-garde novel."[22] The *Library Journal* called *We Fished All Night* "strongly derivative in both content and style of the Dos Passos Trilogy *U.S.A.*"[23] *Time* magazine, too, made a correlation to Great Depression literature, albeit a negative one: "But for the most part its political sermonizing stirs unhappy memories of the 'proletarian fiction' of the 1930s."[24]

In 1952, Motley acquired a house near Mexico City, and announced that he had adopted Sergio Lopez as a son. For the rest of his life he lived a somewhat secretive and isolated existence outside the United States. Return visits and a stream of house guests diminished over time. Following the restrained response among critics and the public to *We Fished All Night*, Motley's literary reputation began to wane. There was a momentary resuscitation, nonetheless, in 1958, when he published *Let No Man Write My Epitaph*. Reviews were severe but sales were satisfactory, and a Columbia pictures movie version was released in 1963.

Let No Man Write My Epitaph was technically a follow-up to *Knock on Any Door* yet furnishes an original viewpoint on varied topics and adds fresh material to Motley's rendition of life among the multiethnic underclass of Chicago. Although there are several flashbacks to episodes from the original saga of Nick Romano, Motley worked diligently to incorporate altogether divergent episodes that address narcotic addiction as well as race relations. The focus of the sequel is on two Romanos, both of whom are related to the original Nick. One is his son, Nick Romano Jr., born to waitress Nellie Watkins after Nick's execution at the conclusion of *Knock on Any Door*. The other is Louie Romano, mentioned in passing in the original novel as the younger brother of Nick.

Nick Jr.'s mother, Nellie, endeavors in each and every manner to safeguard her son from the effects of the urban environment that had shattered his father. Yet the anguish of her life, intensified not only by Nick's calamitous execution but correspondingly by her own disconsolate working conditions, pushes her toward a sexual addiction to a young thug, Frankie Ramponi. Ramponi then hooks Nellie on heroin in order to control her. Over time, Nick Jr., too, becomes enslaved by narcotics. Yet the sequence of addiction ends affirmatively when Grant Holloway returns to the scene, anxious to intervene and make amends by rescuing Nick's son from following his father to an early demise. Holloway is joined by a number of neighborhood friends of Nellie and Nick Jr. who rescue the two addicts and demonstrate the redemptive capacity of the community of Chicago's multiethnic poor.

The parallel narrative in *Let No Man Write My Epitaph* concerns Louie Romano. Louie is roughly a twin of his older brother Nick, and likewise commences to drift toward a life of crime. Nevertheless, he is thrown off course by the appearance of his Aunt Rosa, a character in *Knock on Any Door*. Rosa breaks the family silence about Nick in order to instruct Louie about the dangers that lie ahead. Furthermore, Louie falls in love with Judy, a beautiful African American woman. Although the relationship does not culminate in marriage, the affair assists in bringing about Louie's reform.

Although *Let No Man Write My Epitaph* was a popular novel, the critics were brutal in emphasizing its allegedly nonliterary and even imitative features. *Time* magazine explained that the novel's only virtue was authentic speech, but that even this "recalls Nelson Algren's excursion into the same territory" in *The Man with the Golden Arm* (1949).[25] The *New Yorker* claimed that "the book represents an extension of Steinbeck's soft-boiled Cannery Row characters to Nelson Algren's hardboiled Chicago."[26] Algren himself insisted in the *Nation* magazine that the novel's treatment of drug addicts was a fraud, "plucked, not from the corners where the traffic is plied, but off the national paperback clothesline as it stretches, drug store to drug store, coast to coast."[27]

Mapping out future literary projects in Mexico, Motley hoped to return in his imagination to Chicago for a third volume on the Romano family. Moreover, he had collected research materials for a multivolume saga of his own family history. Yet the labors of his final years of literary productivity were devoted largely to writing up data collected from his Mexican residence of the 1950s. The most finished result was a nonfiction travel book, "My House Is Your House," which was never published outside of four chapters in *Rogue* magazine. Completed in revised form, with four chapters still in outline, was also a novel that he called "Tourist Town"; following alterations and cuts made by Motley's editors at Putnam, Ted Purdy and Peter Israel, the volume was posthumously published in 1966 as *Let Noon Be Fair*.

"My House Is Your House" embodied much material about the food and social customs of Mexico. Yet it also had features of a political commentary. Motley discussed the discrimination suffered by the Native American Indian population, and he also indicted the role of the United States through the impact of U.S. tourism and developers.

Let Noon Be Fair correspondingly provides critical commentary, especially on the Catholic Church and U.S. tourism. Further, Motley delved at length into the negative traits of the Mexican upper class. The town of Las Casas in the novel is mainly a fictionalized version of Puerto Vallarta, with some aspects of Cuernavaca and Acapulco. Initially the future tourist Mecca is still a small fishing village undergoing a transformation. Over the twenty years covered by the novel, a tiny number of visitors escalates to the point where the town metamorphoses into a capital commercial development.

Characters in *Let Noon Be Fair* are drawn from the entire socioeconomic range of the community. This includes a sexually active priest who is in league with the madam of a whorehouse. In the novel, the Mexican government claims to prohibit foreign ownership of beach property. Yet Americans gobble up the major hotels and brothels, sometimes by use of dummy partners. Gradually, the U.S. standard of living comes to predominate, along with the English language and the sexually exploitative practices of the invaders.

Before Motley could revise *Let Noon Be Fair* for publication, he died in Mexico on March 14, 1965. The circumstances appear murky, but newspaper reports and other sources suggest that he had been suffering stomach pains for some time. Motley was then living alone and reluctant to turn to doctors for medical assistance. Apparently he thought he could medicate himself but then lapsed into unconsciousness. By the time he was found by Sergio Lopez, his condition was grave. Lopez took Motley to a hospital near Mexico City, but an examination showed that a section of his intestines was infected with gangrene, perhaps because oxygen had been cut off. Motley never recovered consciousness, and a small group of friends and relatives flew to Mexico for his burial.

Scholarship about Motley has proceeded along two principal axes. The prevailing point of view in print preserves the canonical perspective of appraising him as the author of only one successful novel, *Knock on Any Door*, followed by an undisciplined failure and two potboilers. The tendency here is to affirm Motley's talent in areas of producing case studies and "raceless" novels.[28] These categories place him in the company of the sociological and documentary tradition, as well as among Black writers treating "white life" but also suggest that his work is relatively artless and lacking complexity of thought. Even though his posthumous *Let Noon Be Fair* addressed a new subject, culture clash South of the border, critics charged that Motley had produced "an empty carcass of the panoramic novel" (*Saturday Review*)[29] and that his method of elaboration was "superficial and commonplace" (*New York Times Book Review*).[30]

Developments in the climate of literary scholarship in recent decades, however, have promoted thinking and research that is likely to lead to a second evaluation, one based on a more intricate understanding of the political era from which Motley emerged and a freshly detailed examination of biographical sources. These latter encompass and yet go beyond Motley's vast archives of manuscripts and correspondence in Chicago and Madison. From the ascending perspective, some of which is on the verge of appearing in dissertations and in print, the traumas of Motley's early and intimate life, his sexual orientation, and his growing political commitment in the mid-1940s point in the direction of fresh angles for grasping his literary projects and appraising their underlying philosophy as well as originality.

Coincidentally, the several extant studies of the revisions that occurred prior to actual publication of Motley's novels, especially those addressing the changes and deletions compelled by editors as well as instituted in *Let Noon Be Fair* after his death, tend to confirm issues raised in the latest areas of research. Motley's early drafts indicate the existence of a somewhat hidden and more complex Motley, often struggling to find ways to communicate indirectly with the reader beyond the most sensational elements of his plots. A significant piece of evidence here is William Nelles's 1988 analysis of the posthumous deletions from *Let Noon Be Fair*.[31] These cuts include the elimination of a number of characters who bear partial resemblances to Motley, and who, if they had been left in the published version, might have provided insights into Motley's psychology, as well as into his artistic and political aims that are often short-changed in the edition now available.

One deletion involves five chapters about a fictionalized novelist named Melvin Morrison, through whom Motley had intended to provide commentary on his own creative process. Another set of deletions was directed at heightening the sexual aspects of the novel by toning down considerably Motley's deliberations about racial and religious topics. One group of these cuts was an eight-chapter unit about the racially oppressive experiences of an African American, Charles Jackson, in respect to white residents of Las Casas; and another involved the mention of sex between Euro-American women and Black men.

Some of the material trimmed from *Let Noon Be Fair* embodies direct representations of Motley himself. One of these entails an incident where Charles Jackson challenges an autobiographical Motley for his failure to focus on African Americans in his writing, and Motley reaffirms his Black identity with a folk maxim. Moreover, the cuts made in relation to a homosexual character, Chester, transform a tragic figure into a villain. In this instance, as well as that of another character who is a prostitute, the text that has been cut out is background information about these characters that is crucial to understanding their later sexual behavior.

Most revisionist efforts of Motley's work to date are just now emerging in dissertation form, in specialized journals, and in conference papers at professional organizations such as the Modern Languages Association and American Studies Association. Only *Knock on Any Door* remains in print, so partisans of the other novels are unable to advance discussion by introducing them into classrooms or interacting with informed audiences at conferences. Even more challenging is the project of making censored, edited, and cut versions of texts available to scholars, or of introducing previously unpublished books and stories in venues that will facilitate academic study.

Notwithstanding, in the twenty-first century there is the continued expansion of the literary canon into areas such as gay fiction and relatively neglected topics such as African American writers of the 1940s and 1950s. Therefore it is probable that a burgeoning if partially subterranean circle of scholars will persist in returning to Motley for a deeper understanding of these dimensions of U.S. culture. The final report on Motley's literary achievement is far from registered.

Notes

1. Himes, Chester. *"Lonely Crusade." Chicago Daily Sun-Times*, October 2, 1947, 33.
2. "Stand Up and Be Counted." *Time* (June 7, 1963): 11.
3. "Negro Art in Chicago." *Opportunity* 18, 1 (January 1940): 19–22, 28–31.
4. See the discussion in Adam Meyer, "The Need for Cross-Ethnic Studies," *MELUS* 16, 4 (Winter 1989–Winter 1990): 19–39.
5. Kunitz, Stanley J., ed. "Willard Motley." In *Twentieth Century Authors: A Biographical Dictionary, First Supplement*. New York: H. W. Wilson Co., 1955, 693–94.
6. In 1993 I visited the Motley collections at Northern Illinois University and University of Wisconsin, as well as conducted interviews with Frederica Motley (Chicago), Archibald Motley Jr. (Chicago), Ted Pierce (Madison, Wisconsin), Frank Fried (Berkeley, by phone), Alexander Saxton (Lone Pine, California, by phone), and Milton Zaslow (Laguna Beach, by phone). In 2003 I conducted a phone interview with Zev Braun (Los Angeles). My research in Chicago and Madison was carried out with the assistance of Patrick Quinn of Northwestern University Archives, to whom I am much indebted.
   For this essay, I have combined new information with the standard sources that are cited in footnotes and the bibliography of additional readings. The most widely-available work on Motley is Robert F. Fleming's *Willard Motley* (Boston: Twayne, 1978).
7. See Motley's memoir of his experiences in the *Chicago Defender* (National Edition): "First Bud Billiken Tells about Himself after 15 Years," January 20, 1940, 19; January 27, 1940, 19; February 3, 1940, 19; February 17, 1940, 19.
8. Rayson, Ann. "Prototypes of Nick Romano of *Knock on Any Door." Negro American Literature Forum* 8 (Fall 1974): 248–51.
9. "Hull-House Neighborhood," *Hull-House Magazine* 1, 1 (November 1939): 5–7; "Pavement Portraits," *Hull-House Magazine* 1, 2 (December 1939): 2–6; "Handfuls," *Hull-House Magazine* 1, 3 (January 1940): 9–11.
10. The manuscript can be found in the Motley collection at Northern Illinois University, Dekalb.
11. The manuscript can be found in the Motley papers at Northern Illinois University, Dekalb.
12. Weyant, Nancy Jill. "The Craft of Willard Motley's Fiction." Dissertation, Northern Illinois University, 1975.
13. This manuscript can be found in the Motley papers at University of Wisconsin, Madison.
14. See Margaret B. Hexter, "From Altar-Boy to Killer," *Saturday Review of Literature* 30 (May 24, 1947): 13; and Charles Lee, "Disciple of Dreiser," *New York Times Book Review*, May 4, 1947, 3.
15. Motley, Willard. *Knock on Any Door*. New York and London: Appleton-Century, 1947, 503.
16. Ibid., 60.
17. Ibid., 88.
18. Ibid., 185.
19. Ibid., 189.
20. See Sidney Lens, *Unrepentant Radical: An American Activist's Account of Five Turbulent Decades*. Boston: Beacon, 1980, 150–55.

21. Cain, James M. "Into the Lower Depths." *New York Times Book Review*, November 18, 1951, 4, 34.

22. Swados, Harvey. "Angry Novel." *Nation* 173 (December 29, 1951): 572.

23. Kingery, Robert E. Review of *We Fished All Night*. *Library Journal* 76 (December 1, 1951): 2006.

24. Anonymous. "The '30s Revisited." *Time* 58 (November 26, 1951): 120, 122.

25. Anonymous. "The Wire-Recorder Ear." *Time* 72 (August 11, 1958): 74.

26. Anonymous. Review of *Let No Man Write My Epitaph*. *New Yorker* 34 (August 23, 1958): 92.

27. Algren, Nelson. "Epitaph Writ in Syrup." *Nation* 187 (August 16, 1958): 79.

28. This analysis is promoted in Robert A. Bone's highly influential *The Negro Novel in America*. Revised Edition, New Haven: Yale University Press, 1965, 166–72.

29. Donoso, Jose. "From Heaven to Hilton." *Saturday Review* 49 (March 12, 1966): 152.

30. Coleman, Alexander. "The Farther for Being Near." *New York Times Book Review* 71 (February 27, 1966): 2.

31. Nelles, William. "'Tourist Town' to *Let Noon Be Fair*: The Posthumous Revision of Motley's Last Novel." *Analytical and Enumerative Bibliography* 1988 2 (2): 61–67.

References

Abbott, Craig S. "Versions of a Best-Seller: Motley's *Knock on Any Door*." *Papers of the Bibliographical Society of America* 81 (1987): 175–85.

Abbott, Craig S. and Kay Van Mol. "The Willard Motley Papers at NIU." *Resources for American Literary Study* 7 (Spring 1977): 3–26.

Bayliss, Craig S. "Nick Romano: Father and Son." *Negro American Literature Forum* 3 (Summer 1969): 8–21, 32.

Breit, Harvey. "James Baldwin and Two Footnotes." In *The Creative Present*, edited by Nora Balakian and Charles Simmons. New York: Doubleday and Co., 1963, 6–22.

Giles, James R. "Willard Motley's Concept of 'Style' and 'Material.'" *Studies in Black Literature* 4 (Spring 1973): 4–6.

Giles, James R. and Jerome Klinkowitz. "The Emergence of Willard Motley in Black American Literature." *Negro American Literature Forum* 6 (Summer 1972): 31–34.

Giles, James R. and N. Jill Weyant. "The Short Fiction of Willard Motley." *Negro American Literature Forum* 9 (Spring 1975): 3–10.

Grenander, M. E. "Criminal Responsibility in *Native Son* and *Knock on Any Door*." *American Literature* 49 (May 1977): 221–33.

Jarrett, Thomas D. "Sociology and Imagery in a Great American Novel." *English Journal* 38 (November 1949): 518–20.

Klinkowitz, Jerome and Karen Wood. "The Making and Unmaking of *Knock on Any Door*." *Proof* 3 (1973): 121–37.

Klinkowitz, Jerome, James R. Giles, and John T. O'Brien. "The Willard Motley Papers at the University of Wisconsin." *Resources for American Literary Study* 2 (Autumn 1972): 218–273.

Morgan, Stacey I. *Rethinking Social Realism: African American Art and Literature, 1910–1953*. Athens: University of Georgia Press, 2004.

Robinson, Jontyle Theresa and Wendy Greenhouse. *The Art of Archibald J. Motley, Jr.* Chicago: Chicago Historical Society, 1991.

Schapiro, Paul [pseud. for Paul N. Siegel]. "Workers' Bookshelf: *Knock on Any Door*." *Militant* (January 5, 1948): 4.

Weissgarber, Alfred. "Willard Motley and the Sociological Novel." *Studi American 7* (1961): 299–309.

Weyant, N. Jill. "Lyrical Experimentalism in Willard Motley's Mexican Novel: *Let Noon Be Fair*." *Negro American Literature Forum* 10 (Spring 1976): 95–99.

———. "Willard Motley's Pivotal Novel: *Let No Man Write My Epitaph*." *Black American Literature Forum* 11 (Summer 1977): 35–38.

Wood, Charles. "The Adventure Manuscript: New Light on Willard Motley's Naturalism." *Negro American Literature Forum* 6 (Summer 1972): 35–38.

Papers

Motley's papers reside at Northern Illinois University, Dekalb, and University of Wisconsin, Madison.

Published Novels

Knock on Any Door. New York: Appleton-Century, 1947.
We Fished All Night. New York: Appleton-Century-Crofts, 1951.
Let No Man Write My Epitaph. New York: Random House, 1958.
Let Noon Be Fair. New York: Putnam, 1966.

Selected Other Published Writing by Motley

"The Almost White Boy." In *Soon, One Morning: New Writing by American Negroes*, edited by Herbert Hill. New York: Knopf, 1963. Originally written in 1940.

The Diaries of Willard Motley, edited by Jerome Klinkowitz. Ames: Iowa State University Press, 1979.

"Let No Man Write Epitaph of Hate for His Chicago." *Chicago Sunday Sun-Times*, August 11, 1963, section 2, 1–4.

"Religion and the Handout." *Commonweal* 29 (March 10, 1939): 542–43.

"Small-town Los Angeles." *Commonweal* 30 (June 30, 1939): 251–52.

GORDON PARKS
(November 30, 1912–March 7, 2006)
Elizabeth Schultz

In 1999, Gordon Parks received his fifty-sixth honorary doctorate degree. In accepting this award from Princeton University, the nonagenarian Parks expressed his wish that the white high-school English teacher in Kansas who had told him and his black classmates that their families should not waste their money on sending them to college might have been present for this occasion. Although he did not go on to finish high school, Parks, who died in New York in March, 2006, during his lifetime received accolades, honors, and distinctions from a wide range of national organizations, including the National Medal of Art, presented by President Ronald Reagan in 1988, for his achievements during a long, creative, and socially conscious life. His work as a photojournalist, fashion photographer, art photographer, novelist, poet, memoirist, scriptwriter, filmmaker, and music composer, in which he combined a commitment to social justice with an aesthetic for beauty and tragedy, took him far beyond his Kansas origins and the erroneous and potentially damaging judgment of his high school English teacher. In the course of his long life, during which he moved from Kansas to Minnesota, Chicago, Washington, and New York, to Paris, Barcelona, and Rio, to Africa and Asia, he learned from his own experiences, from his associations with ordinary and extraordinary individuals, and from his continuous desire to create and to experiment with diverse genres and diverse media. While his work was significantly influenced by the social and cultural circumstances wherever he lived, the time he spent in Chicago, where he became familiar with the work of Black Chicago Renaissance writer Richard Wright and his colleagues, provided a formative dimension to his vision as it played out in the variety of genres in which he worked during his long life.

Just as Frederick Douglass rewrote the narrative of his years in slavery and of his escape to freedom in each of his three autobiographies, Parks relives his Kansas experiences in each of his six autobiographical works as well as in numerous interviews. His autobiographies invariably begin with tribute to his parents—Andrew Jackson and Sarah. Born on November 30, 1912, the last of fifteen children, he was raised on the family's farm outside of Fort Scott. He credits his parents' lessons in perseverance and dignity and love to his survival in a racist society and to his decision to choose art—words and pictures, the pen and the camera—as his "weapons" rather than violence and hatred.[1] His experiences with racism, both individual and institutional, began as a boy in Kansas where he was subjected to segregated schools and witnessed the persecution of black acquaintances. Although he attained worldwide renown and respect, Parks never forgot that his beloved parents as well as other members of his family lay in a segregated cemetery in Fort Scott, a fact he recalled frequently in his interviews and autobiographies.

Parks's boyhood was characterized not only by the intimacy and support of his family, but also by his appreciation for the beauty of the Kansas landscape. In 2004, on the occasion of Kansas Governor Kathleen Sebelius's declaring June 12 to be "Gordon Parks Day," Parks commented that "Kansas was [a] marvelous place for me and a terrible place."[2] His poem, "Kansas Land," which appears in several of his books, enumerates the delight he took in the state's natural beauty: "Cloud tufts billowing across the round blue sky. / Butterflies to chase through grass high as the chin. / Junebugs, swallowtails, red robin and bobolink, / Nights filled of soft laughter, fireflies and restless stars." The poem's conclusion, however, indicates that these pleasures were tempered by "the fear, hatred and violence / We blacks had suffered upon this beautiful land."[3] This bifurcated vision—of perceiving tragedy simultaneously with beauty—which he first felt during his Kansas boyhood becomes a primary attribute of his aesthetic.

Immediately following his mother's death, Gordon, at age fifteen, was sent to St. Paul, Minnesota, to live with a sister—a traumatic event that quickly introduced him into a changing and complex urban society, first in St. Paul and then in Chicago. After an altercation with his brother-in-law, he found himself on the street, penniless and homeless, in a frigid climate. "It was," he explains in *Half Past Autumn*, "a frightening leap to a big metropolis that would wash over me like a cold sea."[4] From 1927 to 1934, Parks shifted among a variety of jobs that were available for young black men during the Depression—playing piano in a brothel, washing dishes, busing dishes, writing songs, traveling with a band, working for the Civilian Conservation Corps, waiting on tables for the transcontinental North Coast Limited.

Although these years stimulated his musical sensibility, and his song "No Love" prompted band leader Larry Funk to invite him to join his group, it was Parks's discovery of the Farm Security Administration photographs in a magazine left behind on the North Coast Limited that changed the direction of his life. The FSA photographs moved him to acquire his first camera, a $7.50 Voightlander Brilliant in 1938 in a Seattle pawn shop. The FSA photographs of migrants and desperate farmers by such distinguished photographers as Dorothea Lange,

Arthur Rothstein, Carl Mydans, Walker Evans, and Ben Shahn moved Parks not only because of their subjects—America's dispossessed, men and women, old and young, black and white, in rural and urban settings—but also because of their powerful, stark black-and-white imagery. In the seven decades since Parks was first moved by a photograph and first held a camera, his own photographic record of the world's bigotry and poverty on the one hand, and of its capacity for compassion and beauty on the other, has been the primary basis for his renown.

The impact of the FSA pictures was reinforced by John Steinbeck's novels, by the images in Erskine Caldwell's and Margaret Bourke-White's *You Have Seen Their Faces* (1937), and by the photographs and perspective of Richard Wright's *12 Million Black Voices* (1941). In a 1963 issue of *Popular Photography*, Parks listed *12 Million Black Voices* as one of the two books he valued most; later, he named it the "bible" for this formative stage in his writing and photography careers.[5] Later Parks remembered Wright—for whom he provided a dust jacket photo for Wright's autobiography, *Black Boy* (1945)—as "neat, soft-spoken, well-groomed, and scholarly looking, seemingly free of the scars of his terrible Southern boyhood." Yet a sort of "terror lurked in his soft eyes."[6] Clearly, the aesthetic of Chicago Renaissance figures, such as Wright and Edwin Rosskam, whom Parks "shadowed" during his years in Chicago, impacted Parks's own artistic vision, particularly in the "simplicity, directness, and force" that Horace Cayton, in a November, 15, 1941, review in the *Pittsburgh Courier*, identified as a characteristic of Wright's and Rosskam's work.[7]

In the two years following the acquisition of his first camera, Parks began to explore and reveal the two elements of his complex vision—his perception of the shifting intersections of beauty and tragedy in human life. This dual perspective became apparent as he devoted himself to photographing both women's fashion and the lives of black America, two subjects which continued to occupy him in his long career as a photographer. In Minneapolis, with a young family (he had married Sally Alvis in 1933) and with no steady income, he decided to try his hand at fashion photography, a field in which he later became an acknowledged master. Some of his photographs, appearing in a fashionable Minneapolis women's clothing store, caught the eye of Marva Louis, wife of heavyweight boxing champion, Joe Louis, who encouraged him to move to Chicago in 1940, where through her connections, she believed he could make a profitable living as a fashion photographer and by doing photo shoots of the city's society matrons.

As all six of his autobiographies indicate, Chicago proved to be pivotal in Parks's growth, as the site where he became conscious of the significance of art in human life and of himself as an artist depicting human life. During his brief layovers in Chicago when he was working on the North Coast Limited he saw the despair in the lives of men living in flophouses as well as the luxurious ease of the wealthy. In Chicago, he observed the power of documentary newsreels and repeatedly visited the Chicago Art Institute, where he learned to appreciate the compositions in the paintings of Reubens, Renoir, and Matisse. These two different visual media—contemporary newsreel footage and European paintings—provided important models for him; they showed him equally "the power of a good picture," as he explained in his first autobiography, *A Choice of Weapons.*[8]

Marva Louis also introduced him to Chicago's South Side Community Art Center, where, as he describes in *A Choice of Weapons*, for the first time he met diverse artists who discussed with him art's power to effect change and who encouraged him to exhibit his photographs. Thus while making a living in Chicago by focusing on fashion, Parks also committed himself to showing its antithesis. He began to use his camera to focus on "the dismal acres of the south side, photographing depressed black people and the shacks and brick tenements that entombed them," determined "to strike at the evil of poverty" and, thereby, to illuminate the national tragedy of racism and poverty.[9] Influenced by the FSA pictures, he developed a documentary style of photography in Chicago, which allowed him to show the appalling effects of racism and poverty in explicit and dramatic images. In his early documentary photographs of Chicago's South Side, Parks began to perceive that tragedy could be revealed in combination with the astonishing and beautiful inner lives of his subjects. Later, in direct and forceful narratives in all six of his autobiographies, Parks dramatizes his personal experiences in Chicago, the urban setting where he was introduced to an intensification of the violence and despair, engendered by the racism and poverty he had first witnessed in rural Kansas.

Parks's depictions of Chicago's South Side were the immediate catalyst for his future success as a photographer. In 1941, they earned him the coveted Julius Rosenwald Fellowship, which in turn led to the director of the FSA, Roy Emerson Stryker's bringing him to Washington, D.C., to finish out the fellowship under the umbrella of the FSA itself. Stryker influenced Parks critically, encouraging him not only to look for the story behind his subjects but also to "think in terms of words and images. They can be mighty powerful when they are fitted together properly."[10] Given the visual impact of Parks's descriptive and dramatic language in his six autobiographies, his cinematic career, and the shift in his later years toward the creation of books in which words and images intersect, Stryker's advice was prophetic in Parks's work as an artist and helped to set him on the path of experimenting with the interrelationship of media to convey his messages.

In Washington, Parks was impressed by the capital's monuments, but he rapidly realized that they obscured the racism and poverty he had confronted throughout his life. Advised by Stryker to meet blacks who had intimately experienced these conditions, he became acquainted with Ella Watson, a cleaning woman in the FSA building, and in 1942 he photographed her standing against an immense American flag, flanked by a broom and a mop. His image of this slight, reflective woman in her simple dress, which complements Grant Wood's painting, *American Gothic*, where a white American couple stand with their farm implements, has become iconic, representing the millions of black Americans who perform the nation's tasks with much dignity and little recognition. Parks's acquaintance with Watson led to his creating the first of his black-and-white photographic portfolios focused on a particular family or historical event. His photographs of Watson with her grandchildren and of these children with a large white doll have also become well-known, not only for their compositions, but also for their visual insight into the impact of white standards of beauty on African American children and into the closeness of African American families.

In 1944, Parks returned to fashion photography, recognizing that this work would provide him with a steady income. He resigned from federal employment and moved to New York City, where he continued to live until his death in 2006, with intermittent periods abroad. Although *Harper's Bazaar* refused to hire him because of his race, he secured a recommendation from the renowned photographer, Edward Steichen, which landed him jobs, first doing casual-wear assignments for *Glamour* and then doing evening gowns for *Vogue*, where he would work for the following five years. Parks's photographs of haute couture focus on prominent symbols of wealth and power—sumptuous women and sumptuous clothes. Although he continued to use black-and-white for his fashion work during the 1940s and early 1950s, he increasingly experimented with color. His lavish color pictures of models posed to display their luxurious gowns in contrived and exotic settings contrast emphatically with his black-and-white pictures of lower- and middle-class people. Staged to appeal to a wealthy clientele, these pictures use color to highlight the desirability of both the models and their garments. The success of his work for *Vogue* led to his first European trip, sponsored by *Life*, to photograph the French collections being shown in Paris in 1950. Admittedly Parks was captivated by beautiful women and their clothes and by Paris, which he identified in *Half Past Autumn* as being "a long way from the cornfields of Kansas,"[11] and he continued to photograph the world of haute couture throughout Europe and the United States for many decades. Although later Parks acknowledged that fashion photography was "rewarding," he also realized that it was "rarefied."[12] Although the women in most fashion photography are arranged to appear as exquisite artifacts, Parks's use of lighting as well as gesture often gives a vibrancy to these mannequins and a complexity to their inner lives. His 1960 black-and-white portrait of the heiress, Gloria Vanderbilt, in which he captures her intense brooding as she stands posed in an elaborate dress with a constricting waist, epitomizes his ability to reveal the inner lives of these women.

In the late 1940s, just as Parks was becoming known for his magazine work, he published two instructional books on photography—*Flash Photography* (1947) and *Camera Portraits: Techniques and Principles of Documentary Portraiture* (1948). During this decade, Stryker also invited Parks to join a seventeen-man photography team at New Jersey's Standard Oil Company where he was given the double assignment of photographing corporate executives and documenting life at midcentury throughout the United States. To fulfill the latter part of this project, Parks traveled throughout New England, focusing on ordinary people engaged in ordinary activities. In the majority of these works, Parks, like the well-known French photographer of the 1940s and 1950s, Henri Cartier-Bresson, concentrates on "a decisive moment," a moment that is revealed in the intensity in his subject's expression. He also created three significant photographic portfolios during this period which illuminated different aspects of African American lives: the black fighter pilots of the 332nd Fighter Group; the August 1943 Harlem riot; and a Harlem gang. A visit to Richard Wright landed Parks in the middle of a Harlem riot. His pictures, taken on the spot, document not only the poverty that caused the riot but also a range of emotions—pain, terror, desperation, confusion, exhaustion, patience—in the individual faces of those watching and participating in the riot.

The impact of these images led directly to his appointment at *Life* in 1948, an appointment in which he would be doing both feature and fashion photography, an appointment that would last until 1972. To give focus to his first assignment—on Harlem gangs, Parks again chose a particular individual, Red Jackson, a sixteen-year-old gang leader. "Red's perilous existence," he wrote, "was a far cry from the perfumed houses of high fashion. Such a double-faced reality posed the kind of readjustment that was hard to come by."[13] His powerful photographic essay on Red and members of his gang—staring through a broken window, fighting, looking into the coffin of a slain friend—were the first of over 300 assignments that Parks would produce for *Life*. Of his photographic career in general, Parks writes in *Half Past Autumn*, "Tyrants, dictators, dethroned kings, beggars, queens, harlots, priests, the uplifting and the despoilers—all stared into my camera with eyes that were unveiled. The camera revealed them as they were—human beings imprisoned inside themselves."[14]

During his early years with *Life*, Parks was frequently sent abroad to photograph the world's celebrities as well as its rich and poor. In 1951 he was in Europe for Otto of Hapsburg's wedding, for Marshal Petain's funeral, and for Dwight Eisenhower's Paris visit. But in France and Portugal, he also captured a sleeping couple on a bench, a beggar playing the accordion, a political meeting of grim-faced men in a tavern, a shrewd bespectacled woman shopper, a child opening the doors onto a balcony. In Portugal, he captured a young girl holding a baby, smiling street boys, a destitute woman with her child, a severe matron in fur. *Life* sent Parks to Stomboli to cover the ostensibly scandalous romance between the Italian director, Roberto Rossellini, and the Swedish American actress, Ingrid Bergman. However, his photographs testify to his having discovered instead two human beings, as he felt, troubled by "heartache and uncertainty."[15]

However, Parks's commitment to using his camera to reveal the experiences of American blacks continued to be reflected in *Life* as well, with his autobiographies supplementing his photographs in order to expose American racism and poverty and to explain in succinct words his deepening moral concerns. On assignment in 1949, he returned to Fort Scott to trace the lives of the eleven black members of his junior high-school class and to note the town's changes since his departure twenty-three years earlier. In 1956, he spent weeks in Alabama, preparing a photographic essay on "Segregation in the Deep South." Again, Parks made a single family the centerpiece of his essay, and as a result of his particularizing the effects of racism and poverty through the moving pictures of Willie Causey, his wife, and children in their home, living with courage and dignity in the midst of continuing attempts at degradation, *Life's* editors acknowledged the impact he made on their readership by continuing to give him socially charged assignments.

Parks returned to Chicago in 1957, in conjunction with a story for *Life* on "Crime in America." In *Voices in the Mirror*, Parks designates Chicago as "a mecca of criminal transgression since Al Capone's reign of gangland terror," and in *Half Past Autumn* he calls the city "a mecca for drug addiction, murder, and corruption."[16] In these autobiographies, he re-creates his experiences accompanying Chicago police in their work, even as his colored photographs project the terrifying scenes in which violence and drug usage emerge out of shadows. Using tough vernacular dialogue, he evokes scenes in which the cops prove as violent as the crooks, and in which their credibility as law enforcers is undermined as they seek to set him up for sensationalized photographs. His reflections in *Voices in the Mirror* on his "assignment through the world of crime" lead him to "the realization that I had managed to escape it." Parks's concluding words not only ponder the inequities of the American prison system and capital punishment, but also muse more generally: "So many lives behind prison walls have been stopped forever. It is one thing to place the fault, another thing to point at where the fault lies."[17]

In his autobiographies Parks voices the basic concerns that underlay his powerful photographs of the 1960s and 1970s. In *Voices in the Mirror*, he explains: "I have, for a long time, worked under the premise that everyone is worth something; that every life is valuable to our existence. Consequently, I've felt it was my camera's responsibility to shed light on any condition that hinders human growth or warps the spirit of those trapped in the ruinous evils of poverty. It is not easy to do away with, whether its victims are black or white."[18] Thus through

these socially transformative years, Parks used his camera to change the perceptions of *Life's* readers regarding the lives of the poor and of black Americans
as he used words and story to attempt the same ends in his autobiographies.

During the sixties, his photographic essays focused on images depicting the
poverty and desperation of two families—in 1961 of Flavio da Silva's family in
Rio de Janeiro, and in 1967 of the Fontenelle family in Harlem. During these
decades, he also focused on portraits of such distinguished and controversial
African Americans as Duke Ellington, Elijah Muhammad, Malcolm X, Stokely
Carmichael, and Muhammad Ali, as well as on the lives and work of the Black
Panthers and the Black Muslims. While his portrait photographs of well-known
blacks have become iconic, Parks specifically explained that his photos of the
Fontenelles derived from his attempt to answer the question posed to him by
Life's managing editor as to "why black people were rioting and why they were so
discontent."[19] Parks's recognition of the necessity of addressing social injustices
stemming from racism and poverty as well as his profound commitment to civil
rights and his hope for change is reflected in both the photographic essays of the
unknown da Silva and Fontenelle families, as well as in the portraits depicting
the notorious and newsworthy. In *Born Black* (1971), in which many of these
photographs appear alongside his personal accounts of meeting the people in
them, he explains his commitment: "I came to each story with a strong sense
of involvement, finding it difficult to screen out my own memories of a scarred
past. But I tried for truth, the kind that comes through looking and listening,
through the careful sifting of day-to-day emotions that white America whips up
in black people. My own background has enabled me, I hope, to better share the
experiences of some other black people. I do not presume to speak for them. I
have just offered a glimpse, however, fleeting, of their world through black eyes."[20]

The impact of Parks's photographs of the Fontenelle family and of Flavio da
Silva and his family led to unanticipated and complicated repercussions, about
which Parks writes with compassion. In the "Foreword" to *Flavio* (1979), in which
he recounts the story of his relationship with the Brazilian boy from the time
of their meeting through his later years, he describes the two families and his
relationship to them, "The da Silvas and the Fontenelles lived across the world
from one another, but they shared the same tragedy, a private tragedy but one
at once very public—and I became caught up in their struggle to survive it."[21]
Assigned by *Life* to report on "Poverty in Brazil," Parks found his subject in a
favela outside Rio—Flavio, a twelve-year-old boy, malnourished and suffering a
deadly asthma, who had made himself the principal caretaker of his numerous
brothers and sisters. His pictures of Flavio, his parents, his siblings, the shack
where they lived with its crowded and filthy rooms exposed circumstances otherwise unimaginable to the middle-class American readers of *Life*. In the da Silva
children's spindly bodies, marked with sores, and in their anguished and win-

some faces, he documented the experience of thousands of others. The readers of *Life*, moved by his pictures of the da Silva family in Brazil and the Fontenelle family in the United States, responded by funding new houses for them both, by finding new jobs for the adults, and by paying for Flavio to come to the United States for expensive and long-term medical treatment. *Flavio* was given the Christopher Award for the best biography in 1978, but in his compassionate narrative Parks questions himself about the role of himself and his photographs in "altering human lives." Compellingly, he describes how the changes in the material circumstances of both families, which perhaps propelled them toward "improbable dreams," contributed to subsequent tragedies in their lives.[22]

Parks's autobiographical novel, *The Learning Tree*, published in 1963 and dedicated to his parents, however, inaugurated his second career as a writer and led to his choosing words as well as pictures as his weapons against racism and poverty. Identified as "a novel from life" on its title page, *The Learning Tree* was a Book-of-the-Month Club selection and has gone through several printings, remaining available today. In beginning his narrative with a tornado, Parks follows a pattern established for Kansas-based novels by L. Frank Baum's *The Wonderful Wizard of Oz* (1900) and Langston Hughes's *Not Without Laughter* (1937). The tornado in *The Learning Tree*, which affects both blacks and whites, is the means for the boy Newt Winger, Parks's stand-in for himself, to begin to question the world from multiple perspectives. Although a tornado was not a part of Parks's boyhood, many of the incidents and characters in *The Learning Tree* were directly drawn from his early years in Fort Scott, fictionalized as Cherokee Flats. The words of wisdom that Sarah Winger passes on to her son and by which Parks explains the title for *The Learning Tree* appear rephrased later in *Voices in the Mirror*, as words Parks's own mother, Sarah, spoke to him: "I hope you won't have to stay here all your life, Newt. It ain't a all-good place and it ain't a all-bad place. But you can learn just as much here about people and things as you can learn any place else. Cherokee Flats is sorta like a fruit tree. Some of the people are good and some of them are bad—just like the fruit on a tree. . . . No matter if you go or stay, think of it like that till the day you die—let it be your learnin' tree."[23] As Parks himself was subjected to racial slurs and terrorized by whites in Kansas as a boy, so is Newt. Like other boys coming of age, he and his fictional counterpart also had to overcome the fear of death. Death in racist Kansas, however, was not only an existential situation; it was precipitated by racist law-enforcement officers. His parents' steadfast love and capacity to dream a better life gives Newt the courage, as it did Parks, to prevail.

The shaping experiences in *The Learning Tree* form the springboard for Parks's subsequent autobiographies—*A Choice of Weapons* (1965), *To Smile in Autumn* (1979), *Voices in the Mirror* (1990), *Half Past Autumn* (1997), *A Hungry Heart: A Memoir* (2005), as well as his movie based on *The Learning Tree*—with each autobiography taking him further forward as in an ongoing search for justice and creative means for understanding tragedy and beauty. In *To Smile in Autumn* he claims that he has "been born again and again" and that in *Voices in the Mirror* he has "lived in so many different skins it is impossible for one skin to claim me."[24] In *A Choice of Weapons*, at fifty-four, he explained how he survived his lonely and destitute years following his departure from Kansas and discovered his salvation in the camera; in *To Smile in Autumn*, at age sixty-seven, he can describe his success as photographer, cinematographer, and writer, a success that he balances against the tragic loss of his first son and namesake; in *Voices in the Mirror*, at age seventy-eight, watching his children and his grandchildren mature and embracing diverse creative endeavors, he attains an equanimity with failure, tragedy, time, death. In the "Epilogue" for this autobiography, he writes: "I still don't know what compels me off into different directions. Perhaps the early years on the prairie have something to do with it—my putting a wetted finger up to catch the drifting of the wind, or the feel of oncoming rain or snow. . . . there were so many things to learn. Sometimes now, I go back to the prairie riverbanks to gaze into the water I envied for flowing off to places I would never see, but places I have been to since and learned from."[25] The 1997 retrospective exhibition of Parks's photographic career at the Corcoran Gallery of Art in Washington, D. C., provided the basis for *Half Past Autumn*, his fifth autobiographical work, which allowed him to reflect on the intersection of words and photographs in the course of his long life. The exhibition toured the United States, and the book that accompanied it became the basis for an HBO documentary on his life. *A Hungry Heart*, published shortly before his death, depicts Parks as "a one-man wrecking crew of racial barriers,"[26] yet also shows him as continuing his interest in discovering new ways of perceiving and expressing life's wonders.

In 1981, Parks deviated from his autobiographical narratives to tell the story of an Irish American family in his second novel, *Shannon*. Spanning the twentieth century, *Shannon* is set in New York City, Parks's adopted city. Emphasizing national, religious, and class conflict rather than racial discrimination, he traces the rise of the O'Farrell family, through the twentieth-century's labor problems, to social prominence at the end of the century. As in his two books of photographic essays—*Flavio* and *Born Black*—*The Learning Tree*, and his autobiographically dictated works, Parks sustains an easy narrative style characterized by a keen sense of story, vivid character portrayals, precise images, and lively dialogue. In all of his written works, including the poetry that he increasingly wrote in his later years, Parks took his lesson from Roy Stryker and Richard Wright, balancing specific "words and images" with his large concerns for human problems and writing clearly and forcefully. Consequently, whether he himself is the principal figure in the narrative or whether it is another, his writings appeal to readers of diverse ages and backgrounds.

Given Parks's understanding of the power of both narrative and image, it was perhaps inevitable that he would turn to cinema as a means of sharing his vision with an American audience. Three years after *Life* published his photographic essay on Flavio, Parks wrote the screenplay for and directed a twelve-minute film about the Brazilian boy. In 1968, his photographs of the Fontenelle family became the basis for a television documentary, titled *Diary of a Harlem Family*, for which he provided the narration and for which he received an Emmy Award for best TV documentary. In the same year, he directed the hour-long *World of Piri Thomas*, based on Thomas's *Down These Mean Streets* (1967), a memoir of growing up in Harlem's Puerto-Rican barrio. However, with his 1969 conversion of *The Learning Tree* into a film, Parks was catapulted into Hollywood work, which soon resulted in his gradual resignation from *Life*. The first African American to produce, direct, and write the screenplay and score for a film with a major studio (Warner Brothers), Parks returned once more to Fort Scott to another re-creation of the joys and traumas of his own boyhood. In 1989 *The Learning Tree* was designated one of twenty-five films to be placed on the National Film Registry of the Library of Congress. After *The Learning Tree*, Parks directed a trio of films for MGM—Shaft (1971), *Shaft's Big Score* (1972), and *The Super Cops* (1974); "a grand leap from Kansas to the mean streets of New York," he wrote, describing *Shaft* as "a noisy film about a black, suave, high-powered big-city detective."[27] These films, in which he explicitly sought to provide an alternative model for free-wheeling black masculinity, became international hits. He chose historical and more complex black heroes as the subjects for his subsequent films—*Leadbelly* (1976), the story of the great folk and blues singer; *Solomon Northrup's Odyssey* (1984), a retelling of the narrative of a black freedman, kidnapped, and sold into slavery, from which he escaped after a twelve-year trial; and *Martin* (1989). Parks wrote the scripts for both *Solomon Northrup's Odyssey* and *Martin* as well as the score for *Martin*, a five-act ballet devoted to Martin Luther King Jr. In 1990, *Martin* was shown on King's birthday on national television.

Having learned to play his parents' battered upright piano by ear at six, Parks was always moved by music—gospel and jazz, classical and popular, and since his early days in Minnesota, when he played piano and composed in order to live, he has been involved in making music, even developing his own system of notation. His travels to Europe expanded his interest in music, and his work with film allowed him to develop and express this interest more fully, adapting his film scores—notably for *The Learning Tree* and for *Shaft's Big Score*—for separate release. His compositions include *Concerto for Piano and Orchestra*, *Piece for Cello and Orchestra*, *Five Piano Sonatas*, and *Celebrations for Sarah Ross and Andrew Jackson Parks* in memory of his parents.

In 1968, Parks published *Gordon Parks: A Poet and His Camera*, the first of several books, including *In Love* (1971), *Whispers of Intimate Things* (1971), *Moments without Proper Names* (1975), *Arias in Silence* (1994), *Glimpses Toward Infinity* (1996), and *Eyes with Winged Thoughts* (2005), which, in their integration of his poetry with his imagistic color photographs, move decidedly away from social documentation and toward abstraction, from social tragedy toward natural beauty. Although his photographic essays in *Life* and his books, *Born Black* and *Flavio*, brought his words and his black-and-white pictures powerfully together in the middle of his career, *A Poet and His Camera* reveals Parks's ongoing interest in creative experimentation and in synergistic aesthetic possibilities. In the "Foreword" to *Arias in Silence*, he explains the importance of this shift: "The pictures that have most persistently confronted my camera have been those of crime, racism and poverty. I was cut through by the jagged edges of all three. Yet I remain aware of imagery that lends itself to serenity and beauty, and here my camera has searched for nature's evanescent splendors. Recording them was a matter of devout observance, a sort of metamorphosis through which I called upon things dear to me—poetry, music and the magic of watercolor."[28] Identifying Parks in his preface for *A Poet and His Camera* as "one of the most remarkable living photographers" and as "a poet with his camera as well as with his pen," Stephen Spender praises him for his "concentration on the image."[29] Focusing on single objects, blurring them to create movement, shadowing them to evoke mystery, or juxtaposing them against a contrasting background in this pioneering work, Parks provides pictorial images, which resonate and illuminate the lyrical, imagistic poems that accompany them and which muse on nature, love, and time.

In Parks's two 1971 books—*In Love* and *Whispers of Intimate Things*—he shifted explicitly from Bresson's "the decisive moment" to focus on beautiful moments in both word and picture. In *Moments without Proper Names* (1975), however, his poetry accompanies powerful images from his major photographic essays depicting the struggle characterizing African American life and contrasting with images of poignancy and wonder in the human and the natural world in the concluding pages. Philip Brookman maintains that since 1985 Parks "combined his external vision with his internal feelings to create an extended series of poetic, constructed landscapes."[30] These constructed landscapes have also been called "soulscapes" or "eye music." Always in color, he positions a sculpture or one or more natural objects—a flower, a leaf, a shell, driftwood—against a background of one of his own oil and watercolor paintings—to create sumptuous, multilayered collages. Increasingly, his images evoke sea, land, and sky, with a sun or moon balancing the foregrounded object. Often photographing through glass, he achieves unusual lighting effects and depth. Drenched in color and texture, his recent works resemble Georgia O'Keeffe's desert and flower paintings. *A Star for Noon* (2004) is devoted to nudes and is accompanied by a CD of his compositions. His poetic and imagistic constructions demonstrate his decision to use art—words, pictures, and music—as an explicit expression of peace and loveliness and an implicit expression against racism, poverty, and violence. He believes that "After working so hard at showing the desolation and the poverty, I have a right to show something beautiful as well. . . . It's all there, and you've done only half the job if you don't do that."[31]

In his nineties, Parks was surrounded by his family—his three children (his oldest son, Gordon, also a photographer and filmmaker, died in 1979 on location in Kenya), their spouses, and several grandchildren. Divorced from his first wife, Sally, in 1961, he subsequently married Elizabeth Campbell in 1962, whom he divorced in 1973, and in 1973, he married Genevieve Young, whom he divorced in 1979. Calling his children and grandchildren "a gathering of fine jewels," he rejoiced in the "jumble of bloodlines" reflected in his family, creating "the color of a rainbow."[32]

A cosmopolitan, nonetheless Parks frequently and continually recognized the importance of the lessons gleaned in his formative years in Kansas and in Chicago. Increasingly as the master of diverse genres and media, he was referred to in public as a "Renaissance man," although his son, David, insists that his success lay in his ease with all people, his ability to get "next to his subjects and to stay out of the way, . . . he keyed in on them rather than having them key in on him."[33] The concluding words of *Half Past Autumn*, however, suggest that Parks never rested on his laurels, that he remained vitally engaged in creativity and discovery: "Dreams keep moving in, and the desire is still there to devour them. . . . since my time is so short, there is no room for idleness. At the moment I'm painting, reworking an unfinished novel, editing verse, and composing a piano sonata that reflects the natures of my four children. Naturally, the camera moves in to have its say now and then. . . . At half past autumn I'm all roses, thorns, shadows, and dreams; still touching what exists . . . I keep moving; later is too late."[34] His honors and awards continued until his death; in 2002, he was inducted into the International Photography Hall of Fame; several schools have been given his name.

In the "Epilogue" for *Half Past Autumn*, he states, "I still wait impatiently for that segregated graveyard to become a forgotten memory. Until then, the peace, hovering between me and my birthplace, will continue to be untrustworthy."[35] Although Fort Scott city officials had offered to move the African American graves to the hill where the white elite are buried, Parks demanded instead that the city carefully maintain the black cemetery, keeping it as a historical monument to Fort Scott's stalwart black community. His son, David, reveals that prior to his death, Parks expressed his desire to go "home" to Kansas to be buried.[36] Fort Scott had been working to make amends for its history of prejudice and injustice, recognizing Parks as its most distinguished citizen and in 2004 inaugurating the annual Gordon Parks Celebration of Culture and Diversity with scholarly lectures, exhibitions, musical tributes, trolley rides, and a film festival. The city has beautified "that segregated graveyard," where Parks now makes peace with Kansas at last, resting there with his parents and extended family.

Throughout his long life, Parks revealed in words, pictures, and music his commitment to social activism. His work revealed as well his commitment to an aesthetic nurtured by contemplation, creativity, and experimentation. Often referred to as a "Renaissance man" and a cosmopolitan, he recognized the important lessons gleaned in his formative years in Kansas and in Chicago.

Gordon Parks died on March 7, 2006, at the age of 93, at his home in Manhattan. His funeral at Riverside Church in Morningside Heights was attended by family and associates such as former New York mayor David Dinkins, actor Avery Brooks, and fashion designer Gloria Vanderbilt, as well as numerous photographers, no doubt many his professional heirs. Parks is buried near his parents in Fort Scott, Kansas.

Notes

1. Titling his first autobiography, *A Choice of Weapons* (New York: Harper and Row Publishers, 1965), Parks writes in his conclusion, "Poverty and bigotry would still be around, but at last I could fight them on even terms. The significant thing was a choice of weapons with which to fight them most effectively. . . . I would [choose] those of a mother who placed love, dignity and hard work over hatred" (274).

2. Hurd, Greg. "Fellow Kansans Honor Gordon Parks in Harlem." *Lawrence Journal World* (June 18, 2004): 2D.

3. Parks, Gordon. *A Poet and His Camera*. New York: Viking Press, 1968, n.p.

4. Parks, Gordon. *Half Past Autumn*. Boston: Little, Brown and Company, 1997, 12.

5. Parks, *A Choice of Weapons*, 232.

6. Ibid., 243–44.

7. Gates Jr., Henry Louis and Kwame Anthony Appiah. *Richard Wright: Critical Perspectives Past and Present*. New York: Amistad, 1993, 26–27.

8. Parks, *A Choice of Weapons*, 178.

9. Ibid., 208, 212–13.

10. Ibid., 227.

11. Parks, *Half Past Autumn*, 92.

12. Ibid., 80.

13. Ibid.

14. Ibid., 13.

15. Ibid., 102.

16. Parks, Gordon. *Voices in the Mirror: An Autobiography*. New York: Doubleday, 1990, 171; Parks, *Half Past Autumn*, 180.

17. Parks, *Voices in the Mirror*, 178.

18. Ibid., 179–80.

19. Parks, *Half Past Autumn*, 228.

20. Parks, Gordon. *Born Black*. Philadelphia: J. B. Lippincott, 1971, 12.

21. Parks, Gordon. *Flavio*. New York: W. W. Norton, 1979, 7.

22. Ibid., 7, 8.

23. Parks, Gordon. *The Learning Tree*. New York: Fawcett-Crest, 1963, 35–36.

24. Parks, Gordon. *To Smile in Autumn*. New York: W. W. Norton, 1979, 247; Parks, *Voices in the Mirror*, 340.

25. Parks, *Voices in the Mirror*, 341.

26. Wranovics, John. "Weapon of Choice," *New York Times Book Review*, January 8, 2006, 15.

27. Parks, *Half Past Autumn*, 320.

28. Parks, Gordon. *Arias in Silence*. Boston: Bulfinch Press, 1994, n.p.

29. Spender, Stephen. "Preface," *Gordon Parks: A Poet and His Camera*. New York: Viking Press, 1968, n.p.

30. Brookman, Philip. "Unlocked Doors: Gordon Parks at the Crossroads." In *Half Past Autumn*, 352.

31. "Legends Online," http://www.pdngallery.com/legends/parks/bio.shtml.

32. Parks, *Half Past Autumn*, 324, 326.

33. Rombeck, Terry. "Nearly Year after Father's Death, Son Visits Father's Boyhood Home." *Lawrence Journal World* (January 18, 2007): 2D.

34. Parks, *Half Past Autumn*, 343.

35. Ibid.

36. Rombeck, *Lawrence Journal World*.

For Further Reading

Brierly, Dean. "Renaissance Man: The Photography of Gordon Parks." *Camera and Darkroom* 13 (December 1, 1991): 24.

Doherty, Thomas. "The Black Exploitation Picture: Superfly and Black Caesar." *Ball State University Forum* 24.2 (1983): 30–39.

Henry, Matthew. "He Is a 'Bad Mother': Shaft and Contemporary Black Masculinity." *African American Review* 38.1 (Spring 2004): 119–26.

Houston, Helen R. "Gordon Parks." *Notable Black American Men*, edited by Jessie Carney Smith. Detroit: Gale Research Inc., 1999.

Lyne, William. "No Accident: From Black Power to Black Box Office." *African American Review* 34.1 (Spring 2000): 39–59.

Moore, Deedee. "Shooting Straight: The Many Worlds of Gordon Parks." *Smithsonian* 20.1 (April 1989): 66–72, 74, 76–77.

Myers, Walter. "Gordon Parks: John Henry with a Camera." *Black Scholar* 7 (January–February 1976): 26–30.

Paris, Michael. "Country Blues on the Screen: The Leadbelly Films." *Journal of American Studies* 30.1 (April 1996): 119–25.

Parks, Gordon. *Bare Witness*. New York: Rizzoli, 2006.

———. *Camera Portraits: Techniques and Principles of Documentary Portraiture*. New York: F. Watts, 1948.

———. "A Conversation with Gordon Parks." With Martin H. Bush. In *The Photographs of Gordon Parks*. Wichita, Kans.: Wichita State University Press, 1983.

———. *Eyes with Winged Thoughts*. New York: Atria, 2005.

———. *Flash Photography*. New York: Grosset and Dunlap, 1947.

———. *Glimpses Toward Infinity*. Boston: Little, Brown, and Company, 1996.

———. "Gordon Parks Interview." With Maurice Peterson. *Essence* 3 (October 1972): 62.

———. "Gordon Parks Interview." With Roy Campanella. *Millimeter* 4 (April 1976): 30–32.

———. *A Hungry Heart: A Memoir*. New York: Atria, 2005.

———. *In Love*. Philadelphia: Lippincott, 1971.

———. *Moments Without Proper Names*. New York: Viking Press, 1975.

———. *Shannon*. Boston: Little, Brown, and Company, 1981.

———. *A Star for Noon*. Boston: Bulfinch Press, 2004.

———. "A Talk with Gordon Parks." With B. Thomas. *Action* 7 (July–August, 1972): 14–18.

———. *Whispers of Intimate Things*. New York: Viking Press, 1971.

Schultz, Elizabeth. "Dreams Deferred: The Personal Narratives of Four Black Kansans." *American Studies* 34.2 (Fall 1993): 25–52.

Tidwell, John Edgar. "Gordon Parks and the Unending Quest for Self-Fulfillment." In *John Brown to Bob Dole: Movers and Shakers in Kansas History*, edited by Virgil Dean. Lawrence: University Press of Kansas, 2006. 293–305.

Tidwell, John Edgar and Carmaletta Williams. "Coming of Age in the Land of Uncertainty." *Cottonwood* 56 (2000): 42–59.

JOHN SENGSTACKE
(1912–1997)
Jamal Eric Watson

In chronicling the history of the African American press in the United States, John Sengstacke emerges as one of the nation's most powerful African American newspaper publishers. In 1940, at the ripe age of 27, the young Sengstacke gained national notoriety when he became the second publisher of the *Chicago Defender*, arguably one of the most recognized black newspapers in the country. Founded in 1905 by Sengstacke's uncle, Robert Sengstacke Abbott, the *Chicago Defender* quickly emerged as a powerful voice in articulating the widespread oppression that African Americans throughout the nation faced. It also served as a creative outlet for hundreds of African American writers and artists who gathered in Chicago to hone their creative talents during what has come to be known as the Black Chicago Renaissance. From 1932 through 1950, Chicago's black community witnessed, and participated in, important creative developments in literature, art, music, social science, and journalism that affected not only the literary world but the broader community through its social and political content and commitment. The *Chicago Defender* was one of a handful of newspapers that provided African Americans in Chicago and elsewhere with a platform to challenge forcefully legal segregation and the mistreatment of African Americans. As a result, Sengstacke became an important figure in the civil rights movement and a shaper of public opinion, including the opinions of those writers whose works exemplified the spirit of the Black Chicago Renaissance.

Long before Sengstacke became publisher of the *Chicago Defender*, it was clear that he was being groomed for a life in the newspaper industry. Born in Savannah, Georgia, on May 12, 1912, he graduated from Brick Junior College and later attended Hampton Institute, a historically black college in Virginia that was eventually renamed Hampton University. As a child, Sengstacke was solely responsible for soliciting ads and laying out the news pages for the *Woodville Times*, a weekly newspaper that was founded by his grandfather, John H. H. Sengstacke, and later run by his father, Alexander Sengstacke. It was there that he learned the inner workings of the business, though he admitted frankly back then that he was not "too keen" on the newspaper business. However, he was singled out anyway by his uncle, Robert S. Abbott, who was the publisher of the *Chicago Defender*, and trained as Abbott's successor. In fact, Abbott was so personally impressed by Sengstacke's talent that he financed his nephew's education at Hampton Institute, where he graduated in 1934. He also subsidized his studies at the Mergenthaler Linotype School, The Chicago School of Printing, Northwestern University, and Ohio State University.

In 1934, Sengstacke became vice president and general manager of The Robert S. Abbott Publishing Company, and when his uncle died in 1940, he inherited the paper and became the company's second president and publisher. Almost immediately, Sengstacke had to restructure the newspaper's business operation. Though Abbott had acquired a massive personal fortune as publisher of the paper, the *Chicago Defender* was nearly bankrupt when Sengstacke took control after Abbott's death. But over time, Sengstacke eventually nursed it back to profitability and presided over the paper's circulation boom.

Clearly, Sengstacke had big shoes to fill, and he understood the responsibilities that accompanied running the country's largest black newspaper. Under his uncle's leadership, the *Chicago Defender* had gained a national readership that extended far beyond Chicago. The paper's decision to become a champion of the Great Black Migration was single-handedly responsible for the influx of thousands of black southerners into Chicago from southern states like Mississippi, North Carolina, and Alabama. Beginning in World War I, Abbott used his newspaper as a platform to encourage southerners to come north. He forcefully argued that the destiny of Black Americans was inextricably linked to the North, where factories were desperate for workers. The *Chicago Defender* printed the one-way train schedules from cities in the South to Chicago and blacks responded favorably. Some white southerners, however, were not so happy with the tenor and tone of the newspaper, and a number of African Americans report that the *Defender* had to be read and distributed covertly in parts of the South where its equal rights message and encouragement to migrate north was considered an affront to southern values and economy, as well as a danger to the moral and social fabric of the country as a whole.

In just a few years since taking the helm of the newspaper, John Sengstacke came to realize that his Chicago had also become a destination place for rising African American artists who were looking for an outlet to showcase their talent. As the publisher of the *Chicago Defender*, Sengstacke presided over and watched the formation of the Black Chicago Renaissance, an exciting literary and cultural period for African American writers and artists who were deeply committed to the development of the arts among African Americans. Thousands of black writers would congregate in Chicago to celebrate Black artistic expression. This phenomenon had of course been successful in Harlem many years before, and

Sengstacke and others were confident that Chicago, with its burgeoning Black population and a spirit of cooperation among black and white progressive or radical artists in the city, could experience a similar cultural awakening. For young writers who were looking to begin journalism careers, Sengstacke was the person to see. He offered African Americans an opportunity to write their first bylined story and provided a space for freelance photographers to show-case their photos. In 1943, Langston Hughes, who had been involved with the cultural outpouring in Harlem, introduced his famous character, Jess Semple, in his *Chicago Defender* column. "Simple," as he was called, became a beloved figure whose social and political ideas helped expose issues of race and gender to a popular audience made far more possible by the distribution it garnered in Sengstacke's newspaper. Several volumes of Simple stories followed the popular-ity of the articles in the *Defender*, and helped Hughes to continue concentrating on being a professional writer as opposed to taking on other jobs to supplement his writing income. Gwendolyn Brooks, whose work represented an early poetic flowering of the Chicago Renaissance, signified by the popular acclaim for her first poetry volume and the awarding of the Pulitzer Prize to her second, first published her poetry in the *Chicago Defender* from 1934 to 1936. Others such as Richard Wright and Frank Marshall Davis also found an atmosphere in Chicago that was congenial to writers within the pages of the newspaper. For example, the *Chicago Defender* committed itself to writing about rising African American artists. When mainstream newspapers ignored writers like Lorraine Hansberry, whose *A Raisin in the Sun* would win the 1959 New York Drama Critics Circle Award, Sengstacke allowed his newspaper to publish feature stories on writers like Hansberry and others.

In terms of Black journalism, Chicago, in the period of the Renaissance, was the epicenter of the Black Press. In addition to Sengstacke's centrally im-portant *Chicago Defender*, Chicagoans could also read the Chicago edition of the *Pittsburgh Courier*, the *Chicago Bee*, the *Chicago Whip*, and several smaller community papers. All of these papers printed articles from the national Black wire service, which was also based in Chicago. Magazines were also flourishing in Chicago, largely because of the success of publisher John Harold Johnson. Johnson mortgaged his mother's furniture for a meager $500 so he could pay for his first direct mail advertising about his magazine, *Negro Digest*, which he launched in 1942. He would go on to launch *Jet* and *Ebony* magazines a few years later. During this period, Chicago's black population had soared from 44,000 in 1910 to more than 230,000 by 1930. The tightly knit community of nineteenth-century African Americans was mostly literate and could read the daily publications. It was this group that threw their support behind the various black newspapers and ensured that they survived.

It is important to note that not only did Sengstacke control one of the na-tion's most powerful black newspapers, his influence was far reaching. He was also the founder of the Negro Newspaper Publishers Association (NNPA), a collaborative of dozens of black newspapers that routinely met to show their strength as a collective power in the publishing industry and that had sought to restrict entrance to African Americans. Sengstacke founded the NNPA in 1940 and served seven terms as the group's president. He later witnessed the organization change its name from the Negro Newspaper Publishers Association to the National Newspaper Publishers Association. The NNPA was created to counter the resistance that black newspapers faced from white mainstream newspapers who did not see African American publications as serious enough to serve as conveyors of the news. But the organization, though still in existence today, never really got off the ground, in part because small, family-owned black newspapers resisted the idea of being represented under the umbrella of Sengstacke's enterprise, and many rejected the idea of collaborating with other black newspapers that were viewed primarily as competition. For years, they feuded with each other over everything from advertising dollars to circulation numbers. Despite the tensions, Sengstacke kept the organization together, pointing out that the Black Press, because of its continual attacks on racism, would be the subject of harsh criticisms.

In the realm of politics, Sengstacke demonstrated that he had a keen understanding of the issues that confronted the nation, and he wielded a substantial amount of political clout. Sengstacke inherited the paper from Abbott, who became a millionaire, in large part because of the success of the *Chicago Defender.* Like his uncle, Sengstacke was never shy about being an activist. In fact, he used his position as publisher of the largest circulated black newspaper to push for causes that affected African Americans. He worked with President Franklin D. Roosevelt to jumpstart jobs in the U.S. Postal Service for African Americans and eventually persuaded Roosevelt to include an African American reporter in a White House news conference for the first time in the country's history. More importantly, however, it was Sengstacke's insistence that the armed services during World War II be fully integrated, and he aggressively pressured the Roosevelt administration to change the policies. Like other African American publishers, Sengstacke gained access to Roosevelt through his connection with his wife— Eleanor Roosevelt, who was largely seen as a champion of Negro Rights. Mrs. Roosevelt was seen as a friend to African American leaders, because she had a long track record of advocating civil rights and often supported causes that were not embraced by her husband's administration. In fact, many whites were outraged with Mrs. Roosevelt when in 1943 she penned a column for another publication, *Negro Digest,* called "If I Was a Negro." In the column, Roosevelt challenged the mistreatment that African Americans faced.

Though President Roosevelt resisted listening to Sengstacke's advice, his successor, President Harry Truman named Sengstacke to the commission that he formed to desegregate the military. And in 1956, Sengstacke made a bold move by transforming his popular weekly newspaper into a daily, making it the nation's largest black-owned daily at the time. That year, Sengstacke also purchased the *Pittsburgh Courier*, a newspaper that was at one time owned by Robert Vann. During World War II, Vann's newspaper came under scrutiny after it launched the "Double V" campaign in its pages. The "Double V" campaign called for victory against fascism in Nazi Germany during World War II as well as against racism in the United States. During that period, the Black Press was severely under attack by J. Edgar Hoover, who complained that black newspapers were engaged in acts of sedition aimed at weakening the nation's morale during the time of war. Hoover threatened to put the African American press out of business and had urged Francis Biddle, then U.S. Attorney General, to launch an investigation. Sengstacke, in his capacity as head of the NNPA, traveled to Washington, D.C., and convinced Biddle and other government officials to back down. In an attempt to further solidify his economic base, Sengstacke purchased the *Tri-State Defender* in Memphis and the *Michigan Chronicle* in Detroit and formed a newspaper chain called Sengstacke Enterprises Inc.

During his tenure, Sengstacke was most responsible for recruiting some of the best talents to the newspaper. Most noticeably, he hired Ethel Payne, a feisty African American journalist with little experience to work for the *Chicago Defender*. Payne would later garner a national name for herself by aggressively covering civil rights issues. She would become one of the few black journalists covering national politics in Washington, D.C., in the 1950s. For example, her work in the Black Press was so lauded that she was affectionately called "The First Lady of the Black Press." Payne was the paper's White House correspondent, a job that she secured in large part because of the pressure that Sengstacke placed on the White House to grant press credentials to a reporter representing the Black Press. She also traveled with U.S. presidents overseas, something that was unparalleled in the Black Press. But like Sengstacke, Ethel Payne used journalism primarily as a vehicle for her own social activism. In the pages of the *Chicago Defender*, she tried to train a national spotlight on issues relevant to African Americans, and her column was eventually syndicated in other black newspapers across the country. In 1954, she received national attention when, at a press conference, she asked President Eisenhower when he planned to ban segregation in interstate travel. Visibly irritated, Eisenhower said he refused to support any special interest, and never recognized her at future press briefings. Others said her question helped move civil rights onto the national agenda. That afternoon, the *Washington Evening Star* carried a center box on page one with the caption "Negro Reporter Angers Ike." Sengstacke, who was based in Chicago, called Payne after hearing of the confrontation. "So you're picking on presidents now," he said.[1]

It is important to note that Sengstacke's contributions were not just limited to the publishing industry. His efforts at integrating public spaces in the 1940s, for example, helped to lead to the hiring of Jackie Robinson, who in 1947 became the first black player in major league baseball. Though he was encouraged to run for public office by some who felt that he could use his influence to shape public policy, Sengstacke maintained his position behind the scenes and insisted that he neither yearned for the responsibility or the fame of elected office.

Thomas Picou, a nephew of Sengstacke's who purchased the *Chicago Defender* and Sengstacke's other newspapers in 2003 said that his uncle was responsible for helping to elect Mayor Richard J. Daley and was chiefly responsible for the integration of the school board and fire and police departments.

But in 1983, Sengstacke would develop a contentious relationship with Chicago's first black mayor—Harold Washington. Sengstacke, who was friends with the Daley family—Chicago's political machine—was accused of inadequately covering Washington's tenure in office. Many in the African American community were troubled, particularly since the *Chicago Defender* was a black-owned newspaper. Some African Americans canceled their subscriptions and abandoned the newspaper. Washington felt ignored by the Black daily and was personally hurt by the decision of Sengstacke to endorse his white opponent, Richard Daley, in the Democratic primary. In fact, officials in Washington's administration would often slip scoops to the *Chicago Defender*, in hopes that they would pursue a particular story, often to no avail. Meanwhile, his opposition worked overtime feeding reporters dirt on Washington—with great success. Editorials and news stories routinely attacked Washington, though his popularity in Chicago's African American community soared.

Four years before his death, John Sengstacke stepped down as publisher and turned the reins over to his brother, Frederick Sengstacke. He served as publisher until 2000, when Colonel Eugene Scott, U.S. Army (ret.), assumed the role. John Sengstacke died of a heart attack on May 28, 1999, at the age of 84, after a prolonged illness. He was awarded the Presidential Citizens Medal posthumously by President Bill Clinton in 2000, and the enterprise called the *Chicago Defender* that he developed continues to be the largest African American chain of newspapers operating in the country.

Before his death in 2005, John H. Johnson, the publisher of *Ebony* and *Jet* and one of Sengstacke's contemporaries, said that he was inspired by the journalism that the *Chicago Defender* represented and tried on many occasions to replicate some of the same ideas into his African American magazines. "My mother and I became aware of the opportunities in Chicago for Black people by reading the *Defender*," said Johnson, who headquartered his publications in Chicago as well. "Sengstacke took a great newspaper and made it better," he added.[2]

Sengstacke was philanthropic as well, having served as chairman of the board of Provident Hospital and Training School Association, where he built a new $50 million Provident Medical Center to enable the hospital, in which the world's first heart operation was performed, to continue its life-saving service to Blacks and others on Chicago's South Side.

Notes

1. Interview with Ethel L. Payne by Kathleen Currie, Women in Journalism oral history project of the Washington Press Club Foundation, August 25, 1987 through November 17, 1987, Oral History Collection, Columbia University, 49–50.

2. John H. Johnson, interview with author, Chicago, July 17, 2004.

References

Brooks, Maxwell R. *The Negro Press Re-Examined: Political Content of Leading Negro Newspapers*. Boston: Christopher Publishing House, 1959.

Dawkins, Wayne. *Black Journalists: The NABJ Story*. Sicklerville, N.J.: August Press, 1993.

Finkle, Lee. *Forum for Protest: The Black Press during World War II*. Cranbury, N.J.: Fairleigh Dickinson University Press, 1975.

Higgins, Chester Sr. "Is the Black Press Dying?" *The Crisis* 1980 87 (7): 240–41.

Hogan Lawrence. *A Black National News Service: The Associated Negro Press and Claude Barnett, 1919–1945*. Rutherford, N.J.: Fairleigh Dickinson University Press; London: Associated University Presses, 1984.

La Brie III, Henry G, ed. *Perspectives of the Black Press: 1974*. Kennebunkport, Maine: Mercer House Press, 1974.

Lyle, Jack, ed. *The Black American and the Press*. Berkeley: University of California Press, 1968.

Myrdal, Gunnar, et al. *An American Dilemma: The Negro Problem and Modern Democracy: Volume I*. New York: Harper and Brothers Publishers, 1944.

Penn, I. Garland. *The Afro-American Press and Its Editors*. Salem, N.H.: Ayer Company Publishers, Inc., 1891.

Pride, Armistead and Clint C. Wilson II. *A History of The Black Press*. Washington, D.C.: Howard University Press, 1997.

Senna, Carl. *The Black Press and the Struggle for Civil Rights*. New York: Franklin Watts, 1993.

Staples, Brent. "John H. Sengstacke: Citizen Sengstacke." *The New York Times Magazine*, January 4, 1998, 27–28.

Streitmatter, Rodger. *Raising Her Voice: African-American Women Journalists Who Changed History*. Lexington: University Press of Kentucky, 1994.

Tinney, James S. and Justine J. Rector. *Issues and Trends in Afro-American Journalism*. Washington, D.C.: University Press of America, Inc., 1980.

Washburn, Patrick S. *A Question of Sedition: The Federal Government's Investigation of the Black Press during World War II*. New York: Oxford University Press, 1986.

———. "J. Edgar Hoover and the Black Press in World War II." *Journalism History* 1986 13(1): 26–33.

Wolseley, Roland Edgar. *The Black Press, U.S.A.* Ames: Iowa State University Press, 1971.

MARGARET WALKER
(July 7, 1915–November 30, 1998)
Maryemma Graham

A few months after a little known group of radical black artists and intellectuals assembled to meet on Chicago's South Side in 1936, the youngest member was inspired to write her most famous poem, "For My People." It stunned the group, since the author, Margaret Walker, was a virtual unknown and barely twenty-two. Five years later, fresh from the University of Iowa Writers' Workshop, Walker made history as the first African American to claim the prestigious Yale Series of Younger Poets Award. Those who knew Walker saw a tiny determined woman who broke more barriers by the time she was thirty than most people do in a lifetime. Because she had such early success and for more than sixty years produced work that was alternately brilliant, revolutionary, trendsetting, and inspiring, her shadow falls over much of African American literature without being clearly defined. She was a writer of poetry, fiction, essays, and a biography, all while making her living as a teacher and mentor to generations of students and writers, especially women. When she was no longer young, she became an organizer and an activist, which made her central to the rise of a visible African American literary culture in the 1960s. The range and extent of Walker's work represents an unusual blend of classical and modernist forms and vernacular traditions, appearing in influential journals beginning in the early 1930s. She became best known as a poet, but the publication of her 1966 novel *Jubilee* added significantly to her reputation. It was the first modern work to reclaim the slave narrative tradition that has profoundly influenced contemporary black fiction. Walker's literary legacy is her insistence upon intellectual depth, a certain black sound and feeling tone, and agency, the components of an aesthetic aimed at liberation and transformation.

Margaret Abigail Walker was the oldest of four children born to Sigismund and Marion Dozier Walker. Her birth on July 7, 1915, in a private home in Mason City, a poor community in the West End area of Birmingham, Alabama, was no predictor of her future. The kinetic reality of this all-black Southern community provoked a strong spiritual connection and intellectual identity that Walker retained throughout her life. Sigismund Walker, a Jamaican immigrant, was a formally educated minister, who served the United Methodist churches in Alabama and Mississippi until he began teaching at New Orleans University. In "Epitaph for My Father" published in *October Journey* (1973), Walker remembered "the noble princelike man . . . teaching daily, preaching Sundays / Tailoring at night to give us bread. / His days were all the same—/ No time for fun."[1]

A determined intellectual, Sigismund Walker was a quiet man, homesick for Jamaica, who gave his daughter an intellectual curiosity that accounted for her restless and rebellious youth. In contrast, Marion Dozier Walker, a talented young musician, was an assertive, demanding woman who regretted having given up a promising career to become a minister's wife. Even though the Walkers were no better off financially than most of their barely literate neighbors, they identified strongly as New Negroes whose proudest possessions, according to Walker, were her mother's piano and her father's books.

Walker began school by accompanying her mother to her job as a music teacher. She moved so quickly through the primary grades that by eleven she was ready to enter high school. The family had moved to New Orleans, where her father began teaching college full time, and her mother opened a professional music studio. Walker was encouraged to write as a way to channel the uneasiness she felt as a somewhat sickly, precocious child, whose physical underdevelopment seemed to match her delayed social development. Marion Walker feared a "wild streak" in her oldest daughter and wanted to keep her out of harm's way. Walker was encouraged to write, as long as it was something to keep her busy, her parents believed. It quickly became, however, a preoccupation.

By the time she finished high school at fourteen, Walker had begun to see herself as part of a chosen generation entrusted with the future of the race. The earliest extant essay, published when she was a sixteen-year-old college student at New Orleans University, gives a clear sense of her social awareness and the exacting nature of her judgment. "If we decide to cast our lot in the places where our native talent and equipment can be used in greatest advantage and all in the conquering faith of our fathers," she wrote in "What Is to Become of Us?" (1932), "we may feel sure not only of a high place of intellectual and spiritual growth, but we will know the answer [to] 'What is to become of us?' politically, financially, and economically."[2] Walker was honing her skills as a critic and her sensitivity as an artist, while deepening her commitment to socially engaged writing. By the time she and her sister left for Northwestern University, she had completed an entire manuscript of poems in the journal that had been a cherished gift from her father.

Despite some very unpleasant racial encounters in Evanston while a student at Northwestern, where neither she nor her sister could live on campus, Walker spent her NU years reading and writing with an intensity fueled by her own internal ambitions. After graduation, she elected to remain in Chicago. It was the middle of the Depression and, like so many Americans, she joined the ranks of the unemployed. Finally, after lying about her age, Walker secured an entry-level job with the Chicago branch of the Federal Writers' Project, one of the programs of the Works Progress Administration. For a young black woman reared according to Southern custom and convention in a deeply religious household, living in Chicago and working with the Writers' Project was an education in itself. What she did not realize until much later was that she was a member of a new generation of writers who were giving definition to an as yet unnamed Black Chicago Renaissance. Their youthful revolutionary spirit was filled with hope, a desire for freedom, and the knowledge that these were the times of expanding opportunity for minorities and ethnic groups.

Walker would later write about her experiences in Chicago, especially her encounter with Richard Wright, who was a fellow writer on the Writers' Project, the leader of the South Side Writers Group to which she belonged, and someone with whom she shared a close political and personal friendship between 1937 and 1939. Wright impressed her immediately because of his talent, his intense driving ambition, and discipline, even though she disagreed with many of his ideas and his tastes in books. She believed that she owed much to Wright's influence and interest in her work but was never clear what their relationship meant to him.[3]

Walker saw Chicago from many different angles. She discovered *Poetry* magazine, a leading avant-garde journal, and became acquainted with women writers who were some of the major voices of the modernist movement. She was exposed to a new and vibrant poetry by women such as Edna St. Vincent Millay, Leonie Adams, Eleanor Wylie, and Louise Bogan. She met and read important women on the Left who helped to map a radical activist tradition in women's literature, including Muriel Rukeyser, Genevieve Taggard, and Lola Ridge. For the first time, Walker saw women writers identifying and leading a movement, women who were being heard without having to resort to the parochial, the genteel, and the sentimental, the usual domain for the woman writer.

The most significant event in her life, however, was an invitation from Richard Wright to join a gathering of black writers and students from the University of Chicago. This turned out to be the inaugural meeting of the South Side Writers Group, which began in April 1936 with Walker as one of its founding members. The group found a common sense of purpose as they began to search for a voice with which to represent the dissatisfaction of Black America, doubly betrayed, first by Emancipation and the promise of freedom and then by migration to the North, where they were met only by massive unemployment and poverty. The rhythms of black life were changing, and it was the task of the writer and artist to document this change. At meetings they read and critiqued each other's work, discussed the impact of the Great Depression on African American culture, and actively debated Communist politics. They developed a mission statement and together worked on a special issue of *New Challenge*, edited by Dorothy West and Richard Wright, who moved to New York in 1937. It was mainly the inspiration of the group that led Wright to conceive of "Blueprint for Negro Writing" (1937). The South Side Writers membership roster read like a Who's Who of African American intellectual and cultural history: Frank Marshall Davis, Edward Bland, Theodore Ward, Marian Minus, Fern Gayden, and St. Clair Drake, among others. More importantly for Walker, when Wright left Chicago for New York, it was she who kept the group together until it disbanded in 1939.

Walker's politicization came quickly and intensely, altering the way she viewed the world. She was captivated by Marxist ideas and Russian writers, those whom Wright encouraged her to read; and she regularly attended Communist Party–sponsored programs and associated literary events. She was no newcomer to philosophy and history, owing to the influence of her own family background, and devoured the reading lists she collected from meetings and debates. A larger circle of friendships developed as she completed various assignments for the Writers' Project, and she came to know Nelson Algren, Frank Yerby, Arna Bontemps, Margaret Taylor Goss (Burroughs), and Gwendolyn Brooks. Growing up in the Deep South exposed Walker to assorted forms of discrimination and exploitation, which offered an authentic landscape for exploring ideas derived from the radical Left. Walker's vision of an art "for her people" was the result of her growth and transformation within this political culture as much as it was the by-product of the close working relationship she developed with Richard Wright. Reportedly a love affair that went sour, she suffered an enduring loss that was utterly painful, one that demanded her silence until long after Wright's death.

Nevertheless, by all accounts, the Chicago years were Walker's most productive. Her famous poem, "For My People," which first appeared in 1937, before it was published in a collection, is a direct reflection of the era that gave birth to a radically new literature from modern Black America. It was probably the quality and visibility of the poem in a major literary journal, and the potential that it signaled for its author, that gained Walker admission into the University of Iowa in 1939. Earlier that year, she had known her days on the Writers' Project were numbered and with the breakup of the South Side Writers Group, she needed a new context for moving forward. Going to Iowa would give her access to world-renowned teachers and ensure a national reputation. Not surprisingly, it was in Iowa where Walker developed a stronger sense of connection to her Southern heritage. She was away from a community of black people and homesick, living without any family for the first time, and reading news about Wright and other artists who were gaining in importance. She had much to work out in her own mind about the South; she didn't hate it as Wright did and, in fact, grew increasingly to love it. She could be critical of its savagery and brutality at the same time she was taken by the sense of community, the moral and spiritual strength that its people symbolized. This tension among these different aspects of the South and between her own academic and vernacular experiences animated her work.

Walker suffered fatigue, depression, and generally poor health throughout the year and a half at Iowa, but worked diligently to polish the manuscript she had been working on since college. She was very clear that she wanted her poetry to reflect the communal experiences of African Americans. She wanted to capture the beauty and vitality of the people she had come to know as a child in Mason City, as a teenager in New Orleans, and as a young adult living on Chicago's South Side. By then, Walker had developed an almost intuitive connection to these people so that what might have appeared public was very private. The real problem for her as a student of poetry was finding a form that was not demeaning to African Americans, as many considered dialect poetry to be, but that would showcase her mastery of the modern lyric and the traditional English forms that her teachers demanded. Above all, she wanted to write poems that realized the vision of "I Want to Write," an early published poem that first appeared in a 1934 issue of *The Crisis* magazine and was later collected in *This Is My Century*. "I want to frame their dreams into words: their souls into notes / I want to catch their sunshine laughter in a bowl."[4] The indication of her success came none too soon. Stephen Vincent Benet held the completed manuscript for two years before deciding in 1941 that it was the best work by any emerging younger writer, black or white. *For My People*, a book of twenty-eight poems—a mixture of well-honed lyrics, sonnets, and folk ballads—brought her immediate acclaim when it was published in the fall as the 1942 selection for the Yale Series of Younger Poets Award.

For My People is as much a tribute to Walker's native South as it was a discovery of her own voice in the modernist canon. The volume is a somewhat eclectic rendering that ranges from the often quoted "Lineage," filled with nostalgia and familial piety, to briskly written sonnets like "Whores" that challenge our sense of propriety, and unforgettable ballads like "Molly Means" and "Papa Chicken" that delight as they caustically disclose closely guarded secrets gleaned from the folk past. Of the twenty-eight poems, ten are ballads, a form that gave Walker considerable difficulty at first since the ballads she had been accustomed to writing in the African American tradition were different in form from the traditional English ballad she learned about in her poetry classes at Iowa. Walker's intent—and the ballads were essential in this regard—was to give voice to those who could not speak and, while carefully observing the rules of the craft she had learned so well at Northwestern and Iowa, to force to the surface a deep sense of collective memory. Not content to speak to memory alone, but rather to that which memory can evoke, challenge, and inspire, Walker's inaugural volume was a shock to the conventional poetic sensibility that had an expressed preference for more feminine, romantic lyrics. It was not that Walker did not write romantic poetry—she had pages of it in her journals that would remain unpublished—but she developed in Chicago an almost ceremonial sense of who she was as an artist in relationship to the lived experiences of her people. As a result, Walker's romantic and mystical inclinations, the passion for nature and natural details and her constant evocation of childhood memories, are given real if intangible powers as they are willed into use as powerful imagery. *For My People* was a forceful volume when it appeared and remains so today, making the reader aware that Walker has something to say, and that she is not simply making us privy to a moment of sheer emotion.

In 1969, Stephen Henderson considered "For My People" the most comprehensively soulful poem ever written, because thirty years after the poem's first appearance, it was being used as a rallying cry for the insurgent Black Power Movement.[5] Walker understood early that poetry was part of a sermonic tradition that formed an essential component of African American culture. Writing the poem was only part of its enduring legacy. Her visibility in response to ongoing audience demand for her readings ensured the popularity of her poetry just as it facilitated her return to public life in the late 1960s, after a twenty-five-year absence. It is not surprising that criticism of the single poem exceeds that of all of her other poetry combined. If it remains the centerpiece of her work, it also provides the best example of the formula she crafted and the art for which she is so admired.

The poem's first appearance in *Poetry* gave it a prominent place in the poetry community just as it provided an auspicious beginning for a young black writer. The poem consists of nine stanzas in free verse followed by a final stanza that brings the reader to a sudden halt before changing its tone. Through the nine stanzas, the poet depicts the fragmented world of the American South, its brutal realities in sharp relief as the poem periodizes the black experience for all to see. It is an intergenerational meditation that begins each stanza with the captivating refrain, "For my people." The contrasting scenes of black life emerge through a series of carefully narrated details and biblical cadences, capturing the pain, sorrow, joy, and pleasure that affirm the humanity of a people who refuse to succumb to inhuman conditions. The poem does not single out black people as a race, and the poet insists upon contextualizing the black experience at every turn, as she speaks of "all the adams and eves and their countless generations."[6] That it is a history of black people especially in the American South is unmistakable without ever being made explicit. The tone of the poem shifts completely in the final stanza, beginning with the apocalyptic "Let a new earth rise." In imagining the end of one world and the beginning of a new one, Walker is not negating the past, but allowing it to signify the strength and potential necessary to bring about change.

The best poems in her first volume are those that tell a story in spare, unsentimental free verse form, made that much more powerful through internal rhyme. Typically, the movement of a poem is disrupted by the poet's thoughtful, provocative realization near the conclusion. In "Delta," for example, Walker creates a familiar catalog of images in successive stanzas, using incremental repetition to highlight a history of contrasts: love of land / bloody fields; buzzards / lullabies; death / birth. In the last stanza, what has been evoked through historical, tangible experience is set aside. "Only the naked arm of Time / can measure the ground we know / and thresh the air we breathe." She concludes by allowing the reader no emotional distance. The voice asserts, "Neither earth nor star nor water's host / can sever us from our life to be / for we are beyond your reach O mighty winnowing flail! / Infinite and free!"[7] This ending invites a deeply resonating, soulful affirmation not unlike the sorrow songs that W. E. B. DuBois spoke of so articulately. "Delta," like "For My People," uses words synchronized with the sounds; we are hearing and feeling the images that have been laid bare before us, rather than merely seeing words arranged formally on a page.

For My People gave readers some of Walker's most remembered poems. The volume also establishes the lineage by which Walker identifies herself as an American poet. Her first memories of poetry would have been the recitals of Paul Laurence Dunbar, the most popular African American poet who read and performed his dialect poems in the early decades of the twentieth century, and even later in parts of the South. She would have learned his poems by heart and read them at public programs where elocution and memorization were stressed. Walker also had extensive knowledge of nineteenth century English Romantic poetry early on from her father, who had gone through high school in colonial Jamaica; she, therefore, excelled in her English studies at Northwestern. She read and recited Dunbar just as she did Byron, Shelley, Keats, and Wordsworth. In addition, Walker benefited from the company of modernist women poets whom she had been regularly reading in the pages of literary magazines. By the time she went to Iowa for graduate school in the late thirties, she had behind her a rich knowledge of poetry and exposure to its assorted practitioners—British, Anglo-American and African American, both men and women. She may even have considered herself part of an inner circle of contemporary poets. In the process of assimilating these multiple traditions, especially in the intense political environment of the 1930s, Walker created, as Alicia Ostriker has noted, her own distinct brand of poetry that was at once socially conscious and vernacular-based, innovative and intellectually assertive without being autobiographical.[8] Walker seemed to find compatibility with many of the poets that she admired, the catalogues of Walt Whitman and Carl Sandburg, for example. On the other hand, it was Langston Hughes to whom she owed the most as a poetic mentor. She heard him read in New Orleans when she was sixteen, and he was the first established poet to view her unpublished work. From Hughes, she developed a healthy respect for vernacular traditions and black speech that she never lost, not believing as many in her generation did that black dialect provided limited access to the range of black feeling and thought.

All the poems in *For My People* are reflections, embracing sure and steady rhythms that make them highly quotable, always unpretentious, sometimes deceptively simple, and packed with the details that are the arsenal of a realist. If "For My People" is the most radical and far-reaching of the poems, there are many others that share its stylistic features, tonality, and content. In addition to "Delta," "Southern Song," "Since 1619," and "Today" display a range of emotions and tensions deriving from ancestral memory and continued oppression. Walker had a fondness for the long poem, wrote more of them in later volumes, but rarely reached the quality she did with "For My People" and "Delta." More than anything else, for this first volume she showed herself to be a gifted writer who saw the world through the controlled medium of poetry.

Walker completed her master's degree at Iowa in 1940 and returned to New Orleans for a much-needed vacation before beginning her teaching career at Livingstone College in Salisbury, North Carolina. After a brief courtship, at twenty-seven, she met and married Firnist James Alexander and moved to High Point, North Carolina, to live with her in-laws. For three years she tried to juggle her professional career and her growing family without much success. Eventually, she took a position in the English department at Jackson State University. By the time her last child was born in 1954, Walker had all but given up any semblance of her writing career. She was teaching full time and bore the primary financial responsibility for her family. A rare essay published in 1951, "How I Told My Child about Race," shows her efforts to infuse social consciousness into a life consumed with working and caring for children.

From her unpublished papers and journals, as well as the essays she began to publish later in life, it is clear that Walker was acutely aware of the difficulties of a woman writer and of her position as the mother of four children and wife of a disabled World War II veteran. She also had considerable influence on the campus of Jackson State, where she earned a reputation for being an exacting and exciting teacher, actively promoting curriculum changes and student involvement in the emerging Civil Rights Movement. Walker frequently invited her former friends from the 1930s and 1940s to visit the Jackson community, thus maintaining ties to a literary world that was otherwise lost to her. When Arna Bontemps, Sterling Brown, St. Clair Drake, Gwendolyn Brooks, Robert Hayden, Melvin Tolson, Dudley Randall, Ruby Dee, Ossie Davis, and others appeared in Jackson in the 1950s and early 1960s, it was usually in response to an invitation from Margaret Walker. Her passion for the classroom, where she gave her remarkable lectures on Afro-American literature and history, freely sharing personal anecdotes and memories of the many writers she knew, equaled her passion for the kitchen, where she talked intermittently while cleaning and cook-ing fresh collards or her renowned Louisiana Gumbo. Among the appearances of her early acquaintances, only Richard Wright was missing; She and Wright never spoke to each other again after Wright left the United States for France.

Although the poetry world heard nothing from Walker for twenty-five years, she continued to write privately and found her feminist consciousness rapidly evolving. She worked steadily on the book begun in college that recounted the story of her great-great-grandmother. She had conceived of a fictional work based on the stories told to her by Elvira Ware Dozier, with whom she had spent her earliest years. Her grandmother's death, coupled with the desire to write herself back into existence, provided the impetus Walker needed to finish the book in the early 1960s. As if running a race with time, Walker returned once more to Iowa and worked nonstop for two years to complete the novel, which served as her PhD dissertation. Less than a year later she learned that the manuscript had won the Houghton Mifflin literary award, enabling her to quickly complete the revisions for the 1966 publication date for *Jubilee*.

The timing of *Jubilee's* publication could not have been better. Walker was already active in the Civil Rights Movement and lived down the street from Medgar Evers, one of the movement's early martyrs. Jackson, Mississippi, was a major site for the Southern-based movement as well as for some of the most significant events of the era. If "For My People" became redefined within the context of a movement that promoted resistance and an end to domination, *Jubilee* offered the literary and aesthetic continuity sorely lacking in much of the writing of the Black Arts Movement. Walker would go on to publish three collections of new poetry in the 1970s and 1980s, but none had the impact of *Jubilee*, with its indebtedness to a rich oral tradition, its treatment of shifting notions of power and authority, and its gendered analysis of history. In *How I Wrote Jubilee*, Walker said she "always intended *Jubilee* to be a folk novel based on folk materials: folk sayings, folk belief, folkways . . . I clearly envisioned the development of a folk novel . . . never deviated from that outline."[9] But it is more accurately described as an ancestral novel, a composite of many selves extracted through her maternal kin. Elvira Ware Dozier is the prototype for Vyry, the novel's protagonist, who is the fictionalized equivalent of Walker's great-grandmother in the novel. It is Minna, Vyry's daughter in the novel, who will become Walker's grandmother. Walker did pioneering research to establish the historical accuracy for the story's geographical settings and time periods, since she not only wanted to portray the lives of black people before and during the Civil War, but she also wanted to use the actual sites where her own ances-tors had migrated after the war.

The elements of the traditional slave narrative and the historical novel merge in *Jubilee*, even if the historical sections sometimes overshadow the narrative.

Vyry, the mulatto slave child of the owner of the Dutton plantation, is educated in the "Big House," through a series of violent acts inflicted mainly by an angry plantation mistress. Because she is the bastard child of the Dutton household, barely a shade darker than Dutton's legal daughter, and hence a daily confirmation of her paternity, Vyry is a target for abuse that her father/owner is unable to stop. Nevertheless, she grows to womanhood as the companion to her unacknowledged half sister, learning from and eventually replacing the family's much adored cook. When she falls in love with Randall Ware, a free Negro, she is introduced to the idea of freedom. After the birth of her second child, an unsuccessful escape with children in tow convinces her that she must accept her fate, as the scars from the brutal whipping she received take shape on her back. While other slaves make successful and unsuccessful escapes, Vyry remains on the plantation and vows to wait for her "freeman" to return for his family after the war. Freedom comes to her only after the war ends and Emancipation is proclaimed.

The reversals in the novel become increasingly apparent in the postwar section. Vyry becomes the head of a plantation in fact, a plantation that has suffered the loss of all the white folk except for the evil mistress, who suffers an emotional breakdown after she is raped by enemy soldiers. Walker deftly handles the decline of the Dutton family, physically and psychologically, as Vyry rises to importance and gains her own voice. Lillian's silence and eventual disappearance from the story emphasizes Vyry's evolution into a savvy, independent woman who refuses to carry hate in her heart.

Vyry's strength of spirit is the driving force behind the novel. As the newly freed slaves depart one by one, Vyry remains, ostensibly to wait for Randall Ware, but also because she refuses to leave her incapacitated mistress alone. The narrative negotiates the familiar elements of the woman's novel and historical fiction. There is, for example, a seduction and the plots are triangulated. Vyry's mother, who dies in childbirth, has been the unwilling mistress of John Dutton. Vyry, still committed to Randall Ware, reluctantly returns the affections of Innis Brown, an illiterate black slave with unwavering devotion to her and her two children. Their journey in search of land and the home that Vyry has wanted to call her own is set against the backdrop of Reconstruction, Ku Klux Klan terror, and other acts of violence that force them to restart their lives multiple times. They finally refuse to move again and become part of a community in which everyone, black and white, learns the benefits of mutual respect and support. One of the book's most important climaxes comes when the white neighbors help them rebuild their home and are forced to fully appreciate Vyry's skills as a midwife and farmer.

The final section of the novel explores some of the ideological issues of Reconstruction. Just as things appear to settle down and Vyry has a home and a successful farm, Randall Ware, who has been active in the Reconstruction government, returns. Vyry must decide between the two men—the one from her past and the one from her present—the one with whom she was unable to have a life and the one with whom she has made a life. Her extended monologue about the value of love counters Randall Ware's black, separatist politics. Walker makes sure we see the differences in the two men as choices of the head and not merely of the heart. Ware criticizes Vyry for being a midwife to white women. Brown's belief in the importance of the land and his insistence that Jim learn the culture of the farm counters Randall Ware's offer to send Jim away to a school that will train leaders for the race.

Walker does a lot to revise the traditions of the form within which she was working. In "The Violation of Voice: Revising the Slave Narrative," Amy Levin suggests that Vyry's decision to remain with Innis Brown can be seen as a critique of certain sentimental conventions just as it rewrites the nineteenth-century slave narrative. Typically, the courtship novel concludes with the heroine's choice of a suitor who can give her the most socially acceptable identity. Harriet Jacobs, who makes the reader aware that she is revising the plot line of *Incidents in the Life of a Slave Girl* with her words "Reader, my story ends in freedom; not in the usual way, with marriage," offered one revision of this convention. *Jubilee* suggests yet another alternative, according to Levin, since Vyry's choice, like Harriet Jacobs's, has more to do with her freedom than issues of social acceptability. In slavery choice is not possible, but Vyry's extended monologue explains her choice of Innis Brown over Randall Ware; it is this act itself that is an explicit expression of her liberation.[10]

Jubilee represented reclamation of history and those forms identified with the African American past. As a multigenerational family saga, the novel draws heavily on Walker's research into her maternal kin, the Duggans-Ware-Brown-Dozier family in Georgia, Alabama, and North Carolina. This one family's story became African American history writ large for a generation already engaged in fierce, passionate arguments over the meaning and interpretation of the historical past. Just as *For My People* represented Walker's search for creative synthesis of a rational political analysis and historical memory during the 1930s, *Jubilee* was a testament to Walker's skill as a narrative writer. As a documentary novel, *Jubilee*'s historical accuracy could not be questioned, but it was the novel's spirited protagonist who provided the novel's moral center. As a novel about the excesses and abuses of slavery, it angers and sickens. Yet as a story about the human capacity to triumph over adversity, it inspires and delights. Taking what she had learned from *For My People*, Walker found it easy to disrupt the flow of a conventional historical narrative by exploring more creative, vernacular options, including assorted Africanisms, black folk speech, traditional sermons, folktales, spirituals, and work songs.

Walker was fortunate that her retreat from the public literary world for nearly thirty years did not eclipse her career. Had *Jubilee* not appeared when it did and had it not been so compatible with the new social currents, it might not have had the authority that it began to claim. And while it did not put Walker on the map with her contemporaries Ralph Ellison and James Baldwin, it did allow her to reinvent herself in ways that were beneficial for the remainder of her career. The novel and the three poetry volumes that appeared in the 1970s are routinely identified with the literary productivity of the Black Arts Movement, a movement that sought to bring the arts and political activism together to serve the economic, political, and social interests of black people during the tumultuous period of the 1960s. Walker also proudly accepted responsibility for helping to usher in the era of Black Studies, a related movement and the most important transformation in higher education in the modern era. With so many contradictory cultural forces at work during the 1960s, African American literature became a broad canvas on which to paint these contradictions in sharp relief. Walker had more experience than most in synthesizing conflicting traditions and ideologies. She put her radical legacy from the 1930s and her close relationship to the Jackson, Mississippi–based movement to good use. She was, therefore, highly regarded by the younger more militant writers.

With *Prophets for a New Day* (1970), Walker reentered the world of poetry, which was in the 1970s one of the most highly politicized forms of black written expression. She tried to locate her voice among the fervor and enthusiasm that a particular audience of readers shared. Walker offered the volume to the Detroit-based Broadside Press, an independent black publishing company started by her friend Dudley Randall as an outlet for his own work as well as that of other Black Arts poets. The book shared the company of a large group of poets, among them Sonia Sanchez, Haki Madhubuti (Don L. Lee), and Nikki Giovanni, who were to become her close friends. *Prophets* is as much a memorial to the Civil Rights Movement as it was a rare second chance for Walker to speak with intellectual boldness, to insert her voice into a national conversation about race and social change. Unlike some of her generation who considered the movement too militant, full of rage, and, therefore, wrongheaded, Walker identified strongly with the younger generation. While many poets who become public figures sense a loss of the private self they need for true inspiration, Walker felt renewed in purpose and spirit. It would have been difficult not to connect the literary history of her art with the social and political history of the 1960s. Moreover, the final stanza of her 1937 poem was a true metaphorical rendering of the life of those times. "Let a new earth rise," *For My People* concludes. "Let another world be born. / Let a bloody peace be written in the sky. Let a second / generation full of courage issue forth; . . . / Let a race of men now rise and take control."[11] Her own apocalyptic sensibility assured her that this was indeed a new era.

Walker successfully created a community of memory by synthesizing a consciousness of the past in *For My People*. *Prophets for a New Day*, on the other hand, is more concerned with symbolizing the present. "Street Demonstration," "Girl Held Without Bail," "Sit-Ins," "Birmingham," "At the Lincoln Monument," "For Malcolm X," and "For Andy Goodman, Michael Schwerner, and James Chaney," all capture moments and celebrate heroes of the Civil Rights Movement. There is no title poem for the volume. Instead Walker recasts the well-known prophets in poems, namely "Amos," "Jeremiah," "Joel," "Hosea," and "Micah": modern heroes of the Civil Rights Movement, all noticeably male. The religious scaffolding is the most significant change in this volume that does not allow Walker the luxury of lingering on the more stylized form of the folk ballad, but requires a return to an explicit and deep religious faith. Walker is very much aware of the roots of the Civil Rights Movement in the black religious tradition, but the movement has incurred such losses that Walker's mood is satisfied more by forms such as the elegy and monody, the latter noted by R. Baxter Miller in "The 'Etched Flame' of Margaret Walker: Literary and Biblical Re-creation in Southern History." According to Miller, *Prophets for a New Day* is designed as a metaphorical quest. Walker uses poetry to re-create anthropocentric space, summoning up the courage necessary to confront and transcend the travesties of the real world in creating a more hopeful human community, one where universal freedom prevails. The result is that the poems create certain immediacy, as Walker and her readers share a sense of moral indignation at what has occurred, as well as an abiding faith in the possibility of change.[12] In *Prophets* Walker recalls well-known biblical stories and images: Adam and Eve, Jesus of Galilee, Jacob, and most importantly, Moses, leading the Israelites out of Egypt. Juxtaposing contemporary stories and the stories of faith, or the lack thereof, Walker restores some order to a disorderly, faithless world. If the poems in *For My People* are more like praise songs to a people whose particular history has allowed them to envision the future as a community bound by faith, those in *Prophets* are a collection of cautionary tales, reminders of the trials and obstacles that face those in pursuit of liberty.

There are only two ballads in the volume. "The Ballad of the Free" shows Walker at her best in her ongoing effort to merge the secular spirit of revolution with Christian fundamentalism. The refrain is drawn from the Old Testament: "The serpent is loosed and the hour is come / The last shall be the first and first shall be none / The serpent is loosed and the hour is come."[13] Individual stanzas are devoted to Nat Turner, Gabriel Prosser, Denmark Vesey, Toussaint L'Ouverture, and John Brown. The contrast between the social history that is recounted and the biblical stories creates a dramatic tension that builds up toward the end of the poem. Walker has carefully controlled the flow so that the poet has reclaimed her right to prophesy that "Wars and Rumors of Wars have gone / But Freedom's army marches on. / The hero's list of dead is long. / And Freedom still is for the strong."[14]

Walker's third volume of poetry *October Journey* (1973) is her most personal. She completed it during frequent bouts of poor health, including extended hospital stays that gave her a great deal of time to think and write. Although African American writers were gaining increased access to mainstream publishing outlets and a new generation of black women writers had emerged, Walker remained faithful to Broadside Press, since by that time, she and her work had become almost a cult phenomenon. She was greatly aided by the newfound interest in southern literature. When Jackson, Mississippi, native Eudora Welty won the 1973 Pulitzer Prize, the South received renewed attention, notably because of the contrasting pictures drawn by black and white writers. Although not in the best of health, Walker responded to the demand for and interest in southern black writers. She spent most of her retirement years giving lectures and readings throughout the United States.

Her papers indicate that she had written more than five hundred poems by the early 1970s, but she carved out a slim volume of occasional poems and tributes to make up *October Journey*. The title poem worked extremely well as an overview of Walker's poetic adventures, from which she could draw wisdom. The concept of "October Journey" is physical and symbolic; they denote the cycles and transformations of nature, and the poet's revitalization by full immersion in a specific place, the South, at a specific time, October. She urges us to "take heed for journeys undertaken in the dark of the year," noting the fall journey to be the "safest, brightest, and best."[15] The poem relives those moments when she had returned to the South, her spiritual homeland, by evoking the fear that accompanies such returns. The tributes, like "Epitaph to My Father," and those to literary icons, like "Ballad for Phillis Wheatley," and the poem "For Paul Laurence Dunbar," are a bit stronger than the occasional poems, but show very little that is new or innovative.

October Journey did include, however, several important pieces that reminded readers why Walker was still a poet of considerable stature. "I Want to Write," collected in a volume for the first time since its original appearance in *The Crisis* magazine under the title "Daydream," contains all the elements that had made *For My People* so successful. It exhibits the tension between consciousness and experience and between human will and historical circumstance, the rhythmic repetitions and lyrical phrases that ascend with intensity, coming to a crescendo in the final two lines. It is very likely that as Walker began to review the trajectory of her life, she returned to the twelve-line poem, a typical length for her. The poem moves from the general opening refrain, "I Want to Write," utilizing incremental repetition that had become her forte, to the specific "I Want to Write the Songs of my people." The specificity of context, "my people," and identification of form, "songs," join with a collage of metaphors; these are the raw materials that she must "catch . . . / Then crush and mix."[16] Invoking a routinely feminine activity as a site of artistic creation affirms the importance of Walker as a female writer. Walker, in this her very first poem, reclaimed near the end of her career, has successfully inserted the female voice; her own, as she has synthesized various elements to create a work of art. "I Want to Write," as Eleanor Traylor has noted, is a meditation and a dedication, a public acknowledgment of poetic commitment that Walker needed to be reminded that her poetic journey is nearly complete.[17]

Before retiring from Jackson State University in 1979, however, Walker founded the first national research center for the study of the Black South. In response to the assassination of Martin Luther King Jr. and the political upheaval that it generated, along with her own desire to create some kind of institutional legacy, Walker created one of the first Black Studies programs in the nation, and the first in the South. She named it the Center for the Study of the Life, History and Culture of Black People and used it as a launching pad for organizing conferences and seminars on literary and historical subjects. In 1973, she commemorated the bicentennial of Phillis Wheatley's first volume of poetry. The mammoth conference, coming at a time when the feminist movement was in full sway and concerns about gender inequality were gaining greater visibility, gave Wheatley iconic status. Author of the first published book by a black writer in America, Wheatley signified and highlighted the importance of black women writers. Walker thus understood the timing of the event and convened an international group of black women. Three generations of black women writers came to Jackson, many of whom were only recently published, making this the first ever gathering of its kind. Today many regard the Phillis Wheatley Festival as the inaugural moment of the black women's literary renaissance. Motivated by the sense of authority she had acquired as a 1930s radical, Walker acted in her senior role as a writer, one who brought continuity to a literary tradition, and who could think carefully, but not rigidly, about matters of great significance to black people and the whole of America. If the Black Arts Movement found Richard Wright, Ralph Ellison, and James Baldwin old school, they found in Walker a voice for the twentieth century in her expansive ideas, her philosophical depth, and her passion for socially engaged art.

During the 1970s Walker also became much more conscious of her reputation at a time when black literature was gaining in visibility and stature. While she never identified with radical feminism, her experiences during the later 1970s and the 1980s fueled her outrage at being left out, if not dismissed, by the larger literary world, the source of which she quickly determined to be sexism. The issue that triggered her bitterness and resentment and brought her a significant amount of negative publicity was her suit against Alex Haley, author of *Roots*, a highly influential and best selling novel. Haley capitalized on the public interest in the black historical past, which was at its height when *Roots* was published in 1976. Walker's vitriolic charges against Haley, who she believed had lifted whole passages from *Jubilee*, became very public just as did her strong, detailed case for copyright infringement. As the only woman of the four people who sued Haley—the other three won—she saw her loss as clear evidence of society's systematic exploitation and exclusion of black women.

Once again Walker put her anger and passion to good use. *This Is My Century* is a compilation of her earlier volumes and new poems that appeared in 1989. The collection, showcasing more than four decades of a life in poetry, gives readers what they had come to expect in a Walker volume: psalmlike lyrics, ballads, tributes, and moments of self-reflection. Each of the new poems moves with cameralike intensity pointed inward and outward. She shows her art to be an open-ended process, not a finished product. The poems are public and private at once. "I suffer now from stress," Walker says in "Old Age," "the pain of living too long, / the clash of race and sex and class / against stark hunger of the world / for freedom, peace, and bread."[18] The economic and political realities that have been central to an understanding of struggle are not ignored, and she cites police brutality, inflation, poverty, and disillusionment. For the first time, Walker shows evidence of a triadic relationship—between race, sex, and class—as conflictual and complicated. The last two poems are explicit in their evocation of a search not so much for harmony, but for "Solace," as the title of one of the poems suggests. "Fanfare, Coda, and Finale" has an odelike quality; it is the poet's poet who is compelled at long last to decry her "hurt and bruised dignity . . ." still " . . . bursting in my throat [to] find melody." The struggle of the older poet, battered and abused, unappreciated, and underrecognized, as Walker clearly saw herself in her last decade, is not so much the social struggle, but the struggle to "lift this weight of brick and stone against my neck, and . . . sing."[19] What is worse than lack of recognition is the fear of every poet: the loss of creativity.

Although Walker's poetic energies seemed to wane, she had not lost all creativity, and she was in no way "finished" as a writer. She had always been interested in nonfiction and the essay and published a number of essays during her early years. Often she used the essay to signal an important transition in her life. Her first essay had been published when she was sixteen and a high-school senior during the Depression years. She answered a question that was being posed by many young people at the time: "What Is to Become of Us?" A second had come during the early years of marriage when she was struggling to manage her life as a mother, wife, teacher, and writer. In "How I told My Child about Race" Walker made a private concern more public. In the early 1970s, basking in the success of *Jubilee* and long before she would battle with Alex Haley, she was asked to talk about the composition of the book that had taken her so long to write. *How I Wrote Jubilee* published in 1972 by Third World Press was a widely circulating pamphlet authenticating the novel as a twentieth-century slave narrative, not unlike the prefatory matter that was a stock feature of the original slave narratives. The essay also illuminated Walker's importance as a scholar, giving her greater confidence for the monumental project, the biography of Richard Wright that she would take up in her retirement.

The Black Arts Movement was especially important for expanding Walker's interests from poetry and fiction to psychobiography. Walker was the only person living, or so she believed, who had known Wright during his earlier life other than his wife. No black writer had ever been given permission to write a biography of Richard Wright, whose death in 1960 represented the end of an era he had dominated in African American literature. Returning to Richard Wright, at least the man she knew in the 1930s, brought back a complex of emotions about her personal and political relationship to one of the world's most renowned writers. Amistad Books published *Richard Wright, Daemonic Genius* in 1987, after a lengthy battle with Wright's widow Ellen Wright. The manuscript moved from publisher to publisher, each of them finding the project too costly with legal entanglements. Walker felt she was in a battle for her life. She had fought Alex Haley and lost. Now she was taking on the whole of literary history, arguing her right to write about the man she had known, whose story she believed had yet to be told, despite Michel Fabre's widely circulating *The Unfinished Quest of Richard Wright* (1973). If Walker's intentions had not been mired in subjectivity at the beginning of the project, by the time the book was published in 1989, rescued by Amistad Press, a new imprint of Warner Books, it had suffered repeated delays. The most important had been a nasty suit over copyright infringement brought by Ellen Wright that was finally settled in Walker's favor. Walker seemed justified in her belief that she was being persecuted. Always known as a fighter, now in her late sixties, Walker found her reputation badly damaged after the *Roots* fiasco. Readers and book reviewers saw her as a cynical old woman whose career was not what she wished it had been, who was lashing out against other male writers who had succeeded better than she had. The book achieved its main objective, however, as a study of a man whose imagination Walker saw as gothic and vision, tragic. It was Wright who was able to accomplish a psychological transformation of rage and suffering. "Richard Wright came out of hell," Walker wrote, " . . . anger . . . ambivalence . . . aberration . . . these devils lived in the hell of his daily environment. . . . All his life he agonized, and all his days he searched for meaning."[20] Walker never changed the book's controversial title, *Richard Wright, Daemonic Genius: A Portrait of the Man, A Critical Look at His Work*, hoping to signify the tragedy and trauma—the humanity—of man she had known.

Many critics believed the Wright biography to be Walker's least successful project. Attempting an objective assessment would be extremely difficult in any case as the entire project was an unending series of tragicomic events. The published version reflected heavy deletions, since Walker was required to stay within the provisions of "fair use." As the book's galleys moved from publisher to publisher, Walker became defiant and often impractical, often confusing the battles with the Wright estate and the constructive criticisms from her editors.

Richard Wright, Daemonic Genius is as much about Walker herself as it is about Wright. Walker and Wright had spent a good portion of their apprentice years together, and to expect detachment from her subject was unrealistic. Walker wrote about Wright's anxieties, for she knew them well; she had a clear sense of what it meant to be a black southerner, who knew too much and felt too deeply. Because Wright never had a chance to face his own demons, he internalized them. Yet he lived a life of purpose and intent and sought to impose order on the chaotic psychological and emotional world he inhabited through his fiction. If *Richard Wright, Daemonic Genius* does not read like objective biography, it does read often, not surprisingly, like poetry. The language is condensed, and patterns of repetition abound. Writing the book was a command performance for her; she was the only remaining active member of a generation of writers and intellectuals from the 1930s. The book allowed her to speak about her generation with some of the critical tools they had been trained to use. As the first major biography of an African American writer by another African American writer, it was not what the critics wanted. The public perception that she had unresolved issues after having been rejected by Wright made her an easy target. Yet it remains one of Walker's major accomplishments.

The continuing loss of public approval increased Walker's belief that she was under attack. Slowly, her keen political mind and social vision combined with paranoia and renewed concerns over her financial instability. At 75, after suffering a stroke from which she barely recovered, Walker went on an extensive speaking tour, promoting *This Is My Century* and another book, her first compilation of essays, *"How I Wrote Jubilee" and Other Essays on Life and Literature* (1990). The lead essay had appeared earlier, but the entire volume gave readers much of the style they had encountered in the speeches she so often gave. They show a consistency in Walker's method of thinking and analysis as a Marxist-trained intellectual, who was always questioning assumptions and looking to live rationally in an irrational world.

Although the first essay collection covers a wide variety of topics, including religion, family, racial consciousness, and the role of women, Walker's final essay collection provides full disclosure. *On Being Female, Black, and Free* (1997) was published a year before Walker's death after being diagnosed with cancer. Toward the end of her life, Walker was conscious of shaping an image of herself as a feminist and a radical thinker. *On Being Female, Black, and Free* speaks directly to the nature of Walker's art and her activism as they evolved over her lengthy career. "What Is to Become of Us?" is collected for the first time, and because it was written before she had ever published a single poem, it provides a rare look back at the young woman who has already accepted her self-prescribed role as spokesperson for her people. What she must reconcile, the essay discloses, is the contradiction she sees between the determinism she was taught to respect in religion and the inevitability of historical change.

Walker does not see longevity as simply a blessing, but rather an opportunity to voice continually her bitter opposition to all forms of discrimination and injustice and to remind the artist of her responsibility to help bring about a new vision *and* a new world. Walker spared neither her home state nor her nation in leveling her criticisms. Prophetic in tone, the essays range from a discussion of Clarence Thomas, war, and fascism in America to the transformative role of education in a global society. Alternating between personal testimony and collective outrage, Walker is bolder than ever, sharing the unvarnished truth at the conclusion of the title essay, "On Being Female, Black, and Free": "I am a black woman living in a male-oriented and male-dominated world. Moreover, I live in an American Empire where the financial tentacles of the American Octopus in the business-banking world extend around the globe, with the multinational and international conglomerates encircling everybody and impinging on the lives of every single soul. I have come through the fires of hell because I am a black woman, because I am poor, because I live in America and because I am determined to be both a creative artist and maintain my inner integrity and my instinctive need to be free."[21] She had first written that essay in 1980 after her battle with Alex Haley, the death of her husband, and after having signed the contract to do the Wright biography. It was a particularly appropriate time for her to write an autobiographical piece about life as a black woman poet, little knowing that she would be offering a manifesto for the younger generation of black women.

As the first nationally recognized African American woman poet in the twentieth century, Margaret Walker was known for her intellectual boldness and radical honesty. Coming of age in the 1930s, she gave shape and meaning to the Black Chicago Renaissance as one of its most widely published and longest living writers. In her poetry, fiction, and prose, Walker adopted a representative persona. With a single-minded intensity, she became the voice of her people, consistently affirming their humanistic vision and invincible spirit, and celebrating the dynamism and continuity of their rich literary and cultural heritage.

Unlike many writers who are identified with a particular literary movement, Walker's passion for intellectual engagement renewed itself with each artistic awakening as it mirrored her own expanding consciousness. As a result, Walker's ten published volumes map the evolution of African American literary expression that extends from the Black Chicago Renaissance in the 1930s and 1940s through the Black Arts Movement of the 1960s and 1970s and the Black Women's Literary Renaissance of the 1980s. Walker's concern for socially conscious art that was equally attentive to craft earned her a reputation for being a master artist, an exceptional teacher, and a highly respected public figure.

Her legacy is that of a well-trained intellectual who synthesized traditional and modern elements in her work, who read extensively in classical philosophy, revolutionary theory, psychoanalysis, existentialism, world religions, and Pan-Africanism, and who despised hypocrisy, racism, and gender chauvinism. She was a dedicated modernist, but her project was not so much about extracting language to make it new as it was appropriating through language the eloquence, texture, and soul of the people who gave it meaning. Her literary reputation rests primarily on *For My People*, her first published work. The appearance of *Jubilee* some twenty-five years later put her in the forefront of a new movement in fiction writing that reclaimed the slave narrative for contemporary writers.

Walker's was the committed life of a literary artist; she wrote all the time, publishing only a small portion of this work during her lifetime. When all of the poetry, fiction, essays, journals, and letters are made available, Walker's literary importance may well extend beyond those of her more highly acclaimed contemporary, Richard Wright. Nevertheless, she remains a major twentieth-century writer who never feared speaking the truth as she resisted socially imposed boundaries of race and gender. Her sometimes adversarial relationship with the literary establishment notwithstanding, Walker's forcefulness and passion as "a juggler of words, a dreamer with spoken dreams, a fire-maker who blows the sparks into flame with magic bellows"[22] always endeared her to eager listening audiences and readers alike. Her own sense of justice and the divinely human brought to American literature a vital alternative, signaling both exploration and enlightenment that continues to be one of literature's most important strengths.

Walker was in the forefront of the movement of Afro-modernist aesthetics by creating multivoiced texts that reflected the paradoxical nature of Southern life. Both her poetry and fiction shift and alternate modalities, tonalities, and narrative structures to give voice to the spiritual, secular, and folk-based traditions that makes up the black experience in America. Her turn to the essay and creative nonfiction late in life gave her another platform for exploring ideas that were central to African American life and thought. Though lesser known, *"How I Wrote Jubilee" and Other Essays on Life and Literature* and *On Being Female, Black, and Free*, along with *Richard Wright, Daemonic Genius*, illuminate her further importance to twentieth-century intellectual thought, making her a worthy literary successor to early women writers Ann Plato, Anna Julia Cooper, and Frances Harper. Walker's strategic use of her own experience as a Southern black woman—always overworked, underpaid and passed over—produced some of the earliest and most forceful critiques of racial, class, and gender discrimination. The twelve books she published are a testament to a brilliant if uneven career and to her unusual ability to capture the spirit of the age.

Criticism of Walker remains sparse. Her general reputation is that of a social poet from the 1930s, since she was absent from the literary scene by the time literary criticism began to claim a dominant place in the American academy. With the evolution of the first wave of African American literary criticism, Walker again received short shrift. Negative criticism of her work reached a consensus as a result of her biography of Wright. A generation of women critics often excluded her, since they privileged the younger writers of the 1970s whose radical feminism was more in keeping with the times. The critical assessment of her work has begun in earnest, and critics have become increasingly aware of the important connections Walker makes to gender, racial, and class consciousness.

So fully energized by the Civil Rights and Women's Movements following the publication of *Jubilee* in 1966, only her death at the age of eighty-three would put an end to a Walker's second lucrative career. Even when weak and showing visible signs of dementia, she made a last appearance in Chicago two months before she died, reading the poem that had made her famous. Her last important act was to donate her papers to Jackson State University, understanding well the importance of her exemplary life as a preeminent twentieth-century American. Walker died shortly after Thanksgiving in 1998 and is buried in Jackson, Mississippi. Margaret Walker's life and literary career helps to complete our understanding of the lasting impact of the Black Chicago Renaissance.

Notes

1. Walker, Margaret. *This Is My Century: New and Collected Poems.* Athens: University of Georgia Press, 1989, 103–5.
2. Walker, Margaret. "What Is to Become of Us?" In *On Being Female, Black, and Free: Essays by Margaret Walker*, edited by Maryemma Graham. Knoxville: University of Tennessee Press, 1997, 171–76.
3. Walker, Margaret. "Richard Wright." In *How I Wrote Jubilee and Other Essays on Life and Literature by Margaret Walker*, edited by Maryemma Graham. New York: Feminist Press, 1990, 33–49.
4. Walker, *This Is My Century*, 113.
5. Henderson, Stephen E. "'Survival Motion': A Study of the Black Writer and the Black Revolution in America." In *The Militant Black Writer in Africa and the United States* by Mercer Cook and Stephen E. Henderson. Madison: University of Wisconsin Press, 1969, 68–102.
6. Walker, *This Is My Century*, 7.

7. Ibid., 15–20.
8. Ostriker, Alicia Suskind. *Stealing the Language: The Emergence of Women's Poetry in America*. Boston: Beacon Press, 1986, 1–56.
9. Walker, *How I Wrote Jubilee*, 54.
10. Levin, Amy. "The Violation of Voice: Revising the Slave Narrative." In *Fields Watered with Blood: Critical Essays on Margaret Walker*, edited by Maryemma Graham. Athens: University of Georgia Press, 2001, 283–89.
11. Walker, *This Is My Century*, 7.
12. Miller, R. Baxter. "The 'Etched Flame' of Margaret Walker: Literary and Biblical Re-Creation in Southern History." In *Fields Watered with Blood: Critical Essays on Margaret Walker*, edited by Maryemma Graham. Athens: University of Georgia Press, 2001, 81–97.
13. Walker, *This Is My Century*, 60.
14. Ibid., 61.
15. Ibid., 91.
16. Ibid., 113.
17. Traylor, Eleanor. "'Bolder Measures Crashing Through': Margaret Walker's Poem of the Century." In *Fields Watered with Blood: Critical Essays on Margaret Walker*, edited by Maryemma Graham. Athens: University of Georgia Press, 2001, 110–38.
18. Walker, *This Is My Century*, 63.
19. Ibid., 194–95.
20. Walker, Margaret. *Richard Wright, Daemonic Genius*. New York: Warner, 1989, 13.
21. Walker, *On Being Female, Black and Free*, 4–11.
22. Ibid., 16.

For Further Reading

Berke, Nancy. *Women Poets on the Left: Lola Ridge, Genevieve Taggard, Margaret Walker*. Gainesville: University Press of Florida, 2001, 123–57.
Carby, Hazel. "The Historical Novel of Slavery." In *Slavery and the Literary Imagination*, edited by Deborah E. McDowell and Arnold Rampersad. Baltimore: Johns Hopkins University Press, 1989, 125–43.
Carmichael, Jacqueline Miller. *Trumpeting a Fiery Sound: History and Folklore in Margaret Walker's Jubilee*. Athens: University of Georgia Press, 1998.
Cook, Mercer and Stephen E. Henderson. *The Militant Black Writer in Africa and the United States*. Madison: University of Wisconsin Press, 1969, 68–102.
Giddings, Paula. "'A Shoulder Hunched against a Sharp Concern': Some Themes in the Poetry of Margaret Walker." *Black World* (1971): 20–34.
Graham, Maryemma, ed. *Conversations with Margaret Walker*. Jackson: University Press of Mississippi, 2002.
———, ed. *Fields Watered with Blood: Critical Essays on Margaret Walker*. Athens: University of Georgia Press, 2001.
Walker, Margaret. *For My People*. New Haven: Yale University Press, 1942; reprint, New York: Arno Press, 1968.

————. *Jubilee*. Boston: Houghton Mifflin, 1966.

————. *Prophets for a New Day*. Detroit: Broadside Press, 1970.

————. *October Journey*. Detroit: Broadside Press, 1973.

————. *For Farish Street*. Jackson: Jackson Arts Alliance, 1986.

————. *Richard Wright, Daemonic Genius*. New York: Warner, 1989.

————. *This Is My Century: New and Collected Poems*. Athens: University of Georgia Press, 1989.

————. *"How I Wrote Jubilee" and Other Essays on Life and Literature*, ed. Maryemma Graham. New York: Feminist Press, 1990.

————. *On Being Female, Black, and Free: Essays by Margaret Walker, 1932–1992*, edited by Maryemma Graham. Knoxville: University of Tennessee Press, 1997.

Walker, Melissa. *Down from the Mountaintop: Black Women's Novels in the Wake of the Civil Rights Movement, 1966-1989*. New Haven: Yale University Press, 1991, 13–26.

Williams, Delores S. "Black Women's Literature and the Task of Feminist Theology." In *Immaculate and Powerful: The Female in Sacred Image and Social Reality*, edited by Clarissa Atkinson, Constance Buchanan, and Margaret Miles. Boston: Beacon, 1985, 88–110.

Papers

The Margaret Walker Alexander Papers are housed at the Margaret Walker Alexander National Research Center, Jackson State University Archives, Jackson, Mississippi.

THEODORE WARD
(September 15, 1902–May 8, 1983)

Alan M. Wald

A trailblazing author in African American theater, as well a conspicuous left-wing cultural worker in the 1930s and 1940s, Theodore Ward was a principal contributor in dramatic art to the early stages of the Black Chicago Renaissance. In 1935 he was a founding member of the radical Black South Side Writers Group, and in 1938 his *Big White Fog: A Negro Tragedy in Three Acts* expressed the classic Chicago Renaissance theme of the impact of Northern racism on veterans of the Great Migration.

The triumph of *Big White Fog* launched Ward on a forty-five year career during which his performed plays, a small fraction of his oeuvre, provided vivid renditions of sundry controversial themes and well-researched episodes from African American life and history. Moreover, Ward employed popular forms to address intricate political and social issues without making concessions in his content to popular taste. Although Ward passed much of the 1940s and 1950s in New York City, he returned to Chicago in 1964. There he continued to write and produce plays in relative obscurity for most of the last two decades of his life.

Nearly all of available information about the early years of Ward's life stems from interviews he gave to the Communist press in the late 1940s, and to several academic researchers in correspondence and interviews during the 1960s and 1970s.[1] Little of this data has been independently corroborated, nor has any substantial research been carried out in relation to Ward's private life. The fine points of his association with radical political and cultural organizations are also unascertained. The principal exception has been the controversy surrounding the Federal Theatre Project (FTP) production of *Big White Fog* in Chicago.[2] Even if many of Ward's anecdotes about his family history and itinerant youth cannot be positively validated, such memories played a pointed role in shaping the literary imagination and political engagement that inform his plays.

Furthermore, a general representation of Ward's personal associations and political commitments can be gleaned from correspondence by and about Ward in various archives. There are especially revealing letters in papers held by the

Schomburg Library in New York and the Beinecke Library at Yale University. Besides, there is a small record of some of Ward's own prose writing on politics and culture that can be consulted, as well as the documentary record of editorial positions Ward assumed on politically affiliated publications.

James Theodore Ward, who ceased using his first name when he started writing, was born in Thibodaux, Louisiana, the eighth of eleven surviving children. Thibodaux was the seat of Lafourche Parish, forty miles West of New Orleans in a rich sugarcane and truck-farming delta. Ward's father, Everett Ward, was an upright Christian schoolteacher who peddled religious books and classics along with patent medicine from a horse-drawn wagon. Ward's paternal grandmother, a former slave, had lost her right hand when her master discovered that she had learned to write.

Everett Ward was an enthralling storyteller, and at an early age Ward indulged himself in reading the sample chapters that his father utilized to sell books. However, his father, an admirer of Booker T. Washington, was personally conservative and tried to discourage his children from listening to jazz. Among the books attracting the young Ward was Charles Dickens's *David Copperfield*. Ward was enthralled by the fancy English of the character Mr. Micawber. Often he tried to speak and write letters in this style.

Ward's mother, Mary Louis Pierre Ward, was a housewife. Ward believed that his maternal grandfather was killed while leading a rebellion of hundreds of Lafourche Parish field workers in the post-Emancipation years. Their aim had been to obtain a daily wage increase by requiring planters to come into town to hire their workers. The family legend was that the planters arrived with rifles and sought out Ward's grandfather, gunning him down in front of his house. Ward's mother kept the bullet to show to her children, but refused to reveal the planter's name for fear that they might be tempted to take revenge.

When Ward's mother died in 1915, while giving birth to her eleventh child, the family disintegrated and the thirteen-year-old Ward wandered North. Drawn toward Chicago by the tales of freedom and opportunity that he picked up from Black Pullman porters, Ward ended up in Cairo, Illinois. Although a white couple offered to take him in, Ward jumped a train to St. Louis. There he survived by finding work in a barber shop and shining shoes. Soon he migrated up to Chicago, where his eloquent speaking style attracted the attention of a friend of Chicago Black community leader Ida B. Wells. Wells was a journalist, editor, diarist, autobiographer, lecturer, suffragist, antilynching crusader, and civil rights activist, celebrated for her exposés of race riots North and South. Wells fed Ward and helped him obtain a job at the YMCA while he attended public school and then found him supplementary work delivering jewelry for a shop.

In the 1920s, however, Ward was consumed by wanderlust. He traveled around the Northwest while reading voraciously. In Portland, Ward worked as a boot-black and a housecleaner. In Seattle he shined shoes and gambled. With a background of reading novels by Knut Hamsun, Jack London, and Gustave Flaubert, Ward now immersed himself in the fiction of Theodore Dreiser and Joseph Conrad as well as the Harvard Classics editions of Descartes, Adam Smith, Rousseau, Aristophanes, Voltaire, and Goethe. In due time, Ward landed in Salt Lake City, Utah. With some savings from his success at gambling, he initially spent his time studying English grammar and frequenting a shoe-shine parlor to hear the embittered discourse of its owner on the past and future of African Americans. In the parlor Ward also met Gale Martin, a white labor journalist connected with the NAACP. Martin introduced Ward to Louis Zucker, an English professor at the University of Utah, who encouraged Ward to write fiction based on his experiences. After examining some of Ward's work, Zucker urged that Ward take one of his writing courses through an extension program. He furthermore inspired Ward to apply for a Zona Gale Fellowship in Creative Writing at the University of Wisconsin. Ward enrolled in the course, producing both poetry and fiction, and subsequently recalled selling a piece to *Real Detective Tales and Mystery Stories* for $75.

Ward was successful in winning the Zona Gale fellowship, and he moved to Madison in the fall of 1931. At the end of the year he relocated to Chicago, but his work so pleased Zona Gale that she personally renewed the fellowship and sent an emissary to convince Ward to return for a second year, 1932–33. During these two years in Madison, Ward, still chiefly an aspiring poet and fiction writer, first mastered theatrical reading. On his own local radio show on WIBA he recited verse and sections of plays, with Chekhov and Shakespeare becoming his preferred writers. Ward was then offered the opportunity to stay at the university and enter a degree program, despite his lack of a high-school education. By the summer of 1933, however, he had become disheartened with the isolation of university life for African Americans.

Returning to Chicago, Ward happened to attend a chapter meeting on Michigan Avenue of the John Reed Club, a Communist-led cultural group. There Ward witnessed the performance of a skit treating the right of African Americans to vote in the South. Ward felt that he had the personal capacity to produce a superior writing job and began to formulate the idea for a play called "Sick and Tired."

While meditating on the concept of "Sick and Tired," Ward recalled that he had once attempted to write a play when he was twelve years old and living in Louisiana. Ward's elementary school teacher decided that the class would perform some plays, and Ward won the part of female character, turning out to be the star of the show. Ward was so inspired by the experience that he determined to write his own play. Teachers at the school were enthusiastic about the end result, but his parents responded differently. His mother read the play in silence and then turned it over to Ward's father. After reading the play, Ward's father threw it in the fire and called it the Devil's work. Ward immediately blocked out the experience until it returned to memory following his sojourn at Wisconsin and experiences at the John Reed Club.

Now permanently residing in Chicago, Ward used his friendship with a social worker to secure a job with the federal government's Works Progress Administration (WPA). He became a recreational director for the Abraham Lincoln Center on the South Side, starting in 1934 and lasting until 1938. By 1937 Ward was directing one-act plays at the Center, but, when the Federal Theatre was founded, he also became part of the Chicago Negro Unit as an actor. At this time he revised the dramatic conception he formulated after the John Reed Club meeting into a one-act play called "Sick and Tiahd." The plot of the play, which has not survived in any public archive, dealt with a southern African American poor farmer who had his own family and plot of land to raise cotton.[3] However, the farmer was beaten down by the system. He had been borrowing money from white moneylenders, but now they claimed that he owed more than he actually did. When the Black farmer refused to submit, a fight ensued during which a white man was badly injured by falling on a ploughshare. The white community organized to kill the Black worker, who turned to his Black friends in the hope that they would unite for self-defense. To his surprise, his friends insisted that the situation was hopeless and that he must flee.

Yet the Black worker refuses to flee, announcing that he is "sick and tired." Instead, he sends away his wife and children, preparing to fight. The wife, however, returns and insists on standing by her husband. When the whites knock on the door of the home of the Black couple to demand that poor farmer come out, the Black rebel ends the play by announcing that "You'll have to come and get me."

The play brought Ward to local attention in 1937, when he won second prize in a Chicago Repertory Theater contest. First place was won by Paul Green's *Hymn to the Rising Sun* (1936), a one-act play about a Southern Black chain gang. At this point Ward began to think seriously about a career as a playwright. Although "Sick and Tiahd" was never produced outside of the contest, Ward himself gave a reading at the Lincoln Center. The occasion was a public meeting following the formation of the Communist-led National Negro Congress in 1936, and was attended mostly by several hundred African American students.

By then, Ward had already met the budding Communist poet and fiction writer, Richard Wright. In late summer or early fall of 1935, Ward was sitting in the Main Reading Room of the George Cleveland Hall branch of the Chicago Public Library when Wright came over and introduced himself. Subsequently Ward invited Wright to visit Ward's WPA class in dramatics at the Abraham Lincoln Center. Out of their discussions about the need for a community of Black writers to critically discuss each other's work was born the notion of a "Chicago Negro Writers Group" that would meet in Ward's classroom on Sunday afternoons. The workshop, later called the South Side Writers Group, more or less continued until Wright left Chicago in 1938. The central figures included Wright, Ward, Margaret Walker, Arna Bontemps, Frank Marshall Davis, Marian Minus, Edward Bland, Russell Marshall, and Robert Davis. Many other aspiring writers drifted in and out, and occasionally white writers also attended.[4]

Then, in the spring of 1937, members of the Negro Unit of the Federal Theatre Project of Chicago began to organize a protest against a planned production of Paul Green's play, *Hymn to the Rising Sun*. This work was to be directed by Charles DeSheim, a Jewish American radical with a background in New York City's Group Theater. Wright, who was transferred from the Federal Writers' Project to serve as publicity agent for the production, was allied with DeSheim. It was mainly Black members of the company who insisted that DeSheim be replaced by an African American director and argued that *Hymn to the Rising Sun* was objectionable to Blacks.

Since Ward was known to be sympathetic to both the play and director, Wright felt that Ward could assist him. It was at this time that Wright induced Ward to transfer from the WPA Recreational Project to the Negro Unit of Federal Theatre. Ward later expressed the view that the Black actors antagonistic to DeSheim were being manipulated by those hostile to the more left-wing elements in the Federal Theatre, possibly even at the behest of conservative whites. In Ward's judgment, DeSheim and those around him were unprejudiced whites trying to develop theater in accordance with a vision of the labor movement in which the freedom of Black and white workers was mutually interdependent. Ultimately Wright and Ward were defeated; DeSheim was forced out and the play was canceled.

That same year Ward wrote *Big White Fog: A Negro Tragedy in Three Acts*, his first full-length play. This work would become a landmark production by the Chicago Federal Theatre of WPA in 1938. Ward later recalled that the origin of the play went back to his travels in the 1920s, when his emerging literary sensibility coalesced around a graphic image from nature. In those years, in addition to reading classic and popular literature, Ward followed Black writing in *The Crisis*, *Opportunity*, and *Chicago Defender*. He had also heard about the Harlem Renaissance poets. Then, during a trip to the Pacific Coast, Ward, traveling on a freight train on the Great Northern Railroad, stopped off at a place called Horseshoe Bend.

Before him stretched a tremendous spectacle where trains had to cross a giant canyon. In the center he saw the fog growing, and Ward was stunned by both the magnificence of the countryside as well as his isolation as an African American from his homeland. In trying to grasp this disconcerting relationship, Ward was struck by a feeling that African Americans lacked a clear point of view of their own as to the causes of their dilemma and possible solutions. Instead, Blacks were indoctrinated mainly by the racist views of white people—views that surrounded African Americans like a "big white fog." This image haunted Ward for years and eventually led to his setting out to write a play that would create clarification and even provide a theoretical perspective on the Black situation. In the play, African Americans are lost for a time in the fog of white racism, but ultimately gravitate toward the light of Marxism.

Big White Fog is in no way autobiographical, other than making use of this image from Ward's youth. Ward claimed, however, that the events dramatized were drawn from an incident in Chicago when a Black man was shot during an attempt of the Communist-led Workers Alliance to stop the eviction of an African American family. Ward had read that the man killed was part of the Great Migration, coming North with his family to escape the racism of the South. Moreover, the victim was a hard-working man with some education.

In relation to other aspects of the play, Ward had also observed how young Black saleswomen in Chicago became the object of lecherous white salesmen. The women felt obligated to curry favor out of the financial desperation of their families. Ward additionally had been impressed by the number of educated Black men he knew who were forced to find employment as porters and window-washers. Moreover, Ward adapted the situation of the son, Les Mason, of being denied a college scholarship due to his race, from newspaper articles. Nevertheless, Ward did invent a past for his protagonist, Victor Mason, as a follower of Marcus Garvey. Ward crafted Mason to be a symbol—an honest man who tried to do something for his family and his people.

Ward asked Wright to read over the play and was later dismayed to find that Wright had employed the notion of a "Big White Fog" in three places: "Fire and Cloud," which appeared as part of *Uncle Tom's Children* (1938); the short story "Bright and Morning Star" (originally published separately but incorporated into the 1940 edition of *Uncle Tom's Children*); and *Native Son* (1940). In his 1947 essay on "Five Negro Novelists: Revolt and Retreat," Ward would castigate Wright for his theft of the theme, and also announce that Wright ultimately abandoned it after his 1944 break with Communism because "it allowed too much freedom as well as the Negro's finding his way out." Instead, Ward maintained that Wright chose "to conceive of the Negro as being trapped in a steel cage, cut off from all freedom of movement, choice, or decision—a prisoner in the hands of forces beyond his volition or control."[5]

The production of *Big White Fog* by the Federal Theatre Project was preceded by considerable controversy that has been carefully documented and analyzed by scholar Rena Fraden in *Blueprints for a Black Federal Theatre 1935–1939* (1994). Ward himself wanted to attract a broad, interracial audience, but the acting director of the Chicago Project, Harry Minturn, was nervous about booking a radical Black play into the mainstream Chicago Loop Theater. Minturn preferred a theater on the Black South Side because he thought that the play's social realism might achieve the greatest response in that milieu. To scout out support in the Black community, Minturn dispatched his choice of director for *Big White Fog*, Shirley Graham, a writer who would later marry W. E. B. DuBois.

Nervous about the possible response from the Black community, Graham arranged for Ward to read his play in a "preview" at the South Side YMCA. This would allow her to judge audience reaction. According to a report that Fraden uncovered that was authored by Graham, the audience included NAACP and Urban League representatives, as well as churches, funeral associations, and integrated theater clubs. Although the audience was respectful at the time Ward gave his reading, the subsequent reaction against his depiction of the Black middle class in the play was extreme. Graham reported that the view was widespread that Ward's portrait was not realistic and relied on stereotypes.

Graham concluded that Ward's play, which she had thought to be benign at first, actually contained elements that would offend almost every sector of the Chicago black community—especially the church establishment, businessmen, and followers of Marcus Garvey. Moreover, she concluded that the producing of a play that frankly discussed color prejudice among Blacks would only open up old wounds before the eyes of the white public. Following Graham's disturbing report, Minturn was even more hesitant about the play than before; he was resolved to keep it from a broad public, if it was to be produced at all.

Yet, for reasons that Fraden was unable to determine, there was a last minute turnaround at the Project. Not only was the play produced, but it was performed at the Great Northern Theater at the Loop. To Minturn's surprise, it ran for thirty-seven performances before an enthusiastic, integrated theater crowd. There had even been a fear among some FTP members of possible race riots around the theater, but these did not materialize. Critical responses in the press were positive across the board. Nevertheless, Ward was ever afterward outraged at the treatment his play had received at the hands of Minturn, alleging jealousy and invidious personal motives on the part of *Big White Fog*'s various antagonists. Ward was grateful, however, for the unflagging support of Federal Theatre Project director Hallie Flanagan.

Big White Fog is a dramatized historical allegory of contending social and political forces in the Chicago African American community, and perhaps other urban centers, between 1922 and 1932. Chicago was the second largest African American urban population in the United States, where Blacks, about one-quarter of the total citizenry, were concentrated on the South Side. Historically *Big White Fog* mirrors the rise and fall of the Marcus Garvey movement (organized as the Universal Negro Improvement Association), aimed at uniting the Black Diaspora to encourage agriculture in and migration to Africa.

Although the play centers primarily around choices made by members of one extended family, and the consequences of their decisions, Ward seems to be using the family as a microcosm of the larger community. In this sense, realism was intentionally violated. This equivocal allegorical dimension may have a factor that led to the misunderstanding by opponents of the play on the South Side. Some community members had objected to the production on the grounds that no single family could embody such extreme positions. Others held that it was a slander on Ward's part to imagine that a typical Black family had members who behaved in the ways depicted in *Big White Fog*. There was especially anger at the portrait of the daughter, Wanda, who succumbs to prostitution with a white man. Notwithstanding, in light of Ward's overall aims, the scholarly consensus is that he succeeded admirably in capturing the essence of the principal political choices as they appeared to many radicals in the Depression. Since the 1930s, the play has undergone a number of revivals and has stayed in print up to the present, although more as a period piece than the practical guide to action that Ward intended.

In *Big White Fog*, a pair of brothers-in-law, Victor Mason and Daniel Rogers, represent the failure of two moral and political choices made in the 1920s. When the play opens, Victor is a hod-carrier and Daniel a Pullman porter, both men with dreams of a better life for themselves and their families. At first, Victor seems the sole loser as he pledges allegiance to the Marcus Garvey movement; moreover, after Garvey's shipping line is closed down for using unsafe vessels and Garvey himself arrested, Daniel becomes even more devoted to donating money in an effort to keep his failing fantasy alive. Dan, in contrast, is a budding capitalist who sees an opportunity to make a big profit by purchasing apartment buildings and cutting the rooms into smaller units ("kitchenettes") in order to double his income. By the time of the Great Depression, Victor has lost everything and faces eviction, while Dan has been financially devastated as well, forced to rent out parts of his own house to individuals engaged in prostitution and crime.

A critical figure in the play is Victor's oldest son, Lester, who had hopes of breaking free of the limited circle of choices by going to college. When Lester wins a scholarship, this option seems possible; but then his plans are dashed when he receives news that his African American identity will exclude him as a recipient. Lester subsequently accepts the generosity of his uncle, Daniel, who agrees to help with Lester's tuition if the nephew works for him part time. Soon Lester finds himself attracted to Socialist ideas, through a friendship he develops with a Jewish classmate, Nathan Piszer. As the family's fortunes grow worse, the seeds of this Socialist idea develop into a full-blown identity with the Communist movement in 1932. At the climax of the play, an interracial Communist-led protest is mobilized in a dramatic effort to save the Mason family from eviction.

The women in Ward's tragedy play a paradoxical role. Daniel's mother-in-law, Martha Brooks, is created as a brutal portrait of self-hatred among the Black middle class. She is obsessed with her white ancestry and wholly unsympathetic to the struggles of her son-in-law to find dignity in the racist North. Indeed, Brooks harbors a hatred of Daniel's dark complexion, a sentiment that bursts forth from her in an ugly family explosion. The result is permanent disaffection, and for a time Brooks leaves the Mason household to move in with the Rogers family. Brooks's daughter, Ella, seems loyal to her husband Victor at first, even sharing to some extent in his Garveyite aspirations. Yet Ella is disillusioned earlier and more willing to capitulate to the ideas of her brother-in-law, Daniel. As the crisis deepens, Ella chooses to side with her mother against her husband.

Most complex is the daughter, Wanda, who in some ways is drawn to her father's idealism and even assists him in his work. Nevertheless, in her early twenties Wanda makes a fateful decision to give up on school. She has a talent for academics and there was a possibility that she might find a secure, if poorly paid and undignified, career as a teacher in a segregated institution. Instead, Wanda opts to take immediate employment in a drugstore with the aim of having a salary that will enable her to have a good time in the here and now. In this choice Wanda is somewhat inspired by her uncle, Percy Mason. Percy is a veteran of World War I who was humiliated upon his return from the military and who has since taken refuge in alcohol and cabaret life. Wanda is furthermore pushed forward by her "fast" friend, Claudine, who seems unmoored from the residue of ethics that still lingers in Wanda, inhibiting Wanda about trading sexual favors for money.

As the Mason family's finances unravel, Wanda is eventually drawn into a liaison with an older white drug salesman who frequently visits the drugstore. Although Wanda has apparently been sexually free, and even led on some wealthy white men to obtain gifts, this ultimate act is solely motivated by her belief that she must get money for the family to prevent their eviction. When her liaison is unexpectedly exposed to her family, she is bitterly denounced by her self-righteous brother and father. Victor then determines that he will accept no aid at all from Wanda or the offer of his brother-in-law to put his family up; instead, he joins forces with the Communists to forcibly resist the eviction.

After Victor is shot by the police, however, he rethinks, as he lies wounded, the tragic set of circumstances that have impinged on the choices made by him and his family. He now more fully grasps his own misjudgments and illusions, and comes to forgive and embrace his daughter, regarding her as similarly victimized. Unfortunately, the reconciliation is cut short by Victor's death, and there is no change-of-heart shown by Lester. The son simply points to his interracial group of comrades as the answer to Black oppression. The play ends with Victor achieving status as a martyr to the cause, and the eviction temporarily halted.

Ultimate victory is by no means assured, but the implication of *Big White Fog* is strong that the course of the son and his Communist friends offers the only way out of the "Big White Fog" that had hitherto obscured all choices. The protestors are described as all male, and the women in the cast are silent and marginalized in the closing statements.

The political atmosphere in which *Big White Fog* was produced must be reconstructed in order to judge the likely impact of the play. In the late 1930s, the U.S. Left appeared to be on the ascendancy. Growth in the organization of the industrial working class had been dramatic, with the formation of the Congress of Industrial Organizations in 1936. A year earlier, the turn of the Communist International to the Popular Front strategy had resulted in a dramatic increase in membership and influence for the Communist Party in the United States. In that ambience, the uplifting ending probably seemed plausible—a gesture toward a future of interracial working class unity that would transform the capitalist system of racism and class exploitation into a new world.

In later decades, of course, the ending may well have been read as forced, contrived, anachronistic, and even somewhat perplexing. That is, in the late 1930s, the martyrdom of Victor might seem more admissible as a necessary sacrifice for an ultimate end that was within sight. In post-Depression years, with the absorption of the Communist-led Left into wartime patriotism and then the hegemony of anti-Communism during the Cold War, such a climax was more likely to appear as predictable "agit-prop," and as an unnecessary waste of a decent man's life. Moreover, Victor's son, Lester, constitutes a weak symbol of the bridge to the future. The son's character is never much developed, and his ultimate rage against his sister is never redeemed through the new understanding revealed by his father before the latter's death. Indeed, despite Ward's effort to transcend politically the Garvey movement and to find the necessary light through Communism to escape the big white fog, Victor's spirit remains the "victor" while the son, Les, seems to be very much less of a moral force.

Originally subtitled "A Negro Tragedy," the reference to tragedy is doubleedged. On the one hand, the allegorical aspects of the plot resonate with themes from African American history, suggesting that the lot of the African American people is tragic as a whole. Indeed, from Ward's view, the obscuring of options by a big white fog was the experience of an entire population. At the same time, the tragic figure is clearly Victor. His nobility lies in his commitment to a vision that he believes will provide a collective solution for Africa's lost children in the United States, but his flaw is a pride that renders him slow to admit error and respond to possible alternatives until very late. Yet there is irony in that, in place of his father's Garvey movement and African homeland, Les is substituting the new utopian fantasy of the USSR as a savior for African Americans. There is an implied element of progress in the transition from the father's Garveyism to the son's Communism that may today appear to be more ironic than Ward imagined.

Following *Big White Fog*, Ward was identified in the public eye with Communism. Later in life he would insist that the play was not Communist propaganda but only a realistic assessment of the choices that were accessible at that time. In one sense, Ward's retrospective self-defense had a point in that his Marxist politics were not deduced, top-down, from any ideological or organizational loyalty. He had throughout his life encountered a number of sympathetic, antiracist whites, and he found the Communists championing causes to which he himself had felt drawn. Ward did not need the Communists to tell him that interracial unity of Black and white workers was a politically attractive project in the 1930s and 1940s. Moreover, the strong religious training of Ward's youth may have encouraged a state of mind requiring faith in some ultimate vision of redemption and purpose in life. Finally, the play itself, despite the favorable portrait of Communists, did not fit comfortably into any particular Party line of the moment.

In fact, Ward's choice to represent Communism by means of the Jewish-identified student, Nathan, was somewhat at odds with the Popular Front emphasis on "Americanization," and the Communist effort to center typical working people as the hope of a new future. Besides, even though the play was written during the era when the Communist Party was promoting Popular Front unity among Communists and liberals to stave off fascism and consolidate liberal democracy, Ward decided to set the play in the early 1930s. At that time, different policies, more militant and more focused on proletarian unity, prevailed, and *Big White Fog* suggests that a violent uprising, not support of the liberal New Deal, is the only solution to racial and economic oppression.

Although Ward certainly traveled in Communist cultural circles in the late 1930s and early 1940s, it was only in the postwar era, after the collapse of the Popular Front, that he emerged as an editorial board member in Communist publications and a more direct spokesman for Communist causes. Yet the evidence of Ward's correspondence does not suggest that he was categorically against the Popular Front and nostalgic for the approach of the early 1930s. Rather, like many Left writers drawn to the Communist movement and the spell of the USSR, Ward still reasoned for himself within a Marxist framework. He made his own choices and alliances according to a variety of factors, and his principal aim was always the writing and production of plays.

Following *Big White Fog*, there was no letup in Ward's activity. In 1938 he also completed a brief play about lynching called "Even the Dead Arise." It had some features of a fantasy where the ghosts of lynched men hold a convention to protest the continuation of lynching. Ward even depicts Haitian revolutionary Touissaint L'Ouverture rising in his tomb to dispatch messages to the U.S. Congress. In 1939, no longer affiliated with Chicago WPA, and hoping to launch a career in New York theater, Ward came East while singing in the chorus of the Federal Theatre production of *Swing Mikado*, a popular adaptation of Gilbert and Sullivan's 1885 comic opera, *The Mikado*.

Ward, usually called "Ted," was at that time a trim, slightly built man of thirty-seven, with a soft, handsome face. Once in New York, Ward promptly contacted Richard Wright, who had arrived a year earlier to write for the *Daily Worker*. Wright's departure from Chicago had followed a bitter conflict with Black Communist Party members in the Chicago branch of the Party. Wright felt that they were trying to control or discourage his writing, and they in turn accused him of "Trotskyism," apparently because he had no qualms about talking to individuals critical of the Party. Yet Wright mended his ties to the Party in New York and was a rising figure in cultural circles.

Wright came to see the *Swing Mikado* production as Ward's guest. Subsequently Wright arranged for Ward to move into the apartment building in Bedford-Stuyvesant in which he shared rooms with an interracial Communist couple, Herbert and Jane Newton. After Ward accidentally set a fire by falling asleep with a burning cigarette, he was asked to leave the building. He then moved to the Douglass Hotel in Harlem, where he was immediately joined by Wright. Now that he had settled in New York City, he learned that the Federal Theatre was to be closed down by Congress and that he was out of work.

In 1940, Ward organized and became president of the Negro Playwrights Company in Harlem. On the Board of Directors were Langston Hughes, Powell Lindsay, Owen Dodson, George Norford, and Theodore Browne. Paul Robeson, Richard Wright, Edna Thomas, Max Yergan, Gwendolyn Bennett, Rev. John Robinson, Alain Locke, and George B. Murphy Jr. served as Associate members. A colossal benefit was held at the Golden Gate Ballroom where Wright appeared with Robeson and Hazel Scott to raise funds for the company to pay for the Lincoln Theater at 135th and Lennox Avenue.

Big White Fog was the only production of the Negro Playwrights Company, with a cast featuring Canada Lee, Hilda Offley, Frank Silvera, and Lionel Monagas. The setting of the play was designed by Perry Watkins, and Powell Lindsay served as director. Ward later estimated that 24,000 white New Yorkers attended the performances, but that only 1,500 African Americans came, indicating a failure to develop roots in the community. There was strong support for the play in statements by Langston Hughes, Ralph Ellison, V. J. Jerome, and others on the Left, but the major newspaper reviews were hostile on political grounds. Ward subsequently concluded that the strongly anti-Communist atmosphere of the years of the Hitler-Stalin Pact, 1939–1941, created the basis for the poor reception among critics.

In June of that year Ward married Mary Sangigian, a Euro-American office manager. Ward had known her in Communist circles in Chicago, and in New

York she had left-wing theater connections. Their relationship, however, caused some controversy in the Communist Party milueu. Ward believed that black women in the movement resented his interracial relationship with Mary. Nevertheless, the marriage lasted two decades, and they had two daughters, Elsie Virginia and Laura Louise.

When Wright began planning for a theatrical adaptation of his novel *Native Son*, he approached Ward about scripting the interpretation. Ward, however, required a financial subsidy to support him and his family during the period of preparation. Wright insisted that none was available at that time. Relations between the two men were complicated by Ward's suspicion that Wright was antipathetic to Mary. Ward suspected that Wright believed that Mary had been a party to the Communist efforts to discredit Wright as a "Trotskyist" when Wright was in Chicago. Ward did, however, adapt Wright's short story "Bright and Morning Star," which was performed at a summer resort colony.

In 1941, Ward began doing research and completed a draft of the writing of *Our Lan,'* a play about reconstruction. He read W. E. B. DuBoiss's *Black Reconstruction* (1935), as well as studies of the same era by Communists such as Herbert Aptheker, Elizabeth Lawson, and James S. Allen. He also examined government summaries of the Reconstruction events contained in Freedmen's Bureau reports and Union Army communications in the New York Library. He then manipulated the information for narrative purposes. Ward would later insist that the play was entirely factual, and grew out of his effort to understand the persistence of racist ideology and stereotypes after Emancipation. His research demonstrated to him that many African Americans had understood that land ownership was crucial for economic and political advancement, and some had fought with arms to defend the property to which they thought they had a right. It was this ultimate disempowerment of Blacks during Reconstruction, and the need for the dominant culture to rationalize continued subjugation, that substantially explained the unremitting character of white supremacism over the centuries. By implication, African Americans could finally defeat anti-Black racism through a recontinuation of economic struggle to attain material resources.

With the advent of World War II, Ward went to Washington, D.C. There he unsuccessfully attempted to write plays for the Writers War Board, the goal of which was to promote the war effort. He had already written a play called "Deliver the Goods," produced at Greenwich House in New York, favoring national defense preparation. Now he proposed to dramatize the life of Frederick Douglass to boost the morale of Black troops. The Board, however, seemed to want only escapist entertainment, and Ward suspected that it especially feared any Civil War themes that might antagonize Southern soldiers.

For a while Ward shined shoes, and then he left for the countryside to spend time painting water colors. Finally he returned to Chicago and opened a shoeshine parlor in the hopes of writing in his spare time. When he found that, in fact, all his energy was absorbed by the business, he sold the parlor. He then worked as an inspector of automotive products while he tried to find backers for a production of *Our Lan.'*

Failing in his theatrical entrepreneurial efforts, Ward returned to New York in 1945. There he was able to write some scripts for overseas broadcasts of the Office of War Information (OWI). When the OWI was abolished by Congress, Ward shifted into sales until the Theater Guild gave him a National Theater Conference Fellowship. Subsequently Ward organized a group of antifascist writers into Associated Playwrights: Edmund B. Hennefeld, Nicholas J. Biel, Harry Granick, Haug Monoogian, Samuel Kaiser, Don Huddleston, and Daniel Rudston. *Our Lan'* was one of three plays selected by the group for production at the Henry Street Playhouse.

The first series of performances of *Our Lan'* was such a success that it attracted the attention of Eddie Dowling, who had produced Tennessee Williams's *The Glass Menagerie.* Dowling, along with Louis J. Singer, was determined to bring the play to Broadway. Much of the cast was retained, including William Veasy and Muriel Smith in starring roles, and Julie Hayden as the Yankee schoolmistress. However, Dowling decided that *Our Lan'* should be rewritten as a musical, "floodlighted as would be scenes in a Ziegfeld extravaganza," according to *Phylon* reviewer Miles Jefferson. The result was a clash between the serious theme and the diversionary entertainment that was catastrophic in regard to the critical response. The same reviewers who had once praised *Our Lan'* now condemned it, and the audience disappeared.

Ward's plot of ten scenes concerns the betrayal of Union Army General Sherman's promise of "forty acres and a mule" to the newly freed African Americans. Following Emancipation, a population of Blacks migrate, under the Moseslike leadership of Joshua Tain, to an island off the coast of Georgia. Their aim is to farm collectively the land that they believe was given to them by the Union Army. When the workers find themselves betrayed, it is Joshua who leads them into battle against the Union soldiers who have come to restore the property to the former slavemaster.

As in *Big White Fog*, Ward features a subplot involving a young woman, Delphine, manipulated into a sexual encounter with a more powerful man, Ollie Webster. Webster is described in the list of characters as "a young pre–Civil War Mulatto Freedman," and Webster originally hoped to make money off Joshua and his followers. As the fortunes of the newly emancipated African Americans fall, Webster switches sides. When Joshua, in love with Delphine, learns that she is pregnant with Webster's child, Joshua is enraged. Yet he forgives Delphine just before he is killed during the armed resistance.

As a thoughtful drama of Civil War history from an African American standpoint, *Our Lan'* is a unique achievement for its time in U.S. theater. Owen E. Bady's brilliant 1984 analysis of the drafts of the play reveal the evolution of

Ward's thought as he negotiated a variety of strategies to move the narrative from melodrama to tragedy.[6] The play essentially combines the story of the U.S. government's betrayal of a community, with the more personal story of a love affair between a humble but charismatic leader and a woman trapped among contending pressures. Characters in the background provide a panorama of types from the period—Bady identifies them as representatives of the free Black community, Northern liberals, racist property owners, small businessmen, former Confederate soldiers turned into poor workers, and so forth. Continuity among episodes was provided by African American spirituals, which communicated "coded messages of resistance and rebellion."[7] Ultimately, though, Ward was using African American history analogically in the fashion of many of his contemporaries, such as the novelist Arna Bontemps and the painter Jacob Lawrence. Ward's primary aim was to address the current, post–World War II dilemma of African Americans by disclosing the root causes of their oppression and dramatizing possible role models for sustaining the battle for liberation from racial and economic oppression.

In early drafts, as Brady discloses, Ward assembled his basic raw material for the events but relied on political oratory combined with sensational events. No doubt Ward was trying to adapt the formula he had seen for popular plays that reached out to the broadest audience of a liberal middle class, both white and Black. Among other features, the end of the early draft featured the martyrdom of Delphine, the young woman Joshua loves who has been seduced by the unscrupulous Ollie Webster. Delphine throws herself between Joshua and the guns of the Union soldiers. Stunned by this turn of events the soldiers cease fire. All action comes to a halt as Joshua lifts Delphine's lifeless body and starts to sing "Deep River."

Ward's 1945 revision of the play, carried out in a New York City seminar run by University of Michigan Drama Professor Kenneth Thorpe, was monumental in terms of *Our Lan*'s structure. Ward conflated four sprawling acts into two tight ones. He toned down sensational features, eliminated folksy wit and other aspects of the early draft that suggested stereotypes of Black culture, and transformed the climax. Moreover, young Ollie Webster has become a more complex prefiguration of the Black middle class. Instead of the classical villain of melodrama, he is depicted as torn between personal opportunism and sympathy for the freedom struggle. There is a change in the development of Delphine as well. In the original version she was seduced and impregnated by Ollie through the gimmick of his slipping her a love potion. Now it is suggested that Delphine possibly succumbed to Ollie due to a preliminary confusion about where her long-term personal interests lay. On the one hand, she had to support financially her sister, and Webster was of a superior economic status. Yet she would clearly be dependent on Webster, whereas life with Joshua could offer her a kind of equality in the new, apparently classless, society that he and his community were building.

Still, the ending of the new version of *Our Lan'* remained uncertain, and the matter was never fully resolved. At first Ward reversed the fatal scenario; instead of Delphine sacrificing herself for Joshua, Ward switched to having Joshua die in a failed effort to protect Delphine from the Union army. However, for the experimental Henry Street production, Ward decided to simply end with the final assault of the Union soldiers; the deaths of Joshua and Delphine are implied but not shown. In fact, even the soldiers who carry out the assault are kept off stage, suggesting that a larger system of destruction is responsible for this tragedy than simply malign individuals. As Joshua and Delphine face the army singing "Deep River" together, a chorus joins them. Finally, Ward decided on an experiment devised just as the production moved to the Henry Street stage. The last sound to be heard was powerful cannon shot, one that broke any sense of closure or tragic resolution. Moreover, the shot suggested the continuing threat of violence and oppression into the present.

Yet when *Our Lan'* moved uptown to Broadway, following the original enthusiastic reviews, the new producer Dowling feared the possible audience reaction to the explosive cannon. He felt it might terrify middle class white women in the audience, and that it would certainly clash with his decision to stage the spirituals in an operatic fashion. Thus the cannon blast was eliminated. A decade later, when Kenneth Rowe published a version of *Our Lan'* with commentary in 1960, the disturbing cannon blast was still absent. Only eleven years later, in 1971, was it restored to the text in the edition prepared by Darwin Turner.

In 1948, Ward was the first African American dramatist to receive a Guggenheim Fellowship. His hope was to complete a major work on John Brown, tentatively called "Of Human Grandeur." The intensification of the Cold War, however, limited Ward's opportunities for theatrical work, and he struggled to find further time and support to bring the play to fruition. In 1950 a preliminary version, "John Brown," was produced by a left-wing Theater Company in New York, People's Drama. The focus of the action was three moments in Brown's antislavery campaign. These include the immediate aftermath to Brown's attack on slavers at Pottawatomie; the sojourn in the Adirondacks where Brown prepares for Harper's Ferry; and the night of Brown's momentous raid against the arsenal. The director of the production was Gene Frankel, and Irving Pakewitz played the part of Brown. "John Brown," however, received negative notice in the mainstream press. Even in Communist publications the play was called courageous but a failure in relation to explaining Brown's motivation and those of his followers.[8]

In the late 1940s, Ward wrote yet another play with radical themes. This was "Shout Hallelujah," a slice-of-life drama projected against the background of a famous working-class tragedy. The setting was in the late 1920s, in Gawley Bridge, West Virginia. At that time thousands of Black and white tunnel construction workers had contracted silicosis, which eventually led to their agonizing deaths.

In 1951, while temporarily in Chicago, Ward wrote "Throwback," a remarkable one-act play. This time he made more central his recurring theme of the poor Black woman pressed into illicit sexual relations with a wealthy white man. A production was staged at the 11th Street Theater in New York but received no attention. As was often the case in relation to source material, Ward developed the play from an incident that had been reported to him, this time from the Deep South. The "throwback" of the play is a light-skinned child born to a poor African American couple. The Black husband assumes that the child must be light because of a light grandparent, thus it is a "throwback." However, he learns from his aunt that his wife, Callie, has been sleeping with his white boss on the farm.

Like Wanda in *Big White Fog* and Delphine in *Our Lan,'* Callie had been caught in complicated economic circumstances that set the stage for her victimization. A primary factor is that her husband, Seth, is desperate to earn overtime by working extra hours in the evening. Seth's goal is to eventually own property and imitate his boss, Coffee. Of course, Coffee is glad to oblige, because he is obsessed with Callie and now has extra time to devote to seduction. Due to the neglect of her husband, as well as a desire to protect Seth from Coffee's jealous and violent wrath, Callie succumbs. When the truth comes out, Seth goes into a bitter rage. Yet, faced with a sense of his own guilt and her refusal to abandon the "throwback," Seth forgives Callie and agrees to raise the child as his own. Seth and the aunt then collaborate in hog-tying Coffee so that Seth and Callie can make their getaway from the region.

A second play that Ward composed in Chicago, "Whole Hog or Nothing," addressed aspects of World War II in the Pacific. Structured through episodes, the drama was partly based on a story that Ward heard from a young Black officer who had fought in the U.S. Army against the Japanese. Ward learned from him that, while in training camp in New Jersey, the officer had undergone considerable racist harassment. As an officer, he couldn't technically be barred from the dining room at the base, but the commander arranged to have a screen put around him while he ate. Memories of this incident later produced an illness while the officer was serving in the Pacific.

In another episode of wartime racism in "Whole Hog or Nothing," Ward depicts an incident in New Guinea about which he had heard. There a group of Black engineers failed to get the artillery support they needed, and most were wiped out. The survivors had to find their way back to the coast through the jungle. En route they encountered a group of surviving white soldiers, but this resulted a crisis because the highest ranking officer was Black.

In 1953, Ward wrote a play called "The Daubers," which would wait twenty years before production. In the early 1960s, Ward attempted two musicals. One was "Charity: A Play with Music" (1961), in which the book and lyrics were by Ward, the music by Irving Schlein, and the idea was suggested by Mildred Stock. Another was "Big Money: A Negro Musical" (1961), for which Ward wrote the book and collaborated on words and music with Frank Fields. Both of them were never published and there is no record of production. Another play, "Black Wizard of the Keyboard: A Musical Play for Television," is undated. The music was by Frank Fields, and it was also derived from an idea suggested by Mildred Stock. Other undated and apparently unproduced plays of the post–World War II decades include "The Creole," "Skin Deep," "Falcon of Adowa," "The Life of Harriet Tubman," and "John the Conqueror."

Although Ward's sympathy for Communism and the Soviet Union date from the mid-1930s, he was organizationally at arm's length until the end of World War II. In 1938 Ward did join the Communist-led League of American Writers and attended some public events, but he was never as prominent in the organization as his friends Richard Wright and Ralph Ellison. At the time of the publication of *Native Son*, Ward followed the discussion within the Communist movement closely and seemed to have access to the internal discussions of Party members and leaders. For some years after that, his main preoccupation appears to have been finding time to write his plays and the resources to produce them. However, in early 1944 Ward wrote to Langston Hughes about his enthusiasm for the new political orientation of the Communist Party under the leadership of Earl Browder. He believed that the change was in harmony with and would assist his present writing. Ward's letter, announcing that he would support Browder's report urging cooperation with liberal capitalists in the final years of World War II and the postwar era, is based more on a belief in the superior abilities of the Communist leadership than in the capacity of capitalism to actually cooperate. Moreover, Ward's strong statement of support for the Party seems to have been partly a reaction to Richard Wright's disaffection, announced a few months before in a shocking essay in *Atlantic Monthly* called "I Tried to Be a Communist."[9]

It is conceivable that, despite his tactical support to Browder's policies, Ward still considered himself on the left wing of the Communist movement. Browder was deposed for his deviations to the Right only a year later and expelled from the Communist Party in early 1946. Yet, in 1947, with the Party shifting dramatically to the Left, Ward was among a group of distinguished founding editors of a Communist literary journal, *Mainstream*. This publication was in part a replacement for the Party's *New Masses*, a weekly that combined cultural and political work, which had fallen victim to the hard times of the Cold War. In *Mainstream* Ward published an extraordinary literary essay, "Five Negro Novelists: Revolt and Retreat," with his pro-Soviet views and hopes for the Communist movement clearly expressed. Ward also disclosed considerable skills as a critic, as he treats fiction by Frank Yerby, Chester Himes, Carl Offord, William Attaway, and Ann Petry. Nevertheless, the judgments are subordinated to a sectarian view, substantially fueled by his animosity toward his ex-friend Richard Wright.

Although *Mainstream* folded after four issues, Ward remained on the editorial board of its successor, *Masses & Mainstream*, up until the near-collapse of the U.S. Communist Party in 1956. At that time the Communist movement throughout the world was profoundly divided over the secret report of Nikita Khrushchev to the Twentieth Congress of the Communist Party of the Soviet Union. Khrushchev acknowledged many of Stalin's crimes and yet a few months later ordered Soviet tanks to stage a brutal crackdown against a rebellion in neighboring Hungary. The precise impact of these events on Ward is not known, but he had published sections from his work-in-progress in *Masses & Mainstream* during the years when he was listed as an editor. After the magazine was reorganized, assuming the name *Mainstream* again, Ward was absent from its pages for some few years but then commenced to contribute episodically in the early 1960s.

In 1964, Ward returned to Chicago where he founded the South Side Center of the Performing Arts. There he served as executive director and taught playwriting classes for children. The Center expressed the desire for a Black Community Theater, but funding and an institutional base remained an uncertainty. In the early spring of 1966, the Center produced Alice Childress's play "Florence," followed by Ward's "Whole Hog or Nothing." The performances were followed by animated discussion from the audience. However, these discussions gave rise to a debate among the theater sponsors as to whether the time was really right for a major Black community theater, as opposed to an integrated little theater. When playwright Douglas Turner Ward, himself a veteran of the Communist movement and later the founder of the Negro Ensemble Company of New York, arrived in Chicago for a visit in the mid-1960s, Theodore Ward expected to find an ally. Instead, in meetings held to discuss the future of the theater, he felt that Douglas Ward was actually supporting his integrationist antagonists.

A complete collapse of the Center was averted in 1967. At that time a white Chicagoan gave the Center $5,000 for the purpose of pursing Ward's aims. With the additional support of Black-owned businessmen, Ward launched a new production of *Our Lan'* on October 26, 1967. Notwithstanding, Ward found himself unable to move forward with his additional projects, because the only theater facilities that he could locate were inferior and unattractive to the kind of Black middle-class audience that might provide long-term support.

Still, in 1967 Ward wrote "Candle in the Wind," and in 1973 "The Daubers" was finally produced. In 1978 Ward was invited to serve as Writer-in-Residence at the Free Southern Theater in New Orleans. After returning to Chicago, he received local recognition in 1982 as a recipient of the DuSable Writers' Seminar and Poetry Festival Award for Excellence in Drama. That same year, Ward died of a heart attack at age eighty-one in the Michael Reese Hospital and Medical Center. Earlier, in the 1960s, Ward's contributions to Black theater were discussed in scholarly books by Loften Mitchell and Doris Abramson. In the decade of Ward's death and just after, in the 1980s and 1990s, his relation to the Federal Theatre was treated in books by E. Quita Craig and Rena Fraden. Nonetheless, a collection of his plays has never been published, and the vast majority of his writing remains unknown to scholars in American literature.

Notes

1. Most useful for reconstructing Ward's biography in this essay are Dennis Gobbins, "The Education of Theodore Ward," *New Masses* 25, 3 (October 28, 1947): 10–14; letters from Ward to Constance Webb Pearlstein, November 7, 1966, and January 10, 1967, Schomburg Library, New York; letter from Ward to Langston Hughes, August 29, 1939, Beinecke Rare Book Room, Yale University; and oral history of Ward in Hatch-Billops Collection, New York City.

2. See E. Quita Craig, *Black Drama of the Federal Theater Era: Beyond the Formal Horizons* (Amherst, Mass.: University of Massachusetts Press, 1980); and Rena Fraden, *Blueprints for a Black Federal Theater 1935–1939* (New York: Cambridge University Press, 1994).

3. This description of the play is based on the oral history of Ward in the Hatch-Billops Collection, op. cit., 9–10.

4. See the history of the South Side Writers Group in Alan M. Wald, *Exiles From a Future Time: The Forging of the Mid-Twentieth Century Literary Left* (Chapel Hill: University of North Carolina Press, 2002), 267–76.

5. Ward, Theodore. "Five Negro Novelists: Revolt and Retreat." *Mainstream* 1, 1 (Winter 1947): 100–110.

6. Bady, Owen E. "Theodore Ward's *Our Lan'*: From the Slavery of Melodrama to the Freedom of Tragedy." *Callaloo* 7, 21 (Spring–Summer 1984): 40–56.

7. Ibid., 41.

8. Schneider, Isidor. "'Longitude 49' and 'John Brown.'" *Masses & Mainstream* 3 (June 1950): 91–95.

9. Ward to Langston Hughes, January 24, 1944, Langston Hughes Papers, Beinecke Library, Yale University. See also Richard Wright, "I Tried to Be a Communist," *Atlantic Monthly* 174 (August 1940): 61–70, and (September 1944): 48–56.

For Further Reading

Abramson, Doris E. *Negro Playwrights in the American Theater, 1925–1959*. New York: Columbia University Press, 1969.

An Anthology. Greenwich, Conn.: Fawcett Publications, 1971, 73–145.

Anonymous. "Five New People's Plays Open in 1950," *Daily Worker*, January 3, 1951, 11.

"Big Money: A Negro Musical," 1961.

Big White Fog. London: Nick Hern Books, 2008; also in *Black Theater USA*, edited by James V. Hatch. New York: Free Press, 1974, 278–319.

"Black Wizard of the Keyboard: A Musical Play for Television."

Brown, Fahamisha Patricia. "Theodore Ward." *Dictionary of Literary Biography 76: Afro-American Writers, 1940–1955*, edited by Trudier Harris. Farmington Hills, Michigan: Bruccoli Clark Layman Books, 1988.

Brown, John Mason. "The Uphill Road." *Saturday Review of Literature* (October 18, 1947): 24–27.

"Charity: A Play with Music," 1960.

"Excerpt from 'John Brown.'" *Masses & Mainstream* 2 (October 1949): 36–47.

"Excerpt from 'Shout Hallelujah.'" *Masses & Mainstream* 1 (May 1948): 8–18.

"Five Negro Novelists: Revolt and Retreat." *Mainstream* 1, 1 (Winter 1947): 100–110.

Fraser, C. Gerald. "Theodore Ward, Playwright Who Focused on Blacks, Dies," *New York Times*, May 5, 1983, D23.

Hatch, James V. "Theodore Ward: Black American Playwright." *Freedomways* 15 (1975): 37–41.

Hill, Errol. *The Theater of Black Americans, Volume II.* Englewood Cliffs, N.J.: Prentice-Hall, 1980.

Jefferson, Miles. "The Negro on Broadway." *Phylon* 9, 2 (Second Quarter 1948): 99–107.

Letter from Theodore Ward to Keneth Kinnamon, July 8, 1965, Kinnamon Papers, University of Arkansas.

Lovel, John. "New Curtains Going Up." *The Crisis* 54 (October 1947): 305–7, 315–316.

Mitchell, Loften. *Black Drama: The Story of the American Negro in the Theatre.* New York: Hawthorne Books, 1967.

Nathan, George Jean. "Memoranda on Four Play Categories." *American Mercury* 66 (January 1948): 37–41.

"Of Human Grandeur: A John Simon Guggenheim Fellowship Play," 1949–64.

Our Lan'. In Darwin T. Turner, ed., *Black Drama in America: "Challenge: A One Act Play on John Brown."* *Mainstream* 15 (February 1962): 40–59; and (March 1962): 39–52.

Rowe, Kenneth. *A Theater in Your Head.* New York: Funk and Wagnall, 1960.

"Scene from 'The Daubers.'" In Alice Childress, ed., *Black Scenes.* New York: Doubleday and Company, 1971, 77–89.

Schneider, Isidor. "*Our Lan'*: A Triumph." *New Masses* 25, 3 (October 14, 1947): 12–13.

———. "Theatre." *Masses & Mainstream* 3 (June 1950): 91–95.

Schomburg Center for Research in Black Culture, New York Public Library. This includes manuscripts of plays.

"Songs." *Mainstream* 15 (September 1962): 38–41.

"The South Side Center of the Performing Arts." *Black Theatre* 2 (1969): 3–4.

"Throwback: A Negro Play in One Act," 1951.

Papers

See the Hatch-Billops Collection, New York City. Included are manuscripts of plays and a lengthy oral history.

RICHARD WRIGHT

(September 4, 1908–November 28, 1960)

Robert Butler

When the eminent sociologist Robert Park met Richard Wright in Chicago in 1941 he exclaimed, "How in hell did you happen?"[1] For a relatively conservative thinker like Park who believed character was a function of environment and environment was slow to change, Wright was indeed a puzzle. For Wright, who had a year earlier achieved national prominence as writer with the publication of *Native Son*, had grown up in the worst possible environment, the brutally segregated world of the Deep South, but had somehow risen well above the society that had tried to put severe limitations on his development.

By the time Wright died in 1960 at the age of fifty-two, he had achieved extraordinary success as a writer, political thinker, and cultural critic, becoming one who changed the course of American and African American literatures. He published seven novels, including *Native Son*, a book that transformed the ways Americans envision race by revealing truths that previous writers were either blind to or lacked the courage to confront. His two collections of short stories, *Uncle Tom's Children* and *Eight Men*, are noteworthy for their formal artistry and honest treatments of social problems that continue to startle and disturb their readers. Wright's autobiography, *Black Boy/American Hunger*, has established itself as one of the seminal texts in American autobiographical writing. Moreover, he published more than 250 newspaper articles, book reviews, and occasional essays. His groundbreaking critical articles such as, "Blueprint for Negro Writing," "How 'Bigger' Was Born," and "The Literature of the Negro in the United States," set high aesthetic standards for black literature and established a solid theoretical framework that exerted strong influence over several generations of African American writers. Wright was also one of the first novelists to put American racial dilemmas into a global perspective, publishing three penetrating studies late in his career: *Black Power*, *The Color Curtain*, and *Pagan Spain*. He also achieved success as a poet, writing a powerful series of political poems at the outset of his career and creating a large body of haiku verse at the very end of his life. Very few other major American writers have achieved more success in such a wide variety of literary forms and intellectual inquiry.

Born to Ella and Nathan Wright on September 4, 1908, on Rucker's Plantation near Roxie, Mississippi, Wright was raised in a world of stark poverty and
systematic discrimination, a rigidly segregated society that was designed by
those in power to make sure that he and other black people would stay forever
in their "place." And as Wright would later reveal in all of his writings about the
South, this "place" was calculated not only to deprive him of the education he
needed to rise in American life but was also intended to reduce him to a subhu-
man level and relegate him and his people to the extreme margins of American
life. As Wright stressed in *Black Boy*, the social environment he experienced
growing up in the Deep South put the most extreme limits on him, becoming
a world "ringed by walls,"[2] which would make him feel "forever condemned."
The South, therefore, was to Wright not only a naturalistic trap depriving him
of economic opportunities and social development but also a Dantean hell that
threatened his very soul. But Wright's life, which has been so ably captured by
biographers such as Michel Fabre, Margaret Walker, and Hazel Rowley, can
also be regarded as the extraordinary American success story that astonished
Robert Park. Facing long odds that very few, if any, major American writers had
to face, Wright eventually used his extraordinary talent and will to overcome
the repressive environment, which would have crushed many lesser writers. In
the process, he became a seminal writer who changed the course of American
and African American literatures. As Keneth Kinnamon has observed, Wright
became "one of the most important figures of twentieth-century American fiction."[3] He revolutionized American and African American literatures because
he was courageous enough to attack old taboos that previous writers dared not
approach and created startling new images of black experience that continue
to inspire writers and disturb readers.

His early life was spent shifting back and forth between a bewildering number
of locations in Mississippi, Arkansas, and Tennessee as his family sought suitable
work that would provide them with some degree of security and stability. His
father, an illiterate sharecropper and mill worker, moved the family to Natchez
in 1911 to work in a sawmill and two years later moved them to Memphis, Tennessee, where he became a night porter in a Beale Street drug store. He abandoned his wife and children in 1915, condemning them to desperate poverty.
When Wright's mother contracted a serious illness shortly thereafter, Richard
was placed for a while in a Memphis orphanage, an experience that terrified
him and left in him an enduring sense of his own loneliness and a tendency he
notes in *Black Boy* to "distrust everything and everybody" (*BB*, 34). Wright's
maternal grandmother, Margaret Bolton Wilson, joined the family in Memphis
in 1916, taking them back to her house in Jackson, Mississippi. Over the next few
years Wright, along with his mother and brother Leon, lived in an assortment of
places, staying for a while with his Aunt Maggie in Elaine, Arkansas, and later

in West Helena, Arkansas. After his mother suffered a paralyzing stroke in 1919, which made her a semi-invalid for the rest of her life, the Wrights moved back to Jackson where they were forced again to move frequently because of their problems paying rent. Except for a short and unhappy stay in Greenwood, Mississippi, to live with his aunt and uncle, Clark and Jody Wilson, Wright spent the remainder of his boyhood in Jackson in his grandmother's household.

Wright's childhood thus was characterized by family disorganization, emotional anxiety, and physical deprivation, which often took the form of severe hunger. All of these problems were compounded by the racism he was forced to endure as a young black person living in the Deep South during one of the worst periods of racial discrimination and violence in U.S. history. The intricately fashioned Jim Crow laws of Mississippi, Arkansas, and Tennessee racially segregated all aspects of public life and many aspects of private life, harshly relegating black people to marginal existences, stripped of civil rights, economic opportunities and social equality. White and black children attended altogether separate but absolutely unequal schools. (Black schools were underfunded, poorly equipped, and often staffed by inadequately trained teachers. Jackson, like most southern towns and cities, had no public high school for black children.) Public accommodations, likewise, were completely segregated in restaurants, transit, restrooms, hospitals, and even cemeteries. Black people were also excluded from skilled trades and higher-paying factory jobs, leaving them to work at poorly paid menial jobs in cities and sharecropping on plantations. Jim Crow laws, moreover, strictly forbade marriage and sexual activity between the races.

This vast and intricate system of white dominance over blacks was enforced in a number of ways. First of all, black people were systematically disenfranchised through white primaries, poll taxes, literacy tests, and physical intimidation. Denied the vote, they possessed no legal mechanism by which they could modify or eliminate Jim Crow laws and practices. Secondly, the South's segregated system was upheld by a court system that excluded blacks from juries and extralegal violence in the form of lynchings, beatings, and mob violence. Organizations such as the Ku Klux Klan and white citizens councils severely punished even the smallest deviations from Jim Crow law with terrorist violence. (Between 1882, when records of reported lynchings began to be kept, and 1950, 4,739 Americans, the majority of them black southerners, were lynched. Wright's home state of Mississippi reported 539 lynchings during this period, far more than any other state in the United States.)

Wright experienced what he called the "horror" of southern racism in his own personal life, and it left an indelible mark on his consciousness and shaped his work in all of its phases. As many critics and biographers have pointed out, Wright's southern experiences remained at the core of his personality and even though he traveled widely as an adult and lived in a great variety of places out-side the South, he was never able to shake the alienation, fear, and anger that the segregated South induced in him as a child and young man. His uncle Silas Hoskins was murdered in 1917 by whites who resented his business success and Wright and his family had to flee Hoskins's home in the middle of the night to avoid further violence being inflicted on them. Wright also knew a young black man named Ray Robinson who was castrated when he allegedly had sex with a white prostitute. As Hazel Rowley has pointed out, Wright would "never forget Ray Robinson's fate" (39) and learned at a young age to distance himself from most white people. And Wright himself was once overwhelmed by the fear of being lynched when he worked as a handyman for a white family in Jackson and accidentally witnessed their daughter naked when he entered her room without knocking to deliver firewood. (He later revealed to psychiatrist Albert Wertham that this disturbing episode was the germ of the scene in *Native Son* where Big-ger, fearing a fate similar to Ray Robinson's, panics in Mary Dalton's bedroom.)

As Wright stressed in "The Ethics of Living Jim Crow," his growing up in the Deep South provided him with a series of traumatic experiences that shaped his consciousness and ingrained in him "gems of Jim Crow wisdom,"[4] which always forced him to realize that he was a black outsider in a white-dominated world and that terrible punishments awaited him if he violated the harsh written and unspoken codes of the Jim Crow South. The fear that he knew as a southern black person would later turn into rage but, as John Reilly has pointed out, he would triumph over this potentially "self-destructive rage" by transforming it into powerfully controlled "art."[5]

Wright's sense of himself as a lonely outsider was deepened by chronic fam-ily problems. After his mother became a semi-invalid when Wright was eleven, Wright and his family moved to Jackson, Mississippi, where they became part of his grandmother's household. Wright always felt like an outsider in this ex-tended family, partly because of temperamental differences between him and his grandmother, but also because his grandmother was a staunch Seventh Day Adventist who tried to impose her sternly puritanical religious vision on his rebellious sensibility. This led to Wright distancing himself strongly from all members of his family, with the exception of his mother, and to developing what would become a lifelong distaste for formal religion and other forms of externally imposed authority.

Wright rebelled strongly against being placed in a Seventh Day Adventist grammar school under the tutelage of his equally pious Aunt Addie and by 1921 was enrolled in Jim Hill School, a public elementary school which his grand-mother despised. Although Wright's nomadic life had put him behind in his studies and he was placed at Jim Hill School two years behind his age group, he thrived in public education and began to develop a strong habit of reading, devouring detective magazines, dime novels about the West, and pulp fiction focusing on American success stories, especially the novels of Horatio Alger. Wright's habit of reading opened up a new and liberating world for him that was in stark contrast to the harshly restrictive life he was directed to live by his family and southern society. He entered Smith Robertson Junior High School in 1923 and graduated as class valedictorian on May 29, 1925. While a student at Smith Robertson, Wright published his first short story, "The Voodoo of Hell's Half Acre" in the Spring 1924 issue of the *Southern Register*, Jackson's black newspaper. Wright's growing rebelliousness and individualism was later displayed vividly when he refused to deliver the graduation speech prepared for him by the school principal and instead wrote and delivered his own speech, "The Attributes of Life."

Because Jackson's segregated school system provided no high school for black students, Wright was unable to pursue his education further and worked in a number of odd jobs such as hotel bellboy, movie theater usher, and a janitor and delivery boy at American Optical Company. As he revealed in "The Ethics of Living Jim Crow," he tried to gain the skills necessary to attain better work in the optical company but was severely chided by his white coworkers for aspiring to have "*white* man's work" (*UTC*, 10). Reminded again of the "boundaries" (*UTC*, 11) that black people faced in the segregated South, he became determined to leave Jackson, and in 1925 he went to Memphis, Tennessee, where he boarded with a black family and worked a series of menial jobs as a dishwasher, delivery boy, and porter at the Merry Optical Company.

His experience in Memphis proved to be a turning point in life because he was free at last to read widely without his grandmother's disapproval and was also able to begin imagining for himself alternatives to the "place" prescribed for him by Mississippi whites. Borrowing a library card from a white Catholic coworker who was not threatened by a young black man's desire to educate himself, Wright withdrew many books from the Memphis Public Library, two of which would radically change his life, H. L. Mencken's *Prejudices* and *A Book of Prefaces*. He was immediately impressed by Mencken's iconoclastic mind and was especially intrigued by Mencken's sharp criticisms of the American South as a backward society crippled by mindless prejudice and an irrational fear of modern freedom and individualism. Moreover, Wright found in *A Book of Prefaces* a reading list of modern masterworks, which became for him a program of self-education.

As Wright revealed in *Black Boy*, Mencken's example and the works Mencken approved of convinced him that books could not only become "vicarious cultural infusions" (*BB*, 282), which could revive him after he had been devastated by a static and decadent southern culture, but he also learned from Mencken that words could be "weapons" to fight the "blind ignorance and hate" he had experienced in the South. Such books could provide Wright with "a sense of freedom" that he needed to liberate himself from "southern darkness" (*BB*, 282, 284). The authors whom Mencken cited from the realistic and naturalistic traditions in modern literature proved particularly useful and inspiring to Wright. In *Black Boy* he stressed that "All my life had shaped me for the realism, the naturalism of the modern novel and I could not read enough of them" (*BB*, 295). In particular, he mentioned Theodore Dreiser, Fyodor Dostoevsky (two novelists he would later claim exerted the most influence over his writing), Stephen Crane, Henrik Ibsen, Sinclair Lewis, and Emile Zola as especially strong influences. Such reading provided him with "new ways of looking and seeing" and "a sense of life itself" helping him to understand and artistically shape his own experiences in vital, coherent ways (*BB*, 294, 295).

Wright left Memphis in November, 1927, to go to Chicago with his aunt Maggie where the two would live on the South Side in one of America's largest racial ghettos. From the beginning, Wright perceived Chicago in powerfully ambivalent terms, sensing it both as a coldly mechanical modern environment and also a place of twentieth-century possibility. In "How 'Bigger' Was Born" he would describe it as "a city of extremes," which was both a "huge, roaring, dirty, noisy, raw, stark, brutal" urban environment and also a young and "fabulous" world of American change and modern freedom. However much Wright might criticize northern cities like Chicago, he remained an urbanite for the rest of his life and was never tempted to idealize pastoral locations or return to the South. He certainly endorsed the folk wisdom enunciated by a black man in *12 Million Black Voices* who claimed "We'd rather be a lamppost in Chicago than the president of Dixie."[6]

Arriving in Chicago less than two years before the onset of the Great Depression and forced to live in a massive ghetto that was particularly hard hit by the economic disasters of the 1930s, Wright experienced Chicago as a harshly naturalistic environment, which reduced him and his family to the same hunger and poverty they had known earlier in the South. For nearly ten years, Wright and his mother and brother lived in crowded, overpriced "kitchenettes," which he would later describe in *12 Million Black Voices* as a "prison" for black people, "our death sentence without a trial" (*12M*, 106). Working at a series of low-paying jobs as ditchdigger, hospital attendant, and dishwasher while often times being unemployed and at the mercy of a stingy, demeaning welfare system, Wright lived out in his own life the betrayals of the Great Migration, which promised blacks a new life in the North but delivered new forms of racial discrimination, social injustice, and poverty.

Paradoxically, Chicago also gave Wright many new opportunities for his own development as an individual and as a writer. In 1929 he began work at the central post office as a clerk and mail sorter. Although this monotonous job did not pay very well, it did soften Wright's isolation by bringing him in contact with Joe Brown and other schoolmates from Mississippi who had also found menial jobs as postal workers. Even though Wright lost his position in the aftermath of the Stock Market Crash, he regained it in 1932 and worked intermittently at the post office until he left for New York in 1937. It was a fellow postal worker, Abe Aaron, who helped to change Wright's life dramatically when he recruited him in 1933 to join the Chicago branch of the John Reed Club, an organization of young leftists and Communists. This would prove to be a critically important development in Wright's life because it ended his long personal and intellectual isolation and connected him with a group of like-minded writers and organizers. The John Reed Club offered Wright for the first time in his life a community that welcomed him as a black person and joined him to people of diverse ethnic, racial, and social backgrounds who shared his social vision and encouraged his writing. It became what Hazel Rowley has called "Wright's university" (78), because it made available to him reading lists, books, study groups, and lectures as well as leftist journals that published his writing. (By 1934 Wright had published three poems in *Left Front*, two poems in *Anvil*, and one poem in *New Masses*.) Wright's program of self-education, initiated independently in Memphis, became more organized and disciplined because of his membership in the Chicago branch of the John Reed Club. For the first time in his life, he had become an important part of an intellectual and political community that anchored his restless spirit, shared some of his deepest thoughts and impulses, and formed a foundation for him as a writer.

It was through the John Reed Club that Wright became acquainted with professors from the University of Chicago such as the sociologist Louis Wirth and the literature professor Robert Morss Lovett. The John Reed Club also enabled him to form friendships with novelists Nelson Algren, Jack Conroy, and Michael Gold. And his positive experiences in the club encouraged Wright to become involved with other groups that nourished him artistically and personally. In 1936 he became a member of the South Side Writers Group, a group of African American writers and intellectuals whose regular meetings were of tremendous benefit to Wright as he worked out his social vision and literary strategies. He also became strongly involved in three W.P.A. organizations, the Federal Writers' Project, the Federal Theatre Project, and the Illinois Writers' Project. He joined the League of American Writers in 1935. His activities in these groups enabled him to make important friendships with writers such as James T. Farrell, Langston Hughes, and Margaret Walker. As Walker has stressed, Wright had "a great need for such associations" because they ameliorated the "deep alienation"[7] dating back to traumatic experiences that he had endured growing up in the South, experiences that threatened to blight his spirit and cripple his imagination.

Chicago, therefore, provided Wright with a surprisingly rich cultural environment that nurtured his art and helped him to play a pivotal role in the Black Chicago Renaissance. Unlike its counterpart at the turn of the century, which was catalyzed by Theodore Dreiser, Edgar Lee Masters, and Carl Sandburg and took place in an energetic city undergoing enormous growth, the second renaissance grew out of the sufferings brought on by the Great Depression and was created by African American writers and thinkers. Wright, whom Walker described as "the exciting hot center" (71) of the South Side Writers Group, was also the focal point of the Black Chicago Renaissance. He helped to change the direction of modern African American literature by centering it on militant social protest and a meticulous examination of the dynamics of the American urban environment. This renaissance combined the efforts of older Chicago writers like Fenton Johnson and the work of a new generation of black poets, novelists, and sociologists such as Margaret Walker, Arna Bontemps, Frank Marshall Davis, Theodore Ward, St. Clair Drake, and Horace Cayton. This remarkable rebirth of black culture continued into the 1940s and 1950s, producing what Robert Bone has called the "Wright school" of novelists such as Willard Motley, Chester Himes, Anne Petry, William Demby, each of whom was deeply impressed by Wright's powerful naturalistic techniques and radically new vision of black life in America (Bone 446–68).

But perhaps the most important aspect of Wright's life in Chicago was his involvement with the Communist Party of America, which was headquartered in Chicago where one of the strongest John Reed Clubs in the United States also existed. Wright became interested in Marxist ideas in the early 1930s and finally joined the Communist Party in 1934. Communism provided Wright with what he would later describe in "I Tried to Be a Communist" with "the first total commitment of my life,"[8] a new faith to replace the old beliefs shattered by the disappointments of the Great Migration and the cultural and economic shocks of the Great Depression. Communism helped him to develop as a man and a writer, for it gave him a coherent philosophical vision, "an organized search for truth" that intellectually stabilized him in a world that was rapidly falling apart. It also provided him with an imaginatively potent vision of human unity, "a common vision that bound us all together" (Crossman, 141), which Wright needed both for his writing and his psychological well-being. Indeed, it helped to repair the enormous damage done to Wright by his growing up in the American South, for it replaced southern segregation, which had induced a terrible alienation in Wright, with a colossal vision of human integration, a classless society in which all people would be equal and interrelated.

Although Wright would eventually become disillusioned with Communism and leave the Party in 1942, his commitments to the Socialism underlying Communism would remain with him throughout his life. Some of the literary principles which Wright developed as a Communist would also help to shape some of his best work, particularly *Uncle Tom's Children* and *Native Son*. Wright's "Blueprint for Negro Writing," which he wrote in 1937 as he completed *Uncle Tom's Children* and was beginning to write *Native Son*, was deeply rooted in Marxist thinking and was quite consistent with the literary strictures issued by the Party. It is not only a manifesto of a committed Communist writer but also contains some of the literary beliefs that Wright would adhere to long after he had formally broken with Communism.

"Blueprint for Negro Writing" calls for a radically new form of black American literature, which is centered in the actual experiences of the masses of black people, using "channels of racial wisdom," black folk art as it is expressed in the blues, spirituals, and folktales. The essay also called for an end to the isolation of earlier African American writers, replacing it with a deeply social and political consciousness embedded in the responsibility to express "a collective sense of Negro life in America." For Wright at this point in his career, only "a Marxist concept of reality and society"[9] could truly capture the present and historical experience of African Americans. Wright would, later in his career, reject a narrowly Marxist vision but he would always maintain that the roots of African American literature were deeply set in the experience of ordinary black Americans rather than DuBois's "talented tenth."

Wright left Chicago in 1937, turning down a permanent position in the post office so that he could better pursue his career as a writer in New York. He became the Harlem editor of the Communist newspaper, the *Daily Worker*, a job that deepened his understanding of black urban life and provided him with many opportunities to develop as a politically engaged writer. In his first year alone he wrote over two hundred articles for the *Daily Worker* and over the next three years he would continue to write on an extremely wide variety of topics, including the trials of Angelo Herndon and the Scottsboro boys, Joe Louis's championship fights, racial discrimination in housing, violence in Harlem, and the spread of fascism in Europe. Like the research he did for various W.P.A. agencies in Chicago, his journalism in New York became a powerful form of education for Wright, deepening his awareness of the plight of black people in the United States and helping him to connect their problems to crises developing abroad.

Wright's years in Chicago and New York were crucial for his personal development and offered him a unique training as a writer who would create important new directions in American and African American literatures. Although he wrote a few apprentice pieces while living in the South, his serious writing began in Chicago when he produced a series of free verse poems for leftist journals and began work on a Joycean novel about one day in the life of a Chicago postal worker. (This book, which was originally titled *Cesspool*, was rejected by publishers because of its harsh language and frank treatment of sex and was published posthumously as *Lawd Today!* in 1963.) Wright's first real break as a writer came in 1937, when his story "Fire and Cloud" won the coveted first prize in *Story Magazine*'s annual contest. A year later, this piece was included with four other novellas in Wright's first book *Uncle Tom's Children*, which drew national attention and established Wright as a fresh voice in American literature. It was favorably reviewed by critics such as Lewis Gannett, James T. Farrell, and Sterling Brown, and it drew high praise from Eleanor Roosevelt in her column in the *New York World-Telegram*.

What makes *Uncle Tom's Children* such a groundbreaking work is its brutally ironic style and its unremittingly honest treatment of racial injustice and violence in the American South. Hailed by James T. Farrell as "a new and powerful work by a new American writer,"[10] *Uncle Tom's Children* boldly departs from the traditional ways in which black life had been depicted by earlier generations of American and African American writers. As its title suggests, it aggressively challenges the long-standing stereotype of Uncle Tom, the Negro who is spiritually ennobled by passively enduring with Christian forbearance the sufferings inflicted upon him by racist whites. But in Wright's book, the modern descendents of Uncle Tom often seethe with anger against white people and act upon their deep feelings of resentment by striking out in terrible violence when threatened by white aggression. Moreover, some of this new generation of blacks have translated their rage into political action, becoming Communists who are committed to overturning an unjust social system and replacing it with a revolutionary "classless" society of workers who are racially integrated equals.

The central character of the collection's first story, "Big Boy Leaves Home," for example, kills the white man who murdered his two friends, and the protagonist of the next story, "Down by the Riverside," does likewise when a white man calls him a "nigger," shoots two of his buddies, and threatens to kill him. In "Long Black Song," Silas dispenses similar violent punishment to the white traveling salesman who rapes his wife, first whipping the man and then shooting him. In the book's final two stories, "Fire and Cloud" and "Bright and Morning Star," the black characters go beyond personal resistance to racial injustice and organize themselves politically, joining the Communist Party and engaging in demonstrations and other acts of disobedience designed to make radical changes in the Jim Crow South. In each of these stories, Wright depicts black people confronting an oppressive white system with powerful acts of rebellion. Like Silas in "Long Black Song," they ultimately are "unafraid" and willing to sacrifice their lives as they avoid the passive suffering of characters like Harriet Beecher Stowe's Uncle Tom.

Wright's black characters in *Uncle Tom's Children* are given plenty of good reasons for feeling such negative impulses toward white people since they are imperiled on a daily basis by a social system reducing them to stark poverty and acts of terror if they demonstrate any kind of resistance to this system. Each of the five stories and the autobiographical sketch, "The Ethics of Living Jim Crow," which prefaces the collection, is suffused with brutal violence, which whites administer to blacks. In "The Ethics of Living Jim Crow," Wright laments the fate of a bellhop with whom he worked in a Jackson hotel who was "castrated and run out of town" (*UTC*, 15) when he was caught having consensual sex with a white prostitute. And several stories describe the ultimate form of intimidation and social control devised by southern whites, lynching. In "Big Boy Leaves Home" Wright depicts in graphic detail the beating, burning, and mutilation of a young black man by a white mob. At the end of "Down by the Riverside," Mann is killed in a hail of bullets as he runs away from whites who cry out "Lynch him!" (*UTC*, 89) as they try to satisfy their need for avenging Mann's justified killing of a white man. Reverend Taylor in "Fire and Cloud" is immediately threatened with lynching when he opposes the will of the town's mayor, and he does indeed come close to being lynched when he is later tied to a tree and whipped nearly to death by town officials. "Long Black Song" concludes with a bizarre variation of lynching when vigilantes burn Silas alive by setting fire to his house as they shout "Cook the coon" (*UTC*, 115).

In addition to reducing to absurdity the myth of Uncle Tom, Wright's book also broke away from other conventional ways of representing African American experience in literature. It strongly challenged the tradition of dialect writing established by white authors such as Joel Chandler Harris and black writers like Paul Laurence Dunbar. Whereas these writers presented black vernacular speech as a means of cultivating a soft and picturesque vision of the rural South, Wright used the language of black peasants in a terse, naturalistic manner to achieve powerfully ironic effects. *Uncle Tom's Children* also broke with the tradition of representing the experience of rural blacks as exotic primitives who were somehow immune from the pressures of mechanized modern life. Novels like Sherwood Anderson's *Dark Laughter*, Jean Toomer's *Cane*, and Zora Neale Hurston's *Their Eyes Were Watching God*, while pointing out racial injustices suffered by rural blacks, nevertheless ascribe a unique vitality and spirituality to these people because of their separation from the dehumanizing forces of modern industrialization, technology, and urbanization. Wright, a thoroughgoing modernist who detested the stagnancy and backwardness of southern rural life, presents an altogether unexotic vision of rural life in *Uncle Tom's Children*. There is nothing picturesque about Wright's Mississippi as a bleak landscape serves as an appropriate reflector of the barren lives that his characters are forced to live. The harsh extremities of southern weather—enervating heat and cataclysmic floods—likewise serve as a powerful reflector of his characters' emotional extremes, alternating between fatalistic acceptance and explosive violence. Wright's

South, far from being a lush escape from the ravages of modern life, is, in many ways, a concentrated version of the most crippling forms of modernism, a brutally naturalistic environment stripping people of free will and crushing them with forces beyond their understanding and control.

A guarded and sternly qualified hope, however, is suggested in *Uncle Tom's Children* with the political vision contained in the final two stories, "Fire and Cloud" and "Bright and Morning Star." Reverend Taylor in the former story finally realizes the truth of his earlier intimation that "maybe them Reds is right" (*UTC*, 117), and he joins the march organized by Communists who demand food and social justice for poor people. While he marches, "A baptism of clean joy" (*UTC*, 161) sweeps over him as he realizes that his new faith in leftist politics can provide "the way" to a better life for himself and his people (*UTC*, 161). "Bright and Morning Star" also transforms conventional religious meanings, investing them with new political significance. Its protagonist Sue moves from a faith in Christ to a faith in Communist revolution, a "star that grew bright in the morning of a new hope" (*UTC*, 191). After one son, Sug, has been jailed for his political activities and her other son Johnny-Boy has been tortured to death in a failed attempt to get him to inform on his comrades, she becomes a political martyr by killing Booker, a Judas figure who is about to reveal the names of the people who are organizing political dissent in the area. The story concludes with whites murdering Sue, but her "faith" in the "fight of black men for freedom" (*UTC*, 170) makes her a political martyr who, in the story's final words, becomes part of "the dead that never dies" (*UTC*, 184).

The only significant negative review of *Uncle Tom's Children* came from Zora Neale Hurston, who objected to the book's bleak portrayal of black life and what she felt was the naiveté of its political vision. Her review in *Saturday Review of Literature*, which can be seen as a "tit-for-tat" for Wright's harshly negative review of *Their Eyes Were Watching God* a year earlier, accused Wright of writing a book about hatreds, which failed to fairly represent the broader and more fundamental aspects of Negro life. Moreover, Hurston felt that the solution of the Party that Wright embraced narrowed his vision. She also found *Uncle Tom's Children*, with all its violence and getting even with white people, to be primarily designed to satisfy black male readers. Hurston's criticisms, while not given much notice in the late 1930s, would assume much more prominence with subsequent critics in the late 1940s and throughout the 1950s who would take Wright to task by becoming increasingly critical of his politics and his bleak portrait of black culture. Hurston's criticism of Wright on gender grounds would resurface strongly in the last two decades of the twentieth century when feminist critics would make serious complaints about Wright's portrayal of women.

While still at work on the stories that would comprise *Uncle Tom's Children* and "Blueprint for Negro Writing," Wright was beginning to imagine another book, which would have an even more startling and dramatic effect on American and African American literatures. Keneth Kinnamon estimated that "preliminary notes"[11] for *Native Son* were sketched in 1935 when Wright was in Chicago and counseled troubled youth at the South Side Boys Club. His work on his novel, "Cesspool," poems such as "Between the World and Me," and short stories such as "Big Boy Leaves Home" had forced Wright to place this new book on his back burner where it simmered for several years. But when some of the initial reviews of *Uncle Tom's Children* drew some responses that Wright considered sentimental and blunted the political impact of the book, he returned to his novel and resolved, as he observed in "How 'Bigger' Was Born," to "make it so hard and deep" that "bankers' daughters" would have to face it without "the consolation of tears."[12] He sent a preliminary outline of *Native Son* to his editor, Edward Aswell, in early 1938 and a rough first draft on October 24 of that year. He then engaged in several months of careful research and revision. The research he carried out focused on two notorious Chicago criminal cases: Robert Nixon's murder of a white woman in 1938 and the Leopold/Loeb "thrill killing" of Bobby Franks in 1924. As he stressed in "How 'Bigger' Was Born," he worked hard on the manuscript, substantially reducing its size and weaving into its narrative important motifs that provided the novel with heightened intensity and increased formal unity and coherence. He also revisited the novel's central character, endowing him with a richer, more complex inner life. He completed the novel in the spring of 1939, and it was published as a Book-of-the-Month Club selection on March 1, 1940.

As Irving Howe has exclaimed, "The day *Native Son* appeared, American culture was changed forever,"[13] since the novel revealed long repressed truths about racial relations in the United States and "made impossible a repetition of the old lies." The book opens with a clock sounding its abrasive alarm, which wakes the Thomas family out of their sound sleep and makes them frighteningly aware of a serious problem, a huge rat that has entered their crowded one-room kitchenette. In a similar way, the entire novel is calculated by Wright as a loud wakeup call to Americans, jolting them out of their long "sleep," their lack of consciousness of the serious racial problems that have afflicted the nation from the beginning of its history and threaten to plunge it into widespread chaos and violence during the Great Depression.

The shocking newness of *Native Son* can also be clearly seen in a rough summary of its plot. The opening episode, which in many ways telescopes the entire novel, is a grimly naturalistic scene of entrapment and death that sets the tone of the entire novel and dramatizes its central themes. Just as the rat is cornered and killed, the Thomas family is trapped by the poverty and racism of the ghetto in which they are forced to live. Bigger Thomas reacts to this desperate situation like the rat, lashing out with defiant violence. And this violence takes two forms, the physical crushing of the rat's head and the emotional taunting of his sister Vera by dangling the rat's corpse in front of her terrified eyes, something he does to cover up his own intense fear.

The other major sequences in Book One are artful variations on the opening scene. After Bigger leaves his family's decrepit apartment, he meets up with his friend Gus and later with members of his gang, and they discuss their plans to rob at gunpoint a white-owned delicatessen. To hide his fear of robbing a white man, Bigger again lashes out in reflexive violence, attacking Gus with the sharp point of his knife, in much the same way that the cornered rat had attacked him with its "yellow tusks."[14] The next day, Bigger goes to work for the Dalton family, wealthy white people who are trying to assuage their guilt for being slumlords by offering an impoverished black youth a job as their chauffeur. Feeling like an unwanted intruder in the strange and opulent world of white people, which he perceives as "a cold and distant world" (NS, 44), Bigger again assumes the role of the cornered rat. When he is given the task of chauffeuring the Daltons' daughter Mary around Chicago later that night, he feels emotionally confused and is brought to near panic when she and her boyfriend begin drinking and assuming a forced familiarity with him that triggers all of his pent-up fears and resentments toward white people. The sequence comes to a terrifying climax when Bigger takes Mary home and carries her to her upstairs bedroom. After the two become sexually aroused and Mrs. Dalton enters the bedroom, Bigger is reduced to "hysterical terror" (NS, 85) and accidentally smothers Mary with a pillow to keep her quiet. He then decides to destroy the evidence of his actions by burning her body in the basement furnace and is forced to decapitate her in order to fit her into the furnace.

Book Two and Three are also structured as a series of entrapment episodes culminating in death. After Mary's charred remains are discovered by reporters who question Bigger in the basement of the Dalton home, he escapes and wanders through the South Side, taking refuge in abandoned buildings. Fearing that his girlfriend Bessie would reveal details of his killing of Mary to the police, he takes her with him and, in the novel's most brutal scene, rapes her and crushes her skull with a brick. (In this way he resembles Robert Nixon who also killed his victim by smashing her head with a brick.) He is eventually caught by the police who trap him on the roof of an abandoned building and subdue him by freezing him with water hoses and knocking him unconscious with blows to the head.

The novel's final section, appropriately titled "Fate," describes Bigger's experiences in jail and at the trial, which condemns him to death in the electric chair. While outwardly immobilized, Bigger grows inwardly, becoming more conscious of his world and experiencing guilt for his actions. He also feels strongly connected to his family and, for the first time in his life, develops a positive relationship with white people, especially Boris Max, his lawyer. Wright stresses a powerful irony in Book Three as Bigger is doomed to be executed precisely at the point where his psychological, moral, and emotional growth indicates that he is no longer the environmentally produced killer he was seen as in the novel's first two books. By the end of *Native Son*, the narrative has come full circle with Bigger being treated like the rat in the opening scene. And just as he destroyed the rat by crushing its skull, the state will dispense with him by placing electrodes on his head and reducing him to a corpse with a violent surge of electricity. The novel, which began with Bigger turning on an electric light so that he could better see and think, concludes with him awaiting death by electricity, which will destroy his powers of vision and thought.

What makes *Native Son* such a revolutionary work is not only its sensation-alistic outer plot, which boldly depicts a young black man reduced by society to the level of a rat, but, more importantly, its extraordinary inner narrative, which enabled Wright to explore black psychology as no other previous writer had ever done and to make us see the humanity of the central character which almost all of the figures in the novel are blind to. For Wright always makes us aware of the important fact that there are "two Biggers" (*NS*, 252), a person who performs societally induced monstrous acts and a man with a deeply human inward self. To underscore the powerlessness and futility of the socially constructed Bigger, Wright probes in an altogether honest way his character's most shocking impulses as he experiences a perverse "elation" (*NS*, 107) when he ponders his killing of Mary. (The Nietzschean pride he takes in such a gruesome act certainly resembles the chilling satisfactions that Leopold and Loeb took in their killing of Bobby Franks.) Indeed, Bigger feels that "His crime seemed natural" (*NS*, 106) and expresses "the hidden meaning of his life." Wright clearly is not endorsing Bigger's destructive violence, as some critics have argued, but is pointing out that a pathological environment "naturally" produces murderous behavior and that in a world that strips people of all meaningful forms of action, *any* action, especially violent behavior, will produce a dangerous illusion of empowerment.

Native Son is also a radically new kind of book in several other ways. It was the first American novel to portray in meticulously realistic detail life in an American urban ghetto. And it did so not from the perspective of a privileged omniscient narrator who could supply sociological information about racial ghettos but from the point of view of one of its victims, a young, underedu-cated, and inarticulate black man. Wright's skilled use of third person narration makes us dramatically *experience* Bigger's world instead of clinically analyz-ing it. Wright also explores the complexities of interracial sex more fully than any other previous American writer, brilliantly exploring the sexual fears at the core of segregation. And by making Bigger a representative figure, a "na-tive son," he stressed another disturbing irony, which very few other writers

356 • ROBERT BUTLER

would explore—Bigger, far from being an aberrant monster, was a symbol of all Americans. Wright, who deeply believed that "The Negro is the metaphor of America," confronted his readers with the troubling notion that Bigger was a reflection of them and that his problems were also their problems.

When *Native Son* appeared on March 1, 1940, it was an immediate popular success, selling 215,000 copies in three weeks. Almost overnight, Wright became a nationally prominent figure and in January 1941 he won the Spingarn Medal, the NAACP's prestigious award for outstanding achievement by a black American. Moreover, *Native Son* ignited a firestorm of critical debate, some of which continues to the present day. Many important critics praised it as a groundbreaking novel creating bold new directions in American literature while many other reviewers dismissed it as a crudely written piece of propaganda. Henry Seidel Canby asserted that *Native Son* was "the finest novel written by an American Negro,"[15] and Sterling Brown celebrated the book as a "literary phenomenon" because it was the first novel about American blacks that provided a "psychological probing of the outcast, the disinherited, the generation lost in the slum jungles of American civilization."[16] Harry Hansen remarked that the novel "packs a tremendous punch, something like a big fist through the windows of our complacent lives."[17]

But several other readers were sharply critical of the novel on aesthetic and political grounds. Howard Mumford Jones found too much "dull propaganda"[18] in the book, while leftist critics such as Herbert Gold felt that its politics were not sufficiently in line with Communist ideology. David Cohn, a white Mississippian, argued that *Native Son* was "a blinding and corrosive study of hate"[19] which gave a distorted picture of black American life. Jonathan Daniels saw Wright's novel as "the story of a rat"[20] describing Bigger Thomas as a stereotyped figure who served the needs of a political tract.

What makes these strong reactions to *Native Son* even more remarkable today is the fact that we now know that the text that reviewers responded to was to some extent a watered down version of the novel that Wright intended. Wright's agent, Paul Reynolds, his editor, Edward Aswell, and the editorial board of Book-of-the-Month Club were uncomfortable with the manuscript that Wright had sent to them and convinced him to make a series of revisions designed to tone down the novel's political vision and soften its depiction of sex, especially interracial sex. For example, Wright was persuaded to change substantially the scene in Book One in which Bigger and his friends watch a film in a downtown theater. He deleted that part in the scene where they masturbate, and he also eliminated the crudely sexual comments that they make about Mary Dalton when they see her in a newsreel film clip. Bigger's later sexual encounters with Mary are also carefully revised, downplaying the strong sexual attraction Bigger feels toward Mary and her initiating the sexual foreplay. Wright also partially reduced Max's Communist speeches at Bigger's trial, somewhat blunting the novel's political impact. The novel that Wright intended for publication and Harper agreed to publish was never made available to readers, critics, and scholars until the Library of America edition of Wright's major works appeared in 1991.

In the years following the dramatic appearance of *Native Son* Wright published very little fiction but he was deeply involved in a number of important literary projects. In 1940 he collaborated with Paul Green on a stage version of *Native Son*, which opened a year later in New York. He also wrote "How 'Bigger' Was Born" to answer critics like Cohn and Daniels who charged him with providing an unrealistic, excessively grim portrait of black life to advance the agenda given him by the Communist Party. This essay, which he first presented as a lecture at Columbia University and which later became attached to Harper's editions of *Native Son*, authenticates the novel by proving how it is rooted in Wright's own experiences and the lives of six black youths he knew while growing up in Mississippi who became prototypes for Bigger.

In January 1941 Wright met WPA photographer Edwin Rosskam who suggested that they collaborate on a photo-documentary book which would focus on the history of black people in America. Their work culminated in *12 Million Black Voices*, which was published in October 1941. The book consisted of a series of remarkable photographs taken by Rosskam in Chicago, a series of pictures from the files of the Farm Security Administration, and Wright's written text interspersed among the photographs. Wright's survey of African American history was divided into four parts: 1) slavery, 2) post–Civil War segregation and sharecropping, 3) the migration of blacks from the rural South to the urban North, and 4) a vision of the future. The first three parts stress the enormous sufferings endured by American blacks but the final section, entitled "Men in the Making," is strongly optimistic, stressing a new black militancy and forecasting vast changes in American society, which will enable black people to "share in the upward march of American life" (*12M*, 146). Wright finally envisions his people at a "crossroads" of their history and ends the book with the hopeful statement that "Men are moving! And we shall be with them. . . . (*12M*, 147).

The imagery that Wright uses throughout the book is quite similar to that found in his fiction. Images of entrapment, paralysis, and death are woven throughout the text to describe various forms of injustice and exclusion, which African Americans have experienced in their "nightmare of history" (*12M*, 26). Cotton culture thus is pictured as a "hateful web" (*12M*, 43) and sharecroppers are described as "walled in cotton" (*12M*, 49). The northern urban areas, likewise, create "death on the city pavements" (*12M*, 91) while urban blacks are "boxed in stone and steel" (*12M*, 108). Chicago's kitchenettes are presented as "our prison" (*12M*, 106), a "funnel through which our pulverized lives flow to ruin and death" (*12M*, 111).

What makes *12 Million Black Voices* unique in the Wright canon, however, are its point of view and vision of black folk life. Unlike most of his fiction, which is written using a coldly objective third person or omniscient perspective that sometimes suggests Wright's emotional distance from the black life he describes, *12 Million Black Voices* is narrated with a first person plural perspective. Filtering his vision of African American history through the pronoun "we," Wright achieves an unusual warmth as he closely identifies with his people's struggles and shares their aspirations. While he could be sharply critical of black folk life in other works, particularly *Black Boy* where he speaks of "the cultural barrenness of black life" and "the strange absence of real kindness in Negroes" (*BB*, 43), in this documentary book he consistently praises black people for building a rich folk culture that sustained them through centuries of hardship. He provides a nontypically positive image of black family life, pointing out that "our delicate families are held together by love, sympathy, and pity" (*12M*, 61). And Wright who in most of his earlier and later work rejects African American religion as a destructive opiate, celebrates the fundamentalist faith of southern blacks, seeing their religious faith as providing them with joy and "vision," which "lifted [us] far beyond the boundaries of our daily lives" (*12M*, 73).

Wright also developed three pieces of fiction in the years immediately following the publication of *Native Son*: a novel about the "woman question" entitled *Black Hope*, which remains unpublished; a story about juvenile delinquents, *The Jackal*, which appeared posthumously in 1994 as *Rite of Passage*; and his extraordinary novella, "The Man Who Lived Underground." For reasons that are difficult to understand, Wright was not able to publish "The Man Who Lived Underground" in book form but eventually placed it in the 1942 issue of *Accent*. An expanded version appeared two years later in *Cross Section*. The inspiration for this story about police brutality came partly from Wright's indignation over the savage beating of his friend Herbert Newton at the hands of New York policemen in 1941 because of his political activities and partly from a story Wright read in *True Detective* magazine about a white man who lived under the streets of Manhattan and would surface at night to assume the life of a burglar.

Wright was also influenced by Fyodor Dostoevsky's *Notes from the Underground*. He regarded the Russian novelist as one of the strongest influences on his own writing and once described him to Margaret Walker as "the greatest novelist who ever lived" (75). Like Dostoevsky's nameless antihero, Wright's protagonist, Fred Daniels, is reduced to marginal status by a repressive society, which regards him as barely human. Both characters withdraw into underground worlds where they discover surprising human resources within themselves but are finally unable to translate their underground discoveries into significant action in the aboveground world.

Fred Daniels's story clearly illustrates how conventional society dehumanizes him in a variety of ways. Accusing him of a murder he did not commit and brutally extorting a confession from him, the police have forced Daniels to encounter the fate suffered by Bigger Thomas and most of Wright's central characters in *Uncle Tom's Children*, death at the hands of a racist social system. But Daniels is somehow able to escape police custody and hides for a period of time in the sewers underneath the streets of New York. Once underground, however, he develops a lucid vision of how the aboveground society operates and this new knowledge endows him with a "sense of power" (*Man*, 62) and "freedom" (*Man*, 59), which he has never experienced in his previous life.

Indeed, he discovers a new self while underground, which is a sharp contrast to the blind and passive self he had prior to moving underground. His new life provides him with deepened, expanded vision as he is able to observe clearly from his undetected perspective beneath the streets the forces in his environment that have denied him a full human life. He observes, for example, a black church service and laughs at their "groveling and begging for something they could not get" (*Man*, 30). And he also witnesses an aborted human fetus floating in the sewer, a sign of society's gross indifference to human life. He later observes people in a movie theater being entertained as they laugh at "animated shadows of themselves" (*Man*, 36) rather than doing something to make their empty lives meaningful. By the end of the story he sees even more disturbing images of the brutality and absurdity of conventional society when he watches a policeman forcing a confession from an innocent man who is so humiliated that he commits suicide.

Daniels's response to this new vision is to assume for the first time in his life the role of conscious rebel. He steals a number of items such as a radio, money, jewelry, watches, and a gun from unsuspecting people, protected by their inability to see him. He acquires these goods to experience a sense of control over the kind of people who formerly dominated him and he laughs as he does so, savoring his ironic new status as a man who can manipulate people and events. He papers his underground room with money and gold watches, enjoying "brittle laughter" (*Man*, 55) as he makes a joke of the way the system controls people with money and time management.

He therefore discovers in the underground sewers a place he had earlier equated with death, a "new kind of living" (*Man* 24), which endows his life with knowledge and power denied him in his aboveground existence. But he is unable to solve the problem of how to translate his personal transformation into social action, and when he returns to the streets at the end of the story he blunders badly. He goes back to the police station and confesses to his various thefts. The policemen, fearing that he might cause trouble for them by revealing their earlier framing of him for a crime they now realize he did not commit, bring him back to his underground retreat where they murder him. He dies ignominiously, "a whirling object rushing alone in the darkness in the heart of the earth" (*Man*, 84).

Missing from Wright's novella is the hope created by Marxist values and the promise of Communist revolution in *Uncle Tom's Children* and *Native Son*.

There is no character like Boris Max who can raise Fred Daniels's consciousness with Marxist ideas and point to the "bright and morning star" of revolution that will provide hope in the future. The nonpolitical vision of "The Man Who Lived Underground" represents an important turning point in Wright's career. Even as a member of the John Reed Club in 1933, Wright had some suspicions of radically leftist ideology, and, as the years wore on, he felt increased tensions between pressures from the Party to conform to their vision of the world and his desire to remain true to his experience as an African American artist. The Party's dissolving of all John Reed Clubs in 1934, their harsh punishments of members who were deemed heretical, and their refusal to take a stand on racial discrimination in war industries deeply troubled Wright, and in 1942 he formally broke with the Party. As he would later reveal in "I Tried to Be a Communist," "I had fled from men who did not like the color of my skin and now I was among men who did not like the color of my thoughts" (Crossman, 119). Between 1941 when he began writing "The Man Who Lived Underground" and 1942 when he found a publisher for the story, Wright's thoughts were increasingly colored by philosophical concepts developed by European existentialists who offered Wright possibilities he could not find in Marxist determinism. Existentialism, therefore, enabled Wright to recover an outlook that could serve as a basis for humanistic belief and action. Existentialist ideas are central to "The Man Who Lived Underground," opening up a new range of thematic and technical possibilities that Wright would explore for the remainder of his career.

Rather than being a systematic philosophy centered in one rigorously defined vision of life, existentialism contains a broad range of ideas and assumes many forms, something that was very appealing to Wright in the early to mid-1940s when he felt overly constrained by the absolute formulations of Communist ideology. But it does have two core ideas: 1) The world is "absurd" since it can not be explained in rational terms but operates in unpredictable, often chaotic, ways, and 2) Man is free and through consciously deliberated choice and action can therefore create meaning in an otherwise meaningless world. Wright would have been attracted to both aspects of existentialism. His brutal experiences in the segregated South and the urban North would put him in strong agreement with Fred Daniels's belief that social systems are "crazy" but he also realized that his own triumph over this absurd world provided compelling evidence that human consciousness and will could enable him to construct a meaningful life for himself and others.

Wright's *Black Boy*, the autobiography he had begun to imagine in 1937 when he published "The Ethics of Living Jim Crow" and which gained momentum after he visited his father in Mississippi in 1940 and lectured at Fisk University in 1943, is also centered in an existential vision of life. But unlike "The Man Who Lived Underground," which stresses the absurd environment that victimized its intellectually immature central character, *Black Boy* focuses more sharply on the existential consciousness, will, and action of its protagonist, becoming a heroic narrative of human triumph through self creation. Wright stresses this at the end of Chapter I when he contrasts himself as a writer in 1940 with his aging father whom he sees for the last time in Mississippi. Like Fred Daniels, Wright's father has been crushed by an overwhelming environment that remains an absurd puzzle to him. But Wright, in developing the existential self, which his father lacks, has been "lifted" to "shores of knowing" (*BB*, 41). He is not a "peasant" who is "a creature of the earth" but a writer who freely constructs the book of his own life. He and his father thus live on "vastly different planes of reality" (*BB*, 40).

His task, therefore, is first to understand and then to transcend the irrational environment that defeats the characters who populate Wright's earlier works. From an early age growing up in the Deep South, Wright senses that his social environment does not really make sense to his child's mind and later makes even less sense when analyzed by the penetrating consciousness he develops as a young adult. The book opens with him undergoing a painfully irrational experience as he is confined at age four to a small room with a lit fireplace and told to "keep still" (*BB*, 3) by his mother. When he does what most children of that age would naturally do, play with the fire, he is severely beaten "out of [his] senses" (*BB*, 7) by his mother who comes "close to killing" (*BB*, 8) him. *Black Boy* is filled with such absurd incidents, which shock and alienate young Wright. When he is six years old, he is forced to witness a court hearing in which a white judge allows his father to desert his family without making support payments and concludes that the whole proceeding was "useless" (*BB*, 31). And he is deeply pained by his father laughing throughout the absurd ritual. He is nine when he experiences his "first baptism of racial emotion" (*BB*, 57) when his uncle Silas Hoskins is murdered by whites who are jealous of his successes in business. Unable to discover any good reason for such violence, Wright is reduced to a paralyzing fear of whites, which remained with him for the remainder of his childhood and adolescence.

When Wright asks his mother why they did not fight back against the whites, he is slapped into "silence" (*BB*, 64) by her. In the world of *Black Boy* rational questions are usually answered with irrational responses. Puzzled by the fact that his grandmother is very light-complected and indeed appears to be white, he is again slapped when he asks why she lives in the black community and why she did not marry a white man. Later observing a chain gang composed of black men, he asks his mother "Why don't the white men wear the stripes?" (*BB*, 68) and again gets no satisfactory answer. As he grows older, his questions become more penetrating, but he rarely gets useful replies from people. When he works as a janitor and delivery boy at the American Optical Company in Jackson and inquires about what he needs to know in order to advance in the company, he is physically threatened by white coworkers who want to keep him in his place by denying him access to "*white* man's work" (*BB*, 220). After he moves to Memphis and witnesses a black man named Shorty humiliating himself by allowing white people to kick him in the buttocks for a quarter, he asks Shorty "How in God's name can you do that?" (*BB*, 269). He gets no adequate response to his question other than Shorty's "wild laughter" and his statement "Listen nigger . . . my ass is tough and quarters is scarce" (*BB*, 269–70). Wright is again reduced to silence by a response that supplies no real answer to his question and concludes "I never discussed the subject with him again" (*BB*, 270).

As Wright observes the intricately segregated society he is forced to live in, he comes to regard it as something like Shorty's life, containing rational meanings on the surface that cover up an essentially irrational state of being. (Even if Shorty's ass is tough, quarters do not represent a reasonable payment for kicking it, and Shorty's wild laughter covers up his despair and "rage" [*BB*, 303], which he reveals on the last page of the book.) When Wright tries to "understand" this strangely bifurcated society in which "two sets of people lived side by side" but never touched "except in violence" (*BB*, 54), he can only conclude that such a conflicted society is centered in irrational fear and hatred. As he tries to develop an understanding of "the secret" (*BB*, 55) of southern racial codes, he is never able to assign any rational meanings to them. His grandmother, "who looks white" (*BB*, 55), is defined as a black person and nobody is either willing or able to explain why this is so. When he asks the question "Then what am I?" he is given an arbitrary and meaningless label as a "colored" (*BB*, 57) person, again reducing him to an angry silence.

Wright is able to avoid being ultimately victimized by such an absurd environment by developing the existential will, consciousness, and action that everyone else in his world lacks. After seeing his mother reduced to "meaningless pain and suffering" (*BB*, 117) brought about by deteriorated health and accepting her "place" in southern society, he resolves in his own life to existentially "wring a meaning out of meaningless suffering" (*BB*, 118). From the beginning of *Black Boy* he is endowed with a rich and active inward life, which separates him from all of the book's other characters, and throughout his childhood and adolescence he finds ways of nourishing this inner self. His sensitivity to language plays an especially key role in development of a humane personality. When his mother reads him stories as a child, his "imagination blazed" and "reality changed" (*BB*, 45) and he regards such writing as a "gateway to a forbidden and enchanting land" (*BB*, 47). When he later begins to read pulp fiction as a teenager, he likewise sees these books as a "gateway to the world" (*BB*, 151). This process of liberation through reading culminates at the end of *Black Boy* when he discovers modern writers such as H. L. Mencken, Theodore Dreiser, Sinclair Lewis, and Emile Zola, who finally satisfy his inward "hunger" and give him "new avenues of seeing and feeling," thus helping him "to build a new life" (*BB*, 296).

Coupled with this expanded, deepened consciousness nurtured by his sensitivity to language is an existential rebelliousness, which Wright seems naturally endowed with. He is deeply suspicious of all of the authority figures in his world, and unlike his mother, never accepts the limits that they place on him. As a child he is intent on developing strategies to "get back" (*BB*, 12) at his father and at one point threatens to strike him with a poker. When his grandmother annoys him by giving him a bath and forcing him to bend over so that she can scrub his backside, he tells her "When you get through, kiss back there" (*BB*, 48). And he refuses to read the valedictory speech that the school principal has prepared for him, delivering his own speech "Attributes of Life," instead.

Wright has to be cautious in rebelling against white people since he is fully aware of the terrible punishments they can invoke, but he never accepts the "place" that whites have defined for him and other blacks. When reminded at the optical company he works for in Jackson of the limits of the work he is allowed to do as a black employee, he quits his job and moves to Memphis. As a sixteen-year-old, he develops hopes of "going north and writing books" because his imagination has made the North a symbolic "place where everything is possible" (*BB*, 199) and his writing is a powerful instrument of self-creation and social criticism. Realizing that "My environment contained nothing more alien than writing" (*BB*, 199), he envisions artistic creation as a powerful form of creative rebellion, which can enable him to find answers to his questions and can also supply him with the weapons he needs to effectively fight back at the white society that strips him of manhood and relegates him permanently to the status of a black boy. In the book's final scene, he is sharply contrasted with Shorty who will "never leave this goddamn South" and indeed will die in the South if he ever acts on his desire "to kill everybody" (*BB*, 303). Wright, who is no longer trapped by his fears and hatreds, is poised to assume a liberating new life centered in existential consciousness and action. His rebellious acts are profoundly creative, not destructive.

Black Boy as a Book-of-the-Month Club selection sold well, becoming number one on the best seller list from late April to early June. By May 10, the Harper edition of the book had sold 195,000 copies, and by August, the Book-of-the-Month Club edition had sold 351,000 copies. It drew a wide range of critical responses, most of them positive but several of them sharply negative. Horace Cayton praised the book for its honest probing of the social realities African Americans face in a segregated society. Charles Lee characterized *Black Boy* as "one of the most memorable books of our time"[21] and claimed it was artistically superior to *Native Son*. Orville Prescott, although faulting the book for being "strained" and "overwritten," nevertheless found it "powerful and moving."[22] Ralph Ellison wrote the most sensitive review, likening the book to a blues performance that both explores the pain of African American experience and exults in its joys and triumphs with "a near tragic, near comic lyricism."[23]

Leftist critics, deeply resentful of Wright's departure from the Party, chided Wright for losing sympathy for the black proletariat and cultivating what they considered a self-indulgent individualism. W. E. B. DuBois agreed, complaining about Wright's portraying black people in an excessively negative way and failing to grasp the richness of their folk culture. He found the book to be centered in a "narcissistic" protagonist whose self absorption is "almost pathological."[24] Ben Burns, writing for the *Chicago Defender*, considered *Black Boy* a "sorry slander of Negroes,"[25] because it neglected to account for the positive features of black cultural life and the heroic attempts to achieve justice and equality in the United States. James Ivy's review in *The Crisis* put the case against Wright in even stronger terms, charging that he "put a sword in the back of his race."[26]

These critics might have had even stronger views of the book, both positively and negatively, if they had been able to read the autobiography that Wright had intended for publication. As was the case with *Native Son*, *Black Boy* was a Book-of-the-Month Club publication and that group's editorial board was responsible for pressuring Wright to make significant changes in the manuscript before it appeared in print in March 1945. Wright had originally titled his autobiography *American Hunger* and wrote it in two sections, "Southern Nights," which contained his life in the Deep South, and "The Horror and the Glory," which described his experiences in Chicago. When the Book-of-the-Month Club told Harper that it would accept only the first half of the book, Wright agreed to drop the section on his northern experiences, with the assurance that it would be published later as a separate volume. (It finally appeared in 1977 as *American Hunger.*) But Dorothy Canfield Fisher, an influential member of the editorial board, pressed Wright in private correspondence for more changes that would substantially alter the ending of the book, which was now entitled *Black Boy*. She wanted a more affirmative conclusion that would celebrate positive American values. Wright was extremely uncomfortable with Fisher's suggestions, but he ultimately supplied a new ending that was bittersweet, stressing not only the psychological scars of his growing up in the South but his being awakened to new life in the North. The revised text concluded with the protagonist leaving a dark world of southern racism and gazing at the stars in the northern heavens, which direct him to fresh possibilities in Chicago.

As Arnold Rampersad and others have pointed out, the changes that Wright was pressured to make certainly altered the tone and meaning of his autobiography. By deleting the rather grim second section dealing with Wright's political and personal difficulties in Chicago, the book acquired an affirmative lift that it did not possess earlier. And by cutting the disturbing conversation between Shorty and Wright, which had originally concluded the southern experiences, a conversation in which Shorty expresses a desire "to kill everybody" (*BB*, 303), *Black Boy* clearly acquired a more lyrical conclusion in line with what Fisher considered "American ideals." Wright never recorded his own estimate of these changes and critics continue to debate their merits. The autobiography that Wright had originally written was restored in 1991 in the Library of America series and is now titled *Black Boy/American Hunger*.

With the popular and critical success of *Black Boy*, Richard Wright reached a high point in his career and was widely regarded as an important American writer who had produced three significant books and faced the brightest possible future. The royalties from *Black Boy* and *Native Son* enabled him to purchase a townhouse in Greenwich Village where he, his wife, Ellen Poplar, and his daughter, Julia, enjoyed a lifestyle unimaginable for them just a few years earlier. As Michel Fabre has observed, for Wright, "1945 finished in security, glory and comfort."[27]

Wright's outward success, however, was undercut by a number of serious anxieties, and by 1946 he began thinking of leaving the United States and taking up residence in France, a place he had admired for some time for its cosmopolitan culture and freedom from racial discrimination. New York in the 1940s was still a place of considerable racial tension and de facto segregation and Wright worried that his young family would be damaged if they established roots there. His neighbors were openly hostile to them, and Wright and his white wife were often the targets of racial slurs when they walked the streets of their neighborhood. Even though the Wrights lived in Greenwich Village, he had to go to Harlem to get his hair cut because white barbers in other parts of the city refused to serve him. And, beginning in 1947, gangs of white youths would come to the village to molest interracial couples and throw black people out of restaurants. Wright was deeply concerned about his daughter's schooling and was particularly angered on one occasion when she was refused admittance to restroom facilities in a New York department store.

By 1946 and 1947, therefore, Wright was painfully conflicted, both as a man and a writer. Although in an interview in February 1947 he stressed that his work was in the "particular hell" of the United States where he was "fashioned," he had earlier revealed to Anaïs Nin that " . . . as a writer here I am strangled by petty humiliations, and daily insults. I am obsessed with only one theme. I need perspective. I need to get away from my personal hurts, my personal irritations. I am so completely disturbed that I can not even work. I need to live free if I am to expand" (quoted in Rowley, 352). He was invited by the French government to Paris in 1946 and, after resolving hassles about his passport with American officials, left for France on May 1, arriving in LaHarve eight days later where he was greeted by American expatriate Gertrude Stein, who considered Wright one of the most promising American writers. During this trip, lasting little more than six months, Wright formed friendships with French intellectuals and novelists such as Albert Camus, André Gide, Jean Paul Sartre, and

Simone de Beauvoir, as well as leading figures of the Negritude movement like Léopold Senghor and Alioune Diop of Senegal and Aimé Césaire of Martinique. He helped to create with these three revolutionary thinkers *Présence Africaine*, a journal devoted to Pan-African issues.

Wright's first trip to France, therefore, was an unqualified success. On May 15, 1946, he wrote to Edward Aswell "Paris is all I ever hoped it to be . . . there is an absence of race hate that seems a little unreal" (Fabre, *Quest*, 306). When his visa expired, he sailed back to New York in January 1947, but had strong thoughts of returning to France in the near future. By June of that year, Wright sold his Charles Street home and moved his family back to Paris in what proved to be a permanent exile.

Wright's decision not to return to the United States was fueled by his growing fears from 1947 onward of two disturbing trends he perceived in post–World War II America, an arrogant triumphalism, which he considered a threat to world peace, and an increasing right-wing hostility to liberal ideas and people espousing those ideas. He realized that the progressive spirit of the New Deal era was over and had been replaced by the "Red Scare," which would culminate in hearings held by the House Un-American Activities Committee (HUAC) of the McCarthy period. As the Cold War between the United States and the Soviet Union intensified during the late 1940s and throughout the 1950s, Wright's fears about these matters deepened, especially after he became aware that files were being kept on him by the FBI since 1941 and that the CIA considered him subversive. When he saw former coworkers Benjamin Davis and James W. Ford sent to prison for their political beliefs and when he witnessed Langston Hughes being bullied by HUAC, Wright resolved to make his exile in Europe permanent. After 1947, he would make only one trip back to the United States in order to shoot footage for the film version of *Native Son*, rejecting several invitations to visit his native country throughout the 1950s.

Wright's first five years in France provided him with an excellent opportunity to broaden his vision of his life, which he worried had become too narrowly focused on "only one theme" of racism while he worked in the United States. From the beginning of his exile, he read widely and deeply in the work of European existentialists, studying Kierkegaard's *Concept of Dread* while crossing the Atlantic, and plunging into a serious study of the works of Martin Heidegger, Camus, Sartre, and de Beauvoir after he arrived in Paris. He became actively involved with Camus and Sartre in the formation and conduct of Rassemblement Démocratique Révolutionnaire (RDR), an organization of people on the non-Communist Left who were suspicious both of American capitalism and Soviet totalitarianism. He also took a strong interest in organizations committed to freeing Africa of colonialist domination. Separating so decisively from

America enabled Wright to develop a broader political and cultural vision that was truly global in nature.

His exile, however, was not nearly as fruitful from a literary standpoint. The fiction that Wright produced in France never matched the power and formal artistry of *Uncle Tom's Children, Native Son,* and "The Man Who Lived Underground." He began writing *The Outsider* in 1948 but did not complete the novel until 1953, creating what Rowley has called "an eight-year publishing hiatus" (Rowley, 374), which contrasts so sharply with the unusually productive seven-year period that preceded it. Part of the problem clearly was Wright's unusually busy life in his first eight years of exile when he engaged in a wide range of time-consuming projects, such as the filming of *Native Son* in Chicago and Argentina, his formation of the Franco-American Fellowship, and his writing for journals like *Les Temps Modernes, Présence Africaine, Twice a Year,* and *Ebony.* He also served as the unofficial leader of a group of black American expatriate writers gathering around the Café Tournon and traveled widely in England, Italy, and Africa. But the weakening of Wright's literary output in France must also be explained in terms of his separating his work from the "particular hell" that "fashioned" him, his deeply felt experiences in the American South and northern cities. Ironically, Wright exiled himself from the United States precisely at a time when its turbulent post–World War II history might have provided him with fresh material that could have reenergized his writing.

The Outsider, like much of the fiction Wright wrote during his exile, suffers from his desire to transcend the themes that centered his earlier work in an attempt to reach a broader, more "universal" understanding of the human condition. Its central character, Cross Damon, is black, but his problems are metaphysical, not social or political. He suffers from having what the existentialists called an "inauthentic" life; that is, a life imposed upon him by an absurd environment that causes him to marry a woman he does not love and have three sons by her to whom he feels unrelated. Moreover, he feels shackled to a pregnant mistress for whom he has little genuine feeling and a domineering mother about whom he feels ambivalent. He is released from this inauthentic life when he becomes involved in a train crash and is mistakenly reported as dead.

He then leaves Chicago and goes to New York where he tries to create for himself an existentially authentic life with a series of rebellious actions. His first act of rebellion is to become a member of the Communist Party and to befriend two comrades, Gil and Eva Blount. He shares an apartment with the Blounts in a building owned by a fascist, Langley Herndon. When he tries to moderate a fight between Gil and Herndon, he accidentally kills both and feels a godlike, Nietzschean power in doing so. The book concludes with him being tracked down by Communists intent on avenging Blount's death. He dies affirming his existential freedom, proclaiming his status as an outsider. When asked in the final pages of the book what he found meaningful in life, he reduces all to absurdity by answering "Nothing."

This brief plot summary suggests what is wrong with the book and how it falls so short of the power achieved in Wright's masterpieces. Its melodramatic narrative is grounded in philosophical abstraction rather than lived experience and this reduces the characters to thin stereotypes acting out prescribed roles in an ideological debate. Critics were quick to point out how Wright's work had flattened out since he had produced *Native Son* and *Black Boy*, books that arose from the depths of his experiences as an American black man. Arna Bontemps, who was a strong defender of Wright's work, disapproved of what he called Wright's "roll in the hay with existentialism"[28] because it moved him away from his forte, a relentlessly honest probing of America's racial problems. Milton Rugoff, who had high praise for *Native Son*, saw little to admire in *The Outsider*, faulting the book for its "sheer melodrama," which was a "compost of sex and crime."[29] Orville Prescott argued that Wright's "philosophical novel" had moved him too far away from his own concrete experiences and thus was populated with "unreal characters," making the book "artificial" and lacking the "impact" that was the trademark of his earlier fiction.[30] Lorraine Hansberry offered what was perhaps the most damning criticism of *The Outsider* when she claimed that Wright had "destroyed his talent" because he had forgotten the "beauty and strength" of working-class black people. By centering the novel instead on a monstrously violent black protagonist who had no feeling for his family or any other blacks, Hansberry claimed that Wright had reinforced the worst stereotypes about African Americans, producing a "propaganda piece for the enemies of the Negro people."[31]

Wright's next novel, *Savage Holiday*, which was published a year later, did little to recuperate Wright's declining reputation as it was rejected by both Harper and World publishers and appeared as an Avon paperback, which received no American reviews. The book grew out of Wright's association with Clinton Brewer, a man whom Wright helped to release from prison in 1941 after he had served nineteen years for the fatal stabbing of his teenage wife. Three months after he was paroled, Brewer committed a strikingly similar crime when he stabbed to death a woman who had refused his offer of marriage and was returned to prison for the remainder of his life. Wright dedicated *Savage Holiday* to Brewer and used him as a model for the novel's central character, Erskine Fowler, who also compulsively stabs a woman to death after she turns down his proposal of marriage.

Seeking again to avoid the racial themes of his earlier work and elevating his art to a more "universal" level, Wright made all of the main characters in the novel white and placed them in an upper-class world. Fowler is a wealthy, recently retired insurance executive who employs a black maid and lives in the stylish "upper seventies of Manhattan."[32] Just as *The Outsider* is grounded in the principles of existentialism, *Savage Holiday* is a consciously written "novel of ideas" centered in Freudian psychology. But Wright's attempt to extend his vision of life by moving beyond his own lived experience and infusing his novel with new ideas produced the same disappointing literary results achieved by *The Outsider*. The plot is even more strained and the characters are even less plausible in this abstractly driven novel.

While *The Outsider* suffers from being a kind of philosophical treatise, *Savage Holiday*'s bizarre plot makes it a curious case study in support of Freudian theories. Fowler's problems begin when Tony Blake, the five-year-old son of Mabel Blake, dies after accidentally falling off the balcony of Fowler's high-rise apartment. He then tries to atone for the child's death by somehow convincing himself that he can make things right by marrying Mabel. When she refuses his proposal and eventually learns the circumstances of her son's death, Fowler compulsively stabs her to death. His altogether strange behavior is finally explained in unconvincing Freudian terms by tracing his pathological impulses to a hatred of his mother who at one point in his childhood had punished him for stabbing one of his dolls.

After completing *Savage Holiday* Wright published three works of nonfiction in three years, *Black Power* (1954), *The Color Curtain* (1956), and *Pagan Spain* (1957). These works also reflect his attempts to transcend his American background by focusing on his growing interest in cultures other than his own and in matters of international importance. *Black Power* grew out of his trip to the Gold Coast in the summer of 1953. He met Prime Minister Kwame Nkrumah in Accra, as well as many other African leaders, as he traveled nearly 3,000 miles by automobile throughout the country. *Black Power* expresses his strong ambivalence about post–World War II Africa. Although he celebrated the prospect of independence of African nations from colonial rule and predicted a momentous role for Africa to play in twentieth-century history, he was greatly disturbed by the political divisiveness, diseases, and overall backwardness he observed everywhere he went in what was soon to become Ghana. A confirmed rationalist and modernist, Wright saw Africa's only real hope was to embrace western industrialism, technology, and urbanization. He returned from Africa after only two and one-half months out of a projected six month's stay, disillusioned and painfully aware that he was a westerner who was scarcely at home in his people's ancestral continent.

The next summer Wright toured Spain in hopes of collecting material for a book on a culture that had fascinated him from the time he had read Hemingway in the late 1920s and later when he became acutely interested in the Spanish Civil War. Wright's response to Spain, like his assessment of Africa, was fundamentally ambivalent. He very much admired the Spanish people, finding them, ironically, friendlier and easier to relate to than the Africans he had met. And he enjoyed the Spanish cities, particularly Barcelona and Madrid. Like Hemingway, he was intrigued by the bullfights but was more interested in victimization of the bulls rather than the heroic deportment of the matadors.

Wright, however, was appalled by other aspects of Spanish culture and at many points likened it to the worst features of life in the American South. He objected to the Franco government's treatment of the Protestant minority, sensing that a kind of "slavery" had been imposed upon them. He felt that Spanish gypsies were treated as "white Negroes" who had been stripped of their rights. And he was repulsed by the ways in which women were also treated as marginalized, second-class citizens. Wright's view of the Catholic Church in Spain resembled his condemnation of formal religion in the American South, regarding it as a force that maintained medieval conditions in all aspects of Spanish life. Wright's solution to the problems he witnessed in Spain was identical to the solution he proposed to African problems. He argued strongly that both Africa and Spain, like the American South, must abandon their inhibiting pasts and become part of a progressive modern world.

Wright's next book, *The Color Curtain*, grew out of his attendance in the spring of 1955 at the Congress for Cultural Freedom in Bandung, Indonesia, which brought together twenty-nine independent nations of Asia and Africa to discuss the problems of western colonialism. Wright saw the conference as an event with the potential to initiate a process that could eventually unite colored people from all over the globe, forming a new world free from colonial domination. In a journal entry that he wrote on April 8, 1955, as he was about to take the long flight to Indonesia, he observed that he was "flying from the old world of Spain to the new world of Asia" (Rowley, 461). But he was deeply suspicious of any attempts to revive what he called the "past and dead cultures" (Rowley, 466) by reviving their religious traditions and racial animosities. Rather, he advocated a "welding"[33] of the consciousness of colored peoples to "the techniques of the twentieth century." For this reason, he described Prime Minister Nehru of India, the driving force behind the Bandung Conference, as a great man because he was able to harmonize the best features of eastern and western cultures.

In *The Color Curtain*, Wright expresses a deep fear that nations that were newly liberated from colonial control would become "flooded, drowned in an irrational tide of racial and religious passions" (*CC*, 219) if they did not "shake loose . . . from a static past" (*CC*, 220). He also feared that if the West was either unwilling or unable to assist emerging nations with financial and technical assistance that they would be vulnerable to the "murder and terror" (*CC*, 220) of either Fascism or Communism.

By 1957, therefore, Wright had become detached not only from his earlier commitments to Marxism and Communism, but also had developed substantial anxieties about the new political theories circulating in the Third World, which rejected western modernism. He came to see himself as one of the "lonely outsiders," whom he described in the inscription of his next book, *White Man, Listen!* (1957), who were part of a "westernized and tragic elite" and who "existed precariously on the clifflike margins of many cultures."[34] This new book of literary and cultural essays, which Wright had presented as lectures in Europe over the past four years, attempted to combine "the best of two worlds" by fusing progressive western ideas with the political and social traditions of emerging nations.

In his final five years before his unexpected death in 1960, Wright devoted considerable time and energy to his fiction. In the summer of 1955 he sketched out plans for an ambitious series of novels, including one set in Aztec, New Mexico, which would explore the conflicts between the individual and society. The title for the entire sequence was *Celebration* and one novel, *A Strange Daughter*, focused on a white woman who had several affairs with black men. *Island of Hallucinations* was begun in 1958 and centered on the personal, sexual, and political intrigues of black expatriates in Paris. In the summer of 1960, Wright worked on *A Father's Law*, which dealt with a man who goes on a murder spree after discovering that his fiancée has contracted syphilis. By 1960, Wright had also put together a series of short stories, along with a longer version of "The Man Who Lived Underground," in a new book, *Eight Men*, which was published shortly after his death.

But the only fictional project that Wright was able to complete and publish before his death was *The Long Dream*, a novel set in Mississippi, which drew upon some of his experiences growing up in the South. The central character's mother Emma is modeled to some extent after Wright's own mother Ella, as both women are presented as religionists who constantly warn their sons about the sins of the flesh and the dangers presented by white people. And two of the book's most important events are drawn from actual happenings. Chris Sims, a young black man, is castrated and murdered after he is discovered having consensual sex with a white woman, suffering a punishment similar to that endured by Ray Robinson, the brother of one of Wright's classmates at Smith Robertson Junior High School. And the fire at Grove Dance Hall which is so vividly depicted in *The Long Dream* is based upon a 1940 fire in Natchez's Rhythm Club, which resulted in the deaths of 209 black people. Wright, who once claimed in an unpublished lecture that "All writing is a secret form of autobiography" (Rowley, 410), drew heavily from actual experiences as he wrote *The Long Dream*.

The novel, like *Black Boy*, describes a journey from twentieth-century forms of slavery to existential freedom and self-creation. The book's central character,

Fishbelly Tucker, like Wright, envisions the South as "a kind of purgatory,"[35] which he must first understand and then transcend. His father, Tyree Tucker, resembles Wright's father in certain ways. Although he achieves middle-class status by operating a black funeral home, he is essentially trapped by a segregated world that forces him to behave in a servile manner before whites, and he thus becomes for his son a symbol of black victimhood. When he offends the white system, he, like Wright's Uncle Silas, is murdered. Fishbelly then takes over his father's business and is later sent to prison on trumped-up rape charges. After he is released, he flees the South by taking a path quite similar to the one Wright took, first boarding a train for Memphis and then taking planes to New York and Paris.

The ending of the novel bears a striking resemblance to the conclusion of *Black Boy*. Fishbelly acts upon his friend Zeke's advice to "leave . . . shake the dust off your feet and don't look back once (*LD*, 372). Inspired by the "high blue stars glazing a black velvet sky," he extricates himself from the trap of southern culture and destroys "all the bridges to the past" (*LD*, 375). On the flight to Paris, he has the same perception that Wright had on his train ride to Memphis, believing that "He had fled a world . . . that had emotionally crucified him," and he looks forward to "a new possible life" (*LD*, 383). In the novel's final paragraph, Fishbelly, like the young Wright, feels renewed by "space" (*LD*, 384) as he imagines his life in a world of terrifying new challenges and liberating fresh possibilities.

Wright's final years were characterized by painful self-doubt and a series of personal disasters, which deepened his isolation, making him what Gunnar Myrdal described in his introduction to *The Color Curtain* as "a free and lonely intellectual" (*CC*, 7). His marriage suffered serious strains after his wife had discovered a series of his affairs dating back to 1951 when he became involved with Madelyn Jackson during the filming of *Native Son* in Argentina. By 1960 Ellen and their two daughters lived apart from Wright in London and a divorce was a strong possibility. Wright had also become deeply disillusioned with France as a result of the Algerian War, and only visa problems prevented him from living elsewhere. Moreover, he had lost faith in his earlier political enthusiasms and felt persecuted by the FBI and CIA. And by 1960 several of the friends and relatives he felt most strongly connected to had died. Edward Aswell, his longtime editor and close friend, died suddenly in 1958, and George Padmore, whom Wright greatly admired and saw as one of the few persons who shared his views, died in 1959 at the age of fifty-six. Wright was also deeply shaken by the passing away of his Aunt Maggie in 1957 and his mother in 1959.

His final years were also plagued by serious health problems, perhaps dating back to the amoebic dysentery he had contracted during his visit to the Gold Coast. He became quite ill in August 1959 with a painful gastrointestinal disorder and was treated with heavy medications such as bismuth and emetine hydrochloride, which had dangerous side effects, particularly those pertaining to cardiac problems. The acute stress that Wright experienced as a result of his growing personal and professional difficulties exacerbated his medical problems and he suffered greatly in his final year from exhaustion and pain. Afflicted by what he thought was a heavy flu, he checked himself into the Eugene Gibez Clinic on November 26, 1960, and died of a heart attack a day later. His premature death at age 52 has never been adequately explained.

Wright died, ironically, on the cusp of a great revival of interest in his work as, throughout the 1960s, he was reevaluated as an important writer who had transformed American and African American literary traditions. The increasing militancy of the Civil Rights Movement and a new interest in "Black Power," gave his work new relevance. Whereas the critics of the late 1940s and 1950s were likely to view Wright's aggressive politics as an aesthetic liability, critics from the mid-1960s onward, particularly those connected with the Black Arts Movement, saw him as a model of the politically and socially committed black writer. Earlier critics such as James Baldwin and Lorraine Hansberry were likely to view a character such as Bigger Thomas as a dangerous stereotype of the "bad nigger" who would make people think twice about integration, but sixties' critics such as Amiri Baraka were apt to view Bigger as a revolutionary black hero who wanted to challenge white society rather than integrate with it. While novelists like Ralph Ellison faulted Wright in the 1950s for writing "protest novels," more militant writers of the next decade like John H. Williams praised Wright for writing ideologically charged books loudly protesting American racism.

Several of Wright's important books were published after his death, contributing greatly to a revival of interest in his work. *Eight Men*, a collection of stories written over more than twenty years and which Wright had attempted to publish as a shorter collection in 1944, appeared in 1961. It included "The Man Who Lived Underground" as well as seven other pieces set in a variety of locations. Two of the stories, "The Man Who Was Almost a Man" and "The Man Who Saw the Flood," were set in the South in the 1930s and examined problems quite similar to those explored in *Uncle Tom's Children*, describing how black men are destroyed by a series of overwhelming environmental forces. "Big Black Good Man" and "Man, God Ain't Like That," two of the collection's least successful pieces, are mostly set in Europe. The remaining stories take place in Chicago and New York and rank among Wright's finest achievements in fiction. Taken as a group, the eight stories dramatize a movement from naturalistic victimization to existential triumph over environmental forces by the achievement of enriched consciousness leading to action resulting in existential selfhood.

Contemporary reviewers responded in largely negative terms to *Eight Men*. Irving Howe, a longtime advocate for Wright, complained that the book revealed the literary faults of Wright's later work. He argued that Wright's efforts to break away from an outdated naturalistic tradition were "clumsy" and resulted in sur-realistic writing that was at its best "uneven."[36] Saunders Redding claimed that *Eight Men* "is not one of the works by which Richard Wright deserves to be judged,"[37] because it was mired in a sterile nihilism brought about by his European exile. Richard Gilman called the collection of stories "a dismally stale and dated book," which "reached the lowest point to which Wright's career had ever sunk."[38] Later critics, however, have taken issue with these extremely harsh reviews, assigning *Eight Men* an important position in the Wright canon. Three stories in particular, "The Man Who Lived Underground," "The Man Who Killed a Shadow," and "The Man Who Was Almost a Man," have been cited by many scholars as some of Wright's most accomplished fictions, and they have been frequently anthologized.

Lawd Today!, which was rejected by eight major publishing houses after Wright wrote it in the early 1930s, and which was turned down by World Publishing Co. in 1961, was finally published by Walker and Co. in 1963 through the determined efforts of Ellen Wright. While editors during Wright's lifetime objected to the book because they felt that its harsh subject matter and experimental style made it an economic liability, late twentieth-century readers have responded favorably to the book and regard it as one of Wright's most significant literary achievements. Arnold Rampersad, the editor of The Library of America's editions of Wright's major books, has argued that it is "among Wright's most compelling works.[39]

Like Joyce's *Ulysses*, the novel ironically juxtaposes the antiheroic present with a heroic past. Just as *Ulysses* contrasts Leopold Bloom's bumblings with the heroic achievements of Odysseus, *Lawd Today!* contrasts Jake Jackson's futile actions as a twentieth century "slave" with the heroic story of the emancipation of black people as a result of the Civil War and Abraham Lincoln's heroism. As the radio recounts events from the American past on the national holiday commemorating Lincoln's birthday, Jake's life in Depression America is presented as a very "uncivil" war, which he clearly loses. While the radio broadcast concludes with Lincoln's heroic words "with malice toward none and charity for all,"[40] Jake's story ends with his being consumed by his self-destructive hatreds and his inability to feel love for anyone but himself.

Jake's deterministic narrative comes in three parts, an opening scene in which he awakens from a deep sleep and has a violent argument with his wife; a middle sequence describing his day of work in the Chicago Post Office; and a concluding section where he goes to a whorehouse, gets drunk and beaten up, and then returns home where he has another violent altercation with his wife. The futility of Jake's life is dramatized by this circular structure where he indeed ends, as he tells his friends, "right where I started" (*LT*, 212). The novel opens with Jake resisting his wife's attempts to awaken him, because he prefers the soft world of his dreams to the hard pain of his waking life and ends with him falling into a "drunken sleep" (*LT*, 219) after he is knocked unconscious by his wife when she defends herself against his attack. Throughout the book Jake is presented as incapable of handling the demands of his actual life and retreating into various forms of "sleep" which provide him with the illusion of power.

Jake's violent personal narrative is reinforced by the novel's cultural narrative, which is revealed by the radio broadcasts and newspaper reports interspersed throughout the novel. The news from the outer world always gives evidence of a world which, like Jake's life, is out of control and on the verge of collapse. As Jake argues with his wife, he reads of mounting violence in Germany, gangsters terrorizing innocent people in Chicago, Communists rioting in New York, and black people being lynched in Mississippi. He later hears radio reports of the Japanese army invading Manchuria and enjoys talking with his coworkers at the post office about several women in Chicago who have performed macabre murders. They also discuss the "crime of the century," the Loeb/Leopold murder of Bobby Franks, a "thrill killing" that is a grisly parallel to the pleasure Jake experiences as he contemplates doing violence to his wife, his bosses, and a wide assortment of enemies.

Wright also broadens the significance of Jake's narrative by making his place of work, the Chicago Post Office, a metaphor of modern American society. Like the deterministic environment in which Jake is trapped, the post office is an elaborate "squirrel cage" (*LT*, 159), which dehumanizes workers with mindless routine, low pay, and constant surveillance. The mechanical work of sorting mail produces a "numbing weariness of spirit" (*LT*, 150), which turns people into robots. To make matters worse for Jake and his friends, the post office is a rigidly segregated society controlled by whites, who supervise blacks who have no alternative but to continue working in menial jobs and white college students who regard such work as only a temporary phase in their moving upward in American life. But Jake fully understands that "when a black man gets a job in the Post Office, he's done reached the top" (*LT*, 118). The "top" for African Americans, ironically, turns out to be a Dantean underground. Jake envisions his eight hours of work each day as "a series of black pits" (*LT*, 130), and he has difficulty talking above the din of the sorting machines which are described as "rumbling like an underground volcano" (*LT*, 117).

The only releases that Jake and his friends find from their dreary work, ironically, make their lives even worse in the long run. The movies that entertain them with "action . . . suspense, thrills, and stolen love" (*LT*, 52) provide only temporary escapes from their grim lives and dull their resolve to pragmatically change their environment. And the liquor, hot jazz, and cheap sex, which they find in whorehouses, compound their problems by depleting their stores of money and endangering their health. When Jake tries to solve his problems at the end of the book by borrowing one hundred dollars and going out for a night on the town at Rose's cat house, he is robbed of his money and savagely beaten when he complains. The treatment he gets there turns out to be no better than the treatment he gets at the post office where he is bullied by supervisors and cheated with low pay.

American Hunger, the second part of Wright's autobiography, which was rejected by Book-of-the-Month Club in 1944, was finally published by Harper and Row in 1977. It greatly resembles *Lawd Today!* in terms of its portrait of the social environment, depicting Chicago as a naturalistic world, a city of "steel and stone,"[41] which can reduce its inhabitants to the level of victimized animals. In *American Hunger* Wright faces the same economic and racial problems that defeat Jake Jackson as he is forced to endure extreme poverty and live in a segregated world that makes him feel like a "slave" (*AH*, 51). He describes the discrimination he experiences in Chicago as a "racial attack that went to the root of my life" (*AH*, 5), something which erodes his conception of self and makes him wonder if he can "survive" (*AH*, 1) as a human being.

Like Jake, he works at the Chicago Post Office and feels demeaned and enervated by his work there. When he is laid off from his postal job, he is forced to work at even lower paying, harsher jobs such as sweeping streets, selling fraudulent insurance policies and being an orderly at a large Chicago hospital. His position at the hospital, like Jake's job at the post office, becomes a metaphor of American society, as whites occupy professional and supervisory roles while blacks are relegated an "underground position" (*AH*, 47) in the basement as janitors and orderlies. Like Jake, he feels that the authorities at work do not perceive him as a "human being" (*AH*, 58) but treat him and his black coworkers as animals. The parallels between the two books are also strongly suggested by Wright's careful use of allusions to T. S. Eliot's *The Waste Land*. At the end of *Lawd Today!* Jake is described as a denizen of "Rat's Alley" as he descends into a world of drunkenness, prostitution, and violence, while in the first paragraph of *American Hunger* Wright characterizes Chicago as "an unreal" city (*AH*, 1).

But the two books are altogether different in terms of their central characters' responses to the modern waste land. While Jake lacks the inward resources either to understand or cope with his nightmarish environment, Wright can survive and even triumph in the "machine-city" (*AH*, 2) of Chicago because he possesses the psychological and imaginative powers that enable him to construct a human life. *American Hunger*, far from being a book about human failure, is instead a kind of autobiographical version of a *bildungsroman*, a text celebrating the transformative powers of education. Unlike Jake, who numbs himself with alcohol, cheap fantasy, and "a fever of bitterness" (*LT*, 143), which reduce him to animal rage or a minimal level of human consciousness, Wright experiences life as a powerful learning process. His job selling fraudulent insurance policies to poor blacks provides him with "a new kind of education" (*AH*, 31), which gives him valuable insights into how ghetto life operates. Likewise, his relief job working with delinquent youth at the South Side Boys Club becomes "deeply engrossing" (*AH*, 88), because it teaches him about the social forces that send black youth down the road Jake is traveling, which leads to "the clinics, morgues, prison, reformatories, and the electric chair" (*AH*, 88). Even the grim job he has at the hospital cleaning rat cages and devocalizing dogs provides him with valuable lessons. The dogs become for him "a symbol of silent suffering" (*AH*, 48), which characters like Jake's wife, Lil, endure and which Wright's own mother experienced. The foolishly violent antics that his black coworkers, Brand and Cooke, indulge in are seen by Wright as behaviors to avoid as he envisions a productive new life for himself. While they inadvertently act out the stereo-typed roles that whites have constructed for them, Wright consciously rebels against such roles.

This new life is nurtured by Wright's reading, writing, and political commit-ments. While Jake believes that "Too much reading's bad" because it "addles your brains" (*LT*, 69), Wright regards his reading of books such as Dostoevsky's *The Possessed* and Gertrude Stein's *Three Lives* as life-giving because they lead to "new realms of feeling" (*AH*, 19). Jake has no time for or interest in writing, but Wright follows his long days of work with writing fiction at night. This enables him to transform the chaos of his raw experiments into ordered art. He believes that "wrestling with words gave me moments of deepest meaning" (*AH* 88) and concludes that writing helped him "to build a bridge of words between me and that world outside" (*AH*, 135).

Jake dismisses all politics as useless and labels Communists as "crackbrains" (*LT*, 50), but Wright discovers "a new faith" (*AH*, 45) in leftist ideals. Although by the end of *American Hunger* he rejects Communism as a perversion of Social-ist values, he maintained a strong belief in these values, and they helped him to overcome his despair and feel connected to important matters beyond himself. Jake, in sharp contrast, is finally destroyed by his own egoism and inability to establish sustained meaningful human relationships.

After Wright had completed *American Hunger* in 1944, he was already at work on a short novel, *The Jackal*, which he was unable to publish in his lifetime but which appeared in 1994 as *Rite of Passage*. This book about teenage gangs in New York was rooted in Wright's work with juvenile delinquents during the Depression at the South Side Boys Club in Chicago, and later at the free clinic, which he and Dr. Frederic Wertham had set up in Harlem, as well as his involvement with the Wiltwyck School for Boys in Esopus, New York. Indeed, an actual case study of a boy sent to Wiltwyck provided Wright with the germ of *Rite of Passage*.

Johnny Gibbs, like the boy at Wiltwyck, was placed in a foster home that pro-vided him with a stable, loving family life, but he was arbitrarily removed from that family at age fifteen by authorities at the New York Welfare Department. Both boys then ran away from "home" and entered the sinister and violent world of Harlem street life, becoming members of gangs engaging in crimes ranging from petty theft to violent muggings. *Rite of Passage*, like "The Man Who Was Almost a Man" and so much of Wright's best work, stresses the existential fragility of its protagonist with a narrative that describes how his life is completely transformed by a single dramatic event. Like Dave Saunders who is detached from a relatively stable and familiar life when he accidentally kills his boss's mule, Johnny's whole world falls apart when welfare department authorities attempt to place him with another family. Like Bigger Thomas, Cross Damon, and Fred Daniels, whose lives are forever changed when they are accused of breaking the laws of impersonal societies that deny them any real legal protection, Johnny finds his old life suddenly dissolved when he returns home from school one day to discover that he is in fact a foster child who has been living since infancy with people who are not his real parents. He therefore is confronted with the same dilemma troubling the protagonist of *Black Boy*—should he accept an identity imposed upon him by a social world that refuses to perceive him as a human being, or should he rebel absolutely and begin the task of constructing a new self? Not surprisingly, he chooses the latter alternative and by the end of the book he is described as "alone," attempting "to make a life for himself by trying to reassemble the shattered fragments of his lonely heart."[42]

What makes this book quite different from Wright's other work is the fact that hope is finally created, because Johnny is not really alone since a number of women offer him love, guidance, and kinship. Unlike so many of Wright's works in which women are presented as a threat to male identity, *Rite of Passage* portrays women in a consistently positive way. Johnny's best self is nurtured by feminine values and influence while his worst self is defined by macho violence and egoism. In the novel's final scenes, Johnny's humane self is activated by his desire for contact with women. As he trudges "the empty streets" (*R*, 102) with the gang as they make their way to Central Park to randomly attack white people, his inner self "yearned to sink to his knees to some kind of old black woman" and sob: "Help me . . . I can't go through with this!" (*R*, 102). After he has participated in the mugging, he hears the voice of a "Negro woman" screaming her disapproval of the gang's senseless behavior by shouting "You boys! You boys!" (*R*, 107). Although it is highly unlikely that this woman is objectively real since only Johnny hears her repeated calls, she is crucially important in the story because she is presented as a human voice within Johnny, a moral consciousness that, like his foster mother and his teacher, directs him away from self-destructive violence and encourages him to respond to the world in intelligent, creative ways. They try to motivate him to see his world as a school, not a prison, an educational process leading to human growth.

Late in his life Wright was also engaged in writing two other novels, "Island of Hallucinations" and *A Father's Law*, but his untimely death made it impossible for him to complete either work. "Island of Hallucinations" was planned as a sequel to *The Long Dream*, focusing on African American expatriate life during the Cold War. The core of the book examines Fishbelly Tucker's love affairs with various white women and the Byzantine personal and political intrigues experienced by black American writers and intellectuals. The novel in its uncompleted form stops when Fishbelly is deported after one of his friends betrays him by falsely reporting him to French authorities as a dangerous revolutionary.

A Father's Law, in contrast, is set in Chicago and centers on the struggles of a black middle-class family. Its protagonist, Rudolf Turner, is a successful police chief who lives in Brentwood Park, a neighborhood loosely modeled after Kenwood, an exclusive white suburb of Chicago, which was the setting for the crimes committed in the 1920s by Richard Loeb and Nathan Leopold. Turner has been given the task of solving a series of brutal killings in his neighborhood and comes to suspect his son, Tommy, of being a serial murderer. Although Wright came close to completing the novel in his final days, he was not able to fashion an ending that would identify the killer or resolve the issues raised in the book. *A Father's Law* was eventually published by HarperCollins in its uncompleted form in 2008. Wright's daughter, Julia, provided a brief introduction placing the novel in the context of Wright's previous work and the personal difficulties he faced late in life.

In his final two years Wright engaged in one other unusual literary project, the writing of haiku poetry. In 1959 he became fascinated with Japanese haiku, reading widely in this area, and writing approximately four thousand of these delicate, three-lined poems. For the most part, Wright's haiku are a melancholy reflection of the isolation and illness he experienced at the end of his life, focusing on a lonely individual contemplating a desolate landscape and the prospect of death. As Hazel Rowley has pointed out, they were a form of "meditation" (505), which gave Wright "a modicum of inner peace in the worst period of despair and self-doubt he had ever known." World Publishing Company rejected Wright's book of haiku poems in June 1960, but a substantial collection of his best haiku was edited by Yoshinobu Hakutani and Robert Tener and published in 1998.

In a literary career spanning over twenty-five years and unfortunately cut short by his unexpected death at age fifty-two, Wright achieved remarkable success. Acknowledged by many as the father of modern African American literature, he revolutionized both American consciousness and black writing, because he was courageous enough to challenge old taboos and to boldly articulate disturbing truths about America's racial problems, which previous writers were either unable or unwilling to explore. As Arnold Rampersad has noted, "Compared with him, some of the bravest earlier black writers seem almost timid" (3). Wright's example as a socially committed artist and his writing of masterpieces such as *Uncle Tom's Children*, *Native Son*, "The Man Who Lived Underground," and *Black Boy/American Hunger* helped to inspire a wide range of black writers throughout the 1940s, 1950s, and 1960s. And he continues to exert a strong influence over contemporary novelists such as Albert French,

Jeffrey Renard Allen, and Walter Mosley. Moreover, his novels, stories, and essays have been translated into many languages and are read today all over the world. Wright's best work, while growing out of his own rich experiences that were deeply embedded in the times and places in which he lived, ultimately generates truly universal meanings. In the words of his reluctant admirer, James Baldwin, "Wright's unrelentingly bleak landscape was not merely that of the Deep South or of Chicago, but that of the world, of the human heart."[43]

Notes

1. Rowley, Hazel. *Richard Wright: The Life and Times.* New York: Henry Holt, 2001, 25. All subsequent references are to this edition and page numbers are cited parenthetically after the quote.

2. Wright, Richard. *Black Boy/American Hunger.* New York: Harper Perennial, 1993, 296. All subsequent references are to this edition and page numbers are cited parenthetically after the quote.

3. Kinnamon, Keneth. *The Emergence of Richard Wright: A Study of Literature and Society.* Urbana: University of Illinois Press, 1971, 118.

4. Wright, Richard. *Uncle Tom's Children: Five Long Stories.* New York and London: Harper, 1940, 8. All subsequent references are to this edition and page numbers are cited parenthetically after the quote.

5. Reilly, John M. "Afterword." In *Native Son* by Richard Wright. New York: Harper and Row, 1966, 397.

6. Wright, Richard. *12 Million Black Voices.* 1941. Rpt. New York: Thunder's Mouth Press, 1988, 88. All subsequent references are to this edition and page numbers are cited parenthetically after the quote.

7. Walker, Margaret. *Richard Wright, Daemonic Genius.* New York: Amistad Press, 1988, 284. All subsequent references are to this edition and page numbers are cited parenthetically after the quote.

8. Wright, Richard. "I Tried to Be a Communist." In *The God That Failed* by Richard Crossman. New York: Bantam Books, 1965, 117.

9. Wright, Richard. "Blueprint for Negro Writing." In *The Norton Anthology of African American Literature*, edited by Henry Louis Gates Jr. and Nellie Y. McKay. New York: W. W. Norton, 1997, 1382, 1384.

10. Farrell, James T. "Lynch Patterns." *Partisan Review* (May 4, 1938): 57–58.

11. Kinnamon, Keneth. *New Essays on Native Son.* New York: Cambridge University Press, 1990, 4.

12. Wright, Richard. "How 'Bigger' Was Born." In *Native Son: The Restored Text*. New York: Harper Perennial Classics, 2008, 454.

13. Howe, Irving. "Black Boys and Native Sons." In *A World More Attractive*. New York: Horizon, 1963, 98.

14. Wright, Richard. *Native Son: The Restored Text*. New York: Harper Perennial Classics, 2008, 6. All subsequent references are to this edition and page numbers are cited parenthetically after the quote.

15. Canby, Henry Seidel. "Review of *Native Son.*" *Book-of-the-Month Club News* (February 1940): 2.

16. Brown, Sterling. "Review of *Native Son.*" *Opportunity* (June 18, 1940): 185.

17. Hansen, Harry. "Review of *Native Son,*" *New York World-Telegram,* March 2, 1940, 17.

18. Jones, Howard Mumford. "Uneven Effect," *Boston Evening Transcript Book Section,* March 1, 1940, 1.

19. Cohn, David. "The Negro Novel: Richard Wright." *Atlantic Monthly* (May 1940): 660.

20. Daniels, Jonathan. "Review of *Native Son,*" *Richmond Times-Dispatch,* March 31, 1940, 13.

21. Lee, Charles. "Review of *Black Boy,*" *Philadelphia Record,* March 1, 1945, 20.

22. Prescott, Orville. "Review of *Black Boy,*" *New York Times,* February 28, 1945, 30.

23. Ellison, Ralph. "Richard Wright's Blues." *The Antioch Review* (Summer 1945): 5.

24. DuBois, W. E. B. "Richard Wright Looks Back," *New York Herald Tribune Weekly Book Review,* March 4, 1945, 2.

25. Burns, Ben. "Review of *Black Boy,*" *Chicago Defender,* March 3, 1945, 11.

26. Ivy, James. "American Hunger." *The Crisis* 52 (April 1945): 118.

27. Fabre, Michel. *The Unfinished Quest of Richard Wright.* New York: William Morrow, 1973, 294. All subsequent references are to this edition and page numbers are cited parenthetically after the quote.

28. Bontemps, Arna. "Review of *The Outsider,*" *Saturday Review,* March 28, 153, 15.

29. Rugoff, Milton. "Review of *The Outsider,*" *New York Herald Tribune Book Review,* March 22, 1953, 14.

30. Prescott, Orville. "Review of *The Outsider,*" *New York Times,* March 18, 1953, 29.

31. Hansberry, Lorraine. "Review of *The Outsider.*" *Freedom* (April 1953): 7.

32. Wright, Richard. *Savage Holiday.* Jackson: University Press of Mississippi, 1995, 34. All subsequent references are to this edition and page numbers are cited parenthetically after the quote.

33. Wright, Richard. *The Color Curtain: A Report on the Banding Conference.* Jackson: University Press of Mississippi, 1995, 219. All subsequent references are to this edition and page numbers are cited parenthetically after the quote.

34. Wright, Richard. *White Man, Listen!* Garden City, N.Y.: Doubleday, 1957, iv. All subsequent references are to this edition and page numbers are cited parenthetically after the quote.

35. Wright, Richard. *The Long Dream.* Chatham, N.J.: The Chatham Bookseller, 1969, 164. All subsequent references are to this edition and page numbers are cited parenthetically after the quote.

36. Howe, Irving. "Richard Wright: A Word of Farewell." *The New Republic* 114 (February 13, 1961): 17.

37. Redding, Saunders. "Richard Wright's Posthumous Stories," *New York Herald Tribune Book Review,* January 22, 1961, 33.

38. Gilman, Richard. "The Immediate Misfortunes of Widespread Sympathy." *Commonweal* (April 28, 1961): 130.

39. Rampersad, Arnold. "Too Honest for His Own Time," *The New York Times Book Review,* December 29, 1991, 3.

40. Wright, Richard. *Lawd Today.* Boston: Northeastern University Press, 1986, 201. All subsequent references are to this edition and page numbers are cited parenthetically after the quote.

41. Wright, Richard. *American Hunger.* New York: Harper and Row, 1977, 2. All subsequent references are to this edition and page numbers are cited parenthetically after the quote.

42. Wright, Richard. *Rite of Passage.* New York: HarperCollins, 1994, 115. All subsequent references are to this edition and page numbers are cited parenthetically after the quote.

43. Baldwin, James. *Nobody Knows My Name: More Notes of a Native Son.* New York: Dial Press, 1961, 149.

For Further Reading

Primary Sources

Uncle Tom's Children: Four Novellas (New York: Harper, 1938; London: Gollanz, 1939); enlarged as *Uncle Tom's Children: Five Long Stories* (New York: Harper, 1940; London: Gollanz, 1940).

Native Son. New York: Harper, 1940; London: Gollanz, 1940.

How "Bigger" Was Born. New York: Harper, 1940.

Native Son (The Biography of a Young American): A Play in Ten Scenes, by Wright and Paul Green (New York: Harper, 1941); revised by Green in *Black Drama, An Anthology,* edited by William Brasmer and Dominic Consola (Columbus, Ohio: Merrill, 1970), 70–178.

Twelve Million Black Voices: A Folk History of the Negro in the United States. New York: Viking, 1941; London: Drummond, 1947. Reprinted by Thunder's Mouth Press, 2002.

Black Boy: A Record of Childhood and Youth. New York: Harper, 1945; London: Gollanz, 1945.

The Outsider. New York: Harper, 1953; London: Angus and Robertson, 1953.

Savage Holiday. New York: Avon, 1954. Reprinted by University Press of Mississippi, 1994.

Black Power: A Record of Reactions in a Land of Pathos. New York: Harper, 1954. Reprinted by Harper Perennial, 1995.

The Color Curtain: A Report on the Bandung Conference. Cleveland: World, 1956; London: Dobson, 1956. Reprinted by University of Mississippi Press, 1994.

Pagan Spain: A Report on the Journey into the Past. New York: Harper, 1957; London: Bodley Head, 1960. Reprinted by Harper Perennial, 1995.

White Man, Listen! Garden City, N.Y.: Doubleday, 1957. Reprinted by Harper Perennial, 1995.

The Long Dream. Garden City, N.Y.: Doubleday, 1958; London: Angus and Robertson, 1960.

Eight Men. Cleveland: World, 1961. Reprinted by Harper Perennial, 1996.

Lawd Today! New York: Walker, 1963; London: Blond, 1965. Reprinted by Northeastern University Press, 1986.

American Hunger. New York: Harper and Row, 1977; London: Gollanz, 1978.

Richard Wright, Early Works: Lawd Today!, Uncle Tom's Children, and Native Son. New York: Library of America, 1991.

Richard Wright, Later Works: Black Boy/American Hunger, The Outsider. New York: Library of America, 1991.
Rite of Passage. New York: HarperCollins, 1994.
A Father's Law. New York: HarperCollins, 2008.

Play Productions

Native Son, by Wright and Paul Green, New York, St. James Theatre, March 24, 1941.
Daddy Goodness, by Wright and Louis Sapin, New York, St. Mark's Playhouse, June 4, 1968.

Screenplay

Native Son (Classic Films, 1951), screenplay by Wright.

Other

"The Ethics of Living Jim Crow, an Autobiographical Sketch." In *American Stuff: An Anthology of Prose & Verse* by Federal Writers' Project. New York: Viking Press, 1937, 39–52.
"I Tried to Be a Communist." In *The God That Failed*, edited by Richard Crossman. New York: Harper, 1950, 115–63.
"Introduction to George Padmore's *Pan Africanism or Communism?* London: Dobson, 1956.
"Five Episodes." In *Soon One Morning*, edited by Herbert Hill. New York: Knopf, 1963, 149–64.
"The American Problem—Its Negro Phase." In *Richard Wright: Impressions and Perspectives*, edited by David Ray and Robert Farnsworth. Ann Arbor: University of Michigan Press, 1973, 9–16.

Periodical Publications

"Blueprint for Negro Writing." *New Challenge II* (Fall 1937): 53–65.
"Not My People's War." *New Masses* 39, 13 (June 17, 1941): 8–9.
"US Negroes Greet You," *Daily Worker*, September 1, 1941, 7.
"Richard Wright Describes the Birth of *Black Boy*," *New York Post*, November 30, 1944, 36.
"Psychiatry Comes to Harlem." *Free World* 12 (September 1946): 49–51.
"How Jim Crow Feels." *True: The Man's Magazine* (November 1946): 25–27, 154–56.
"Urban Misery in an American City: Juvenile Delinquency in Harlem." *Twice a Year* 14–15 (Fall 1946–Winter 1947): 339–45.
"American Negroes in France." *The Crisis* 58 (June–July 1951): 381–83.
"The Shame of Chicago." *Ebony* 7 (December 1951): 24–32.
"Harlem." *Les Parisiens* 1 (December 1960): 23.

Bibliographies

Davis, Charles T. and Michel Fabre. *Richard Wright: A Primary Bibliography*. Boston: G. K. Hall, 1982.
Kinnamon, Keneth, with the help of Joseph Benson, Michel Fabre, and Craig Werner.

A Richard Wright Bibliography: Fifty Years of Commentary and Criticism, 1933–1982. Westport, Conn.: Greenwood Press, 1988.

Kinnamon, Keneth. *Richard Wright: An Annotated Bibliography of Criticism and Commentary, 1983–2003.* Jefferson, N.C.: McFarland and Sons, 2006.

Biographies

Fabre, Michel. *The Unfinished Quest of Richard Wright.* New York: Morrow, 1973.

Gayle, Addison, Jr. *Richard Wright: The Ordeal of a Native Son.* New York: Anchor Books, 1980.

Rowley, Hazel. *Richard Wright: The Life and Times.* New York: Henry Holt, 2001.

Walker, Margaret. *Richard Wright, Daemonic Genius: A Portrait of the Man and a Critical Look at His Work.* New York: Amistad, 1988.

Webb, Constance. *Richard Wright: A Biography.* New York: Putnam's, 1968.

Williams, John A. and Dorothy Sterling. *The Most Native of Sons: A Biography of Richard Wright.* Garden City, N.Y.: Doubleday, 1970.

Critical Studies

Baldwin, James. "Alas, Poor Richard." In *Nobody Knows My Name.* New York: Dial Press, 1961, 181–89.

———. "Everybody's Protest Novel." In *Notes of a Native Son.* Boston: Beacon, 1955, 85–114.

Bloom, Harold. *Bloom's Modern Critical Views: Richard Wright.* New York: Infobase Publishing, 2009.

———, ed. *Richard Wright.* New York: Chelsea House, 1987.

Butler, Robert. "The Loeb and Leopold Case: A Neglected Source for Richard Wright's *Native Son,*" *African American Review* (Winter 2005): 555–67.

———. *Native Son: The Emergence of a New Black Hero.* Boston: Twayne Publishers, 1991.

———. "Signifying and Self-Portraiture in Richard Wright's *A Father's Law.*" *College Language Association Journal* 51:1 (September 2008): 55–73.

———, ed. *The Critical Response to Richard Wright.* Westport, Conn.: Greenwood, 1995.

Callaloo 9 (Summer 1986): 21–30. [Issue devoted to Wright].

Capetti, Carla. "Sociology of an Existence: Richard Wright and the Chicago School." *MELUS* 12 (Summer 1985): 25–43.

Cayton, Horace. "Fear and Hunger in Black America," *Chicago Sun Book Week*, March 4, 1945, 3.

DuBois, W. E. B. "Richard Wright Looks Back," *New York Herald Tribune Weekly Book Review*, March 4, 1945, 2.

Ellison, Ralph. "Richard Wright's Blues." *The Antioch Review* (Summer 1945), 1–13.

Fabre, Michel. *Richard Wright: Books and Writers.* Jackson: University Press of Mississippi, 1990.

———. *The World of Richard Wright.* Jackson: University Press of Mississippi, 1985.

Gates, Henry Louis Jr., and K. A. Appiah, eds. *Richard Wright: Critical Perspectives Past and Present.* New York: Amistad, 1993.

Gibson, Donald B. "Wright's Invisible Native Son." *American Quarterly* 21 (Winter 1969): 728–39.

Graham, Maryemma. "Richard Wright." *Callaloo* 9 (Summer 1986): 21–30.

Green, Tara. "The Virgin Mary, Eve, and Mary Magdalene in Richard Wright's Novels." *College Language Association Journal* (December 2002): 168–93.

Griffiths, Frederick. "Ralph Ellison, Richard Wright and the Case of Angelo Herndon." *African American Review* 35 (Winter 2001): 615–36.

Hakutani,Yoshinobu. *Richard Wright and Racial Discourse.* Columbia: University of Missouri Press, 1996.

———, ed. *Critical Essays on Richard Wright.* Boston: G. K. Hall, 1982.

Higashida, Cheryl. "Aunt Sue's Children: Reviewing the Gender(ed) Politics of Richard Wright's Radicalism." *American Literature* 75, 2 (June 2003): 395–425.

Kinnamon, Keneth. *The Emergence of Richard Wright: A Study of Literature and Society.* Urbana: University of Illinois Press, 1972.

———. *New Essays on 'Native Son.'* New York: Cambridge University Press, 1990.

Kinnamon, Keneth and Michel Fabre. *Conversations with Richard Wright.* Jackson: University Press of Mississippi, 1993.

Miller, James, ed. *Approaches to Teaching Richard Wright's Native Son.* New York: Modern Language Association, 1997.

Mitchell, Hayley R., ed. *Readings on 'Native Son.'* San Diego: Green Haven Press, 2000.

Rampersad, Arnold. "Too Honest for His Own Time," *The New York Times Book Review*, December 29, 1991, 17–19.

Redding, Saunders. "Home Is Where the Heart Is." *The New Leader* 44 (December 11, 1961): 24–25.

Reilly, John. *Richard Wright: The Critical Reception.* New York: Burt Franklin, 1978.

Smethurst, James. "Invented by Horror: The Gothic and African American Literary Ideology in *Native Son.*" *African American Review* 35 (Spring 2001): 29–40.

Smith, Virginia Whatley, ed. *Richard Wright's Travel Writings: New Reflections.* Jackson: University Press of Mississippi, 2001.

Ward, Jerry W., Jr. "The Wright Critical Paradigm: Facing a Future." *Callaloo* 9 (Summer 1985): 25–43.

Ward, Jerry W., Jr. and Robert J. Butler. *The Richard Wright Encyclopedia.* Westport, Conn.: Greenwood Press, 2008.

Wertham, Albert. "An Unconscious Determinant in *Native Son.*" *Journal of Clinical Psychopathology and Psychotherapy* 6 (Winter 1944): 111–15.

Wright, Julia. "Introduction to *A Father's Law.*" In *A Father's Law.* New York: HarperCollins, 2008.

Papers

The major collection of Wright's papers is in the Richard Wright Archive in the Beinecke Rare Book and Manuscript Library at Yale University. A manuscript of *Black Power* is held at Northwestern University. Eighteen letters by Wright are collected at Kent State University. Many magazines and newspapers that include Wright's work are in the Schomburg Collection of the New York Public Library, the American Library in Paris, and the Harvard University libraries.

FRANK GARVIN YERBY
(September 5, 1916–November 29, 1991)
James L. Hill

From the Jim Crow section of Augusta, Georgia, to voluntary expatriation in Europe, from automobile plant technician during World War II to recipient of honorary doctorate degrees, from social protest writer in the 1940s to American King of the Costume Romance, and from Chicago Works Progress Administration (WPA) writers' colony to international celeb novelist translated into twenty-three languages, Frank Garvin Yerby did indeed make history both as an African American and American writer, becoming one of the most commercially successful and popular writers of the twentieth century. Seminal to each of these Yerby journeys were his work with the Federal Writers' Project in Chicago and his becoming acquainted with WPA writers and artists, including Richard Wright, Willard Motley, Margaret Walker, William Attaway, and Arna Bontemps, all of whom would eventually make their mark in American literature and help define the developing Black Chicago Renaissance. For Yerby, the Chicago WPA experience was an opportune apprenticeship, and as he told *Current Biography* in 1946, the brief period he spent with other Chicago Renaissance writers was the best literary training he had received.[1]

One of the most prolific writers of the twentieth century, Yerby was the first African American to write a best-selling novel and have a book purchased by a Hollywood studio for a film adaptation. During his prolific career as a writer, he published thirty-three novels between 1946 and 1985, almost one a year. Many of his novels were bestsellers and book club selections, and sales of his novels during his career totaled more than 62,000,000 copies hardback and paperback. Three of his early novels, *The Foxes of Harrow*, *The Golden Hawk*, and *The Saracen Blade*, were made into movies, and a fourth, *Bride of Liberty*, was adapted as a one-hour television show. According to Russell B. Nye in *The Unembarrassed Muse*, Yerby ranks as one of the five most popular writers of the second half of the twentieth century.[2] Despite these unprecedented achievements, however, Yerby never enjoyed the critical acclaim of many of his contemporaries of the Chicago Renaissance.

Frank Garvin Yerby, the second child and the first of three sons of Rufus Garvin and Wilhelmina (Smythe) Yerby, was born in Augusta, Georgia, on September 5, 1916. A well-established and influential black family in the Augusta community, the Yerbys lived in a two-story frame house on the corners of Eighth and Hall Streets, just outside the heart of Augusta's largest predominantly black residential area, "The Terry." Yerby's birth home, located originally at 1112 Eighth Street, has now been moved to the campus of Paine College, where it is being restored as a Yerby historic site. Rufus Yerby, the writer's father, worked as an itinerant hotel doorman in Miami and Detroit and traveled periodically to and from Augusta. Consequently, Yerby, his older sister, Ellena, and his two younger brothers, Paul and Alonza, were raised primarily by their mother, Wilhelmina, a former teacher, and by three aunts, Louise, Fannie, and Emily Symthe, who also were teachers.

As a young man, Yerby developed two strong propensities that occupied most of his time. At an early age, he became a voracious reader, and he also enjoyed tinkering with mechanical and electronic devices. Two interesting anecdotes about his early formative years are indicative of his boyhood penchant toward literacy. Sometimes when given money for lunch at school, he would save it until he accumulated enough to purchase a particular book he wanted, and Yerby frequently fabricated stories that he related to his aunts. Once, when he was reprimanded by his Aunt Emily for inventing stories, his Aunt Fannie remarked prophetically, "Oh, let him alone! He might be a writer some day."[3]

The Yerby children attended Haines Institute, then a private black school in Augusta with both elementary and high school grades, and now a public secondary school renamed Lucy Laney High School. Yerby quickly acquired a reputation among his classmates for being an avid reader and a studious youth. In an interview, Rebecca Zealey, one of his teachers at Haines, revealed that Yerby preferred reading to taking advantage of the school recess periods and sometimes had to be forced to go outside with the other students.[4] After graduation from Haines Institute, Yerby attended Paine College, a black undergraduate college in Augusta, where he majored in English and minored in foreign languages. While still an undergraduate, he transferred to the City College of New York; however, illness forced him to return to school in Augusta. At Paine, Yerby was active in the English Club and the Dramatics Club and was on the staff of the school newspaper, *The Paineite*. Pursuing his inclination toward the arts, he also assisted in the production of several plays and performed the lead role in *Hamlet*. Yerby in retrospect, however, remembered his high school and college days as unexciting, for as he said to Harvey Breit in 1951: "I was a fairly dreadful kind of student. Nonathletic, very studious, took scholastic honors, what the boys today would call a grind."[5]

It was during his early "dreadful school years" that Yerby developed an interest in writing. As early as his high school years, he showed promise as a writer and was encouraged by his teachers; and as a college student, he wrote short stories, poetry, and editorials for the school paper. Some of his first poems were published in "little magazines" such as *Challenge, Shard,* and *Arts Quarterly*; and in 1937, "Love Story," the first of nine short stories he published, appeared in *The Paineite.* He also cowrote the Paine College Alma Mater; and in collaboration with one faculty member, Miss Emma C. W. Gray, he wrote "March On," a historical pageant that celebrated the college's fiftieth anniversary, while also recounting the history of Black Americans and of Paine College. More significant encouragement for the aspiring writer came, however, from a well-known black writer. "The late James Weldon Johnson," Yerby said in *Current Biography,* "approved some verses of mine shown to him by my sister, then a student at Fisk University."[6]

With this type of encouragement, Yerby continued to develop his writing skills, periodically publishing poetry and short stories. After graduation from Paine in 1937, he headed to graduate school at Fisk University, and one of the ambitions he expressed as he prepared to leave Paine was the desire to walk down the aisle of his Alma Mater in doctoral regalia. At this too he almost succeeded. In 1977, Paine College invited Yerby to serve as its Spring Commencement speaker, and at the commencement, his Alma Mater conferred on him an honorary Doctorate of Humane Letters. That same year, Yerby also became an honorary citizen of the State of Tennessee by Governor's Proclamation.

Yerby continued his development as a writer at Fisk, publishing two stories, "A Date with Vera" and "Young Man Afraid," in the *Fisk Herald* in 1937. The former story focuses on race relations in the South and North, while the latter is introspective, exploring a youth's fear of death after an automobile accident. At Fisk, Yerby majored in English, was active in the Little Theater group, and wrote and produced several plays, one of which toured several states on the Little Theater Circuit. Additionally, he wrote his master's thesis, "The Little Theatre in the Negro College," under the direction of noted scholar Lorenzo D. Turner. After receiving his Master of Arts degree in Dramatic Arts in 1938 at the age of twenty-one, Yerby enrolled in the University of Chicago to pursue a doctorate degree in English.

The American South in general and the Augusta community in particular greatly influenced some of Yerby's early convictions, shaping him in at least two distinctly different ways. Typical then of the racial climate of most towns of its size in the Deep South, Yerby's hometown Augusta was controlled politically by the Cracker Party, a local reactionary political organization in power; and as in other Southern communities, segregation and social and economic oppression of blacks were the order of the day. Favorably, Yerby spent the first twenty years of his life in Augusta and gained a firsthand knowledge of Southern mores and customs—the subject he eventually chose for much of his fiction. While living in the South shaped the realistic perspective from which he views the traditions and culture of the South, Yerby was, on the other hand, adversely affected by the South's racism and segregation. He was fortunate enough to have avoided working in the Augusta community, unlike many Paine College students did, thus escaping some of the harsher realities of racial discrimination then prevalent in Augusta.

Yerby did not, however, totally escape the indignities of black life in the Jim Crow South. Occasionally, he received affronting stares from whites when he and his lighter complexioned sister Ellena were together; and as he told this author in a letter,[7] the police in several Southern states and even in the state of New York harassed him when they mistakenly thought his first wife, Flora Helen Claire, was white. Indeed, the first twenty years of Yerby's life in the South may well have been as he describes them in a letter to the author: "I lived (existed is a better word, for I dwelt spiritually an alien and a stranger, in a totally foreign land) in Augusta, from 1916 to 1936."[8] Yerby eventually migrated to the North to escape the harsh realities of Southern life; and in the same letter, he indicates his attitude toward the South: "I was fed to the backeye teeth with Augusta, and the South, and believed (poor young fool that I was!) that the North would be better."[9] Subsequently, Yerby's attitude about life in the South became a powerful motivation in his literary decision to chronicle the inglorious legends of the "Old South."

Although he migrated to Chicago in 1938 to continue his education, Yerby could not have chosen a more propitious time to arrive in the "Windy City." As the famed Harlem Renaissance was winding down, Michael Flug observes, a new cultural flowering was erupting on the South Side of Chicago, more commonly known as Bronzeville. Fueled by the Great Migration and the Great Depression that followed, Flug continues, the new "Chicago Renaissance"—the term was coined decades later—produced startling developments in literature, art, music, social science, and journalism.[10] Among the many emerging African American literary talents that helped shape the 1930s and 1940s Chicago Renaissance were Richard Wright, Frank Yerby, Arna Bontemps, Frank Marshall Davis, Marita Bonner, Gwendolyn Brooks, Margaret Walker, Willard Motley, Theodore Ward, Fenton Johnson, and John H. Johnson. "What they did not dream," Arna Bontemps observed, "was that a second awakening, less gaudy but closer to realities, was already in prospect."[11] In *Bronzeville: Black Chicago in Pictures, 1941–1943*, Maren Stange identifies several overlapping groups that nurtured and supported the Chicago Renaissance; and included among these groups were the South Side Writers Project, variously led by Richard Wright and Margaret Walker, and the Illinois Writers' Project, which included the celebrated Negro in Illinois Project directed by Bontemps and employing Wright,

Katherine Dunham, and others.[12] As part of the "Negro in Illinois Project," Yerby worked for a while with a group of writers supervised by Dunham.

During his stint with the Chicago Renaissance writers, Yerby also wrote and published his fourth short story "The Thunder of God." Published in *The New Anvil* in 1939, "The Thunder of God" is set in Yerby's hometown of Augusta, Georgia, and depicts black life and social conditions of the period. The story incorporates Augusta's great flood of 1939 as a backdrop, and narrated by a young man enrolled at Haines Institute, it describes the scene of torrent rain and a rising river threatening to break the levee and flood the entire city. Two white policemen have corralled young men from Haines Institute to help control the levee, and the police force the Haines students and other black men at gunpoint to work the levee, repairing it wherever it breaks. While they prevent destruction of white neighborhoods, the men are forced to watch their own neighborhoods being flooded and destroyed. Only the divine intervention of a loud clap of thunder and accompanying lightning extricates the men from this tense situation. Lightning strikes the levee, killing some of the men and leaving the white boss who held the men at gunpoint hanging onto the broken levee and screaming for help. The other men make no attempt to save the white boss, and as the river swiftly carries him away, they leave the levee, walking though the flooded streets of their town.

Yerby was with the Chicago WPA, however, for only nine months. Financial problems forced him to discontinue his education and leave Chicago in search of a teaching position, but his early departure may also have resulted in part, as Arna Bontemps suggested, from his being overly conscious of the subtle racism to which WPAers were occasionally subjected. Yerby's discontinuance of his education in Chicago may also, however, have been providential. Second-guessing his fate years later, he said in retrospect: "Had I gotten the degree, I'd probably still be stuck in some small school teaching."[13]

Yerby's departure from Chicago in 1939 took him back to the South. On June 12, 1939, he accepted a teaching position in the Department of English at Florida A&M University, and from 1939 to 1941, he worked as an English professor, one year in Tallahassee, Florida, and a subsequent year at Southern University in Baton Rouge, Louisiana. Additionally, pursuing his interest in black college theater developed during his undergraduate and graduate school experiences, Yerby also published "Problems Confronting the Little Theater in the Negro College" in the *Quarterly Journal of Florida A & M University*, and "A Brief Historical Sketch of the Little Theater in the Negro College" in the *Southern University Bulletin*. While he was teaching at Florida A&M University, Yerby met Flora Helen Claire Williams, and after he relocated to Louisiana the next year, the two were married on March 1, 1941. At the end of the year, Yerby left his teaching position and with his wife moved to New York. In New York, however, he experienced difficulty securing a job and moved several months later to Detroit, where he found work as a laboratory technician in the Ford Motor Company's Dearborn, Michigan, plant. Working in Michigan from 1942 through 1944, Yerby again found time to be creative and renewed his lagging interest in writing, working on a serious novel and several short stories, all of which were influenced by his experiences among Chicago Renaissance writers.

In June, 1944, the Yerbys and their three children, Jacques Loring, Nikki Ethlyn, and Faune Ellena, moved to Long Island, New York, as Yerby began work at Ranger (Fairchild) Aircraft in Jamaica, New York. In the Long Island community where Yerby lived, he again encountered racism. The first few months his family lived in the Valley Stream community were entirely peaceful; but his neighbors, who offered information and assistance, apparently did not know that the light-skinned Yerbys were the only blacks in the neighborhood. Several months later, the quietude was disrupted when a black friend began visiting the Yerbys, leading to the Valley Stream neighbors' discovery of the racial heritage of the Yerbys. Immediately, Yerby and his family became outcasts in the community. Some neighbors threatened them, ostracized them, and offered to buy their house at triple its value. However, in 1946 when Yerby published his first novel, which he had completed while continuing to work at the aircraft factory, the accompanying publicity caused a change of heart in the community. The Yerbys were showered with apologies, and after the writer deposited $150,000 in a local bank some months later, the Yerbys became the community's favorite citizens. Despite protestations from his Valley Stream neighbors, Yerby chose to move to Jackson Heights, Queens, where in 1950 the family was expanded by the birth of Jan Keith, Yerby's second son.

Although he began writing as early as age seventeen, Yerby actually began his professional career as a writer in the 1940s. From 1944 to 1946, while living and working in Dearborn, Michigan, and New York, he published five of his most popular and frequently anthologized short stories; and he wrote a social protest novel that he submitted to a *Redbook* literary contest. A protest story about a Northern black steel mill worker turned professional boxer, the novel explored discrimination and injustices against blacks in the North. *Redbook* editors rejected Yerby's novel but not without encouragement. In a letter to this author, Yerby said that *Redbook*'s Muriel Fuller wrote: "This is a lousy novel, but you sure can write! Send me something else."[14] The "something else" was an early story by Yerby entitled "Health Card"; but deciding that it was not *Redbook*'s kind of material, Fuller sent "Health Card" to *Harper's* magazine, where it was published in 1944, and became Yerby's first nationally publicized short story, eventually winning the O. Henry Memorial Award for the best short story of the year. "Health Card," like Yerby's protest novel written in the Richard Wright tradition of social protest, is a narrative about the injustices visited upon a black couple by the military police. In "Health Card," the military police harass Johnny Green and his wife because they automatically assume that Green's wife is a prostitute and demand to see her health card. In addition to providing Yerby his first national recognition, "Health Card" also brought Yerby invitations from other publishers.

Like "Health Card," Yerby's other published short stories focus on the mistreatment of blacks as they seek to negotiate racially hostile environments. "White Magnolias," published in *Phylon* in 1944, explores the incongruities between the myths and realities of the customs of the Old South, but in addition to its import as a social protest story, it actually prefigures Yerby's historical novels. Racial conflict arises in "White Magnolias" when a Southern white girl, Beth Thomas, invites black Fisk graduate Hannah Summers to afternoon tea. Having met previously at an interracial conference in the North, Hannah and Beth have initiated a friendship, which is forbidden by Southern social conventions. "Roads Going Down" and "The Homecoming" were published in the Summer 1945 and Spring 1946 issues of *Common Ground*, respectively, and both stories depict racial and social circumscription of black life in the South. In "Roads Going Down," similar in theme and incident to Wright's "Big Boy Leaves Home," Robert is forced to leave home after accidentally intruding on nude whites who are swimming. "Homecoming," like "Health Card," explores the racial indignities that a black soldier suffers. When Sergeant Willie Green returns home after fighting in World War II, he is expected to resubmit to the oppressive racial conventions of the South, an expectation he finds unacceptable. In "The Homecoming," Green says: "I done fought and been most killed and now I'm a man. Can't be a boy no more. Nobody's boy."[15]

In 1946, Yerby's last published short story, "My Brother Went to College," appeared in *Tomorrow*. "My Brother Went to College" depicts the lives of two brothers who took different paths, one a quest to find complete freedom and the other a quest for materialistic success. The narrator of the story, Mark Johnson, has spent the past ten years wandering across the country in search of an elusive freedom, and his brother, Matthew Johnson, has achieved his goal of becoming a successful, reputable physician. Happily reunited, the brothers reexamine their paths in life. Although he realizes the severe restrictions that middle-class life places on his brother Matthew, Mark is impressed with the luxuries of Matthew's middle-class life and eventually gravitates toward his brother's path to success. Contrary to popular opinion, however, "My Brother Went to College" was not the last social protest story Yerby wrote; he continued to write protest stories until the midfifties, although they remain unpublished. Yerby's identity as a popular writer, his publishers, his expanding literary interests, and perhaps even his earlier antiprotest stance—all seem to have conspired to keep him from actually publishing more protest stories.

The formative years of Yerby's development as a writer, including his WPA and Chicago Renaissance days, undeniably shaped his perspective. Like most African American writers of his era in America, Frank Yerby began his career writing protest stories, and like other writers, he illustrates in his stories the imposition of social and racial conventions on the lives of Black Americans and the limited responses available to them. His characters are alienated socially, economically, and politically from mainstream American life, cumulatively emphasizing their marginality. While the South as subject is as important in most of his short stories as it would become in his costume novels, his stories are more overtly racial and are written from the perspective of an embittered Black American. In fact, along with contemporaries such as Richard Wright, Ann Petry, Chester Himes, John Henrik Clark, and Ralph Ellison, Yerby contributed to a significant transition in the development of short stories written by African American writers. First, in the late thirties and early forties, African American writers collectively eliminated pathos from black protest stories and introduced new themes and insights; and second, in addition to *The Crisis* and *Opportunity*, which served as the major proving grounds for black writers, these writers found acceptance for their stories in some mainstream publications. Although Yerby had previously published in "little magazines" as a teenager, it is significant that most of his racial protest stories were published in the forties, a period in American letters when mainstream publications generally became more liberal in their acceptance of stories by black writers.

In fact, it was social protest fiction that actually prompted Yerby's entrée into the world of the new vogue of historical romance popularized in the thirties. After his first attempt to publish a protest novel failed, Yerby decided he could best employ his talents as a writer in another arena of fiction; and deserting the ranks of black protest writers, he turned to historical fiction. When he talked with George Joel of Dial Press, the only publisher who had shown any interest in his protest novel, Yerby convinced Joel to let him try writing a historical novel. On the basis of twenty-seven pages Yerby wrote one night after working twelve hours in a Long Island airplane plant, Joel gave him a book advance of $250. The result was, of course, the popular, widely read historical novel *The Foxes of Harrow.* Thus began Yerby's long and profitable relationship with Dial Press. Explaining his transition to popular fiction in "How and Why I Write the Costume Novel" in *Harper's* in 1959, Yerby commented: "The idea dawned on me that to continue to follow the route I had mapped out for myself was roughly analogous to shouting one's head off in Mammoth Cave."[16] Though his novels are set in historical periods and based on historical data, Yerby prefers to call them costume novels, and in the *Harper's* article, he defines the costume novel as a genre of light, pleasant fiction intended merely to entertain. Notwithstanding Yerby's entertainment declaration, his novels are intentionally written both to entertain and instruct.

In 1946 with the publication of his first novel, *The Foxes of Harrow*, Yerby made an abrupt transition from protest to popular fiction writer, prompting many of his contemporaries to question his motives. With the success of "Health Card," they reasoned, why did Yerby abandon protest fiction? Initially, Yerby responded that he was not equipped to write protest fiction; however, his real motivations no doubt lay somewhere between the economics of publishing and his desire to succeed as a writer. Despite the misgivings of some about his venture into popular fiction, the reception of *The Foxes of Harrow* brought Yerby immediate success never before equaled by an African American writer; and the popularity of the book reached unprecedented heights for a novel written by an African American. Within two months, *The Foxes of Harrow* sold over 500,000 copies, and by the end of 1946, its sales had exceeded one million copies. Additionally, the novel was reprinted in condensed form in *Negro Digest*, *Omnibook*, and *Liberty*. Twentieth Century Fox purchased the screen rights for the novel and sought internationally known actors to portray the roles. Though Yerby did not particularly like the film version of his novel, *The Foxes of Harrow* became his passport to national prominence, to the "fast lane" in American popular fiction and to unparalleled literary success, however jaded. Additionally, *The Foxes of Harrow* is historically important because it established a commercially successful formula for Yerby's novels and set the stage for his reception in the United States.

Covering the historical period from 1825–65, *The Foxes of Harrow* relates the story of Stephen Fox, an Irish immigrant and gambler who rises from poverty to wealth in New Orleans. After marrying into an aristocratic Creole family, Fox sets out to become a wealthy man. Between 1825 and 1865, he succeeds in becoming the owner of two huge plantations and amasses a fortune from gambling, conniving, working his slaves, and selling cotton. Fox, however, is an outcast who gains recognition in aristocratic New Orleans society but remains on the margins of that society, because he neither shares its beliefs nor conforms to the traditions of the South. In fact, Fox espouses political views that reflect a national perspective, not the regional perspective of the South; and in actuality, Fox becomes the prototype for subsequent Yerby protagonists.

Like many writers of first novels in the popular fiction genre, Yerby establishes an identifiable fiction formula in *The Foxes of Harrow*, one he replicates variously but consistently in subsequent novels. Amid the trappings and conventions of the Southern historical romance, Yerby's first novel introduces a fictional pattern that generally includes 1) a protagonist who is alienated from society by misfortunes of birth or personal convictions, 2) a villainous antagonist, 3) a loyal companion or friend who understands and aids the protagonist, 4) several beautiful women who are attracted to the protagonist, 5) one or more oppressed minority groups—blacks, poor whites, slaves, serfs, etc., and 6) a significant historical focus—an important historical event or issue. Cementing the ingredients of Yerby's success formula are an adventurous protagonist, ex-teriorized conflict, and literary sex. In *The Foxes of Harrow*, as indeed in many of his subsequent novels, Yerby portrays characters who resemble the common person, even as their bizarre exploits, fascinating sex lives, heroic struggles, and efforts to gain respect and make a name for themselves exact the suspension of the reader's disbelief.

Critical reactions to *The Foxes of Harrow* and Yerby as a new author were generally favorable. When the sales of the novel skyrocketed in 1946, Yerby emerged overnight as a successful American writer. Immediately, many black intellectuals and writers concluded that Yerby, because of his success in popular fiction, possessed the potential for championing the cause of racial justice to the masses of the American public. They pointed to his talent and lauded his achievement as a black pioneer in the arena of popular fiction, but they were cautious. In the *Chicago Sun Book Week*, Arna Bontemps described Yerby's achievement as a significant first but concluded that Yerby was actually stifling his talent by restricting his writing to popular fiction.[17] Similarly, in *Phylon* in 1948, Alain Locke praised Yerby's ability to free himself of the conventional confinement to racial themes,[18] but like other black intellectuals, he hoped that Yerby would turn his attention to social issues. Thus, while not actually satisfied with Yerby's choice of subject matter in *The Foxes of Harrow*, most black intel-lectuals and writers were generous in their reviews of the novel; at least they reserved their judgment.

White critics' reviews of *The Foxes of Harrow* were more mixed but also gen-erally favorable. In the *New York Herald Tribune*, for example, Hartnett Kane said: "This first novel indicates that Mr. Yerby has talent, a way with words. He needs, primarily, restraint."[19] Some reviewers concluded, however, that Yerby's first novel amassed all of the stock characters and situations found in Southern historical romance novels, including the picaresque adventure, fragile but beau-tiful women, gambling and dueling, and the idyllic romance of the Southern plantation. Another critic in the *New Yorker* said: "Mr. Yerby has packed ev-erything in—passion, politics, Creole society, sex, the clashes of the races, and war—but he never captures the faintest flutter of the breath of life."[20] Although some reviewers criticized *The Foxes of Harrow* as mediocre fiction, most were optimistic and lauded Yerby's trailblazing performance as a black author, sug-gesting that it was soon to pass judgment on him.

Shortly after the publication of *The Foxes of Harrow*, Yerby announced that he was working on a second novel about Reconstruction in the South, and black and white intellectuals and critics alike awaited the publication of his second major literary effort. Written initially under the title "Ignoble Victory" but published as *The Vixens* (1947), Yerby's second novel was a sequel to *The Foxes of Harrow* and tilled the same historical materials Yerby used in his first novel. Set during the years 1866–74, *The Vixens* focuses on Reconstruction politics in the South. Laird Fournois, son of a Creole planter, returns to New Orleans after fighting with the Union Army during the Civil War. Typical of Yerby protagonists, he enjoys acceptance in New Orleans society but remains an outcast. At the end of the novel, he rejects the South and goes to the North in search of a better life. *The Vixens* enjoyed a reception similar to that of *The Foxes of Harrow*. While it too made the bestseller list, the major significance of this novel for white reviewers was Yerby's continued success in popular fiction. "What gives *The Vixens* special interest," one reviewer said in a 1947 *Time* article, "is the fact that its author is the first Negro to make an unqualified success in the slick-writing field."[21] For black intellectuals, however, it was still too soon to judge Yerby. Though *The Vixens* followed the fiction pattern established in *The Foxes of Harrow*, they still harbored other expectations for the young, black successful author who had become, temporarily, a heroic symbol. For some, Yerby's second novel had an even greater significance. Touting the significance of Yerby's achievement, Hugh Gloster asserted in *The Crisis* that Yerby's success demonstrated the black writer's ability to "shake himself free of the shackles of race and to use the treasure trove of American experience. . . ."[22]

The real test of Yerby's significance as a symbol depended, however, on the publication of subsequent novels. Like other popular fiction writers who break into print, Yerby continued to adhere to his proven fictional blueprint established in *The Foxes of Harrow*, and reviews of his subsequent novels primarily emphasized the extent to which he adapted and manipulated the conventions of popular fiction. In the *New York Times*, one reviewer of *The Golden Hawk* (1948) said: "Certainly, Mr Yerby's roaring prose belongs in a cartoon balloon, rather than between the covers of a full-priced novel."[23] Published in 1949, *Pride's Castle* had a similar reception, and a *Chicago Sun* reviewer concluded that Yerby's fifth novel, *Floodtide* (1950), showed little artistry.[24] Although most magazine and newspaper reviewers routinely conceded that Yerby would probably continue to be successful and praised the black writer who could perform consistently in popular fiction, the aura of success surrounding Yerby was already losing its luster. Reviewers showed signs of becoming weary of Yerby's costume formula and found little social relevance in his writing.

For black intellectuals, however, the heroic symbolism associated with Yerby's achievement in popular fiction died much sooner. Though black intellectuals had hoped that Yerby, once established, would produce fiction that commented on contemporary social issues, Yerby steadfastly maintained his apolitical stance, refusing to embrace racial ideology or lend the prestige of his name or stature to racial causes. Yerby's refusal to embrace racial ideology in his writing was unacceptable, and black intellectuals soon discarded the early heroic symbolism associated with his career. The comments of noted scholar Darwin T. Turner in a 1968 *Massachusetts Review* article appropriately describe the eclipse of the Yerby's symbolic image: "Yerby did not prove effective as a symbol. He refused to plead for the race; he abandoned America without shrieking that bigotry exiled him from home; he earned a fortune writing books, and spent his time racing sportscars and lolling on beaches. So corpulent an achiever of the American dream can never personify the Negro intellectual, for the charm of the symbol is its aura of failure."[25]

Published in 1951, a pivotal time in the development of Yerby's career, *A Woman Called Fancy* is his sixth novel and his first with a female as the central character. Set in Yerby's hometown of Augusta, Georgia, the novel covers the period from 1880 to 1894 and traces the life of Fancy Williamson, a beautiful woman from the hills of South Carolina who rises from poverty to prominence among aristocrats in Augusta. Like other Yerby protagonists, Fancy is an outcast, and Yerby devotes most of the novel to her rise in society. In his portrayal of Fancy, however, he emphasizes pointedly the ignoble origins of most Southern aristocrats. Not only does Fancy symbolize the accepted ideals of southerners; she in fact possesses nobler qualities than the southerners with whom she aspires to identify. Significantly, the year following his publication of *A Woman Called Fancy*, Yerby concluded that he had firmly established himself as a productive writer, and he quietly left America for France.

Unlike some black expatriates who decried American racism upon their departure, Yerby created no fanfare; however, his voluntary exile should not have been a surprise. A year earlier in *A Woman Called Fancy*, he had already declared his feelings about living in America. A sympathetic white character in the novel states:

> I have to admit that blacks and whites can't really live together. Not now, not ever. A Negro is just too damned physically, visibly different from a white man. Notice I said physically. I've known black boys who were in the first rank intellectually, which makes life damned miserable for them, the poor bastards, . . . What do you think it does to a bright boy to know it would cost him his life if he ever reared up on his haunches and acted like a man? Being bought and sold like mules did something to them. And even after that was over, the system we worked out to bolster up our uncertain vanities kept up the dirty work. It's like Dred was saying: you don't ever call a black man, "Mister." Up to forty-five, he's a "boy"; and after that he's "Uncle." The ones you know, you call by their first name—no matter how slightly you know 'em. The women are Mary Jane while they're young, and after that they're "Mammy" or "Antie." We carry the thing even to such extremes of pure damned pettiness. We put them in places like the Terry and keep them there. We deny them anything like comfort. Heck, we've

got it fixed so they don't even get enough to eat. Then, when they rear up and act like the beasts we've made of them, we lynch them with a barbaric savagery that would disgrace a Sioux.[26]

It seems clear that Yerby considered himself one of those intelligent blacks; thus his expatriation. Though his quiet abandoning of the United States was directly related to its racial situation, Yerby resolved politically to ignore the issue of race altogether. Understanding the pettiness of American racism, he decided that prejudice based on the color of one's skin is totally irrational; and in his 1969 *Ebony* interview with Hoyt Fuller, he stated his unwillingness to tolerate racism:

> To put it as an oversimplification, I just don't have time to waste on such nonsensical questions as casing a joint, or this or that restaurant to find out whether I will go in there and sit for three hours before some stupid ass of a waitress comes to spill a glass of water down my neck. I just don't have time. It's ridiculous. I should, if I were a combative, courageous-type militant who would put himself at the front of The Movement and go out and get himself shot in the belly a couple of times to advance things. So, I'm a coward. Let's face it.[27]

Like other African American expatriates—Richard Wright, Chester Himes, and James Baldwin—Yerby left the United States to escape the psychological burden of racism and find refuge from racism in a foreign land, a goal he later concluded was impossible. Yerby's exile from the United States was, too, a logical extension of his refusal to make race the central focus of his fiction. Unlike other African American expatriates, he was not prepared to commit his fiction to racial causes, and in a 1968 *Detroit News and Times* interview, he admitted his compromise:

> If I'd stayed here, I would have been forced by emotional pressures to write about race, to write propaganda. I was arrested once for walking down the street with my sister; her skin is lighter than mine. I was unwilling to put up with a million annoyances here. I wanted to be able to write without thinking about race or politics or religion. I wanted to be able to write without rage.[28]

After leaving the United States, Yerby and his family settled in France, where he continued to write and develop his hobbies, including deep sea diving, sports car racing, and tinkering with electronic devices. Living in Nice on the Riviera, the Yerbys traveled extensively in Europe, while their children attended school in Switzerland. Traveling also afforded Yerby opportunities to gather historical data for future novels. During this period, however, he began having marital problems, and his wife and children returned to the States. In July 1956, his wife Flora Claire Helen filed for divorce in Mobile, Alabama, charging that Yerby had abandoned her in February 1955. The divorce was finalized in 1956.

While separated from his wife in 1955, Yerby met the woman who eventually became his second wife. During one of his visits to Madrid to see a friend in April 1955, Yerby met Blanquita Calle-Perez, a secretary employed at an American military corporation in Spain. Although born in Spain, Blanquita had spent her childhood in France, where she learned French before she completely mastered her native language. Several months after she met Yerby, she resigned her job to go to Italy to work, but Yerby became desperately ill and had to be hospitalized. Showing her devotion to him, she scarcely left his side until he recovered. They were married a year later on July 27, 1956, in Mexico City and honeymooned in Acapulco. Subsequently, Blanquita Calle-Perez became her husband's secretary, translator, researcher, and general manager.

Following his marriage to Blánquita in 1956, Yerby returned to the United States with his new bride. Unaccustomed to the racial climate in America, his wife was extremely disturbed by the open hostility and curiosity white Americans displayed toward them. Yerby, however, was less perturbed by the inquisitiveness of Americans. Recalling their visit to the United States thirteen years later, he explained his views to Hoyt Fuller in the 1966 *Ebony* article: "Why do I have to have such things as to walk down the street with my wife and have somebody bump into a lamp post looking at us? Nonsense. I don't have to put up with this. Why? One of the inalienable rights is that of the pursuit of happiness, and as of now, well, I've never been particularly happy in the States. So, I will probably visit the States with increasing frequency from now on, but to live there, I don't think so. . . ."[29]

Thus, Yerby's attitude toward living in the United States had not changed. Though he visited the United States on a number of other occasions, he concluded that he would never return to live permanently in his country. After 1956, Frank and Blanquita Yerby lived only in Madrid, Spain, where they owned a house in a neighborhood on the outskirts of the city. Although their marriage produced no children, it was a very satisfying union according to Yerby.

Although the sales of Yerby's novels did not indicate it, serious critical attention to Yerby's fiction was already waning by the midfifties. Black intellectuals and writers had accepted the fact that Yerby would remain oblivious to contemporary social issues, and they devoted little attention to his writings. White reviewers, on the other hand, could not so easily dispose of Yerby, for he continued to produce best-selling novels. However differently assessed by reviewers, Yerby's literary productivity exemplified the makings of a legend in the publishing industry, especially for an African American writer. In general, therefore, reviewers continued to track Yerby's successive best-sellers and expertly analyzed his magic formula in such novels as *A Woman Called Fancy* (1951), *The Saracen Blade* (1952), *Bride of Liberty* (1954), and *The Treasure of Pleasant Valley* (1955). Sometimes they criticized Yerby's failure to depart from his well-established fiction formula, finding little redeeming value in his novels; other times they labeled him a pulpster writing only for the money. Of the novels Yerby published in the last half of the fifties, *Fairoaks* (1957) received more critical acclaim than *Captain Rebel* (1956), *The Serpent and the Staff* (1958), or *Jarrett's Jade* (1959). In the *Chicago Tribune* (August 25, 1957), William Yates called *Fairoaks* "Yerby's most ambitious novel, his best by far. . . ."[30] Yet in leading newspapers and magazines, especially the *New York Times*, there was a noticeable decrease in the import, regularity, and length of reviews of Yerby's novels.

Though Yerby had indicated an interest in writing more serious fiction as early as 1949, it was not until the sixties that he became noticeably concerned about the critical reception of his novels. Perhaps it was his own doubts about his place in the literary canon, his concern for his literary reputation, his increased artistic consciousness or all three combined, but in the sixties, Yerby demonstrated greater concern about the quality of his novels. The precipitous decline in his reputation as a popular novelist in the sixties also concerned his publishers. While his publishers were more interested in the sales of his novels, Yerby was no longer satisfied just to write novels. In a letter to his editors, he not only expressed displeasure with Dial Press' editorial policies but also with the promotion and critical reception of his novels. His suspicions about the decline in the reception of his novels were indeed well-founded. After routine reviews of *The Garfield Honor* (1961) and *Griffin's Way* (1962), the *New York Times* generally omitted reviews of his works until the publication of *Judas, My Brother* in 1968. Thus, the lack of serious critical consideration of Yerby's novels in the late fifties and sixties is directly related to his recurrent use of his fiction formula and less significant novels.

In addition to less significant novels, however, one of the more persistent veins of critical opinion about Yerby's fiction, especially among African Americans, was that he provided little or no interpretation of black life. A closer examination of his novels, however, reveals evidence to the contrary. Although Yerby purposefully avoided writing overtly about contemporary racial issues in his fiction during the first two decades of his career, he did not completely omit commentary on race. A substantial number of Yerby's novels focus on historical periods before, during, and after the Civil War, and there are numerous images of blacks in the historical contexts of these novels, i.e., slaves, house servants, field workers, stablemen, breeders, slave children, and freedmen. Additionally, there are negative images of blacks that have historical significance, including servile, cringing slaves and slaves betraying their fellow slaves. In the panorama of images of blacks in Yerby's fiction, however, it is not difficult to distinguish positive black images and history-bound images, positive or negative; and any careful evaluation of the images of blacks in Yerby's fiction reveals more positive black images than critics have acknowledged. In fact, in his survey of American best-sellers written between 1900–1960, Donald Baker cites Yerby as one of only a few novelists who provide positive images of blacks.[31]

In *The Foxes of Harrow*, for example, La Belle Sauvauge is a rebellious slave, but Yerby chooses to portray her as a dignified and noble character, one who refuses to submit to the inferior role of the slave. Depicted as a paragon of virtue in *The Foxes of Harrow*, Inchcliff becomes a respected leader of his people during Reconstruction in the sequel *The Vixens*. In *Griffin's Way*, there is further evidence of the progressive development in Yerby's depiction of black characters. The most important black character in this novel is Dr. Bruce Randolph, an idealistic Harvard graduate who comes to the South to educate his people and eventually becomes a dedicated black leader. Positive and socially relevant images of blacks in *Benton's Row* are evident as Yerby chronicles four generations of the white Benton family from 1842–92; using the literary technique of parallel characters, Yerby depicts positive images of black characters juxtaposed to each of the white male successors of the Benton family. Additionally, black physician Mose Johnson is the literary double for Duncan Childers, the protagonist and white physician in *The Serpent and the Staff*. In fact, most of Yerby's novels of the South incorporate a secondary plot that usually depicts positive images of blacks, often in juxtaposition or in stark contrast to white characters.

Yerby's growing concern with his reputation in the 1960s also spawned his interest in writing about contemporary issues. Though he did not participate, Yerby followed the Civil Rights Movement closely, and the turbulent sixties affected him personally. Consequently, the sixties were the impetus for what Yerby calls one of his best novels. In 1963, he wrote "The Tents of Shem," a Civil Rights novel about a black family that integrates an all-white neighborhood. When his publishers rejected "The Tents of Shem," he revised the novel and submitted it again in 1969; however, it is still unpublished. Neither Yerby nor his publishers ever explained why "The Tents of Shem" was not published. It is quite probable, however, that Yerby's editors decided that the novel lacked the popular appeal of his previous novels and that it would damage his noncontroversial image. Despite the fate of "The Tents of Shem," Yerby's newfound willingness to demonstrate race consciousness in his writing subsequently influenced his writing of two of his most important novels, *Speak Now* (1969) and *The Dahomean* (1971).

Motivated by the amelioration of racial conditions in the United States during the sixties, Yerby concluded that the climate for the reception of novels about race had improved; and in *Speak Now* and *The Dahomean*, he abandons his apolitical stance on race, focusing on an African American and an African protagonist, respectively. As indications of Yerby's increased willingness to demonstrate his racial consciousness, *Speak Now* and *The Dahomean* present different aspects of black history, many of which Yerby had actually presented in previous novels. Reviewers of *Speak Now* were quick to point out that Yerby deserted the historical romance genre, although it is not Yerby's first contemporary novel; but some critics found Yerby's contemporary novel a welcomed departure from the historical romance. One *New York Times* (Nov. 30, 1969) reviewer, noting Yerby's treatment of his first black protagonist, said: "Harry's peppery convictions are welcomed seasoning for the saintly role he plays in the novel. I hope we have not seen the last of him."[32]

A restatement of some of the racial themes addressed in "The Tents of Shem," *Speak Now* is a contemporary novel about Harry Forbes, a black musician who has lived alternatively in Europe and the United States since age thirteen. Seeking refuge from racism, he has resigned himself to the invisible role of the black jazz musician in Paris, France. Then Forbes meets Kathy Nichols, a white woman bigot from the American South, and the remainder of the novel explores the vicissitudes of racism and interracial relations between the two. In Paris, Forbes avoids racial frustrations by acquiescing to the role that Frenchmen expect of him as a black musician; however, his affair with Kathy forces him to confront the reality of his blackness again. He vents his frustrations by vengefully tormenting Kathy, but when he falls in love with her, he struggles to separate his bigotry and his genuine feelings for her. Though an alien in exile, Forbes cannot escape his racial identity or the American psychology of race.

Yerby's best novel, *The Dahomean*, is the story of Nyasanu (Hwesu), second son of the village Chief Gbenu, who succeeds his father as Chief of the Alladah. After marrying a beautiful Dahomean woman, he goes to war and distinguishes himself as a warrior. Following the deaths of his father who is fatally injured in the war and his wife who dies during childbirth, he becomes the Chief of the Alladah people, inheriting his father's wives and children; but Nyasanu struggles to maintain rule over dissenting factions of his province. After he is betrayed by a jealous stepbrother and a vengeful wife, he is sold into slavery. The perfect platform for Yerby to demonstrate both his racial consciousness and his penchant for detailed research, *The Dahomean* far exceeded *Speak Now* in critical acclaim. In the novel, through a re-creation of nineteenth-century Dahomean culture, Yerby probes the richness and variety of the culture of Dahomey, creating noteworthy historical fiction. While Lael Pritchard praised the novel in *Best Sellers* in 1971, observing "*The Dahomean* is a rare book indeed. . . . The book does not glamorize; it describes with insight what was,"[33] Darwin T. Turner concluded in *Black World* in 1972 that *The Dahomean* was Yerby's most satisfying novel.[34]

The Dahomean is a contemporary African American novel with an African setting, and as Dave Khune concludes, it is perhaps the most detailed descriptions of African culture in American fiction.[35] Between the novel's prologue and the concluding scene, both of which are set in America, Yerby acquaints his readers with the intricate complexities of Dahomean culture. In an introductory note to the novel, Yerby admonishes his readers: "The purpose of the

The Dahomean is admittedly to correct, so far as it is possible, the Anglo-Saxon reader's historical perspective. For among the countless tragedies caused by North American slavery was the destruction of the high, and in many ways, admirable, culture of the African." As the novel unfolds, Yerby explores in detail Dahomean religion, magic, family life, rituals, war, and technology. Additionally, providing a balanced view of the culture, he focuses on such negatives as polygamy, female genital mutilation, and absolute power. Most objectionable to Yerby is the latter, which also informs his characterization. At the end of the novel, Nyasanu is captured, sold into slavery and transported to the United States; and as the novel ends, Nyasanu, now called Wesley Parks in America, declares that he will one day reveal the horrors of life in slavery. In 1976 when this author interviewed Yerby and engaged him in a conversation about his protagonists, particularly his failure to write about an African American protagonist in an American setting, Yerby declared that he planned to do so in the future. In *A Darkness at Ingraham's Crest* (1979), the sequel to *The Dahomean*, he did. An excoriating indictment of the slaveholding antebellum South and its impositions on the slave and the master, *A Darkness at Ingraham's Crest* is the story of the conflict between Wes Parks, a slave yearning for freedom, and Pamela Bibbs, a transplanted Northerner, who becomes the embodiment of the brutality and inhumanity of slavery.

Yerby's growing concern for his literary reputation coupled with his living and traveling abroad also converged as he searched for significance in his writing. In his *Ebony* interview, Yerby pronounced that his most recent novels, *The Old Gods Laugh* (1964) and *An Odor of Sanctity* (1965) were historical novels and therefore different from his previous costume novels. Additionally, he characterized *Goat Song* (1967) and *Judas, My Brother* (1969) as serious novels. Reflecting his extensive travels and painstaking research of subjects for his novels, *Goat Song* is set in ancient Greece; and *Judas, My Brother*, a re-creation of the beginnings of Christianity, variously explores the locales of Galilee, Jerusalem, and Rome. Admittedly controversial, *Judas, My Brother*, according to Yerby, is the result of thirty years of research, and it did significantly improve the critical reception of his fiction. Reviewers discerned a more serious effort in his fiction and praised his accomplishment. In 1969, black scholar Darwin T. Turner wrote: " . . . although he may disappoint enthusiasts and literary purists, Yerby has developed his most significant theme. . . ."[36] Instead of merely entertaining his readers in *Judas, My Brother*, therefore, Yerby deliberately provokes thought about Christian myths.

Though many of his novels are Southern historical romances, Yerby was also cognizant of his becoming too provincial as a writer. Thus, while continuing to examine the myths and legends of the South, he increasingly explored other regions of America and the Western world. Yerby demonstrated that he could write convincingly about other cultures as early as his third novel, *The Golden Hawk* (1948), which chronicles the piratical adventures of Kit Gerado in the seventeenth-century West Indies. Although it retains a pronounced southern flavor, Yerby's fourth novel *Pride's Castle* (1949) tells the story of a transplanted southerner in the North. Another three years passed before *The Saracen Blade* (1952), Yerby's fourth novel with a foreign setting; and one year after his self-exile from the United States, he published *The Devil's Laughter* (1953), a novel about the turbulent years of the French Revolution. In 1964, 1965, 1967, 1968 respectively, he published *The Old Gods Laugh, An Odor of Sanctity, Goat Song,* and *Judas, My Brother,* followed by *Speak Now* (1969) and *The Dahomean* (1971), all with foreign settings. Spanish-speaking countries are the subject of Yerby's last two novels about cultures other than America. While *A Rose For Ana Maria* (1976) explores revolutionary activities in Spain, Yerby's adopted home country, *Hail the Conquering Hero* (1977) focuses on government corruption in Latin American Costa Verde. It is not surprising, however, that Yerby's fiction increasingly portrays characters in other cultures, for his voluntary self-exile, his expanding interest in other cultures, and his popularity abroad no doubt combined to influence his choices of literary materials.

In fact, Yerby published only five novels set in the United States after 1962, but he never really abandoned America or the South, his favorite literary settings. Both *A Darkness at Ingraham's Crest* (1979) and *McKenzie's Hundred* (1985), written during the latter years of Yerby's career, are set in the United States. While the former exposes the ills of American slavery in the South, the latter tells the story of a Virginia woman spy for the Confederate Army during the Civil War. In between these two novels, Yerby also published two novels with a Southern flavor but set in other regions of America. *Western, A Saga of the Great Plains* (1982) is the story of a Civil War veteran who migrates to Kansas in search of peace, and *Devilseed* (1984) features another Yerby female protagonist who migrates from Louisiana to San Francisco during the gold rush days and rises to the highest level of society.

In the genre of popular fiction in which he chose to carve his niche, it was inevitable that Yerby would quickly become an anomaly in African American fiction. Although his overwhelming success in the field of popular fiction did not establish him as the first black American to write historical fiction or to write about white protagonists, what distinguishes him from other African American writers is that he, adopting almost totally the vernacular of popular fiction, restricted himself to writing predominantly about whites. Thus, his decision to write for a popular fiction audience precluded the visibility of overt, traditional racial protest in his writing, placing him squarely outside the mainstream of African American fiction. Although writing popular fiction for the larger predominantly white audience promised Yerby greater popularity and success, it simultaneously placed restrictions on the type of fiction he could write.

On the surface, the absence of an overt protest seems another glaring distinction between Yerby and his contemporaries of African American fiction. The costume romances Yerby chose to write, however, were not entirely outside the pale of protest fiction. In lieu of the overt racial protest of mainstream African American fiction, Yerby's novels reveal a distinct transformation of the protest aim. Modifying the protest impulse evident in his early short stories and using history and social and philosophical commentary, Yerby retains in various modified ways the original aim of protest fiction. His social criticism includes but transcends matters of race, exposing injustices perpetrated against blacks, debunking myths of American and Western cultures, arguing the realities of history and commenting on human values. Not surprisingly, the same racial attitudes Yerby conveys in his black protest stories pervade his popular fiction, sometimes in obvious and sometimes in disguised ways.

In his transition from protest to popular fiction, there is little doubt but that Yerby effected a compromise, however large or small; but it was a compromise he was obviously willing to make. At the same time, the price of succeeding as a popular fiction writer commanded his subversion of racial concerns, resulting in even greater compromise. In pursuit of his career in popular fiction, Yerby elected to write historical romances because they brought money and fame, though they obviously cost him literary respect. Yerby, apprenticed in the tradition of protest fiction, adapted protest to the medium of popular fiction and continued to attack racism, hypocrisy, and oppression. In fact, as he established himself in the arena of popular fiction, Yerby adopted a special mission—use of historical data to debunk the inaccuracies of myths and legends in the historical periods and cultures about which he wrote. In his use of historical data, Yerby reveals gross historical inaccuracies, corrects common misconceptions, reaffirms historical truths, and comments on human nature. Avoiding the label of historical novelist, he preferred to call his fiction "costume novels" because, as he said, Dial Press often excised much of the historical data he included. Any careful perusal of his costume novels, however, reveals that historical data in Yerby's novels is as important if not more than the trappings of historical romance.

Thus, Yerby's costume novels are not the traditional romances of hearts and flowers. In addition to entertaining the reader, his costume novels incorporate a modern realistic perspective, a spirit of protest, and the author's philosophical views. Unlike the typical hero of the historical romance, however, Yerby's protagonists are not all brave men and women who achieve honor, fame, and happiness; and while almost all struggle to secure a place in an alien culture, they often remained alienated. Yerby's protagonists, like the heroes in the picaresque novel, are also alienated by circumstances of birth or their past; and as they seek to establish themselves in alien cultures, they are not always patriotic or heroic. More often than not, they resist conformity to societal codes and victimize all who stand between them and their goals. While they engage in perilous adventures, they find little honor or glory in them. Like other writers of traditional picaresque fiction, Yerby is implicitly satirical of the heroic ideal, and thus his novels contain two poles of interest—one, the protagonist and his adventures and the other, the society that the protagonist pillories.

During his brief time in Chicago, Yerby established himself as one of the emerging writers of the Chicago Renaissance. The "most typical as well as the famous example of the Depression-bred Chicago Renaissance writers," Bontemps declares in "Famous WPA Writers," "was Richard Wright"(43–47); and early in his career, Frank Yerby was expected to follow Wright's example. Yerby opted, however, for another route to literary success. Though he never achieved the critical acclaim of other Chicago Renaissance writers, Yerby's achievements as a popular fiction novelist propelled him into a singularly unique position in the history of African American literature. As an African American writer, he captured the imagination of his readers for almost a half century writing entertaining fiction, and his venture into popular fiction provided him with the best of two worlds. He could enjoy the financial rewards and popularity of a writer read by the millions, and he could execute his own sense of mission by pointing out the weaknesses of the very cultures he was re-creating. Yet, it was not by way of the latter but the former image of the popular writer that Yerby became known to Americans.

If Yerby was slow in admitting his concessions as a popular writer, his critics were not; for it was primarily the social, political, and economic issues, not the literary, which dominated critical reactions to Yerby in America. Most of the critical reactions to Yerby's fiction relate, as might be expected, to his varying public images. It was not long after he began publishing, however, that critics began to call for more from Yerby—black critics for more racially relevant fiction and white critics for more meaningful novels. When Yerby did not meet either of these expectations, critical reviews of his novels waned in later years, causing Yerby to develop a search for meaning in his writing. While he did eventually write more meaningful fiction, namely *Judas, My Brother*, *Speak Now*, and *The Dahomean*, he never again achieved the level of success he enjoyed early in his career, and critical literary acclaim always eluded him. Even though most critics either lauded his accomplishments or dismissed him, no significant history of American popular fiction or African American literature can completely ignore him.

The significance of Yerby's historical fiction cannot really be determined by the millions of novels he sold or his enduring popularity as a costume novelist. Any serious assessment of his fiction must involve the motivations of the writer, for although the ideas in his novels have often been misread or simply ignored, the import of Yerby's fiction is not romance but actually historical and social criticism. In his transition from protest to popular fiction, Yerby effected his own dual isolation as a writer in the American literary world—isolation from the African American literary tradition in which he was apprenticed and isolation within the very literary genre in which he achieved unprecedented success. Confronted with his growing isolation in popular fiction, Yerby developed his own sense of a mission in his writing; and incorporating the original critical and satirical aims of protest fiction into his popular fiction, he became perhaps America's greatest debunker of its legendary past.

Frank Yerby died of conjunctive heart failure in Madrid on November 29, 1991, at the age of 76 and is buried in the Almudena Cemetery. Like his expatriation, however, his death created little fanfare. His wife Blanquita Calle-Perez was the only person who attended the burial ceremony held on Sunday, a day not normal for funerals in Spain, and notice of his death came several weeks later. In fact, on his death bed, Yerby exacted a promise from his wife that his funeral would have no guests except her and that she would not announce his death until five weeks later.

Notes

1. "Frank Yerby." *Current Biography*, edited by Anne Rothe. New York: Wilson Company, 1947, 672–74.

2. Nye, Russell B. *The Unembarrassed Muse*. New York: Dial Press, 1970, 47–54.

3. Richardson, Josephine, personal interview, January 23, 1974.

4. Zealey, Rebecca, personal interview, January 24, 1974.

5. Breit, Harvey. *The Writer Observed*. Cleveland, Ohio: World, 1960, 127–29.

6. "Frank Yerby." *Current Biography*, 672–74.

7. Yerby, Frank. Letter to the author, February 24, 1974.

8. Yerby, Frank. Letter to the author, September 7, 1973.

9. Ibid.

10. Flug, Michael. "Chicago Renaissance 1932–1950, A Flowering of Afro-American Culture." http://www.chipublib.org/digital/chiren/ (Accessed December 29, 2004).

11. Bontemps, Arna. "Famous WPA Authors." *Negro Digest* 7 (June 1950): 43–47.

12. Stange, Maren. *Bronzeville: Black Chicago in Pictures, 1941–1943*. New York: The New Press, 2003, xxix–xxx.

13. "Mystery Man of Letters." *Ebony* 10 (February 1955): 31–32, 35–38.

14. Yerby, Frank. Letter to the author, January 28, 1974.

15. Yerby, Frank. "The Homecoming." *Common Ground* 6 (1946): 41–47.

16. Yerby, Frank. "How and Why I Write the Costume Novel." *Harper's* 219 (1959): 145–50.

17. Bontemps, Arna. "From Lad of Ireland to Bayou Grandee," *Chicago Sun Book Week* 4, February 10, 1946, 1.

18. Locke, Alain. "Race and Reason: A Review of the Literature of the Negro for 1946." *Phylon* 8 (1947): 20.

19. Kane, Harnett. "Author of 'Plantation Parade,'" *New York Herald Tribune Weekly Book Review* 22, February 24, 1946, 8.

20. "Briefly Noted Fiction." *New Yorker* 21 (February 1946): 96–97.

21. "Scarlet Splash." *Time* 29 (May 5, 1947): 111.

22. Gloster, Hugh. "The Significance of Frank Yerby." *The Crisis* (1948): 55.

23. Watson, Wilbur. "Balloon Prose," New York Times, May 2, 1949, 22.

24. "Bookshelf: Recent Novels," *Chicago Sun Book Week*, October 14, 1950, 15.

25. Turner, Darwin T. "Frank Yerby as Debunker." *Massachusetts Review* 20 (1968): 569–77.

26. Yerby, Frank. *A Woman Called Fancy*. New York: Dial Press, 1951, 280–81.

27. Fuller, Hoyt. "Famous Writer Faces a Challenge." *Ebony* 21 (1966): 188–190.

28. Schaap, Dick. "Frank Yerby, Expert in Pap Comes Up with An Angry Novel," *Detriot News and Times*, 1968, 1-E.

29. Fuller, Hoyt. "Famous Writer Faces a Challenge." *Ebony* 21 (1966): 188–90.

30. Yates, William. "Yerby's Most Ambitious Novel," *Chicago Tribune*, August 25, 1957, 5.

31. Baker, Donald. "From Apartheid to Invisibility: Black Americans in Popular Fiction, 1900–1960. *Midwest Quarterly* 13 (July 1972): 365–85.

32. "*Speak Now*," *New York Times*, Nov. 30, 1969, 67.

33. Pritchard, Lael. "*The Dahomean*." *Best Sellers* 31 (1971): 255.

34. Turner, Darwin T. "*The Dahomean*." *Black World* 21 (1972): 87.

35. Khune, Dave. "Black on Black: African-American Novels with African Settings." In *African Settings in Contemporary American Novels*. Westport, Conn.: Greenwood Press, 1999, 57–60.

36. Turner, Darwin T. "Judas, My Brother." *Negro Digest* (1969): 80–82.

For Further Reading

"Back in U.S., "Frank Yerby Tells Why He Hates Racial Tags." *Jet* (1960): 4–5.

Bell, Bernard W. *The Afro-American Novel and Its Traditions*. Amherst: University of Massachusetts Press, 1987.

Benson, Brian J. "Frank Yerby." In *Southern Writers*, edited by Louis Rubin, Robert Bain, and Joseph M. Flora. Baton Rouge: Louisiana State University Press, 1979, 510–11.

Benson, Joseph. "*The Dahomean*: An Historical Novel." In *Masterpieces of African American Literature*, edited by Frank N. Magill. New York: HarperCollins Publishers, 1992, 131–33.

Bone, Robert. "Richard Wright and the Chicago Renaissance." *Callaloo* 9, no. 3 (Summer 1986): 446–68.

Butcher, Phillip. "In Print: Our Raceless Writers." *Opportunity* 26 (1948): 113–15.

Campenni, Frank. "Frank Yerby." *Contemporary Novelists*. New York: St. Martin's Press, 1972, 1416–19.

Chandler, Lewis G. "Coming of Age: A Note on American Negro Novelists." *Phylon* 9 (1948): 25–29.

Crawford, Valerie Mathews. "Middle Ground: Frank Yerby's Novels in the African American Literary Tradition." Dissertation, University of North Carolina, Chapel Hill, 1999.

"Five American Negro Authors." *Salute* 3 (1948): 48–49.

Ford, Nick Aaron. "Four Popular Novelists." *Phylon* 25 (1954): 29–39.

Glasrud, Bruce A. and Laurie Champion. "The Fishes and the Poet's Hands: Frank Yerby, A Black Author in White America." *Journal of American and Comparative Cultures* 23 (2000): 15–22.

Gloster, Hugh. "The Significance of Frank Yerby." *The Crisis* 55 (1948): 12–13.

"The Golden Corn: He Writes to Please." *Time* 64 (1954): 97.

Graham, Maryemma."Frank Yerby, King of the Costume Novel." *Essence* 6 (October 1975): 70–71, 88–92.

Hill, James L. "An Interview with Frank Garvin Yerby." *Resources for American Literary Study* 21 (1995): 206–39.

———. "The Anti-Heroic Hero in Frank Yerby's Historical Novels." In *Perspectives of Black Popular Culture*, edited by Harry B. Shaw. Bowling Green, Ohio: Popular Culture Association, 1990, 5–16.

———. "Anti-Heroic Perspectives: The Life and Works of Frank Garvin Yerby." Dissertation, University of Iowa, 1976.

———. "Between Philosophy and Race: Images of Blacks in the Fiction of Frank Yerby." *Umoja* 4 (1980): 5–16.

———. "Frank Yerby." In *Oxford Companion to African American Literature*, edited by William L. Andrews, Frances Smith Foster and Trudier Harris. New York: Oxford University Press,1997, 797–98.

Hill, William W. "Behind the Magnolia Mask: Frank Yerby as Critic of the South." Master's Thesis, Auburn University, 1968.

Hughes, Carl M. *The Negro Novelist, 1940–1950*. New York: Citadel Press, 1953, 149–59, 236–38.

Jarrett, Thomas. "Recent Fiction by Negroes." *College English* 16 (1954): 85–91.

———. "Toward Unfettered Creativity: A Note on the Negro Novelist's Coming of Age." *Phylon* (1950): 313–17.

Klotman, Phyllis R. "A Harrowing Experience: Frank Yerby's First Novel to Film." *CLA Journal* 31 (1987): 210–22.

Locke Alain L. "A Critical Restrospect of Literature of the Negro for 1947." *Phylon* 9 (1948): 3–12.

Lupac, Alan C. "Frank Yerby's Wisdom." *Notes on Contemporary Literature* 7 (1977): 8.

Middleton, Laura Ferguson. "Shifting Perspectives: A Reevaluation of Frank Garvin Yerby." Master's Thesis, Baylor University, 1996.

Moore, Jack B. "The Guilt of the Victim: Racial Themes in Some Frank Yerby Novels." *Journal of Popular Culture* 8 (1975): 746–56.

Morgan, Gwendolyn. "Challenging the Black Aesthetic: The Silencing of Frank Yerby." *Florida A&M University Research Bulletin* 35 (1993): 19–30.

Parker, Jeffrey. "Frank Yerby." In *Afro-American Writers, 1940–1955*, edited by Trudier Harris and Thadious M. Davis. Detroit: Gale Research Inc., 1988, 222–31.

Penkower, Monty Noam. *The Federal Writers' Project*. Urbana: University of Illinois Press, 1977, 66, 133, 146, 227.

Pratt, Louis Hill. "Frank Garvin Yerby." In *Contemporary African American Novelists: A Bio-Bibliographical Critical Sourcebook*, edited by Emmanuel S. Nelson. Westport, Conn.: Greenwood Press, 1999, 505–11.

——. "Frank Yerby." In *Critical Survey of Short Fiction*, edited by Frank N. Magill. Englewood Cliff, N.J.: Salem, 1981, 2475–80.

Reedy, Daniel R. "Vision Del Caribe en Las Novelas De Frank Yerby." In *Homenaje A Lydia Cabrera*, edited by Reinaldo Sanchez and Jose A. Madrigal. Miami: Ediciones Universal, 1978, 229–40.

Runton, Gloria Cecelia. "The Life and Novels of Frank Garvin Yerby." Master's Thesis, Florida State University, 1959.

Shockley, Ann A. and Sue P. Chandler. *Living Black American Authors*. New York: Bowker Company, 1973, 177.

Smiles, Robin V. "Uncovering Frank Yerby." *Black Issues in Higher Education* 21 (2004): 28.

Thomas, Will. "Negro Writers of Pulp Fiction." *Negro Digest* 8 (1950): 81–84.

Turner, Darwin T. "Frank Yerby: Golden Debunker." *Black Books Bulletin* 1 (1972): 4–9, 30–33.

——. "The Negro Novelist and the South." *Southern Humanities Review* 1 (1967): 21–29.

Ward, Theodore. "Five Negro Novelists: Revolt and Retreat." *Mainstream* (1947): 100–110.

Woodley, Lisa. *American Voices of the Chicago Renaissance*. Dekalb: Northern Illinois University Press, 2000, 12–13, 121–50.

"Frank Yerby." *African American Writers, A-Z*, edited by Philip Bader. New York: Facts on File, Inc., 2004, 263–65.

"Frank Yerby." *Beacham's Encyclopedia of Popular Fiction*, edited by Kirk H. Beetz. Osprey, Fla.: Beacham Publishing Company, 1996, 2003–7.

"Frank Yerby." *Black Literary Criticism*, edited by James P. Draper. Detroit: Gale Research Inc., 2022–31.

"Frank Yerby." *Black Writers: A Selection of Sketches from Contemporary Authors*, edited by Linda Metzger. Detroit: Gale Research Inc., 1989, 613–16.

"Frank Yerby." *Contemporary Authors*. Detroit: Gale Research Inc., 1974, 985–86.

"Frank Yerby." *Contemporary Authors, New Revision Series*, edited by Linda Metzger and Deborah Straub. Detroit: Gale Research Inc., 1986, 466–71.

"Frank Yerby." *Contemporary Literary Criticism*, edited by Sharon R. Gunton and Jean C. Stine. Detroit: Gale Research Inc., 1982, 487–91.

"Frank Yerby." *Major 20th-Century Writers: A Selection of Sketches from Contemporary Authors*, edited by Bryan Ryan. Detroit: Gale Research Inc., 1991, 3267–69.

Yerby, Frank. "A Brief Historical Sketch of the Little Theatre in the Negro College." *Quarterly Journal of Florida A&M University* 10 (1940): 27–32.

——. *A Darkness at Ingraham's Crest: A Tale of the Slaveholding South*. New York: Dial Press, 1979; London: Grenada, 1981.

——. "A Date with Vera." *Fisk Herald* 31 (1937): 16–17.

——. "All I Have Known." *Fisk Herald* 31 (1937): 14.

——. *An Odor of Sanctity: A Novel of Medieval Moorish Spain*. New York: Dial Press, 1965; London: Heinemann, 1966.

———. *A Rose for Ana Maria.* New York: Dial Press, 1976; London: Heinemann, 1976.

———. *A Woman Called Fancy.* New York: Dial Press, 1951; London: Heinemann, 1952.

———. *Benton's Row.* New York: Dial Press, 1954; London: Heinemann, 1955.

———. "Bitter Lotus." *Fisk Herald* 31 (1937): 22.

———. "Brevity." *Challenge* 1 (1934): 27.

———. *Bride of Liberty.* Garden City, N.Y.: Doubleday, 1954; London, Heinemann, 1955.

———. "A Calm after Storm." *Shards* 4 (1936): 20.

———. *Captain Rebel.* New York: Dial Press, 1956; London, Heinemann, 1957.

———. *Devilseed.* Garden City, N.Y.: Doubleday, 1984; London: Grenada, 1984.

———. "Drought." *Challenge* 1 (1935): 15.

———. *Fairoaks.* New York: Dial Press, 1957; London: Heinemann, 1958.

———. *Floodtide.* New York: Dial Press, 1950; London: Heinemann, 1951.

———. *Gillian.* New York: Dial Press, 1960; London: Heinemann, 1961.

———. *Goat Song: A Novel of Ancient Greece.* New York: Dial Press, 1967; London: Heinemann, 1968.

———. *Griffin's Way.* New York: Dial Press, 1962; London: Heinemann, 1963.

———. *Hail the Conquering Hero.* New York: Dial Press, 1977; London: Heinemann, 1978.

———. "Health Card." *Harper's* 188 (1944): 448–53.

———. "How and Why I Write the Costume Novel." *Harper's* 219 (1959): 45–150.

———. *Jarrett's Jade.* New York: Dial Press, 1959; London: Heinemann, 1960.

———. *Judas, My Brother: The Story of the Thirteenth Disciple.* New York: Dial Press, 1968; London: Heinemann, 1969.

———. "Love Story." *The Paineite* (1937): 15–16.

———. *McKenzie's Hundred.* Garden City, N.Y.: Doubleday, 1985; London: Grafton, 1986.

———. "Miracles." *Challenge* 1 (1934): 27.

———. "My Brother Went to College." *Tomorrow* 5 (1946): 9–12.

———. *Pride's Castle.* New York: Dial Press, 1949; London: Heinemann, 1950.

———. "Problems Confronting the Little Theatre in the Negro College." *Southern University Bulletin* 27 (1941): 96–103.

———. "Roads Going Down." *Common Ground* 5 (Summer 1945): 67–72.

———. *Speak Now: A Modern Novel.* New York: Dial Press, 1969; London: Heinemann, 1973.

———. *The Dahomean: An Historical Novel.* New York: Dial Press, 1971. Republished as *The Man from Dahomey.* London: Heinemann, 1971.

———. *The Devil's Laughter.* New York: Dial Press, 1953; London: Heinemann, 1954.

———. "The Fishes and the Poet's Hand." *Fisk Herald* 31 (1938): 10–11.

———. *The Foxes of Harrow.* New York: Dial Press, 1946; London: Heinemann, 1947.

———. *The Garfield Honor.* New York: Dial Press, 1961; London: Heinemann, 1962.

———. *The Girl from Storyville: A Victorian Novel.* New York: Dial Press, 1972; London: Heinemann, 1972.

———. *The Golden Hawk.* New York: Dial Press, 1948; London: Heinemann, 1949.

———. "The Homecoming." *Common Ground* 6 (1946): 41–47.

———. "The Little Theater in the Negro College." Master's Thesis, Fisk University, 1938.

———. *The Old Gods Laugh: A Modern Romance*. New York: Dial Press, 1964; London: Heinemann, 1964.

———. *The Saracen Blade*. New York: Dial Press, 1952; London: Heinemann, 1953.

———. *The Serpent and the Staff*. New York: Dial Press, 1958; London: Heinemann, 1959.

———. "The Thunder of God." *New Anvil* 1 (1939): 5–8.

———. *The Treasure of Pleasant Valley*. New York: Dial Press, 1955; London: Heinemann, 1956.

———. *The Vixens*. New York: Dial Press, 1947; London: Heinemann, 1948.

———. *The Voyage Unplanned.* New York: Dial Press, 1974; London: Heinemann, 1974.

———. "Three Sonnets." *Challenge* 1 (1936): 11–12.

———. "To a Seagull." *Challenge* 1 (1935): 15.

———. *Tobias and the Angel*. New York: Dial Press, 1975; London: Heinemann, 1975.

———. "Weltschmerz." *Shards* 4 (1936): 9.

———. *Western: A Saga of the Great Plains*. New York: Dial Press, 1982; London: Grenada, 1983.

———. "White Magnolias." *Phylon* 5 (1944): 319–26.

———. "Wisdom." *Arts Quarterly* 1(1937): 34.

———. "You Are a Part of Me." *Fisk Herald* 31 (1937): 15.

———. "Young Man Afraid." *Fisk Herald* 31 (1937): 10–11.

BLACK WRITERS AND THE FEDERAL THEATRE PROJECT

August 1935–June 1939

Angelene Jamison-Hall

Chicago's black cultural life in the 1930s and 1940s was as vital as New York's during the Harlem Renaissance. Literature, art, music, theater, and other creative activities thrived and developed into what has recently been referred to as the Chicago Renaissance. The migration of African Americans during the twenty years before the Depression had contributed to the development of a spirited Black community. By 1930 it was estimated that Chicago's black population reached 230,000 people, and many of these migrants were generally segregated to the South Side or what became known as "Bronzeville."

Chicago boasted of many organizations that added to the vitality of the African American communities. Rena Fraden notes in her book, *Blueprints for a Black Federal Theatre, 1935–1939*, that there were "167 churches, 47 college clubs, 97 fraternal orders, and over 18 local and national college fraternities and sororities in existence in 1927."[1] In addition to women's clubs, service organizations, and social networks, there were also business and professional clubs in which Blacks participated and supported. Theater, too, with its vaudeville, minstrels, comedies, dramas, and musical shows represented a rich tradition in African American culture in Chicago.

Theater was part of the strong cultural tradition among blacks in Chicago. In 1861, the first stock theater was founded. Robert T. Motts who had traveled in England and seen theater presentations, returned to Chicago to initiate a comparable program. According to Fraden, after opening the Pekin Theater in 1905, which seated twelve hundred people, Mott was successful until 1911, when he found himself in competition with white theaters doing vaudeville.

There were, however, other achievements in Chicago's black theater history. Tony Langston, an actor, was dramatic editor of the historic *Chicago Defender*. Billy King not only produced shows, but wrote hundreds of plays and sketches, and the list of actors included Evelyn Preer, who began her career with the

Lafayette Players in Chicago, and Clarence Muse, another member of the Lafayette Players.[2] Given the city's background in black theater, with performers,
technicians, and artistic activists, the creative energy that permeated the South
Side during the thirties and forties suggested great possibilities for the Federal
Theatre Project (FTP).

The Federal Theatre Project was one of the four arts projects of the Works
Progress Administration (WPA) developed by President Franklin D. Roosevelt
in response to the high unemployment among creative artists during the Great
Depression. Along with the other arts projects—writing, art, and music—theater
suffered greatly during the 1930s. Although it had been in decline prior to the
thirties, with the introduction of the motion picture industry and other cheaper
forms of entertainment, actors, designers, stagehands, writers, and craftsmen
now had little choice but to go on relief. Fraden asserts that the Federal Theatre
Project not only intended for these artists to acquire employment, allowing them
to continue to develop their skills, it also suggested that theater was an integral
part of American culture and should not be allowed to die.

As the Federal Theatre sought to provide employment for theater professionals, additional goals became important when Hallie Flanagan became director
of the Project. President Roosevelt and Harry Hopkins, deputy administrator of
New York's Federal Emergency Relief Act (FERA) and later head of the WPA,
recruited her from Vassar, where she had been involved in noncommercial theater. Flanagan had revolutionary ideas about the Federal Theatre Project. She
wanted the FTP to provide employment opportunities for people with theater
experience and to encourage them to expand their talents. Moreover, she wanted
the project to bring theater to the people, to use local talent and exercise local
control, and to include issues in the plays that exemplified diversity and social
significance. In his essay, "The Role of Blacks in the Federal Theatre," Ronald
Ross points out that Flanagan "wanted the forgotten man . . . to be a major
concern of the Federal Theatre Project."[3]

Flanagan's commitment to a theater of and for the people led her and Rose
McClendon, one of the major black actresses of the time, to come together in
1935 to talk about the establishment of separate units for blacks. McClendon
and Flanagan both believed that the only way to achieve equality of opportunity
and racial parity was to establish autonomous separate black units. McClendon
was highly concerned that as these units acquire autonomy, they also portray
Black life realistically. She had been working with Dick Campbell, a singer-actor,
to organize a Negro People's Theater, but after her death, many of the theater
employees gravitated to the Negro Unit of the Federal Theatre.[4] Loften Mitchell
asserts that in keeping with Flanagan's goal to bring theater to the people, some
of the New York groups presented productions at the YMCA, African American
churches, "ballrooms and halls," and other social arenas.[5]

These Negro Units of the Federal Theatre Project provided significant opportunities for African Americans. In Chicago, identified by Flanagan as "one of the five great regions," she supported the Negro unit and wanted to see it succeed.[6] *Swing Mikado*, the most successful production of the Chicago Negro Unit, gave blacks many opportunities for creative work. Lafayette Theater in Harlem, another example, provided the people a burst of enthusiasm about the possibilities of a theater where blacks could determine their own creative direction. Meeting nightly to discuss directions for the theater, share ideas, and examine possible plays, the Negro Units were encouraged by the support garnered from the Federal Theatre.

In addition to employment, some theater scholars have noted that the Federal Theatre was partly responsible for helping black playwrights develop their skills and write about black life. Fraden, however, informs us that John Houseman, a white producer Rose McClendon asked to run the Negro Unit in Harlem, pointed out that his major problem in the role was no "performable Negro scripts."[7] Apparently, Houseman was either unaware of or misinformed about the existence of significant plays such as Joseph Seamon Cotter Jr.'s *On the Fields of France* (1921), May Miller's *The Bog Guide* (1925) or *Scratches* (1929), and Willis Richardson's *Rooms for Rent* (1926).

Although these plays existed, many of the Negro units performed white plays adapted for a black cast. For example, the voodoo *Macbeth* was performed at the Lafayette Theater in Harlem in 1936 and *Swing Mikado*, an adaptation of Gilbert and Sullivan's *The Mikado*, was staged in Chicago in 1938. Though each of these plays were commercially successful and later moved to the commercial stage, W. E. B. DuBois, Theophilus Lewis, Alain Locke, and other black critics wanted the Negro units to move toward a realistic portrayal of black life and experiences, such as those found in Theodore Ward's *Big White Fog*, which initially opened in Chicago. White directors and producers, however, sought out white scripts, because they were more readily available. Blacks were now more responsible for the kind of drama they wanted to produce, but they needed to develop their skills.

The objective of the FTP to help black playwrights develop their skills was slow in coming to fruition. The Negro Dramatists' Laboratory, organized in New York by George Zorn and lasting from November 1936 to February 1937 is just one program instituted by the Federal Theatre Project to develop and train Black playwrights. Ronald Ross points to the intense lectures and workshops on "script forms, research techniques, technical requirements, and copyright laws," and credits the Negro Dramatists' Laboratory as invaluable to helping Black writers compete as artists in American culture.[8] In providing training opportunities for Black playwrights, this program fulfilled one of the objectives of the FTP.

While the Negro Dramatists' Laboratory was part of the New York scene, and many of the preliminary theater initiatives occurred there, New York was not the only vibrant area where Negro units existed. Among the many units throughout the country were those in Seattle, Boston, New Jersey, Dallas, Los Angeles, North Carolina, Oklahoma, Durham, and Chicago. The Chicago Unit of the FTP was one of the largest, boasting of three successful original productions—*Swing Mikado, Big White Fog*, and *Little Black Sambo*. With government support, Blacks, who had already been interested and involved in theater, had some assurance they would have a chance to use their talents. Moreover, since Chicago had a memorable Black theater history, there was no problem finding talented technicians, stagehands, and performers such as Herman Green, Maurice Cooper, and William Franklin, who were capable of performing a variety of entertainment from musicals to realistic drama.

Since realistic drama was less accessible and therefore, less popular during the Chicago Renaissance, some white directors turned to musicals, classical plays, and even minstrels. Flanagan praised Shirley Graham's adaptation of Charlotte Chorpenning's *Little Black Sambo*, for its "skill and understanding of its direction and the vivid jungle quality of its sets and music."[9] Shirley Graham, later Shirley Graham Dubois, had amassed impressive credentials in music and theater. Under the auspices of the Federal Summer Theatre, convening at Vassar in the mid-1930s, she participated in a gathering of theater professionals, studying and working for six weeks. She returned to work in Chicago and later received a fellowship from the Rosenwald Foundation to study at Yale. According to Flanagan, Graham wanted to devote her talents to "the development of Negro theater in this country."[10]

It is not certain if *Little Black Sambo* met this objective or was designed for this purpose. It is, nonetheless, the story of an African boy who must outwit tigers to get home. Flanagan notes that the show, "designed, composed, and directed" by Graham, was well-received by both critics and audiences. The jungle motif, which Flanagan referred to, obviously did not influence the reception of the show since the Negro unit performed before healthcare facilities, schools, parks, Boy Scouts, and other youth groups. While the FTP advocated the abolition of black stereotypes and did not support negative images that permeated much of black theater, the Negro unit in Chicago also performed *Little Black Sambo*, as part of Puppet Theater, to audiences of children.[11] Although Blacks were not limited to the theatrical forms that helped to keep black stereotypes alive, they nevertheless found the show entertaining.

When the Chicago unit abandoned much of the minstrel form, they, like other units across the country, began to focus on white plays, such as *Androcles and the Lion, The Taming of the Shrew*, and of course, *Macbeth* and *The Mikado*, adapted for black performers. When black casts performed European plays revamped for them, critics responded enthusiastically because blacks demonstrated their abilities to work in categories usually relegated to white actors. *Voodoo Macbeth*, one of the major successes of the Lafayette Theater in Harlem, is one such example.

In Fraden's discussion of the response to *Voodoo Macbeth*, she notes that there were a variety of comments, "critical and appreciative." One Black reviewer had high expectations that this production would "define a black audience." Roi Ottley wrote that the production was "spectacular" and proved the importance of the FTP and black actors. Moreover, he believed the performance was characteristically Harlem, which suggests that the performance represented the people.

The most successful play in Chicago, though, was the 1938 production of *Swing Mikado*, a musical comedy adapted from Gilbert and Sullivan's 1885 *Mikado*. Although there have been many adaptations of *The Mikado*, the Chicago unit's version was the most commercially successful. Attracting many black professional actors with a history in the business, *Swing Mikado* showcased the talents of several outstanding vaudevillians, such as Herman Green, who played the role of Ko-Ko, the tailor in the musical; Maurice Cooper, the lead character; and William Franklin, who was experienced in opera. The musical ran in Chicago for "five months to 250,000 people and made $35,000; in the weeks before Christmas, it grossed between $5,000 and $5,500 a week."[12] Receiving high marks from both black and white reviewers, *Swing Mikado* showed that blacks could do Gilbert and Sullivan and bring something special to it. While most of the white reviewers wanted more of the "exotic and primitive," the production so excited the theater industry that New York tried to buy *Swing Mikado* from the Chicago Theater.

Swing Mikado was directed by Harry Minturn, who, in 1937, was the white acting assistant director to Hallie Flanagan, charged with the responsibility of finding a play for the Chicago Negro Unit. With a background primarily in "vaudeville and popular shows as theatrical manager and producer, actor and director," he had no particular cultural or New Deal mission.[13] Less interested in making a political statement about the importance of blacks in the FTP, Minturn was more interested in showcasing his talents and those of the performers. Minturn chose to present an adaptation of the Gilbert and Sullivan success, *The Mikado*, a comic opera about a young girl, Yum-Yum, who falls in love with the Mikado's son, but is promised to an older man, Ko-Ko. The Mikado, however, has sworn that anyone who is unmarried and eyes or flirts with another will be beheaded. Ko-Ko has been condemned to death for "such crimes to humanity." Nevertheless, the people release him because the next person to be decapitated "Cannot cut off another's head / Until he's cut his own off."[14]

While *The Mikado* focuses on bizarre situations, *Swing Mikado* showcases both the actors' talents and the director's. Minturn changed the setting from Japan, which had been controversial, to the South Pacific. He also catered to some of the actors' dancing skills and singing talents by rearranging three of the songs to swing versions and by keeping other songs true to the original script, respectively.

The show opened in the fall of 1938 as part of the new season, and received enthusiastic reviews from both white and black audiences. Black reviewers believed the success of this musical comedy would bring people to the theater in

Chicago and throughout the nation with eager anticipation to see such a great production. Although most white reviewers wanted a more stereotyped black presentation and more swing, they were nevertheless impressed with the performance and gave it high marks. The production demonstrated the gifts of the black cast and showed that black casts could do wonders with an exceptional play, such as the one by Gilbert and Sullivan.

The successful production of *Swing Mikado* fulfilled the needs of several groups, as Fraden clearly notes. Minturn was pleased with his ability to direct successfully a black cast without making too many changes and still appeal to the black audience. The cast was pleased with the opportunity to perform in a musical comedy with the reputation of *The Mikado*. The FTP director applauded the performance's bringing theater to a number who, without the government's help, would be unable to experience theater. The FTP was especially pleased with the jobs provided for blacks with theatrical skill and the unit's helping people to build and maintain their skills.

The Chicago unit's success with *Swing Mikado* and other white productions tailored to black casts generally eclipsed the work of the black playwright. Though producers and directors were still calling for better plays by blacks, and one of the objectives of the FTP was to develop black playwrights, there were few opportunities in Chicago for writers to master the discipline and skills to write good plays, as in the case of the Negro Dramatists' Laboratory in New York. Theodore Ward, the black playwright and author of *Big White Fog*, however, had collaborated with Richard Wright and learned from him and the group of writers with whom Wright associated. When Wright worked for a while with the Chicago Negro unit, he tried to assist playwrights and actors, but his ideas were not readily accepted, particularly by the actors who objected to what they perceived as Wright's radical form of theater.

Flanagan had the idea of uplift as the focus of the Negro units and was not opposed to rejecting some of the plays, especially if she deemed them too violent or potentially upsetting for the audience. Although she rejected Hughes Allison's *Panyared*, a play about miscegenation and the violence of slavery, black playwrights continued to submit material to the FTP. While the FTP wanted opportunities and self-determination for blacks in the units, the federal administration was not beyond censorship.

With some censorship but greater opportunities under the government-sponsored program, black playwrights were willing to take their chance with the FTP. Among the list were Hall Johnson, Frank Wilson, Hughes Allison, John Silvera, Abram Hill, Augustus Smith, Paul Morrell, Rudolph Fisher, Theodore Brown, and Theodore Ward. While the reviewers looked at the plays with a cautious eye, and sometimes allowed FTP politics and confusion to obstruct their critical vision, some of the plays were produced by one or more Negro units of the

FTP. The most popular play written for the FTP and initially produced by the Chicago unit is Theodore Ward's *Big White Fog*, a striking example of dramatic realism, which first appeared in 1938. Set in Chicago during the years between 1922 and 1932, the play was Ward's attempt to create a realistic portrayal of African American life. Unlike some of the plays submitted to the FTP, which did not always get a favorable response from the administration, *Big White Fog* was one of the plays Flanagan strongly supported. It was also a play that dealt with racism and injustice in the urban north, something absent in many of the plays produced by the FTP. Ward's play made money during its ten-week run in Chicago, and gave the city a strong presence in the revival of black theater.

Theodore Ward's experiences were fodder for his creativity. Louisiana-born, he left at the age of thirteen and traveled throughout the United States. Working odd jobs, he eventually settled in Chicago, after attending the University of Utah and the University of Wisconsin. In Chicago, he met Richard Wright, joined the John Reed Club, and began working for the WPA. In a short while, Ward had become an active part of the creative and cultural group of the South Side of Chicago, or Bronzeville.

Keenly aware of the racism and Jim Crow practices that existed not just in small southern towns, but in big northern cities as well, Ward believed in a coalition of working-class blacks and whites as an effective way of dealing with the racial and class injustices with which he was familiar. One of his goals as a playwright was to write about the injustices confronting the black family, and how the family can be devastated by racism and capitalism. Ward's journey from the South to the industrialized North represents an important chapter in black social history, and as Fraden asserts, *Big White Fog* dramatizes "what happens to their dreams once they hit the big northern city."[15]

Big White Fog is a play reflecting the life of an African American family living in Chicago in the twenties. Through Victor Mason, the patriarch, his wife and children—particularly his son, Les, and daughter, Wanda—his in-laws, and Les's Jewish friend, Pizer, the play reveals the ideological, political, and economical struggle of the Mason family as they wander in a "big white fog." A three-act play, *Big White Fog* describes Victor Mason and his family during the years blacks were rapidly immigrating to Chicago from the south. Vic Mason, a single-minded Garveyite, demonstrates the commitment of some blacks to Marcus Garvey's self-help, independence, and back-to-Africa program, which had a branch in Chicago.

The play opens in 1922, in the living room of the Mason home on Dearborn Street, Chicago, the setting of the entire play. Like many African Americans who had migrated to the cities during WWI, Vic uproots his family from the Mississippi cotton fields in search of a dream, only to find it illusive. Spending his time "carrying a hod by day and wrestling in the movement all night," Vic is determined to follow through on the promises he made to his family. Like others, he dreams of a place where his children can be educated, his wife can live without being victimized by prejudice, and he can experience self-worth as a black man.

Instead of realizing his dream, Victor Mason watches his family endure economic and social inequalities. His older son is rejected for a scholarship, for which he is qualified, because blacks are ineligible. His older daughter drops out of school, takes a job, and ends up supporting the family, sometimes by questionable means. Vic, himself, foolishly invests the family's $1500 in Garvey's Black Star Line, leaving his wife unable to take care of the younger children. Finally, reaching the breaking point, the Mason family unravels under the pressures, which in the end reveal themselves in domestic hostilities, self-hatred, and acrimonious insults.

While Garveyism does not save Victor, he remains a loyal follower until the Depression hits and the family faces eviction. When his son encourages him to join hands with the resistance forces that have organized to fight the powerful bosses, Vic is unwilling. But when the bailiff calls for the policeman to enforce the eviction notice, Vic stands his ground. He does not, however, acknowledge the value of the resistance struggle until he lay dying, the victim of a policeman's bullet.

The act of resistance by a coalition of left-wing blacks and whites at the conclusion of *Big White Fog* seems to be Ward's answer to the economic and social injustices faced by blacks in Chicago and throughout the country. The play took a position on political and social issues facing those who left *de facto* slavery seeking the mythic north. Ward's re-creation of this part of black life reflected what W. E. B. DuBois, Sterling Brown, and Richard Wright outlined in their discussions about the need for more realistic portrayals. Exploring issues common to black families in a racially and economically hostile environment was categorically different from anything about blacks that had been produced in Chicago by the FTP.

In spite of its originality and promise, *Big White Fog* had a rather tumultuous journey to the stage. Harry Minturn, who was then acting director of the Chicago Project in 1937, agreed with the position of W. E. B. DuBois that the play should be presented somewhere on the South Side. Though Ward wanted his play presented before a broader audience, Minturn asked Shirley Graham to find a theater in the Black community. Fraden notes that part of Shirley Graham's responsibility was to find out what the black community was thinking, to interpret it for Minturn, and to garner their support. Graham, who knew the tastes of black Chicago audiences, recognized the problems the play presented to some of the people. According to Graham, issues addressed in the play—coalition among blacks and whites, which they interpreted as Communism, black women taking money from white men, blacks' support of their own businesses exclusively, and even the Garvey failure would be troublesome to black audiences.

There were other concerns about *Big White Fog*. Blacks were not a homogeneous audience. Some wanted the re-creation of material socially and politically relevant, while others preferred to be entertained with singing, dancing, jokes, and considerable artifice. Some members of the audience didn't want to be reminded of the struggle, while others wanted it reinforced in the theater. These differences, along with Graham's commitment to racial uplift, did not imbue her with enthusiasm for the play. Moreover, she was disappointed with Chicago blacks whom she believed lacked interest in culture. When the play was previewed at the YWCA on the South Side, the reception was polite, but not enthusiastic, and responses later collected were unfavorable. After Graham reread the play, she decided it should not be produced. *Big White Fog* did finally reach the stage, the political controversies notwithstanding. Fraden suspects the Chicago city administration put pressure on the WPA, and the play was produced at the Great Northern theatre, the setting of many of the FTP's experimental plays. Flanagan had urged the FTP to produce the play, and so had a well-known African American woman who told the downtown bureaucrats Blacks wanted to see *Big White Fog*. After the successful run in Chicago to a mixed audience, the play went to locations in the Bronzeville area. When the government cut the funds of the WPA and the FTP ended, *Big White Fog* went to New York and was revived by the Negro Theater Company.

The Federal Theatre Project ended on June 30, 1939, by an Act of Congress. Flanagan writes that the Federal Theatre ended because of political issues. She also notes that she had read in a New York paper that the Federal Theatre was "dominated by Communists and that you had to belong to the Workers' Alliance in order to get on the project."[16] Members of Congress were not willing to put their careers on the line for the Federal Theatre, the budget of which they had been shaving for two years. Eventually the FTP became the victim of Congressional legislation.

The Federal Theatre Project, like the other three arts projects of the WPA, was created out of the need to respond to the high unemployment among creative artists. By the early 1930s African Americans who had migrated to Chicago had established a culturally vital community, which they tried to maintain in spite of the economic climate. A significant part of this culture was the theater, which had begun to decline in the late 1920s with the arrival of cheaper forms of entertainment and the onset of the Depression. The Chicago Negro Unit of the FTP became invaluable to Chicago's black theater and helped to shape it into one of the most important creative outlets of the Chicago Renaissance.

The Black Chicago Renaissance benefited significantly from the activities of the Negro unit. The unit assured Blacks employment opportunities in the theater, while it helped them to hone and conserve their skills. Black technicians, stagehands, actors, designers, and writers were able to participate in the productions supported by the government. *Little Black Sambo, Swing Mikado*, and *Big White Fog* were three of the most successful productions of the Chicago Negro unit, bringing attention to black Chicago and its theater tradition. The success of both *Swing Mikado* and *Big White Fog*, principally, helped to shape the cultural and artistic achievement of Chicago during the thirties and forties, and all who contributed to the accomplishments are now part of the history of the FTP and the Chicago Renaissance.

Notes

1. Flanagan, Rena. ARENA: *The History of the Federal Theatre*. New York: Cambridge University Press, 1965, 111.
2. Ibid., 111.
3. Ross, Ronald. "The Role of Blacks in the Federal Theatre, 1935–39." In *The Theater of Black Americans Vol. II: in The Presenters/the Participators*, edited by Errol Hill. Englewood Cliffs, N.J.: Prentice-Hall, 1980, 35.
4. Fraden, Rena. *Blueprints for a Black Federal Theatre, 1935–39*. New York: Cambridge University Press, 1994, 3.
5. Mitchell, Loften. "The Depression Year: Propaganda Plays, the Federal Theatre, Efforts Toward a New Harlem Theater." In *Black Drama: The Story of the American Negro in the Theatre*. New York: Hawthorne Books, 1967, 100.
6. Flanagan, *ARENA: The History of the Federal Theatre*, 21.
7. Fraden, *Blueprints for a Black Federal Theatre, 1935–39*, 96.
8. Ross, "The Role of Blacks in the Federal Theatre, 1935–39," 45–46.
9. Flanagan, *ARENA: The History of the Federal Theatre*, 144.
10. Ibid., 215.
11. Ibid.
12. Fraden, *Blueprints for a Black Federal Theatre, 1935–39*, 189.
13. Ibid.
14. Ibid., 187.
15. Ibid., 117.
16. Flanagan, 335.

For Further Reading

Abramson, Doris E. "The Thirties: The Job We Never Had," and "The Forties: Did Somebody Die?" In her *Negro Playwrights in the American Theatre*. New York: Columbia University Press, 1969, 44–164.

Brown, Lorraine and the Staff of the Fenwick Library, George Mason University. *The Federal Theatre Project: A Catalog-Calendar of Productions*. New York: Greenwood Press, 1986.

Brown, Lorraine. "Federal Theatre: Melodrama, Social Protest and Genius." *Journal of the Library of Congress* 36, 1 (Winter 1979): 18–37.

Brown, Sterling. "Realistic and Problem Drama." In his *Negro Poetry and Drama and the Negro in American Fiction*. New York: Atheneum, 1972, 124–42.

Chicago Renaissance 1932–1950, Chicago Public Library Digital Collections. http://www.chipublib.org/digital/chiren/introduction.html.

http://www.chipublib.org/digital/chiren/artpage.html; http://www.chipublib.org/digital/chiren/institutions.html; http://www.chipublib.org/digital/chiren/literature.html.

Fraden, Rena. "A National Negro Theater That Never Was: A History of African American Theater Production, Performance and Drama in the US—Includes a Directory of National and Regional African American Theater Companies." *American Visions* (October–November 1994). http://www.findarticles.com/p/articles/mi_mi_m1546/isn5_v9/ai15875048/print.

Hamalian, Leo and James V. Hatch. *Lost Plays of the Harlem Renaissance: 1920–1940*. Detroit: Wayne State University Press, 1966.

Hatch, James V. and Omanii Abdullah, comp. and eds. *Black Playwrights, 1823–1977: An Annotated Bibliography of Plays*. New York: R. R. Bowker, 1977.

The Living Newspaper. http://www.thirteen.org/pressroom/pdf/fedtheatre/Living Newspaper.pdf.

Mitchell, Loften. "The Depression Year: Propaganda Plays, the Federal Theatre, Efforts toward a New Harlem Theatre." In his *Black Drama: The Story of the American Negro in the Theatre*. New York: Hawthorne Books, 1967, 91–110.

Ponce, Pedro. "An Hour upon the Stage: The Brief Life of the Federal Theatre." http://www.neh.gov/news/humanities/2003-07/federaltheatre.html.

Reardon, Patrick T. "Can Bronzeville Reclaim Its Soul? After Redevelopment, the Name May Be All That's Left of the Community's Rich Heritage," *Chicago Tribune*, May 21, 2000. http://www.palmtavern.bizland.com/palmtavern/000521 Can_Bronzeville_Reclaim_Its_Soul_full. http://www.chfestival.org/education.cfm?Action=EdLessons.

Ross, Ronald. "The Role of Blacks in the Federal Theatre, 1935–1939." In *The Theater of Black Americans Vol. II: The Presenters/the Participators*, edited by Errol Hill. Englewood Cliffs, N.J.: Prentice-Hall, 1980, 33–48.

Trumbull, Eric W. "The Federal Theatre Project" (1998–2001). http://www.novaonline.nv.cc.va.us/eli/spd130et/federaltheatre.htm.

AFRICAN AMERICAN MUSIC IN CHICAGO DURING THE CHICAGO RENAISSANCE

Robert H. Cataliotti

While the Black Chicago Renaissance is primarily recognized for the flourishing of African American literature, during this era the city played host to a flourishing of African American music. Chicago's black musicians applied their creative talents and technical mastery to jazz, blues, gospel, an emerging form, rhythm and blues, and European classical music. One distinction, however, that existed between the literature and the music was that Chicago had already established itself as a crucial center for African American music during the New Negro Renaissance era of the 1920s, when the earlier white Chicago Renaissance was in full swing.

Throughout the evolution of the African American literary tradition, black writers have often been drawn to African American music's ability to function as a cultural conduit and attempted to infuse their texts with its spiritual essence. Certainly the writers of the Chicago Renaissance were working in an environment suffused with black musical creativity. One of the writers whose work served as a bridge between the New Negro Renaissance and the Chicago Renaissance was Frank Marshall Davis. He first moved to the city for a two-year stay as a journalist in 1927 and returned in 1934. Davis clearly found his cultural identity in the music: "But I feel the blues walked into my life when I first heard them and have never left me. That's why I call my autobiography *Livin' the Blues.*" He wrote about the new, black urban experience and considered the free verse he employed in his poetry as the literary equivalent of jazz improvisation: "So I put down my roots to live in Chicago, and I think I had some success in my attempt to mirror Aframerican Chicago in particular.... There is no law preventing the ancient muse from blowing a saxophone."[1] Margaret Walker, in the title poem to her 1942 volume *For My People*, begins the poem with an evocation of the variety and importance of African American music, and draws on music for a number of important poems in the collection. The writers who worked during the Chicago Renaissance, Frank Marshall Davis, Margaret Walker, Richard Wright, Frank London Brown, and Gwendolyn Brooks among them, may be seen as aesthetically coexisting with and in many cases drawing upon the spirit and energy of the music in order to generate their own artistic productions.

The foundation for Chicago's African American music scene was laid during the turn of the nineteenth century when a career in music came to be regarded as a reputable pursuit for members of the city's black upper class. In *From Jazz to Swing*, Thomas J. Hennessey states: "In 1890, Chicago's black musicians were clearly tied to the respectable establishment's institutions and emphasis on appearances and traditions. Those institutions—the black lodges, churches, and the Eighth Illinois National Guard regiment—provided most of the opportunities for musicians."[2] There was an emphasis on formal musical training, and in 1902 an African American union, Local 208 of the American Federation of Musicians, was formed. During the next two decades, professional opportunities multiplied for African American musicians in Chicago. Theaters opened, requiring pit bands to perform for silent movies and vaudeville artists. In addition, black musicians found work in clubs and for dances.

The Great Migration that was leading African Americans out of the South toward northern urban centers, such as Chicago, included many musicians. Jazz, an amalgam of brass bands, ragtime, blues, spirituals, and European forms, found particularly fertile ground for its inception in New Orleans and was carried to Chicago during the early years of the 1920s. These New Orleans jazz men included pianist Jelly Roll Morton, clarinetist Johnny Dodds, cornetist Joe "King" Oliver, trombonist Edward "Kid" Ory, and cornetist Louis Armstrong (switching to trumpet in Chicago). This infusion of new talent combined with the opportunity to perform with established local musicians, such as bandleader and educator Erskine Tate, created an environment that would spur the evolution of jazz. In the 1920s, the Chicago's jazz scene was making a major contribution to the New Negro Renaissance, even though its locus may have been Harlem. The recordings made by Armstrong with his Hot Five and Hot Seven bands and Morton's Red Hot Peppers band cemented Chicago as the preeminent center of the jazz world. While Morton is recognized for his innovative compositions, Armstrong's recorded work in Chicago during this era is nothing short of revolutionary as he switched the emphasis of jazz performance from collective ensemble playing to a focus on the structured, individual improvisation in dialogue with a group underpinning, infused with an uplifting energy dubbed "swing." By the close of the 1920s, the economics of the music business changed, and with Armstrong's move East in 1929, the center of the jazz world shifted from Chicago to New York.

Despite this shift to the East Coast, new venues opened in Chicago during the final years of the 1920s that insured African American musicians would continue to create a viable and innovative jazz scene in the city throughout the era now known as the Black Chicago Renaissance. In 1928, the Grand Terrace Café opened on South Parkway and Thirty-Ninth Street with a stage show and former Armstrong associate, Pittsburgh-born pianist Earl "Fatha" Hines, at the helm of a ten-piece orchestra. Hines worked at the club for ten years, and he became the first black bandleader in Chicago to be broadcast nightly on a national radio network. As Thomas J. Hennessey asserts in *From Jazz to Swing*: "Hines's Grand Terrace Band became the major Chicago band of the 1930s with a style strongly tied to national trends."[3] Over the years, the Hines band became a proving ground for many Chicago-reared jazz artists. The band's tenure at the Grand Terrace marked the nightclub as one of the city's landmark musical venues, and it continued (at a new location after 1937) to book African American musical artists into the 1950s.

The Regal Theater was another major venue for black music that opened in 1928. Located next to the Savoy Ballroom (which had opened in 1926), at Forty-seventh and South Parkway, the Regal was part of a series of showcases, along with the Royal in Baltimore, the Howard in Washington, D.C., the Apollo in New York, the Fox in Detroit, and the Uptown in Philadelphia, that became known as the "chitlin' circuit," booking stellar revues of black entertainment through the 1960s. The Savoy experienced its ups and downs throughout its twenty-two years of operation. A hot spot during the 1920s, it presented prize-fights and roller-skating along with local bands during the 1930s. The Savoy was revivified during the later years of the decade with the booking of premiere, nationally renowned, African American swing bands, such as Duke Ellington, Count Basie, Chick Webb, Andy Kirk, Jimmy Lunceford, Erskine Hawkins, and Fletcher Henderson.

During the 1930s, the establishment of a large number of clubs on the city's South Side, which came to be known as "Bronzeville," played a significant role in nurturing African American jazz artists in Chicago. Many of these clubs were located along East Garfield Boulevard. In *An Autobiography of Black Jazz*, Dempsey J. Travis recalls the scene: "Most of the nightclubs and lounges along Garfield Boulevard were open twenty-four hours a day, so there was a lot of all-night sidewalk traffic. Neon signs hung in front of the showplaces that were strung like pearls along the Boulevard." These clubs, which featured a mix of local Chicago and national talent, included Rhumboogie, Three Deuces, Ciro's, the El Rado Café in the Garfield Hotel, Herb "Speedy" Bruce's Lounge, the It Club, and Booker Ashford's 65 Club.[4] It is likely that the sounds he heard in clubs such as these inspired Frank Marshall Davis's 1935 poem, "Jazz Band." The opening stanza reflects the emotive, rhythmic energy of a jazz club: "Play that thing, you jazz mad fools! / Boil a skyscraper with a jungle / Ahhhhhhhh / Rip it open then sew it up, jazz band!"[5] One of the premiere clubs on Chicago's South Side featuring African American musical artists was the Club DeLisa, which opened in 1934 and relocated in 1941. With its floor show, often featuring a chorus line, dance teams, comedians, and top-flight musicians, the Club DeLisa attracted celebrities, both black and white, and provided a springboard to national recognition for such performers as vocalists Billy Eckstine (with Hines) and Joe Williams (with Basie), bassist Israel Crosby (with Henderson) and comedian George Kirby. In *An Autobiography of Black Jazz*, Dempsey J. Travis describes the scene at Club DeLisa: "The musical and artistic talent found at Club DeLisa made it the "in" place to go whether you were a native or a visitor to Chicago. To make certain that everybody got into the act, the club furnished souvenir table knockers to every patron. Every night at Club DeLisa was a holiday like Christmas or New Year's Eve."[6]

In 1940, another major Chicago Renaissance era jazz institution opened its doors, the DuSable Hotel, and a year later, the DuSable Lounge began featuring live music in the basement. The DuSable's impact, however, went beyond the music scene. Located at 764 East Oakwood Boulevard, the hotel served as an agent of social change as it spearheaded the expansion of the South Side African American community east of Cottage Grove and south of Oakwood. The hotel became a central location for African Americans visiting Chicago, particularly jazz musicians and entertainers. The Lounge was open twenty-four hours a day and was a prime destination for jam sessions when both local and touring musicians finished their performances at other venues.[7]

During the Chicago Renaissance, a remarkable amount of jazz talent emerged from the city, participating in both the local and national music scenes. A great deal of credit for this new generation of African American musicians must be given to educator Captain Walter Henri Dyett, who taught at Wendell Phillips (1931–35) and DuSable (1936–69) High Schools. Dyett carried on the tradition of quality music education in Chicago's black community that reached back to the nineteenth century. He picked up the mantle of Nathaniel Clark Smith, who had mentored the previous generation of black musicians, including bassist Milt Hinton, drummer/vibraharpist Lionel Hampton, bassist Eddie Cole, and trumpeter/violinist Ray Nance, at Wendell Phillips and in the *Chicago Defender* band. In addition to his career as an educator, Dyett was the bandmaster in the U.S. Eighth Infantry band and led the bands around the city. Dorothy Donegan remembers Dyett's influence in Dempsey J. Travis's *An Autobiography of Black Jazz*: "Captain Dyett was an excellent musician and a hard taskmaster. He would always say, 'When you're right, you can afford to be quiet.' But he also made you very conscious of being a good musician."[8] The jazz artists who participated in DuSable's music program during the Chicago Renaissance and emerged as major figures on the national jazz scene include pianists Donegan, Nat "King" Cole, and John Young; trumpeter Raymond Orr; drummer Floyd

Campbell; singer Austin Powell; bassist Richard Davis; saxophonists Johnny Board, Gene "Jug" Ammons, Von Freeman, Clifford Jordan, John Gilmore, and Johnny Griffin, among many others.

Even though the city was no longer the primary seat of jazz innovation, the musicians who emerged from the local scene went on to play central roles in the development of the tradition. Cole is by far the most renowned jazz artist to emerge from the Chicago Renaissance. Ironically, his stature as a jazz musician is overshadowed by the popularity he achieved as a singer later in his career. He left Chicago in 1936 and settled in Los Angeles, where he established the highly influential and successful King Cole Trio. He continued to perform and record as a pianist and vocalist with the trio until 1951, and his jazz work was also featured both on record and in concert with Norman Granz's Jazz at the Philharmonic. Donegan built a career as a club and cabaret artist with a reputation for virtuoso technique as a jazz, boogie-woogie, and classical pianist. Ammons became known as the main bop soloist in Eckstine's big band and through his fabled saxophone battles with Sonny Stitt. Griffin established his reputation through associations with pianists Bud Powell and Thelonious Monk, drummer Art Blakey, and as coleader of a quintet with fellow tenor saxophonist Eddie "Lockjaw" Davis. Jordan made a name for himself through his work in the bands of drummer Max Roach, pianist Horace Silver, and bassist Charles Mingus. Richard Davis's bass playing brought him associations with a wide variety of stylists, including singer Sarah Vaughan; pianist Hank Jones; reed men Eric Dolphy, Booker Ervin, Stan Getz, and Ben Webster; and the Thad Jones–Mel Lewis Orchestra. Freeman often performed on the local scene in bands with his brothers, guitarist George and drummer Bruz. During the 1940s, he worked in Chicago as a sideman with artists like Horace Henderson, Charlie Parker, Roy Eldridge, and Lester Young, and in the 1950s, he performed with Ahmad Jamal and members of the younger generation who formed the nucleus of the emerging avant-garde scene. After touring with blues and R&B acts in the 1960s, he returned to working regularly on the local scene, and in late 1970s, his son, Chico, established himself on the New York scene. Clearly, during the Chicago Renaissance the city's music scene produced world-class musicians who sustained the jazz tradition, both locally and nationally.

During World War II, the Chicago area experienced a massive influx of African American musical, particularly jazz, talent due to the U.S. Navy's establishment of a special camp for training black recruits at the Great Lakes base. Before 1942, African Americans could serve in the navy only as mess attendants and stewards, but antidiscrimination policies were instituted during World War II, and the navy organized, ironically, the segregated Camp Robert Smalls. Eventually, two other "black camps" were established, Camp Moffet and Camp Lawrence, and each camp had its own band. The recruits included some of the best African American musicians, including veterans of the Hines, Ellington, Henderson, and Jay McShann big bands, as well as musicians and singers with chorus, movie, and Broadway show experience. The best band at Great Lakes, the Camp Smalls "A" Band, played concerts on a regular basis in Grant Park in Chicago, and the best musicians from each camp's band were joined together to create a radio band and presented a CBS network "Men O' War Radio Show" every Saturday night from Chicago's WBBM.[9]

Over five thousand African American servicemen were trained in the music programs at the Great Lakes base. When the bandsmen completed training, they were organized into twenty-five member bands and assigned to bases throughout the country. As Eileen Southern states in *The Music of Black Americans*: "They performed so ably that the Great Lakes camps earned a well-deserved reputation for producing some of the finest musicians in the armed services."[10] During the war, African American soldiers and sailors, including many of the men stationed at Great Lakes, congregated at USO Serviceman's Center #3, which was established because the other two Chicago-area centers were designated for whites only. In an interview with Charles Walton, trumpeter Clark Terry recalled his Great Lakes experience: "When we were in the navy, in 1942, we were a new breed as far as the Black Man was concerned. Earlier, all Black people associated with the navy were assigned as chief cooks, bootblacks and stokers, but in 1942, we came into a program that was inaugurated in 1941. When we finished our boot camp we received our ratings, which was displayed by having a lyre sewn on our sleeve. To see a Black man in the U.S. Navy with a lyre on his sleeve instead of a C, which meant cook, was quite an oddity. We literally took over Chicago. The old Bacon's Casino, on Forty-ninth and Wabash, used to be our headquarters after it became a USO."[11] Following the war, the Navy bandsmen, including many Chicago musicians, returned to prominent positions on the jazz scene.

While Chicago had lost its place as the center of the jazz tradition's development at the close of the 1920s, the city's African American music scene kept pace with the evolution of jazz during the Chicago Renaissance. Big band swing played an integral role in the theaters and dance halls in the 1930s, and as the big bands broke up in the 1940s, their star soloists appeared with their own small groups or with local rhythm sections in South Side clubs and theaters. Also, during the 1940s, the new sounds of bebop found a home in the music venues of Bronzeville.

As the Chicago Renaissance era was coming to a close in the early 1950s, the city's musicians were at the forefront of laying a foundation for a new approach to jazz, the avant-garde. One of the Chicago-based explorers of this new music was pianist Sun Ra (Herman "Sonny" Blount), who came to the city in 1946 to work with the Henderson big band at the Club DeLisa and continued working in the area. In 1949, he was back at the DeLisa working as the pianist and arranger for drummer Red Saunders's house band. During this time, he went through some kind of spiritual transformation, and, in 1952, he declared that he was a citizen of Saturn and a member of an angel race. He changed his name to Le Sony'r Ra.[12] His band, which he renamed the Arkestra, included core members who would remain with him for decades, including saxophonists Gilmore, Pat Patrick, and Marshall Allen. They began performing at Cadillac Bob's Budland in the basement of the Pershing Hotel. The Arkestra was playing hard swinging, bebop-influenced compositions and made their first recordings in 1956. Sun Ra's music became increasingly free-form over the rest of the decade, and when the band moved to New York in 1961, his music had clearly pioneered a path for the avant-garde.[13] Foremost among the new generation of musicians that was emerging on the Chicago scene to contribute to the development of the jazz avant-garde in the following decade were pianists Muhal Richard Abrams and Andrew Hill. Abrams, who studied at the Chicago Musical College, worked professionally as a sideman and arranger on the local scene beginning in 1948. He went on to form one of the first free jazz ensembles and founded the Association for the Advancement of Creative Musicians in 1965. Hill studied with the composer Paul Hindemith and worked around the Chicago club scene beginning in 1950, where he backed up soloists such as Miles Davis, Charlie Parker, and Griffin. He moved to New York in 1961 as an accompanist for Dinah Washington and went on to garner recognition as an avant-garde improviser and composer. Other young musicians who emerged from the city's jazz scene during the final years of the Chicago Renaissance era and went on to play a significant role in the evolution of the avant-garde were trombonist Julian Priester, bassist Malachi Favors, violinist Leroy Jenkins, and reed players Anthony Braxton, Joseph Jarman, Roscoe Mitchell, and Henry Threadgill.[14]

The blues, like jazz, traveled north to Chicago in the Great Migration during the first two decades of the twentieth century. Female singers, such as Alberta Hunter and Lucille Hegamin, who melded blues with popular, vaudeville material, a style that came to be called "Classic Blues," were living in the city and performing in South Side clubs prior to 1920. Other Classic Blues singers, such as Gertrude "Ma" Rainey, Ida Cox, and Lucille Bogan, came to Chicago during the 1920s to perform at vaudeville theaters and record for labels like Paramount and Brunswick. Bertha "Chippie" Hill moved to Chicago in the midtwenties, after touring as a singer and dancer with the Rabbit Foot Minstrels. She performed and recorded with many of the city's leading jazz musicians, including Armstrong and Oliver. In *Black Pearls: Blues Queens of the 1920s*, Daphne Duval Harrison states that although Hill never achieved a large national following, she developed a unique approach to the Classic Blues idiom: "Hill's style does not evoke images of the bereft, helpless female. Instead, one hears a woman who has seen and heard it all, who can be down, but refuses to be counted out." Over the next two decades, Hill worked in venues like the Club DeLisa.[15]

Toward the end of the 1920s, Southern male blues musicians started to migrate to Chicago, drawn to the opportunities to record and perform for the African American community that was rapidly developing on the city's South Side. Two of the earliest of these blues men to arrive in Chicago were the guitarist Tampa Red (Hudson Whitaker) and pianist Thomas A. "Georgia Tom" Dorsey. They teamed up and had a profound influence in shaping the Chicago blues scene that would blossom during the Chicago Renaissance. According to Mike Rowe in *Chicago Breakdown*, the piano/guitar format contributed to the urbanization of the blues sound: "Piano disciples were already beginning to curb the rough zeal of the blues guitarist and this trend towards a more uniform blues sound was the first effect of the transition of the blues from the country to the city." In 1928, Dorsey and Red recorded "It's Tight Like That" for the Vocalion label, and it became a huge national hit. With its bawdy lyrics and good time, rocking "hokum" sound, the success of "It's Tight Like That" represented a major transitional event for Chicago blues. It had clear connections back to the rural culture from which the blues was migrating but also captured the up-tempo, rhythmic drive of the evolving, modern African American, urban experience.[16]

During the early 1930s, Dorsey left the blues behind and applied his talents to shaping the newly emerging gospel idiom. Red, however, played a major role in sustaining the Chicago blues scene as he employed and mentored the next wave of blues men migrating into the city. In fact, he opened his home to many of these new arrivals who were responsible for the blossoming of the city's blues during the Chicago Renaissance, including guitarist William "Big Bill" Broonzy, pianist Memphis Slim (Peter Chatman), harmonica player John Lee "Sonny Boy" Williamson, singer Peter "Doctor" Clayton, and pianist Major "Big Maceo" Merriweather. It was the sound of blues crafted by the likes of these bluesmen that probably played on the jukebox of the South Side fried chicken joint on the fateful night that Bigger Thomas spent with Mary Dalton and her boyfriend Jan in Richard Wright's 1940 novel, *Native Son*.[17]

Although he was firmly rooted in the blues of the Mississippi Delta, Broonzy epitomized the new, urbanized sound produced in Chicago and came to be recognized as the most influential blues man on the scene during the first decade of the Chicago Renaissance era. As Paul Oliver states in *The Story of the Blues*: "In his voice could be heard a quality that recalled the field holler and an authority that suggested the city dweller. Both were present because his life was spent between Chicago and his Arkansas farm, and with his continued contact with both rural and urban living, Broonzy sang of each with feeling."[18] His career reached a watershed moment in 1938 when he was asked to replace the recently deceased Mississippi blues man Robert Johnson at impresario John

Hammond's "From Spirituals to Swing" concert at New York's Carnegie Hall. A versatile and innovative artist, Broonzy could perform solo, rural, Delta blues, "hokum" style good-time music with artists like Georgia Tom, and, increasingly during the 1930s, swing-influenced blues with small bands including horns, piano, bass, and drums. He was also one of the first blues men to use an electric guitar. Working regularly in South Side clubs and recording extensively as both a leader and sideman, Broonzy, like Red before him, became a mentor to many of the blues musicians who arrived from the South. When the Chicago blues style shifted to a raw, driving, electrified sound after World War II, Broonzy continued to record the urban blues he pioneered, but he also went back to his roots and recast himself as an acoustic, rural blues man and resuscitated his career by appealing to the fledgling folk music revival.

Another musician who had a major impact on the evolution of blues during the first half of the Chicago Renaissance was Sonny Boy Williamson, often referred to as No. 1, so he is not confused with another harmonica player/singer, Sonny Boy Williamson (No. 2), who migrated to Chicago in the 1950s. Williamson No. 1 arrived in Chicago in 1934, and often worked with Broonzy. Using an innovative, "crossed" harp style, he is almost single-handedly responsible for making the harmonica (harp) a central solo instrument in the Chicago blues sound. As Giles Oakley asserts in *The Devil's Music*: "Harps had always played their parts in the blues, especially the jug bands, but Sonny Boy (No. 1) was identified as the lead man, completely tied to the sound of his instrument. The fast interplay between little instrumental riffs and voice, the upfront drive of his blowing and his vocal mannerisms were much admired, bringing him a rapid rise to pre-eminence in Chicago." Williamson No. 1's career was cut short in 1948 when he was murdered, yet his work represents a major link with the post–World War II blues scene in Chicago.[19]

Although female Classic Blues singers had ruled the Chicago scene during the 1920s, by the Chicago Renaissance era, the blues had become a male-dominated form. One woman, guitarist Memphis Minnie (Lizzie Douglas), however, established herself as an important Chicago-based blues artist during the 1930s. Born in New Orleans, she launched her career on Beale Street in Memphis during the 1920s and headed to Chicago early in the next decade. She held her own alongside the blues men on the scene and is reputed to have bested Broonzy in a South Side blues contest. A pioneer in the use of the electric guitar, she was the subject of a January 1943 *Chicago Defender* review by Langston Hughes. He describes a New Year's Eve performance with post–Depression-era patrons flush with money from national defense work: "Memphis Minnie, at year's end, picks up those nuances and tunes them into the strings of her guitar, weaves them into runs and trills and deep steady chords that come through the amplifiers like Negro heartbeats mixed with iron and steel. The way Memphis Minnie swings, it sometimes makes folks snap their fingers, women get up and move their bodies, men holler, 'Yes!' When they do, Minnie smiles."[20] The Blue Monday parties that she hosted for over a decade at Ruby Lee's Gatewood Tavern, which featured both established stars and up-and-coming artists, testify to Memphis Minnie's prominence on the Chicago Renaissance era blues scene.

During the 1920s, a highly rhythmic style of piano blues called "boogie-woogie" garnered widespread popularity. The phenomenon was largely due to the success of a 1928 record, called "Pine Top's Boogie Woogie," recorded in 1928 by Chicago-based pianist Clarence "Pine Top" Smith. Boogie-woogie features a percussive approach, which is comprised of blues chord progressions played by the right hand in dialogue with the left hand playing a repetitive, "rolling" bass pattern.[21] Although the title of Smith's record most prominently associated him with the style, there were many pianists in Chicago (and in other cities) during the 1920s who featured this approach, including Albert Ammons (father of the bebop saxophonist Gene), Meade "Lux" Lewis, "Cripple" Clarence Lofton, Eur-real "Little Brother" Montgomery, and Jimmy Yancey. This piano music literally found a home in Chicago and other African American urban communities as the soundtrack for "rent parties," where the music attracted admission-paying revelers to help the host raise money for rent. As Giles Oakley declares in *The Devil's Music*: "The aggression and tension of ghetto life could sometimes be briefly sublimated by boogie-woogie into the joy of physical release through the pounding excitement of the piano. The ritualistic insistence of the dance could affirm a sense of sharing and participation in a community that sanctioned expressive needs. If there is a 'message' in boogie it is an old one, that there is nothing wrong or sinful about having a good time and that there is human warmth in coming together."[22]

Boogie-woogie piano enjoyed its own renaissance in Chicago during the late 1930s, thanks largely to Hammond booking a boogie-woogie trio of Ammons, Lewis, and Kansas City–based pianist Pete Johnson in his "From Spirituals to Swing" concert. After the concert, the trio worked regularly at New York's Café Society. The renewed interest in boogie-woogie piano revived the careers of the other original, Chicago practitioners, including Yancey and Lofton, and many of them continued to perform and record into the 1950s. Boogie-woogie also was absorbed into the standard, musical vocabulary of jazz, blues, and R&B.

In the heart of the Chicago Renaissance era, during the early 1940s, the Great Migration was bringing a new generation of musicians out of the South, and the blues began to undergo a major transformation. The journey that had the most significant impact on the blues in Chicago and, ultimately, popular music world-wide was in the summer of 1943, when the guitarist Muddy Waters (McKinley Morganfield) quit his day job on the Stovall Plantation outside of Clarksdale, Mississippi, and headed north. Waters had been singing and playing slide guitar in the juke joints of the Delta for years, but in 1941 and 1942, folklorists Alan Lomax and John Work made field recordings of his performances. When he finally heard the recordings, Waters recognized the power of his singing and playing and soon decided to leave sharecropping behind and head for Chicago and its legendary blues scene.

During World War II, Chicago was a boomtown, and the African Americans pouring in from the South found plenty of employment opportunities in defense work, in steel mills, in slaughterhouses, and other industries. While Waters worked in a paper factory and drove a truck, he was building a reputation for the fiery, powerful intensity of his Delta-style blues. His talent was welcomed on the scene, and Waters found an early supporter in Broonzy, just as he had been encouraged by Tampa Red two decades earlier. The young blues man appreciated the older man's encouragement, and in 1959, he recorded a tribute album to his mentor, *Muddy Waters Sings Big Bill Broonzy*. In *Can't Be Satisfied*, Robert Gordon records comments Waters made on Broonzy in the 1970s: "But Big Bill, he don't care where you from. He didn't look over you 'cause he been on records a long time. 'Do your thing, stay with it, man. If you stay with it, you going to make it.' That's what Big Bill told me. Mostly I try to be like him."[23]

Switching to electric guitar, Waters worked around the club scene with a small band and made his first recordings in 1946 with little success. Eventually, Waters was introduced to the brothers Leonard and Phil Chess, Polish immigrants who owned a string of bars on the South Side. They recognized the popularity of the music among their African American clientele and started Aristocrat Records in 1947. The Chess brothers recorded Waters in the spring of 1948, and the first single, "I Can't Be Satisfied" / "I Feel Like Going Home," was an immediate success. The sound was filled with a raw, searing energy and a driving, menacing rhythmic groove that revolutionized the sound of Chicago blues over the following decade.

The Chess brothers bought out their partner and formed Chess Records in 1949, and Waters, their first star, produced an unrivaled series of Classic Blues records for them. He developed his band, incorporating many of the best musicians on the scene, men who often left to become blues stars in their own right, and the format that he devised, featuring electric guitars and bass, piano, harmonica and drums, formed the template for modern blues, R&B, and rock and roll bands. As Francis Davis asserts in *The History of the Blues*: "Muddy so dominated Chicago blues in the wake of such hits as 'Rolling Stone' and 'Hoochie Coochie Man' that we tend to categorize other Chicago bluesmen as Muddy's forebears, Muddy's rivals, Muddy's progeny, and those from his own generation whom he completely overshadowed."[24] Little wonder that Frank London Brown, who moved to the South Side of Chicago at age 12, used the blues of Muddy Waters, as well as Joe Williams's "Every Day I Have the Blues," in his 1959 novel

Trumbull Park. Like Broonzy in the previous generation, Waters came north steeped in the traditional, rural, Southern blues idiom and adapted the music to reflect and harness the intensity and energy that he found in the rapidly transforming, modern, urban environment of Chicago.

One of the blues men from the postwar generation who helped Waters forge the new sound of Chicago blues was harmonica player Marion "Little Walter" Jacobs. Arriving from Louisiana in 1947, Jacobs was a regular at the Maxwell Street market, an area that was a central gathering place for blues musicians in Chicago. Blues men who arrived in the city without musical connections built their reputation on the highly competitive street. Building upon the work of Williamson No. 1, Jacobs developed a harmonica style that made him a blues star, and he went out on his own in 1952, following his instrumental hit on Chess, "Juke." In *Chicago Breakdown*, Mike Rowe states that "so big was the sound of Walter's amplified harp and so revolutionary his phrasing that it seemed at times as if he was blowing a sax. He played with a control, range, fluency, and imagination that was breathtaking; each solo was brilliantly constructed and pushed to its logical conclusion."[25]

Chess found another star in the Memphis-based singer/guitarist/harmonica player Howlin' Wolf (Chester Burnett), who moved to Chicago in 1952. He had been one of the most popular blues men on the Memphis scene, thanks largely to a live radio show he broadcast daily on KWEM in West Memphis. His music was brought to the attention of Memphis disc jockey, fledgling recording studio operator, and eventual founder of Sun Records, Sam Phillips, who brought Wolf into the studio for the first time in 1951. The results were staggering; with his deep, gravely voice and signature, falsetto howl, he created blues that were simple, visceral and overpowering. As Mark A. Humphrey states in "Bright Lights, Big City": "Wolf has been called primitive, but his primitivism was willful and might be likened to that of the cubist painters who, by juxtaposing 'primitive' elements in unexpected ways, created the art of the avant-garde. Wolf understood what he was doing with his blues deconstructions. In order to rebuild this music, he first had to raze it to its very foundations."[26] Wolf moved to Chicago after Phillips sent the tape to the Chess brothers, and he became one of the city's most distinctive postwar blues stylists and Waters's greatest rival.

The Chess brothers added one last major blues artist to their roster before the ascendancy of R&B and rock and roll, when they bought the contract of Sonny Boy Williamson No. 2 (Aleck "Rice" Miller). The veteran harmonica player and vocalist had made a name for himself in the Delta during the 1940s through his daily live performance on the "King Biscuit Time" show broadcast of radio station KFFA in Helena, Arkansas. Older than Waters, Wolf, or even Williamson No. 1, he never recorded until 1951 in Jackson, Mississippi, but he was undoubtedly a blues master who wrote catchy, often mystifying lyrics and possessed the ability to conjure an irresistible groove. As Paul Oliver states in *The Story of the Blues*: "He had an uncanny sense of timing, marked by short sung phrases, finger-snaps and tongue clicks which crackled against the rhythmic-melodic phrases of his harp."[27]

With artists like Waters, Jacobs, Wolf, and Williamson No. 2 on their roster, Chess certainly played a pivotal role in the development and exposure of the city's blues scene during the Chicago Renaissance. Aside from the unparalleled talents of the individual artists, Chess recordings had a distinctive sound. A good deal of credit for creating that sound must be given to bassist, songwriter, and producer, Willie Dixon. His family came to Chicago from Vicksburg, Mississippi, in 1935. Dixon's first experiences in the music business came in the 1940s when he led "jump" blues groups that were influenced by the swinging approach of the King Cole Trio. He produced his first records for Chess in 1951 and by 1954 became a prolific songwriter, supplying hit material, producing, and often playing acoustic bass on the recordings of Chess artists. As Francis Davis states in *The History of the Blues*: "He helped to reshape the blues into a style of pop, combining a Delta blues man's flair for plain expressive language with a pop songwriter's sense of what made for a great hook."[28] Dixon composed over two hundred songs, and some of the most well known include: "My Babe," "Close to You," "Wang Dang Doodle," "Bring It On Home," "I'm Ready," "I Ain't Superstitious," "The Life I Love," and "The Red Rooster."

As the Chicago Renaissance drew to a close in the midfifties, Chess and its four major blues men were not alone in shaping the sound of postwar Chicago blues. Other independent labels were formed and drew upon the talent from this thriving scene, including J.O.B., Chance, United/States, Sabre, Blue Lake, and Parrot. With the thriving blues scene, there were many blues artists who established themselves both as sidemen and leaders, including pianists Sunnyland Slim (Albert Luandrew), Otis Spann, and Eddie Boyd; harmonica players Amos "Junior" Wells, James "Snooky" Pryor, and "Big" Walter Horton; guitarists Elmore James, Johnny Shines, Robert Lockwood Jr., Hubert Sumlin, J. B. Lenoir, "Homesick" James Williamson, John Brim, Louis Myers, Dave Myers, and Jimmy Rogers; and drummers Fred Below and Odie Payne Jr. During the late 1950s, a new source of blues activity developed on the city's West Side. This next generation of young gun immigrants from the South, such as guitarists George "Buddy" Guy, Otis Rush, and "Magic" Sam Maghett, created a new variation on the Chicago blues with a stripped-down sound featuring extended, often flamboyant solos. In addition, the next wave of artists on Chess, guitarists Chuck Berry and Bo Diddley (Ellas McDaniel) essentially made the Delta-based sound obsolete as they created a more lighthearted, upbeat sound that would be dubbed rock and roll.

The independent record labels that grew out of the Chicago blues scene began to catch hold of a new genre of African American music, rhythm and blues

(R&B), which was emerging in the early 1950s. Coined to replace the term "race records," "rhythm 'n' blues" (R&B) first appeared in *Billboard* magazine in 1949 as a catchall category for African American secular recordings. It gradually came to be identified with a style of popular music that was a melding of influences: blues grooves, jazz solos, and gospel vocals. The impact of this fledgling R&B scene is testified to in Gwendolyn Brooks's 1953 novel, *Maud Martha*, in which the teenage protagonist attends a frenzied performance by the fictional singer, Howie Joe Jones, at the Regal Theater. Although the character is turned off by the show, she recognizes how this new music seduces the crowd: "The audience had applauded. Had stamped its strange, hilarious foot. Had put its fingers in its mouth—whistled. Had sped a shininess up to its eyes."[29]

In the early 1950s, the center of the fledgling R&B recording scene was a South Side neighborhood that came to be called "Record Row." Located near Cottage Grove and Forty-seventh Street, the area was home to Chess, United, Chance, Parrot, Sheridan, and in 1954, Vee Jay, which had moved from Gary, Indiana. Formed in 1953, by Vivian Carter and James Bracken, who were married shortly after the move to Chicago, Vee Jay became a major rival to Chess and eventually the largest African American–owned record label in America prior to the rise of Motown in the early 1960s. They made inroads into the blues market, especially with guitarist/harmonica player Jimmy Reed, but the emergence of Vee Jay had its most significant impact in the developing Chicago R&B scene.

The style of R&B that was attracting the attention of Vee Jay and other black music–oriented, independent labels was a vocal style called "doowop." Named after two of the characteristic, nonsensical syllables that provide the rhythmic underpinning for its smooth vocal harmonies, doowop could trace its roots back through African American harmony groups, like the Mills Brothers and the Ink Spots, to gospel quartets. According to Barry Hansen in "Doo-Wop," the dramatic change that the early 1950s doowop groups brought to African American harmony singing was a combination of "liberated gospel-style lead singing with a beat far heftier than any previously heard behind a black vocal group."[30] The proving grounds for these groups were the street corner, and the competition was often intense.

The Spaniels was the group that set the pace for Chicago's early 1950s doowop scene. They were organized for their high school talent show in Gary, Indiana, and auditioned for Carter's nascent Vee Jay label in her record shop. A few weeks later they recorded "Baby It's You," and within months the record was on the *Billboard* R&B chart. National stardom hit the following year with "Goodnite Sweetheart, Goodnite." With a string of hits, including "You Gave Me Peace of Mind," "Let's Make Up," and "Everybody's Laughing," lead vocalist James "Pookie" Hudson went on to be regarded as one of the great doowop singers of the decade. According to Robert Pruter in *Doowop: The Chicago Scene*, they were one of the outstanding exponents of the new style: "What the Spaniels did with a song lifted them from the level of fine craftsmen to the level of exceptional artists. With deep feeling, the Spaniels managed to evoke the emotions and sensibilities of youth growing to adulthood in the fifties."[31] Vee Jay followed up the success of the Spaniels with releases from the El Dorados, the Kool Gents, and the Dells. A floodgate opened, and young African American vocal talent poured out of the Chicago independent labels, including records by the Five Chances, the Flamingos, the Moonglows, the Danderliers, and the Five Echoes. Even Sun Ra wrote four-part harmony tunes for teenage doowop groups called the Cosmic Rays, the Nu Sounds, and the Clockstoppers, which he recorded on his own label.

During the Chicago Renaissance, the city was also home to many of the most influential artists in the evolution of the gospel music tradition. This new form of African American sacred music, gospel, emerged during the early decades of the twentieth century through a melding of spirituals and hymns with musical techniques borrowed from the blues and jazz. Gospel, in turn, influenced its secular cousins. By the middle decades of the century, this music that had been heard exclusively in the context of religious worship was crossing over to clubs and concert halls and making significant inroads in the radio, recording, and music publishing industries.

The single most important factor in establishing the primacy of Chicago's gospel scene was the arrival of the blues pianist Thomas A. "Georgia Tom" Dorsey in 1918. He composed gospel tunes occasionally during the 1920s, but in 1928 he experienced a religious conversion and within two years renounced the blues and turned his attention to the composition of sacred music. Regarded as the "Father of Gospel Music," Dorsey organized the first ever gospel chorus at Ebenezer Baptist Church and was a founder of the National Convention of Gospel Choirs and Choruses (NCGCC). He established the first African American gospel publishing company and composed over one thousand gospel songs, including such classics as "Take My Hand, Precious Lord," "There'll Be Peace in the Valley," "Search Me, Lord," and "I'm Going to Live the Life I Sing About in My Song." During the 1930s and 1940s, his compositions played such a definitive role that gospel songs were often referred to as "Dorseys." Particularly during the Depression, Dorsey's songs, which often incorporated the infectious, rhythmic energy of jazz and the emotive power of the blues, resonated for the African American community because they addressed the trials and tribulations with an uplifting sense of faith and hope. As Horace Boyer states in *The Golden Age of Gospel*: "Marked by catchy titles, many of which became part of the religious rhetoric of African American Christians, these songs had simple but beautiful melodies, harmonies that did not overshadow the text, and open spaces for the obligatory improvisation that identified gospel."[32] He toured regularly under the banner of "Evenings with Dorsey," featuring such Chicago-based soloists as Sallie Martin, Theodore Frye, and Mahalia Jackson, who, as "demonstrators" under his tutelage, spread the popularity of his compositions.

Frye and Martin were two of Dorsey's main collaborators in developing gospel in Chicago. With his close friend Dorsey as his accompanist, Frye created a sensation with his highly emotive singing. He was codirector of the Ebenezer junior choir and a cofounder of the NCGCC and became an important figure on the scene as a singer, director, composer, and producer. Martin joined Dorsey's chorus in 1932 and soon assumed a pivotal position in the management and promotion of his musical endeavors. She was a powerful singer, whose performances were filled with raw emotion. In 1940, she moved to Los Angeles where she established a following for Dorsey's approach to the gospel idiom. Martin's business acumen led her to join with Kenneth Morris in establishing one of the most successful gospel publishing companies.

In addition to his success as a pianist, choir director, composer, and publisher, Morris, who arrived in Chicago as an aspiring jazz musician, had a major impact on the gospel sound when he convinced his pastor, Revered Clarence Cobb, to purchase a Hammond electric organ. As Bernice Johnson Reagon explains in *African American Gospel: The Pioneering Composers*: "Morris stated that while he was criticized as too worldly, people nevertheless flocked to the church to hear the new sound. Musicians were particularly taken with the versatility and rapid response of the Hammond, and it was adopted throughout the gospel world."[33]

Singer and pianist Roberta Martin (no relation to Sallie) was another Dorsey protégé who helped shape the gospel sound during the Chicago Renaissance. Her musical training at Wendell Phillips High School enabled Martin to introduce elements of European classical music into her gospel accompaniment. After joining Dorsey's chorus in 1932 and coleading a chorus of young, male vocalists with Frye, she formed the Roberta Martin Singers in 1936. At the start of the next decade, she made a major innovation when she became the first leader of a gospel chorus to mix men and women singers. According to Boyer in *The Golden Age of Gospel*: "The Martin style was one of refinement in songs, singing style and piano and organ accompaniment. Although her inspiration came from the Pentecostal shouters, she felt that she could not duplicate this fiery kind of singing and instead attempted, with great success, to capture their zest with well-modulated voices."[34] She was also a highly successful composer, publisher, and recording artist, and a series of significant Chicago gospel figures emerged from her group, including Eugene Smith, Robert Anderson, Norsalus McKissick, and Willie Webb.

The most renowned and influential singer to emerge from the Chicago Renaissance era gospel scene was Mahalia Jackson. She was raised in New Orleans and moved to Chicago in 1927. Jazz and blues and the "shouting style" of singing of the Sanctified Church that she heard in New Orleans influenced Jackson's unbridled, improvisational approach, and she was met with resistance from the established churches in Chicago. Yet, it was her spontaneous, down-home fervor that resonated with the dispossessed African American population that had made its way north in the Great Migration. Rather than become affiliated with a church choir, Jackson joined the city's first organized group, the Johnson Singers, who often performed in storefront churches, and built a reputation as a soloist. Although she was first associated with Dorsey in 1929, she did not begin to collaborate with him regularly until 1939, when he wrote "There'll Be Peace in the Valley" with her in mind. They toured together regularly through the mid-1940s.

Jackson signed a contract with Apollo Records in 1946, and the following year, with Frye coordinating her second session, Jackson recorded the two-part, "Move On Up a Little Higher." It was a best-seller and propelled her to national stardom. After a series of hits for Apollo, she signed with Columbia Records in 1954 and, more than any other gospel artist, Jackson took gospel out of the realm of the African American church and into mainstream America. As Anthony Heilbut asserts in *The Gospel Sound*: "If America knows no other gospel singer, she has conferred a blessed status on Mahalia Jackson. All by herself, Mahalia was the vocal, physical and spiritual symbol of gospel music."[35] She recorded "sacred" music with Duke Ellington and appeared on national radio broadcasts, on network television, in films, at the Newport Jazz Festival, and at an inaugural event for President John F. Kennedy.

As the Chicago Renaissance era drew to a close, a new generation of gospel stars was emerging in the city. Albertina Walker and the Caravans split off from former Roberta Martin Singer Robert Anderson's group in 1952. In addition to Walker, the original group included Ora Lee Hopkins, Elyse Yancey, and Nellie Grace Daniels. According to Horace Boyer in *The Golden Age of Gospel*, the Caravans featured "close, earthy harmony, percussive attacks, and a precise rhythm unlike any other female gospel group."[36] During the 1950s and 1960s, the Caravans were a Chicago institution, and a succession of outstanding soloists joined the group and shared center stage with Walker. Many of these women went on to become stars in their own right, including Bessie Griffin, Shirley Caesar, Inez Andrews, Dorothy Norwood, Cassietta George, and Imogene Green.

Pianist, vocalist, arranger, and composer James Cleveland was another emerging gospel star associated with the Caravans. Born in Chicago in 1931, Cleveland's roots grew deeply into the soil of the city's gospel tradition. He was a member of Dorsey's youth choir and was profoundly influenced by Roberta Martin's piano playing and the singing of her group. By 1946, he was leading his own group, and, in 1950, he was backing up the Gospelaires, two former Martin Singers, McKissick and Bessie Folk. In the mid-1950s, he was writing songs for Martin and had joined Walker and the Caravans. He went on to sign a contract with Savoy Records and become a gospel superstar. Cleveland transformed the world of gospel choirs in 1968 when he organized the Gospel Music Workshop of America.

Following his service in World War II, singer/composer Professor Alex Bradford came to Chicago and immersed himself in the gospel scene, forging associations with Dorsey, Jackson, Roberta Martin, and Sallie Martin. In 1953, he organized the Bradford Specials and scored a major hit with "Too Close to Heaven." Bradford was one of the gospel performers during this era who was blurring the line between the sacred and the secular. As Anthony Heilbut states in *The Gospel Sound*: "The song sold over a million copies and established Bradford as the 'Singing Rage of the Gospel Age.' His huge, rough voice shook listeners, but what turned America on most was the Bradford Specials choreography. 'I'm too close,' Bradford would sing, answered by the resonant tenor of Little Joe Jackson, the group's spark plug. Then the two men would gracefully swirl off together, while the other Specials would simultaneously dip in unison."[37] He left Chicago in 1961 to perform the Langston Hughes–inspired *Black Nativity* on Broadway.

In the late 1940s, the Staple Singers, a gospel group that featured a down-home, back-to-the-roots sound was formed by Roebuck "Pops" Staples with his children. Staples was a guitarist and singer who migrated to Chicago from Winone, Mississippi, in 1935 with his wife, Oceola, and oldest daughter, Cloeotha. Four more children—Pervis, Yvonne, Mavis, and Cynthia—were born in Chicago. They were the first widely renowned gospel group to consist of a father and his children, and his blues-inflected guitar work helped to bring the instrument to prominence in gospel. They made their first recording for the United label in 1953 and scored their first hit in 1956 on Vee Jay with "Uncloudy Day." They went on to achieve widespread, crossover success in R&B on the Stax label during the 1960s and 1970s.

The South was undoubtedly the breeding ground for the "a cappella" harmonies of the gospel quartets; however, the Great Migration brought the foremost exponent of this style, the Soul Stirrers, to Chicago. The group, which formed in Texas, made their first recordings in 1936 and shaped the modern quartet sound. According to Eileen Southern in *The Music of Black Americans*: "The Soul Stirrers are credited with establishing most of the practices of modern gospel quartet style: they were the first to add a fifth man to the quartet, thus creating four-part harmony support for the lead singer; the first to use guitar accompaniment; and the first to give concerts consisting solely of gospel music."[38] By the early 1940s, they had established themselves on the Chicago scene and broadcast on radio station WIND on Sundays for more than a decade.

When the Soul Stirrers arrived in Chicago, the driving force behind the group was lead singer Robert H. Harris, who was responsible for initiating many of their innovations. He was a dynamic performer who injected a spiritual fervor into the quartet style. In 1947, Harris was instrumental in forming and leading the National Quartet Association of America. He left the group in 1950, and the following year singer Sam Cooke joined and took the Soul Stirrers to unprecedented heights in the both gospel and popular music. Cooke's family moved to Chicago's South Side from Clarksdale, Mississippi, in 1931 when he was an infant, and his singing first garnered attention as a student at Wendell Phillips High School. When he joined the Soul Stirrers, Cooke, at first, stood in Harris's shadow, but he soon developed an individual style as both a lead singer and composer. As Horace Boyer explains in *The Golden Age of Gospel*: "Cooke brought the Stirrers to the forefront again but with a difference: no longer were they the reverent semirural 'a cappella' quartet of Harris's day, but a sophisticated, pop-oriented performing group, accompanied by guitar in concerts and by guitar, piano and organ on recordings."[39] He was a handsome man who became, even in the realm of sacred music, a teen heartthrob. Cooke played a major role in crafting a series of hit records for the Specialty label during the first half of the 1950s. He began recording R&B as a solo artist for the Keen label and later for RCA at the close of 1950s and was elevated to the status of pop superstar until his tragic death in 1964.

During the Chicago Renaissance, the city's African American population made some significant achievements in European classical music. The city's African American musical community had established itself in the realm of classical music, like the jazz scene, during the New Negro Renaissance era. In 1919, Nora Holt, the music editor of the *Chicago Defender* was instrumental in founding the National Association of Negro Musicians (NANM), which held its first convention in Chicago in July of that year. The first recipient of the organization's scholarship was the opera singer Marian Anderson. Both Holt and her successor as music editor, Maude Roberts George, used their column in the *Defender* to promote classical music education and performances.

Chicago boasted an extensive tradition of choral groups that reached back to the early decades of the twentieth century. James Mundy and J. Wesley Jones founded two of the most enduring choruses. Their "Battles of the Choirs" were major events in the city during the 1930s. Florence Price, who is considered to be the first African American woman to be recognized for her work as a classical composer, studied in Chicago at Chicago Musical College and American Conservatory of Music during the 1920s. She wrote concertos and symphonies, as well as teaching pieces for which she found publishers in Chicago. Her *Symphony in E Minor* was premiered in 1933 at the Century of Progress International Exposition in Chicago. According to Eileen Southern's *The Music of Black Americans*: "Although Price's music became known only in the postwar world, she belonged to an older generation in terms of training and experience, and her style is best defined as neoromantic, which was rather conservative for her time. She was also a black nationalist in that she drew freely upon folk idioms in her compositions."[40] A Chicago native, pianist Margaret Bonds, who was educated at Northwestern and Julliard, performed Price's Piano Concerto with the Women's Symphony Orchestra of Chicago in 1934. Bonds also went on to a distinguished career as a composer, often incorporating African American folk elements and texts from Langston Hughes. William Levi Dawson, another native Chicagoan, also studied at Chicago Musical College and American Conservatory of Music during the 1920s. The Philadelphia Orchestra, directed by Leopold Stokowski, premiered Dawson's *Negro Folk Symphony* in 1934. He revised the symphony to include African rhythms in 1952, after a journey to West Africa.

African American artists also made important inroads in opera in Chicago. Mary Cardwell Dawson, a North Carolina native, studied at the Chicago Musical College and went on to found and manage the National Negro Opera Company. According to Raoul Abdul in *Blacks in Classical Music*: "For two decades beginning in 1941, she carried forward almost single-handedly the banner of Black opera."[41] In addition, Dawson organized the Cardwell Dawson Choir, which was featured at the Century of Progress International Exposition in Chicago in 1933. Dawson was also the founder of the National Association of Negro Musicians, and she brought their production of *Aida* to the Chicago Civic Opera House in 1942. Chicago natives La Julia Rhea and William Franklin sang with the National Negro Opera Company. Rhea made her concert debut in 1929 at Chicago's Kimball Hall and her operatic debut in 1937, singing the lead role in *Aida* with the Chicago City Opera Company. Franklin, who sang the male lead in the premiere of Dawson's production of *Aida* in Pittsburgh, was known for his performances of the lead role in *The Mikado* by Gilbert and Sullivan and in 1944 sang the lead in a revival of *Porgy and Bess*. Zelma Watson George, a Cleveland native, studied voice at Chicago's American Conservatory of Music. She went on to become the first African American woman to perform a lead role of a white character on Broadway, when she sang in Gian Carlo Menotti's *The Medium* in 1950.

The Black Chicago Renaissance witnessed a tremendous outpouring of African American musical talent and innovations. Taking hold of the baton passed on by the artists of the New Negro Renaissance, Chicago's black musicians extended the traditions of jazz, blues, and gospel. In his 1941 book *12 Million Black Voices: A Folk History of the Negro in the U.S.*, Richard Wright clearly recognizes the tremendous blossoming and significance of African American music during this era in Chicago: "On the plantations our songs carried a strain of otherwordly yearning which people called 'spiritual'; but now our blues, jazz, swing, and boogie-woogie are our 'spirituals' of the city pavements, our longing for freedom and opportunity, and expression of our bewilderment and despair in the world whose meaning eludes us."[42] Like the writers who lived in the city during the middle decades of the twentieth century, African American musicians captured the spirit of a vibrant community and opened myriad artistic possibilities, which laid the foundation for the whirlwind of social, political, and artistic forces that would transform America beginning in the late 1950s and continue through the 1960s.

The avant-garde jazz that was emerging from the city's jazz scene flourished and provided an outlet for the expression of the frustration and the rage felt by the younger generation. The Black Arts Movement of the 1960s embraced the probing nature and the premium placed on freedom of expression that were characteristic of the avant-garde jazz created by jazz artists like Abrams and his Association for the Advancement of Creative Musicians (AACM), associates, the Art Ensemble of Chicago.

The blues scene of Waters, Wolf, Jacobs, Williamson No. 2, and their postwar cohorts reached into the next decade as they became the musical idols of the 1960s blues rock revivalists, including the Butterfield Blues Band, Bob Dylan, The Band, Taj Mahal, Jimi Hendrix, the Rolling Stones, Canned Heat, and Eric Clapton. Music that had existed almost completely within the insulated worlds of the Mississippi Delta and Chicago's South Side broke down racial barriers, transformed popular music, and gained international renown. The second wave of doowop groups in the late 1950s included such young Chicago artists as Jerry Butler and Curtis Mayfield, who were at the forefront as R&B was recast as "soul" music. Mayfield went on to become a composer of socially conscious, Civil Rights anthems, such as "People Get Ready," "This Is My Country," "Choice of Colors," and "Move On Up."

Gospel also became associated with the Civil Rights Movement, providing many of the musical building blocks for the "freedom songs" of the marches, protests, and sit-ins. The Staple Singers became closely identified with the movement and incorporated many of these topical, protest songs into their repertoire. Mahalia Jackson, like so many black musicians, lent her voice to the struggle. She sang the old spiritual "I Been 'Buked and I Been Scorned" prior to Martin Luther King's classic "I Have A Dream Speech" at the 1963 March on Washington and Dorsey's "Take My Hand, Precious Lord" at King's funeral in 1968. The legacy of the music produced in Chicago by African Americans during the Chicago Renaissance was certainly profound and far-reaching.

Notes

1. Hill, Patricia, et al., eds. *Call & Response: The Riverside Anthology of the African American Literary Tradition*. Boston: Houghton Mifflin Company, 1998, 1007–10.

2. Hennessey, Thomas J. *From Jazz to Swing: African American Jazz Musicians and Their Music 1890–1935*. Detroit: Wayne State University Press, 1994, 81.

3. Ibid., 134.

4. Travis, Dempsey J. *An Autobiography of Black Jazz.* Chicago: Urban Research Institute, 1983, 113.

5. Davis, Frank Marshall. *Black Moods: Collected Poems*, edited by John Tidwell. Urbana: University of Illinois Press, 2002, 20.

6. Travis, *An Autobiography of Black Jazz*, 138.

7. Walton, Charles. "Bronzeville Conversation: The DuSable Hotel and the Drexel Square Area." *Jazz Institute of Chicago* (July 19, 2004). http://jazzinchicago.org.

8. Travis, *An Autobiography of Black Jazz*, 300.

9. Walton, Charles. "Clark Terry and Sykes Smith: A Bronzeville Conversation." *Jazz Institute of Chicago* (July 19, 2004). http://jazzinchicago.org.

10. Southern, Eileen. *The Music of Black Americans: A History, 3rd Ed.* New York: Norton, 1997, 468.

11. Walton, "Clark Terry and Sykes Smith: A Bronzeville Conversation."

12. Campbell, Robert L. "From Sonny Blount to Sun Ra: The Birmingham and Chicago Years." *Saturn Web* (March 1995). http://www.dpo.uab.edu/~moudry/camp1.htm.

13. McFarland, Scott. "Sun Ra and His Intergalactic Harmonies." *Perfect Sound Forever* (February 1997). www.furious.com/perfect/sunra.html.

14. Kernfield, Barry. *The New Grove Dictionary of Jazz.* New York: St. Martin's Press, 1994.

15. Harrison, Daphne Duval. *Black Pearls: Blues Queens of the 1920s.* New Brunswick, N.J.: Rutgers University Press, 1990, 232–34.

16. Rowe, Mike. *Chicago Breakdown.* New York: DaCapo Press, 1979, 13–14.

17. Wright, Richard. *Native Son.* 1940. New York: Harper Perennial, 1993, 73.

18. Oliver, Paul. *The Story of the Blues.* Radnor, Pa.: Chilton Book Company, 1969, 101.

19. Oakley, Giles. *The Devil's Music: A History of the Blues.* New York: Harcourt Brace Jovanovich, 1976, 197.

20. Hughes, Langston. "Happy New Year! With Memphis Minnie." *Martin Scorsese Presents The Blues: A Musical Journey.* New York: HarperCollins, 2003, 202–3.

21. Kernfield, *The New Grove Dictionary of Jazz.*

22. Oakley, *The Devil's Music: A History of the Blues*, 175.

23. Gordon, Robert. *Can't Be Satisfied: The Life and Times of Muddy Waters.* Boston: Little, Brown and Company, 2002, 73.

24. Davis, Francis. *The History of the Blues.* New York: Hyperion, 1995, 188.

25. Rowe, *Chicago Breakdown*, 91.

26. Humphrey, Mark A. "Bright Lights, Big City: Urban Blues." In *Nothing But the Blues: The Music and the Musicians*, edited by Lawrence Cohn. New York: Abbeville Press, 1993, 190.

27. Oliver, *The Story of the Blues*, 146.

28. Davis, *The History of the Blues*, 195.

29. Brooks, Gwendolyn. *Maud Martha.* 1953. Chicago: Third World Press, 1993, 20.

30. Hansen, Barry. "Doo-Wop." In *The Rolling Stone Illustrated History of Rock & Roll*, edited by Jim Miller. New York: Random House, 1976, 82.

31. Pruter, Robert. *Doowop: The Chicago Scene*. Urbana: University of Illinois Press, 1996, 106.

32. Boyer, Horace Clarence. *The Golden Age of Gospel*. Urbana: University of Illinois Press, 1995, 61.

33. Reagon, Bernice Johnson, Pearl Williams-Jones and Lisa Pertillar Brevard. *African American Gospel: The Pioneering Composers*. Liner Notes. Washington, D.C.: Smithsonian/Folkways Recordings, 1994, 8.

34. Boyer, *The Golden Age of Gospel*, 67–68.

35. Heilbut, Anthony. *The Gospel Sound: Good News and Bad Times*, Revised and updated. New York: Limelight Editions, 1985, 55.

36. Boyer, *The Golden Age of Gospel*, 219.

37. Heilbut, *The Gospel Sound: Good News and Bad Times*, 154.

38. Southern, *The Music of Black Americans: A History*, 483.

39. Boyer, *The Golden Age of Gospel*, 198.

40. Southern, *The Music of Black Americans: A History*, 425.

41. Abdul, Raoul. *Blacks in Classical Music: A Personal History*. New York: Dodd, Mead and Company, 1977, 148.

42. Wright, Richard. *12 Million Black Voices: A Folk History of the Negro in the U.S.* 1941. Edited by Ellen Wright and Michel Fabre. New York: Harper and Row, 1978, 227.

For Further Reading

Bastin, Bruce. Liner Notes, *Jimmy & Mama Yancey Chicago Piano*. New York: Atlantic Records, 1972.

Chicago Renaissance 1932–1950, Chicago Public Library, December 8, 2004. http://www.chipublib.org/digital/chiren/musicpage.html

Dance, Stanley. *The World of Earl Hines*. New York: DaCapo Press, 1977.

Feather, Leonard. *The Encyclopedia of Jazz*. New York: Horizon Press, 1969.

Harris, Michael W. *The Rise of Gospel Blues: The Music of Thomas Dorsey in the Urban Church*. New York: Oxford University Press, 1992.

Harris, Sheldon. *Blues Who's Who: A Biographical Dictionary of Blues Singers*. New York: DaCapo Press, 1979.

Jackson, Jerma. *Singing in My Soul: Black Gospel Music in a Secular Age*. Chapel Hill: University of North Carolina Press, 2004.

Kenney, William Howland. *Chicago Jazz: A Cultural History 1904–1930*. New York: Oxford University Press, 1993.

Lowry, Pete. Liner Notes, *Blues Piano: Chicago Plus*. New York: Atlantic Records, 1972.

McEwen, Joe. "Sam Cooke." In *The Rolling Stone Illustrated History of Rock & Roll*, edited by Jim Miller. New York: Random House, 1976, 114–17.

O'Neal, Jim. "I Once Was Lost, But Now I'm Found: The Blues Revival of the 1960s." In *Nothing But the Blues: The Music and the Musicians*, edited by Lawrence Cohn. New York: Abbeville Press, 1993, 347–88.

Pruter, Robert. *Chicago Soul*. Urbana: University of Illinois Press, 1991.

Shaw, Arnold. *Honkers and Shouters: The Golden Years of Rhythm & Blues*. New York: Collier Books, 1978.

Spottswood, Richard K. "Country Girls, Classic Blues and Vaudeville Voices: Women and the Blues." In *Nothing But the Blues: The Music and the Musicians*, edited by Lawrence Cohn. New York: Abbeville Press, 1993, 87–106.

Stearns, Marshall. *The Story of Jazz*. New York: Mentor, 1958.

Tooze, Sandra B. *Muddy Waters: The Mojo Man*. Toronto: ECW Press, 1997.

Travis, Dempsey J. *An Autobiography of Black Chicago*. Chicago: Urban Research Institute, 1981.

Ward, Geoffrey C. and Ken Burns. *Jazz: A History of America's Music*. New York: Alfred A. Knopf, 2000.

Young, Akan. *Woke Up This Morning: Black Gospel Singers and the Gospel Life*. Jackson: University of Mississippi Press, 1997.

THE BLACK PRESS AND THE
BLACK CHICAGO RENAISSANCE
Zoe Trodd

In February 1927, Matilda McEwan of Hubbard Woods, Illinois, read an issue of the *Chicago Defender*, America's leading black newspaper of the day. She took particular notice of an item in The Bookshelf, the *Defender's* book review column and self-styled "literary club."[1] The item was a request from a reader in Dallas, Texas, for information on a half-remembered poem.[2] Matilda's response ran in The Bookshelf on February 19, 1927: "I saw in 'The Bookshelf' where someone is asking for the complete poem 'The Face on the Barroom Floor.' Having memorized it years ago, I shall be glad to send it to the person as I remember it." She included her address.[3]

A month later the column ran another letter from Matilda: "Dear Readers of 'The Bookshelf,' I only meant to send the poem to the person who asked for it in the column. But to date I have received over 50 letters asking that a copy be sent to them. Since I am only a working girl and haven't much leisure time, it would be impossible for me to answer them all." She added: "If there are those who are very anxious for a copy and will send a small contribution with their letters, I shall be glad to make a special effort to send it to them."[4] A literary club was in full swing.

On May 14, 1928, the anonymous editor of The Bookshelf announced in the column that "the West" was finally speaking "in the realm of letters."[5] The Bookshelf's contribution to this realm in fact dated back to November 14, 1925, when the column, then three years old, began to offer a question-and-answer forum for readers alongside its existing selection of book reviews and literary gossip. The new forum included sections called "Defender Forum" and "Who Can Answer This?" And, after its introduction, readers immediately used the new question-and-answer feature to support their own book clubs, perhaps inspiring the official metamorphosis of the column into a "literary club" in January 1926. On December 26, 1925, a reader wrote to The Bookshelf about "a speaker at our forum" and in the following issue a reading group began to use the column as a source for its selections, writing: "Our literary club is planning a birthday program the last Sunday in this month. Can you tell us which poets were born in January?"[6] Two weeks after publishing this request, The Bookshelf's editor removed the part of the column's banner that had proclaimed: "In the small space allotted we will try to touch upon subjects generally of interest to readers."[7] Instead appeared a new line: "If you are a book lover and like the idea of a literary club that meets through 'The Bookshelf' column, you are welcome."[8] The column's new status as a literary club was official.

The imaginative space of a "literary club" then expanded the "small space allotted," as the earlier banner put it, to make room for Matilda, the fifty readers who wanted her poem, and potentially hundreds of thousands of others. By 1920 the *Defender* was the most widely read black newspaper in America, with a circulation of 283,571, according to a circulation pamphlet distributed by the newspaper. No other black newspaper of the time claimed a circulation of more than half this number. The issue of March 14, 1925, apparently ran to 247,867 copies (though the Audit Bureau of Circulations, which guarantees newspaper circulation, did not then include the Black Press, so the accuracy of this figure is impossible to verify) and each copy of the newspaper sold was likely read by four to five African Americans, putting its actual readership at close to a million people each week. In 1931 black newspaper circulation reached 1,600,000 and by 1950 it was at 2,440,000, with the *Defender* still prominent. Robert Sengstacke Abbott, who had produced the first issue of the *Chicago Defender* on May 5, 1905, became the first black publishing millionaire.[9]

In 1922 Frederick Detweiler compared the Black Press to a public work of art and a church or lodge, a symbol of aspiration and an embodiment of group life.[10] Black newspapers did not just reflect life but helped to create it. This was still the case in 1944, Gunnar Myrdal believed. The press defined black people to themselves, so that the individual shared in the lives of the millions beyond the local community: "The press, more than any other institution, has created the Negro group as a social and a psychological reality to the individual Negro," he argued.[11] And the *Defender* was particularly active in helping to create this race consciousness.[12] The newspaper's motto was "American Race Prejudice must be destroyed" and advertisements for the newspaper proclaimed that "if you have race pride you can't afford to miss it." Other advertisements described the *Defender* as the "Mouthpiece of 14 Million People," echoing the founding editorial of *Freedom's Journal*, America's first black newspaper, which famously declared in 1827: "Too long have others spoken for us." A black migrant interviewed by the Chicago Commission on Race Relations in 1922 recognized that the *Defender* fostered race feeling, stimulating "self-respect, character and initiative" and the Commission's report went on to trace the origins of the Chicago riots of 1919 in feelings of race consciousness emphasized by a defiant and assertive Black Press.[13] Certainly *Defender* editorials were fiery, especially during the race riots (for example, instructing black people to kill any member of a white mob that attacked them).

Both Abbott's tone and style were groundbreaking. His was the first black newspaper to have bold large print for headlines, and he added the parenthesis "white" to any mention of a white person, in answer to white newspapers' practice of including the word "Negro" as a prefix. The *Defender* referred to African Americans as "Race men and Race women" and Abbott banned the word "Negro." He frequently declared himself for the "masses" not the "classes," printed editorials questioning why black people should fight for a country that did not protect them, during World War I, and called until his death in 1940 for a black cabinet member in the White House. He campaigned relentlessly for antilynching legislation, pushed for fair housing and equal employment for blacks, and protested against institutionalized racism and Franklin Roosevelt's discriminatory New Deal relief initiatives throughout the 1930s. This radicalism prompted articles in the white press and scholarly journals attacking it as antisocial. A reader's letter to the *Defender* on May 3, 1930, even asked if the newspaper was produced "with the sole object in view of fomenting, maintaining and perpetuating the hatred of the white and Negro race for one another."[14]

But while it was important on a national level, the *Defender* was also famously committed to the local black community of Chicago, in part because of the newspaper's role in the Great Migration. The black population of Chicago increased by 148.5 percent between 1910 and 1920, and had doubled again by 1930. Reaching more than 500,000 southern readers a week by 1917, the *Defender*'s migration campaign played a role in stimulating the exodus of an estimated one million to northern cities. Editorials encouraged African Americans in the South to migrate north, and, as a result, the newspaper was banned in numerous southern cities. Abbott asked railroad porters to carry his newspaper down nonetheless and published train schedules and job listings to further assist migration. The Chicago Commission on Race Relations highlighted the newspaper's role: "the *Defender*'s policy prompted thousands of restless Negroes to venture North, where they were assured of its protection and championship of their cause. Many migrants in Chicago attribute their presence in the North to the *Defender*'s encouraging pictures of relief from conditions at home. . . . [The newspaper was] largely responsible for stimulating migration to the North."[15]

During the peak years of the migration (1916–18), the *Defender*'s circulation rose from 50,000 to 125,000. Many new readers were the migrants, now segregated in the Black Belt, on the South Side of Chicago. Abbott, dubbed the "Black Joshua," thought they needed what he frequently called "acclimatization." He committed his newspaper to instructing and guiding the newcomers, offering a legal help column and advertising fund drives. Even the newspaper's first attempt at a book review, before the launch of The Bookshelf, opened with a description of "the thousands of books annually thrust upon an unsuspecting public," as though the new community might need defense from literary as well as civil and physical assaults.[16] Then, once acclimatized, Abbott thought the migrants needed race pride to gel as a community. So he set about creating "Defenderland," his new name for a South Side bound together in its identity by the newspaper. Eugene F. Gordon, in the New York–based black magazine *Opportunity*, commented in January 1927 that the Black Press was doing more than any other agency to cultivate race consciousness in its readers and the *Defender* remained a voice for the city's black community throughout the Chicago Renaissance.[17]

The Bookshelf, which usually ran on the front page of the features section, was a popular item in this race-conscious *Defender* and a significant cultural gatekeeper during the early years of the Chicago Renaissance. Many of the other major black newspapers did not print book columns, and Chicago's black *Half-Century Magazine* ran only one book review throughout its entire existence.[18] Gordon's *Opportunity* article of January 1927 listed the *Defender* as one of the best black newspapers, highlighted The Bookshelf as a good original feature, and expressed hope that it would be a permanent fixture. It would end up being one of the longest running book-review columns of the twentieth-century Black Press (only coming to an end in 1948), with new additional sections like "Observations: The Trend of Current Thought and Discussion."

The column was important because—far from the Harlem's hub—black Chicagoans seemingly felt their relative cultural poverty. In *The New Negro*, Alain Locke had described Harlem as the epicenter of "common consciousness," "the greatest Negro city in the world," the race capital where "Negro life is seizing upon its first chances for group expression and self-determination."[19] And in one column of 1926, a Bookshelf reader asked wistfully: "Is it true that a large New York bookstore recently gave over its entire display window to books concerning the Race?"[20] A few months later, another reader expressed envy of "Harlem, with its intimate contacts with liberal-minded men and women of letters."[21] But the editor of The Bookshelf believed that the *Defender*'s imaginary book club could furnish Chicago with intimate contacts and perhaps a renaissance and literary scene of its own. He knew that "many of the best books by Race authors some of the guests see here [in the column] for the first time," as he put it in January 1928, and he strove to offer Chicago the equivalent of Harlem's literary salons and group expression. He painted a picture for his readers: "On the walls, lettered artistically, a quotation from Cullen's *The Dark Tower* and Langston Hughes's *The Weary Blues* are read as the diners sip their ginger ale." The Bookshelf was a place where black Chicagoans might find "pleasure and freedom, culture and refinement" and explore a "cabinet, with 'Books by Negro Authors.'"[22] On other occasions he further encouraged readers to imagine themselves coming together to share time with books.

This community-building through literature accompanied an encouragement of literary kinship through reading. The editor wrote of acquaintance and
friendship with literary characters, saying of one character: "if you do not know
her you ought to be acquainted at once." Another review recommended a book
because it would make "you feel as though you were being introduced personally at tea and then having the advantage of being led off into a quiet corner to
hear the intimate gossip that follows." Yet another promised the reader would
feel as anxious about the characters "as if they were your own kith and kin."[23]

In the nation's biggest black newspaper, which was the South Side's major
exponent of race pride, the column was fostering a collective consciousness
through literature. Readers responded to this attempt. Their published letters
included details about their identities and the literary discussions in which they
engaged person-to-person, creating a sense of real-life community beyond the
printed page. They wrote of their upcoming talks before high school public
speaking classes, described the quotations on the reading rooms of their local
libraries, and inquired about the existence of free evening schools on the South
Side. Frequently they would request details on books mentioned by other readers
the previous week. As Chicago's black readers answered each other's questions
and shared information on their favorite books, reading became more of a social
practice than a solitary activity. The Bookshelf also assisted in the creation of an
alternate creative space. Readers asked for advice on writing style and requested
information on publishers, one seeking an audience for a 100,000-word novel.
Others submitted poems for publication in the column itself.

The literary club of The Bookshelf, though without a common fireplace beyond the pages of the *Defender*, was becoming the kind of "knot" described
by *Opportunity* in 1926: "We who clink our cups over New York fireplaces,"
the writer noted, "are wont to miss the fact that little knots of literary devo-
tees are in like manner sipping their 'cup o' warmth' in this or that city in the
'provinces.'"[24] And the Bookshelf's imaginary literary club seemed also to bring
about *real* communal "fireplaces," where Chicagoans might sip together a cup
of their burgeoning Renaissance. As Matilda and the birthday-author letters
demonstrate, the *Defender* apparently helped form numerous other book clubs
in black Chicago as the Renaissance flourished. The reader who wanted a list
of writers born in January for a book club birthday program wrote again to
ask for the names of writers born in March, and repeated her request in May,
June, September, October, and December. Eventually, perhaps inspired by the
example of this reader's real literary club, a second reader seemed to launch a
similar book club, suddenly writing to ask which literary characters had *died*
in the month of December. More real book club activity was evident when a
reader asked for information on how to conduct literary clubs, or when another
requested material that might help the organization of a reading group and was

told to send a self-addressed envelope to The Bookshelf. The editor sometimes suggested that a book be the subject of club discussions, and the readers asked for the correction pronunciations of authors' names, as though really in conversation. Many readers used The Bookshelf as the arbiter in literary debates, asking the editor to settle arguments about authors and novels, as though he was the host of a bookish gathering.

Through the pages of the newspaper a community had developed. And, as the column evolved, it charted the growth of the Black Chicago Renaissance and watered the seeds of what Locke called in 1929, the "second . . . crop" of black expression.[25] Before 1925, an average of only 25 percent of the books discussed each month were by or about blacks and three-quarters of this small percentage were studies by white authors of black life, Africa, or the West Indies.[26] This focus was not necessarily at odds with the newspaper's tone. In addition to racial equality, the complex Abbott also championed polite society, good manners, and the gradual acquisition of culture. He would occasionally offer a Blue Ribbon Prize to readers who kept their lawns tidy. In a regular feature entitled "Things That Should Be Considered" he would editorialize on correct language and manners, and the newspaper's column "Better English" was full of what he considered to be current idiomatic expressions of the white middle class.

Yet the focus on white literature *was* at odds with much of the Black Press. Only slightly higher than the percentage of books about or by African Americans reviewed in the *New York Times*, The Bookshelf's early average contrasted the 90 percent black literature content of contemporaneous book-review columns in Harlem Renaissance periodicals like *The Crisis* or *Messenger*. *The Negro World*, a radical black New York newspaper, ran a short-lived book column that focused almost all of its reviews on books by or about African Americans, and another major black New York newspaper, the *Amsterdam News*, ran a column called "The Negro in World Literature," which reviewed only black writers. The Bookshelf was initially the antithesis of such columns and of those like the *Pittsburgh Courier*'s "Your History," which listed black cultural and political achievements. The *Defender*'s column also seems incongruous when set next to contemporary black publishing houses. For example, the founding statement of Associated Publishers from 1921 reads: "During the recent years the Negro race has been seeking to learn more about itself. . . . The Negro reading public has been largely increased and . . . any creditable publication giving important facts about the race now finds a ready market."[27]

From 1925 onward, however, this "ready market" did begin to include Chicago. Throughout the whole period of the question-and-answer forum, seven out of every ten questions that readers asked and tried to answer were about black literature. They asked for histories of "the Race's leading men," lists of "the best Negro historians," and books "dealing exclusively with Race poets."[28] Frequently they queried whether an author was a member of "the Race." Eventually, in the same issue that ran Matilda's second letter, a reader wrote: "I think it would be a good idea to print lists of books written by Race writers from the earliest known to the contemporary. By doing this, the readers of your column could select books written by Race men or women."[29] This persistent interest of his readers in black writers struck the editor of the column powerfully. Immediately after the introduction of the readers' forum in 1925, the review percentage of black writers rose from a monthly average of 25 to 65 percent. The reviews gradually came to echo the readers' questions and interests, so that by 1926 a book review would regularly follow on the heels of a reader's inquiry about that book. By the end of the decade the editor was acknowledging in the column that an amazing number of books discussing black life and thought were being printed and that what had seemed a mere fad for books by and about black Americans was in fact a permanent interest.

He had encountered in his readers a desire for access to black art and literature. Not only adjusting the ratio of black to white books reviewed, he also revised the column's explicit attitudes. For example, in January 1926, as the column was establishing the readers' forum and first included the "literary club" banner, one review expressed satisfaction that *The Weary Blues* allowed readers to forget that Hughes was black. But a year later, after thirteen months of reader interaction and influence, the editor reviewed Hughes's newest work with a different kind of satisfaction: "We have needed someone to interpret the emotions . . . of the great masses of us who are so far down in the scale of things," he wrote.[30]

By the early 1930s, the column would often recommend books by white authors only if they had clearly influenced black literature (New Negro poetry drew on Robert Frost's New England poems, for example). As well, under the influence of the readers' forum, The Bookshelf was noticeably more critical of books that valued too highly the perceived cultural standards of white Americans. The column expressed dislike for the black desire to imitate whites and railed against black shame of Africa and the folk tale heritage. It declared that a cultural revolution was in progress and explicitly relegated to an earlier cultural moment the tendency toward imitation. It celebrated the recent discovery by black Americans of their own self-consciousness and distinct means of self-expression. In the early 1920s, before the introduction of the readers' forum, a book review would express distaste for poor black people and call for books to represent rags-to-riches stories of uplift, but now, as the Black Chicago Renaissance got underway, the editor criticized narratives of passing as unfortunate choices of subject: "just because we live in a white man's country, eat his food, wear his clothes . . . work his factories and fight his battles is no reason why we should stand in his window and look wistfully into his house, thus giving the impression that we want to come in," he insisted in one review.[31]

Once dismissive of what it termed the "eternal race problem," and enthusiastic about Americanization societies, the column began to recommend books on segregation, lynching, and black labor, and ran three reviews of a book called *What the Negro Thinks*.[32]

But The Bookshelf did retain an ambiguous approach to the black literature associated with the Harlem Renaissance. Reviews repeatedly expressed a dislike of modernist literature and instead recommended books that made "pleasant as well as profitable reading" or were "both popular and excellent."[33] In one issue a review condemned "pretentious" and "meaningless" literature that was "handled far too consciously" and "incoherent" books that showed "a straining for effect" and necessitated "wading through [a] mass of words." The books to which this particular review referred were James Weldon Johnson's *The Autobiography of an Ex-Colored Man* and Countee Cullen's *Copper Sun*. Both books represented, as far as the column was concerned, the incoherent "spirit of the modernist."[34] The Bookshelf also avoided the white modernists, never mentioning writers like John Dos Passos or Gertrude Stein. One review asked: "Is it part of today's realism to believe that discordance is necessary? Keats . . . did not do it."[35] Another referred scathingly to the "rampant activities of more modern writers" of which "New York has been the hotbed . . . as a rule," going on to state a preference for "inspiration" over "literary value."[36] While black periodicals like *The Crisis* focused on experimental black literature, The Bookshelf reviewed outlines of black history and biographies of black leaders. It repeatedly recommended Will Durant's *The Story of Philosophy*, the great middlebrow Book-of-the-Month Club (BOMC) success, which the editor felt would "capture the interest of the layman" as well as commanding "the respect of the most erudite PhD."[37]

In fact, The Bookshelf was to the black avant-garde literary scene what the contemporaneous BOMC was to experimental white modernists. The Bookshelf may even have modeled itself on the BOMC: the literary club format was introduced just after the first phase of controversial and widespread advertising for the BOMC, and by the 1930s the column listed the Club selections and ran occasional reviews by Christopher Morley, one of the Club's first board members. No evidence survives about the racial makeup of the BOMC's membership but the editorial board's responses to novels like Richard Wright's *Native Son* indicate that they thought their members were mainly white.[38] The Bookshelf therefore functioned as its middlebrow black counterpart—as well as being Chicago's answer to Harlem's literary salons. The editorial policies of The Bookshelf and the BOMC were similar: both tried to avoid books that depicted immoral characters, sought books that inspired emotion, and aimed themselves at what the column's banner and the BOMC's board described as "book-lovers."[39]

Of course, the major middlebrow feature that The Bookshelf shared with the BOMC was its identity as a literary club. The idea of an interactive club appears in the column's logo: a bookshelf with a small pile of books and some partially used leaves of note-paper, suggesting note-taking and preparation for discussion, or perhaps something unfinished to which the reader might participate. Offering to the Chicago Renaissance a middlebrow literary society, The Bookshelf's logo contrasted the logo of "Turning Pages," an early column in the *Defender* that ran for a month in 1922. This featured an open book lit by a single candle, indicating solitary bedtime reading and the personal and private experience of turning the pages of a book—the opposite of a literary club. It also contrasted the logo of the books column "What Books Tell Us," in *Abbott's Monthly*. This showed a book on a display stand, an authority to be respected but not challenged. In this Chicago Renaissance-era periodical, books "tell us" things.

Abbott had launched *Abbott's Monthly* in 1930, and its circulation soon reached 100,000. Much of the magazine focused on gossip, photographs of racially indeterminate people, sensationalist hack writing, romance serials, and lowbrow detective fiction, including "the strange case of Anton La Rue" (which needed no literary merit to solve, as the banner in the issue of October 1930 promised). But Richard Wright published the story "Superstition," his first Chicago publication, in the April 1931 issue, and the magazine featured J. Max Barber, Hughes, Robert Hayden, and Chester Himes. The 1930s and 1940s also saw the *Defender* itself publish the writings of W. E. B. DuBois, Hughes, Wright, and Margaret Walker. Walter White wrote a regular column; and Gwendolyn Brooks's first published poems appeared in the newspaper between 1934 and 1936.

After Abbott's death in 1940, his more culturally progressive heir and nephew John Sengstacke took over the *Defender*. In an early editorial, Sengstacke declared black artistic achievement a weapon in the fight for equality of opportunity, and on September 12, 1942, after Paul Robeson's performance in *Othello* in Cambridge, the *Defender* affirmed victory for black America on the cultural front. Under Sengstacke, the newspaper featured a regular column written in jive talk, and another in rhyme. More famously, Hughes (who had published his early poems in the *Defender* on a page called "Lights and Shadows: A Little Bit of Everything") now began a weekly column "From Here to Yonder," which appeared from 1942 through 1962. Here he wrote sympathetically of the Soviet Union and printed radical verse, and in 1943 he introduced his famous working-class black character, Jesse Semple, into the column. Along the same lines, staff writer Bruce Reynolds contributed a serial weekly story, usually a topical and factual account of working-class life on the South Side. The *Defender* also showcased essays, short stories, and poetry by unknown authors: black schoolteachers, ministers, and others.

The Depression hit the Black Press hard, and more than half of all black periodicals went out of business. But while the *Defender*'s circulation declined, it remained Chicago's leading black newspaper, with branch offices across the country and in Europe. During the 1930s and 1940s, the editors maintained readership with long-running gossip columns, numerous illustrations, exciting front-pages headlines, serializations of novels, and popular sports columns. Social scientists from the Chicago School of Sociology contributed regular commentaries, and humorous anecdotes appeared in a column called "Adventures in Race Relations," to which readers contributed. Articles listed music, literature, and art events, women's and social club meetings. The newspaper ran a regular "Mayor of Bronzeville" contest, which awarded a column and symbolic office to personalities in the black community, and staged the annual Billiken festival, parade, and picnic, linked to its "Billiken Page" and Club. The *Defender*'s writers campaigned for integrated sports and editorialized on the Scottsboro boys, the war in Ethiopia, and World War II—in particular on racism in the military. To bring attention to the campaign for admittance of black men into the air force, the newspaper cosponsored the flight of two black pilots to Washington in 1939. Metz Lochard, editor-in-chief of the *Defender*, then published a controversial one-time supplement in 1942, the "Victory Edition," with articles by black and white leaders on the two fronts of the war: fascism abroad and racism at home. The *Defender*'s war coverage boosted circulation, and the newspaper began to forge links with radio and TV stations, sponsoring a radio show until 1952.

Then, on February 6, 1956, Sengstacke turned the *Defender* into the Chicago *Daily Defender*, the largest black-owned daily in the world. He continued as the *Defender*'s publisher until his death in May 1997. He also founded the National Negro Publishers Association, known today as the National Newspaper Publishers Association (NNPA). This Association unified publishers of black newspapers across the country, and Sengstacke noted in the founding documents of February 1940 that: "The Black press believes that America can best lead the world away from racial and national antagonisms when it accords to every person, regardless of color or creed, full human and legal rights. Hating no person, and fearing no person, the Black press strives to help every person in the firm belief that all are hurt as long as anyone is held back."[40] In the week of Abbott's death, during a year when national circulation for black newspapers reached the all-time high of 1,265,000, seventy-five publishers from across the country met in Chicago to affirm these sentiments. Several months later, in June 1940, the Association was permanent and had its own trade magazine, *The American Negro Editor*. By 1944 the NNPA had a feature on NBC and CBS called "Newspaper Week Broadcasts," which included music, drama, and political commentary.

In addition to the National Negro Publishers Association, the *Defender*, *Abbott's Monthly*, and the Associated Negro Press (Claude Barnett's highly respected Chicago-based national wire service), Chicago also boasted black weeklies like the *Bee* (published by Anthony Overton, with an all-women staff and a national circulation of 50,000) and the muck-raking *Whip*. Published by William C. Linton and edited by Yale Law School graduates Joseph D. Bibb and Arthur Clement MacNeal, the *Whip* sold 65,000 copies weekly. Its editors criticized white politicians, launched successful "Don't Buy Where You Can't Work" and "Spend Your Money Where You Can Work" campaigns that lasted throughout the Depression (and helped to create more than two thousand jobs in South Side stores), and increased the *Whip's* Chicago circulation to almost that of the *Defender*.

Though it didn't carry a books column, the *Whip* regularly reviewed theater and music and imitated the *Defender's* columnist format, running widely read gossip columns like "Nosey Knows" and "Under the Lash." Its sensationalist editorials, and a variety of legal and health sections, were also popular. But the *Whip* did not survive its own successes. White advertisers responded to its "Don't Buy Where You Can't Work" campaign by taking their business to the *Defender*, and the *Whip* folded in 1939. In his autobiography, the journalist Enoch Waters noted that the newspaper was a "victim of its own ingenuity and vigor."[41] Two other black newspapers that had endorsed local boycotts, *The Negro World* and the New York *Interstate Tattler*, also went out of business. The more conservative *Chicago Bee*, which largely ignored civil rights, weathered the Depression only to collapse in the wake of Overton's death in 1946 after a brief tabloid-size reinvention.

Overton, an ex-slave and businessmen who founded and published the *Bee*, was pro-education, antisuperstition, and supportive of the National Negro Business League, racial improvement, and interracial cooperation. With *Bee* editor Olive Diggs, he was committed to what the newspaper termed "wholesome and authentic news."[42] The "honeybees," as Waters remembered calling the all-female staff of the *Bee*, resisted sensationalism, wrote thoughtful and well-researched editorials, and championed decorum and refinement.[43] Nurturing the development of a coherent black community in Chicago, they printed details of black Chicagoans serving in the army and a monthly supplement with glossy photographs of the South Side's high-profile figures, and also sponsored the original "Mayor of Bronzeville" contest in the 1930s that gave rise to the name "Bronzeville" for the South Side. Like the *Defender's* Bookshelf, the *Bee* encouraged literary community, selling black history and literature books directly to its readers. While the *Defender* brought local women's groups together to form the National Council of Negro Women, the *Bee* covered the activities of the Black Women's Club Movement.

Black magazines also thrived in Chicago. *Negro Story* was the first magazine to publish stories only by or about black Americans. Editors Alice C. Browning and Fern Gayden had ties to the South Side Writers Group and also to the *Defender* via Browning's husband (who organized publicity for Sengstacke's newspaper) and Sengstacke's wife (who contributed to *Negro Story*). In addition, Browning had written a fashion column for the *Defender* in the late 1930s. Browning and Gayden used these connections to promote the magazine, sending regular press releases to the *Defender* and announcing the 1945 anniversary issue of the magazine in the pages of the newspaper. Around seventy pages long and costing forty cents an issue, *Negro Story* was subtitled "A Magazine for All Americans." It featured Hughes in its masthead as an editorial advisor and included the column "Current Town Talk," which at one point detailed Ralph Ellison's activities in the marines. During its short existence between 1944 and 1946, it featured poems and stories by Himes, Wright, and Frank Marshall Davis, politically radical pieces by Hughes and Ellison, and some of Brooks's first prose, including a series called "Chicago Portraits . . . Sketches of Chicago Life." It also showcased unknown black and white working-class writers.

The editors theorized a new kind of documentary-style literature. They wrote in their inaugural issue of their belief that "among thirteen million Negroes in America, there must be many who were eager to write creatively if they had a market," and expressed a faith that "good writing may be entertaining as well as socially enlightening." The magazine was an "opportunity to participate in the creation of a better world," and this world was one for which they felt "an obligation to work and to struggle."[44] In their fourth issue they asked "What Should The Negro Story Be?" and printed responses by *Defender* columnist Earl Conrad, white radical Jack Conroy, and Harlem Renaissance veteran Alain Locke. Over the next two years the editors then gave space to stories about current affairs and poems that used newspaper headlines, a literature that combined news and art to make what the magazine termed "plotless realism."

In 1947 Conrad placed *Negro Story* at the center of what he called the "Blues School of Literature," adding that this school showed "the negative in Negro life, with a view to reaching the positive conclusion of indicting a white supremacist society."[45] He believed that *Negro Story* had launched several writers and was widely read in the publishing world. Beyond this magazine, Browning continued her cultural politics as president of the National Negro Magazine Publishers Association, suggesting to members in 1945 that they encourage the adaptation in story and article form of black case histories, covering civil liberties, housing, socialized medicine, and fascism. Browning also planned what would have been the real equivalent of the *Defender's* imaginary book club, in the form of "Negro Story Book" clubs.

Another important Chicago-based figure in the world of the Black Press was John H. Johnson, who in 1940 launched his first periodical, *Negro Digest*. In the style of *Reader's Digest*, this sold 150,000 monthly copies by 1944. Johnson followed his success with *Ebony* in 1945, which again followed a tried-and-true formula and imitated *Life*. *Ebony* reached a circulation of half a million by 1950, and Johnson added the pocket news weekly *Jet* to his stable in 1951. Ben Burns, one of the first editors at both *Negro Digest* and *Ebony*, put the magazines' popular success down to their focus on "four basic subject areas: interracial marriage, Negroes passing as whites, sex, and anatomical freaks."[46] In addition, white advertisers willingly brought their business to a publisher who announced in *Ebony* that his editorial policy was "to mirror the happier side of Negro life—the positive, everyday accomplishments from Harlem to Hollywood."[47] Johnson Publishing Company emerged from the Chicago Renaissance a powerful force in American journalism. Other pioneers in the field of publishing began and remained in Chicago, and city officials and candidates for political office began to woo the Black Press.

Throughout the Chicago Renaissance, the city's black newspapers and periodicals had printed and reviewed thousands of stories and poems, and forged a tangible literary community on the South Side. Enoch P. Waters, who worked for the *Defender* between 1930 and 1945, noted in his autobiography that "Chicago Negroes did not have an atmosphere that encouraged cultural pursuits as Harlem had . . . because Chicago did not." He insisted that the "ego of the Southside . . . was always in the shadow of Harlem."[48] Yet a 26-week investigative series that Waters spearheaded for the *Defender* during the Chicago Renaissance detailed a vast array of cultural activities and interests on the South Side. The editors titled the series "Is the South Side Doomed?" and concluded that it most certainly was *not*.[49] Matilda McEwan, fielding requests from more than fifty readers for her poem in 1927, could have told them that.

Notes

1. From January 1926 onward, the following banner ran each week beneath the logo for The Bookshelf: "'The Bookshelf' is for the benefit of those of our readers who are interested in things literary. If you are a book lover and like the idea of a literary club that meets through 'The Bookshelf' column, you are welcome. You are urged to write in to this department any comments on current or past literature that you have in mind. If you see questions in this column you care to answer by all means do so. If you have questions to ask pertaining to prose, poetry or fiction in modern or ancient literature, send them in."

2. The letter from S. B. A. of Dallas, Texas, ran in The Bookshelf on February 5, 1927, A1.

3. *Chicago Defender*, The Bookshelf, February 19, 1927, A1.

4. The Bookshelf, March 19, 1927, A1.

5. The Bookshelf, May 14, 1928, A1. The first few editions of The Bookshelf, in 1922, listed A. L. Jackson as the column's editor. From 1922 onward, however, no editor's name was attached to the column or listed in the newspaper. The *Defender* archives contain no clue as to the editor's name after 1922. Because most of the newspaper's editors were male, it is to be presumed that The Bookshelf editor was male too.

6. The Bookshelf, December 26, 1925, A1; The Bookshelf, January 2, 1926, A1.

7. See, for example, The Bookshelf, December 26, 1925, A1.

8. The Bookshelf, January 16, 1926, A1.

9. Circulation figures given in Allan H. Spear, *Black Chicago: The Making of a Negro Ghetto* (Chicago: University of Chicago Press, 1967), 185. For more on Abbott, see Alan D. DeSantis, "A Forgotten Leader: Robert S. Abbott and the *Chicago Defender* from 1910–1920," *Journalism History* 23.2 (1997): 63–71, and C. K. Doreski, "From News to History: Robert Abbott and Carl Sandburg read the 1919 Chicago Riot," *African American Review* 26.4 (1992): 637–50.

10. Frederick G. Detweiler. *The Negro Press in the United States.* Chicago: University of Chicago, 1922.

11. Myrdal, Gunnar. *An American Dilemma: The Negro Problem and Modern Democracy.* New York: Harper and Brothers, 1944, 911.

12. For one discussion of the newspaper's racial politics, see T. Ella Strother, "The Black Image in the *Chicago Defender*, 1905–1975." *Journalism History* 4.4 (1977–78): 137–41, 156.

13. *The Negro in Chicago: A Study of Race Relations and a Race Riot, by the Chicago Commission on Race Relations.* Chicago: University of Chicago Press, 1922, 461, 477.

14. Lemos, Justo Fide. Letter to the Editor, *Defender*, May 3, 1930, 14. See also Gladstone H. Yeuell, "The Negro Press as a Factor in Education," *Journal of Educational Sociology* 2.2 (1928): 92–98. In this analysis of three different black newspapers, the *Defender* was ranked the lowest for "social betterment" (37.11 percent of its copy, where *The Age* has 65.69 percent) and the highest for "antisocial" (25.32 percent to *The Age*'s 11.34 percent).

15. *The Negro in Chicago*, 86–87.

16. *Defender*, April 2, 1921, 16.

17. See Eugene F. Gordon, "Survey of the Negro Press," *Opportunity* (January 1927): 7–11, 32.

18. *The Age*, the *Pittsburgh Courier*, and the *Savannah Tribune* did not run book columns during this period. Nor did any of *Defender*'s black competition in Chicago: the *Whip*, the *World*, the *Searchlight*, the *Metropolitan Post*, the *News Ledger*, the *Chicago Enterprise*, the *Chicago Globe*, the *Idea*, the *Chicago Bee*, and the monthly *American Eagle*.

19. Locke, Alain. *The New Negro: An Anthology.* New York: Atheneum, 1925, 14.

20. The Bookshelf, June 19, 1926, A1.

21. The Bookshelf, September 11, 1926, A1.

22. The Bookshelf, January 28, 1928, A1.

23. The Bookshelf, March 25, 1922, A1; The Bookshelf, December 30, 1922, A1; The Bookshelf, April 15, 1922, A1.

24. *Opportunity: A Journal of Negro Life* (October 1926): 322.

25. Locke, "1928: A Retrospective Review," *Opportunity* (January 1929): 8–11 (8). Locke noted of New Negro literature that "as with many another boom, the water will need to be squeezed out of much inflated stock and many bubbles must burst. . . . The real significance and potential power of the Negro renaissance may not reveal itself until after this reaction, and the entire topsoil of contemporary Negro expression may need to be ploughed completely under for a second hardier and richer crop" (8).

26. Calculation made with reference to all the published columns, based on books

reviewed each month with adjustments made for length of review (lines of space allocated).

27. Statement made in July 1921, quoted in Donald Franklin Joyce, "Reflections on the Changing Publishing Objectives of Secular Black Book Publishers, 1900–1986," in Cathy N. Davidson ed., *Reading in America: Literature and Social History* (Baltimore: Johns Hopkins University Press, 1989), 226–39.

28. The Bookshelf, March 5, 1927, A1; The Bookshelf, April 30, 1927, A1; The Bookshelf, April 2, 1927, A1.

29. The Bookshelf, March 19, 1927, A1.

30. The Bookshelf, February 5, 1927, A1.

31. The Bookshelf, June 8, 1929, A1.

32. For "eternal race problem" see The Bookshelf, April 15, 1922, A1.

33. The Bookshelf, August 20, 1927, A1.

34. The Bookshelf, September 17, 1927, A1.

35. The Bookshelf, November 12, 1927, A1.

36. The Bookshelf, November 26, 1927, A1.

37. The Bookshelf, June 19, 1926, A1.

38. For a detailed discussion of the Book-of-the-Month Club's response to *Native Son*, see Janice A. Radway, *A Feeling for Books: The Book-of-the-Month Club, Literary Taste, and Middle-class Desire* (Chapel Hill: University of North Carolina Press, 1997), 286–87.

39. Quoted in Radway, 93.

40. Quoted in Roland E. Wolseley. *The Black Press, U.S.A.* Ames: Iowa State University Press, 1971, 118.

41. Waters, Enoch P. *American Diary: A Personal History of the Black Press.* Chicago: Path Press, 1987, 120.

42. Quoted in Henry Lewis Suggs, ed. *The Black Press in the Middle West, 1865–1985.* Westport, Conn.: Greenward Press, 1996, 33.

43. Waters, 122.

44. Browning, Alice C. and Fern Gayden. "Letter to Our Readers." *Negro Story* 1.1 (August–September 1945): 1.

45. Conrad, Earl. *Jim Crow America.* New York: Duell, Sloan and Pearce, 1947, 59.

46. Burns, Ben. *Nitty Gritty: A White Editor in Black Journalism.* Jackson: University Press of Mississippi, 1996, 114.

47. Quoted in Bill Mullen. *Popular Fronts: Chicago and African-American Cultural Politics, 1935–46.* Urbana: University of Illinois Press, 1999, 186.

48. Waters, 69, 190.

49. The *Defender*, October 21, 1939, 14.

For Further Reading

Abbott's Monthly Microfilm, 1930–33.
American Eagle Microfilm, 1921–25.
Appeal Microfilm, 1885–1923.
Associated Negro Press Microfilm, 1919–67.

Bee Microfilm, 1925–47.

Broad-Ax Microfilm, 1895–1935.

Chicago Defender Microfilm, 1905-present.

The Crisis Microfilm, 1920–29.

Danky, James P. and Wayne A. Wiegand, eds. *Print Culture in a Diverse America.* Urbana: University of Illinois Press, 1998.

DeSantis, Alan D. "A Forgotten Leader: Robert S. Abbott and the *Chicago Defender* from 1910–1920." *Journalism History* 23.2 (1997): 63–71.

De Santis, Christopher C., ed. *Langston Hughes and the Chicago Defender: Essays on Race, Politics, and Culture, 1942–62.* Urbana: University of Illinois Press, 1995.

Doreski, C. K. "From News to History: Robert Abbott and Carl Sandburg read the 1919 Chicago Riot." *African American Review* 26.4 (1992): 637–50.

Drake, St. Clair and Horace R. Cayton. *Black Metropolis: A Study of Negro Life in a Northern City.* New York: Harcourt, Brace and Company, 1945.

Eagle Microfilm, 1889–1930.

Ebony Microfilm, 1945-present.

Free Lance Microfilm, 1895–1926.

Grossman, James R. *Land of Hope: Chicago, Black Southerners, and the Great Migration.* Chicago: University of Chicago Press, 1989.

Half-Century Magazine Microfilm, 1921–25.

Headlines and Pictures Microfilm, 1944–46.

Idea Microfilm, 1926.

Jet Microfilm, 1951-present.

Johnson, Abby Arthur and Ronald Maberry Johnson. *Propaganda and Aesthetics: The Literary Politics of African-American Magazines in the Twentieth Century.* Amherst: University of Massachusetts Press, 1979.

McHenry, Elizabeth. *Forgotten Readers: The Lost History of African-American Literary Societies.* Durham, N.C.: Duke University Press, 2002.

Messenger Microfilm, 1919–28.

National Negro Publishers Association/National Newspaper Publishers Association Microfilm, 1940-present.

Negro Digest Microfilm, 1940–51.

Negro Story Microfilm, 1944–46.

Ottley, Roi. *The Lonely Warrior: The Life and Times of Robert S. Abbott.* Chicago: H. Regnery Co., 1955.

Pride, Armistead S. and Clint C. Wilson II. *A History of the Black Press.* Washington, D.C.: Howard University Press, 1997.

Scott, Emmett J. "Letters of Negro Migrants of 1916–1918." *Journal of Negro History* 4.3 (July 1919): 290–340.

———. "More Letters of Negro Migrants of 1916–1918." *Journal of Negro History* 4.4 (October 1919): 412–65.

Searchlight Microfilm, 1910–32.

Simmons, Charles A. *The African-American Press: A History of News Coverage during National Crises, with Special Reference to Four Black Newspapers, 1827–1965.* Jefferson, N.C.: McFarland and Co., 1998.

Star Microfilm, 1920–52.

Strother, T. Ella. "The Race-Advocacy Function of the Black Press." *Black American Literature Forum* 12.3 (Autumn 1978): 92–99.

Vincent, Theodore G. *Voices of a Black Nation: Political Journalism in the Harlem Renaissance.* San Francisco: Ramparts Press, 1973.

Vogel, Todd, ed. *The Black Press: New Literary and Historical Essays.* New Brunswick, N.J.: Rutgers University Press, 2001.

Washburn, Patrick S. *A Question of Sedition: The Federal Government's Investigation of the Black Press during World War II.* New York: Oxford University Press, 1986.

Whip Microfilm, 1919–39.

World Microfilm, 1900–32.

THE CHICAGO SCHOOL
OF SOCIOLOGY AND THE
BLACK CHICAGO RENAISSANCE
William R. Nash

The Chicago School of Sociology and the Black Chicago Renaissance represent two defining elements of the African American experience in early twentieth-century Chicago. On an empirical level, methods and attitudes developed in the sociology department of the University of Chicago during the first decades of the twentieth century helped shape local and federal policy on racial matters, and thereby affected black-white race relations in the city. On an artistic level, black authors writing in and/or about the city of Chicago in the period between 1935 and 1959 (a slight modification of Robert Bone's definition of the era) brought the landscape of the South Side to life with a richness and intensity matched only in descriptions of Harlem in classic texts of the Harlem Renaissance. While equal in power to the best Harlem works of Langston Hughes, Claude McKay, Nella Larsen, and Rudolph Fisher, Chicago texts by authors like Richard Wright, William Attaway, Willard Motley, and Gwendolyn Brooks also convey a quality of grittiness largely absent from the best-known works of the Harlem Renaissance. For critics like Bone and Carla Cappetti, the grittiness of the writing provides evidence of the influence that Chicago sociology, which focused on how environmental factors in the city determined human behavior, had over the writers of the Chicago Black Renaissance.

Certainly one can learn much from pairing this sociological methodology with literary works from the Black Chicago Renaissance era. As Bone and Cappetti have argued, Wright's fiction and his fictionalized autobiography, *Black Boy/American Hunger*, lend themselves well to Chicago sociological readings. As Wright himself notes in the introduction to Horace Cayton and St. Clair Drake's landmark sociological study of Chicago, *Black Metropolis* (1945), he saw the principles of Chicago sociology as defining his experience and giving it meaning. He further suggests that one can best understand his writing by first understanding basic principles of the Chicago School. This approach works well for reading Wright, who aligns himself with the Chicago sociologists and seeks to give their ideas about environment and behavior life in his literary renderings of the city. For all of that, however, the Wright model becomes a Procrustean bed if one attempts to read other Chicago authors of the era through the same lens. Close consideration of work by Brooks, Motley, Frank Marshall Davis, Theodore Ward, and Frank London Brown complicates the notion that black Chicago writers working between 1935 and 1959 felt the influence of the sociology department at the University of Chicago on their work in any unified sense. Ultimately, then, one best understands the sociologists and writers as making common cause around understanding Chicago life but taking a variety of approaches to achieve that shared end.

In order to best understand this relationship, one must grasp some of the basic principles traditionally grouped under the heading of the Chicago School. Arguably, at least, the term is itself problematic, according to University of Chicago alumnus Howard S. Becker's history of the sociology department. He suggests that one can use the term "Chicago School of Sociology" in its narrowest sense to refer to the Department of Sociology at the University of Chicago; more often, though, students and scholars use the term to reference a coherent body of ideas about urban life generated by faculty and graduate students of the Sociology Department and a concomitant pattern of research practices developed to implement those ideas. In fact, the diverse body of scholars who made up the department pursued their various interests, sometimes in direct conflict with the work of their peers. This detail demonstrates the simplification and mythologizing of the Department of Sociology's scholars and their work—which in turn reinforces the notion of how difficult it is to assess the influence of the sociological school on the literary work.

In all fairness, however, one can point to certain methodological innovations that arose at Chicago as hallmarks of the department's work. One can also identify prominent individuals whose ideas and undertakings advanced the department's status. In the case of Louis Wirth (1897–1952), Cayton, and Wright, one can even draw specific connections between particular individuals whose relationships provide the foundation for Bone's and Capetti's arguments.

To be sure, Wirth is an important figure in the development of the Chicago School; his contributions build, however, on the foundations established by Ernest Burgess (1886–1966), W. I. Thomas (1863–1947), and Robert Park (1864–1944), the scholars who took the department Albion Small (1854–1926) founded in 1892 and transformed it in the 1910s and 1920s into the leading national institution for sociological study. Prior to Burgess's, Park's, and Thomas's ascendancy at Chicago, the fledgling discipline of American sociology concerned itself primarily with theorizing about social conditions and formulating abstract models upon which to test hypotheses. Early scholars in the field, with the notable exception of Small, largely rejected empirical research in favor of generating broad theoretical foundations that would help establish sociology as a viable, independent field of study.

Small saw the need for empirical research, though he was not himself an empiricist. He found in Burgess, Thomas, and Park collaborators who brought empirical research to the forefront of their department's methodology. Under their guidance, the department emphasized methodologies of qualitative analysis, including relying on subject's personal accounts, conducting field work, undertaking social mapping, and performing "ecological analysis," the study of how factors in the environment determine human behavior.

As a part of this ecological analysis, or human ecology, approach, members of the department looked on the city of Chicago itself as a laboratory. In studies like Park's "The City: Suggestions for the Investigation of Human Behavior in the Urban Environment" (1915), Thomas and Znaniecki's *The Polish Peasant in Europe and America* (1918–1920), Charles Johnson's *The Negro in Chicago* (1922, with considerable input from Park), Nels Anderson's *The Hobo* (1923), Burgess's "The Growth of the City" (1925), and Wirth's *The Ghetto* (1928), members of the department focused on understanding the features of the city, particularly its racial and ethnic composition and the resultant local communities that formed within it, the social problems that arose within and among the local communities, and the impact of these conditions on human behavior. The dual ends of this approach were to increase knowledge about the city as an entity and to provide some means of countering the social malaise that these researchers believed the urban environment fostered.

In Park's case, this orientation resulted at least partially from his prior experience as a journalist. Working in that capacity for over a decade before pursuing his career in sociology at Chicago, Park developed an acute sense of the usefulness of careful observation and close contact with the subjects of one's analysis. He also learned firsthand that other sorts of observers, including writers of fiction, could provide useful insights into urban life. One writer whom Park particularly admired was Theodore Dreiser, whose novel *Sister Carrie* (1900) paints Chicago almost as a character itself, a powerful force in the drama of Carrie Meeber Madenda's fall and rise. In Carrie, as in his other works, Dreiser advances the principles of American literary naturalism, which recognizes the increasing mechanization and urbanization of American life as forces too powerful for individual characters to either control or even escape. In many ways, Dreiser's writing has a sociological cast, which makes Park's receptivity to it unsurprising; it also points to one of the major connecting points between Chicago sociology and the Black Chicago Renaissance. When Park identified Dreiser as a legitimate source of information about Chicago, he laid the foundation for relationships between sociologists like Wirth and novelists like Wright.

468 · WILLIAM R. NASH

As biographer Michel Fabre notes, the immediate cause for Wright's in-depth exposure to Chicago sociology was the chance assignment of social worker Mary Wirth, Louis Wirth's spouse, to the Wright family's case. She introduced the aspiring author to her husband, who provided Wright with an informal curriculum in sociology and, along with his research assistant Cayton, discussed the readings with his new protégé at some length. As a part of this discussion, Wirth introduced Wright to the concept of "urbanism," which the sociologist defined in a landmark study entitled "Urbanism as a Way of Life" (1938). Building on Park's 1915 "The City," Wirth suggests the existence of a mode of experience that unites the denizens of a particular urban environment and thereby shapes patterns of behavior in the given city.

At the heart of this idea of urbanism is the conviction that individuals experience greater alienation and isolation in urban environments because, although they interact with larger numbers of people than rural residents do, their interactions tend to be highly specialized and superficial. In Bone's view, Wright's exposure to urbanism and his influence as the primary figure among the writers of the Chicago Black Renaissance makes Wirth's theory the foundation of all the work (or at least all the work Bone deems significant) produced by Wright and his Chicago compatriots.

Whether or not Bone's characterization is accurate, recognition of Wright's bond with Wirth, and through him indirectly with Park, illuminates elements of two of Wright's most sociological works: his best-selling *Native Son* (1940) and his commentary on the Great Migration, *12 Million Black Voices* (1941). The recognition of these elements shows, in turn, Wright's resistance to simply adopting sociological principles that either excused white society too easily or too fully dehumanized blacks.

Native Son chronicles the life of Bigger Thomas, whose attempted transgression of racial and class boundaries in Depression-era Chicago proves lethal for Bigger's two victims, Mary Dalton and Bessie Mears, and leads to Bigger's own demise. Generations of readers have reacted with horror to Bigger's crimes; however, the novel resists simplistic interpretation. Even as Wright demonstrates Bigger's brutality, he emphasizes the impact of racist socioeconomic forces on his character's development. This orientation, which draws on Wirth and Park's human ecological claims that environment determines behavior, suggests an almost exculpatory lack of agency on Bigger's part. While Wright certainly sees the importance of environment in his tale, he also recognizes that to give Bigger over entirely to that line of argument negates his individuality. As Wright sought not only to chronicle the horrific conditions under which blacks lived but also to emphasize blacks' humanity, complete acceptance of this sociological orientation proves untenable. The author's struggle with this paradox provides much of the energy that propels the narrative.

As a condition of his family's maintaining their public assistance income, Bigger takes a job as chauffeur to the wealthy Dalton family. Mr. Dalton, a successful businessman whose holdings include Bigger's slum tenement, and his blind wife see themselves as philanthropists, although their actual help to African Americans is in fact quite limited. Their daughter, Mary, aspires to philanthropy of her own, as she dallies with Communism and with a particular Communist organizer named Jan Erlone. Mary and Jan's well-intentioned but fundamentally misguided attempts to befriend Bigger take a tragic turn the first night of his employment. The white couple insists on eating with Bigger in a South Side restaurant, insensitively overlooking Bigger's discomfort with this transgression of the social code. In an attempt to relax, Bigger shares a bottle of rum with Jan and Mary. When he later takes Mary home, she is so intoxicated that Bigger must carry her up to her room. Once again frightened, but also aroused, by another violation of the social code, Bigger fondles and kisses Mary as she lies drunk on her bed. When her blind mother enters the room, Bigger's overwhelming sense of transgression leads him to cover Mary's mouth with a pillow. He accidentally kills her and then, to avoid detection, burns her corpse in the Dalton's furnace.

The heart of Bigger's difficulties in Book One lie in Chicago sociological theory. Wright attributes Bigger's inarticulate rage and his tendencies toward violence to his environment, although he complicates that notion by distinguishing Bigger's predisposition for violence from the milder hostilities that his peers Gus, Jack, and G. H. feel. The author also further tests the principles of human ecology by moving his subject into a foreign realm within the city. Because of his socialization on the South Side, Bigger can only see the Daltons and Jan Erlone in the most superficial terms, as extensions of the white mass that he has feared and hated his entire life. Similarly, the Daltons and Jan view Bigger superficially, although one can argue that the young Communists at least want to bridge the gap. These notions, which echo the work of Park, Burgess, and Wirth, propel the narrative forward to the moment of the first murder and set up further sociological consideration of both the protagonist and his environment.

Book Two describes Bigger's being identified as the murderer, his flight through Chicago's slums and his eventual capture by the police. Bigger's flight affords Wright numerous opportunities to chronicle the particular conditions under which black Chicagoans lived during the 1930s. In recounting difficulties finding housing, describing the frustrations of being forced to buy overpriced, substandard food in South Side markets, and chronicling the police force's terrorizing of the black community, Wright incorporates elements of the life history that is a foundational element of the Chicago School's methodology.

Even as Wright makes use of these features of Chicago sociology, he resists the temptation to simply embrace them wholesale. One sees this clearly in the representation of newspapers in the novel. In "Urbanism as a Way of Life," (1938)

Louis Wirth argues that the media outlets of a city must necessarily serve as a "leveling influence." In contrast, Wright notes that the manipulation of the media to racial ends prevents any meaningful leveling from occurring. From after he murders Mary until he has been jailed for his crime, Bigger obsessively seeks out and reads newspapers. Clearly, his primary objective is to determine what the authorities know about his actions and whereabouts. In going consistently to the *Tribune*, though, Bigger effectively makes the paper the authority on who and where he is. In the court of public opinion, the paper tries and convicts him immediately, thereby shaping how the general public sees him as well. In the process of detailing his saga, the paper also relies on racist formulations of identity that shape perceptions of Bigger that are often contrary to reality. Although he did not rape Mary, for instance, the paper brands him as "rapist" and "Negro sex-slayer," labels that "exclude him utterly from the world."[1] From this point on, his reality is determined entirely by the impact of that terminology, as he is captured, tried, and sentenced to death.

The third section of the novel, which recounts Bigger's incarceration and his trial, lacks the emphasis on physical flight that drives the first two sections of the narrative. Nevertheless, it takes the reader on another sort of sociological tour, this time in the shape of attorney Boris Max's argument that Bigger's environment is entirely responsible for his actions in murdering both Mary Dalton and Bessie Mears. For much of this section, Wright gives himself over to the human ecology argument, making a strong case for Bigger's being a product of his environment. Ultimately, however, he pulls the reader back from that, affording his character a moment of individual awareness that comes from the creation of a meaningful human relationship. That does not, of course, change the outcome of Bigger's story, but it does complicate the narrative. Had Bigger known this real connection earlier, then what might his life have been? With that question hanging unresolved at the end of the narrative, the reader cannot rest easily with the notion that human relationships in the urban environment are necessarily superficial. In the end, then, *Native Son* is undeniably a sociologically inflected novel, but it is not at all a wholesale adoption of Chicago sociological principles.

In his introduction to Drake and Cayton's *Black Metropolis* (1945), Wright notes that Chicago has "an open and raw beauty . . . that seems either to kill or endow one with the spirit of life."[2] If *Native Son* reflects the killing edge of Chicago, then *12 Million Black Voices* brings the spirit of life to the black community. To be sure, Wright brings many of the grim details of Cayton's Chicago research to bear in his account of the Great Migration, a text which once again employs the life history model of reportage, although Wright blends particular life histories together into the overarching narrative of a community "we." In his discussion of the power of the Lords of the Land and the Bosses of the Buildings, and most pointedly in his lyrical assessment of the kitchenette apartment as "the funnel through which our pulverized lives flow to ruin and death on the city pavements," one sees the darkness of determinism, the suggestion that the human ecology of the South Side harms, perhaps irreparably, black youth.[3] And yet, for all of that, the narrative does not end here, but moves instead to a final note of hope that counters the pervasive despair of *Native Son*: "We are with the new tide. We stand at the crossroads. We watch each new procession. The hot wires carry urgent appeals. Print compels us. Voices are speaking. Men are moving! And we shall be with them. . . . ."[4] In this formulation, where the media notably is something of a leveler, Wright shows a hopeful outcome to the urbanist way of life, suggesting in the process that while environment may shape experience, it does not determine fate—indeed, transcendence is not only possible, it is also inevitable.

In examining these two texts, which appeared within a year of one another, one can see the complexities of Wright's own relationship to Chicago sociology; fascinated with its theories and its methodology, he nevertheless cannot fully embrace the implications of its principles because of what they cost him and his fellow blacks in individuality and agency. Recognition of his situation necessarily complicates scholarly readings of him as the conduit of Chicago sociological theory and methods to his peers in the South Side Writers Group and to successive generations of Chicago writers.

Among Wright's fellow participants in the South Side Writers Group were poet Frank Marshall Davis and playwright Theodore Ward. Ward's best-known work of this period, *Big White Fog* (1938), was selected for production by the Federal Theatre Project's Chicago unit in 1938 and then ran again in New York in 1940. This important, if somewhat cumbersome, play recounts the misfortunes of the Mason family, who struggle against the largely invisible backdrop of Chicago's South Side to achieve and sustain individual dignity and empowerment in the face of persistent white oppression. Victor Mason, the central character, is a Garveyite, so disillusioned by American racism and so desperate to believe in Garvey as a messiah that he squanders his family's fortunes on stock in the Black Star Line on the very day that officials deem the first Black Star liner unseaworthy. His brother-in-law, Dan Rogers, is a ruthless capitalist, who makes a significant fortune by opening a kitchenette building, loses his money to the Depression, and loses his wife, Juanita, to the boarders that she takes in to make ends meet. Ella, Vic's long-suffering wife and Juanita's sister, defends her husband from Juanita's mockery about his Garveyite beliefs and from her mother Martha Brooks's color-struck hostility toward the "black, evil fool" that took her and her daughters from the security of the South to Chicago and now aspires to move them to Africa.

In the course of the play, Vic rises through the ranks of Garvey's Universal Negro Improvement Association while his family experiences a parallel decline.

His daughter, Wanda, turns eventually to prostitution to provide the rent money that will keep the family from finally being evicted. His son, Les, moves from the disillusionment of being denied a college scholarship because of his race, through involvement in his Uncle Dan's real estate scheme, to radicalization and membership in the Communist Party, which he sees as the only chance to save his family. Ironically, it is the presence of Communist eviction-resisters that leads the police to open fire on the Masons in the final scene of the play, and Victor falls, shot in the back while wearing his now tattered Garvey uniform. As he lies dying, Victor resigns himself to despair and declares the white oppressor victorious. In a move consistent with leftist drama, Ward answers this outcry with the image of Les's comrades, black and white, gathered at Victor's bedside to comfort him as he dies and to lead his family into a brighter future. Although he clearly sees something appealing in this image, Ward resists the complete fix, as Victor declares that his vision has failed him and he cannot see the unity of the races. This might well be the final proof of the character's blindness, the ultimate illustration of his overblown and destructive fidelity to Garvey; alternately, it might well foreshadow the impermanence of the American Communist Party's commitment to racial equality, a sea change that was well underway by the time Ward wrote *Big White Fog*.

Ward's ambivalent resolution of *Big White Fog*, like Wright's mixed picture of Max and Jan in *Native Son*, suggests again literary Black Chicago's uneasy relationship with the Communist Party. Ward breaks with Wright, however, in that his characters all have agency; their suffering is not determined by their environment so much as it is the result of their individual choices. At several points during the play, Victor has opportunities to sacrifice his Garveyite beliefs for the good of his family; but he never makes that choice. This stubbornness on his part costs him the love of his wife, his son's education, and his daughter's virtue, which gives the play a sense of tragedy not unlike what one sees in the deterministic landscape of Wright's most sociological texts. The key difference, and the one that marks Ward outside the boundaries of the sociological school, is that arguably little, perhaps none, of this suffering is inevitable. If he has a scientific model behind his play, it is more likely the scientific Socialism that the American leftist Popular Front brought to Chicago in the 1930s and 1940s.

As the relative obscurity of Ward's play demonstrates, critics interested in the influence of Chicago sociology on the Black Chicago Renaissance often focus their attention primarily on the fiction of that era, perhaps because Wright was himself primarily a fiction writer. But Wright began his literary career as a poet, and several of his most prolific associates in the South Side Writers Group were poets. One among them, Davis, bears close assessment in relation to this question of how Chicago sociology affected black Chicago writers.

Davis's *Black Man's Verse* (1935) demonstrates two features of Chicago sociological methodology: close empirical observation of an environment, and reliance on the personal stories of informants in the studied environment. And yet, Davis does not restrict himself to dry reportage, as one sometimes finds in *Native Son*. Poems like "Chicago's Congo" and "Gary, Indiana" render close observation of regional phenomena in aesthetic terms that at least complicate and at most dismantle any sense of "science" in the work. The notion of Gary's steel mills as "hoboes," for instance, undermines the sense of the mechanistic forces of a social order at work against its residents. This might well be attributable to formal differences, as the demands on the poet, even one who works in free verse as Davis does, necessarily shape the work away from the clear-cut empiricism of the sociological study. Given that, one must turn to the underlying message of the verse to determine what, if any, sympathies Davis might have with Park, Wirth, and their peers.

Davis's poetic universe does show signs of diversity, as indicated in poems like the ebullient "Jazz Band," the starkly grim "Lynched," and "Five Portraits of Chicago at Night." This last poem proves particularly noteworthy in this light, as it moves from the splendor of the Loop to the squalor of the South Side. His black community is hardly monolithic, and in the "Ebony under Granite" section of the work (which clearly resonates to Edgar Lee Masters's *Spoon River Anthology*), he provides the life histories of a surprisingly broad cross section of the black community. And yet, for all of their diversity, they have met the same fate—this speaks to the human condition, of course, but it also points to a pervasive undertone in Davis's work, a suggestion that race determines the broad contours of individuals' experiences and a concomitant intimation that while the particulars of various black lives in Chicago might differ, the city becomes for its black residents an environment that breeds suffering and frustration. One sees that undertone again in "Mojo Mike's Beer Garden," where the visible diversity of the population underscores their common disillusionment and reliance on the "two yellow gals" who deliver the "beer and wine and gin." In this poetic universe, environment does indeed seem to determine human behavior.

For Ward, Davis, and the Wright of *Native Son* and *12 Million Black Voices*, their temporal context is as important as their geographic locale. By 1945, after the end of World War II, Chicago saw heightened racial tensions as the participants in the Second Great Migration clashed with returning soldiers who sought their old jobs and comfortable homes for their families. At the same time, the institution of the G. I. Bill brought an influx of students to the University of Chicago generally, and to the Department of Sociology in particular. This boost of student population, many of whom were schooled about human behavior in the theater of war, gave rise to a second wave, or a Second School, of Chicago

sociology. This represents a refinement of Wirth, Park, and Burgess's innovations in response to an increasingly complicated environment. Black creative
writers similarly modified their reactions to the pressures of the sociological
worldview, yielding an even greater diversity of responses to the questions of
human ecology driving their predecessors.

How different a picture from Davis's one gets in the poetry of Chicago's most
famous black woman writer, Gwendolyn Brooks. Like Wright, and more so than
Davis or Ward, she carefully examines the social conditions shaping the lives
of blacks in her city. Unlike Wright, however, she resists a simple correlation of
environment and action and provides strong evidence for the argument that
Chicago Sociology's influence on Chicago's black literati was more limited than
Bone and Capetti suggest.

Brooks was born in Topeka, Kansas, to David and Keziah (nee Wims) Brooks,
residents of Chicago's South Side, who had returned home for the birth of their
first child. They subsequently moved back to Chicago, where Brooks lived for
most of her life. Despite her family's poverty, which necessitated both of her
parents' foregoing career aspirations, Brooks grew up in a nurturing home environment. Unfortunately, her community experience was not similarly positive. In the face of intraracial prejudice aimed at her because of her appearance, Brooks found solace and self-confidence in her writing. Her mother was
especially sensitive to her daughter's plight and encouraged Brooks to develop
her creative talents. She also took Brooks to readings by authors such as James
Weldon Johnson and Langston Hughes; Hughes strongly encouraged her in her
attempts to establish a poetic career.

By the age of 13, Brooks had already published a poem, "Eventide," in *American Childhood* magazine. At the age of 17, she became a regular contributor to
the *Chicago Defender*, where eventually she published 75 poems. Heartened by
her early success, Brooks continued to hone her craft, enrolling in Inez Cunningham Stark's poetry workshop at the South Side Community Art Center.
That extremely challenging and supportive work environment yielded her a
first prize for her work in the Poets' Class contest, her first publication in *Poetry* magazine, and many of the pieces for her first book of poetry, *A Street in
Bronzeville* (1945).

In that volume's series of polished, graceful poems, Brooks takes readers
inside the world of the black poor, portraying the harsh realities of economic
injustice without ever losing sight of the basic human dignity of her subjects.
Arguably, Brooks shares Wright's goal in *12 Million Black Voices* of striking a
balance between portraying the collective hardships of black life in Chicago and
affirming the dignity of individuals responding to those tribulations. Through
her portrayals of the individuals who inhabit her nameless street, she succeeds
where Wright struggles, perhaps because of the absence of sociological theory

undergirding her work. As she chronicles the difficulties and injustice woven into the fabric of South Side life, she maintains a focus on the individuals who inhabit that landscape; this orientation provides a strong counter to the sense of alienation that marks *Native Son*.

The second poem of Bronzeville, "kitchenette building," establishes the volume's tone. The speaker is, as Brooks was, a resident of a tenement on Chicago's South Side; furthermore, like Brooks the speaker experiences creative urges—the reader sees her wondering whether or not a dream could "sing an aria" in the confines of rooms marked with the stench of "onion fumes . . . fried potatoes / And yesterday's garbage ripening in the hall." For all of her wondering, however, the speaker ultimately recognizes the futility of her speculation. First of all, there are practical needs to be met: "Since Number Five is out of the bathroom now, / We think of lukewarm water, hope to get in it." Secondly, the speaker understands herself and her fellow residents as "things," a notion that the reference to a fellow resident as "Number Five" strongly reinforces. So long as she accepts this vision of herself, the speaker cannot really afford to dream, especially not of a world that values aesthetic sensitivity. Not so for Brooks. As this and the other poems of *A Street in Bronzeville* demonstrate, Brooks sees making art as a viable, even a crucial, response to this environment. In short, making beauty in this world where it is so scarce becomes for the poet one means of surviving it.

Unfortunately, many of Bronzeville's residents are not so lucky as the poet. From the aborted babies of "the mother," to De Witt Williams, whose funeral procession the reader observes, to "poor Percy," the victim of his brother's violence in "the murder," the number of characters who die in the volume is so-bering. Of the ones who do survive, most are scarred by their experiences. One sees, for instance, Matthew Cole, a reclusive bachelor who "never will be done / With dust and his ceiling that / Is everlasting sad" or the subject of "obituary for a living lady," who like Cole is among the dead living. These are adults so broken by events in their lives that they do not live, but only exist. As poignant as these portraits are, the children of Bronzeville are even more heart-wrenching. Percy perishes in flames of his brother, Brucie's, creation. The fires of poverty and intraracial oppression burn others. Of these, none is better known or more moving than Mabbie, the subject of "the ballad of chocolate Mabbie."

A shy seven-year-old whose dark skin suggested to others that she "was cut from a chocolate bar," Mabbie develops a crush on classmate Willie Boone. Innocent enough to think "that the world was heaven," Mabbie believes that declaring her feelings will win her young Boone's devotion. What she does not realize is that he is prone to the intraracial prejudice about skin color that makes light-skinned blacks reject those with darker complexions. Waiting outside the schoolhouse, she encounters Boone and the new object of his affections, "a lemon-hued lynx / With sand-waves loving her brow." The poem ends with an image of Mabbie's isolation, her belief that she is most fit for "chocolate companions" like herself. Although not directly autobiographical, the poem does reflect a crucial part of Brooks's experience: her own feelings of rejection and isolation associated with her darkness. Here, as in "kitchenette building," the experiencing consciousness in the poem can ill afford beauty as solace: chocolate Mabbie faces a life of isolation because of her color, a reality that simple beauty cannot ameliorate. For Brooks, however, the opportunity to make art out of this painful experience is much more effective, perhaps even the best response that she has to injustice.

The ability to make art brings a balance to Bronzeville, as it shows in the lives of individuals who are not beaten by their environment, who instead make beauty in their lives despite the ugliness of their neighborhood. Such is the case for Satin-Legs Smith, the subject of "The Sundays of Satin-Legs Smith." An undistinguished member of the community during the workweek, Smith dons his finery on Sundays and strolls through Bronzeville like a king among his subjects. Though perhaps petty in some aspects, such as in his fixation on the precision of his zoot-suit pants' cuffs, Smith's attitude is one of gentle beneficence and resistance to an environment that brings others around him to despair. Although different in her exterior, Hattie Scott has a similar attitude. Although burdened with a menial job doing day work for a thoughtless white woman, Scott resists resignation, choosing instead to nurture an interiority defined by her determination to enjoy the hours of her life over which she has control and her concomitant sense of herself as a person of worth, not simply a thing who does her employer's bidding.

Perhaps the most moving portrayal of individual agency and human connection in Bronzeville appears in "when you have forgotten Sunday: the love story." This poem, in which the poetic persona addresses her lifetime companion, is a testimonial to the power of meaningful human connection to overcome dire environmental straits. Details in the poem convey the sense that the lovers reside in a South Side kitchenette, as indeed Brooks and her husband Henry Blakely did for the first several years of their marriage. In the context of that environment, however, theirs is a world of clean sheets, satisfying food, intimate conversation, and enduring passion. This image of an oasis of life and love in the midst of Bronzeville undercuts the notion that environment determines human behavior; after all, if that were the case, then how can the same street in Bronzeville house the couple from "when you have forgotten Sunday" and the subjects of the collection's first poem, "the old-marrieds," a pair so beaten by life that even under the most romantic circumstances they do not speak?

Such variation is only possible in a world where individuality and agency profoundly matter; and Bronzeville presents precisely this type of poetic universe. For Brooks, the street as environment proves secondary to the residents it comprises. By taking this approach, she emphasizes the humanity and dignity of all members of this community, from the sufferers to those who succeed. In doing so, she provides a strong counterpoint to the deterministic worldview that typifies sociologically inflected black Chicago literature.

These motifs from *A Street in Bronzeville* resonate through her Pulitzer Prize–winning collection of poems, *Annie Allen* (1948), and through her only novel, *Maud Martha* (1953). The great strength of the novel (which has been largely overlooked by critics) is its sustained examination of the impact of the Bronzeville environment on a single individual. Like chocolate Mabbie, Maud Martha knows the pain of color-based rejection; like the speaker of "kitchenette building," she struggles to keep her aesthetic dreams alive in the oppressive environment of a South Side tenement. Her struggle is powerful, as her poverty, her color, and her increasingly sterile marriage to her inadequate husband, Paul, threaten to overcome her and force her down into resignation, perhaps even despair. And yet, for all of those forces, Maud Martha's individuality and the strength of her character persistently rescue her from that fate. Her persistent resilience and hope, best embodied in her daughter, Paulette, and in the unborn child she carries at the novel's end, move her past the limitations of her environment and inspire her to create a strong sense of self. She maintains that self against the relentless pressure of her environment, and by doing so she undermines the urbanist notions that largely drive novels like Wright's *Native Son*.[5]

As a long-time resident of the South Side and a loving chronicler of her community, Brooks hews somewhat closely to the line of her earlier counterparts in the Black Chicago Renaissance tradition. One finds significantly different circumstances in the life histories of two other Black Chicago Renaissance writers, Willard Motley and Frank London Brown. As each man moved outside the conventional confines of Chicago's Black Belt, he developed a relationship to and a reliance on Chicago sociology that varied in emphasis and orientation according to his place in the broader racial community of Chicago.

Of all the authors named in this study, none fall farther from the mainline of expectations about black writers and black writing in Chicago than Willard Motley. Hailing from an established middle-class family, Motley grew up on the South Side, but his family was the first black family to rent in their neighborhood around 60th Street. Motley was the only African American in his grammar school; when he got to Englewood High School, he found himself thrust together with other black students whose home environments and life experiences were radically different from his. Motley's experiences in this range of diverse environments taught him early on to see people in terms of their common humanity, with little regard for their racial designation. This conviction that "people are just people" would inform most of his significant literary output, especially his first and best-known novel, *Knock on Any Door* (1947).

By the time he published that first novel, Motley was already a seasoned writer and traveler. Having begun his professional literary career at age thirteen writing a "Kid's Column" for the *Chicago Defender*, Motley found upon graduation from high school that his range of experiences was too narrow to provide material for mature fiction. He responded to this recognition by taking a bicycle trip to New York City. Along the way, he encountered disadvantaged people of several racial and ethnic groups, and he gathered material that found its way first into travel articles that he published in his early twenties and, eventually, into his fiction. Of particular importance to his literary career were his encounters with Joe, a young Mexican American man in Colorado who was turning from innocence to a life of crime. As Motley later noted, it was meeting Joe that set him on the path toward writing *Knock on Any Door*.

The novel recounts the transformation of Italian American youth Nick Romano from an upstanding, devout, middle-class altar boy to a streetwise hoodlum whose increasing involvement in Chicago's criminal world leads to his murdering a police officer and being sentenced to die in the electric chair for this crime. Nick's increasing corruption and his concomitant rejection of all the good influences in his life proceeds directly as a result of his moving from a middle-class Denver neighborhood to a slum, and from there to a stint in the reformatory for possessing a stolen bicycle (though Nick himself did not steal it). Brutalized by his experiences in the reformatory, Nick emerges and joins his family, now in Chicago, a greatly changed young man. He drifts into a life of petty crime, passes in and out of incarceration, and eventually becomes a full-fledged hoodlum, rolling drunks and committing armed robberies. In the course of one robbery, Nick kills his old nemesis, a policeman named Riley. Sentenced to death, he goes to the electric chair reflecting on his earliest sufferings at the Denver reformatory. The novel ends "Nick? Knock on any door down this street," an assertion that conveys Motley's sense of the inevitability of environments working on individuals.

In addition to this message, which ties Motley's novel firmly to the concepts of urbanism that drive much Chicago sociology, *Knock on Any Door* also bears the marks of Motley's extensive scientific research on his story. Critic Robert Fleming notes that Motley went to great lengths to try to get an accurate sense of the institutions of the criminal justice system that he treats in his novel. Furthermore, he drew on his personal history, particularly some time that he spent in jail in the course of his bicycle trip to New York. Motley's purpose in drawing all of this material together is to make a statement about the harmful impact of environmental pressures on the lower classes and to illustrate the inevitability of Nick's downfall from the moment that his family leaves the relative safety of the middle class. With this formulation, Motley builds on Wright's example in

Native Son; by paralleling Bigger's experience with Nick's, he also complicates the issue of the role of race in this sociological process, demonstrating the destructive nature of class-based environmental difficulties as the foundation of the trouble in the novel.

Knock on Any Door won Motley broad critical acclaim, the devotion of a public who consumed not only the novel but also comic strip and movie versions of the story; perhaps the most important accolades for our purposes come, though, from sociologist Cayton, the coauthor of *Black Metropolis*. In a series of reviews that he wrote for publications ranging from the *Chicago Tribune* to *New Republic*, Cayton praised Motley for the accuracy of his sociology and embraced the notion that submission to environmental pressures was not a racially based experience. Of all the other writers cited in this study, only Wright shares the distinction of having had his work publicly deemed sociologically significant by a member of Chicago's Sociology Department.

One other author of this period who was locally significant, Frank London Brown, shares with Wright the distinction of having been directly exposed to and influenced by sociologists from the University of Chicago. Brown's urban realist account of the violence accompanying integration of a housing project in the South Deering neighborhood, *Trumbull Park* (1959); the existentially inflected meditation on isolation and community in *The Myth Maker* (1969); and his body of short fiction indicate both the range of his literary abilities and the scope of his social vision.

Brown's direct exposure to the ideas and methodologies of the Chicago School likely began during his undergraduate study at Roosevelt University, where St. Clair Drake, coauthor of *Black Metropolis*, was a faculty member for years. In his introduction to that volume, Wright notes that Cayton and Drake's work "pictures the environment out of which the Bigger Thomases of our nation come." One sees the impact of this seminal study on Brown throughout his body of work, as he repeatedly examines the impact of the urban environment on Chicago's black population.

Trumbull Park, an account based on Brown's own experiences as one of the early integrators of the Trumbull Park Homes in the South Deering neighborhood of Chicago, paints in relentless detail a picture of the protracted violence and outrage that greeted the new black residents of a housing project that was, according to deals supposedly made with the city on its construction in 1938, to have remained ethnically homogenous until the neighborhood agreed to integration (*Chicago Human Relations*, Document I). In Brown's story, Louis "Buggy" Martin, his wife, Helen, and their daughters, Louella and Diane, brave the attack and work to make a home in the midst of the conflict engulfing the project. Though the ending implies they will ultimately succeed, the majority of the story concerns their entry into the struggle and the toll it takes on them individually and on their relationships with the other African American families engaged in the battle.

One might well wonder why these citizens would bear this onslaught; the answer has much to do with the conditions they were escaping on the South Side, where African American families were restricted to unspeakably crowded and inadequate housing and charged exorbitant rents. Arnold Hirsch reports that in the late 1940s, "375,000 blacks resided in an area equipped to house no more than 110,000"; furthermore, many lived in conditions as squalid as those in the basement of 3106 Wentworth, where "ten families occupied cardboard cubicles in 1947. The 'apartments' had no windows or toilets and shared a single broken stairway and stove."[6] Brown evokes this reality in *Trumbull Park* through repeated references to the Gardener Building, the South Side slum where Buggy and Helen Martin grow up, meet, marry, and raise their daughters until this new opportunity presents itself. "We called the building we lived in the Gardener Building, after Mr. Gardener, the owner. . . . the . . . building was real old, like Mr. Gardener, and rotten from the inside out. . . . The Gardener building had its own special smell: baby milk and whiskey, fried chicken and cigarette smoke, perfume—and the sick smell of rotten porches." Having described the environment, Brown shows its impact on the black community as a child falls through one of these rotten porches to her death. Her mother, distraught by her daughter's death, tries to kill herself in the same manner, figuring that self-destruction is a better option than a continued existence in the rat-infested hovel of her tenement apartment.

Once ensconced at Trumbull Park, the Martins face a wave of violent protest, physical and psychological assault, and egregious mob activity by white residents, suffering broken windows, death threats, stonings, and a consistent nightly barrage of fireworks directed at their homes. The novel's account of day-to-day conflict in the development clearly resonates with the actual historical record. When the Donald Howard family leased a Trumbull Park Homes apartment in July 1953, a feat accomplished because of Mrs. Howard's light skin and the absence of her dark-skinned husband from the leasing office, those segregationist agreements were broken. Rather than evict the Howards, which they had no legal grounds for, the Chicago Housing Authority opened Trumbull Park Homes to other African American families. One result was a slow influx of blacks into the project, including the Frank London Brown family, who moved into Trumbull Park Homes in April 1954. Another consequence was a wave of violent protest, physical and psychological assault, and egregious mob activity perpetrated unrelentingly against the new black residents from August 1953 through December 1955. The Howard and Brown families, as well as the other twenty-five African American families who moved into the project, suffered broken windows, death threats, stonings, and a consistent nightly barrage of fireworks directed at their homes.

In the novel, one result of this onslaught is conflict among the integrators of Trumbull Park. As each of the black families in the development descends into its separate struggle to survive, Brown alludes to another important premise of the Chicago School of Sociology. This infighting reflects the theories of W. I. Thomas and Florian Znaniecki, who argue that individual development comes only through inevitable struggle with the community. For each of these families to advance, according to this argument, they must break with one another as they have broken with their home communities in moving to Trumbull Park. Wright adopts a similar pattern in both *Native Son* and *Black Boy/An American Hunger*. Brown brings this struggle to a different resolution, however, as he posits a means of survival for the struggling individuals through community building: the collective celebration of African American cultural markers, one of which is music.

Music is, as many scholars have noted, a critically important element of Brown's life and work. One of his most recognized publications is his 1958 *Down Beat* interview with Thelonious Monk, and Brown's professional highlights include his reading short fiction to the live accompaniment of Monk's music in a New York jazz club. As Sterling Stuckey notes, Brown's interest in jazz dates to his childhood when, after migrating with his family from Kansas to Chicago, he "battered his way into manhood. . . . on the 58th Street 'Stroll'" and spent countless hours listening to music at Morrie's Record Shop, where he was exposed to the blues and jazz evolving in Chicago at the time.[7]

In *Trumbull Park*, music restores Buggy's sense of himself and establishes the community foundation he seeks. Whenever Buggy feels fragmented, he sustains himself with music; when he wants to connect with another black resident of Trumbull Park, he does so by playing records. His first real bonding with Arthur Davis, the first of the black migrants, comes when he plays Billie Holiday records while the two men talk; a shared appreciation for her voice enables them to set aside their present stress and explore their common experiences on "the 58th street 'Stroll.'" Also, as Maryemma Graham notes, when Buggy and a new black resident of Trumbull Park assert their humanity at the end of the novel by walking to the bus stop rather than riding in a squad car and sustain themselves by singing Joe Williams's blues, the music becomes a "new form of collective resistance to oppression."[8]

This scene also illustrates Brown's ultimate response to the primary impulses of the Chicago School. Although he employs sociological methodologies in his chronicling of black life in the city, he resists the deterministic conclusions that the social scientists drew about the impact of environment on individuals and on the community. For him, the structures and traditions of African American culture provide an effective counter to the oppressive urban environment his characters inhabit, a cause for hope rather than despair.

One sees a similar pattern at work in *The Myth Maker*. Ernest Day, the protagonist, is a solitary African American student with no home and no identity. When the novel opens we see him having abandoned his wife and daughters to take up the quest for an intellectual ideal he cannot achieve. In a moment of despair he kills a man who treats him kindly and spends the rest of the novel fleeing the consequences of his actions. Near the end of the story, however, he finds some hope and immediately transforms it into a celebration of his heritage. In this moment, Day heads for 58th Street and Morrie's Record Mart, which "seemed to be the place to go now that Ernest wanted to live." His desire for the place extends into a desire for the music of a litany of performers Brown names, including "Bird, Diz, Prez, Ella, Sarah, Dakota, Horace Silver, Count Basie, Joe Williams, Jackie McLean, Thelonious, Ornette Coleman . . . Muddy Waters, Blind Lemon, and Harry Belafonte."[9] A cavalcade of jazz and blues greats, the names represent both the rich cultural heritage of the African American community and a means of further healing for Day. As he listens eagerly and carefully to a Thelonious Monk recording, Day gains a new perspective on his life and his role in the community, a level of insight enabling him to step away from his intellectual despair and toward a place of human connection.

As Day hears Monk move "history forward," he recognizes "the cyclic circularity of history, and of the future of man, and the end of the bad things, and the beginning of the good things" and feels "free, loose, weightless, yet not in need of wings! In need of nothing but his will to be free."[10] This ability to "move history," and the concomitant hopefulness associated with it, further reinforces Brown's assertion of African American cultural forms as a counter to the determinism of Chicago sociology. Although he vividly chronicles ghetto life in *The Myth Maker*, addressing the social and economic forces that conspire to perpetuate this oppressive existence, he once again suggests that environment alone does not entirely determine the future of the African American urban community. So long as individuals within that group embrace traditional cultural forms, there is a chance to build something better for the group.

In addition to his novels, Brown wrote a number of significant stories that also illustrate his views about heritage as a means of countering isolation, alienation, and oppression. Two bear special mention in this context—"Singing Dinah's Song" and "McDougal." In many ways, "Dinah's Song" picks up directly on themes appearing in *Trumbull Park*. By contrast, "McDougal" makes a bold new statement about the possibilities for harmony between the races.

"Singing Dinah's Song" is the story of a drill press operator whose coworker and friend, Daddy-O, sustains his work at the plant by singing Dinah Washington's songs as he works. The music gives him a sense of self and makes the work bearable, at least in the moment. The larger issues behind the work sur-face when Daddy-O comes to work beautifully dressed and insisting he has bought his machine with his ten years of work. Refusing to either operate it or allow anyone else to touch it, Daddy-O asserts his rights and holds the plant manager at bay until the police come and force him to surrender. With that he breaks down and is led away, leaving the narrator to reflect on his actions. He understands that the blues has been a shield for Daddy-O, but he also sees that the blues alone are not enough. As he recognizes that "being in the plant made [Daddy-O] sing those songs and like finally the good buddy couldn't sing hard enough to keep up the dues on his machine," he knows that the blues are only part of the solution.[11] In addition to the music, Daddy-O needs the community that sustains it; he needs the friendship of the narrator, who stands up for him and tries to help him deal with this crisis. Furthermore, he also needs the nar-rator to remember him and his trials, something the narrator does by singing one of Dinah Washington's songs himself as he works after Daddy-O's removal. Though it comes perhaps too late for Daddy-O himself, the community he needs grows in the wake of his blues lesson to sustain the narrator.

Community and music are even more intertwined in "McDougal," one of Brown's most respected stories. A brief impressionistic account of a jazz per-formance, the story raises the issue of whether or not the white trumpeter, Mc-Dougal, has any legitimate right to be on the bandstand with the black members of the jazz combo they all play in. One might well expect this to be simply a statement of the racial exclusivity of legitimate jazz or some sort of condemna-tion of the presumptuousness of white culture. That McDougal has a black wife apparently suggests a complicated and problematic fusion of cultures. Certainly the fact that McDougal and his wife suffer racial slights, that they cannot find a place to live, and that he cannot support her and their three children point to the difficulties of interracial marriage. More importantly than that, however, these experiences become for McDougal the raw material of the superb jazz that he plays. As the bassist, Little Jug, explains, "he knows the happenings . . . I mean about where we get it, you dig? I mean like with Leola and those kids and Forty Seventh Street and those jive landlords, you dig? The man's been burnt, Percy. Listen to that somitch—listen to him!"[12] His bandmates respect him and distinguish him from a cadre of white imitators who seek to soullessly copy the accomplishments of black musicians. McDougal is acceptable to them because he is living their life, and the music that he plays is born from a version of the suffering that they have known.

This story marks an important step for Brown with regard to his thought about race and the possibility for community. In his novels, the hope of community rests primarily within racial groups, and racial antagonism exists simply as a matter of course. In "McDougal," the white character's ability to share a sense of black experiences and to make authentic art from them, art that is acceptable to black people, offers hope for meaningful connections that transcend racial boundaries. McDougal simultaneously maintains his white identity and experiences black life. His openness to connection across societal boundaries suggests that the difficulties Brown's other characters suffer under need not be permanent. True McDougal is only one man, but he represents a great potential, the hope that fulfills the positive undertones recurring throughout Brown's body of work.

McDougal gains acceptance among his fellow jazz musicians because they can grasp the veracity of his experience and understand that he does indeed know the troubles they see. Furthermore, he sees the value of their heritage and the cultural forms it generates as a means of expressing that experience. In the process of sharing his art, he helps forge a community among the initiated. The racial mixture of this new community suggests that the small steps of this beginning will eventually be expanded to encompass the broader human community. This is the message of hope that Brown builds toward throughout his body of work. Always well aware of the difficulties and injustice that African Americans face at the hands of power-maddened whites with no regard for their humanity, Brown also knows that blacks can and must resist that power and create collective, coherent responses to the injustice and oppression visited on them. As the bonds of that resistance are forged, the growing community can supplement its strength and reach out farther, eventually embracing all people in an acknowledgment of a collective human heritage.

Brown's emphasis on community building reflects his complete commitment to social reform. In addition to his literary career, Brown also worked to effect social change in Chicago through his roles of social activist and union organizer. In his life, as in his art, Brown resisted the notion that the sociological conditions documented by the Chicago School defined African American experiences in the city. As his fiction demonstrates, he believed instead that a positive awareness of heritage and a strong sense of group identity were the tools that African Americans could use to build themselves a new life in Chicago. Widely known in his home city during his life, Brown was in a sense a prophet who was honored in his own country. His modification of the sociological vision associated makes his a significant voice in the city's African American literary tradition and a figure worthy of further scholarly attention.

As the various authors cited in this study demonstrate, the job of determining the influence of Chicago Sociology on writers of the Black Chicago Renaissance is both vast and complex. On the continuum of author's responses from Wright's almost total fealty to Wirth's and Park's ideas to Brooks's almost complete rejection of the basic principles of urbanism, one finds many shades of gray, many writers who see some use in sociological observation but variously resist or reject the conclusions that the social scientists drew about black Chicago using those principles. Perhaps the simplest thing to say is that the work of sociologists at the University of Chicago and the work of black authors writing in and/or about the city during the Renaissance era shared the goal of illuminating black life in the city; the varieties of use that these authors make of sociological methodology in their work, then, represents the richness and complexity of their personal responses to their intellectual and cultural environment.

Notes

1. Wright, Richard. *Native Son*. New York: Harper and Brothers, 1940, 243, 256.
2. Ibid., "Introduction," xvii.
3. Wright, Richard. *12 Million Black Voices: A Folk History of the Negro in the United States*. New York: Viking Press, 1941, 111.
4. Ibid., 147.
5. In drawing this distinction between Brooks and Wright, I must acknowledge the critical view that Wright tempers his deterministic view in *Native Son* by having Bigger insist that his actions are more than a product of his environment. I do not believe that Bigger's resistance of this characterization conveys Wright's message about the deterministic power of race and class to define Bigger's existence.
6. Hirsch, Arnold. *Making the Second Ghetto: Race & Housing in Chicago 1940–1960*. Chicago: University of Chicago, 1983, 19, 23.
7. Stuckey, Sterling. "Frank London Brown—A Remembrance." In *Black Voices*, edited by Abraham Chapman. New York: New American Library, 1968, 670.
8. Graham, Maryemma. "Bearing Witness in Black Chicago: A View of Selected Fiction by Richard Wright, Frank London Brown, and Ronald Fair." *CLA Journal* 33 (March 1990), 292.
9. Brown, Frank London. *The Myth Maker*. Chicago: Path Press, 1969, 97.
10. Ibid., 100.
11. Brown, Frank London. "Singing Dinah's Song." In *The Best Short Stories by Negro Writers*, edited by Langston Hughes. Boston: Little, Brown and Company, 1967, 300.
12. Brown, Frank London. "McDougal." In *Black Voices*, edited by Abraham Chapman. New York: New American Library, 1968, 204.

For Further Reading

Becker, Howard S. "The Chicago School, So-called." http://home.earthlink.net/~hsbecker/chicago.html.
Bone, Robert. "Richard Wright and the Chicago Renaissance." *Callaloo* 28. Richard Wright: A Special Issue (Summer 1986): 446–68.
Brooks, Gwendolyn. *A Street in Bronzeville*. New York: Harper and Brothers, 1945.
———. *Maud Martha*. New York: Harper and Brothers, 1953.
Brown, Frank London. "McDougal." In *Black Voices*, edited by Abraham Chapman. New York: New American Library, 1968, 202–4.

———. "Singing Dinah's Song." In *The Best Short Stories by Negro Writers*, edited by Langston Hughes. Boston: Little, Brown and Company, 1967, 295–300.

———. *The Myth Maker*. Chicago: Path Press, 1969.

———. *Trumbull Park: A Novel*. Chicago: Regnery, 1959.

Bulmer, Martin. *The Chicago School of Sociology: Institutionalization, Diversity, and the Rise of Sociological Research*. Chicago: University of Chicago Press, 1984.

Cappetti, Carla. *Writing Chicago: Modernism, Ethnography, and the Novel*. New York: Columbia University Press, 1993.

Davis, Frank Marshall. *Black Man's Verse*. Chicago: Black Cat Press, 1935.

Drake, St. Clair and Horace Cayton. *Black Metropolis: A Study of Negro Life in a Northern City*. Chicago: University of Chicago Press, 1945.

Fabre, Michel. *The Unfinished Quest of Richard Wright*. Urbana: University of Illinois, 1993.

Fleming, Robert E. *Willard Motley*. Boston: Twayne Publishers, 1978, 302.

Graham, Maryemma. "Bearing Witness in Black Chicago: A View of Selected Fiction by Richard Wright, Frank London Brown, and Ronald Fair." *CLA Journal* 33 (March 1990): 280–97.

Hirsch, Arnold. *Making the Second Ghetto: Race & Housing in Chicago 1940–1960*. Chicago: University of Chicago, 1983.

Motley, Willard. *Knock on Any Door*. New York: E. P. Dutton, 1947.

Person, Stow. *Ethnic Studies at Chicago 1905–45*. Urbana: University of Illinois Press, 1987.

Stuckey, Sterling. "Frank London Brown—A Remembrance." In *Black Voices*, edited by Abraham Chapman. New York: New American Library, 1968, 669–76.

Ward, Theodore. *Big White Fog*. In *Black Theatre USA: Plays by African Americans, The Early Period (1847–1938)*, edited by James V. Hatch and Ted Shine. New York: Free Press, 1996.

Wirth, Louis. "Urbanism as a Way of Life." *American Journal of Sociology* (1938). Rpt. in *On Cities and Social Life*, edited by Albert J. Reiss Jr. Chicago: University of Chicago Press, 1981, 60–83.

Wright, Richard. *Native Son*. New York: Harper and Brothers, 1940.

———. *12 Million Black Voices: A Folk History of the Negro in the United States*. New York: Viking Press, 1941.

JOHN REED CLUBS/
LEAGUE OF AMERICAN WRITERS
James Smethurst

The John Reed Clubs (JRC) and its successor, the League of American Writers (LAW), played crucial roles in the development and direction of the Chicago Renaissance. Both organizations were major institutions of the cultural world of the Communist Left during the 1930s and early 1940s. Though the national images of the two groups reflected quite different political and cultural moments, in practice both played much the same role with respect to black artists in Chicago. Each actively sought the participation of African American artists and intellectuals, breaching the walls of Jim Crow in a notoriously segregated city and providing black artists a connection to their literary counterparts beyond the South Side. At the same time, both groups provided models and networks of support for the organizations and activities of Left African American arts groups and institutions, such as the South Side Writers Group and *Negro Story*, which formed much of the base of the Chicago Renaissance.

The JRC grew out of attempts in the late 1920s to merge the legacy of the so-called "lyrical Left" associated with Greenwich Village and the *Masses* and *Liberator* magazines during the teens and the early twenties with a newer "Proletarian literature" impulse greatly influenced by European (especially Soviet and German) Communist artistic movements. Much of the impetus for this merger emerged from the movement to save the anarchists Nicola Sacco and Bartolomeo Vanzetti from execution, a movement that brought together older radicals and liberals with younger (and not so young) activists associated with the new Communist Party of the United States of America (CPUSA). The *New Masses* magazine was founded in 1926 in part as an attempt to keep this Left-liberal alliance together. It included as contributors and/or editorial board members a considerable number of black artists and intellectuals associated with the New Negro Renaissance, among them Langston Hughes, James Weldon Johnson, George Schuyler, Alain Locke, Claude McKay, Jean Toomer, and Eric Walrond. Countee Cullen, an activist in the effort to free Sacco and Vanzetti, also fell within this circle. As the name suggests, the journal was posed as successor to the *Masses*. A stalwart of the old "lyrical Left" (and a close friend of Jean Toomer), Waldo Frank, was initially elected editor-in-chief. However, Frank quickly departed as editor, leaving the younger writers, Michael Gold and Joseph Freeman (who, too, despite their relative youth, had come of age in the "lyrical Left" of Greenwich Village and the *Masses*) to take the editorial lead. As the 1920s wore on, Gold (a native of the Lower East Side most famous as a writer for his 1930 novel *Jews without Money*) became increasingly dominant, taking the journal more and more into the "proletarian literature" movement.

Essentially, the proletarian arts movement, including activists in literature, theater, the visual arts, dance, music, photography, and the relatively new medium of film, sought to break with established artistic forms and institutions and to allow workers and farmers to create new art forms, journals, organizations, and so on, that both expressed current identities and concerns of the working class as well as prefigured or heralded what a new proletarian culture might look like when the international working class has (as "The Internationale" predicts) become all and the state has withered away. It also looked to the CPUSA, the Communist International (Comintern), and the Soviet Union for political and ideological leadership.

This movement took root in the United States during the "Third Period" ideological era of the late 1920s and early 1930s. The term *Third Period* referred to a formulation of Stalin in which he saw the revolutionary moment during and immediately after the Bolshevik Revolution (the "First Period") as being followed by a phase of relative capitalist stability (the "Second Period"). However, Stalin predicted in the late 1920s that the Second Period would soon end and be followed by another (and deeper) era of capitalist crisis (the "Third Period") in which the working class around the world would be receptive to the leadership of the revolutionary parties associated with the Comintern. However, Stalin and the Comintern also concluded that the workers might be misled by various sorts of liberal and non-Communist Left groups, especially the various Social Democratic groups. As a result, what became known as Third Period ideology (which in fact was a product of the so-called Second Period) emphasized the establishment of countercultural "workers'" institutions, such as workers' theaters, bookstores, visual arts groups, writers' groups, journals, and so on, that were formally, thematically, and institutionally distinct from "bourgeois" culture, whether conservative or liberal. This ideology also discouraged the sorts of political and cultural alliances that in fact led to the founding of *New Masses*, attacking such organizations as the Socialist Party and the NAACP and causing the departure of a considerable number of editors and contributors.

By 1928, *New Masses* focused its attention on the development of "worker-writers," many the children of so-called "new immigrants" from Southern and Eastern Europe. Because many were from the Midwest and other regions outside the usual literary precincts of New York and Boston, these correspondents from the class war were encouraged to tell their stories in their own regional and class voices and in their own styles. Of course, the journal and the new literary Left did not totally sever its sentimental and practical ties with its predecessors. In 1929, a group of artists associated with *New Masses*, the CPUSA, and proletarian literature founded the John Reed Club in New York City. The club was named after the stalwart of the *Masses* and pre-Bolshevik Greenwich Village Left bohemia who famously chronicled the Bolshevik Revolution and was one of the leaders of the 1919 split in the Socialist Party that resulted in the beginnings of the CPUSA (originally in two different parties). The new club attempted to further Gold's and *New Masses'* efforts to encourage the development of worker-artists and new types of working class or proletarian art through classes, formal and information discussions, debate, networking, art shows, poetry reading, and so on.

The New York club became a prototype for other John Reed Clubs across the country, with an initial convention in 1932. Within a couple of years, the JRC had a membership of over 1,200 artists and writers in at least 30 chapters, many with their own journals—though only the *Partisan Review* of the New York chapter and *Left Front* of the Chicago chapter survived more than a couple of years. As a member of the International Union of Writers and Artists, basically a Comintern cultural umbrella organization, the JRC had links to like-minded organizations internationally. Again, it should be emphasized that the JRC (and *New Masses*, the CPUSA, and the Comintern) did not lay down definitive strictures about what proletarian literature might be (or even whether a sympathetic middle-class author could write it or not). Rather, it was a place where developing artists in many media and genres could showcase their work, study, and discuss politics and aesthetics (and the relation of politics to aesthetics). It also provided a place where they could network with their more- and less-established counterparts while participating in the larger political struggles of the day, particularly the unemployed movement and the efforts to organize unions in mass production industries that would culminate in the formation of the Committee for Industrial Organization (CIO), later renamed the Congress of Industrial Organizations. The general artistic tenor of the JRC is summed up in its slogan, "Art Is a Class Weapon."

The chapter in Chicago was probably the most influential and most stable local JRC organization outside of New York City, with separate subgroups for visual artists, writers, and musicians, as well as a study group. It also shared a South Michigan Avenue headquarters with a JRC spin-off, the Film and Photo League, and the Chicago Workers Theatre. The Chicago JRC and its journal *Left Front* anchored the organization throughout the Midwest region, which included chapters in Milwaukee, St. Louis, Cleveland, Detroit, Grand Rapids,

Indianapolis, Davenport, and the left-wing Commonwealth College in Mena, Arkansas, many of which published their own local journals (such as Detroit's *New Force* and Grand Rapids's *The Cauldron*). In addition to *Left Front* and the more short-lived official JRC journals, *The Anvil*, one of the most influential and long-lived of the Left journals of the 1930s, was edited by another midwestern JRC member in Moberly, Missouri, Jack Conroy. Conroy later moved to Chicago as a member of the Federal Writers' Project, where he (and *The Anvil*) became a strong supporter of the Black Chicago Renaissance.

Another ideological development on the Left spurred by the Comintern in the late 1920s came to have a great impact on the shape of the JRC and the Left in the United States generally. Quite a few African American artists, intellectuals, and activists, such as W. E. B. DuBois, A. Philip Randolph, Chandler Owen, Claude McKay, W. A. Domingo, Cyril Briggs, Richard Moore, Eric Walrond, Jean Toomer, Alain Locke, Langston Hughes, Countee Cullen, William Patterson, and Harry Haywood, had some relationship to Left organizations like the Socialist Party, the CPUSA, and the Industrial Workers of the World (IWW) in the 1910s and the 1920s. However, by and large the Left before the late 1920s considered the category of race to be a sort of false consciousness that would basically wither away when the class question was solved through Socialist (or anarchist) revolution. It is true that some black leftists, particularly the pro-Bolshevik African Blood Brotherhood that included in its leadership or membership Briggs, Moore, and Haywood, mixed Marxism with black nationalist ideology, and that the international Communist movement increasingly began to use Lenin and Stalin's theorization of the "national question" of the former "prison house of nations" that had been the Russian Empire to come to understand the relationship of African Americans to working-class struggles in the United States. However, it is not until the Sixth Comintern Congress in 1928 that the "Negro Question" in the United States is finally adjudicated to be a "national question," with African Americans in the southern "Black Belt" deemed to be a nation with the right to self-determination up to and including the right to form a separate republic, and in the urban North to be a "national minority" that needed to be integrated into "mainstream" society on the basis of full equality. Equally important as far as the work of the CPUSA and the organizations it influenced were concerned, the Comintern concluded that this national question was not peripheral to the struggle for working-class power, but absolutely central. Instead of being something that could wait, or that would take care of itself after the revolution, the question of "Negro liberation" was posited as something that must be addressed if the working class was going to make any fundamental advances. This position was not universally hailed by CPUSA leadership and rank and file, black and white—though at least one black Communist, Harry Haywood, was instrumental in its formulation. However, by the time the JRC took shape as a national organization in 1932, the centrality of Negro liberation to all aspects of Party work was entrenched in the CPUSA.

This had a number of important practical consequences. One was the concerted effort that the CPUSA made to recruit African Americans and promote them to positions of leadership in both the Party and the groups over which it exerted leadership or significant influence. Another was that the Left attempted to push what it saw as the issues confronting African Americans to the fore, from the fight to save the defendants in the infamous Scottsboro, Alabama, rape case from legal or extralegal execution to the battle against Jim Crow in public accommodations, housing, employment, and education. In the trade union movement, particularly with the formation of the CIO, the Communist Left pushed strongly for the inclusion of black workers under the slogan, "Black and White Unite and Fight," helping to create a cadre of Left African American trade union activists, particularly in the electrical and packinghouse industries, which would organize considerable institutional support for the Chicago Renaissance. Perhaps even more importantly so far as the Chicago Renaissance is concerned, black and white leftists, including former JRC members like Jack Conroy and Richard Wright, led the struggle for the inclusion of black artists in the Federal Arts Project (FAP), the Federal Theatre Project (FTP), and the Federal Writers' Project (FWP), and for the public support of cultural initiatives in the African American community, such as the South Side Community Art Center.

The JRC followed the general CPUSA and Comintern admonition to recruit African Americans and to put the issues of African Americans in the forefront. The initial membership of the JRC in the Midwest was overwhelmingly white—more so than the local organizations of the CPUSA itself. However, JRC worked hard to attract the attention of the black community in the Midwest. In St. Louis, the white painter Joe Jones conducted JRC community art classes in which half his students were African Americans. Chapters put on productions of Langston Hughes's one-act "mass chant" *Scottsboro Limited*—Hughes, a native midwesterner, had close ties to the JRC in New York, the Midwest, and California. The JRC journals devoted a large proportion of their pages to work about and aimed at African Americans. For example, in 1933 and 1934 *Left Front* printed reportage detailing Jim Crow practices at the 1933 World's Fair in Chicago, a strike by black nut-pickers in St. Louis, and the unemployed movement on the South Side, as well as sketches of the daily life of black workers, a one-act play about John Henry as a working-class hero, graphics about lynching and racist (and anti–working class) police violence, and poetry by a young black writer, Richard Wright.

While the membership of the JRC remained largely white, a core of black writers, including Wright in Chicago; Robert Hayden in Detroit; Langston Hughes in New York City and Carmel, California; Eugene Gordon in Boston; Eugene

Clay Holmes in Washington, D.C.; and Frank Ankenbrand in Philadelphia were drawn into its orbit. Wright was introduced to the JRC in 1933 through fellow workers at the Chicago Post Office, a longtime hotbed of black and white political activism. Within a few months, Wright was elected executive secretary of the Chicago JRC chapter, in part because of the CPUSA imperative to promote black leadership and in part because of an internal leadership struggle within the chapter. Not long after, Wright became a member of the editorial board of *Left Front*. Wright's membership in the JRC and later the CPUSA led to his first publications in *Left Front*, *The Anvil*, and *New Masses*. Within the Chicago JRC, not only did his discussions about politics and art generally, and his own work in particular, allow Wright to develop his craft as a writer, but his leadership role in the chapter and ultimately the national organization allowed him to build a national network of contacts. These translated into an international reputation as his poetry and essays appeared in *International Literature*, the journal of the International Union of Revolutionary Writers, the cultural wing of the Comintern, with which the JRC was affiliated.

The JRC was disbanded in 1934, largely at the behest of the CPUSA leadership. In part, the dissolution of the group came as part of a new international policy of the Comintern that led to the Popular Front. The triumph of the Nazis in Germany in 1933 and the rapid and near-total destruction of what had been the largest Communist Party outside of the Soviet Union shocked the international Communist movement, especially as other fascist organizations quickly gained in strength internationally, with fascist governments in Portugal and Austria joining those of Germany and Italy. Part of the Comintern's assessment of these fascist successes, especially in Germany, was that Third Period sectarianism inhibited the development of a potential antifascist coalition among Communists, Socialists, and liberals of various stripes. Also, there was a sense that the Nazis and the Italian fascists had been extremely adept in their use of nationalism and popular culture to consolidate and mobilize a mass political base that allowed them to seize and maintain power. So the Comintern directed its member parties to abandon the sort of countercultural approach that characterized Third Period ideology and activities and seek to build alliances with liberals and others on the Left in a "popular front" against fascism. This involved the abandonment or transformation of many Left institutions that had been set up as alternatives to their less radical counterparts. The CPUSA, for example, disbanded the "revolutionary unions" of the Trade Union Unity League (TUUL), a Left-led labor federation set up in opposition to the American Federation of Labor (AFL), and instructed TUUL members to join the AFL.

The CPUSA leadership considered the JRC as another Third Period sectarian organization and many of its members "ultraleftists" who saw even Mike Gold as a sort of "right opportunist" promoting "middle-class" writers. Despite the

JRC's rapid growth, its membership and the publication of its journals other than *Partisan Review* and *Left Front* were extremely unstable—and *Left Front* lacked the resources to survive past 1934. Even *New Masses* had to recast itself drastically in 1934, moving away from the "proletarian literature" model toward something more like *The Nation* or *The New Republic* in format, as much or more for reasons of financial survival as any directive from the CPUSA leadership or the Comintern. JRC meetings and lectures were characterized by endless argument about politics and aesthetics—arguments that were stimulating to some, but alienating and arcane to others. Such arguments reflected the persistent struggles between "left" and "right" within the local leadership of the clubs, such as the fight that was in part responsible for Wright's advancement in Chicago. Despite the fears of the "ultraleftists" about liberal cooptation of the JRC and the urgings of the International Union of Revolutionary Writers to reach out to the broader literary community, the JRC made little headway among established writers not already committed to the Left, even though the CPUSA believed that the notion of an antifascist alliance would find a receptive audience among many authors in the United States. As a result, the CPUSA and its cultural apparatus attempted to create a new sort of writers' group that would replace the JRC.

However, one initial problem with the incipient Popular Front approach in the United States was the lack of developed liberal-Left institutions that could form the basis of such progressive antifascist alliances. While the CPUSA dissolved the TUUL, for example, and directed its militants to join the AFL, the fact was that in many of the mass production industries in which the TUUL had been active, there were either no AFL unions or just union jurisdictions that existed only on paper. Even trades that had a long tradition of labor organizing, such as longshoring and coal mining, were dominated in many areas by company unions in the early 1930s. As a result, labor activists in such industries as auto, steel, rubber, and electrical—many, if not most of them leftists—had to organize more or less independent organizations under "federal charters" from the AFL, with the result that the workers in those industries received little attention and less respect from the conservative leaders of the building trades and craft unions that dominated the AFL. Ultimately, dissatisfaction with this neglect and the unwillingness of AFL leaders to devote energy and resources to organizing workers who might threaten their control of the federation led to the formation of the CIO by a handful of established industrial unions and the "federal locals," breaking from the AFL in 1935 to form the rival organization. While some of the CIO's initial leaders, such as the United Mine Workers Union's John L. Lewis and the International Ladies Garment Workers' Union's David Dubinsky, had long histories as anti-Communists, many of the leaders of new CIO affiliates had connections to the CPUSA—even Lewis showed a new willingness to work closely with Communists. In short, Left labor militants abandoned their radical unions to join the AFL, only to leave the AFL a few years later. The point is not that these activists, and the CPUSA, were ideologically fickle, but that in the end the AFL was not a suitable Popular Front "mass organization" vehicle.

Similarly, there was no obvious organizational replacement for the JRC. The few "mainstream" writers' groups that existed, such as the Authors Guild and its parent organization, the Authors League of America, were generally conservative and focused narrowly on issues of copyright, royalties, tax codes, and so on, allowing little room for advancing the sort of antifascist, prounion progressive politics that characterized the Popular Front. A more radical counterpart to the Author's Guild, the Writers Union, was organized in New York in 1935, but did not really get very far until it became the official labor representative of Federal Writers' Project workers—and even then it did not achieve the institutional strength of its counterpart in the Federal Arts Project, the Artists Union.

So the CPUSA proposed that a new group be created that would focus its organizing efforts on professional writers and attempt to situate itself within the tradition (albeit a broadly progressive tradition) of American culture rather than outside or against it. During the second and final convention of the JRC in Chicago in 1934, the chief CPUSA cultural official Alexander Trachtenberg (head of the CPUSA press International Publishers) met with a caucus of CPUSA activists in the JRC, informing them of the Party's decision to dissolve the group and replace it with what would become the LAW. There were immediate objections to the proposal from JRC members. Some rightly felt that to disband a group without consulting its membership (or even its leadership, really) was authoritarian and bureaucratic—centralist without the democracy. There was also considerable feeling that the CPUSA was abandoning the development and support of new working-class writers in favor of a more elitist, middle-class (or petty bourgeois, to use the CPUSA idiom) approach—an issue that Wright raised at the meeting with Trachtenberg. Where, he asked, would incipient writers, such as he was when he came into the JRC, find a place in the movement? Nonetheless, Trachtenberg and the CPUSA carried the day. Even though some of the clubs attempted to carry on for some months, the JRC fell apart and its journals vanished except for the *Partisan Review*, which continued for a few more years as a journal of the Communist Left, merging with Jack Conroy's *The Anvil* in 1936, before its transformation into an independent journal of the anti-Stalinist Left by its editors Phillip Rahv and William Phillips in the late 1930s.

One result of the dissolution of the JRC was Wright's desire to replicate it in the South Side of Chicago in a more strictly African American vein. This desire led to Wright's instigation of the South Side Writers Group as a combination of workshop, discussion circle, and study group, much like the JRC. Interestingly, though, in some ways the South Side Writers Group had the sort of range of writers within its orbit that the CPUSA intended for the LAW, including older writers with long careers, such as Fenton Johnson, Arna Bontemps, and Langston Hughes (when he was in Chicago); younger writers who had begun to establish a wider reputation, such as Wright himself and Frank Marshall Davis; and emerging authors, such as Margaret Walker, Marian Minus, and Edward Bland. Even though the South Side Writers Group was to some degree set up in opposition to dissolution of the JRC and the creation of the LAW, it helped draw a cadre of black artists and intellectuals into the cultural and political life of the Communist Left in Chicago, giving the LAW an advantage in recruiting African Americans that the JRC had lacked.

The LAW was established at the first American Writers Congress in 1935. To a large extent, the LAW never completely realized the dreams of Trachtenberg and the CPUSA or the fears of Wright. Relatively few well-established non-Communist writers became very active in the organization—though Van Wyck Brooks and Ernest Hemingway were for a time League officers. Some higher profile writers who lent their support to the LAW at one time or another, such as Sherwood Anderson, John Dos Passos, Waldo Frank, and Upton Sinclair, had been among the comparative handful of well-known authors who had similarly backed the JRC. Some others, such as Dashiell Hammett, Lillian Hellman, and such successful Hollywood screenwriters as John Howard Lawson, Ring Lardner Jr., Budd Schulberg, and Dalton Trumbo were members or strong supporters of the CPUSA. It is true that the LAW had more success in convincing such authors and intellectuals as William Faulkner, James Weldon Johnson, Edgar Lee Masters, Marianne Moore, and Katherine Porter to sign its antifascist statements, particularly in favor of the Spanish Republic. However, despite the appearance of such relative stars as Gwendolyn Brooks and Ernest Hemingway as officers at different times (especially immediately after the third LAW convention in 1939), the national LAW leadership generally looked a good deal like that of the JRC, including many who had been active, or the sort of writers who would have been active had they been around, in the JRC and the "worker-writer" movement. Despite his objections to the disbanding of the JRC, Richard Wright was one of the original signers to call for the Congress and was elected to the LAW's National Council.

There were some major differences between the two organizations. The central principle of the LAW was developing a prounion antifascist front of writers, while the JRC had been devoted to creating a counterculture of working-class artists in many media and genres promoting international proletarian revolution. Another major difference was that LAW never developed the strong grassroots local organizations and journals as did the JRC. LAW was far more diffuse, held together largely through national and regional congresses and the efforts of the national office. Unlike the JRC, which made a major priority the development of branches in such industrial centers as Chicago, Milwaukee, Grand Rapids, Cleveland, St. Louis, Detroit, Newark, and Indianapolis, local LAW organizations tended to take shape only in the traditional literary centers of New York, Boston, Connecticut (to which many New York writers had decamped), and Chicago, and in the newer center of Los Angeles (really Hollywood), where many authors from the older centers were drawn to work in the film industry. And only New York, Los Angeles, and Chicago developed any real stability—in part because particular CPUSA units (or "clubs") and "sections" comprised of writers and other artists in those cities concentrated much of their energy on the local LAW chapters.

However, the LAW chapter in Chicago closely resembled its JRC counterpart in many respects. Though Chicago had a considerable history as a literary center, playing a particularly important part in the development of literary modernism in the United States during the first couple of decades of the twentieth century, it was also famously a city of basic industry, of steel mills, metal fabricating plants, stock yards, slaughterhouses, meatpacking plants, and railroads—and a center for the new industrial unions of the CIO. Despite a wealth of talented and productive writers, there was virtually no "mainstream" publishing industry and relatively few "star" writers in Chicago as compared with New York and Hollywood. Many of the white LAW members (and Wright) were veterans of the JRC and the worker-writer movement—though some, such as Wright and Nelson Algren, would achieve stardom or near stardom in the 1940s. Probably the most financially successful was Meyer Levin, but that success was much more based on his position as an editor and writer at *Esquire* magazine than for the novels of working-class Jewish life in Chicago that he wrote during the 1930s. So if one had to present some credentials as a writer to join the LAW, in Chicago the bar for young writers was considerably lower than it was in, say, Hollywood. There also seems to have been less ideological conflict within the Chicago chapter (at least before the German-Soviet Non-Aggression Pact in 1939), though at times, members of the chapter were at odds with the national LAW office—a sort of regional conflict between New York and the Midwest that also typified the JRC.

One difference between the JRC and the LAW in Chicago, however, was that black writers had an even higher profile in the latter than they had in the former. In part, this was because with the rise of the CIO and Left-led campaigns for unemployment insurance, tenants' rights, civil rights, and so on, the CPUSA's base in the South Side African American community was far larger than it had been in the early 1930s. Another factor was the creation of the WPA arts projects, especially the Federal Writers' Project, the Federal Theatre Project, and the Federal Arts Project that after considerable struggle, often through the Left-led unions of WPA arts project workers, hired many African American writers and artists in Chicago. Among the writers were Wright, Bontemps, Katherine Dunham, Fenton Johnson, Willard Motley, Margaret Walker, Theodore Ward, and Frank Yerby. In the Federal Writers' Project, these authors worked with many of the white radicals who would join them in the local LAW chapter, including Nelson Algren and Jack Conroy (whose *New Anvil* now replaced his older *Anvil* that had disappeared through its merger with *Partisan Review*).

The Left literary community anchored by the LAW and such institutions as the South Side Community Art Center, the National Negro Congress, *The New Anvil*, the WPA arts projects, and the writers club of the CPUSA, provided emerging African American writers with the opportunity to network with other writers outside of the black community of the South Side. Nearly all the members of the South Side Writers Group and the black workers at the FWP and FTP joined the LAW or participated in its local activities, bringing in other black writers. For example, Wright introduced the journalist and poet Frank Marshall Davis to the LAW circle; soon Davis was the treasurer of the Chicago chapter. Davis later credited the League as the means by which he began to escape the social and artistic walls of the ghetto. Such networking had happened before in Chicago. Fenton Johnson had been active in the earlier Chicago Renaissance, especially Harriet Monroe's journal *Poetry*, and in the related bohemia around Washington Square Park (also known as "Bughouse Square") on the Near North Side during the early twentieth century. And, of course, Wright had made like connections in the JRC. Still, such crossing of racial boundaries by black and white writers took place on a whole new scale in the Left milieu of LAW, the CPUSA, and the Popular Front in the late 1930s.

Like the JRC, LAW was characterized by considerable debate over policy and mission, though perhaps on a less open basis than in the jawboning sessions of the JRC in many cities. The source of the debates came in part from outside the group with the rise of such "anti-Stalinist Left" organizations and journals as the Committee for Cultural Freedom and the new incarnation of the *Partisan Review*, led largely by Trotskyists (many of whom were former members of the JRC whose original alienation from the CPUSA grew of out the preemptory disbanding of the writers' group) who, rather than making antifascist alliances with the Communist Left, grouped the Communists together with fascists as fellow totalitarians. While this view generally received a tepid response from non-Communist artists and intellectuals in LAW, issues of Stalinist repression raised by the anti-Stalinists, particularly the "Moscow show trials," did have a considerable impact.

Perhaps the closest that the LAW came to realizing fully its dream of organizing a broad antifascist coalition of writers that would prominently feature well-known non-Communist writers, at least on paper, was at its Third Congress in June 1939, when Van Wyck Brooks, Louis Bromfield, Malcolm Cowley, Dorothy

Canfield Fisher, Ernest Hemingway, Langston Hughes, George Seldes, Vincent Sheean, Upton Sinclair, and John Steinbeck were elected as vice presidents of the organization. However, the nonaggression pact between Germany and the Soviet Union a couple of months later, followed by the Soviet occupation of what was then eastern Poland and the Soviet invasion of Finland, threw the organization in crisis. No doubt from Stalin's perspective it was possible to explain these events as realpolitik maneuvers designed to ensure the survival of the U.S.S.R. and to reverse territorial concessions forced on a weakened nation in the Treaty of Brest-Litovsk. However, the Soviets gave the CPUSA and the Left of the United States no inkling that such a drastic change of policy was in the works. When the antifascist coalition was so quickly abandoned by the CPUSA and the groups it led, it rankled many inside and outside the LAW, strengthening the disquiet that many within the cultural world of the Communist Left already felt over Stalin's trials and purges of leading revolutionaries, intellectuals, and artists. Quite a few LAW activists resigned; others became more or less inactive. The Chicago chapter ceased to function as a local organization—though the national organization survived until 1942.

This crisis was not the end of the Left cultural circles in the Midwest. Despite the consternation that the pact caused among many Left artist and intellectuals, especially among Jewish participants in the Popular Front, it had less of an impact on black artists. Though they, too, felt some discomfort with the pact, the continuing commitment of the Communist Left to African American empowerment and the fight against Jim Crow tended to carry more weight with them. In fact, the early to mid-1940s was in many respects the period of greatest public Left influence within the black community in the Midwest and elsewhere, despite the decline of some major Popular Front organizations, such as the National Negro Congress and the LAW. It was the period in which the Ford Motor Company's huge River Rouge plant in Dearborn, Michigan, (with the largest concentration of black industrial workers of any workplace in the world) was successfully organized by the United Automobile Workers, forming the Left-led Local 600. It was also the era when the African American Communist leader, Benjamin Davis, was elected as a city councilperson in New York City.

It was also between 1939 and 1945 that the Chicago Renaissance really took off, gaining a national profile through Left political and cultural network forged through the JRC, the LAW, the South Side Writers Group, the Abraham Lincoln School, the WPA arts projects, the CIO, and the CPUSA. This period saw the publication of Wright's *Native Son* and *12 Million Black Voices*, William Attaway's *Let Me Breathe Thunder* and *Blood on the Forge*, Margaret Walker's *For My People* (which won the Yale Younger Poets Award in 1942), Gwendolyn Brooks's *A Street in Bronzeville*, and Arna Bontemps and Jack Conroy's sociological collaboration on the Great Migration, *They Seek A City*. It also included the production of

Theodore Ward's play *Big White Fog* (first staged by the Chicago "Negro unit" of the Federal Theatre Project in 1938) in New York City to nationwide acclaim. Furthermore, it was the era of perhaps the most stable Left African American cultural journal of the 1930s and 1940s, the Chicago-based *Negro Story* (which, despite its name, published much poetry).

The early career of Gwendolyn Brooks is a good example of how this network promoted the work of young black writers. Like her friends and contemporaries Margaret Burroughs and Margaret Danner, Brooks came of artistic age in the milieu of such interlocking political and cultural institutions of the LAW, the National Negro Congress, the NAACP Youth Council, the South Side Community Art Center, the Abraham Lincoln School (a Popular Front educational institution largely initiated by the black Communist William Patterson and bankrolled by the department store scion Marshall Fields), the *Chicago Defender* (whose staff had a distinct Left influence then), *Negro Story*, and the CIO in Chicago. Some of Brooks's earliest publications came in *Negro Story*. A prominent black Communist activist, Ishmael Flory, convinced the Left-leaning United Electrical, Radio, and Machine Workers Union to fund a *Negro Story* poetry prize to support Brooks's work. Brooks's career also demonstrates how even those alienated from the CPUSA often continued to maintain the network of associations and contacts, as well as the literary interests in race, class, and ethnicity, forged in the JRC and LAW. Richard Wright, by then out (or on his way out) of the CPUSA largely over the Communist backpedaling on Negro Liberation during World War II, was (along with Langston Hughes) an enthusiastic reader of Brooks's manuscript for *A Street in Bronzeville*, ensuring the book's publication. Edwin Seaver, a stalwart of the Communist literary Left estranged by the German-Soviet pact, published Brooks's poetry in his influential *Cross Section* anthologies in the 1940s.

When the LAW finally collapsed in 1942, no national Left writers or artists group rose to take its place. However, again, the networks created by the JRC, the LAW, and other cultural institutions of the Popular Front remained in place to a large extent, facilitating the continued advancement of Chicago Renaissance participants as novelists, playwrights, visual artists, poets, critics, and editors. In some cases, these participants remained quite overtly Left in orientation, such as those who joined the circles around Paul Robeson's newspaper *Freedom* in the 1950s and the journal *Freedomways* from the 1960s to the 1980s. Others moved considerably from their old ideological moorings, but still maintained many of the old ties, albeit in different political and cultural contexts. However, it is clear that without the JRC and the LAW and the cultural worlds of the Third Period and Popular Front Left, the development and career paths of nearly all the Chicago Renaissance authors, particularly those who came of artistic age in the 1930s and 1940s, would have happened far differently, if at all.

References

Aaron, Daniel. *Writers on the Left*. New York: Harcourt, Brace, 1961.

Bone, Robert. "Richard Wright and the Chicago Renaissance." *Callaloo* 9.3 (Summer 1986): 446–68.

Conroy, Jack and Curt Johnson. *Writers in Revolt: The Anvil Anthology, 1933–1940*. New York: L. Hill, 1973.

Davis, Frank Marshall. *Livin' the Blues: Memoirs of a Black Journalist and Poet*. Madison: University of Wisconsin Press, 1992.

Denning, Michael. *The Cultural Front: The Laboring of American Culture in the Twentieth Century*. New York: Verso, 1997.

Folsom, Franklin. *Days of Anger, Days of Hope: A Memoir of the League of American Writers, 1937–1942*. Boulder: University Press of Colorado, 1994.

Homberger, Eric. *American Writers and Radical Politics, 1900–1939: Equivocal Commitments*. New York: St. Martin's Press, 1986.

Kutulas, Judy. *The Long War: The Intellectual People's Front and Anti-Stalinism, 1930–1940*. Durham, N.C.: Duke University Press, 1995.

Morgan, Stacy I. *Rethinking Social Realism: African American Art and Literature, 1930–1953*. Athens: University of Georgia Press, 2004.

Mullen, Bill V. *Popular Fronts: Chicago and African-American Politics, 1935–46*. Urbana: University of Illinois Press, 1999.

Smethurst, James Edward. *The New Red Negro: The Literary Left and African-American Poetry, 1930–1946*. New York: Oxford University Press, 1999.

Wald, Alan M. *Exiles from a Future Time: The Forging of a Mid-Twentieth-Century Literary Left*. Chapel Hill: University of North Carolina Press, 2002.

Walker, Margaret. *How I Wrote Jubilee and Other Essays on Life and Literature*. New York: Feminist Press, 1990.

———. *Richard Wright, Daemonic Genius*. New York: Warner, 1988.

Wright, Richard. *Later Works*. New York: Library of America, 1991.

MATERIALS FOR FURTHER STUDY
Steven C. Tracy

Abramson, Doris E. *Negro Playwrights in the American Theatre, 1925–1959.* New York: Columbia University Press, 1969.

An, Jee Hyun. "Chicago Renaissance." In *The Greenwood Encyclopedia of African American Literature.* Westport, Conn.: Greenwood Press, 2005: 262–65.

Baldwin, Davarian. *Chicago's New Negroes: Modernity, the Great Migration, and Black Urban Life.* Chapel Hill: University of North Carolina Press, 2007.

Bolden, Barbara Jean. *Urban Rage in Bronzeville: Social Commentary in the Poetry of Gwendolyn Brooks, 1945–1960.* Chicago: Third World Press, 1999.

Bone, Robert. "Richard Wright and the Chicago Renaissance." *Callaloo* 28 (Summer 1968): 446–68.

Brooks, Gwendolyn. *Report from Part One.* Detroit: Broadside Press, 1972.

Butler, Robert J., ed. *The Critical Response to Richard Wright.* Westport, Conn.: Greenwood Press, 1995.

Cappetti, Carla. "Sociology of an Existence: Richard Wright and the Chicago School." *MELUS* (Summer 1985): 25–43.

———. *Writing Chicago: Modernism, Ethnography, and the Novel.* New York: Columbia University Press, 1993.

Cheney, Anne. *Lorraine Hansberry.* Boston: Twayne, 1984.

Craig, E. Quita. *Black Drama of the Federal Theatre Era: Beyond the Formal Horizons.* Amherst: University of Massachusetts Press, 1980.

Davis, Frank Marshall. *Livin' the Blues: Memoirs of a Black Journalist and Poet*, edited by John Edgar Tidwell. Madison: University of Wisconsin Press, 1992.

Demlinger, Sandor and John Steiner. *Destination Chicago Jazz.* Chicago: Arcadia, 2003.

Denning, Michael. *The Cultural Front: The Laboring of American Culture in the Twentieth Century.* London: Verso, 1998.

Fabre, Michel. *The Unfinished Quest of Richard Wright.* Urbana: University of Illinois Press, 1993.

Fleming, Robert E. *Willard Motley.* Boston: Twayne, 1978.

Fraden, Rena. *Blueprints for a Black Federal Theatre 1935–1939.* New York: Cambridge University Press, 1994.

Graham, Maryemma. "Bearing Witness in Black Chicago: A View of Selected Fiction by Richard Wright, Frank London Brown, and Ronald Fair." *CLA Journal* 33 (March 1990): 280–97.

———, ed. *Fields Watered with Blood: Critical Essays on Margaret Walker*. Athens: University of Georgia Press, 2001.

Grossman, James. *Land of Hope: Chicago, Black Southerners, and the Great Migration*. Chicago: University of Chicago Press, 1989.

Grossman, James R., Ann Durking Keating, and Janice L. Reiff, eds. *The Encyclopedia of Chicago*. Chicago: University of Chicago Press, 2004.

Guzman, Richard R. *Black Writing from Chicago: In the World, Not of It?* Carbondale: Southern Illinois University Press, 2006.

Harris, Michael W. *The Rise of Gospel Blues: The Music of Thomas Andrew Dorsey in the Urban Church*. Oxford: Oxford University Press, 1992.

Hricko, Mary. *The Genesis of the Chicago Renaissance*. New York: Routledge, 2009.

Hughes, Langston. *Langston Hughes and the Chicago Defender*. Ed. Christopher De Santis. Urbana: University of Illinois Press, 1995.

Jones, Kirkland C. *Renaissance Man from Louisiana: A Biography of Arna Wendell Bontemps*. Westport, Conn.: Greenwood Press, 1992.

Kenney, William Howland. *Chicago Jazz: A Cultural History, 1904–1930*. New York: Oxford University Press, 1994.

Kent, George E. *A Life of Gwendolyn Brooks*. Lexington: University Press of Kentucky, 1990.

Klinkowitz, Jerome, ed. *The Diaries of Willard Motley*. Ames: Iowa State University Press, 1979.

Knupfler, Anne Meis. *The Chicago Black Renaissance and Women's Activism*. Urbana: University of Illinois Press, 2006.

Kramer, Dale. *Chicago Renaissance: The Literary Life in the Midwest, 1900–1930*. New York: Appleton-Century, 1966.

Langston Hughes Review 14 (Spring–Fall 1996). Special Issue on Frank Marshall Davis.

Mayer, Harold M. and Richard C. Wade. *Chicago: Growth of a Metropolis*. Chicago: University of Chicago Press, 1973.

Miller, Wayne F. *Chicago's South Side, 1946–1948*. Berkeley: University of California Press, 2000.

Mootry, Maria K. and Gary Smith. *A Life Distilled: Gwendolyn Brooks, Her Poetry and Fiction*. Urbana: University of Illinois Press, 1989.

Morgan, Stacy I. *Rethinking Social Realism: African American Art and Literature, 1930–1953*. Athens: University of Georgia Press, 2004.

Mullen, Bill V. *Popular Fronts: Chicago and African-American Cultural Politics, 1935–1946*. Urbana: University of Illinois Press, 1999.

Pinkerton, Jan, and Randolph K. Hudson. *Encyclopedia of the Chicago Literary Renaissance*. New York: Facts on File, 2004.

Rowe, Mike. *Chicago Blues: The City and the Music*. New York: Da Capo, 1981.

Rowley, Hazel. *Richard Wright: The Life and Times*. New York: Henry Holt, 2001.

Semmes, Clovis E. *The Regal Theater and Black Culture*. New York: Palgrave Macmillan, 2006.

Sengstock, Jr., Charles A. *Jazz Music in Chicago's Early South-Side Theaters*. Northbrook, Ill.: Canterbury Press, 2000.

Smith, Carl S. *Chicago and the American Literary Imagination, 1880–1920*. Chicago: University of Chicago Press, 1984.

Smethurst, James. *The Black Arts Movement: Literary Nationalism in the 1960s and 1970s*. Chapel Hill: University of North Carolina Press, 2005.

———. *The New Red Negro*. New York: Oxford University Press, 1999.

Spear, Allan H. *The Making of a Negro Ghetto, 1890–1920*. Chicago: University of Chicago Press, 1969.

Storch, Randi. *Red Chicago: American Communism at its Grassroots, 1928–1935*. Urbana: University of Illinois Press, 2007.

Tidwell, John Edgar, ed. *Writings of Frank Marshall Davis: A Voice of the Black Press*. Jackson: University Press of Mississippi, 2007.

Travis, Dempsey J. *An Autobiography of Black Chicago*. Chicago: Urban Research Institute, 1981.

Vaillant, Derek. *Sounds of Reform: Progressivism and Music in Chicago, 1873–1935*. Chapel Hill: University of North Carolina Press, 2003.

Vogel, Todd. "Introduction." *The Black Press: New Literary and Historical Essays*. New Brunswick: Rutgers University Press, 2001.

Walker, Margaret. *Richard Wright, Daemonic Genius: A Portrait of the Man and a Critical Look at His Work*. New York: Warner, 1988.

Webb, Constance. *Richard Wright: A Biography*. New York: Putnam's, 1968.

Wooley, Lisa. *American Voices of the Chicago Renaissance*. DeKalb: Northern Illinois University Press, 2000.

Wright, Richard. *12 Million Black Voices: A Folk History of the Negro in the U.S.* New York: Viking, 1941.

Wright, Stephen Caldwell, ed. *On Gwendolyn Brooks: Reliant Contemplation*. Ann Arbor: University of Michigan Press, 1996.

Selected CDs and Videos

Related to Black Chicago Renaissance Writers

Brooks, Gwendolyn. *Essential Brooks*. Caedmon VACD 1244 (1).

Various. *Black Diamonds*. Cambria CD 1097 (includes compositions by Margaret Burroughs and others).

———. *Dreamer: A Portrait of Langston Hughes*. Naxos 05537 (two settings by Margaret Burroughs).

Walker, Margaret. *Margaret Walker Alexander Reads Poems of Paul Laurence Dunbar, James Weldon Johnson, and Langston Hughes*. Folkways 9796.

———. *Margaret Walker Reads Margaret Walker and Langston Hughes*. Folkways 9797.

———. *The Poetry of Margaret Walker*. Folkways 9795.

Selected DVDs Related to Chicago Renaissance Writers

Dunham, Katherine. *Best Dancers of All Time in Movies: Mambo DVD*. Quality Information Publishers.

Parks, Gordon. *Half Past Autumn: The Life and Works of Gordon Parks*. HBO Home Video.

Wright, Richard. *Great Books: Native Son*. Cronkite Ward, 1996 (Discovery Channel documentary).

———. *Native Son*. Xenon (VHS).

———. *Richard Wright: Writing Is His Weapon*. History on Video EDU 2000.

———. *Richard Wright's Almos' a Man*. Monterey Video.

A Brief Discography of CDs of African American Music in Chicago:

There are many CDs devoted to Chicago musicians from 1904–59. The anthologies listed below offer a broad sampling of that music. Following each genre listing of anthologies is a brief selection of recommended CD recordings by major figures in each genre.

General

Vee Jay: Celebrating 40 Years of Classic Hits, 1953–1993. Vee-Jay NVS2-3-400.

Blues

Blues Is Killing Me. Paula PCD 19.
The Blues World of Little Walter. Delmark 648.
Chess Blues. MCA Chess 9340 (4 CDs).
Chess Blues Classics, 1947–1956. MCA Chess 9369.
Chess Blues Classics, 1957–1967. MCA Chess 9368.
Chess Blues Guitar: Two Decades of Killer Fretwork. MCA Chess CHD2-9393 (2 CDs).
Chess Blues Piano Greats. MCA Chess CHD2-4385 (2 CDs).
Chicago Blues Vol. 1 (1939–1951). Document 5270.
Chicago Blues Vol. 2 (1941–1944). Document 5444.
Chicago Blues Masters Vol. 3. Capitol CDP7243 8 36288 (2 CDs).
Chicago Blues of the 1950s. Paula PCD 22.
Chicago Blues: The Chance Era. Charly 146 (2 CDs).
Chicago Blues: The Vee-Jay Era. Charly 145 (2 CDs).
Chicago Boogie. P-Vine PCD 1888.
Chicago Is Just That Way. JSP 7744 (4 CDs).
The Cobra Records Story. Capricorn 42012 (2 CDs).
Drop Down Mama. MCA Chess 93002.

Broonzy, Big Bill. *Volume 2, 1937–1940*. JSP 7750.
———. *The War and Post-War Years, 1940–1951*. JSP 7767.
Memphis Minnie. *Queen of the Delta Blues Vol. 2*. JSP 7741.7741.
Meriweather, Big Maceo. *The King of Chicago Blues Piano*. Arhoolie 7009.
Tampa Red. *The Bluebird Recordings, 1934–1936*. RCA 07863 66721-2.

Weldon, Casey Bill. *Complete Recorded Works in Chronological Order Vol. 3.* Document 5219.
Williamson, Sonny Boy. *Complete Recorded Works in Chronological Order Vol. 5.* Document 5059.

Jazz

Black Chicago Big Bands. Frog DGF 28.
Chicago 1929–1930: That's My Stuff. Frog DGF 7.
Chicago 1928–1930: Get Easy Blues. Frog DGF 9.
Chicago Black Small Bands. Acrobat 186.
Jazz Classics in Digital Stereo: Chicago. BBC CD 589.
Jazz from the Windy City. Timeless CBC 1021.
Juke Box Jazz from the Southside of Chicago. Empire Musicwerks 545 450 696-2.

Ammons, Albert. *Boogie Woogie Man.* ASV 5305.
Ammons, Gene. *Greatest Hits: The Fifties.* OJC 6013.
———, and Sonny Stitt. *All Star Sessions.* OJC 014.
Armstrong, Louis. *The Hot Fives and Sevens.* JSP 100 (4 CDs).
———. *New Orleans in Chicago.* Zoom (6 CDs).
Beiderbecke, Bix. *Bix and Tram.* JSP 913 (4 CDs).
Hines, Earl. *Piano Man!* ASV 5131.
Morton, Jelly Roll. *Volume 2: The Red Hot Peppers (Chicago).* Smithsonian RD 044.
Nicholas, Albert and Art Hodes Quartet. *The New Orleans–Chicago Connection.* Delmark 207.
Oliver, King. *Off the Record: The Complete 1923 Jazz Band Recordings.* Off the Record OTR-MM6-C2 (2 CDs).
South, Eddie. *Black Gypsy, 1927–1934.* Frog DGF 36.
Sun Ra. *The Singles.* Evidence 22164-2.

Gospel

All God's Sons and Daughters: Chicago Gospel Legends. Shanachie 2306.
Working the Road: The Golden Age of Chicago Gospel. Delmark DE 702.

Dorsey, Thomas A. *Georgia Tom: Complete Recorded Works in Chronological Order Vol. 2.* Document 6022 (late blues and early gospel).
———. *Precious Lord: The Great Gospel Songs of Thomas A. Dorsey.* Sony 32151.
Jackson, Mahalia. *The Apollo Sessions.* Pair PCD-2-1332.
The Sallie Martin Singers. *Precious Lord.* Vee-Jay 5021.
The Soul Stirrers. *The Last Mile of the Way.* Specialty SPCD 7052.
The Staple Singers. *The Best of the Vee-Jay Years.* Shout Factory 310641.

Classical

Dawson, William Levi. *The Spirituals of William L. Dawson.* St. Olaf Records 2159.
Dawson, William Levi, and Johannes Brahms. MCAD 2/9862A.

Price, Florence B. *Florence Price.* Koch CD 3-7518-2-111.
Various. *Black Diamonds.* Cambria CD 1097.
———. *Kaleidoscope: Music by African-American Women.* Leonardo LE 339.
———. *Soulscapes: Music by African American Women.* Albany: TROY 857.
———. *You Can Tell the World: Songs by African American Women Composers.* Senrab 2000.

Blues and Jazz DVDs

American Experience—Chicago: City of the Century. PBS Paramount AMER 6505.
American Folk Blues Festival Vol. 2. Hip-O B0000751-09.
American Folk Blues Festival: The British Tours. Hip-O B0008353-09.
Ammons, Albert et al. *Boogie Woogie.* Storyville 16013.
Armstrong, Louis. *Masters of American Music: Satchmo—Louis Armstrong.* Columbia Music Video Legacy CVD 49024.
Beiderbecke, Bix. *Bix: Ain't None of Them Played Like Him Yet.* Playboy Jazz PBV9043.
Gillespie, Dizzy. *Jivin' in Be-Bop.* Idem DVD 1018 (with Dan Burley).
Hines, Earl, et al. *20th Century Jazz Masters.* Idem DVD 1049.
Howlin' Wolf. *The Howlin' Wolf Story.* Bluebird DVD 9.
Jackson, Mahalia. *Give God the Glory.* Kultur D1499.
———. *The Power and the Glory.* Xenon XE XX 3026DVD.
Muddy Waters. *Classic Concerts.* Hip-O B0005842-09.
Roosevelt Sykes and Big Bill Broonzy. Yazoo DVD 518.
Sun Ra. *The Cry of Jazz.* Atavistic MVD DJ 865.

Books on Visual Art

Adams, Robert Henry. *African American Art in Chicago, 1900–1950.* Chicago: Robert Henry Adams Fine Art, 1999.
African Americans in Art: Selections from the Art Institute of Chicago. Chicago: Art Institute of Chicago, 1991.
Bearden, Romare, and Harry Henderson. *A History of African American Artists: From 1792 to the Present.* New York: Pantheon, 1993.
Lewis, Samella. *African American Art and Artists.* Berkeley: University of California Press, 2003.
Patton, Sharon. *African American Art.* New York: Oxford University Press, 1998.
Powell, Richard J. *Black Art: A Cultural History.* London: Thames and Hudson, 2002.

CONTRIBUTORS

ROBERT BUTLER is professor of English at Canisius College in Buffalo, New York, where he teaches American, African American, and modern literature. He is the author of *Native Son: The Emergence of a New Black Hero* (1995), *The Critical Response to Richard Wright* (1995), *Contemporary African American Literature: The Open Journey* (1998), and *The Critical Response to Ralph Ellison* (2001). He has coauthored with Jerry Ward Jr. *The Richard Wright Encyclopedia* (2008), as well as two books with Yoshinobu Hakutani, *The City in African American Literature* (1995) and *The Critical Response in Japan to African American Writers* (2003).

ROBERT H. CATALIOTTI, PhD, is a professor in the Department of Humanities at Coppin State University in Baltimore, where he teaches American and African American literature. Winner of a 1983 ASCAP–Deems Taylor Award, he has written two books: *The Music in African American Fiction* (Garland, 1995) and *The Songs Became the Stories: The Music in African American Fiction, 1970–2007* (Peter Lang, 2007). He produced and annotated the CD that accompanies *Call & Response: The Riverside Anthology of the African American Literary Tradition* and the Smithsonian Folkways compact discs *Classic Sounds of New Orleans; On My Journey: Paul Robeson's Independent Recordings*, and *Every Tone A Testimony: An African American Aural History*, and annotated *A Voice Ringing O'er the Gale! The Oratory of Frederick Douglass*.

MARYEMMA GRAHAM is a professor of English at the University of Kansas and founder/director of the Project on the History of Black Writing. She has published extensively on American and African American literature and culture and has directed numerous national and international workshops and institutes on literature, literary history, criticism, and pedagogy. Her most recent books include *Fields Watered with Blood: Critical Essays on Margaret Walker* (2001) and *Conversations with Margaret Walker* (2002). She is currently completing the authorized biography of Walker.

JAMES C. HALL is director of New College at the University of Alabama, and author of *Mercy, Mercy Me: African American Culture and the American Sixties* (Oxford, 2001) and editor of *Approaches to Teaching the Narrative of the Life of Frederick Douglass* (MLA, 1999).

DR. JAMES L. HILL is professor of English and chair of the Department of English, Modern Languages and Mass Communication at Albany State University, Georgia. In his professional affiliations, Professor Hill has served as Chair of the Conference on College Composition and Communication, NCTE College Section and the Georgia Humanities Council; and he has published in a number of journals and other publications, including the *Oxford Companion to African American Literature, African American Review, Journal of Negro History, Forum on Public Policy*, and *Resources for American Literary Study*. A former dean of Arts and Sciences and assistant vice president for Academic Affairs at his university, Professor Hill was selected as a 2008 Visiting Fellow for the Twentieth Anniversary Oxford Round Table, Oxford, England.

MICHAEL D. HILL is an assistant professor at the University of Iowa. With his wife, Lena Hill, he has cowritten *Ralph Ellison's "Invisible Man": A Reference Guide* (2008). He has also completed "Toni Morrison and the Post-Civil Rights African American Novel," a chapter for *The Cambridge History of the American Novel* (2011). His research interests include twentieth-century African American fiction, contemporary black culture (especially hip-hop), and the drama of August Wilson and Suzan-Lori Parks. Currently, he is working on *The Ethics of Swagger*, a book about prize-winning African American novels between 1977 and 1993.

LAWRENCE JACKSON is professor of English and African American Studies. Professor Jackson earned his PhD at Stanford University in 1997 and he began his teaching career at Howard University in Washington, D.C. He joined Emory's faculty in 2002, the year his biography, *Ralph Ellison: Emergence of Genius*, was published. His most recent book is called *The Indignant Generation: A Narrative History of African American Writers and Critics, 1934–1960* (Princeton, 2010). His forthcoming books include *From the Staunton to the Dan: Slavery, the Civil War and an Afro-Virginian Family* and a biography of Chester Himes.

DR. ANGELENE JAMISON-HALL is professor emerita of Africana Studies in A&S College at the University of Cincinnati. Having taught courses in the Black Cultural Studies concentration, she specialized in twentieth-century African American women's literature, and published in such collections as *World Literature Criticism, 1500 to the Present* (ed. James P. Draper, Gale Research, Inc.), *Censored Books: Critical Viewpoints* (eds. Burress, Karolides, and Kean), *Critical Essays* on *Phillis Wheatley* (ed. William Robinson), and *Black Women Writers (1950–1980)* (ed. Mari Evans). Her work also appeared in several academic journals, including *Obsidian II: Black Literature in Review, Sage: A Scholarly Journal of Black Women, Western Journal of Black Studies* and *Journal of Negro Education.*

LOVALERIE KING is director of the Africana Research Center and associate professor of English, African American Studies, and Women's Studies at Penn State University. She has authored or coedited six volumes, including *James Baldwin and Toni Morrison: Comparative Critical and Theoretical Essays* (2006), *Race, Theft, and Ethics: Property Matters in African American Literature* (2007), *New Essays on the African American Novel* and *The Cambridge Introduction to Zora Neale Hurston* (2008), and *African American Culture and Legal Discourse* (2009). She is a regular co-planner of a conference series on African American literature and moderator of the Contemporary African American Literature listserv.

KEITH D. LEONARD is the chair of the Literature Department at American University. He is the author of *Fettered Genius: The African American Bardic Poet from Slavery to Civil Rights* (2005). His current research interests include African Americans in Paris, jazz in African American culture, and black writers' conceptions of love, sexuality, and family as political ideals.

LISBETH LIPARI is an associate professor of Communication at Denison University. She is the author of "Hansberry's Hidden Transcript," forthcoming in the *Journal of Popular Culture* and "The Rhetoric of Intersectionality: Lorraine Hansberry's Letters to the Ladder," in Charles Morris III (ed.), *Queering Public Address: Sexuality and American Historical Discourse*, (University of South Carolina Press, 2007); and" Fearful of the Written Word: White Fear, Black Writing, and Hansberry's Raisin in the Sun Screenplay" in the *Quarterly Journal of Speech.*

BILL V. MULLEN is professor of English and American Studies at Purdue University. He is the author of *Popular Fronts: Chicago and African American Cultural Politics, 1935–1946* and *Afro-Orientalism.* He is coeditor with Fred Ho of *Afro-Asia: Revolutionary Connections between African Americans and Asian Americans,* and coeditor with Cathryn Watson of *W. E. B. Du Bois on Asia: Crossing the World Color Line.* He is currently at work on a political biography of Du Bois.

PATRICK NAICK is an assistant professor of English at Coe College in Cedar Rapids, Iowa, where he also serves as coordinator for the American Studies and African American Studies programs. His research interests include twentieth-century African American literature and American urban studies. He is currently working on a book project about African American literature from Chicago's South Side.

WILLIAM R. NASH is professor of American Studies and English at Middlebury College, Middlebury, Vermont. He is the author of *Charles Johnson's Fiction* (Illinois, 2002) and coeditor of *Charles Johnson: The Novelist as Philosopher* (Mississippi, 2007). He is currently completing a project on space and place in Chicago Renaissance–era visual and verbal art and music.

Currently, **CHARLENE REGESTER** is an associate professor in the Department of African & Afro-American Studies at the University of North Carolina–Chapel Hill. Recent publications include *African American Actresses: The Struggle for Visibility, 1900–1960* (Bloomington: Indiana University Press, 2010) Her other publications include essays on early black film stars and filmmakers that have appeared in journals such as *Film Literature Quarterly, Popular Culture Review, Western Journal of Black Studies, Studies in American Culture, Film History, Journal of Film and Video*, etc. Additionally, she serves on the editorial board of the *Journal of Film and Video* and *Screening Noir*.

KIMBERLY N. RUFFIN is assistant professor of English at Roosevelt University and the author of *Black on Earth: African American Ecoliterary Traditions* (University of Georgia, 2010). She has taught a broad spectrum of ecoliterary perspectives (from U.S. canonical nature-writers to global contemporary ecoliterature) in courses such as "Reading and Writing American Ecological Literature," "Writing Social Justice," "African-American Ecological Perspectives," "African and Diasporic Ecological Literature," and "Environmental Literature, Theory, and Justice."

Retired from the University of Kansas in 2001, **ELIZABETH SCHULTZ** was the first teacher of African American literature there. She has published widely on African American fiction and autobiography as well as on nineteenth-century American literature, with major works on Herman Melville. She now spends her time writing poetry and essays on nature as well as attending and organizing conferences around the world on ecocriticism.

Professor **JOYCE HOPE SCOTT** is associate professor of American Studies and Humanities at Wheelock College, Boston. A former Fulbright professor to Burkina Faso and the Republic of Bénin, Professor Hope Scott has presented numerous conferences, lectures, and scholarly papers in Africa, Europe, Australia, India, South America, and the Caribbean, as well as across the United States She is the recipient of many awards and recognitions and author of numerous publications on African American writers and African diaspora literatures and culture. Professor Hope Scott's current research projects include 1) translation of texts on the Sacred Ancestral Sciences of Sub-Saharan Africa, 2) Traditional African Spirituality in African American and Diaspora literatures, and 3) Black Women's Travel Narratives as Subversive Discourse.

JAMES SMETHURST teaches in the W. E. B. Du Bois Department of Afro-American Studies at the University of Massachusetts Amherst. He is the author of *The New Red Negro: The Literary Left and African American Poetry, 1930–1946* (1999) and *The Black Arts Movement: Literary Nationalism in the 1960s and 1970s* (2005), and *The African American Roots of Modernism: From Reconstruction to the Harlem Renaissance* (2011). He is also the coeditor of *Left of the Color Line: Race, Radicalism and Twentieth-Century Literature of the United States* (2003) and *Radicalism in the South since Reconstruction* (2006).

KIMBERLY STANLEY is a doctoral candidate in History and American studies at Indiana University. She is currently working on her dissertation, "Pulling Down the House and Tearing Up the Yard: Constructing, Policing and Containing Black Masculinity, 1920–1960," which is a social and cultural historical examination of how the Black Press discursively constructed black middle-class masculinity from the 1920s until the1960s in hopes of shoring up a cohesive black middle class that would serve in advancing the cause of racial equality.

KATHRYN WADDELL TAKARA, 2010 recipient of an American Book Award by Before Columbus Foundation, retired University of Hawaii professor, is currently a writer and public scholar. She has taught Ethnic Studies and Africana Studies. She earned an MA in French (UC Berkeley); a PhD in Political Science (University of Hawaii) and published various academic articles; three books of poetry—*New and Collected Poems, Pacific Raven: Hawaii Poems,* and *Tourmalines: Beyond the Ebony Portal;* and over 300 poems. She was born in Alabama and educated in a Quaker school and Tufts University on the East Coast and in Bordeaux, France.

STEVEN C. TRACY is professor of Afro-American Studies at the University of Massachusetts Amherst. He has written, edited, coedited, general coedited, or introduced 29 books (with two more currently under contract), including *Langston Hughes and the Blues* (1988), *Going to Cincinnati* (1993), *A Historical Guide to Ralph Ellison* (2004), and *After Winter: The Art and Life of Sterling A. Brown* (2009). He has performed and recorded with his band, Steve Tracy and the Crawling Kingsnakes, Pigmeat Jarrett, Big Joe Duskin, Albert Washington, and the Cincinnati Symphony Orchestra, and has served as opening act for B. B. King, Muddy Waters, Sonny Terry and Brownie McGhee, Albert King, and many others.

ZOE TRODD is a Faculty Fellow at Columbia University in the departments of English and African American Studies, where she teaches courses on protest literature, historical memory, and visual culture. She has a PhD from Harvard University and her books include *Meteor of War: The John Brown Story* (2004), *American Protest Literature* (2006), and *To Plead Our Own Cause* (2008).

ALAN M. WALD is the H. Chandler Davis Collegiate Professor of English Literature and American Culture at the University of Michigan. He is most recently author of a trilogy published by the University of North Carolina Press; *Exiles from a Future Time: The Forging of the Twentieth Century Literary Left* (2002), *Trinity of Passion: The Literary Left and the Anti-Fascist Crusade* (2007), and *American Night: The Literary Left in the Era of the Cold War* (forthcoming 2011).

JAMAL ERIC WATSON is a PhD student in the W. E. B. Du Bois Department of Afro-American Studies at the University of Massachusetts, Amherst. A native of Philadelphia, Mr. Watson attended Georgetown University and Columbia University before enrolling at UMASS. He is a contributor to *Diverse: Issues in Higher Education* magazine.

DONYEL HOBBS WILLIAMS is currently completing her dissertation (University of Illinois Urbana-Champaign) on twentieth-century Black women writers. Having taught composition and literature for ten years, Williams is currently dean of Instruction at Harold Washington College—One of the City Colleges of Chicago.

STEPHEN CALDWELL WRIGHT received his PhD from Indiana University of Pennsylvania. He is the editor of *On Gwendolyn Brooks: Reliant Contemplation* (University of Michigan Press), and his work has appeared in a variety of scholarly journals. He has authored numerous chapbooks and three poetry collections: *Making Symphony: New and Selected Poems* (Middle Atlantic Writers Association Press, Baltimore, 1987); *Inheritance* (The Cloverdale Library, Bristol, Indiana, 1992); and *From the Archives: Perhaps, On A Sunday Afternoon* (2009). Founder and President of the Gwendolyn Brooks Writers Association of Florida, and editor of *Revelry: The Literary Voice of The Gwendolyn Brooks Writers Association*, Wright served as one of the founding members on the National Planning Committee for the Hurston Festival of the Arts and Humanities.

RICHARD YARBOROUGH is professor of English and Faculty Research Associate with the Ralph J. Bunche Center for African American Studies at UCLA. His work focuses on race and American culture, and he has written on authors such as Frederick Douglass, Charles Chesnutt, Harriet Beecher Stowe, and Richard Wright. He is the associate general editor of the *Heath Anthology of American Literature* as well as the director of the University Press of New England's Library of Black Literature series.

INDEX

The University of Illinois Press
is a founding member of the
Association of American University Presses.

Composed in 10.5/13 Adobe Minion Pro
with Trade Gothic display
by Jim Proefrock
at the University of Illinois Press
Manufactured by Thomson-Shore, Inc.

University of Illinois Press
1325 South Oak Street
Champaign, IL 61820-6903
www.press.uillinois.edu